GOVERNMENT INFORMATION ON THE INTERNET

Sixth Edition

GOVERNMENT INFORMATION ON THE INTERNET

Sixth Edition

Edited by Peggy Garvin, MLS
Introduction by Greg R. Notess, MA, MLS

BERNAN
Lanham, Maryland

#52253922

ISBN: 0-89059-622-0

ISSN: 1529-594X

Printed by Automated Graphic Systems, Inc., White Plains, MD, on acid-free paper that meets the American National Standards Institute Z39-48 standard.

2004 2003   4 3 2 1

BERNAN
4611-F Assembly Drive
Lanham, MD 20706
800-274-4447
email: info@bernan.com
www.bernan.com

Contents

Chapter 4: Census and Other Statistical Sources

Chapter 5: Congress

Chapter 6: Education

Chapter 7: Environment

Chapter 8: General Reference Sources

Chapter 9: Health Sciences

Chapter 16: White House

Chapter 17: State and Local

Chapter 18: International

Indexes

Editorial Advisory Board

About the Editor

With over 15 years of experience in library and information science, Peggy Garvin has a keen awareness of government information and technology. Peggy has served as Bernan's Product Development Manager and also has experience working with an Internet e-commerce firm, the Library of Congress Congressional Research Service (CRS), and law firm libraries. At CRS, Peggy managed researchers' use of government information in electronic formats; developed Web reference products; assisted with the migration of congressional mainframe databases to the Web; and evaluated commercial databases for the Library of Congress. She has also served as a user liaison with federal agencies and private companies to provide beta testing and feedback for developing new information products.

Peggy is a member of the Special Libraries Association (SLA), where she is Chair of the Information Technology Division Government Information Section, and is a member of the American Society for Information Science and Technology. She has been an adjunct lecturer at University of Maryland, College of Library and Information Services, and has made professional presentations at meetings such as Computers in Libraries, Online World, and the SLA Annual Meeting. She is also a contributing author for *Congressional Deskbook 2003–2004* (Alexandria, VA: TheCapitol.Net). Peggy earned her MLS from Syracuse University.

Preface

This sixth edition of *Government Information on the Internet* identifies federal, state, local, international, and intergovernmental Web sites. It extends coverage to also include a selection of educational and commercial sites with government-related information and sites that serve as finding aids for government information. Entries include descriptions and evaluations of the sites, and list many of the full-text government publications they host.

At the back of the book, this edition continues the practice of offering multiple indexes for researchers. The cited government publications are indexed by title and by Superintendent of Document number. New to this edition, the Web sites of agencies are also indexed by their home department name. At the end of the book, a Master Index for the Web sites indexes them by site name, subject, and sponsoring agency.

An online edition of *Government Information on the Internet* is also available. For the first time, Bernan is offering free single-user online access with the purchase of this book. (Network subscriptions are available for a fee.) The print edition of *Government Information on the Internet* has long been a staple at reference desks and government documents libraries. The online edition has been reviewed as "recommended for all libraries" in the November 15, 2001 edition of *Library Journal*. We believe there is a role for both the print and online versions, and invite you to try them.

Greg Notess, editor of the first three print editions, provides an introduction to this edition and to the evolving world of online government information. We would like to thank Greg and the other members of the Editorial Advisory Board for their interest and assistance. As with previous editions, thanks also go to the many dedicated government employees, contractors, and librarians who build and maintain the information-rich Web sites described in this book. Additionally, we are grateful to the Illinois Institute of Technology for allowing us to use its Government SuDoc database to enhance the publication listings in this edition.

I also would like to thank Bernan's managing editor Tamera Wells-Lee, staff editor Jacalyn Houston, production team leader Kara Gottschlich, and production assistant Chris Jorgenson for their assistance in creating this directory. Finally, thanks are due to Bernan's IT department for their ongoing programming and database support.

Peggy Garvin, MLS

Introduction

Governments in the United States and around the globe produce a wealth of information. Now that the Internet has become a common publishing medium, governments have put much of this wealth—laws, regulations, maps, consumer pamphlets, technical reports, medical and science research, history and policy, press releases, grants information, and statistics of every kind—on the Web. The U.S. federal government is one of the largest publishers in the world, and a significant portion of its publication activity now occurs online. Governments are also going beyond static Web publications to provide online services, tools for interactive information analysis, and mechanisms for receiving information from the public over the Web.

Government Information on the Internet, sixth edition, is a gateway and guide to this enormous wealth. We have defined "government information" broadly. Resources described in this guide include both government publications and interactive services. Most of the resources are created and made available by governments, but others are the work of academia, nonprofits, or commercial services. The non-government sources integrated into this book include Web sites that complement or supplement the official sites. They provide finding aids for government information, digitize or archive government information not otherwise available online, or present government information with value-added features such as improved indexing. Some sites are included because even though they are privately run, the project is funded by the government. Overall, government and other Web sites are selected and annotated here because they meet the research and reference needs of citizens, consumers, businesses, librarians, teachers, students, and others. Although the main focus of this directory is on U.S. government information, international governmental organizations are included, as well as the main government sites from many other countries.

A continuing theme in online research is the mutability of the resources. This past year has been no different. The federal government has removed from public military and civilian government sites material that is deemed to be a national security risk. The Energy Department's PubScience site was judged to be duplicative of several commercial Web sites and was shut down. Resources from the Bureau of Indian Affairs Web site have been unavailable because of litigation related to online Indian trust fund databases. And the Education Department provoked controversy with a major Web site redesign that involved pulling substantial content from the site. In addition to unique political and policy challenges, government Web sites are subject to the same conditions as other online resources: content can be altered or deleted easily and no permanent record is left behind.

Government Information on the Internet serves as a fixed point from which to navigate this change. Entries include Web site finding aids and sites where archived content can be found. The scope of each site is described, and descriptions often include notes on intended audience, alternative sources, and important background information. One challenge for government Web users this year is following what has been called the largest government reorganization since the creation of the Defense Department in 1947. The Homeland Security Act of 2002 (Public Law 107-296) created the Department of Homeland Security (DHS). The law transfers many existing agencies to DHS and shifts others. Just as the transition of personnel and operations will take time, the transition of Web sites will likely be gradual. This transition is just beginning as *Government Information on the Internet* goes to press. To help, we have provided a special Homeland Security Reorganization section following this Introduction.

The remainder of this Introduction presents some of the history of the online dissemination of government information, a description of the scope of this directory, and an explanation of its entries and organization.

The Government on the Internet

The federal government has long made efforts to provide information to the public. The Federal Depository Library Program, with libraries in every state, was established to give the public access to government documents. However, as the Paperwork Reduction Act and other federal legislative and regulatory efforts have demonstrated, Congress has expressed a growing concern over the bulk of print publications and the expense of producing them. In response, the Government Printing

Office (GPO) and the Superintendent of Documents have explored many options for transforming printed government publications into electronically disseminated documents.

At the same time that concern has been rising over the excess of paper publications, computer and networking technologies have evolved to allow faster, more convenient electronic dissemination to a larger audience. The GPO began distributing floppy disks and CD-ROMs in the 1980s, but both disk formats share many of the same production, distribution, and storage problems that print sources face. Multiple copies of each publication must be created for physical distribution to depository libraries, government agencies, and interested private citizens.

Electronic bulletin boards (BBS) presented an alternate dissemination model. Data could be produced just once in electronic format and then uploaded to the BBS. Using a computer and modem, one could dial into the BBS to retrieve the data. Beginning in the 1980s, government bulletin boards were established for this purpose. Unfortunately, most BBS interfaces were not easy to use, and retrieving the data could be quite complex for users not familiar with BBS software. For users who lived outside of the Washington, DC area, access to most federal BBS was a long distance phone call.

The evolution of the Internet provided a new and more efficient publication and communication mechanism. Superseding early Internet Gophers, FTP servers, and telnet services, the World Wide Web (hereafter referred to simply as the Web) has become synonymous with the Internet. While gaps in access remain, the meteoric rise in accessibility of the Web within the commercial, government, education, and consumer sectors makes it a very attractive medium for the dissemination of government information. There is no long distance charge (beyond any associated with the Internet connection itself), and the popularity of the Web provides a common and easily understood interface to information resources.

For the U.S. federal government, the Web—sometimes supplemented with email alert services— is now the obvious choice for the publication and dissemination of information. Since U.S. federal government information is free of copyright restrictions, it may be distributed online without the digital rights management concerns facing commercial publishers. In addition, the Web allows federal agencies to reach targeted user groups, as well as the general public, without incurring traditional distribution costs. As a result of these advantages, the Web has become a major avenue for government information. Many government Web sites are now in their second, third, or fourth generation. The current Bush administration has re-launched a redesigned FirstGov site (entry #1) and renewed the commitment to FirstGov as the central site for U.S. government outreach to its constituencies. In addition, the administration has launched an array of new single-purpose sites, such as Regulations.gov and Ready.gov (entry #1263 and entry #1261, respectively).

The proliferation of government Web sites raises the need for a print directory—a source that categorizes government information available on the Web. But why bother creating a directory like *Government Information on the Internet* when the Internet changes so quickly? Is it needed alongside centralized online sites like FirstGov and convenient search tools like Google™?

This print directory presents some key advantages. It provides the *context* that an alphabetical list of agency links or the mixed results of a search engine do not. It allows users to search and plan offline, rather than surf and hope. And it provides a snapshot of government resources on the Internet at this time.

Even if a site is no longer at a specified Web address, knowing that a resource was available at one time means that it likely still exists on the Internet, and might require a bit of work to find it. In addition, we have provided special features for librarians and savvy library users, including an emphasis on publications available at sites and the inclusion of Superintendent of Documents (SuDoc) class numbers for many publications and resources. Unfortunately, any directory compiled by human effort, despite the format, suffers the same problems of upkeep. One thing obvious to the compilers of this work is that all of the online directories are incomplete and contain errors. This print directory is also vulnerable to those problems.

Scope

Government Information on the Internet enables users to access a significant portion of the U.S., state, local, and international governments' online world by providing subject and agency access to nearly 5,000 governmental Internet resources. These resources include publicly accessible Internet sites sponsored by any part of the U.S. government. They also include non-governmental sites presenting government data or offering the tools to find it.

This book focuses primarily on the U.S. federal government, including departments, agencies, and commissions from all three branches of the federal government. Two chapters go beyond U.S. federal government resources. The chapter on state and local government resources lists the primary sites for the three branches of U.S. state governments, as well as the URLs for many city and county governments, arranged by state. The international chapter includes selected sites from major intergovernmental organizations, and the addresses for the primary government and parliamentary sites for other countries.

Government Information on the Internet is not limited to resources that are hosted on government-owned computers and thus have the .gov or .mil top-level domain. It also includes resources containing information originating from the government but that is hosted on a non-governmental site. For example, the version of the United States Code (entry #1264) provided by Cornell University's Legal Information Institute is included in this directory even though it is hosted on a university Web site. Some government agencies also use different top-level domains, like the U.S. Forest Service at http://www.fs.fed.us.

Selecting government resources to include raises a difficult question: What distinguishes a single Internet resource? A book or a CD-ROM is easy to identify as a single, unique published item. On the Internet, identifying the boundaries of a unique resource is much more complex. For example, a government agency may provide the same information through multiple access options. In other instances, multiple organizations may post the same publication or data in different network locations, and some documents are published in different formats on the same site.

Differentiating between one resource and many introduces another difficulty in indexing Internet resources. A book generally is complete in one volume, although there are the more complex cases of monographic series, multi-volume works, and books with separately authored chapters. A Web site typically contains a much more diverse collection of materials. One Web page might consist of links to external sites, an electronic journal, press releases, multi-megabyte data sets, photographic images, and a virtual video tour of a location. Each item may be located on the same server, on different servers within the same agency, or even on servers hosted by other agencies. Sites with a hierarchical structure are more easily defined as a single site at the top-level page (the "home page"), but these sites often feature pages or sections that could be considered as separate resources in their own right.

We address this problem through several approaches. Where multiple sites include the exact or very similar information, one record is used and the alternative access points are included. If the information content is significantly different, separate records are used. A second approach involves describing a site rather than individual documents. While defining limits to a site in the wide-open realm of hypertext is an amorphous task, the sense of order present on many government sites helps designate collections of pages as a single resource. At the most basic level, the group of Web pages from and about a specific agency is considered a distinct site, especially when it has a unique host name. Finally, we take the approach of considering the user. If a resource located within a much larger site is particularly valuable, we may highlight it with its own entry. With millions of Web pages in the .gov domain alone, cataloging every single page is impossible. Instead, *Government Information on the Internet* concentrates on identifying distinct and useful resources and sites. These descriptions of federal government Web sites and other resources will launch the government information seeker's exploration of the separate, individual Web pages included on these sites.

Understanding Uniform Resource Locators

One problem that was evident in the early days of tracking information resources on the Internet was the citation difficulty. How should one cite, or even describe, the exact access method for getting to a specific resource? The Uniform Resource Locator (URL) offers a solution to identifying specific resources and providing sufficient information in a citation so that another Internet user can find it. A URL designates the Internet protocol to be used for access, the address of the host computer, the path name or login name to be used, and the file name of a specific document.

The standard example of a URL for a Web site is now quite common, thanks to advertising from the commercial sector. In its simplest form, the http://www.agency.gov/, syntax refers to a hypertext transport protocol (http) connection to the computer at the address www.agency.gov. A more complex URL might be http://www.agency.gov/office/pub.html, which gives the directory path of office and a specific file name of pub.html.

Http is the common Web protocol, but other Internet protocols are designated with URLs as well. This directly still includes a handful of FTP and telnet resources; these all start with their names as the protocol name.

Organization and How to Use the Directory

Government Information on the Internet is organized by topics. Each of the chapters covers a particular broad topic and begins with a brief introduction. In this sixth edition, we have included a new feature at the start of each chapter called Bookmarks and Favorites. These lists highlight the most basic or valuable federal government Web sites or non-government finding aids that are representative of the chapter's topic. Also at the start of each chapter, you will find a Featured Sites section. This section describes one or more Web sites that are particularly helpful, noteworthy, or well designed. They are often some of the best starting points for finding information in the broad subject area.

Following the Featured Sites, most chapters are divided further into subject-oriented sections. The first subdivision is always the General section, which includes resources related to the broad topic as well as more specific resources that do not fall under the other subdivisions. The scope of each of the other subsections is outlined at the beginning of each chapter.

Each record in the directory begins with an entry number. Note that the index refers to entry numbers, rather than page numbers, to help pinpoint the exact entry to which the index term refers. In addition to the entry number, records include a title, URL, alternate URL, sponsors, description, subjects, and publications, as appropriate to the resource. Records for members of Congress include their party affiliation, email address, and district for Representatives. For further information on each field within the records, see the following detailed descriptions.

Entry Number: Each record starts with an entry number. These numbers run sequentially from the first finding aid records to the last records in the final chapter. The entry numbers are used in all of the indexes to refer back to specific records.

Site Name: Directly following the entry number is a site name or title for the resource. Determining the site name of an Internet source is not as easy as finding the title of a book. For Web sites, the site name might be that designated on the top page by the HTML <title> tag or it might be the title included in a top banner graphic. While the HTML <title> designation is the preferred choice for Web resources, it is often not used by Web masters or is poorly used.

For the purposes of this directory, the listed site name generally is derived from the HTML title element, as long as it is descriptive. In some cases, the site name is manufactured from the initial headings or graphics when they more closely represent how the site is commonly referenced. To avoid redundancy, phrases such as "Welcome to the. . .," "The Official Site. . .," and "home page" have been left off of most site names.

Because names of Web sites are subject to ambiguity or change and do not always uniquely identify a site, they are just one way to refer to a resource. The URL is the best way to uniquely identify a resource, although that can change as well.

Primary URL: Uniform Resource Locators are used to denote the primary location of resources and the principal entryway to a site's contents. URLs can be written in many ways and still refer to the same site. Not all permutations are included, but only the most prominent and stable ones.

Alternate URL: Some of the resources have multiple Internet access points, mirror sites, or related resources. Additional URLs are listed for these sites and to highlight any complementary sites. Given the changeable nature of the Web, some of the primary URLs may stop working. In that case, try an alternate URL if one is available. The site's description will usually include additional information about the alternate URL.

Sponsors: This field lists the organization that hosts a site. Sponsors are most often federal government agencies, but commercial, educational, and non-profit organizations will be listed here as well when they host or sponsor a specific resource. Most of the government agencies listed are U.S. federal agencies, so "United States" has usually been dropped from the start of the sponsoring agency names, unless it is an integral part of the name.

For U.S. government agencies, the sponsor name in the entries usually includes a full or partial organizational hierarchy, such as "Agriculture Department—Economic Research Service." In some cases, the full hierarchy has been collapsed. Consult *The United States Government Manual*, entry #1046, (Washington, DC: Government Printing Office) or other resources for official organizational information.

Due to this book's press time, agencies that have been affected by the Homeland Security reorganization may not have their new hierarchy reflected in the Sponsor line. Check the Homeland Security section following this Introduction for a table of changes made.

A uniform entry is used for sponsoring governmental agencies in the State Governments and International chapters. The name of the state or country is followed by a descriptive term for the governmental body. For example, "Ohio. Legislature" and "Mozambique. Government" represent the state legislative body in Ohio and the executive branch of government in Mozambique.

Description: The resource description field explains a site's organization, principal features, menu items, and significant links. For many agencies, a brief description of the agency's mission is included to help explain the site's subject coverage. The description may mention significant publications available on the site in electronic form, or which sections of the site include online documents. The utility of the site, its ease of use, and the potential audience may be evaluated as well, usually as the last paragraph of the description.

Subjects: In general, the subject headings describe the primary focus of the resource and particularly useful subsections of the site. The subject headings may relate to both the subject of the agency and the major sections of available information. Some of the subject terms contain subheadings to more accurately represent the topic. The subject headings are included in the Master Index. For broad subjects, see also the appropriate chapter or chapter subsection.

Publications: This field lists publications that are available from the Internet site. The types of publications listed include important titles, series, and periodicals, but not every available monograph or pamphlet is listed. The Superintendent of Documents (SuDoc) number at the end of most of the titles is used by the Federal Depository Library Program to identify and often to shelve print publications from the Government Printing Office. The SuDoc numbers are useful for finding online counterparts of print publications in a Federal Depository Library collection, as well as for tracking down older print counterparts of online publications. The root SuDoc number is most often used rather than the full SuDocs for each individual item. Selected publications without SuDoc numbers are also included in this field. The Publications Indexes provide access to the entries containing listed publications by both publication title and SuDoc number.

Multiple indexes are available at the back of the book to provide access by site name, sponsor, subject terms, publication titles, and SuDoc numbers:

- The Sponsor Name/Site Name Index lists entries by their sponsoring department or organization, using the top level of the organizational hierarchy. For example, entries from the Internal Revenue Service are listed under Treasury Department along with sites from other Treasury agencies and bureaus. Excluded from this index are entries for the Web sites of members of Congress, states, localities, and countries.
- The Publication Index lists government publications referenced in the individual entries. They are in alphabetical order and include the Superintendent of Documents number (SuDoc) if available.
- The SuDoc Index includes the same information as the Publication Index, but lists the publications in Superintendent of Documents number order.
- The Master Index provides access by subject, sponsor name (at the agency, bureau, division, or department level), and site name. All entries—including those for members of Congress, states, localities, and countries—are included in the Master Index.

—Greg Notess
Reference Librarian and Associate Professor
Montana State University–Bozeman Libraries

Homeland Security Reorganization

The Homeland Security Act of 2002 (Public Law 107-296) mandates the largest federal government reorganization since the establishment of the Department of Defense in 1947. It creates the Department of Homeland Security (DHS), a new member of the Cabinet. It also transfers some existing agencies, offices, and programs to the DHS.

The Department of Homeland Security Web site has been established at http://www.dhs.gov. As this book goes to press, many transferred agencies still maintain their original Web sites. Others have posted a notice regarding the reorganization, have modified their site to reflect their new DHS organization name, or have posted a link to redirect users to the DHS site.

Because this book was going to press as many of the changes were taking place, we have provided a table of Agencies, Offices, and Programs Transferred to DHS, which appears at the end of this Homeland Security section. This table lists the pre-DHS agencies and programs in alphabetical order, noting the department they have been transferred from and the section of DHS to which they are being transferred. Entries in *Government Information on the Internet* may not reflect their new organizational status.

The transfer of such a large number of agencies and agency responsibilities is necessarily complex. The Agencies Transferred table does not cover the entire content of the Homeland Security Act, but can serve as a starting point when trying to locate a transferred function. The table was compiled from several official sources including the text of Public Law 107-296, the November 2002 "Homeland Security Reorganization Plan," and material provided by the Department of Homeland Security on their Web site. As the transition continues and as DHS proceeds through its first years of budget justification and congressional oversight, further changes may occur.

Government Web sites that will carry news of the department's status include:
- The White House, http://www.whitehouse.gov/
- Department of Homeland Security, http://www.dhs.gov/
- House Select Committee on Homeland Security, http://hsc.house.gov/

In addition, both the House and Senate Appropriations Committees have added a Homeland Security Appropriations Subcommittee for the 108th Congress.

A preliminary organization chart for the DHS is provided below. The table of transferred agencies and programs follows.

Peggy Garvin, Editor
Government Information on the Internet

Department of Homeland Security

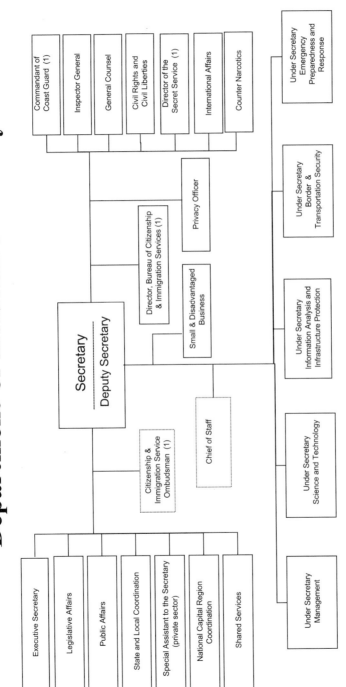

Note (1): Effective March 1st, 2003

Source: http://www.dhs.org

Agencies, Offices, and Programs Transferred to DHS

Agency, Office, or Program	Previous Department	New DHS Directorate or Section
Animal and Plant Health Inspection Service (in part)	Agriculture	Border and Transportation Security Directorate
Coast Guard	Navy and Transportation	Coast Guard
Critical Infrastructure Assurance Office	Commerce	Information Analysis and Infrastructure Protection Directorate
Customs Service (except revenue functions)	Treasury	Border and Transportation Security Directorate
Domestic Emergency Support Team	Justice	Emergency Preparedness and Response Directorate
Energy Assurance Office	Energy	Information Analysis and Infrastructure Protection Directorate
Energy Department research programs (several) related to nuclear nonproliferation and verification, chemical and biological weapons countermeasures, advanced computing, and related areas	Energy	Science and Technology Directorate
Environmental Measurements Laboratory	Energy	Directorate of Science and Technology
Federal Computer Incident Response Center	General Services Administration	Information Analysis and Infrastructure Protection Directorate
Federal Emergency Management Agency	Independent	Emergency Preparedness and Response Directorate
Federal Law Enforcement Training Center	Treasury	Border and Transportation Security Directorate
Federal Protective Service	General Services Administration	Border and Transportation Security Directorate
Immigration and Naturalization Service (citizenship, asylum, and refugee services)	Justice	Bureau for Citizenship and Immigration Services
Immigration and Naturalization Service (enforcement activities)	Justice	Border and Transportation Security Directorate
Integrated Hazard Information System (to be renamed FIRESTAT)	Commerce/National Oceanic and Atmospheric Administration	Emergency Preparedness and Response Directorate
Metropolitan Medical Response System	Health and Human Services	Emergency Preparedness and Response Directorate
National Bio-Weapons Defense Analysis Center	Defense	Science and Technology Directorate

Agency, Office, or Program	**Previous Department**	**New DHS Directorate or Section**
National Communications System	Defense	Information Analysis and Infrastructure Protection Directorate
National Disaster Medical System	Health and Human Services	Emergency Preparedness and Response Directorate
National Domestic Preparedness Office	Justice/Federal Bureau of Investigation	Emergency Preparedness and Response Directorate
National Infrastructure Protection Center (except Computer Investigations and Operations Office)	Justice/Federal Bureau of Investigation	Information Analysis and Infrastructure Protection Directorate
National Infrastructure Simulation and Analysis Center	Energy	Information Analysis and Infrastructure Protection Directorate
National Pharmaceutical Stockpile Program	Health and Human Services/Centers for Disease Control and Prevention	Emergency Preparedness and Response Directorate
Office for Domestic Preparedness	Justice	Emergency Preparedness and Response Directorate
Office of Emergency Preparedness	Health and Human Services	Emergency Preparedness and Response Directorate
Plum Island Animal Disease Center	Agriculture	Science and Technology Directorate
Secret Service	Treasury	Secret Service
Transportation Security Administration	Transportation	Border and Transportation Security Directorate

CHAPTER 1
Finding Aids and Starting Points

Much of the federal government information on the Internet is organized by agency name. If a researcher knows that the information exists on the Web and knows which agency published the information, the search is made easier. Since that is not always the case, a number of finding tools have been developed by the government, academic institutions, and the private sector to fill the gap.

The first chapter of this book highlights a variety of portals, search tools, and other starting points for discovering the sources and scope of government information on the Internet. These sites meet a diversity of needs, as demonstrated by the featured sites described below. FirstGov is a centerpiece of the current administration's strategy for e-government, and InfoMine is a key tool for academic research in government resources.

Other resources in this chapter represent unique or well-known finding aids. As is the case with Internet directories, many of the sites are not comprehensive and may not be consistently up-to-date. They do, however, represent some of the best starting points.

Bookmarks & Favorites

Current Government Sites
- Federal Agency Directory, http://www.lib.lsu.edu/gov/fedgov.html
- FirstGov, http://www.firstgov.gov
- GPO Finding Aids, http://www.access.gpo.gov/su_docs/tools.html
- Grants.gov, http://www.grants.gov

Archived Government Sites
- CyberCemetery, http://govinfo.library.unt.edu

Featured Sites

1. FirstGov
`http://www.firstgov.gov`
Sponsor: General Services Administration
Description: Labeled "the U.S. Government's Official Web Portal," FirstGov is an Executive Branch initiative offering multiple routes to government Web pages and sites. Aiming to focus on the information itself rather than the agency originating it, FirstGov links are most prominently organized by audience: citizens, business, and governments. Links for citizens include E-File Your Taxes and Apply for Student Loans, while links for business include Tax and Wage Reporting and Subcontracting Opportunities. Links for governments include sites for federal employees and for state and local governments.

The two other major tools offered are the FirstGov search engine and an Agencies section. The search engine searches over 50 million federal and state government Web pages. Many federal Web sites also have an option to use the FirstGov search engine locally, searching just their site. The Agencies section features quick lists of unannotated links divided into three categories: Federal; State, Local, Tribal and U.S. Territory; and International. FirstGov also features a variety of links grouped by special topic. A Reference section includes links to sites with federal government phone directories, forms, news releases, libraries, and laws and regulations. It also has sections highlighting sources of federal statistics, publications, and maps.

Originally launched by the Clinton administration in 2000, FirstGov was redesigned and relaunched by the Bush administration in 2002. The site's current search engine and Agencies section are useful for those who know what they are looking for, and the current citizens/business/government gateways serve those who may be less aware of what the government already has online. Only the search engine offers a comprehensive approach at present, however, so FirstGov may not be the researcher's first or last stop. Those interested in administration goals for use of the Web, including FirstGov, may wish to see the Office of Management and Budget Report *E-Government Strategy: Simplified Delivery of Services to Citizens.*

Subjects: Government Information; Finding Aids

Publication: *E-Government Strategy: Simplified Delivery of Services to Citizens*

2. INFOMINE Government Information

http://infomine.ucr.edu/cgi-bin/search?govpub

Sponsor: University of California, Riverside. Library

Description: INFOMINE is an extensive catalog of Internet resources selected for their scholarly or educational value. Coordinated by the University of California Riverside Library, it is a cooperative project involving contributors from UC campuses and elsewhere. This particular portion of the INFOMINE site focuses on government-related information with scholarly or educational value. Access to the Web resources is by fielded search or through browsing. The search function allows users to search by subject, author, title, keyword, or description, and it supports Boolean searching and truncation. Alternatively, users can browse by subject, author, title, keyword, or the "table of contents" option with links arranged by an alphabetical list of subjects.

The subject headings used are fairly detailed, allowing for more precise retrieval. The selected resources are often specific online publications or data sets. The detailed subject indexing combined with records for specific resources makes INFOMINE's government section particularly valuable for finding resources by subject.

Because this is a campus-specific site, some of the listed resources point to non-Internet accessible titles available locally at the UC Riverside Library, such as CD-ROM databases. In addition, the scope of government information is defined broadly; resources in this section include some private interest group Web sites. Despite those entries, this is an excellent catalog for finding specific government research resources by subject.

Subjects: Government Information; Finding Aids

The finding aids in this chapter are divided into one section, spanning the entry numbers indicated here:

> *General   3–24*

General

3. Database List on GPO Access

http://www.access.gpo.gov/su_docs/databases.html

Sponsor: Government Printing Office (GPO) — Superintendent of Documents

Description: The many databases available from the Superintendent of Documents GPO Access Web site offer a wealth of legislative, regulatory, reference, and other government information. This page lists the databases and links to specialized search pages for each. In addition, it offers an option to search across multiple databases. Most of the databases start in 1994 at the earliest, but the *Congressional Record Index* goes back to 1983.

Originally rather limited, GPO Access now features specialized search pages with detailed instructions, database-specific search options, and even the ability to browse for some of the publications. Search queries must use the proper syntax, such as having Boolean operators in all uppercase letters and putting quotation marks around phrases. For additional search help, see the Training Manual link on the side panel of the Database List page. Core databases include *Congressional Directory, Congressional Record, Code of Federal Regulations, Federal Register, Public and Private Laws, Public Papers of the Presidents, U.S. Government Manual, United States Code*, and *Weekly Compilation of Presidential Documents.*

GPO Access databases use the WAIS search engine, which may produce unexpected results for the inexperienced user. Also, search capabilities vary from database to database, in part because of the variety of databases offered. See the "helpful hints" sections linked from individual database search pages for suggestions on constructing an effective search in that database.

Subject: Government Publications

Publications: *Budget of the United States Government*, PrEx 2.8:
Calendar of United States House of Representatives and History of Legislation, Y 1.2/2:
Code of Federal Regulations, AE 2.106/3:
Congressional Bills, Y 1.6:
Congressional Record (Daily), X 1.1/A:
Congressional Record Index, X 1.1/A:
Davis-Bacon Wage Determinations, L 36.211/2:
Decisions of the Comptroller General, GA 1.5:
Deschler's Precedents of the United States House of Representatives, Y 1.1/2:
Economic Indicators, Y 4.EC 7:EC 7/
Economic Report of the President, Pr 42.9:
Federal Register, AE 2.106:
GAO Reports, GA 1.5/A:
Hinds' Precedents of the House of Representatives
House Bills, Y 1.4/6:
House Documents, Y 1.1/7:
House Journal, XJH:
House Reports, Y 1.1/8:
House Rules and Manual, Y 1.2:R 86/2/
LSA, List of CFR Sections Affected, AE 2.106/2:
Official Congressional Directory, Y 4.P 93/1:1/
Privacy Act Issuances, AE 2.106/4:
Privacy Act Issuances Compilation, AE 2.106/4-2:
Public Papers of the President, AE 2.114:
Senate Bills, Y 1.4/1:
Senate Calendar of Business. Daily, Y 1.3/3:
Senate Documents, Y 1.1/3:
Senate Manual, Y 1.1/3:
Senate Reports, Y 1.1/5:
U.S. Constitution, Analysis and Interpretation, Y 1.1/2:
U.S. Government Manual, AE 2.108/2:
U.S. Public Laws, AE 2.110:
United States Code, Y 1.2/5:
Weekly Compilation of Presidential Documents, AE 2.109:

4. FCIC National Contact Center

http://www.info.gov/
Sponsor: General Services Administration
Description: This GSA site is the Web version of a toll-free telephone reference service that answers questions about programs, benefits, and services provided by the government. Users may call 1-800-FED-INFO between 9 a.m. and 8 p.m. eastern time and speak with specially trained GSA staff. The resources used by this staff are available through this site. Information is arranged by topic, such as Social Security, Medicare and Medicaid, Federal Grants, Consumer Topics, Recalls, The Draft, and more. Links to membership lists for the House and the Senate, federal toll-free numbers, and federal agency telephone directories are presented. Also available are links to government agencies that distribute government publications, Federal Press Release Gateway, and FirstGov for Kids.
Subjects: Government Information; Finding Aids

5. Federal Telephone Directories

http://www.info.gov/phone.htm
Alternate URL: http://www.pueblo.gsa.gov/call/phone.htm
Sponsor: General Services Administration
Description: This section of the National Contact Center Web site features direct links to telephone directories for cabinet agencies, independent agencies and commissions, and the members of Congress. It even includes central phone numbers for some that do not have an online phone directory.

Subjects: Federal Government; Directories

6. FedForms
http://www.fedforms.gov/
Sponsor: General Services Administration
Description: This portal site provides "one-stop shopping" for forms commonly needed for federal government services. Links to forms are arranged alphabetically by the issuing department or agency. In addition, there are links to other Web sources of forms and information: FirstGov, the General Services Administration, and the U.S. Postal Service. At the bottom of the page, graphical links direct users to the FedForms title/agency search function, IRS forms, and Small Business Administration forms.
Subject: Government Forms

7. FedWorld Information Network
http://www.fedworld.gov/
Alternate URLs: telnet://fedworld.gov/
ftp://ftp.fedworld.gov/pub/
Sponsor: Commerce Department — Technology Administration (TA) — National Technical Information Service (NTIS)
Description: FedWorld is a government information gateway managed by the National Technical Information Service (NTIS). The Web site, ftp archive, and the telnet version all differ slightly in information content. The Web site functions largely as a portal to other government Web sites. It includes search interfaces to resources including government jobs announcements, archived IRS forms, FirstGov.gov, and EPA's database on repairing auto emission systems. Fedworld Web also features a locator for "Top Government Web Sites."

The ftp FedWorld features access to the FedWorld file libraries, which include more than 10,000 data files, including information on business, health and safety, the environment, and satellite images. The telnet version, which is the original FedWorld, has very little current content that is not available elsewhere.

Although FedWorld was a federal Web pioneer, it now includes a rather eclectic selection of resources, and by no means does it demonstrate the entire breadth of government resources.
Subject: Government Information

8. Finding Aids
http://www.access.gpo.gov/su_docs/tools.html
Sponsor: Government Printing Office (GPO) — Superintendent of Documents
Description: This page offers access to a suite of tools developed for the Federal Depository Library Program to direct librarians and the public to federal government information on the Internet. The resources are divided into two types, Search and Browse. Search links include Databases Online via GPO Access, Catalog of U.S. Government Publications, Sales Product Catalog, Government Information Locator Service, Search the Federal Government through FirstGov, Agency Publication Indexes, and Depository Library in Your Area. Under Browse, the site offers U.S. Government Subscriptions Catalog, U.S. Government Bookstores, New Electronic Titles, FDLP Electronic Collection, Federal Web Sites Hosted by GPO Access, Federal Bulletin Board Files, and Browse a Topic (GPO Subject Bibliographies).

Several Browse links point to university library sites working cooperatively with GPO. The Federal Agency Internet Sites list is hosted by Louisiana State University Libraries. The Cybercemetery is the online archive of selected former federal government entities that is maintained by the University of North Texas (UNT) libraries.

The Finding Aids page is a useful top-level search tool, centralizing access to a variety of current catalogs and directories supported by the Government Printing Office. Documents librarians should have no problem with the site; less experienced users may wish there were more guidance than this unannotated list of links provides.
Subjects: Government Information; Finding Aids
Publications: *Subject Bibliographies*, GP 3.22/2:
U.S. Government Subscriptions, GP 3.9:

9. Google's Unclesam
http://www.google.com/unclesam
Sponsor: Google Inc.
Description: This subsection of the popular Google search engine focuses on Web sites in the .gov, .mil, and .us domains. Unclesam searches enjoy all of the benefits of the Google search approach. Google ranks sites based, in part, on the number of links from other sites, so top search results tend to be the most popular pages on the searched term.

Google's Unclesam is a quick way to locate information on the .gov, .mil, and .us domains, particularly when you are looking for a known item or are familiar with the specific terminology of your search topic. Note that the Advanced Search and Preferences links on the Unclesam page link to regular Google, which is not limited to the .gov, .mil. and .us domains. Advanced Search, however, can be used to limit a search to any of those domains.
Subject: Search Engines

10. GovEngine.com
http://www.govengine.com/
Sponsor: GovEngine.com
Description: GovEngine is a directory of federal, state, and local government and court Web sites. There is no word search engine. Instead, the site provides access through menu listings of government sites for each state or by categories such as federal courts or local governments.

This site's strength is in providing links to sites not often covered by general government directories, such as federal boards and commissions, municipal courts, and state legislative support agencies.
Subjects: Directories; Finding Aids

11. Government Information—Vanderbilt University
http://www.library.vanderbilt.edu/romans/govt/
Sponsor: Vanderbilt University. Library
Description: This collection of Web links follows a model developed by the Government Documents Roundtable (GODORT) of the American Libraries Association. Links to government Web sites are arranged both by level of government and by broad topic. Topical sections include a Reference Shelf, Consumer Information, Maps and Geography, and Resources for Government Information Librarians. The links include a selection of U.S. federal, state, and local sites as well as international organizations.

By offering both hierarchical access to the three branches of government and subject access, this site makes an excellent starting point for general government information searches.
Subjects: Government Information; Finding Aids

12. Government Periodicals
http://library.louisville.edu/government/periodicals/periodall.html
Sponsor: University of Louisville. Ekstrom Library
Description: This university library site offers a subject directory of U.S. government bulletins, journals, and other periodicals. Links to the periodicals on government Web sites are arranged by such subject groupings as Business, Employment, Science, and Military. Each list of periodical links is supplemented with a list of links on related topics. All periodical links can also be listed in alphabetical order.

The site's simple interface provides quick access to hundreds of government periodicals online.
Subjects: Government Publications; Finding Aids

13. GovSpot
http://www.govspot.com/
Sponsor: StartSpot Mediaworks Inc.
Description: This commercial site is one of several StartSpot sites. Under Government Online, it features Executive Branch, Judicial Branch, Legislative Branch, Local Government, State Government, World Government, and Government Employees. Each section then links to top-level government sites. For subject access GovSpot has such categories as The Library, Social

Services, Justice and Military, Matters of Money, Science and Travel, World Affairs, and Politics. GovSpot also features selective lists in sections such as Must-See Sites, Shortcuts, Lists, Government Reports, Issues, and more.

GovSpot can be a good starting point, but it lacks depth of access. On the plus side, it provides a simple interface to some of the more popular and frequently requested government resources.
Subject: Finding Aids

14. GPO Access: Official Federal Government Information at Your Fingertips
http://www.access.gpo.gov/su_docs/
Sponsor: Government Printing Office (GPO) — Superintendent of Documents
Description: Established by Public Law 103-40, GPO Access is a service of the U.S. Government Printing Office that provides free electronic access to federal government information products. Most of these are offered as searchable databases. Under the main category What's Available, the site divides its content into the following sections: Legislative, Executive, Judicial, Regulatory, Administrative Decisions, Core Documents of U.S. Democracy, and Hosted Federal Web Sites. The second main category, Quick Links, provides direct access to the *Code of Federal Regulations, Federal Register, Congressional Record, U.S. Code, Congressional Bills*, and Catalog of U.S. Government Publications databases.

A Library Services section offers information on the Federal Depository Library Program and the Library Programs Service. Under the Online Bookstore section, the site features a variety of sources to help in identifying specific documents available for purchase including the Sales Product Catalog (SPC). On this page, under Browse a Topic, GPO *Subject Bibliographies* are available with annotations and links to online ordering of items.

As the official source for electronic formats of core U.S. government documents, GPO Access is an essential resource.
Subjects: Government Publications; Databases
Publications: *Biennial Report to Congress on the Status of GPO Access*, GP 1.1/2:
Budget of the United States Government, PrEx 2.8:
Calendar of United States House of Representatives and History of Legislation, Y 1.2/2:
Code of Federal Regulations, AE 2.106/3:
Congressional Bills, Y 1.6:
Congressional Record (Daily), X 1.1/A:
Congressional Record Index, X 1.1/A:
Decisions of the Comptroller General, GA 1.5:
Economic Indicators, Y 4.EC 7:EC 7/
Economic Report of the President, PR 43.9:
Federal Depository Library Directory (Online), GP 3.36/2-2:
Federal Register, AE 2.106:
GAO Reports, GA 1.5/A:
Government Paper Specifications Standards, Y 4.P 93/1:7
House Bills, Y 1.4/6:
House Documents, Y 1.1/7:
House Reports, Y 1.1/8:
House Rules and Manual, Y 1.2:R 86/2/
LSA, List of CFR Sections Affected, AE 2.106/2:
Official Congressional Directory, Y 4.P 93/1:1/
Privacy Act Issuances, AE 2.106/4:
Privacy Act Issuances Compilation, AE 2.106/4-2:
Public Papers of the President, AE 2.114:
Senate Bills, Y 1.4/1:
Senate Calendar of Business. Daily., Y 1.3/3:
Senate Documents, Y 1.1/3:
Senate Reports, Y 1.1/5:
Subject Bibliographies, GP 3.22/2:
U.S. Government Manual, AE 2.108/2:
U.S. Government Subscriptions, GP 3.9:
U.S. Public Laws, AE 2.110:

United States Code, Y 1.2/5:
Weekly Compilation of Presidential Documents, AE 2.109:

15. Grants.gov
http://grants.gov/
Sponsor: Health and Human Services Department
Description: Grants.gov is the federal government portal to grants information. The main section of the site, Grants Topics, is essentially an index to agency Web pages that include grants information. An Other Grants Services section lists links to several federal Web sites related to grants, such as the Catalog of Federal Domestic Assistance site. Background information on Grants.gov describes the federal E-Grants initiative, led by the Health and Human Services Department, to provide more integrated online grants management service to grants recipients.
    At this stage in its development, Grants.gov is a simple, usable finding aid for agencies' grants information on the Web.
Subject: Grants

16. LSU Libraries Federal Agencies Directory
http://www.lib.lsu.edu/gov/fedgov.html
Sponsor: Louisiana State University. Library
Description: This finding aid is the product of a partnership between Louisiana State University and the Federal Depository Library Program. The site has an unannotated list of links to federal government Web sites. The list can be searched and displayed in several ways: alphabetically, hierarchically, by a word search, or by browsing categories such as Executive, Judicial, or Legislative. Not every level of an organization may be displayed hierarchically; the site also recommends checking the parent agency's Web site for further levels and offices. A Frequently Asked Questions section is actually a subject guide to selected popular government Internet sites. Featured subject categories include Grants and Funding, Government Sales and Auctions, Military Records, and Jobs.
Subjects: Federal Government; Finding Aids

17. Naval Postgraduate School Resources By Topic
http://library.nps.navy.mil/home/resources.html
Sponsor: Navy — Naval Postgraduate School (NPS)
Description: Resources by Topic, from the Naval Postgraduate School Dudley Knox Library, provides topical access to a selection of links to government and related Web sites. It goes beyond military information to include sections on such topics as Congressional Information Sources, Law, Maps, and Reference Works. But it also includes military resources within these general topics, filling a gap that is often left by more general government information portals. Other sections include Defense Budget, Environment, Health and Medical Resources, Libraries, Military, Military Equipment, National Security, Terrorism, and the branches of the armed services.
Subjects: Military Information; Finding Aids

18. Selected Indexes to Publications of Federal Government Agencies
http://www.library.unr.edu/depts/bgic/guides/government/fed/indexes.html
Sponsor: University of Nevada Reno. Libraries
Description: This useful page lists various federal government bibliographic indexes, catalogs, and databases—such as ERIC and PubMed—that identify hundreds of thousands of government publications. Those with an asterisk (*) may only be available for University of Nevada use. It provides a basic list of more than thirty databases and then offers an annotated listing below that.
Subject: Databases

19. Ten Most Wanted Government Documents
http://www.cdt.org/righttoknow/10mostwanted/
Sponsor: Center for Democracy and Technology
Description: This site is a joint effort between two public interest groups, the Center for Democracy and Technology and OMB Watch. The "ten most wanted" are categories of government information that, in 1999, were selected by a variety of respondents as the government information most

needed on the Web but not yet available on the Web. Three of the targets, most prominently a U.S. Supreme Court Web site, have since become available and are marked on the site as "captured." The site explains the Ten Most Wanted Project, identifies five government sites that are "on the right track," and makes policy recommendations for posting government information online.

When so much information is available online, this site is helpful for pointing out what is not. The goal of the site is to advertise these absences and encourage the agencies that create the information to make it available, so you will not find detailed tips on alternative sources.
Subject: Government Publications — Policy

20. U.S. Blue Pages
http://www.usbluepages.gov/
Sponsor: General Services Administration
Description: The U.S. Blue Pages Project creates both this site and the blue pages sections of local telephone directories, listing phone numbers and some Web links for government agencies and services. Under the section Give Me Local Information, one can access local listings of federal services through a state and city drop-down menu in combination with the selection from a list of a particular area of interest/governmental function. For national information, use only the list to retrieve information. Other sections include About Blue Pages; Government Offices, which is a partial list of government offices ranging from the Administration on Aging to the Veterans Affairs Department; America Anywhere, which is a partial directory of toll-free numbers for federal services and organizations; and In the News.
Subjects: Government Services; Directories

21. U.S. Government Documents Ready Reference Collection
http://www.columbia.edu/cu/lweb/indiv/dsc/readyref.html
Sponsor: Columbia University
Description: This is a subject arrangement of the most frequently used depository document titles at Columbia University Libraries. Although some references are to items housed in the library, most include links to online versions of the titles. Items are arranged by subject. The Web format, link, and frequency are provided for each title.

This site provides a focused, selective list of the best and most popular government resources. The title listings, with print-equivalent call numbers when relevant, are particularly helpful for those who are familiar with a reference book and are looking for the online version.
Subjects: Government Publications; Reference

22. UMich Documents Center
http://www.lib.umich.edu/govdocs/
Sponsor: University of Michigan. Library
Description: This extensive compilation of Web links is maintained at the University of Michigan Library's Document Center. In addition to the alphabetic site index, links are organized into divisions including Federal, Foreign Governments, International, Local, and State. Each division is further organized with an index appropriate to the resources in that area. Special sections focus on Documents in the News, Government Documents Librarianship, Political Science Resources on the Web, and Statistical Resources on the Web. The resources themselves include government, nonprofit, and commercial Web sites related to government and political information. Because a primary audience is the University, cited resources also include some only available to the University of Michigan campus.

Resources created at the University of Michigan but available to all are highlighted in the Special Projects section. These include a frequently updated list of email addresses for U.S. Senators and Representatives, a list of state Governors' email and Web addresses, and the full text of President John F. Kennedy's Executive Orders.

Coordinated by Grace York of the Documents Center, this site is one of the more comprehensive online finding aids for government and political information on the Internet. Links are not strictly to government sources, and they appear to be selected and annotated based on frequently asked reference questions.
Subjects: Government Information; Finding Aids

23. Uncle Sam Migrating Government Publications
http://exlibris.memphis.edu/govpubs/mig.htm
Sponsor: University of Memphis. Library
Description: This site identifies printed government publications that have been made available on, or migrated to, the Internet. The list can be browsed by title or by SuDoc (Superintendent of Documents) number. Each record contains the publication title and SuDoc number, and a link to the source or to the nearest search screen. Some links point directly to the source URL, while others are routed through the GPO PURL (Persistent URL) service. The scope of Migrating Government Publications is limited to serials and periodicals and it includes both official and some unofficial sites. A section titled Rationale, Scope, and Similar Sites explains how this site fits into the wider world of government documents.

This finding aid is tailored to the needs of documents librarians and users of U.S. federal depository libraries. For example, a key indicating that a document is in "electronic format only" means that depository libraries are not receiving a print version, but a print version may exist. While the list is not comprehensive, it can supplement GPO's own Catalog of U.S. Government Publications that includes both monographs and serials but lacks the ability to browse titles.
Subjects: Government Publications; Finding Aids

24. Yahoo! U.S. Government
http://dir.yahoo.com/Government/U_S__Government/
Sponsor: Yahoo! Inc.
Description: Yahoo! is one of the best known and most frequently used general Internet finding aids. Its subject classification approach features sites rather than individual pages, making it an excellent starting point for many searches. Yahoo! Government includes official and unofficial sites at the federal, state, and local levels. The government section is substantial, updated frequently, and broad in scope. There are links to current U.S. government news, and site listings include such links as Project Vote Smart and Ben's Guide to U.S. Government for Kids.

Yahoo! U.S. Government can be a good place to start when exploring sites on a government or political topic. The broad scope and inclusion of non-governmental sites help when beginning research on topics like citizen participation or model congresses. Because of the mix of sites, however, a researcher needs to remember to consider the source of the information and evaluate it independently.
Subject: Finding Aids

CHAPTER 2
Agriculture

In existence for 141 years, the U.S. Department of Agriculture has long been a producer of agricultural statistics and information. Much of their information is now available on the Web. USDA Web sites dominate this chapter. Reflecting the Department's work, these sites cover topics as diverse as weather data, community development, foreign trade, and crop statistics.

Though not the only resource on government agricultural topics, the USDA Web site can be the best starting point for research and is this chapter's featured site.

Bookmarks & Favorites

Agriculture Research and Statistics
- AGRICOLA, http://www.nal.usda.gov/ag98/
- Agriculture Network Information Center, http://www.agnic.org
- National Agricultural Statistics Service, http://www.nass.usda.gov
- USDA Economics and Statistics System, http://usda.mannlib.cornell.edu

Major Agencies
- Agriculture Department, http://www.usda.gov

Featured Site

25. U.S. Department of Agriculture
`http://www.usda.gov/`
Sponsor: Agriculture Department (USDA)
Description: The main USDA Web site provides access to a wealth of governmental agricultural information. The home page offers Events, recent National News Releases, and Top Stories. Listed under Issues are additional primary topics from various sections of the site. From the home page, users may link to other main sections of the Web site, including a Welcome page; the Newsroom; What's New; Agencies, Services, and Programs; USDA Offices, a list of Subjects covered by the USDA Web site; and a Search/Help page (a Search box is provided on the Home page, as well).

The Agencies page is designed in a hierarchical fashion with links to departmental and agency Web sites. In addition, this page points to USDA support programs and affiliates, providing a basic yet easy navigation structure for finding component agencies within the Department of Agriculture. The Newsroom serves as a portal for news from USDA agencies, and provides access to information in a variety of media. The Subject and Search pages provide extensive coverage of the entire site for users who are looking for specific data.

This is a well organized site with easy access to more detailed agricultural information. It is an excellent starting point for finding a variety of agricultural information.
Subject: Agriculture
Publications: *Agriculture Fact Book*, A 1.38/2:
Broadcasters Letter, A 21.34:
Census of Agriculture, State and County Data, Geographic Area Series, Volume 1 (Alabama), A 92.53/1:
Educational and Training Opportunities in Sustainable Agriculture, A 17.32:
List of Materials Acceptable for Use on System of RUS Electrification Borrowers, A 68.6/2:
List of Materials Acceptable for Use on Telecommunications Systems of RUS Borrowers, A 68.6/5:
Molasses Market News, A 88.23:
The Natural Inquirer, A Research and Science Journal, A 13.155:
The People's Department—A Poster About USDA, A 1.32:
USDA News, A 1.57:

The agricultural resources in this chapter are divided into four sections, spanning the entry numbers indicated here:

General	*26–44*
Business Sources	*45–53*
Extension Service	*54–58*
Research	*59–67*

General

26. AGRICOLA
http://www.nalusda.gov/ag98/
Sponsor: Agriculture Department (USDA) — National Agricultural Library (NAL)
Description: AGRICOLA is a large bibliographic database covering literature from all aspects of agriculture and related fields. The database indexes journal articles, short reports, book chapters, and other materials. A facility to search the book collection of the National Agricultural Library is also included. Cited materials are not available online in full text through AGRICOLA. The Web site describes document delivery options; most remote users will need to find the materials through their local libraries.

Due to its quality, size, scope, and historical coverage, AGRICOLA is a key resource for conducting literature searches on any topic related to agriculture.
Subjects: Agriculture Information; Databases

27. Agricultural Outlook Archives
http://usda.mannlib.cornell.edu/reports/erssor/economics/ao-bb/
Sponsor: Cornell University. Mann Library
Description: *Agricultural Outlook*, which was a primary source for USDA's farm and food price forecasts, ceased publication in December 2002. This site has archival issues of the magazine going back to 1995. It also explains and links to the USDA Economic Research Service publications that take over from *Agricultural Outlook*. The magazine issues have data on individual commodities, the general economy, U.S. farm trade, farm income, production expenses, input use, prices received and paid, per capita food consumption, and more.
Subjects: Agricultural Economics; Agriculture — Statistics
Publication: *Agricultural Outlook*, A 93.10/2:

28. Agriculture Network Information Center
http://www.agnic.org/
Sponsor: Agriculture Department (USDA) — National Agricultural Library (NAL)
Description: The Agriculture Network Information Center "(AgNIC) is a guide to quality agricultural information on the Internet as selected by the National Agricultural Library, Land-Grant Universities, and other institutions" (from the Web site). AgNIC is a distributed network that provides access to agriculture-related information, subject area experts, and other resources. From the home page, users may perform simple or advanced searches of the information database, or browse its contents by subject. A Calendar of Events lists conferences, meetings, and seminars in various agricultural fields. The Ask a Question link allows users to pursue reference questions through institutions that specialize in listed topics.
Subject: Agriculture Information

29. Amber Waves
http://www.ers.usda.gov/Amberwaves/
Sponsor: Agriculture Department (USDA) — Economic Research Service (ERS)
Description: The USDA magazine *Amber Waves* began publication in February 2003, replacing *Agricultural Outlook*, *FoodReview*, and *Rural America*. The new magazine includes feature articles covering information and economic analysis about food, farms, natural resources, and rural community issues. An Indicators section provides data and charts on crop and livestock cash receipts, farm household income, agricultural imports and exports, food spending, and other topics. Links at the bottom of the Indicators section lead to further information and to the statistical tables formerly provided by *Agricultural Outlook* magazine. *Amber Waves* is published five times

a year. A print version is available by subscription or can be downloaded in PDF format from the site. The Web version is to be updated more frequently.
Subject: Agricultural Economics

30. Animal and Plant Health Inspection Service
http://www.aphis.usda.gov/
Sponsor: Agriculture Department (USDA) — Animal and Plant Health Inspection Service (APHIS)
Description: The APHIS Web site menu features sections on Programs, Hot Issues, and News. Programs cover the scope of the APHIS role in enforcing regulations governing the import and export of plants and animals and certain agricultural products. The Hot Issues warn against items such as Anthrax, Citrus Canker, BSE ("mad cow disease"), and West Nile Virus. The News section presents press releases, publications, and videos. An APHIS Services menu at the top of each Web page points directly to information on such tasks as finding traveler's information, searching regulations, downloading permit forms, and reporting a pest or disease.

Certain functions of APHIS are being transferred from USDA to the new Department of Homeland Security. At present, this is a useful site for anyone with questions about plant and animal diseases and transporting plant and animal products into and out of the country.
Subjects: Agriculture — Regulations; Animals — Regulations; Imports — Regulations; Plants — Regulations
Publications: *Animal Welfare Report Fiscal Year*, A 101.22/2:
APHIS Fact Sheets, A 101.31:
APHIS Technical Reports, A 101.30:

31. Carl Hayden Bee Research Center
http://gears.tucson.ars.ag.gov/
Sponsor: Agriculture Department (USDA) — Agricultural Research Service (ARS)
Description: This site focuses on the honey bee, with information and software for beekeepers and for teachers and students. Sections include Atlas of a Honey Bee, Online Pollination Handbook, Africanized Honey Bees, and Bee Diversity. A Links section has a selection of links to related Internet sites, including those of the USDA.
Subjects: Beekeeping; Entomology

32. Forest Service
http://www.fs.fed.us/
Description: The USFS Web resources are extensive. Sections include Employment, Fire and Aviation, Maps and Brochures, Passes and Permits, Recreational Activities, Research and Development, and State and Private Forestry. The Publications section includes the full text of USFS directives, manuals, and handbooks, and other publications.

The site is well organized with a substantial amount of information about the agency, its component forests, and publications.
Subject: Forestry
Publications: *Annual Report (Southern Research Station)*, A 13.150/1:
Fire Management Today (formerly Fire Management Notes), A 13.32:
Forest Health Highlights, A 13.154:
Forest Insect and Disease Conditions in the United States, A 13.52/2:
Forest Insect and Disease Conditions, Intermountain Region, A 13.52/12:
Forest Insect And Disease Leaflets (numbered), A 13.52:
Forest Products Laboratory: Lists Of Publications, A 13.27/7:
Grazing Statistical Survey, A 13.83:
Gypsy Moth News, A 13.141:
International Programs Newsletter, A 13.153:
Learning Link, A 13.131:
Recent Publications of the Pacific Northwest Research Station, A 13.66/14:
RMRScience, A 13.151/6:
Rocky Mountain Research Station: New Publications, A 13.151/2-2:
Science Findings, A 13.66/19:
Southern Research Station Employee Directory, A 13.150/4:
U.S. Forests Facts and Historical Trends, A 13.2:F 76/

33. Invasive Species: The Nation's Invasive Species Information System

http://www.invasivespecies.gov/

Sponsor: Agriculture Department (USDA) — National Agricultural Library (NAL)
Description: This is a gateway site for federal information on invasive (non-native and harmful) species including plants, animals, and microbes. Resources include profiles of common invasive species, educational resources, and information on the economic impact of invasive species. There are links to lists of invasives by state, to laws and regulations, and to a variety of plant databases. The site also has information from and about the National Invasive Species Council, an inter-Departmental group.
Subjects: Animals; Fish; Invasive Plant Species
Publication: *Meeting the Invasive Species Challenge: Management Plan* , I 1.2:

34. Joint Agricultural Weather Facility (JAWF)

http://www.usda.gov/oce/waob/jawf/

Sponsors: Commerce Department — National Oceanic and Atmospheric Administration (NOAA); Agriculture Department (USDA) — World Agricultural Outlook Board
Description: The JAWF collects global weather and agricultural information to determine the impact of growing season weather conditions on international crops and livestock production prospects. The JAWF site features National Weather, International Weather, Drought Monitor, Monthly Reports, Crop Calendars, Climate Info, Special Projects, and Agricultural Weather Links. The *Weekly Weather and Crop Bulletin* is posted to this site each Wednesday.
Subjects: Agriculture — International; Weather
Publication: *Weekly Weather and Crop Bulletin*, C 55.209:

35. National Center for Agricultural Law

http://nationalaglawcenter.org/

Sponsor: University of Arkansas. School of Law
Description: The National Center for Agricultural Law is funded by the USDA and operated by the University of Arkansas School of Law. The Web site has summaries of legal decisions and federal regulatory news related to agriculture. It also carries PDF copies of USDA Judicial Officer decisions. A Web Library section features selected links to agricultural law information on the Internet.
Subject: Agriculture — Laws

36. National Organic Program

http://www.ams.usda.gov/nop/

Sponsor: Agriculture Department (USDA) — Agricultural Marketing Service (AMS)
Description: This site presents USDA regulations and policies concerning growing, labeling, and marketing farm produce as "organic." A Questions and Answers section addresses the definition of "organic," production requirements, certification, and the national list of allowed and prohibited substances.

This informative site should be of practical benefit to both producers and consumers of organic food.
Subject: Food — Regulations

37. National Plant Data Center

http://npdc.usda.gov/npdc/index.html

Sponsor: Agriculture Department (USDA) — Natural Resources Conservation Service (NRCS)
Description: NPDC focuses resources on the acquisition, development, integration, quality control, dissemination and access of plant information. Their site features a fully-searchable Plants Database and a Plants Photo Gallery. The site also presents information about the center, links to additional resources, and the NPDC activities.
Subject: Plants

38. Natural Resources Conservation Service

http://www.nrcs.usda.gov/

Sponsor: Agriculture Department (USDA) — Natural Resources Conservation Service (NRCS)

Description: The USDA's Natural Resources Conservation Service provides expertise in conserving soil, water, and other natural resources. The site's Technical Resources section points to information, models, and data on such topics as air quality, nutrient management, soils, streams, and wildlife biology. Other sections of the site include information on agritourism, conservation buffers, erosion protection, forestry, animal waste management, and range and pasture ecology. Audience-specific pages are available for communities, farmers and ranchers, homeowners, policy makers, and students and teachers.

This site leads to far more information on resource conservation programs and practices than is readily apparent from the home page. The sections on programs, technical resources, and audience-specific pages are particularly information-rich.

Subjects: Conservation (Natural Resources); Environmental Protection

Publications: *Alaska Basin Outlook Reports*, A 57.46/13:
Arizona Basin Outlook Report, A 57.46:
Basin Outlook Reports (Colorado), A 57.46/19:
Basin Outlook Reports (New Mexico), A 57.46/18:
Basin Outlook Reports (Washington), A 57.46/7:
Basin Outlook Reports (Wyoming), A 57.46/10:
Fish & Wildlife Habitat Management Leaflets, A 57.56/2:
Idaho Basin Outlook Report, A 57.46/11:
National Engineering Handbook (NEH) 20, A 57.6/2:EN 3/
National Handbook of Conservation Practices, A 57.6/2:C 76

39. Pesticide Impact Assessment Program
http://ipm.ncsu.edu/

Sponsors: North Carolina State University (NCSU); Agriculture Department (USDA) — Pest Management Policy Office

Description: This USDA site serves as a gateway to the agency's pest management programs and resources and to related programs of other government agencies, including the EPA. Features of the site include Crop Profiles (with an emphasis on pest management needs), Pest Management Strategic Plans (transition strategies), and Pesticide Databases. Also available are lists of PIAP Programs and Personnel, a calendar of events, and publications.

Subject: Pesticides

40. Plants National Database
http://plants.usda.gov/

Sponsor: Agriculture Department (USDA) — Natural Resources Conservation Service (NRCS)

Description: The Plants National Database features standardized information about plants. The focus is on vascular plants, mosses, liverworts, hornworts, and lichens of the U.S. and its territories. It includes names, checklists, automated tools, identification information, species abstracts, distributional data, crop information, plant symbols, plant growth data, plant materials information, plant links, and references. In addition, the database can generate reports such as lists of endangered and threatened plants, invasive and noxious plants, and state-specific lists of plants. This database is an excellent source for verifying plant names and other plant information.

Subjects: Plants; Databases

41. Small Farms @ USDA
http://www.usda.gov/oce/smallfarm/sfhome.htm

Sponsor: Agriculture Department (USDA)

Description: This gateway provides information on resources, benefits, and services offered by USDA for small farms. In addition to general information of interest to small farms, a database of recommendations and action plans proposed by the National Commission on Small Farms is presented.

Subject: Farms and Farming

42. U.S. State Fact Sheets
http://www.ers.usda.gov/StateFacts/

Sponsor: Agriculture Department (USDA) — Economic Research Service (ERS)

Description: The fact sheets contain basic demographic and farm statistics for each state. The Web version makes the fact sheets accessible by state name and through an image map of the U.S. The same statistics are also available for the U.S. as a whole. They include population, employment, income, farm characteristics, and farm financial indicators.

This is a useful service for getting basic demographic and agricultural information at the state level.

Subject: Farms and Farming — Statistics

43. USDA Office of Community Development
http://www.rurdev.usda.gov/ocd/
Sponsor: Agriculture Department (USDA) — Rural Development
Description: The Office of Community Development is a part of the U.S. Department of Agriculture's Rural Development program. OCD operates special community development initiatives and provides technical support to USDA Rural Development's community development staff in offices throughout the United States. The site provides detailed information on the Rural Empowerment Zone and Enterprise Community Program and the Rural Economic Area Partnership program.

Aside from the limited information on the Office itself, this site will primarily be of use for the sections on the Office's specific programs.

Subject: Rural Development

44. USDA Regional Pest Management Centers
http://www.pmcenters.org/
Sponsor: Agriculture Department (USDA) — Cooperative State Research, Education, and Extension Service (CSREES)
Description: The USDA has regional pest management centers for the North Central, Northeastern, Western, and Southern regions. This Web site pulls together national resources on pest management strategies and links to sites for the four regional centers. National information includes a database of experts, crop-specific pest management profiles, and a directory of funding sources related to pest management.

Subject: Pest Management

Business Sources

45. Agricultural Marketing Service
http://www.ams.usda.gov/
Sponsor: Agriculture Department (USDA) — Agricultural Marketing Service (AMS)
Description: The Agricultural Marketing Service Web site provides information on the agency's programs and current market news. Features include programs on Cotton, Dairy, Poultry, Fruit and Vegetable, Livestock and Seed, Science and Technology, Tobacco, Transportation and Marketing, and Civil Rights (ensuring agency compliance with federal laws). Other sections of the site provide information about AMS, current Hot Topics, What's New, and Opportunities. Additional resources are provided under the following headings: Direct Marketing, Farmers Markets, Food Purchases, Market News, and Federal Rulemaking. A search function allows for keyword searching of the entire site or of sections. The Newsroom section presents news releases, video features, and publications. From this page, users may search the news and information section for specific documents. The Market News section reports up-to-the minute information on commodity prices, condition, volume, and quality.

This excellent site for agricultural market statistics is current, designed well, and easy to navigate. It is a valuable resource for consumers and experts alike.

Subjects: Agricultural Commodities — Statistics; Agricultural Trade; Food Safety
Publications: *Daily Spot Cotton Quotations*, A 88.11/4:
Dairy Market Statistics, Annual Summary, A 88.14/13:
Dairy Plants Surveyed and Approved for USDA Grading Service, A 88.14/12:
Federal Milk Order Statistics for..., A 88.14/11:
Food Purchase Reports & Invitations to Bid, A 88.67:

Grain Transportation Prospects , A 88.68/2:
Grain Transportation Report, A 88.68:
Items of Interest in Seed Control, A 88.63:
Market News Reports, A 88.66:
Pesticide Data Program Annual Summary, A 88.60:
PlantBook (Voluntary Poultry and Egg Grading and Certification Services Directory), A 88.15/23:
Standards for (Fruits, Vegetables, etc.) (irregular), A 88.6/2:
United States Quality of Cotton Classed Under Smith Doxey Act, A 88.11/23:
Weekly Cotton Market Review, A 88.11/2:

46. Farm Credit Administration

http://www.fca.gov/
Sponsor: Farm Credit Administration (FCA)
Description: The FCA is an independent agency responsible for enforcement and regulation of the Farm Credit System, which includes the Federal Agricultural Mortgage Corporation (Farmer Mac). The FCA Web site features detailed information about the agency, including Procurement Opportunities and Career Opportunities. Other sections cover News and Events; Publications; FCA Handbook, which contains FCA regulations and statutes, board policies, pending regulations, and ethics regulations; and information on other institutions in the Farm Credit System.
Subjects: Farm Loan Programs; Finance — Regulations
Publications: *Annual Report*, FCA 1.1:
Annual Report on the Financial Condition and Performance of the Farm Credit Administration, FCA 1.1/2:
FCA Accountability Reports, FCA 1.1/4:
FCA Annual Performance Plan, FCA 1.1/3:
FCA Newsline, FCA 1.26:
FCA Quarterly Report, FCA 1.23/2-2:
FCA Strategic Plan, FCA 1.1/5:
Financial Performance Indicators, FCA 1.28:

47. Farm Service Agency Online

http://www.fsa.usda.gov/pas/default.asp
Sponsor: Agriculture Department (USDA) — Farm Service Agency (FSA)
Description: The FSA assists farmers in income stabilization, resource conservation, credit services, and disaster recovery. The home page of this Web site presents important program dates and quick links to information of interest to citizens and industry. A side bar on the home page provides access to much of the other information on the site. The Services/Programs section includes sections on Farm Loans, Price Supports, Conservation, Disaster Assistance, and Commodities. Other menu items are FSA office directories and links to information resources such as fact sheets, online forms, and agency communications to Congress.

This site provides much information to its constituents. The site's detailed subsections pull together resources to address many concerns of the American farmer.
Subjects: Agricultural Commodities; Conservation (Natural Resources); Farm Loan Programs
Publications: *FSA Commodity Fact Sheets*, A 112.15:
FSA Farm Loan Program Forms, A 112.19:
U.S. Warehouse Act Licensed Warehouses, A 112.22:

48. FAS Online

http://ffas.usda.gov/
Sponsor: Agriculture Department (USDA) — Foreign Agricultural Service (FAS)
Description: The Foreign Agricultural Service represents U.S. interests in foreign markets. FAS Online features information about the Service and on agricultural exporting. The home page presents new items online and articles from the current issue of *AgExporter*. Main sections of the site include information on: Countries; Commodities; Trade Policy; Export Programs; Exporter Assistance; Buying U.S. Products; Food Aid; Import Programs; and Development and Training. The About FAS section provides background information, strategic plans, FAS divisions, student work programs, and more. Publications, reports, fact sheets, congressional testimony, *Federal Register* notices, trade circulars, and news releases are available through the News and Information section.

Additionally, users may search for publications under the FAS Directory section, which also provides a database of subject experts, links to home pages of FAS divisions, and a directory of field offices.

FAS Online contains all the elements of an excellent Web resource, including an advanced search feature, a logical design, authority data, and useful information.

Subject: Agricultural Trade
Publications: *AgExporter*, A 67.7/3:
Agricultural Export Assistance Update Quarterly Report, A 67.46:
Monthly Summary of Export Credit Guarantee Program Activity, A 67.47:
Trade Leads, A 67.40/2:
Tropical Products: World Markets and Trade, A 67.18:FTROP
U.S. Export Sales, A 67.40:
U.S. Planting Seed Trade, A 67.18/3:
World Agricultural Production, A 67.18:WAP
World Horticultural Trade and U.S. Export Opportunities, A 67.18:FHORT
World Markets and Trade, A 67.18:FG Grain:
World Markets and Trade, A 67.18:FL&P Livestock:
World Markets and Trade, A 67.18:FOP Oilseeds:
World Markets and Trade, A 67.18:FC Cotton:
World Markets and Trade, A 67.18:FD Dairy:
World Markets and Trade, A 67.18:FS Sugar:
World Markets and Trade, A 67.18:FT Tobacco:

49. Grain Inspection, Packers, and Stockyards Administration (GIPSA)

http://www.usda.gov/gipsa/
Sponsor: Agriculture Department (USDA) — Grain Inspection, Packers, and Stockyards Administration (GIPSA)
Description: GIPSA facilitates the marketing of grains, livestock, poultry, and meat for the overall benefit of consumers and American agriculture. The GIPSA home page features services provided by the Federal Grain Inspection Service and information on Packers and Stockyards Programs. The About Us section provides the agency's organizational chart and directories, a budget summary, and an interactive map to local service providers. Links to related acts are under the section entitled Laws and Regulations. The Rulemaking section provides selections from the *Federal Register* back to 1997. Additional resources are located under the Newsroom and Publications sections. A site index allows users to browse through the wealth of information available from this useful site.

This site provides easy access to the full text of relevant regulations and documents.
Subjects: Grains — Regulations; Livestock — Regulations
Publications: *Annual Report of the Grain Inspection, Packers and Stockyards Administration*, A 113.1:
Official United States Standards for Beans, A 113.10/3:
Official United States Standards for Grain, A 113.10:
Official United States Standards for Rice, A 113.10/2:
Official United States Standards for Whole Dry Peas, Split Peas and Lentils, A 113.10/4:

50. Risk Management Agency

http://www.act.fcic.usda.gov/
Sponsor: Agriculture Department (USDA) — Federal Crop Insurance Corporation
Description: The Risk Management Agency at the Federal Crop Insurance Corporation features access to crop insurance and other risk management related information. The home page presents current news, a Weather Watch feature, and Other Crop Weather Links. Its sections include Crop Policies, Pilot Programs, Participation Data, Regulations, Tools and Calculators, Agent Locator, Producer Training, Crop Weather, Publications, and About RMA. Find Hot Topics and recently-released publications under the News section. A FAQ section provides definitions and help on using the site.
Subjects: Crop Insurance; Disaster Assistance
Publications: *Crop Insurance Manager's Bulletins*, A 112.20:
Crop Insurance Research and Development Bulletins, A 112.17:

51. Rural Utilities Service
http://www.usda.gov/rus/
Sponsor: Agriculture Department (USDA) — Rural Utilities Service (RUS)
Description: The Rural Utilities Service supports the expansion and maintenance of electric, telecommunications, water and waste disposal utilities in rural areas. Information on the RUS Web site is divided into sections covering the Electric Program, Water and Environmental Program, and Telecommunications. Each major section includes relevant regulations, publications, and contacts.
Subjects: Rural Development; Rural Utilities

52. Small and Disadvantaged Business Utilization
http://www.usda.gov/da/smallbus/
Sponsor: Agriculture Department (USDA) — Small and Disadvantaged Business Utilization Office
Description: With the intent of assisting small businesses in dealing with the Department of Agriculture's programs and contracting process, OSDBU Online features sections such as Contract Opportunities, Business Support Programs, Marketing Information, and Useful links.

Although the design of the site is lacking, this site provides useful information for "small, small disadvantaged, and small women-owned businesses."
Subjects: Government Procurement; Small Business

53. USDA Procurement
http://www.usda.gov/procurement/
Sponsor: Agriculture Department (USDA)
Description: This procurement site from the USDA's Departmental Administration features information on Business Opportunities, Acquisition Toolkit, Related Links, Integrated Acquisition System, Policy and Regulations, Purchase and Fleet Card, and What's New. Procurement and Property Information outlines the procurement process for individuals new to the USDA.
Subject: Government Procurement

Extension Service

54. Cooperative State Research, Education, and Extension Service
http://www.reeusda.gov/
Sponsor: Agriculture Department (USDA) — Cooperative State Research, Education, and Extension Service (CSREES)
Description: The site features information about the mission, partners, and programs of the Cooperative State Research, Education, and Extension Service (CSREES). Major sections include Program Information, State Partners, Legislation/Budget, Human Resources, Funding Opportunities, Award Administration, News and Information, and Job Opportunities. The News and Information section links to recent news releases and some newsletters.

This site is an excellent gateway for much research and education information about many agricultural subjects. The Program Information section is useful for finding subject-specific information.
Subjects: Agricultural Education — Grants; Agricultural Research — Grants; Extension Services
Publications: *CSREES — Update*, A 94.20:
National Research Initiative Competitive Grants Program, A 94.24:
Small Farm Digest, A 94.23:

55. Extension Disaster Education Network (EDEN)
http://www.agctr.lsu.edu/eden/
Sponsor: Agriculture Department (USDA) — Cooperative State Research, Education, and Extension Service (CSREES)
Description: "The Extension Disaster Education Network (EDEN) links members from across the U.S. and various disciplines—so they can use and share resources to reduce the impact of disasters" (from the Web site). This Web site provides access to resources on disaster preparedness, recovery, and mitigation. It is aimed at Extension agents and educators. Users can search the EDEN Resource

Database, view state disaster information, read working documents, and browse disaster-related links. A directory of EDEN delegates is also available.
Subjects: Disasters and Emergencies; Extension Services

56. Journal of Extension
http://www.joe.org/
Sponsor: Agriculture Department (USDA) — Cooperative State Research, Education, and Extension Service (CSREES)
Description: Journal of Extension (JOE), a peer-reviewed journal for Extension Service personnel, is published only in electronic format. The print version ceased publication in 1994. This online version goes back to 1979. Issues published in 1984 forward are in HTML; those prior are in PDF format.
Subject: Extension Services
Publication: *Journal of Extension*

57. Rural Information Center
http://www.nal.usda.gov/ric/
Sponsor: Agriculture Department (USDA) — National Agricultural Library (NAL)
Description: The Rural Information Center (RIC) is a specialized information and referral service within the National Agricultural Library. It is particularly helpful in areas related to rural economic development and can be of assistance to rural governments, grant-seekers, small farms, and nonprofit organizations.The RIC Web site offers a form for submitting a reference request. It also includes answers to frequently asked questions, which may obviate use of the form. The Rural Resources section links to numerous online sources of information, organized by topic. The Funding Resources section points to general resources but also features pages on seeking funding relating to such specific needs as rural fire departments, rural housing, and rural child care centers.

The Rural Information Center site is an excellent starting point for those researching rural development topics for grant-writing or other purposes.
Subject: Rural Development — Research
Publication: *Rural Information Center Publication Series*, A 17.29:

58. State Partners of the Cooperative State Research, Education, and Extension Service
http://www.reeusda.gov/1700/statepartners/usa.htm
Sponsor: Agriculture Department (USDA) — Cooperative State Research, Education, and Extension Service (CSREES)
Description: This site offers a directory of land-grant universities that are state partners of the Cooperative State Research, Education, and Extension Service. Links are provided to the Web sites for schools of forestry, higher education, home economics, veterinary science, state extension services, and state experiment stations. Also available are the CSREES Online Directory of Professional Workers in Agriculture and the State Extension Service Directors and Administrators Directory. Another link brings users to the *Partners* video magazine, which highlights the programs and accomplishments of the agricultural research, education, and extension systems nationwide.
Subject: Extension Services

Research

59. Agricultural Research Service
http://www.ars.usda.gov/
Sponsor: Agriculture Department (USDA) — Agricultural Research Service (ARS)
Description: The Agricultural Research Service leads USDA's research projects in agriculture, nutrition, technology, and the environment. The site features News and Information, Offices and Programs, National Research Programs (under the section entitled Research Programs), Other Research (links to related endeavors), and a Search function (which also contains the Search ARS on the Web feature and a Personnel Directory). The ARS Spotlight section on the home page highlights new initiatives and hot topics. The bulk of the information on the ARS site is located under

the Research heading. Here, national programs are organized under three major areas: Animal Production, Product Value and Safety; Natural Resources and Sustainable Agricultural Systems; and Crop Production, Product Value and Safety. Under the News and Information heading is actually a full sub-site, containing an archive of News Releases, a Publication Locator, the periodical *Agricultural Research*, a Photo Gallery, a children's section entitled Sci4Kids, and a dedicated search engine.

The disjointed design and structure of this site makes finding information difficult. However, users who are able to navigate the site successfully are rewarded with valuable information resources applicable to everyone from children to novices to expert researchers.

Subject: Agricultural Research

Publications: *Agricultural Research*, A 77.12:
Food & Nutrition Research Briefs (irregular), A 77.518:
Healthy Animals (newsletter)
Methyl Bromide Alternatives, A 77.517:
Quarterly Report of Selected Research Projects, A 77.32/2:

60. Beltsville Agricultural Research Center (BARC)

http://www.barc.usda.gov/

Sponsor: Agriculture Department (USDA) — Agricultural Research Service (ARS)

Description: This site provides links to the institutes, centers, divisions, and laboratories at BARC. The main headings include the Animal & Natural Resources, the Beltsville Human Nutrition Research Center, the Plant Sciences Institute, and the National Arboretum. Each research section profiles the work of BARC laboratories. The site also offers an explanation of the agency's mission, an Internet Classroom, and a directory of personnel.

Subjects: Agricultural Research; Nutrition — Research; Veterinary Medicine — Research

61. Economic Research Service

http://www.ers.usda.gov/

Sponsor: Agriculture Department (USDA) — Economic Research Service (ERS)

Description: The Economic Research Service analyzes food and commodity markets and produces related economic and social indicators. Research areas include global competitiveness for agriculture, food safety, nutrition, the relationship between agriculture and the environment, and the quality of life in rural America. The Publications and Data sections include items in HTML and PDF, and point to ERS hosted publications as well as the collection of ERS publications at the USDA Economics and Statistics System site maintained by Cornell University's Mann Library. The Publications section of the ERS site has the agency's publications since 1996 online and searchable by title, topic, or date. An "ERS elsewhere" link leads to summaries of articles ERS staff have published in professional journals. The Data section describes and links to the agency's data products, available online as databases, spreadsheets, and Web files.

Subjects: Agricultural Economics; Agriculture — Statistics; Rural Development — Statistics

Publications: *Agricultural Income and Finance Situation and Outlook Report*, A 93.9/8:
Agricultural Outlook, A 93.10/2:
Agriculture Information Bulletin (AIB Series), A 1.75:
Aquaculture Outlook, A 93.55:
AREI Updates, A 93.47/3:
Food Consumption, Prices and Expenditures, A 1.34/4:
Food Review, A 93.16/3:
Fruit and Tree Nuts Outlook and Yearbook, A 93.12/3:
Products and Services from ERS-NASS, A 93.39:
Rice Outlook, A 93.11/3:
Rice Yearbook, A 93.11/4:
Rural Conditions and Trends, A 93.41/3:
U.S. Agricultural Trade Update, A 93.17/7-5:

62. GrainGenes

http://wheat.pw.usda.gov/

Sponsor: Agriculture Department (USDA) — Agricultural Research Service (ARS)

Description: GrainGenes, a database for small grains, is a compilation of molecular and phenotypic information on wheat, barley, oats, rye, and sugarcane. Access to the actual data is available by an alphabetical browse by category and name and also by a variety of keyword searches. Forms are available to researchers to add to the database data, bibliographic reference, and contact information. The home page lists Hot Topics, which are links to conferences, program announcements, and other news related to grain research.

The database contains both a substantial amount of genetic information and many links to other genome databases. The interactive and collaborative capabilities of the Internet are used to good advantage by allowing researchers to submit data for entry into the database as well as browse through data that is already included.

Subjects: Germplasms; Grains — Research; Plant Genetics

63. National Agricultural Statistics Service (NASS)

http://www.usda.gov/nass/

Sponsor: Agriculture Department (USDA) — National Agricultural Statistics Service (NASS)

Description: The NASS publishes a broad range of U.S. state and national statistics on crops, livestock, and farming. The agency's site is divided into two sections, for Statistical Information and Agency Information. The Agency Information section links to News and Coming Events, Customer Service, the NASS Kids site, and a list of Other Links. The Agency Information link leads to detailed information about NASS, including Directories and an Organizational Chart. The Statistical Information section contains the bulk of data on the site. In addition to the current day's reports, it includes sections on NASS publications, crop and livestock charts and maps, historical data, statistical research tools, and the Census of Agriculture. The site also features the Agriculture Statistics Database, also known as QuickStats, for querying by commodity, state, and year.

This site, in combination with the USDA Economics and Statistics System hosted by Cornell University, provides a substantial amount of agricultural and crop related statistical publications.

Subjects: Crop Production — Statistics; Farms and Farming — Statistics; Livestock — Statistics

Publications: *Agriculture Statistics*, A 1.47:

Alaska Farm Reporter, A 92.45:

Census of Agriculture, A 92.53:

Census of Agriculture (Vol. 2, Subject Series), A 92.54:

Census of Agriculture, State and County Data, Geographic Area Series, Volume 1 (Alaska), A 92.53/2:

Census of Agriculture, State and County Data, Geographic Area Series, Volume 1 (Arizona), A 92.53/3:

Census of Agriculture, State and County Data, Geographic Area Series, Volume 1 (Arkansas), A 92.53/4:

Census of Agriculture, State and County Data, Geographic Area Series, Volume 1 (California), A 92.53/5:

Census of Agriculture, State and County Data, Geographic Area Series, Volume 1 (Colorado), A 92.53/6:

Census of Agriculture, State and County Data, Geographic Area Series, Volume 1 (Connecticut), A 92.53/7:

Census of Agriculture, State and County Data, Geographic Area Series, Volume 1 (Delaware), A 92.53/8:

Census of Agriculture, State and County Data, Geographic Area Series, Volume 1 (Florida), A 92.53/9:

Census of Agriculture, State and County Data, Geographic Area Series, Volume 1 (Georgia), A 92.53/10:

Census of Agriculture, State and County Data, Geographic Area Series, Volume 1 (Hawaii), A 92.53/11:

Census of Agriculture, State and County Data, Geographic Area Series, Volume 1 (Idaho), A 92.53/12:

Census of Agriculture, State and County Data, Geographic Area Series, Volume 1 (Illinois), A 92.53/13:

Census of Agriculture, State and County Data, Geographic Area Series, Volume 1 (Indiana), A 92.53/14:

Census of Agriculture, State and County Data, Geographic Area Series, Volume 1 (Iowa), A 92.53/15:

Census of Agriculture, State and County Data, Geographic Area Series, Volume 1 (Kansas), A 92.53/16:

Census of Agriculture, State and County Data, Geographic Area Series, Volume 1 (Kentucky), A 92.53/17:

Census of Agriculture, State and County Data, Geographic Area Series, Volume 1 (Louisiana), A 92.53/18:

Census of Agriculture, State and County Data, Geographic Area Series, Volume 1 (Maine), A 92.53/19:

Census of Agriculture, State and County Data, Geographic Area Series, Volume 1 (Maryland), A 92.53/20:

Census of Agriculture, State and County Data, Geographic Area Series, Volume 1 (Massachusetts), A 92.53/21:

Census of Agriculture, State and County Data, Geographic Area Series, Volume 1 (Michigan), A 92.53/22:

Census of Agriculture, State and County Data, Geographic Area Series, Volume 1 (Minnesota), A 92.53/23:

Census of Agriculture, State and County Data, Geographic Area Series, Volume 1 (Mississippi), A 92.53/24:

Census of Agriculture, State and County Data, Geographic Area Series, Volume 1 (Missouri), A 92.53/25:
Census of Agriculture, State and County Data, Geographic Area Series, Volume 1 (Montana), A 92.53/26:
Census of Agriculture, State and County Data, Geographic Area Series, Volume 1 (Nebraska), A 92.53/27:
Census of Agriculture, State and County Data, Geographic Area Series, Volume 1 (Nevada), A 92.53/28:
Census of Agriculture, State and County Data, Geographic Area Series, Volume 1 (New Hampshire), A 92.53/29:
Census of Agriculture, State and County Data, Geographic Area Series, Volume 1 (New Jersey), A 92.53/30:
Census of Agriculture, State and County Data, Geographic Area Series, Volume 1 (New Mexico), A 92.53/31:
Census of Agriculture, State and County Data, Geographic Area Series, Volume 1 (New York), A 92.53/32:
Census of Agriculture, State and County Data, Geographic Area Series, Volume 1 (North Carolina), A 92.53/33:
Census of Agriculture, State and County Data, Geographic Area Series, Volume 1 (North Dakota), A 92.53/34:
Census of Agriculture, State and County Data, Geographic Area Series, Volume 1 (Ohio), A 92.53/35:
Census of Agriculture, State and County Data, Geographic Area Series, Volume 1 (Oklahoma), A 92.53/36:
Census of Agriculture, State and County Data, Geographic Area Series, Volume 1 (Oregon), A 92.53/37:
Census of Agriculture, State and County Data, Geographic Area Series, Volume 1 (Pennsylvania), A 92.53/38:
Census of Agriculture, State and County Data, Geographic Area Series, Volume 1 (Rhode Island), A 92.53/39:
Census of Agriculture, State and County Data, Geographic Area Series, Volume 1 (South Carolina), A 92.53/40:
Census of Agriculture, State and County Data, Geographic Area Series, Volume 1 (South Dakota), A 92.53/41:
Census of Agriculture, State and County Data, Geographic Area Series, Volume 1 (Tennessee), A 92.53/42:
Census of Agriculture, State and County Data, Geographic Area Series, Volume 1 (Texas), A 92.53/43:
Census of Agriculture, State and County Data, Geographic Area Series, Volume 1 (U.S. Summary), A 92.53/51:
Census of Agriculture, State and County Data, Geographic Area Series, Volume 1 (Utah), A 92.53/44:
Census of Agriculture, State and County Data, Geographic Area Series, Volume 1 (Vermont), A 92.53/45:
Census of Agriculture, State and County Data, Geographic Area Series, Volume 1 (Virginia), A 92.53/46:
Census of Agriculture, State and County Data, Geographic Area Series, Volume 1 (Washington), A 92.53/47:
Census of Agriculture, State and County Data, Geographic Area Series, Volume 1 (West Virginia), A 92.53/48:
Census of Agriculture, State and County Data, Geographic Area Series, Volume 1 (Wisconsin), A 92.53/49:
Census of Agriculture, State and County Data, Geographic Area Series, Volume 1 (Wyoming), A 92.53/50:
Cheddar Cheese Prices, A 92.10/8:

64. National Arboretum
http://www.usna.usda.gov/
Sponsor: Agriculture Department (USDA) — Agricultural Research Service (ARS)
Description: The Web site of the National Arboretum is more than an online brochure to the nation's official garden in Washington, DC. The site presents information about the Arboretum, such as exhibits, an interactive map of the grounds, calendars of blooms and of educational events, and internship opportunities. In addition, the site provides information of interest to the general gardening public, including horticultural facts, pest management, new hybrid plant releases, research activities, lists of state trees and flowers, and a plant hardiness map depicting the lowest expected temperatures in the United States.

This well-designed site is a great resource for serious nonprofessional gardeners and plant enthusiasts.
Subjects: Gardening and Landscaping; Trees
Publication: *Arboretum Plant Introduction and Winners (fact sheets)*, A 77.38/2:

65. National Genetic Resources Program
http://www.ars-grin.gov/
Sponsor: Agriculture Department (USDA) — Agricultural Research Service (ARS)
Description: The National Genetic Resources Program is responsible for acquiring, characterizing, preserving, documenting, and distributing scientific information on germplasms of all lifeforms important for food and agricultural production. The site includes a link to the Germplasm Resources Information Network, which has germplasm information about plants, animals, microbes, and invertebrates within the National Genetic Resources Program. Each of the germplasm databases varies in terms of scope and access points. The four databases available are the National Plant Germplasm System, National Animal Germplasm, National Microbial Germplasm, and National Invertebrate Genetic Resources Program. Also available is an explanation of the National Genetic Resources Advisory Council (NGRAC).

This site will be primarily of interest to those researching the germplasm of plants and animals.
Subjects: Germplasms; Plant Genetics

66. SOILS

http://soils.usda.gov/
Sponsor: Agriculture Department (USDA) — Natural Resources Conservation Service (NRCS)
Description: The SOILS Web site is part of the National Cooperative Soil Survey, a cooperative federal-state-academic project. The site has a broad range of scientific, applied, and educational information on soils. The centerpiece of the site is the Soil Survey, which has survey maps, soil characterization data, and soil climate data. Other major sections have soil images, information on soil use, classification standards, current research topics, and K-12 educational material on soils.
Subject: Soil Surveys
Publications: *Keys to Soil Taxonomy*, A 57.2:K 52/
NCSS (National Cooperative Soil Survey) Newsletter, A 57.78:
Soil Quality Information Sheets, A 57.77:

67. USDA Economics and Statistics System

http://usda.mannlib.cornell.edu/
Sponsor: Cornell University. Mann Library
Description: This site features a huge collection of nearly 300 reports and datasets from USDA economics agencies, including the Economic Research Service, the National Agricultural Statistics Service, and the World Agricultural Outlook Board. It includes current and historical data and reports on national food and agricultural developments and forecasts the effects of changing conditions and policies on domestic and international agriculture.

Users may search the entire database or a combination of its components for reports or datasets, or may browse by such topics as: Agricultural Baseline Projections; Farm Sector Economics; Field Crops; Food; Inputs, Technology, and Weather; International Agriculture; Land, Water, and Conservation; Livestock, Dairy, and Poultry; Rural Affairs; Specialty Agriculture; and Trade Issues. In addition, information may be browsed alphabetically by agency by following the links at the top of the home page.

Materials cover both U.S. and international agriculture topics. Most reports are PDF or ASCII text files. Most data sets are in spreadsheet format. These include time-series data that are updated yearly. The Calendar section organizes reports and datasets by expected release date. While some of these reports are also available in full from USDA Web sites, the value of this Cornell site is that it provides a standard interface, centralized access, and historical back files.
Subjects: Agriculture — Statistics; Agriculture Information
Publications: *Acreage*, A 92.39:
Agricultural Chemical Usage, A 92.50:
Agricultural Income and Finance Situation and Outlook Report, A 93.9/8:
Agricultural Outlook, A 93.10/2:
Agricultural Prices, A 92.16:
Agricultural Prices Annual, A 92.16/2:
Agricultural Statistics of the Former USSR Republics and the Baltic States, A 1.34:863
Agriculture Statistics of the European Community, A 1.34:770
Almond Production, A 92.11/2-5:
APEC (Asia-Pacific Economic Cooperation) Situation and Outlook Series, International Agriculture and Trade Reports, A 93.29/2-19:
Aquaculture Outlook, Supplement to Livestock, Dairy and Poultry Situation and Outlook, A 93.46/3-6:
Broiler Hatchery, A 92.46:
Capacity of Refrigerated Warehouses, A 92.21/3:
Catfish Processing, A 92.44:
Catfish Production, A 92.44/2-2:
Cattle, A 92.18/6-2:
Cattle and Sheep Outlook, A 93.46/3-5:
Cattle on Feed, A 92.18/6:
Cattle Predator Loss, A 92.2:C 29/2

Cherry Production, A 92.11/3:
Chickens and Eggs, A 92.9/16:
China International Agriculture and Trade Reports, Situation and Outlook Series, A 93.29/2-11:
Citrus Fruits, A 92.11/8:
Cold Storage, A 92.21:
Cold Storage Annual, A 92.21/2:
Cotton and Wool Outlook, A 93.24/2:
Cotton Ginnings, A 92.47:
Cranberries, A 92.11/6:
Crop Production, A 92.24:
Crop Production Annual, A 92.24/4:
Crop Production—Prospective Plantings, A 92.24:/2
Crop Values, A 92.24/3:
Dairy Outlook, A 93.46/3-3:
Dairy Products, A 92.10/7:
Dairy Products Annual Summary, A 92.10/5:
Egg Products, A 92.9/4:
Europe, Situation and Outlook Series, International Agriculture and Trade Reports, A 93.29/2-9:
Farm Labor, A 92.12:
Farm Production and Expenditures, A 92.9/15:
Farm Production Expenditures Summary, A 92.40:
Farms and Land in Farms, A 92.24/5:
Feed Situation and Outlook, A 93.11/2:
Floriculture Crops, A 92.32:
Food Review, A 93.16/3:
Food Spending in American Households, A 93.52:
Grain Stocks, A 92.15:
Hatchery Production, A 92.9/6:
Hazelnut Production, A 92.14/3:
Hog Outlook, A 93.46/3-4:
Hogs and Pigs, A 92.18/7:
Honey, A 92.28/2:
Hop Stocks, A 92.30:
International Agriculture and Trade, A 92.29/2-7:
Layers and Egg Production, A 92.9/13:
Livestock Slaughter, A 92.18/3:
Livestock Slaughter Annual, A 92.18:
Livestock, Dairy and Poultry Situation and Outlook, A 93.46/3:
Meat Animals, Production, Disposition and Income, A 92.17:
Milk Production, A 92.10:
Milk Production, Disposition and Income, A 92.10/2:
Mink, A 92.18/11:
Mushrooms, A 92.11/10-5:
NAFTA, Situation and Outlook Series, International Agriculture and Trade Reports, A 93.29/2-20:
NASS Reports, A 92.
Newly Independent States and the Baltics, International Agriculture and Trade Reports, Situation and Outlook Series, A 93.29/2-7:
Noncitrus Fruits and Nuts, A 92.11/2-2:
Oil Crops Situation and Outlook, A 93.23/2:
Outlook for U.S. Agricultural Trade, A 93.43:
Peanut Stocks and Processing, A 92.14:
Potato Stocks, A 92.11/11:
Potatoes, A 92.11/4:
Poultry Outlook, A 93.46/3-2:
Poultry Production and Value, A 92.9/3:
Poultry Slaughter, A 92.9/5:
Prospective Planting, A 92.24/2:

Rice Stocks, A 92.43:
Sheep, A 92.18/9:
Sheep and Goats, A 92.18/8:
Situation and Outlook Report, A 93. ERS
Sugar and Sweetener Situation and Outlook, A 93.31/3:
Tobacco Situation and Outlook, A 93.25:
Trout Production, A 92.44/3:
Turkey Hatchery, A 92.9/17-2:
Turkeys, A 92.9/17:
U.S. Agricultural Trade Update, A 93.17/7-5:
United States and Canadian Cattle, A 92.18/6-3:
Vegetables, A 92.11:
Vegetables and Specialties Situation and Outlook, A 93.12/2:
Vegetables Annual Summary, A 92.11/10-2:
Walnut Production, A 92.11/2-4:
Wheat Situation and Outlook, A 93.11:
Wheat Yearbook, A 93.11/2-3:
Winter Wheat and Rye Seedings, A 92.42:
Wool and Mohair, A 92.29/5:
World Agricultural Supply and Demand Estimates, A 93.29/3:

CHAPTER 3

Business and Economics

The federal government both regulates and supports U.S. businesses, and monitors and influences the national economy. These roles drive much of the business and economic information published by the government, which has long been a major authoritative source of industry and financial data. The popularity of the Web has enabled U.S. agencies to make this data and information directly accessible to a wide audience.

The Web sites described in this chapter offer financial statistics, market research, tax forms, contracting opportunities, and more. Despite this breadth of coverage, researchers will also want to check the Census and Statistics chapter of this book for the economic statistics sites listed there. The featured sites for this chapter, the Department of Commerce Web site and the Small Business Administration's U.S. Business Advisor, each have a topical arrangement that makes them both good starting points.

Bookmarks & Favorites

Business Research
- Patent and Trademark Office Electronic Business Center, http://www.uspto.gov/ebc/indexebc.html
- SEC Filings (EDGAR), http://www.sec.gov/edgar.shtml
- U.S. Government Export Portal, http://www.export.gov

Government Business
- Federal Business Opportunities, http://www.fedbizopps.gov
- FirstGov Shopping and Auctions, http://www.firstgov.gov/shopping/shopping.shtml
- Selling to the Government, http://www.gsa.gov/Portal/selling.jsp
- USA Jobs, http://www.usajobs.opm.gov/

Major Agencies
- Commerce Department, http://www.commerce.gov
- Federal Reserve Board, http://www.federalreserve.gov
- Labor Department, http://www.dol.gov
- Securities and Exchange Commission, http://www.sec.gov
- Small Business Administration, http://www.sba.gov
- Treasury Department, http://www.treasury.gov

(Also see Chapter 4, Census and Other Statistical Sources)

Featured Sites

68. Department of Commerce
`http://www.commerce.gov`
Sponsor: Commerce Department
Description: The Department of Commerce site is an excellent starting point for finding government information related to the world of business, as well as population totals, weather forecasts, and the time of day—since the Census Bureau, National Weather Service, and National Institute of Standards and Technology all fall under the Commerce Department. The Commerce site serves as a gateway to information provided by this Executive Branch department and its agencies. The components of the Commerce Department are linked under About Commerce—Organization. The site groups other information into four main categories. Free Trade has links to trade opportunities, compliance information, and export regulations. Innovation links to Commerce offices concerning

technology, telecommunications, and patents and trademarks. Economic Growth includes economic analysis, economic development, and grants and contracting opportunities. Under Stewardship, the sections are Coastal and Marine Resources and Weather.

The site provides easy access to the many other Department of Commerce Internet information sources, both by agency and by topic.

Subjects: Business Information; International Trade
Publications: *Budget and Annual Performance Plan of the U.S. Department of Commerce,* C 1.1/8: *STAT-USA,* C 1.91:

69. U.S. Business Advisor
http://www.business.gov/
Sponsor: Small Business Administration (SBA)
Description: The U.S. Business Advisor provides businesses with one-stop access to a wide variety of federal government information, services, and transactions for the business community. Major sections of the site include Business Development, Financial Assistance, Taxes, Laws and Regulations, International Trade, Workplace Issues, Buying and Selling, Agencies and Gateways, E-Services, and Info Desk.

E-Services offers information about online transaction capabilities including sections for Online Applications, Online Tutorials, Online Stores, Online Counseling, and E-Commerce Sites. The Info Desk includes access to Publications by Agency and a Publications Gateway. Agencies and Gateways functions as a finding aid for government Web sites of interest to the business community. It offers its selections under Agency Home Pages, Agency Business Pages, and One-Stop Gateways.

Very easy to navigate, this site is an excellent starting point and finding aid for business users searching for government information.

Subjects: Business Information; Finding Aids

The business and economic resources in this chapter are divided into three sections, spanning the entry numbers indicated here:

General	70–94
Employment	95–111
Finance	112–140
Government Business	141–172
International Commerce, Exporting & Importing	173–198

General

70. 1040.com: Tax Information for Everyone
http://www.1040.com/
Sponsor: Drake Software, Inc.
Description: While not an official source, this commercial site provides IRS forms and publications. All forms are available in PDF format, some back to the 1992 tax year. In addition to federal information, this site provides tax information at the state level, including addresses of state departments of revenue and links to state tax Web sites. General information is also provided for tax payers, including a newsroom covering tax-related issues and tax-related links.

This site is a nice backup to the IRS site, and it is a useful finding aid for Internet-accessible state tax forms.

Subject: Tax Forms
Publication: *Tax Forms,* T 22.2/12:

71. Alcohol and Tobacco Tax and Trade Bureau
http://www.ttb.gov/
Sponsor: Treasury Department — Alcohol and Tobacco Tax and Trade Bureau (TTB)
Description: The Alcohol and Tobacco Tax and Trade Bureau (TTB) was created by the Homeland Security Act of 2002, which moved the law enforcement functions of the Bureau of Alcohol, Tobacco, and Firearms (ATF) to the Justice Department and established TTB to manage the ATF functions that remain at Treasury.

TTB administers and enforces the federal laws and tax code provisions related to the production and taxation of alcohol and tobacco products. TTB also collects all excise tax on the manufacture of firearms and ammunition. The current TTB site is under construction but includes news, organizational information, services for the regulated industries, and legal and regulatory information. A Frequently Asked Questions section addresses such queries as "what must I do if I want to start a business that imports tobacco?" and "is it legal to buy home distilling equipment?"
Subjects: Taxation; Tobacco — Regulations

72. Baldrige National Quality Program
http://www.quality.nist.gov/
Sponsor: Commerce Department — Technology Administration (TA) — National Institute of Standards and Technology (NIST)
Description: The Malcolm Baldrige National Quality Award, sponsored by the Department of Commerce, is the centerpiece of the Baldrige National Quality Program (BNQP). This award recognizes performance excellence and focuses on an organization's overall performance management system. It does not, however, certify product or service quality. The award is presented for five categories: manufacturing, service, small business, education and health care. The Web site presents detailed information about the award, the awards process, performance criteria, past winners, and the Foundation for the Malcolm Baldrige National Quality Award. The site also has information about the Quest for Excellence, the official conference of the Baldrige Award.
Subject: Business Management — Awards and Honors

73. Bureau of Engraving and Printing
http://www.bep.treas.gov/
Sponsor: Treasury Department — Bureau of Engraving and Printing
Description: The Bureau of Engraving and Printing Web site features information about the Bureau, Locations and Tours, Procurement, the BEP Kids' Page, and the BEP Store with collectible products and souvenirs. Other sections cover the redesigned U.S. paper currency, counterfeit deterrence, money history and trivia, what to do with damaged currency, and information for collectors.
This site is particularly strong in its education and outreach efforts.
Subject: Money

74. Bureau of the Public Debt
http://www.publicdebt.treas.gov/
Sponsor: Treasury Department — Bureau of the Public Debt
Description: The Bureau of the Public Debt borrow the money needed to operate the federal government and to account for the resulting debt; they sell Treasury bills, notes, and bonds and U.S. Savings Bonds. This Web site features information on the U.S. federal debt, as well as on investments in government bonds. Some of the available categories include: The Public Debt; Savings Bonds; T-Bills, Notes, Bonds; Government Securities Market Regulations; and SLGS Securities. The Public Debt page includes a daily debt figure, a monthly statement on the debt, and historical debt figures. The redemption values for savings bonds are available on the Savings Bonds page. The site also offers a savings bond calculator, a savings bond wizard (which helps manage savings bond inventory), and a link to the TreasuryDirect electronic services, where customers can purchase treasury securities online.
Subjects: National Debt; Treasury Bills; Treasury Bonds; Treasury Notes
Publications: *Monthly Statement of the Public Debt of the United States,* T 63.215:
Tables of Redemption Values for $25 Series Bonds, T 63.209/5:
Tables of Redemption Values for $50 Series EE and Series E Savings Bonds, T 63.209/5-2:
Tables of Redemption Values for U.S. Savings Bonds, Series E, T 63.209/6:
Tables of Redemption Values for U.S. Savings Notes, T 63.210:
Tables of Redemption Values for United States Savings Bonds, Series EE, T 63.209/7:
The Bond Teller, T 66.24/2:
U.S. Savings Bond Comprehensive Savings Bond Value Tables, T 63.210/3:

75. Business and International Trade Online Bookstore
http://tradecenter.ntis.gov/
Description: This online NTIS bookstore site provides access to trade and business publications from the government and selected nonprofit organizations. Users may search the entire bookstore collection, or search by specific commercial, government, or non-profit publishers. Searchers may limit results by topic, keywords, or date. Other sections of the site include NTIS Bestsellers, Audiovisual Business Products, Computer Business Products, and Online Databases.
Subjects: Business Information; Government Publications

76. Consumer Protection
http://www.ftc.gov/ftc/consumer.htm
Sponsor: Federal Trade Commission (FTC) — Bureau of Consumer Protection
Description: This site features well over a hundred full-text pamphlets with advice for consumers and businesses from the Federal Trade Commission. These online versions of Facts for Consumers are available in text or PDF format in categories such as: Telemarketing; Automobiles; At Home; Credit; Investments; Diet, Health, and Fitness; Identity Theft; Privacy; E-Commerce and the Internet; Products and Services; Children's Issues; and Media Resources, under which one can access the section Consumer and Business Alerts. Pamphlets are found under each category, with links to publications in Spanish. The site also has a link to file a complaint online.

Although brief, these consumer and business information brochures can be excellent sources of information. It would be helpful to have a keyword search option of all the publications.
Subject: Consumer Information
Publication: *Facts for Consumers,* FT 1.32:

77. Department of Labor
http://www.dol.gov/
Sponsor: Labor Department
Description: The Labor Department uses the front page of its Web site to expose the variety of information in its networks. A side bar called Find It organizes access by Topic, Audience, Top 20 Items Requested, Regional Location, and Online Forms. Another side bar links to reference information such as labor law compliance information, press releases and speeches, state labor offices, Research Library (with links to publications), and links to each of the DOL agencies. The latest economic indicators from DOL's Bureau of Labor Statistics are featured toward the bottom of the page. The site also has a search feature and A-Z Index.The DOL Wirtz Library, under Research Library, hosts a number of finding tools for labor information, including a table of statistics available on the Web with links to current and historic data.

This site provides effective access to Labor Department information and related Web sites by providing multiple paths for accessing that information and by highlighting the most frequently consulted topics.
Subjects: Employment; Labor Law; Labor Statistics; Labor-Management Relations
Publications: *O*NET Online,* L 1.96:
Semiannual Report of the Inspector General, L 1.74:
Senior Executive Service, Forum Series, L 1.95:

78. Economic Development Administration (EDA)
http://www.doc.gov/eda/
Sponsor: Commerce Department — Economic Development Administration (EDA)
Description: This site contains descriptive information on the EDA and links to EDA services, including the Economic Development Information Clearinghouse (EDIC), which provides information about programs and resources available to assist communities with their economic development needs. Major sections of the site include: a list of Regional Offices; Programs and Funding; Grant Requirements; Laws and Regulations; News, Speeches, and Testimony; and EDA Reports and Publications. The EDA Reports and Publications page links to several PDF versions of Research and National Technical Assistance Reports. The EDIC section links to Tools of the Trade, Planning, Federal Agencies, State and Local Economic Development, Related National Organizations and Foundations, and a set of Glossaries.
Subject: Economic Development — Grants

79. E-Stats: Measuring the Electronic Economy

http://www.census.gov/eos/www/ebusiness614.htm

Sponsor: Commerce Department — Economics and Statistics Administration (ESA) — Census Bureau

Description: E-Stats is a central location for reports and data from the Census Bureau's effort to define and measure electronic commerce across multiple economic sectors. The site has quarterly reports on online retail sales and annual reports comparing e-commerce sales to total sales.

Subject: Electronic Commerce — Statistics

80. Federal Citizen Information Center (FCIC)

http://www.pueblo.gsa.gov/

Sponsor: General Services Administration

Description: In February 2000, the Consumer Information Center joined with the Federal Information Center to create the Federal Citizen Information Center. This site provides access to numerous consumer-oriented resources on a variety of topics. It is essentially an online version of the well-known *Consumer Information Catalog*. Unlike the print catalog, which simply lists the various free federally-produced consumer publications, the Web version includes many of the publications in online versions in HTML or PDF formats. The order form for the publications can be downloaded and sent to order print copies of any publication. In addition, the ads (print, radio, and at least one TV ad) that have been used to advertise the *Consumer Information Catalog*, are available in the Press Room section under the Multimedia Gallery link. Other available resources include the *Consumer Action Handbook*, the National Contact Center, and news updates concerning product recalls, scams, and fraudulent schemes.

This is a treasure trove for consumer information. By providing the full text of the publications themselves, it makes it much easier to simply browse the publications instead of browsing the catalog and then ordering the documents.

Subject: Consumer Information

Publications: *Consumer Focus*, GS 11.9/3-2:
Consumer Information Catalog, GS 11.9:
Consumer's Resource Handbook, GS 11.9/3:

81. Federal Trade Commission (FTC)

http://www.ftc.gov/

Sponsor: Federal Trade Commission (FTC)

Description: The FTC Web site presents a number of consumer publications and FTC rulings. The section entitled Formal Actions, Opinions, and Activities includes FTC actions (current and past), rules and guides, advisory opinions, public comments, and adjudicative proceedings, among other resources. Another section presents news releases, publications, and speeches. The home page also organizes information under the topical headings Consumer Protection, Antitrust/Competition, Business Guidance, Economic Issues, and Legal Framework. Some consumer information is available in Spanish. The site also has a form for online filing of a complaint against a particular company or organization.

A separate section of the site named KIDZ Privacy explains to children, adults, teachers, the media, and business operators the FTC's approach to Internet privacy concerns.

The FTC's Web site serves a valuable public function by clearly presenting fresh, timely information. The multiple ways to access information ensure that consumers will be able to find what they are looking for.

Subjects: Business — Regulations; Consumer Information

Publications: *Facts for Business*, FT 1.33:
Federal Trade Commission Decisions, FT 1.11:

82. Internal Revenue Service: The Digital Daily

http://www.irs.gov

Alternate URL: http://www.irs.ustreas.gov

Sponsor: Treasury Department — Internal Revenue Service (IRS)

Description: The official Web site of the IRS has the average U.S. taxpayer as its intended audience. Special sections also lead to information for businesses, charities and nonprofits, government entities, and tax professionals. A Spanish language version is also available. The section for individuals includes instructions, forms and publications, and resources for electronic filing through the IRS e-file program. The top menu bar of the IRS site also has links to tax statistics from the Statistics of Income (SOI) program; information about the agency's history and structure; and a newsroom with press releases, tips on tax-related scams, and a Facts & Figures section highlighting data from the tax statistics reports.The major resources on the IRS Web site are the full-text tax forms, publications, and instructions. The Forms and Publications page offers a variety of ways to search, browse, and display those documents. Most are available in PDF format. Forms and instructions for prior years are available back to 1992. Many forms are also available in a fill-in format. The fill-in forms allow you to enter information while the form is displayed online and then print out the completed form.

One of the most heavily used federal Web sites, the IRS Digital Daily site is well organized and provides multiple points of access to major sections and resources.

Subjects: Income Tax; Tax Forms; Taxation
Publications: *Federal Tax Forms, includes non-calendar year products,* T 22.51/4:
Individual Income Tax Returns, T 22.35/8:
Internal Revenue Bulletin, T 22.23:
Internal Revenue Cumulative Bulletin, T 22.25:
IRS Annual Data Book, T 22.1:
Publication 78, Cumulative List of Organizations (annual), T 22.2/11:
Tax Forms, T 22.2/12:
Tax Information, IRS Publications, T 22.44/2:

83. Minority Business Development Agency

http://www.mbda.gov/
Sponsor: Commerce Department — Minority Business Development Agency (MBDA)
Description: The Minority Business Development Agency features information organized into categories for new, home, small, medium, and large businesses. Resources are also organized into sections for Access to Markets, Access to Capital, Management and Technical Assistance, and Education and Training.
Subject: Minority-Owned Businesses

84. National Labor Relations Board (NLRB)

http://www.nlrb.gov/
Sponsor: National Labor Relations Board (NLRB)
Description: The NLRB conducts secret-ballot elections to determine whether employees want union representation and investigates unfair labor practices by employers and unions. The NLRB site features sections entitled Facts, Organization, Weekly Summary, Press Releases, Public Notices, Forms, Rules and Regulations, Decisions, Other Publications, Manuals, Procurement and Contracts, as well as information on the FOIA and Job Opportunities. Spanish language versions of some sections are also available. Slip opinions and decisions are available in PDF format back to 1993 under the Decisions section. They are arranged by volume number, and are actually housed on the GPO Access server.
Subject: Labor Unions — Regulations
Publications: *Decisions and Orders,* LR 1.8:
Forms, LR 1.17:
Regulations, Rules, Instructions, LR 1.6:
Weekly Summary of NLRB Cases, LR 1.15/2:

85. Online Women's Business Center

http://www.onlinewbc.gov/
Sponsor: Small Business Administration (SBA)
Description: This site, sponsored by the SBA, is designed to provide information for women in business on such topics as how to start your business and how to operate in the global market place. Sections include News, a directory of Women's Business Centers, a database of Local Services, Business Basics, Networking, a list of Hot Topics, and links to Major Partners. The Business Basics section features resources such as Starting your own Business, Financing Your Own Business, Running Your Business, and more. Some information is available in Spanish, Chinese, Japanese, Russian, Arabic, and Icelandic.

This site serves as a decent gateway to information of interest to women in business, although most of the links lead to SBA Web sites.

Subject: Women-Owned Businesses

86. Patent and Trademark Office

http://www.uspto.gov/

Sponsor: Commerce Department — Patent and Trademark Office (PTO)

Description: This site provides a substantial amount of information from the Patent and Trademark Office in the following sections: About USPTO, How to..., Patents, Trademarks, Check Status, Emergencies and Alerts, Activities and Education, Addresses and Contacts, and News and Notices. An online business center is designed for performing electronic business transactions with the USPTO. There are also quick links to the electronic filing systems for patents and trademarks.

The Patents and Trademarks sections, respectively, are each set up with a similar interface and content. They each provide business guides, information on international protection, and other resources. The online search for patents searches against the full-text of patents since 1976, the full-page images since 1790, and patent applications since March 2001. The Trademark Electronic Search System (TESS) has pending, registered, and dead trademarks.

Consistent interfaces for the How To..., Patents, and Trademarks section assist in finding information at this information-dense site. The site map, which actually is an alphabetical index, is also helpful.

Subjects: Intellectual Property; Patent Law; Trademarks

Publications: *Attorneys and Agents Registered to Practice Before U.S. Patent Office,* C 21.9/2:

Basic Facts About Registering a Trademark, C 21.2:R 26/

Cassis Currents Newsletter, C 21.31/12:

General Information Concerning Patents, C 21.26/2:

Index to the U.S. Patent Classification, C 21.12/2:

Manual of Patent Classification, C 21.12:

Manual of Patent Examining Procedure, C 21.15:

Official Gazette of the United States Patent and Trademark Office: Patents (weekly), C 21.5:

Patent and Trademark Office Review (annual), C 21.1/2:

Products and Services Catalog, C 21.30:

PTO Pulse, C 21.33:

Roster of Attorneys and Agents Registered to Practice Before U.S. Patent Office, C 21.9:

U.S. Patent Applications Database, C 21.31/17:

USPTO Today Monthly, C 21.33/2:

USPTO Today Quarterly, C 21.33/2-2:

87. Patent and Trademark Office Electronic Business Center

http://www.uspto.gov/ebc/indexebc.html

Sponsor: Commerce Department — Patent and Trademark Office (PTO)

Description: The Electronic Business Center links to patent and trademarks databases, online document ordering services, and electronic filing systems. It also links to the online Official Patent Gazette and Official Trademark Gazette and has an interface for managing deposit accounts with the Patent Office.

Subjects: Patent Law; Trademarks; Databases

88. Search for Charities

http://www.irs.gov/charities/article/0,,id=96136,00.html

Sponsor: Treasury Department — Internal Revenue Service (IRS)

Description: This an online version of IRS Publication 78 *Cumulative List of Organizations.* It can be searched to see if a particular organization is exempt from federal taxation and if contributions to them are tax deductible. It can be searched by name, city, and state or by browsing an alphabetical list of organizations. This page also links to the Treasury Department list of terrorist groups or those who support them; most contributions to such organizations are prohibited even if they appear in the Cumulative List of Organizations.

Subjects: Charities; Databases

Publication: *Publication 78, Cumulative List of Organizations (annual),* T 22.2/11:

89. Small Business Administration (SBA)

http://www.sba.gov/
Alternate URL: http://www.sbaonline.sba.gov/
Sponsor: Small Business Administration (SBA)
Description: The Small Business Administration site provides a variety of resources for small business. Featured pages include Starting Your Business, Financing Your Business, Business Opportunities, Your Local SBA Offices, SBA Programs, Laws and Regulations, Disaster Help, and Library. The Library includes numerous publications, especially under the Forms and Publications section. This area notes whether the full-text version is available in PDF, ASCII, PostScript, or HTML format. The Your Local SBA Offices page provides links by state with detailed categories of information and links for each. These can include Service Corps of Retired Executives, Small Business Development Centers, Small Business Investment Companies, and Certified Development Companies. The Small Business Classroom is an online resource for training and informing entrepreneurs and other students of enterprise.

This award-winning site provides plenty of useful and interesting resources for those involved with small businesses. For business users in need of timely assistance, the most useful section may be the local contacts for each state.
Subject: Small Business
Publications: *Directory of Small Business Lending in the U.S.*, SBA 1.13/4:
Forms, SBA 1.40:
Listing of SBIR Awardees, SBA 1.42:
Semiannual Report of the Inspector General, SBA 1.1/3:
Small Business Advocate, SBA 1.51:
Small Business Economic Indicators, SBA 1.1/2-2:
Small Business Lending in the United States, SBA 1.52:
State Small Business Profiles, SBA 1.50:
The Facts About..., SBA 1.49/2:

90. Small Business Development Centers

http://www.sba.gov/SBDC/
Sponsor: Small Business Administration (SBA)
Description: This site provides an overview and information on state Small Business Development Centers (SBDCs). This includes a complete state-by-state roster of all SBDCs. The list gives quick and easy access for identifying local Small Business Development Centers. In addition, the page includes tips on Starting Your Business, Financing Your Business, and Expanding Your Business. It also has sections for an SBDC National Clearinghouse and Business Development.
Subject: Small Business

91. U.S. Industry and Trade Outlook News

http://www.ita.doc.gov/td/industry/otea/outlook/webnotice.html
Sponsor: Commerce Department — International Trade Administration (ITA)
Description: The Commerce Department is building a Web-only version of the classic business reference publication *U.S. Industry and Trade Outlook*. There was no 2001 edition of this publication, and the Web version will have to be phased in over time. This page provides status information on the project and refers users to other Commerce Web pages that can provide industry data while the e-Outlook is being developed.

Frequent users of industry statistics will want to monitor developments in this new Web-based product.
Subject: Industries — Statistics
Publication: *U.S. Industry and Trade Outlook*, C 61.48:

92. United States Mint

http://www.usmint.gov/
Sponsor: Treasury Department — United States Mint
Description: The U.S. Mint site features the following main sections: About the Mint, Buy Online, Mint Programs, Consumer Awareness, Pressroom, and Mint Tours. The home page highlights special initiatives and offers, such as the 50 State Quarters program. History In Your Pocket (H.I.P.) Pocket

Change is designed for kids and uses games, stories, and other activities to study coins. The online store makes available for purchase gift sets and commemorative coins. The Pressroom presents press releases and applicable legislation. Publications are available from the About the Mint section.
Subjects: Coins; Money
Publications: *Annual Report of the Director of the United States Mint*, T 28.1:
United States Mint Strategic Plan, T 28.2:

93. WomenBiz.gov
http://www.womenbiz.gov/
Description: This government gateway pulls together information for women-owned businesses intending to sell products and services to the federal government. The sections of the site include Meeting the Basics, Finding Your Market, Getting Started, Finding Business Opps, and Key Contacts. The site also provides links to related federal agencies.
Subjects: Government Procurement; Women-Owned Businesses

94. Women's Business Ownership
http://www.sbaonline.sba.gov/womeninbusiness/
Sponsor: Small Business Administration (SBA)
Description: In addition to links to other sites related to women in business and some conference announcements, this site features numerous programs and resources under the following main sections: Services to Help Women, Procurement, Lending Programs, and Venture Capital. Programs include the Women's Network For Entrepreneurial Training, Women's Business Centers, the Online Women's Business Center, and Women's Business Ownership Representatives. Much of the information at this site refers to financial assistance and grant programs available to women in business.
Subject: Women-Owned Businesses

Employment

95. America's Job Bank
http://www.ajb.dni.us/
Sponsor: Labor Department
Description: The America's Job Bank computerized network links state employment service offices to provide job seekers with the largest pool of active job opportunities available anywhere and nationwide exposure for their resumes. For employers it provides rapid, national exposure for job openings and an easily accessible pool of candidates. The site includes sections designed for Job Seekers and Employers, both of which require users to register. The database may be searched by job title, keyword, military code, or job number. The AJB is one of the Labor Department's suite of tools known as the America Career Kit. The other tools are Career InfoNet, which "helps people make better, more informed career decisions," and Service Locator, which provides "information on service providers that are relevant to employment and training."
Subject: Job Openings

96. Bureau of International Labor Affairs
http://www.dol.gov/ilab/welcome.html
Sponsor: Labor Department — International Labor Affairs Bureau (ILAB)
Description: The Bureau of International Labor Affairs (ILAB) coordinates programs, policies, research, and technical assistance related to international labor issues such as international child labor. The ILAB Web site has information on the bureau and its activities, international labor news, information on grants and technical assistance, and the full text of relevant laws, regulations, and agreements.
Subjects: Child Labor — International; Labor Law — International

97. Davis-Bacon and Related Acts Home Page
http://www.dol.gov/esa/programs/dbra/index.htm
Sponsor: Labor Department — Employment Standards Administration (ESA)
Description: This site includes information on the forms and surveys relevant to the construction contractors complying with the Davis-Bacon Act. The Help section explains many of the Davis-Bacon

provisions and will be of assistance to others learning about these regulations. The site also includes regional contact information for Labor's Wage and Hour Division and has a set of related links to other Web sites.

The information on this site will be of most use to the construction contractors complying with the Davis-Bacon Act.

Subjects: Construction Industry — Regulations; Wages — Regulations

98. Davis-Bacon Wage Determinations

http://www.gpo.gov/davisbacon/

Sponsor: Labor Department — Employment Standards Administration (ESA)

Description: The Department of Labor under the mandate of the Davis-Bacon Act and related legislation determines prevailing wage rates for construction-related occupations in most counties in the United States. All federal government construction contracts and most contracts for federally assisted construction over $2,000 must contain the wage determinations. With this database hosted at the GPO Access site, users may search all determinations, browse all determinations by state, view wage determinations that will be modified in the next week, or browse the current week's modification by determination. The database is updated weekly.

Subjects: Construction Industry — Regulations; Wages — Regulations

Publication: *Davis-Bacon Wage Determinations*, L 36.211/2:

99. Employee Benefits Security Administration (EBSA)

http://www.dol.gov/ebsa/

Sponsor: Labor Department

Description: The Employee Benefits Security Administration (EBSA), formerly the Pension and Welfare Benefits Administration, assists the participants, beneficiaries, and sponsors of pension, health, and other employee benefit plans. The site explains pension rights and employer compliance programs. Major sections include: Consumer Health Plan and Pension Plan Information, Laws and Regulations, and Frequently Asked Questions. Consumer publications at the site include some materials in Spanish.

Subjects: Health Insurance; Pensions

100. Employment and Training Administration

http://www.doleta.gov/

Sponsor: Labor Department — Employment and Training Administration (ETA)

Description: The ETA supports the training of the workforce and the placement of workers in jobs through employment services. The ETA Web site offers sections on Adult Programs, Youth Programs, Workforce Security, Dislocated Workers, Grants and Contracts, Employer Services, Workers, and About ETA. The site includes information on Trade Adjustment Assistance, Senior Community Service Employment Program, migrant and seasonal farmworker programs, and other national ETA programs.

Subjects: Job Training; Unemployment Insurance

Publications: *Comparison of State Unemployment Insurance Laws*, L 37.212: *Unemployment Insurance Weekly Claims Reports*, L 37.12/2-2:

101. Employment Standards Administration

http://www.dol.gov/esa/

Sponsor: Labor Department — Employment Standards Administration (ESA)

Description: ESA is responsible for enforcing and administering laws governing legally-mandated wages and working conditions including child labor, minimum wages, overtime, family and medical leave, equal employment opportunity, workers' compensation, internal union democracy and financial integrity, and union elections. The Web site links to ESA's four component programs: the Office of Federal Contract Compliance Programs, the Office of Labor-Management Standards, the Office of Workers' Compensation Programs, and the Wage and Hour Division departments of labor. Other main sections include Law and Regulations, Minimum Wage, Overtime, Required Posters, and Forms.

Subjects: Labor Law; Minimum Wage

102. FedWorld Federal Government Job Search
http://www.fedworld.gov/jobs/jobsearch.html
Sponsor: Commerce Department — Technology Administration (TA) — National Technical Information Service (NTIS)
Description: FedWorld's Federal Job Search database uses files created by the Office of Personnel Management, gathered from human resource offices throughout the federal government. The database is updated daily. It can be searched by keyword, with a scripted boolean feature, and limited to selected U.S. states or territories.

FedWorld uses the same job announcements database as OPM's USA Jobs Web site, which has more features and information. Searchers may wish to supplement their USA Jobs searches with FedWorld searches due to FedWorld's boolean keyword searching.
Subjects: Government Employees; Job Openings; Databases

103. Job Accommodation Network
http://www.jan.wvu.edu/
Sponsor: Labor Department — Office of Disability Employment Policy
Description: The Job Accommodation Network (JAN) is an Americans with Disabilities Act information service sponsored by the Labor Department and operated by West Virginia University. The focus of the service is on the free JAN consulting service, accessible through their 800 number. The Web site provides information on the consulting service and on the employability of people with disabilities. Information is targeted to audiences including private employers, state and local governments, and individuals with disabilities. The site includes compilations of disability-related legislation and Web sites related to the employment and accommodation of the disabled. Some information is available in Spanish.
Subject: Americans with Disabilities Act (ADA)

104. National Mediation Board
http://www.nmb.gov/
Sponsor: National Mediation Board (NMB)
Description: The NMB is an independent U.S. government agency whose principal role is to foster harmonious labor-management relations in the rail and air transport industries and thereby minimize disruptions to the flow of interstate commerce. Its site features What's New; Mediation, which includes Presidential Emergency Boards; Representation; Arbitration; and Documents and Forms sections.
Subjects: Airlines; Labor Mediation; Railroads
Publications: *Annual Performance Report*, NMB 1.1:
Determinations of the National Mediation Board, NMB 1.9:

105. O*Net—The Occupational Information Network
http://online.onetcenter.org/
Sponsor: Labor Department — Employment and Training Administration (ETA)
Description: O*Net, the Occupational Information Network, is a database system developed by the U.S. Department of Labor to replace the Dictionary of Occupational Titles (DOT). O*Net contains comprehensive information on job requirements and worker competencies. O*Net is aligned with the new Standard Occupational Classification (SOC) System. The site has a Find Occupations section to search the database by keyword and other criteria, and a Skills Search that allows users to select from a list of skills and match them to occupations. It also has a crosswalk between the O*Net classifications and others, such as the Military Occupation Classification.
Subjects: Job Skills; Occupations; Databases

106. Occupational Outlook Handbook
http://www.bls.gov/oco/
Sponsor: Labor Department — Bureau of Labor Statistics (BLS)
Description: The most recent version of the Handbook is available on this site direct from the BLS. It is available in full HTML format, with many hypertext links from within the text to definitions of terms and links to other occupations. A PDF version of each section is also available. Entries for each occupation can be found using the "Search by occupation" feature, which supports Boolean

operators; by browsing the occupational clusters menu; or by using the alphabetical index at the top of the page. Material that supplements the occupation profiles is available from the section Other OOH Info. This includes the overview, Tomorrow's Jobs, and sections on Sources of Career Information and Finding a Job and Evaluating a Job Offer.

This is an excellent implementation of an online version of a standard reference source. The hypertext links to definitions and cross references to other occupations make this source easy to browse online. The option PDF files for printing is a great addition to this already useful resource.

Subjects: Career Information; Occupations; Workforce
Publications: *Occupational Outlook Handbook*, L 2.3/4:
Occupational Outlook Quarterly Online

107. Office of Personnel Management
http://www.opm.gov/
Sponsor: Office of Personnel Management (OPM)
Description: As the federal government personnel office, OPM is a primary source for information on working for the federal government, employment benefits, wages, and federal job listings. Featured sections include Headlines, What's New, Site Index, News Releases, Publications, Speeches, Events, Contact Us, and What's Hot. Under What's Hot, current topics of interest are listed, including the official General Schedule salary tables for the current year. Other salary schedules are also available including the Executive Schedule, Special Salary Rates, Law Enforcement Special Salary Rate, and Wage Schedules. Most include the locality differentials. The Quick Index section links to OPM information by subject.

Subjects: Government Employees; Personnel Management
Publications: *¿Está pensando en su retiro?*, PM 1.10:RI 83-11 SP/
Beneficios de sobreviviente para los hijos, PM 1.10:RI 25-27 SP/
Court Ordered Benefits for Former Spouses, PM 1.10:RI 84-1/
CSRS and FERS Handbook for Personnel and Payroll, PM 1.14/3-3:
Demographic Profile of the Federal Workforce, PM 1.10/2-3:
Employment and Trends as of... (bimonthly), PM 1.15:
Eventualidades de la vida y sus beneficios de retiro y seguro (para pensionados),
   PM 1.10:RI 38-126 SP/
Federal Employees Retirement System (An Overview of Your Benefits), PM 1.10:RI 90-1/
Federal Employees Retirement System Transfer Handbook, PM 1.10:RI 90-3/
Focus on Federal Employee Health Assistance Programs, PM 1.55:
Guide to Personnel Data Standards, PM 1.14/3:
Guide to Processing Personnel Actions, PM 1.14/3-4:
Handbook for Attorneys, PM 1.10:RI 83-116/
Información para los pensionados, PM 1.10:RI 20-59 SP/
Información para los sobrevivientes pensionados, PM 1.10:RI 25-26 SP/
Information for Survivor Annuitants, PM 1.10:RI 25-26/
Occupations of Federal White-Collar and Blue-Collar Workers (bienniel), PM 1.10/2-2:
Position Classification Standards, PM 1.30:
Survivor Benefits for Children, PM 1.10:RI 25-27/
Thinking About Retirement, PM 1.10:RI 83-11/
Work Years and Personnel Costs, PM 1.10/4:
Work-Related Injuries and Fatalities, PM 1.10:RI 84-2/

108. Standard Occupational Classification (SOC) Home Page
http://www.bls.gov/soc/
Sponsor: Labor Department — Bureau of Labor Statistics (BLS)
Description: "The Standard Occupational Classification (SOC) system will be used by all federal statistical agencies to classify workers into occupational categories for the purpose of collecting, calculating, or disseminating data. All workers are classified into one of over 820 occupations according to their occupational definition. To facilitate classification, occupations are combined to form 23 major groups, 96 minor groups, and 449 broad occupations. Each broad occupation includes detailed occupation(s) requiring similar job duties, skills, education, or experience." (From Web site, 12/13/02) This site allows users to search the SOC database, browse its contents, or order a copy of the printed edition of the

Standard Occupational Classification Manual. Related reference material is provided as well, including the SOC User Guide and an SOC Implementation Schedule.
Subject: Occupations
Publication: *Standard Occupational Classification Manual*

109. Studentjobs.gov

http://www.studentjobs.gov
Sponsors: Education Department — Federal Student Aid Office; Office of Personnel Management (OPM)
Description: Studentjobs.gov is a clearinghouse for information about student employment and internships in the federal government. The site features a searchable database for various types of job openings: summer employment, Student Temporary Educational Program (STEP) employment, co-op education, university work-study, volunteer service, student internships, and Outstanding Scholars opportunities. An Agency Information Gateway facilitates browsing with direct links to the relevant employment pages at the agencies' sites. "Create a Profile" for email notification of job openings and "Create a Resume" are two interactive services available.
Subjects: Internships; Job Openings; Students

110. USA Jobs

http://www.usajobs.opm.gov/
Sponsor: Office of Personnel Management (OPM)
Description: The core of the USA Jobs site is a database of current employment opportunities in the federal government. These can be searched by keyword or by other criteria, including agency, occupational grouping, and state. There are also special lists of summer, part-time, student, information technology, skilled trades, and manual labor jobs. A Hot Jobs section lists federal jobs that hard to fill or for which a large number of applicants is needed. Other services on USA Jobs include a resume-building feature, stored searches for email alert notices, and copies of standard federal employment forms.
Subjects: Government Employees; Job Openings

111. YouthRules!

Alternate URL: http://www.youthrules.dol.gov/
Description: The Labor Department's YouthRules! Program seeks to promote safe work experiences for young workers. The Web site has information on federal and state laws and regulations governing child labor. The four main sections are targeted to information needed by teens, parents, educators, and employers. Wages, work hours, state work permits, and safety and health issues are covered. Special sections discuss employment in specific occupations, such as newspaper delivery, door-to-door sales, entertainment, and agriculture.

Finance

112. Commodity Futures Trading Commission

http://www.cftc.gov/cftc/cftchome.htm
Sponsor: Commodity Futures Trading Commission (CFTC)
Description: The CFTC Web site features a variety of information on commodities trading. Sections include: Commitments of Traders, Customer Protection, Exchanges & Products, Market Oversight, Before You Trade, Law & Regulation, Press Office, Federal Register & Comments, International Affairs, FOIA, Reports & Publications, How to Register, and Filing a Customer Complaint. The Commitments of Traders area includes Commitments of Traders in Futures reports in a compressed, comma delimited format for loading into a spreadsheet. Both the long form and short form data reports are available. Some of the reports are available back to 1986. Offering press releases, Weekly Advisories, and the Commitments of Traders in Futures reports, this well-organized site should be of interest to anyone following the commodity futures market.
Subject: Securities and Investments — Regulations
Publications: *Annual Report / Commodity Futures Trading Commission*, Y 3.C 73/5:1/
Commitments of Traders in Futures, Y 3.C 73/5:9-3/

113. Comptroller of the Currency - Administrator of National Banks

http://www.occ.treas.gov/

Sponsor: Treasury Department — Comptroller of the Currency (OCC)

Description: An independent bureau of the Treasury Department, the Office of the Comptroller of the Currency oversees the nation's federally chartered banks and financial regulations pertaining to those banks. The site features information on banking regulations, community development investments of national banks, and electronic banking, among other topics. The Issuances section has news releases, speeches, advisory letters, alerts, and OCC Bulletins. The Public Information section explains how to find information on the Web about individual banks. The Publications section has an order form and list of publications for sale, as well as links to the full text of those publications that are available online.

Subject: Banking Regulation

Publications: *Economic Working Papers*, T 12.22:
OCC Advisory Letters, T 12.23:
OCC Alerts, T 12.21:
OCC Bulletins, T 12.20:
Quarterly Journal, Comptroller of the Currency, T 12.18:

114. EDGAR - SEC Filings and Forms

http://www.sec.gov/edgarhp.htm

Alternate URLs: http://www.tenkwizard.com/
http://www.edgariq.com/
http://www.freeedgar.com/
http://www.secinfo.com/

Sponsor: Securities and Exchange Commission (SEC)

Description: The Electronic Data Gathering, Analysis, and Retrieval (EDGAR) database performs automated collection and indexing of submissions by companies and others who are required by law to file forms with the U.S. Securities and Exchange Commission. The EDGAR Search page includes options to find companies and their current associated filings, browse the latest filings, or search archived EDGAR documents. The site includes a tutorial, a guide to SEC filings, and detailed information on the database content.

Various private companies have sought to improve upon the SEC's EDGAR system by offering the same or more content with a different interface or indexing. While some services are only available for a fee, others offer all or some of their content for free. Of the free services, some may require registration. We have listed several of these free services under the alternate URLs above. These are 10K Wizard, EdgarIQ, FreeEDGAR, and SEC Info.

Subjects: Companies and Enterprises; Databases

115. Fed in Print

http://www.frbsf.org/publications/fedinprint/

Sponsor: Federal Reserve — Federal Reserve Bank of San Francisco

Description: Fed in Print is an index to Federal Reserve economic research. Sponsored by the Federal Reserve Bank of San Francisco, it covers Federal Reserve publications from all the system's banks. The search form supports keyword, title, author, bank, publication year, and publication name searches. A search of publications may also be sorted by category, by type, by topic, and alphabetically.

Subjects: Economics — Research; Databases

116. Federal Deposit Insurance Corporation

http://www.fdic.gov/

Sponsor: Federal Deposit Insurance Corporation (FDIC)

Description: Featuring a large collection of banking information and publications, the FDIC site offers sections such as Deposit Insurance, Bank Data, Regulations and Examination, Consumers and Communities, Buying From and Selling to FDIC, Newsroom, Events, and FOIA, and About FDIC. The sections are repeated along the left side of the home page, with subsections displayed as well. The home page also contains sections on What's New and Topics of Interest. Many resources are available under the topical pages of the Bank Data section, including analytical, statistical, and historical reports. Information on individual FDIC insured institutions can be found under the

Individual Banks heading of this page. The FDIC Financial Institutions and Branch Office Data link on that page connects to a searchable database with demographic and classification information on active and inactive institutions and active branch offices. It also contains total assets and deposits for the institutions.

The FDIC site appeals to both the professional and the consumer with its offerings. For the professional, the detailed statistics and various full-text reports provide opportunities for research into banking trends and specific institutions. For the consumer it offers advice, referrals to rating services, and statistics on individual institutions.

Subject: Banking Regulation
Publications: *FDIC Banking Review*, Y 3.F 31/8:27/
FDIC Consumer News, Y 3.F 31/8:24/
FDIC Data Book, Summary of Deposits, Y 3.F 31/8:22
FDIC Quarterly Banking Profile, Y 3.F 31/8:29/
Financial Institution Letters, Y 3.F 31/8:34
Historical Statistics on Banking, Y 3.F 31/8:26/
Report on Underwriting Practices, Y 3.F 31/8:35
Statistics on Banking, Y 3.F 31/8:1-2:/
Survey of Real Estate Trends, Y 3.F 31/8:28/

117. Federal Financial Institutions Examination Council
http://www.ffiec.gov/
Sponsor: Federal Financial Institutions Examination Council (FFIEC)
Description: "The Council is a formal interagency body empowered to prescribe uniform principles, standards, and report forms for the federal examination of financial institutions by the Board of Governors of the Federal Reserve System, the Federal Deposit Insurance Corporation, the National Credit Union Administration, the Office of the Comptroller of the Currency, and the Office of Thrift Supervision, and to make recommendations to promote uniformity in the supervision of financial institutions." (From Web site, 12/13/02) In addition to links to the other agencies, this site features Information about the FFIEC, Press Releases, Reports, Reporting Forms, Handbooks and Catalogues, Enforcement Actions and Orders, and On-line Information Systems.
Subject: Banking Regulation
Publications: *HMDA Aggregate Reports*, FR 1.63/54:
HMDA Disclosure Reports, FR 1.63/55:

118. Federal Reserve Bank of Atlanta
http://www.frbatlanta.org/
Sponsor: Federal Reserve — Federal Reserve Bank of Atlanta
Description: The Atlanta Fed examines banking institutions in the Sixth Federal Reserve District: Alabama, Florida, Georgia, Louisiana, Mississippi, and Tennessee. The main sections of this site are About the Fed (including information about the Atlanta Fed and the Federal Reserve System); Banking Information; Services for Financial Institutions; Community Development; Consumer Information; Economic Research and Data; News and Events; and Publications. The Publications section includes Periodicals, Annual Reports, Working Papers, Books and Brochures, Catalogs, Forms, and Archives.
Subjects: Banking Regulation; Monetary Policy

119. Federal Reserve Bank of Boston
http://www.bos.frb.org/
Sponsor: Federal Reserve — Federal Reserve Bank of Boston
Description: The Boston Fed serves the First Federal Reserve District, which includes the six New England states: Connecticut, Massachusetts, Maine, New Hampshire, Rhode Island, and Vermont. Their site has information about the Federal Reserve Bank of Boston, along with sections for Banking Information, Community Development, Economic Research, Education Resources, Financial Services, and Publications. The Publications page includes a number of newsletters, research publications, and banking publications. The Economic Research section concentrates on New England economic conditions.
Subjects: Banking Regulation; Monetary Policy

120. Federal Reserve Bank of Chicago
http://www.chicagofed.org/
Sponsor: Federal Reserve — Federal Reserve Bank of Chicago
Description: The Federal Reserve Bank of Chicago features a wide range of banking information for the Seventh Federal Reserve District, which includes all of Iowa and most of Illinois, Indiana, Michigan, and Wisconsin. The main sections of the site are About the Fed; Economic Research and Data; Publications and Education Resources; News and Events; Consumer Information; Banking Information and Regulations; and Services for Financial Institutions. The home page also presents links to special features of the Web site, including Financial Access for the UnBanked; Payment Systems Resource Center; Consumer and Economic Development Research Info Center; Commercial Bank and Bank Holding Company Database; and more.
Subjects: Banking Regulation; Monetary Policy

121. Federal Reserve Bank of Cleveland
http://www.clev.frb.org/
Sponsor: Federal Reserve — Federal Reserve Bank of Cleveland
Description: This site serves the Fourth Federal Reserve District, which includes Ohio, western Pennsylvania, eastern Kentucky, and the northern panhandle of West Virginia. In addition to a general description of the Federal Reserve Bank of Cleveland, this site includes sections entitled General Information, Banking / Services, Economic Research, Publications, and Financial Services. The Economic Research section includes some consumer price indexes and publications. Most of the regional data is under the Publications section, which includes the Annual Report, and Operating Circular Letters. The site also has a link to the Central Bank Institute of the Federal Reserve Bank of Cleveland, which was established to promote greater understanding of central bank practices and institutions.
Subjects: Banking Regulation; Monetary Policy

122. Federal Reserve Bank of Dallas
http://www.dallasfed.org/
Sponsor: Federal Reserve — Federal Reserve Bank of Dallas
Description: This site provides information about the Federal Reserve Bank of Dallas, the Federal Reserve System, and the regional, national and global economies. It covers the 11th Federal Reserve District, which comprises Texas, northern Louisiana, and southern New Mexico. It includes pages on The Federal Reserve, The Dallas Fed, Economic Research, Economic and Financial Data, Banking Supervision, Financial Services, Publications, Center for Latin American Economics, Community Affairs, Economic Education, and Consumer Info. It also offers a special Expand Your Insight section providing highlights on such subjects as Money and Banking, Global Economy, Technology, Free Enterprise, U.S. Economy, and Regional Economy. A section entitled Greenspeak presents recent quotes from Fed Chairman Alan Greenspan. Employment, Savings Bonds/Treasuries, Events, and links to Other Fed Web sites are also featured. Under Economic & Financial Data, this site offers a number of statistics unique to the Southwest regional economy. The Publications page includes access to annual reports and a number of other periodicals, including Banking and Community Perspectives. This sections includes links to publications hosted on this site as well as others.
    This is one of the best, most informative Web sites in the Federal Reserve System.
Subjects: Banking Regulation; Monetary Policy

123. Federal Reserve Bank of Kansas City
http://www.kc.frb.org/
Sponsor: Federal Reserve — Federal Reserve Bank of Kansas City
Description: This site serves the 10th Federal Reserve District, including Colorado, Kansas, Nebraska, Oklahoma, Wyoming, northern New Mexico, and western Missouri. The main sections of the site include About the Fed; Banking Information; Community Development; Consumer Information; Economic Research and Data; News and Events; Services for Financial Institutions; and Publications and Education Resources.
Subjects: Banking Regulation; Monetary Policy

124. Federal Reserve Bank of Minneapolis

http://woodrow.mpls.frb.fed.us/

Sponsor: Federal Reserve — Federal Reserve Bank of Minneapolis

Description: This site features a variety of resources for the Ninth Federal Reserve District, which includes Montana, North Dakota, South Dakota, Minnesota, the Upper Peninsula of Michigan, and northwestern Wisconsin. Primary sections include Banking Supervision, the Economy, and Financial Services. Economic data is available for the United States, with a focus on the Ninth District states. The site also has a searchable database called BancSearch with financial data for each of the banks in the Ninth District. Publications online include the *fedgazette*, *The Region*, and the *Annual Report*.

Well organized and easy to navigate, this site is a rich resource for nationwide banking information and for region specific information.

Subjects: Banking Regulation; Monetary Policy

Publications: *fedgazette*

The Region

125. Federal Reserve Bank of New York

http://www.ny.frb.org/

Sponsor: Federal Reserve — Federal Reserve Bank of New York

Description: Covering the Second Federal Reserve District—which encompasses New York state, Puerto Rico, the Virgin Islands, and parts of New Jersey and Connecticut—the site features Banking Information, Economic Education, Economic Research and Data, News and Events, Publications, and Statistics. The Publications page includes access to online Annual Reports; Board of Governors' Reports, Speeches, and Testimony; General Publications; Research Publications; and Special Reports. The home page provides a link to the Federal Reserve System Search Engine, which allows keyword searches of one or more Web sites of the Federal Reserve Banks.

Subjects: Banking Regulation; Monetary Policy

126. Federal Reserve Bank of Philadelphia

http://www.phil.frb.org/

Sponsor: Federal Reserve — Federal Reserve Bank of Philadelphia

Description: The Federal Reserve Bank of Philadelphia is responsible for eastern Pennsylvania, southern New Jersey, and the state of Delaware. Their Web site provides a variety of information on the Bank and regional statistics. Available sections include Community Development; Supervision, Regulation, and Credit; Publications and Educational Resources; Employment Opportunities; Economic Research; and Consumer Information. The Publications page includes the Annual Report, News Releases, and Speeches.

More regional in focus than the other Federal Reserve Banks sites, this site provides useful information for those interested in the region, the Third Reserve District which comprises two-thirds of Pennsylvania, the southern half of New Jersey, and all of Delaware.

Subjects: Banking Regulation; Monetary Policy

127. Federal Reserve Bank of Richmond

http://www.rich.frb.org/

Sponsor: Federal Reserve — Federal Reserve Bank of Richmond

Description: Serving the Fifth Federal Reserve District—which includes the District of Columbia, Maryland, Virginia, North Carolina, South Carolina, and most of West Virginia—this site features Economic Research and Data, Publications, Banking Information, Financial Services, Community Affairs, Consumer Information, and Speeches and News. The Publications page includes Research and Policy, Regional Economic Information, Economic Education, Community Affairs, and links to online Catalogs.

Subjects: Banking Regulation; Monetary Policy

128. Federal Reserve Bank of San Francisco

http://www.frbsf.org/

Sponsor: Federal Reserve — Federal Reserve Bank of San Francisco

Description: This site serves the 12th Federal Reserve District, which comprises Alaska, Arizona, California, Hawaii, Idaho, Nevada, Oregon, Utah, and Washington. The San Francisco Federal

Reserve Bank Web site features sections on About the Fed, News and Events, Economic Research and Data, Publications, Educational Resources, Community Development, Consumer Information, Banking Information, and Services for Financial Institutions. The Publications section allows users to sort publications by category, type, topic, and alphabetically. Each topic section also provides access to publications, reports, and other resources.

Subjects: Banking Regulation; Monetary Policy

129. Federal Reserve Bank of St. Louis

http://www.stls.frb.org/

Sponsor: Federal Reserve — Federal Reserve Bank of St. Louis

Description: The Federal Reserve Bank of St. Louis represents the Eighth Federal Reserve District covering Arkansas, Illinois, Indiana, Kentucky, Mississippi, Missouri and Tennessee. Its Web site includes Banking Information, Community Affairs, Economic Research, Education, Financial Services, and Publications. The Economic Research section provides easy access to over 800 U.S. economic time series through the Federal Reserve Economic Data (FRED®) system. Under Publications, the site offers PDF copies of the *Federal Reserve Bank of St. Louis Review* going back to 1967.

This is one of the easiest Federal Reserve sites to use. Much of the statistical data are national figures, so this site can be used by those interested in the nation as a whole and not just for the states covered in this district.

Subjects: Banking Regulation; Monetary Policy

Publications: *Federal Reserve Bank of St. Louis Review*
Inside the Vault

130. Federal Reserve System Board of Governors

http://www.federalreserve.gov/

Sponsor: Federal Reserve — Board of Governors

Description: This main site of the Federal Reserve Board includes information about the Federal Reserve System, Federal Open Market Committee, and their publications. Available sections about the Board include General Information, Press Releases, Monetary Policy, Banking System, Regulation and Supervision, Research and Data, Consumer Information, Community Development, Reporting Forms, and Publications. The Monetary Policy section features a section for the Federal Open Market Committee and access to the *Summary of Commentary on Current Economic Conditions*, commonly known as the *Beige Book*. This section also features the *Monetary Policy Report to the Congress*. The Publications section features access to PDF versions of selected *Federal Reserve Bulletin* articles and the *Annual Report*.

This site offers a substantial body of information and statistics from the Board. It is a good starting point for users seeking information on the system as a whole. However, valuable data are also available from the individual Federal Reserve Banks. One limitation of this main site is that links to the member bank Web sites are hidden on the page entitled The Structure of the Federal Reserve System, under the General Information section.

Subjects: Banking Regulation; Monetary Policy

Publications: *Annual Report*, FR 1.1:
Federal Reserve Bulletin, FR 1.3:
Summary of Commentary on Current Economic Conditions (Beige Book)

131. Federal Reserve System's Public Information Catalog

http://app.ny.frb.org/cfpicnic/frame1.cfm

Sponsor: Federal Reserve — Federal Reserve Bank of New York

Description: This site presents a comprehensive guide and online ordering facility for all publications and materials available from the Federal Reserve System (FRS). Most items are free of charge, many as Adobe Acrobat PDF files. Publications are listed by the following topics: Banking System, Consumer Finance, Economics, Federal Reserve System, Financial Markets and Instruments, International Economics, Money, and Payment Systems. Also available are subscriptions from each FRS District, and a selection of Teaching Materials. The database may be searched by keyword, audience type, Federal Reserve Bank, media type, and Journal of Economic Literature subject codes.

Subjects: Banking; Monetary Policy; Publication Catalogs

132. Financial Management Service
http://www.fms.treas.gov/
Sponsor: Treasury Department — Financial Management Service (FMS)
Description: The Financial Management Service manages the daily cash flow into and out of federal accounts. The agency collects debt owed to the federal government and issues the Treasury checks for social security, veterans' benefits, income tax refunds, and other purposes. The FMS Web site is divided into sections for consumer questions and answers (e.g., How do I replace a lost Treasury check?); publications and financial statements; information about FMS; and information on FMS programs.

FMS issues the *Daily* and *Monthly Treasury Statement*, reporting the government's receipts, outlays, and deficit or surplus. Current issues are available at this site, and users are referred to GPO's Web site for archival issues of the *Daily Treasury Statement*. Starting with Fiscal Year 2001, what was previously known as the *United States Government Annual Report* and *Annual Report Appendix* were combined and renamed the *Combined Statement of Receipts, Outlays, and Balances of the United States Government*. The *Combined Statement* is recognized as the official publication of receipts and outlays of the U.S. government. The current report and the annual reports back to 1995 are available at this site. The monthly *Treasury Bulletin*, another important reference publication from FMS, contains statements on federal fiscal operations, the federal debt, U.S. savings bonds, federal securities, U.S. claims and liabilities with foreigners, and the status of federal trust funds.
Subject: Government Finance
Publications: *Combined Statement of Receipts, Outlays, and Balances of the United States Government*, T 63.101/3:
Daily Treasury Statement, T 63.113/2-2:
Financial Connection, T 63.128:
Financial Reports of the United States Government, T 63.113/3:
Monthly Treasury Statement of Receipts and Outlays of the United States Government, T 63.113/2:
Status Report of U.S. Treasury-owned Gold, T 63.131:
Treasury Bulletin (quarterly), T 63.103/2:
Treasury Reporting Rates of Exchange, T 63.121:
United States Government Annual Report, T 63.101/2:

133. National Bankruptcy Review Commission
http://govinfo.library.unt.edu/nbrc/default.html
Sponsor: University of North Texas. Libraries
Description: This collection contains the archive of meeting minutes, the final report, commission membership, and information about the NBRC. This site contains all documents available on the World Wide Web site of the National Bankruptcy Review Commission when the agency closed in November 1997.
Publication: *Report of the National Bankruptcy Review Commission*, Y 3.2:B 22/B 22/

134. National Credit Union Administration
http://www.ncua.gov/
Sponsor: National Credit Union Administration (NCUA)
Description: The National Credit Union Administration is an independent federal agency that supervises and insures credit unions. Their Web site offers statistics and publications from the NCUA. Some of the available sections include About Credit Unions and NCUA, Credit Union Data, and Reference Information.The site has a searchable directory of credit unions available under the Credit Union Data section; entries provide information including assets, membership, and type of credit union. The directory is also available as a full text file, in PDF or ASCII format. Most of this site's online publications can be found under the Reference Information section. Types of documents available include Handbooks, Rules and Regulations, Statistics, Legal Opinion Letters, and Administrative Orders, among many others.
Subject: Credit Unions — Regulations
Publications: *Accounting Manual for Federal Credit Unions*, NCU 1.8:
Annual Report, NCU 1.1:

Annual Report of the National Credit Union Administration, NCU 1.1:
Federal Credit Union Bylaws, NCU 1.8:B 99/
NCUA Credit Union Directory, NCU 1.16:
NCUA Letters to Credit Unions, NCU 1.19:
NCUA News, NCU 1.20:
Regulatory Alert, NCU 1.6/2:
Your Insured Funds, NCU 1.2:F96/

135. National Information Center (NIC)
http://www.ffiec.gov/nic/
Sponsor: Federal Financial Institutions Examination Council (FFIEC)
Description: NIC provides "comprehensive information on banks and other institutions for which the Federal Reserve has a supervisory, regulatory, or research interest, including both domestic and foreign banking organizations operating in the United States. The NIC includes the organizational structure of financial institutions and financial information for some of those institutions. Historical information is available on the structure of all the institutions. Financial information is available for selected time periods." (From the NIC Web site, 12-16-02)
    This site is a great first stop for users seeking basic information about domestic and foreign banks. The data provided, which is slightly more than directory information, is organized under the following sections: Institution Search, Institution History, Organization Hierarchy, Financial and Performance Reports, and Top 50 BHCs/Banks. Institution Search offers a search by head office (United States and foreign), foreign branch of U.S. bank, and U.S. address of foreign bank.
Subjects: Banks; Databases

136. Office of Thrift Supervision
http://www.ots.treas.gov/
Sponsor: Treasury Department — Office of Thrift Supervision (OTS)
Description: The OTS is the primary regulator of all federal and many state-chartered thrift institutions, including savings banks and savings and loan associations. The Web site presents descriptive information on the OTS, Application Status Reports, Laws and Regulations, Publications, Consumer Inquiries, Data and Research, and Thrift Financial Report forms. The Data and Research section includes information on the industry's financial performance, searchable databases of institutions and holding companies, and related papers and statistical information.
Subjects: Savings and Loan Institutions; Thrift Institutions
Publication: *Office of Thrift Supervision News*, T 71.7:

137. SavingsBonds.gov
http://www.savingsbonds.gov/
Sponsor: Treasury Department — Bureau of the Public Debt
Description: This site is a portal for information on United States Savings Bonds. It includes product information on specific bonds, links for online purchase of bonds, and a savings bond calculator. A Frequently Asked Questions section covers topics such as maturity periods and interest rates, lost or stolen bonds, and transferring bond ownership. The site also has audience-specific sections for financial institutions, businesses, employers, and teachers.
Subject: Treasury Bonds

138. Securities and Exchange Commission
http://www.sec.gov/
Sponsor: Securities and Exchange Commission (SEC)
Description: The SEC site features financial information for investors. While a major offering is the EDGAR database of company information, described separately in this work, this site provides additional informational sections, including About the SEC, Investor Information, Regulatory Actions, Staff Interpretations, News and Public Statements, Litigation, and SEC Divisions. Information is also arranged by audience, such as accountants, broker dealers, EDGAR filers, funds and advisers, municipal markets, and small businesses. Links to publications are scattered throughout the site. The *SEC Annual Report* is located under the About the SEC section, while the *SEC News Digest* is accessible from the News and Public Statements page, and the Investor Information

section contains the bulk of the online titles. Investor Information has consumer education materials; some material is available in Spanish.

Subject: Securities and Investments — Regulations
Publications: *Annual Report*, SE 1.1:
Final Report of the SEC Government-Business Forum on Small Business Capital Formation,
 SE 1.35/2:
SEC Rules of Practice
SEC Special Studies, SE 1.38:
Security and Exchange Commission News Digest (daily), SE 1.25/12:

139. Treasury Department

`http://www.ustreas.gov/`
Alternate URL: `http://www.treas.gov/`
Sponsor: Treasury Department
Description: The Treasury Department's Web site provides a public face for the department with current news, links to its bureaus and offices, and direct links to popular topics such as seized property auctions, Treasury securities, and Savings Bonds. The site also provides a subject approach to its activities with Key Topics: Accounting and Budget, Currency and Coins, Financial Markets, International, Law Enforcement, Taxes, and Technology. An Education section includes a history of the Treasury and a virtual tour of the historic Treasury Building. The Press Room section has access to news releases and other publications arranged by topic, by date, and by type (news, testimony, speeches, statements, reports, photographs, and U.S. International Reserve Position statements).
Subject: Government Finance
Publication: *Treasury Inspector General For Tax Administration (semiannual)*, T 1.1/6:

140. TreasuryDirect

`http://www.treasurydirect.gov/`
Sponsor: Treasury Department — Bureau of the Public Debt
Description: TreasuryDirect allows customers to set up an account with the Treasury; to purchase Treasury bills, bonds, and notes; and to manage their accounts. A side bar links to Treasury securities information from the Bureau of the Public Debt.
Subjects: Treasury Bills; Treasury Bonds; Treasury Notes

Government Business

141. ABM Online

`http://www.abm.rda.hq.navy.mil/`
Sponsor: Navy
Description: ABM (Acquisition and Business Management) Online provides access to recent Navy policy, procedures, information, data, and tools of interest to the Navy acquisitions and procurement community. The site offers sections for Policy, Organization, Business Opportunities, Business Practices, and more.
Subject: Military Procurement
Publication: *ABM (Acquisition & Business Management) Online*, D 201.44:

142. AcqNet

`http://www.arnet.gov/`
Sponsor: General Services Administration
Description: AcqNet is intended to facilitate access to multi-agency contracting information. At present, it is a central collection point for the type of reference, legal, and regulatory information needed by those involved in government contracting and procurement. It links to the Federal Acquisition Regulations in various formats, and to federal and non-government Web sites relevant to contract awards, bid protests, individual agency procurement, and professional development for government contracting personnel.

This site appears to be unevenly maintained but is still a helpful starting point for procurement and contracting information.

Subjects: Government Procurement; Military Procurement
Publication: *Federal Acquisition Regulation*, GS 1.6/10:

143. Assistant Secretary of the Army for Acquisition, Logistics, and Technology
https://webportal.saalt.army.mil/
Sponsor: Army
Description: This site is intended to be a central location for regulations, policies, memorandums, briefings, and other documentation for the Army Acquisition Community. It has information about the office's organization and directorates, and quick links to procurement reference material.
Subject: Military Procurement
Publication: *Army RD&A Bulletin*, D 101.52/3:

144. Chief Information Officers Council
http://www.cio.gov/
Sponsor: Chief Information Officers Council
Description: The Chief Information Officers Council is the principal interagency forum focused on federal agency management of information technology (IT). The CIO Council's role includes developing recommendations for IT management policy, procedures, and standards; identifying opportunities to share information resources; and assessing the needs of the federal government IT workforce. The Web site sections include About the Council (with a membership list and meeting minutes), Calendar of Events, Documents, and Links. Documents include CIO Council reports and other government statements on such topics as Accessibility, Best Practices, IT Security, and IT Workforce.
Subject: Information Technology

145. COMMITS
http://www.commits.doc.gov/
Sponsor: Commerce Department
Description: COMMITS (Commerce Information Technology Solutions) system is a Government Wide Agency Contract reserved for small businesses in the information technology sector. Its site includes What is COMMITS?, Why Should I Use COMMITS?, How Can I Get Involved With COMMITS?, I'm a COMMITS Customer, and I'm a COMMITS Team Member. Also covered are COMMITS Vendor Profiles and the COMMITS Balanced Scorecard. The Business Opportunity Page provides access to the COMMITS' databases.
Subjects: Government Contracts; Information Technology

146. Defense Reutilization and Marketing Service, Surplus Property
http://www.drms.dla.mil/
Sponsor: Defense Department — Defense Reutilization and Marketing Service (DRMS)
Description: This site features a publicly accessible searchable database of items available at public auctions and sales. DRMS offers the site to help people obtain original U.S. government surplus property. To search the inventory, browse property catalogs, submit requests, or place a bid, the site provides three separate versions: one for private company or individual users; a second for users from the government, non-profit, or Public Service Agency sectors; and a third for those who are a "Generator/Installation of Government Excess Personal Property For Turn-In."

Anyone interested in buying from the government or just investigating what is available should check out this site.
Subject: Surplus Government Property

147. Defense Supply Center, Columbus
Alternate URL: http://www.dscc.dla.mil/
Sponsor: Defense Department — Defense Supply Center, Columbus (DSCC)
Description: The DSCC, a DoD procurement and supply center, offers information on military procurement and on buying from and selling to DSCC. The section on selling to DSCC includes the DSCC Internet Bid Boards (DIBBS) system and a Vendor Assistance page.

This site is primarily of interest to those in the DoD procurement business.
Subject: Military Procurement

148. Department of Energy's e-center

http://e-center.doe.gov/

Sponsor: Energy Department

Description: The Department of Energy's (DOE's) e-center is its site for obtaining information on doing business with DOE. Sections include current business opportunities, registration for notification of new business opportunities, information and guidance on the acquisition and financial assistance award process. This last section offers information on DOE's use of sealed bid purchases and requests for proposals, contract performance and payment, small business and other preference programs, the unsolicited proposal system. The Professionals Homepage link provides regulatory and organizational guidance in procurement, financial assistance, personal property, contractor human resources management, professional development, and business practices.

This is a useful resource for those wanting government contracts with the DOE.

Subject: Government Contracts

149. FARSite (Federal Acquisition Regulation Site)

http://farsite.hill.af.mil/

Sponsor: Air Force — Hill Air Force Base

Description: This site provides access to the Federal Acquisition Regulation as well as the Defense FAR Supplement (DFARS) and other links to federal regulations for the Navy, Army, Air Force, NASA, and DOE. It provides regulation status, manuals, changes, and electronic forms as well as a forum for questions and help.

FARSite is a one-stop site for contracting regulations.

Subject: Government Procurement — Regulations

Publications: *Air Force Acquisition Regulation Supplement (AFFARS),* D 301.6/2:
Army Federal Acquisition Regulation Supplement (AFARS), D 101.6:
Defense Federal Acquisition Regulation Supplement (DFARS), D 1.6:
Department of Energy Acquisition Regulations Supplement (DEARS)
Federal Acquisition Regulation, GP 3.38/2:
NASA FAR Supplement, NAS 1.6:
Navy Acquisition Procedures Supplement (NAPS)

150. FedBizOpps

http://www.fedbizopps.gov/

Sponsor: General Services Administration

Description: FedBizOpps (FBO) is the central clearinghouse for information on federal government procurement notices in excess of $25,000. Beginning January 2002, federal agencies are required to post these notices to FedBizOpps and are no longer required to submit them to the Commerce Business Daily database. Vendors seeking government business opportunities on FBO can browse postings by agency, agency office, posted date or classification code, and can also see information on awards made. Users can search the full text of postings by word, solicitation number, classification code, and a variety of other options. A Vendor Notification Service provides subscribers with free email notification of procurement announcements.

Subjects: Government Contracts; Government Procurement

151. Federal Acquisition Institute

http://www.gsa.gov/Portal/content/offerings_content.jsp?channelId=-13607&programId=8521&contentOID=117967&contentType=1004&cid=1

Sponsor: General Services Administration

Description: The Federal Acquisition Institute presents its Web site for the acquisition career management program. Categories of information include Events, Publications, and Policies.

This site specifically targets its materials at training federal employees in the acquisitions and procurement realms. The site also contains useful information for non-federal personnel with interests in procurement training information.

Subject: Government Procurement

152. Federal Acquisition Regulations
http://www.acqnet.gov/far/
Sponsor: General Services Administration
Description: This version of the Federal Acquisitions Regulation (FAR) provides access to HTML, zipped HTML, and PDF versions of the regulations. It includes *Federal Acquisition Circulars* in PDF, in their looseleaf and *Federal Register* printing formats. There are also special sections for proposed rules and for Small Entity Compliance Guidelines. Users can subscribe to a FAR News email service to receive news of FACs, proposed rules, public meetings, and other FAR-related issues.
Subject: Government Procurement — Regulations
Publications: *Federal Acquisition Circular,* D 1.6/11-2:
Federal Acquisition Regulation, D 1.6/11:

153. Federal Procurement Data System: U.S. Government Acquisition Contracts Statistics
http://www.fpdc.gov/
Sponsor: General Services Administration
Description: The Federal Procurement Data Center (FPDC) operates and maintains the Federal Procurement Data System (FPDS). The FPDS is the central repository of statistical information on Federal contracting. It contains detailed information on contract awards over $25,000 and summary data on procurements of less than $25,000. The FPDC Web site provides information about its products and services.
Subject: Government Contracts
Publication: *Federal Procurement Report*, PREX 2.24/13:

154. Federal Supply Service
http://www.gsa.gov/Portal/content/orgs_content.jsp?contentOID=22892&con
tentType=1005
Description: The FSS supports supply and procurement, fleet management, excess property disposal, and travel and transportation services for the federal government. This Web site is a central location for those in the federal government seeking information on procuring items from the FSS. The page includes the following categories: Personal Property Management; Travel and Transportation Services; Schedule Sales Query; GSA's Marketing Partnership; GSA Customer Supply Center; Vehicle Acquisition and Leasing Services; Publications; Environmental Programs; and Vendor Support Center.
Subject: Government Procurement
Publications: *Federal Motor Vehicle Fleet Report for Fiscal Year*, GS 2.18:
MarketTips, GS 2.17:

155. FirstGov Shopping and Auctions
http://www.firstgov.gov/shopping/shopping.shtml
Sponsor: General Services Administration
Description: The FirstGov section covering government sales and auctions uses this tag line: "Buy new, seized, and surplus merchandise from government." This portal to other government Web resources is divided into the following sections: Auctions; Cars and Transportation; Loans and Investments; Real Estate; Souvenirs, Books, and Gifts; Supplies and Equipment; For Government and Non-Profit Buyers; and Find Sales by Agency. It also features subscription access to a free email newsletter called Government Sales that provides daily notice of government surplus property and asset sales currently offered across all federal agencies.
Subjects: Government Auctions; Surplus Government Property

156. General Services Administration
http://www.gsa.gov/
Description: The General Services Administration procures and manages federal office space, vehicles, technology, and supplies. The agency also sells off surplus government property. Key sections of this site include Selling to the Government and Buying from GSA. A Policy section has guidance on agency business practices in such areas as mail management, real property, employee travel, and electronic government. Key Information on the home page has quick links to popular topics such as per diem rates, GSA product and service schedules, and IT outsourcing. A drop down menu linking to each GSA division and regional office is available from all pages at the site.

GSA is involved in a 2003 redesign of their site. Top-level links to popular pages, such as in the Key Information section, have improved this site's usability for those in the federal government and for vendors selling to the federal government.

Subjects: Government Administration; Government Procurement; Public Buildings
Publications: *Annual Report / [General Services Administration]*, GS 1.1:
Federal Supply Schedule (by Group), GS 2.7/4:
FirstGov, GS 1.40:
Forms, GS 1.13:
Information Technology Newsletter, GS 1.37/2:INTERNET
Publications of the General Services Administration, GS 1.17:P 96/
Summary Report on Real Property Owned by United States Throughout the World, GS 1.15:
Worldwide Geographic Location Codes, GS 1.34:

157. GSA Advantage!
`https://www.gsaadvantage.gov/advgsa/main_pages/start_page.jsp`
Sponsor: General Services Administration
Description: This GSA site, for use by federal government agencies only, is an online shopping and supply site. Authorized users can use government credit cards to purchase products from the Federal Supply Service.
Subject: Government Procurement

158. HUBzone Empowerment Contracting Program
`https://eweb1.sba.gov/hubzone/internet/`
Sponsor: Small Business Administration (SBA)
Description: The HUBzone Empowerment Contracting program provides federal contracting opportunities for qualified small businesses located in distressed areas. A HUBzone is a Historically Underutilized Business Zone. Their site features areas such as Who We Are, Frequently Asked Questions, Library and Resources, Are You in a HUBZone, and Certified HUBZone Concerns. There is also an online utility for applying for certification as a qualified HUBZone Small Business Concern.
Subjects: Government Contracts; Small Business

159. Javits-Wagner-O'Day
`http://www.jwod.gov/`
Sponsor: Committee for Purchase From People Who Are Blind or Severely Disabled
Description: Through federal procurement policies, The Javits-Wagner-O'Day (JWOD) Program generates jobs and training opportunities for people who are blind or who have other severe disabilities. The site features sections such as About Us, Products and Services, How to Participate, Library (Press Releases, Publications), and Contacts.
Subjects: Disabilities; Government Procurement — Policy
Publication: *Working Together: Federal Customers and the Javits-Wagner-O'Day Program*, Y 3.P 97:8

160. NASA Acquisition Internet Service
`http://prod.nais.nasa.gov/cgi-bin/nais/index.cgi`
Sponsor: National Aeronautics and Space Administration (NASA)
Description: The NASA Acquisition Internet Service (NAIS) site provides a central point of Internet contact for businesses interested in NASA acquisitions and procurement opportunities. The site includes information on NAIS and links to other NASA sites, such sections as Business Opportunities, Reference Library, Center Procurement Sites, and Email Notification. The Center Procurement Sites section provides links to NASA procurement Web sites, including the NASA Office of Procurement, the Kennedy Space Center, and the Marshall Space Flight Center.
Subject: Government Procurement

161. NASA Commercial Technology Network
`http://www.nctn.hq.nasa.gov/`
Sponsor: National Aeronautics and Space Administration (NASA)

Description: The NASA Commercial Technology Network (NCTN) provides access to a wide array of information resources covering research and development, technology, patents, technical expertise, technology partnering, licensing, and commercialization opportunities. The site has information on NASA's Small Business Innovation Research and Small Business Technology Transfer programs, and links to the online versions of *Aerospace Technology Innovation*, which provides information on current NASA projects, and the *Spinoff*, an annual publication featuring the successful commercial and industrial application of NASA technology.
Subjects: Small Business — Grants; Technology Transfer
Publications: *Aerospace Technology Innovation*, NAS 1.95:
Spinoff, Annual Report, NAS 1.1/4:

162. Notices of Funding Availability
http://199.128.89.11/scripts/dbml.exe?Template=/admin/nofa/nofa2.dbm&orderchoice=pub&keyword=all
Sponsor: Agriculture Department (USDA) — Rural Development
Description: The Notices of Funding Availability (NOFA) are announcements that appear in the *Federal Register* inviting applications for federal grant programs. This site allows the generation of a customized listing of Notices of Funding Availability. Users can create the report by choosing a list order (by date of publication or deadline), keyword, and agency. The keywords are preselected and only include very general terms such as Housing, Public Safety, Youth, Education, Technology, Health, and Environment.
Subject: Grants

163. Office of Government Ethics
http://www.usoge.gov/home.html
Sponsor: Office of Government Ethics (OGE)
Description: The Office of Government Ethics coordinates activities in the executive branch related to preventing conflicts of interest on the part of government employees and to resolving conflicts of interest that do occur. Its Web site features sections such as About OGE; What's New; Training Workshops and Seminars; Computer and Web-based Training; Forms, Publications, and Other Ethics Documents; Videos and Software; Laws and Regulations; Advisory Opinions; International; Technical Assistance, and Frequently Asked Questions. Forms are available in either Internet Forms (which may be filled out online) or PDF versions (which must be printed and completed). Other publications are available in PDF format. Laws and Regulations provides the complete text of applicable Executive Orders, Federal Register issuances, statutes and regulations related to the executive branch ethics program.

This site will be useful to government employees concerned with possible conflict of interest situations. It is also an excellent starting point for members of the general public interested in exploring topics in government ethics.
Subjects: Ethics in Government; Government Employees — Regulations
Publication: *Government Ethics Newsgram*, Y 3.ET 3:15

164. Office of Governmentwide Policy
http://www.gsa.gov/Portal/content/orgs_content.jsp?contentOID=22887&contentType=1005
Sponsor: General Services Administration — Office of Governmentwide Policy (OGP)
Description: The Office of Governmentwide Policy (OGP) was created to consolidate all of GSA's governmentwide policy-making activities within one central office. These activities include acquisitions, government travel, and internal management systems. The site links to OGP's component offices and information, such as the Office of Real Property, Federal Vehicle Policy Division, Regulatory Information Service Center, and domestic per diem rates for federal agency travelers while on official business for the government.
Subjects: Government Administration — Policy; Government Procurement — Policy
Publications: *GSA's Federal Travel Regulation*, GS 1.6/8-2:
Intergovernmental Solutions Newsletter, GS 1.38:
U.S. Per Diem Rates, GS 1.36:

165. PRO-Net
http://pro-net.sba.gov/
Sponsor: Small Business Administration (SBA)
Description: SBA's Procurement Marketing and Access Network, PRO-Net, presents a database of procurement information for and about small businesses. For agencies seeking contractors, this site includes information on over 195,000 small, disadvantaged, and women-owned businesses. Users can search by NAICS codes, keywords, location, quality certifications, business type, ownership race and gender, EDI capability, and other criteria. Small business contractors can use the site to promote their businesses, as well as to browse for procurement opportunities. The Web site includes categories entitled What is PRO-Net, How to Use PRO-Net, Update Profiles, Search Database, Register, Opportunities & Resources, and Subcontracting Opportunities.

This powerful tool should be used by all small businesses seeking to do business with the federal government, and by all agencies seeking small business contractors.
Subjects: Government Contracts; Small Business

166. Rates and Allowances
http://www.dtic.mil/perdiem/rateinfo.html
Alternate URL: http://www.policyworks.gov/org/main/mt/homepage/mtt/perdiem/travel.shtml
Sponsors: Defense Department; General Services Administration
Description: Designed for civilian Defense Department employees, this page provides easy access to federal per diem rates, meal rates, and cost of living allowances (COLA) and housing allowances for travel and living arrangements within the United States or throughout the world. The Per Diem Rates page includes charts for official federal government rates and divides the charts into Continental United States (CONUS), Outside Continental United States (OCONUS), and Overseas. The page also covers Overseas Housing Allowances, Basic Allowance for Housing, and Overseas Cost of Living Allowances.

GSA makes per diem rates for federal employees available on its Office of Governmentwide Policy/Per Diem Rates site (see the Alternate URL listed above).
Subject: Civilian Defense Employees

167. Salaries and Wages
http://www.opm.gov/oca/payrates/
Sponsor: Office of Personnel Management (OPM)
Description: This official OPM site for government-wide pay programs for federal employees has information on the General Schedule (GS), Law Enforcement Pay Schedules, and the Federal Wage System (FWS) and provides a variety of resources. Most of the schedules are in PDF format. The following schedules are available: General Schedule and Locality Pay Tables, Law Enforcement Special Salary Rate and Locality Pay Tables, Locality Pay Area Definitions, Executive Schedule, Senior Executive Schedule, Special Salary Rate Tables, Administrative Law Judges, Employees in Senior-Level and Scientific or Professional Positions, and Members of Boards of Contract Appeals. There are also links to the past pay schedules and to information on the Federal Wage System, which includes the section Minimum Wage Notice, and Wage Schedules.
Subjects: Government Employees; Pay and Benefits

168. SBIR and STTR Programs and Awards
http://www.sbaonline.sba.gov/sbir/indexsbir-sttr.html
Sponsor: Small Business Administration (SBA)
Description: The Small Business Innovation Research and Small Business Technology Transfer programs are competitive funding programs to encourage innovative research and development in small businesses and nonprofit research institutions. They are offered by agencies with large research and development budgets, and coordinated by the Small Business Administration. This site describes the programs, lists past winners, and has a handbook for preparation of SBIR/STTR proposals.
Subject: Small Business — Grants

169. Selling to the Government
http://www.gsa.gov/Portal/selling.jsp
Sponsor: General Services Administration
Description: This is the General Services Administration portal for vendors and contractors wishing to do business with the federal government. Information is organized by type of product or service, such as furniture, tools, documents management, transportation, scientific services, or law enforcement. For each category, the site identifies the GSA contacts and relevant acquisition programs. The portal also provides basic information on how to sell to the government and how to get on the Federal Supply Schedule.
Subject: Government Procurement

170. SUB-Net
http://web.sba.gov/subnet/
Sponsor: Small Business Administration (SBA)
Description: The site is designed primarily as a place for large businesses to post solicitations and notices. Prime contractors can use SUB-Net to post subcontracting opportunities. These may or may not be reserved for small business, and they may include either solicitations or other notices—for example, notices of sources sought for teaming partners and subcontractors on future contracts. Small businesses can use this site to identify opportunities in their areas of expertise. The site features About SUB-Net, Search for Solicitation, and Post Solicitation.
Subjects: Government Contracts; Databases

171. U.S. Chief Financial Officers Council
http://www.cfoc.gov/
Sponsor: U.S. Chief Financial Officers Council
Description: Members of the U.S. Chief Financial Officers Council (CFOC) are the CFOs of the largest federal agencies and senior officials of the Office of Management and Budget and the Department of the Treasury. The CFOC Web site includes current membership and committee lists, Council meeting minutes, and the Council history and charter.
Subject: Government Finance

172. UNICOR: Federal Prison Industries, Inc.
http://www.unicor.gov
Sponsor: Federal Prison Industries, Inc.
Description: The UNICOR Web site enables the federal government and contractors to buy goods and services from Federal Prison Industries, whose primary mission is the productive employment of inmates. The UNICOR Web site offers an online product catalog with ordering and browsing capabilities. Sections of the site include What's on Sale, Schedule of Products, Customer Service, Online Store, Order Status, and What is UNICOR.
Subjects: Government Procurement; Prisoners

International Commerce, Exporting & Importing

173. AESDirect
http://www.aesdirect.gov/
Sponsor: Commerce Department — Economics and Statistics Administration (ESA) — Census Bureau
Description: AESDirect (Automated Export System Direct) allows shippers to report exports directly to the U.S. government at no cost to the exporter. The site offers a Tour, registration information, and instructions for use. It is used to file electronically Shipper's Export Declarations (SED) to the government.
Subjects: Exports — Regulations; Shipper's Export Declarations

174. BISNIS: Business Information Service for the Newly Independent States
http://www.bisnis.doc.gov
Sponsor: Commerce Department — International Trade Administration (ITA)

Description: BISNIS is a resource center for doing business in Russia and the other states of the former Soviet Union. This Web site features such sections as Latest News, Country Reports, Industry Reports, Leads, Events, Customs Corner, Sources of Finance, and *BISNIS Bulletin*. Users may register to receive by email industry reports and country reports.

BISNIS is a useful resource for businesses or individuals wishing to learn more about trade with Russia and business opportunities in that region.

Subjects: Emerging Markets; International Business; Eurasia
Publications: *BISNIS Bulletin*, C 61.42:
BISNIS Search for Partners, C 61.42/2:

175. Bureau of Industry and Security

http://www.bxa.doc.gov/
Sponsor: Commerce Department — Bureau of Industry and Security (BIS)
Description: The Department of Commerce Bureau of Industry and Security (BIS) regulates the export of sensitive goods such as weapons technologies and encryption software, and it regulates exports to certain countries in accordance with U.S. policy. Prior to April 2002, BIS was known as the Bureau of Export Administration. The BIS Web site links to major regulations, export licensing guidelines, news, and training courses on export restrictions. The primary audience for the site is the U.S. exporter community. Topical sections include Antiboycott Compliance, High Performance Computer Export Controls, and the Chemical Weapons Convention. A new section called SNAP allows exporters to submit export applications and other requests online. The site also has a page of links to other offices within U.S. government agencies that have export control responsibilities.

While geared toward the practical needs of exporters, the BIS site is also a good source for general research on U.S. export controls.

Subject: Exports — Regulations
Publications: *Annual Report*, C 63.1:
Bureau of Export Administration Fact Sheets, C 63.24:

176. CEEBICnet: Central and Eastern Europe Business Information Center

http://www.mac.doc.gov/ceebic/
Sponsor: Commerce Department — International Trade Administration (ITA) — Market Access and Compliance
Description: CEEBICnet presents economic, commercial, and financial information on the countries of Central and Eastern Europe, intended for use by U.S. firms interested in expanding into the Central and Eastern European markets. Information includes: trade and investment leads; market research; *Country Commercial Guides*; lists of U.S. companies operating in the profiled countries; small business support; specialized email newsletter services; and a calendar of trade fairs.

Countries covered include Albania, Bosnia & Herzegovina, Bulgaria, Croatia, Czech Republic, Estonia, FR Yugoslavia, FYR Macedonia, Hungary, Latvia, Lithuania, Poland, Romania, Slovak Republic, and Slovenia.

The site contains extensive information for those interested in Central and Eastern Europe markets or in profiles of the individual countries included in the program.

Subjects: Emerging Markets; Eastern Europe
Publication: *Central and Eastern Europe Commercial Update*, C 61.43:

177. Commercial News USA

http://www.cnewsusa.com/
Sponsor: Commerce Department — International Trade Administration (ITA)
Description: This site is the online version of Commercial News USA, an official export catalog-magazine of the U.S. Commerce Department. The magazine and Web site are designed to assist importers around the world in their efforts to find the American products or services they would like to buy. The site features separate sections for U.S. exporters and non-U.S. importers, with such resources as trade leads for exporters and a directory of American exporters.

Although an official publication of the Commerce Department, this site is operated by Associated Business Publications International, and accepts advertising.

Subject: Exports
Publication: *Commercial News USA*, C 61.10:

178. Customs Service
http://www.customs.ustreas.gov/

Sponsor: Treasury Department — Customs Service

Description: The Customs Service is becoming part of the new Department of Homeland Security. Its current Web site features sections on importing and exporting, traveler information, enforcement, and careers. A Legal section has Customs rulings, Customs Bulletins and Decisions, and references to customs laws and regulations. Other featured links include a Newsroom and contact information for ports.The Import and Export sections have extensive information for traders, from current trade issues to a regularly updated table of wait times at the U.S. border entry points. They also include information on exporting a vehicle, international mail shipments, and importing goods purchased over the Internet from foreign sources.

This site provides a wealth of practical information about Customs for travelers and the business community.

Subjects: Customs (Trade); Homeland Security

Publications: *Accountability Report*, T 17.1:

Customs Today, T 17.16:

Customs Valuation Encyclopedia 1980–1996, T 17.2:EN 1/980-96

Legal Precedent Retrieval System, T 17.6/3-7:

179. Export-Import Bank of the United States
http://www.exim.gov/

Sponsor: Export-Import Bank of the United States

Description: The Export-Import Bank offers export financing for U.S. businesses. The site presents information on the Bank's services and programs. Sections include About EX-IM, What's New, New & Small Business, Products, Services, Country/Fee Info, Environment, Seminars, and more. Country Fact Sheets, Foreign Language Fact Sheets, and other reports are listed under the Country/Fee section. Additional documents are located under What's New, including press releases, speeches, and more reports.

This site presents valuable information despite an awkward site design. The Index section may provide an easier interface to the site's content than the home page does at present. The Frequently Asked Questions section is helpful and also links to related Web pages for each question.

Subjects: Finance; International Trade

Publication: *Annual Report / Export-Import Bank of the United States*, Y 3.EX 7/3:1/

180. Foreign Exchange Rates (Monthly)
http://www.federalreserve.gov/releases/G5/

Sponsor: Federal Reserve — Board of Governors

Description: This monthly publication from the Federal Reserve, also known as Federal Reserve Statistical Release G.5, provides the average exchange rates for the previous month and comparable figures for earlier months. The averages, which are released at the first of each month, are based on daily noon buying rates for cable transfers in New York City. It does not include rates for all countries and is not as current as some of the nongovernment sources for daily exchange rates on the Web. The releases are available back to June 1996.

Subject: Exchange Rates

Publication: *Foreign Exchange Rates*, FR 1.32/2:

181. Import Administration
http://ia.ita.doc.gov/

Sponsor: Commerce Department — International Trade Administration (ITA) — Import Administration

Description: The Import Administration enforces laws and agreements to prevent unfairly traded imports. The IA home page presents an alphabetical list of information on its site, including: Antidumping Manual; Document Library; Expected Wages of Selected NME Countries; *Federal Register Notices*; Foreign Cases Against U.S. Firms; Foreign-Trade Zones Board; Introduction To Trade Remedies; Laws and Regulations; Litigation; Policy Bulletins; Remand Redeterminations; Subsidies Enforcement Office; Statistics (Antidumping and Countervailing Duties Cases); and Suspension Agreements Reference Prices.

Subject: Trade Laws and Regulations

182. International Trade Administration
http://www.ita.doc.gov/
Sponsor: Commerce Department — International Trade Administration (ITA)
Description: The ITA Web site is divided into three sections: ITA's Key Links, Press Releases, and Upcoming Trade Missions. Key Links lists some of the ITA's bureaus as well as portal Web sites. Links include Export.Gov. BuyUSA.com, Trade Advocacy Center, and Trade Compliance Center. The link to the Office of Public Affairs leads to the online publications catalog.

The numerous links to substantial information repositories make this site a good first choice for export related information.
Subject: International Trade
Publications: *Addressing the Challenges of International Bribery and Fair Competition*, C 61.2:
Export America, C 61.18/2:
Monthly Trade Update, C 61.46:
U.S. Foreign Trade Highlights, C 61.28/2:

183. International Trade Commission
http://www.usitc.gov/
Sponsor: International Trade Commission (ITC)
Description: The International Trade Commission is an independent federal agency concerned with unfair trade practices and the impact of imports on U.S. industries. Major sections of the ITC site include: Publications, Investigations, Dockets, Information Center, and About the USITC. The home page also features Headlines, Today's Events, and New and Notable. Listed under New and Notable is DataWeb, an interactive trade and tariff database.

On the Publications page, users will find the most popular titles listed at the top, including *Harmonized Tariff Schedules*, the *International Economic Review*, and the *Industry, Trade, and Technology Review*—followed by a list of other publications. Users may also search the catalog for reports and other documents. Reports of ITC activities are located under Investigations. In addition to forms, rules, statutes, a calendar, and petitions and complaints filed with the USITC, the Dockets section includes a link to EDIS On-Line. EDIS provides Internet access to public documents filed with the Secretary's Office in USITC investigations. Finally, the Information Center section of the site presents a quick index of site highlights, a reference shelf, and a spotlight section on additions to the site.

Despite the understated presentation, the availability of the tariff schedules and the serials in full-text formats make this an important resource for international trade information.
Subject: International Trade
Publications: *Harmonized Tariff Schedule of the United States, Annotated for Statistical Reporting Purposes*, ITC 1.10:
Industry and Trade Summaries, ITC 1.33:
Industry Trade and Technology Review, ITC 1.33/2:
International Economic Review (monthly), ITC 1.29:
International Trade Commission Investigative Reports, ITC 1.12:
Report to Congress and Trade Policy Committee On Trade Between the United States and Nonmarket Economy Countries, ITC 1.13:
U.S. International Trade Commission Annual Report, ITC 1.1:
Year in Trade: Operation of Trade Agreements Program, ITC 1.24:

184. Market Access and Compliance
http://www.mac.doc.gov/
Sponsor: Commerce Department — International Trade Administration (ITA) — Market Access and Compliance
Description: Market Access and Compliance (MAC) supports U.S. access to foreign markets. In addition to information about MAC and its regional U.S. offices, links are provided to export promotion programs such as the Central and Eastern Europe Business Information Center (CEEBIC) Online, China Gateway, BISNIS Online, Office of Japan, NAFTA, and more.

This site is primarily useful as a link to the individual programs and to see the range of programs sponsored by this agency.
Subjects: Exports; Trade Laws and Regulations

185. NAFTA and Inter-American Affairs Office

http://www.mac.doc.gov/nafta/

Sponsor: Commerce Department — International Trade Administration (ITA) — Market Access and Compliance

Description: The Office of NAFTA and Inter-American Affairs provides information to U.S. exporters experiencing market access barriers in Canada or Mexico. This site contains the full text of the North American Free Trade Agreement (NAFTA) in HTML format, and detailed sections on NAFTA Implementation and NAFTA Compliance. The site also has relevant *Federal Register Notices*, reports, speeches, and statistics, as well as a link to the related MAC site on the Free Trade Area of the Americas program.

Subject: North American Free Trade Agreement (NAFTA)

186. Office of Defense Trade Controls

http://pmdtc.org/

Sponsor: State Department — Defense Trade Controls Office

Description: The Office of Defense Trade Controls Web site provides information on the rules governing U.S. exports of defense materials and services. For manufacturers, exporters, and brokers of defense articles, the site has sections such as Register Your Company, Licensing, and Get Forms. A Reference Library section has the text of relevant regulations, a Country Embargo Reference Chart, and other documents. The Learning Center section has relevant instructions and guidelines.

Subject: Trade Laws and Regulations

187. Office of Textiles and Apparel

http://otexa.ita.doc.gov/

Sponsor: Commerce Department — International Trade Administration (ITA)

Description: The OTEXA site features information about the Office, as well as on exporting U.S.-made textile and apparel products. Primary sections include Trade Data, Import Quotas, the Trade Act of 2000, Trade Agreements, Trade Shows, the Textile Correlation, Publications, *Federal Register Notices*, Bilateral Agreements, and more. The Publications section provides information on ordering documents, while most of the online publications are under Trade Data. The home page highlights new and important sections of the site, and provides links to related organizations such as textile trade associations.

Subjects: Exports; Textile Industry

Publications: *Major Shippers Report*, C 61.53:

Textile and Apparel Trade Balance Report, C 61.51:

U.S. Exports of Textile and Apparel Products, C 61.50:

U.S. Imports of Textile and Apparel Products, C 61.52:

U.S. Textile and Apparel Category System, C 61.54:

188. Office of Trade and Economic Analysis

http://www.ita.doc.gov/td/industry/otea/

Sponsor: Commerce Department — International Trade Administration (ITA)

Description: OTEA prepares and publishes data, research, and analysis on trade and investment issues to support U.S. trade promotion and trade policy. Its site features two key resources for summary trade data: *U.S. Foreign Trade Data Highlights* and *Monthly Foreign Trade Data*. The site also has monthly and yearly summary tables reporting quantity and value of U.S. exports and imports, by country, for each 10-digit code from the *Harmonized Tariff Schedule*. Other sections present state and metropolitan area export data. Table formats are varied throughout the site, including Lotus, Excel, ASCII, HTML, and PDF formats.

Subject: Trade Statistics

Publications: *Monthly Trade Update*, C 61.46:

U.S. Foreign Trade Highlights, C 61.28/2:

U.S. Trade In Perspective

189. Overseas Private Investment Corporation

http://www.opic.gov/

Sponsor: Overseas Private Investment Corporation

Description: The Overseas Private Investment Corporation (OPIC) is an independent U.S. government agency that assists U.S. companies investing in emerging economies around the world. Pages on this site include What Is OPIC; Insurance, Finance and Funds; Investors' Info Gateway Links; Publications and Press; Small Business Center; OPIC and the Environment; OPIC for Kids; and more.
Subjects: International Business; International Economic Development
Publications: *Annual Report / Overseas Private Investment Corporation*, OP 1.1:
OPICNews, OP 1.10:

190. SABIT Training Program
http://www.mac.doc.gov/sabit/sabit.html
Alternate URL: http://www.sabitprogram.org/
Sponsor: Commerce Department — International Trade Administration (ITA) — Market Access and Compliance
Description: The Special American Business Internship Training (SABIT) Program assists U.S. companies and organizations working in the New Independent States of the former Soviet Union by funding training programs for managers and scientists from this area. The program is intended to facilitate U.S.-Eurasian business partnerships. There is a Russian-language Web site for SABIT at the alternate URL listed above.
Subjects: Emerging Markets; Eurasia; Russia

191. Trade Compliance Center
http://www.export.gov/tcc/
Sponsor: Commerce Department — International Trade Administration (ITA)
Description: The TCC helps U.S. exporters understand and abide by the more than 250 U.S. trade agreements. The TCC monitors trade agreements, addresses compliance issues, and provides access to information on the opportunities created by the agreements. The site features Report a Barrier, Trade Agreements, Country Market Research, Bribery, and News.
Subjects: Trade Agreements; Trade Laws and Regulations
Publications: *Addressing the Challenges of International Bribery and Fair Competition*, C 61.2:IN
National Trade Estimate Report on Foreign Trade Barriers, PrEx 9.10:
Trade Policy Review Summaries

192. Trade Development
http://www.ita.doc.gov/td/td_home/tdhome.html
Sponsor: Commerce Department — International Trade Administration (ITA)
Description: Trade Development Unit, within Commerce's International Trade Administration, offers services to promote U.S. exports, with special expertise in U.S. industry sectors. The site has a searchable directory of trade development analysts for specific products and industries. It also links to assorted pages created by the individual ITA offices representing industry sectors, such as the Office of Automotive Affairs and the Forest Products and Building Materials Division.
Subject: Exports

193. Trade Information Center
http://www.trade.gov/td/tic/
Alternate URL: http://www.ita.doc.gov/td/tic/
Sponsor: Commerce Department — International Trade Administration (ITA)
Description: The U.S. Department of Commerce's Trade Information Center links to information about all federal export assistance programs, as well as country and regional market information. It includes sections such as Answers to Your Export Questions, Country Information, Tariff and Tax Information, Export Resources, Trade Offices Nationwide, Trade Events, and Industry Information. The Export Resources section contains a list of publications. The National Export Directory is accessible from the Trade Offices page.
Subjects: Exports; Market Research — International
Publication: *National Export Directory*, C 61.44:

194. U.S. - China Commission

http://www.uscc.gov/

Sponsor: United States-China Security Review Commission

Description: United States-China Security Review Commission (USCC) was created to review the national security implications of trade and economic ties between the United States and the People's Republic of China. Major sections of the Commission's site include Hearing Schedule, Written Testimony, Press Releases, and Hearing Transcripts. The site also has photos and biographies of Commission members, and copies of research papers prepared at the request of the Commission.

Subjects: International Economic Relations; China

195. U.S. - Israel Science and Technology Commission (USISTC)

http://www.ta.doc.gov/International/MideastAfrica/Israel/USISTC.html

Alternate URL: http://www.us-israel.org/jsource/US-Israel/usistc.html

Sponsor: Commerce Department — Technology Administration (TA)

Description: The USISTC promotes cooperation between the high tech sectors in the U.S. and Israel to create jobs and stimulate economic growth in both countries through the awarding of grants. These sites offer general information about the committee.

Subjects: Technology — International; Israel

196. U.S. - Northern Ireland Technology Cooperation

http://www.ta.doc.gov/International/Europe/nireland.html

Commerce Department — Technology Administration (TA)

Description: The U.S.-Northern Ireland technology cooperation initiative is intended to bring opportunities for job growth and economic prosperity in both regions that will help ensure a stable and lasting peace for Northern Ireland. The site describes the initiative, links to the memorandum of understanding, and presents a few links.

Subject: International Economic Development

197. U.S. Government Export Portal

http://www.export.gov

Sponsor: Commerce Department — International Trade Administration (ITA)

Description: This site, also known as Export.gov, is a portal for information relevant to U.S. exporters. The main page has links to information on trade assistance programs, export news, new market reports, U.S. trade missions and delegations, and the U.S. government BuyUSA.com Web site. Other sections bring together export-related links under the categories Information Channels (Export Counseling, Finance and Insurance, Market Research), Export Quick Reference (Export Basics, International Contacts, Tariffs and Taxes), and Helpful Links (Export.gov email newsletter, Webcasts on Exporting).

As with other subject-oriented government Web portals, this site provides one-stop access to resources available from a variety of government agencies. While it is intended for those in the export business, the site is also a useful entry point and reference resource for international trade researchers in general.

Subject: Exports

198. United States Trade Representative

http://www.ustr.gov/

Sponsor: Trade Representative (USTR)

Description: The U.S. Trade Representative (USTR) is America's chief trade negotiator and the principal trade policy advisor to the president. This site offers information on USTR programs and resources in support of this role. Sections include WTO and Multilateral Affairs, World Regions, Sectors, Monitoring and Enforcement, Trade and Development, Outreach, About USTR, and Trade and Environment. Featured thematic sections include Tariff Free World, Agriculture, Steel, Trade Promotion Authority, and the Free Trade Area of the Americas. Press releases, *Federal Register Notices*, speeches and testimony, and reports are in a Resources section.

The USTR provides a starting point for research on U.S. international trade policies, agreements, and disputes. The World Regions section, which compiles relevant documents by region, can be particularly helpful. Two key document are available back to 1995, providing a useful history: *National Trade Estimate Report on Foreign Trade Barriers* and *Trade Policy Agenda and Annual Report of the President of the United States on the Trade Agreements Program.*

Subject: International Trade — Policy

Publications: *National Trade Estimate Report on Foreign Trade Barriers*, PrEx 9.10:

Trade Policy Agenda and Annual Report of the President of the United States on the Trade Agreements Program, PrEx 9.11:

CHAPTER 4

Census and Other Statistical Sources

The ability to collect information through many regulatory programs, surveys, and census studies makes the federal government an excellent source of statistical data. While the government has phased out some familiar printed reports, federal Web sites are a rich source of formatted data tables and downloadable data sets.

This chapter includes many Census Bureau Web sites, but also includes significant resources from other agencies and from the education sector. There are sections for sites that specialize in demographics or economics statistics. The three featured sites listed below are all starting points for the most frequently requested government statistics. From the Census Bureau, there are the American FactFinder and the Census 2000 Gateway sites. From an interagency statistics forum, there is the FedStats site, a government statistics portal.

Bookmarks & Favorites

Census

- American FactFinder, http://factfinder.census.gov
- Census Bureau Economic Programs, http://www.census.gov/econ/www/
- Federal, State, and Local Governments (Census),
     http://www.census.gov/govs/www/
- State and County Quickfacts, http://quickfacts.census.gov/qfd/

Other Statistics

- FedStats, http://www.fedstats.gov
- Statistical Abstract of the U.S., http://www.census.gov/statab/www/

Major Agencies

- Census Bureau, http://www.census.gov
- Bureau of Labor Statistics, http://www.bls.gov

(Also see topical chapters, such as Agriculture or Education.)

Featured Sites

199. American FactFinder
http://factfinder.census.gov/servlet/BasicFactsServlet

Sponsor: Commerce Department — Economics and Statistics Administration (ESA) — Census Bureau

Description: American FactFinder is a major Census Bureau effort to make it easier for the public to retrieve, print, and download Bureau statistics. Users can select data tabulations and maps from the currently available data sets. Data sources include the Decennial Census, the Economic Census, the American Community Survey, and the Population Estimates Program. Some statistics are available down to the block level, depending on the data source. Data tables can be printed or saved as comma-delimited, spreadsheet, or Rich Text Format (RTF) files.

A simple Search option in the upper left corner of the page leads to a surprisingly substantial number of data and reporting options. It will search for tables by keyword or geographic area and display available quick tables, detailed tables, demographic profiles, and reference and thematic maps. A Basic Facts feature allows users to jump to popular tables and maps for the United States, states, counties, cities, towns, and American Indian reservations. For Puerto Rico, basic population, housing, and geographic comparison tables and maps are available with a Spanish-language interface. A Data Sets section provides more options, including creating detailed tables and custom tables. Other features include FactFinder Data Sources, Reference Maps (showing boundaries and features), Thematic Maps (mapping statistical data), and a Site Tour.

American FactFinder supplements its easy interface with extensive hypertext help. The help section can be accessed by choosing either FAQs, Glossary, or Help from the top menu bar. The Frequently Asked Questions section includes a useful finding tool for the beginner: "Where are the data about…" This has direct links to the data on such listed topics as health insurance coverage, immigration, population changes, and state rankings.

American FactFinder accesses enough data and has enough functionality to be the first and last stop for many users, especially those looking for population and housing statistics in the form of basic tables and geographic comparisons. For other approaches to decennial census data, see the Census 2000 Gateway site.

Subjects: Census; Economic Statistics; Population Statistics

200. Census 2000 Gateway

`http://www.census.gov/main/www/cen2000.html`

Sponsor: Commerce Department — Economics and Statistics Administration (ESA) — Census Bureau

Description: As its name implies, the Census 2000 Gateway site is a starting point for finding products, data sets, news, documentation, and other information relating to latest decennial census of population and housing. There are three main approaches to the data itself. The American FactFinder has tables and maps of Census 2000 data for all geographies to the block level. State and County Quick Facts has summaries of the most requested data for states and counties. The third approach, Data Highlights, links to a variety of information at the state, county, and place level, including: American FactFinder tables and maps, FTP access to data sets, technical documentation, news releases, state data center contacts, redistricting data, and other statistics. Other data reports include rankings and comparisons, briefs and special reports, and selected historical Census data.

The Census Gateway also has data release schedules, Census operations information, teaching materials, the Census Store, PDF copies of the short and long form questionnaires, and contact information for Bureau subject experts and state and local resource centers. A Census in Schools section includes teaching resources and lesson plans.

Subjects: Census; Population Statistics

201. FedStats

`http://www.fedstats.gov/`

Sponsor: Federal Interagency Council on Statistical Policy

Description: The FedStats site was established so that users could access statistics from over 100 federal agencies without having to know which agency makes the data available. FedStats is a portal. For the most part, it points to statistical information that is maintained and updated by federal agencies on their own Web servers.

References on this site are arranged in two main groups, Links to Statistics and Links to Statistical Agencies. Links to statistics are organized in several ways: Topic Links A to Z; MapStats (statistical profiles of states, counties, and congressional or federal judicial districts); Statistics by Geography; Statistical Reference Shelf; and a keyword search. Agency links are listed alphabetically and by subject. In addition, FedStats links to statistical agency news releases and to some of the major interactive data tools offered at federal agency Web sites.

FedStats serves as a central starting point for finding government statistics. The fact that the site points to the originating agency server rather than duplicating statistics at its own site reduces the likelihood of getting out-of-date numbers from this intermediary. Once an originating agency has been identified, however, researchers may want to search that site directly to be certain not to miss new or supplemental information.

Subjects: Statistics; Finding Aids

The census and statistical resources in this chapter are divided into three sections, spanning the entry numbers indicated here:

General	*202–217*
Demographics	*218–228*
Economic Statistics	*229–239*

General

202. Bureau of Justice Statistics

http://www.ojp.usdoj.gov/bjs/

Sponsor: Justice Department — Bureau of Justice Statistics (BJS)

Description: The Justice Department's Bureau of Justice Statistics collects and reports data on crime, offenders, victims, and the criminal justice system. Its Web site features quick access to frequently requested statistics on these topics. Justice system statistics highlighted on the main page cover prosecutors, courts, sentencing, corrections, criminal justice employment and expenditures, and criminal records systems. The site hosts and points to a number of other reports and data in spreadsheet and other formats. The site's Press Releases section highlights BJS publications as they are released, and links to the full text of the reports as well as associated spreadsheet files. The Publications section lists reports in alphabetical order and links to the full electronic version when one is available. For source data and codebooks, the site links to the BJS-sponsored National Archive of Criminal Justice Data Web site at the University of Michigan.

BJS also supports grants programs for state, local, and tribal governments to assist with criminal justice statistics programs at those levels. The programs are described under the heading Justice Records Improvement Program.

The BJS site provides well organized access to its own reports but also links to related statistics from other sites, such as the United Nations or other Justice bureaus including the FBI.

Subjects: Criminal Justice — Statistics; Prisons — Statistics

Publications: *Background Checks for Firearm Transfers*, J 29.11:F

Bureau of Justice Statistics Fiscal Year: At A Glance, J 29.1/2:

Bureau of Justice Statistics Publications Catalog, J 29.14/2:

Capital Punishment, J 29.11/3:

Correctional Populations in the United States, J 29.17:

Criminal Victimization (A National Crime Victimization Survey Report), J 29.11/10:

Federal Criminal Case Processing, with Reconciled Data, J 29.2:C 26

Federal Justice Statistics Program (annual), J 29.30:

Federal Law Enforcement Officers, J 29.11:L

Felony Defendants Large Urban Counties, J 29.2:F

Felony Sentences in State Courts, J 29.11/11:

Felony Sentences in the United States, J 29.11/11-2:

HIV in Prisons and Jails, J 29.11:P 93/

Indicators of School Crime and Safety, ED 1.347:

Jails in Indian Country, J 29.2:J

National Corrections Reporting Program, J 29.11/13-2:

Presale Handgun Checks, J 29.11:H 19/

Prison and Jail Inmates at Midyear, J 29.11/5-2:

Prisoners, J 29.11/7:

Prosecutors in State Courts, J 29.11/15:

Sourcebook of Criminal Justice Statistics, J 29.9/6:

State Court Sentencing of Convicted Felons, J 29.11/11-3:

Survey of DNA Crime Laboratories, J 29.13:

Survey of State Criminal History Information Systems, J 29.9/8:H 62/

Survey of State Procedures Related to Firearm Sales, J 29.2:F

203. Bureau of Transportation Statistics

http://www.bts.gov/

Sponsor: Transportation Department — Bureau of Transportation Statistics (BTS)

Description: The Bureau of Transportation Statistics Web site is a central source for U.S. transportation data collected by BTS and other agencies. With its Data Gaps Project, it has also become a resource for finding what data is not being collected. A new intermodal transportation database, called TranStats, is featured prominently on the main page along with a link to the Transportation Research Information Services (TRIS) bibliographic database. Links to major online reports, such as Airline On-Time Performance and Transportation Indicators are also featured on the front page.

An alphabetic and unannotated menu provides access to all of the information at the site, mixing publications, programs, data from BTS, data from other sources, and information about BTS. Main menu items include: Airline Information, Commodity Flow Survey, Data Gaps, Geographic Information Services, Grants, Journal of Transportation and Statistics, Motor Carrier Financial and Operating Statistics, National Household Travel Survey, Speeches, Statistical Policy and Research, and Transportation Studies.

Strong points for the BTS site include detailed airline on-time statistics, summary reports on U.S. transportation, and insight into the government statistical programs on this topic.

Subject: Transportation — Statistics

Publications: *Airport Activity Statistics of Certified Air Carriers,* TD 4.14:

Directory of Transportation Data Sources, TD 1.9/4:

FAA Statistical Handbook of Aviation, TD 4.20:

Journal of Transportation and Statistics, TD 12.18:

National Transportation Statistics, TD 12.1/2:

Telephone Contacts for Users of Federal Transportation Statistics

Transportation Indicators

Transportation Statistics Annual Report, TD 12.1:

TranStats, TD 12.19:

204. Census Bureau

`http://www.census.gov/`

Sponsor: Commerce Department — Economics and Statistics Administration (ESA) — Census Bureau

Description: The Census Bureau Home Page provides topical and alphabetic access to a wide variety of information from and about the bureau. Main categories include Census 2000, People, Business, Geography, Newsroom, At the Bureau, and Special Topics. Special Topics includes information on the newly-released individual records from the 1930 Census.

Data may also be reached through an alphabetic index named Subjects A to Z, under the Publications section, or by the Search section. The Access Tools section provides links to Internet data tools, software, databases, and the American FactFinder (which is described elsewhere in this title). Other features of the site include Population Clocks, State and County QuickFacts, Latest Economic Indicators, and links to other federal statistical sites. Data sets are presented in text, comma delimited, HTML, or PDF formats. Users may order data products in physical formats using the Catalog section.

Overall, the Census Web site offers one of the largest collections of readily accessible statistical data and recent statistical press releases on the Web. This should be one of the first sites to check for demographic and economic statistics.

Subjects: Census; Economic Statistics; Population Statistics

Publications: *1997 Economic Census,* C 3.277:CD-EC 97

1997 Economic Census. Accommodation and Foodservices, C 3.277/2:

1997 Economic Census. Administrative and Support and Waste Management and Remediation Services, C 3.277/2:

1997 Economic Census. Arts, Entertainment, and Recreation, C 3.277/2:

1997 Economic Census. Construction, C 3.277/2:

1997 Economic Census. Educational Services, C 3.277/2:

1997 Economic Census. Finance and Insurance, C 3.277/2:

1997 Economic Census. Health Care and Social Assistance, C 3.277/2:

1997 Economic Census. Management of Companies and Enterprises, C 3.277/2:

1997 Economic Census. Manufacturing, C 3.277/2:

1997 Economic Census. Mining, C 3.277/2:

1997 Economic Census. Other Services, C 3.277/2:

1997 Economic Census. Professional, Scientific, and Technical Services, C 3.277/2:

1997 Economic Census. Real Estate and Rental and Leasing, C 3.277/2:

1997 Economic Census. Retail Trade, C 3.277/2:

1997 Economic Census. Transportation and Warehousing, C 3.277/2:

1997 Economic Census. Utilities, C 3.277/2:

1997 Economic Census. Wholesale Trade, C 3.277/2:

Advance Report on Durable Goods, Manufacturers; Shipments and Orders, C 3.158/2:
American FactFinder, C 3.300:
American Housing Brief (AHB) from the American Housing Survey, C 3.215/20:
America's Families and Living Arrangements, C 3.186/17-2:
Annual Benchmark Report for Retail Trade, C 3.138/3-8:
Annual Benchmark Report for Wholesale Trade, C 3.133/5:
Annual Capital Expenditures, C 3.289:
Annual Survey of Manufactures, C 3.24/9
Census and You, C 3.238:
Census Brief, C 3.205/8:
Census Catalog and Guide, C 3.163/3:
Census of Construction Industries: Geographic Area Series, C 3.245/7:
Census of Construction Industries: Industry Series, C 3.245/3:
Census of Governments, C 3.145/4:
Census of Retail Trade: Geographic Area Series (Alabama), C 3.255/2:
Census of Retail Trade: Geographic Area Series (Alaska), C 3.255/2:
Census of Retail Trade: Geographic Area Series (Arizona), C 3.255/2:
Census of Retail Trade: Geographic Area Series (Arkansas), C 3.255/2:
Census of Retail Trade: Geographic Area Series (California), C 3.255/2:
Census of Retail Trade: Geographic Area Series (Colorado), C 3.255/2:
Census of Retail Trade: Geographic Area Series (Connecticut), C 3.255/2:
Census of Retail Trade: Geographic Area Series (Delaware), C 3.255/2:
Census of Retail Trade: Geographic Area Series (District of Columbia), C 3.255/2:
Census of Retail Trade: Geographic Area Series (Florida), C 3.255/2:
Census of Retail Trade: Geographic Area Series (Georgia), C 3.255/2:
Census of Retail Trade: Geographic Area Series (Hawaii), C 3.255/2:
Census of Retail Trade: Geographic Area Series (Idaho), C 3.255/2:
Census of Retail Trade: Geographic Area Series (Illinois), C 3.255/2:
Census of Retail Trade: Geographic Area Series (Indiana), C 3.255/2:
Census of Retail Trade: Geographic Area Series (Iowa), C 3.255/2:
Census of Retail Trade: Geographic Area Series (Kansas), C 3.255/2:
Census of Retail Trade: Geographic Area Series (Kentucky), C 3.255/2:
Census of Retail Trade: Geographic Area Series (Louisiana), C 3.255/2:
Census of Retail Trade: Geographic Area Series (Maine), C 3.255/2:
Census of Retail Trade: Geographic Area Series (Maryland), C 3.255/2:
Census of Retail Trade: Geographic Area Series (Massachusetts), C 3.255/2:
Census of Retail Trade: Geographic Area Series (Michigan), C 3.255/2:
Census of Retail Trade: Geographic Area Series (Minnesota), C 3.255/2:
Census of Retail Trade: Geographic Area Series (Mississippi), C 3.255/2:
Census of Retail Trade: Geographic Area Series (Missouri), C 3.255/2:
Census of Retail Trade: Geographic Area Series (Montana), C 3.255/2:
Census of Retail Trade: Geographic Area Series (Nebraska), C 3.255/2:
Census of Retail Trade: Geographic Area Series (Nevada), C 3.255/2:
Census of Retail Trade: Geographic Area Series (New Hampshire), C 3.255/2:
Census of Retail Trade: Geographic Area Series (New Jersey), C 3.255/2:
Census of Retail Trade: Geographic Area Series (New Mexico), C 3.255/2:
Census of Retail Trade: Geographic Area Series (New York), C 3.255/2:
Census of Retail Trade: Geographic Area Series (North Carolina), C 3.255/2:
Census of Retail Trade: Geographic Area Series (North Dakota), C 3.255/2:
Census of Retail Trade: Geographic Area Series (Ohio), C 3.255/2:
Census of Retail Trade: Geographic Area Series (Oklahoma), C 3.255/2:
Census of Retail Trade: Geographic Area Series (Oregon), C 3.255/2:
Census of Retail Trade: Geographic Area Series (Pennsylvania), C 3.255/2:
Census of Retail Trade: Geographic Area Series (Rhode Island), C 3.255/2:
Census of Retail Trade: Geographic Area Series (South Carolina), C 3.255/2:
Census of Retail Trade: Geographic Area Series (South Dakota), C 3.255/2:
Census of Retail Trade: Geographic Area Series (Tennessee), C 3.255/2:

Census of Retail Trade: Geographic Area Series (Texas), C 3.255/2:
Census of Retail Trade: Geographic Area Series (U.S. Summary), C 3.255/2:
Census of Retail Trade: Geographic Area Series (Utah), C 3.255/2:
Census of Retail Trade: Geographic Area Series (Vermont), C 3.255/2:
Census of Retail Trade: Geographic Area Series (Virginia), C 3.255/2:
Census of Retail Trade: Geographic Area Series (Washington), C 3.255/2:
Census of Retail Trade: Geographic Area Series (West Virginia), C 3.255/2:
Census of Retail Trade: Geographic Area Series (Wisconsin), C 3.255/2:
Census of Retail Trade: Geographic Area Series (Wyoming), C 3.255/2:
Census of Transportation, Communications, and Utilities, C 3.292:
Census Product Update, C 3.163/7-2:
Company Summary, 1997: 1997 Economic Census, C 3.277/3:
Consolidated Federal Funds Report, C 3.266/3:
Construction Reports: Housing Completions, C22, C 3.215/13:
Construction Reports: Housing Units Authorized by Building Permits, C40, C 3.215/4:
Construction Reports: New One-Family Homes Sold and For Sale, C25, C 3.215/9:
Construction Reports: Value of Construction Put in Place, C30, C 3.215/3:
County Business Patterns, C 3.204/4:
County Business Patterns - Alabama, C 3.204/3-2:
County Business Patterns - Alaska, C 3.204/3-3
County Business Patterns - Arizona, C 3.204/3-4:
County Business Patterns - Arkansas, C 3.204/3-5:
County Business Patterns - California, C 3.204/3-6:
County Business Patterns - Colorado, C 3.204/3-7:
County Business Patterns - Connecticut, C 3.204/3-8:
County Business Patterns - Delaware, C 3.204/3-9:
County Business Patterns - District of Columbia, C 3.204/3-10:
County Business Patterns - Florida, C 3.204/3-11:
County Business Patterns - Georgia, C 3.204/3-12:
County Business Patterns - Hawaii, C 3.204/3-13:
County Business Patterns - Idaho, C 3.204/3-14:
County Business Patterns - Illinois, C 3.204/3-15:
County Business Patterns - Indiana, C 3.204/3-16:
County Business Patterns - Iowa, C 3.204/3-17:
County Business Patterns - Kansas, C 3.204/3-18:
County Business Patterns - Kentucky, C 3.204/3-19:
County Business Patterns - Louisiana, C 3.204/3-20:
County Business Patterns - Maine, C 3.204/3-21:
County Business Patterns - Maryland, C 3.204/3-22:
County Business Patterns - Massachusetts, C 3.204/3-23:
County Business Patterns - Michigan, C 3.204/3-24:
County Business Patterns - Minnesota, C 3.204/3-25:
County Business Patterns - Mississippi, C 3.204/3-26:
County Business Patterns - Missouri, C 3.204/3-27:
County Business Patterns - Montana, C 3.204/3-28:
County Business Patterns - Nebraska, C 3.204/3-29:
County Business Patterns - Nevada, C 3.204/3-30:
County Business Patterns - New Jersey, C 3.204/3-32:
County Business Patterns - New Mexico, C 3.204/3-33:
County Business Patterns - New York, C 3.204/3-34:
County Business Patterns - North Carolina, C 3.204/3-35:
County Business Patterns - North Dakota, C 3.204/3-36:
County Business Patterns - Ohio, C 3.204/3-37:
County Business Patterns - Oklahoma, C 3.204/3-38:
County Business Patterns - Oregon, C 3.204/3-39:
County Business Patterns - Outlying Areas, C 3.204/3-53:
County Business Patterns - Pennsylvania, C 3.204/3-40:

County Business Patterns - Rhode Island, C 3..204/3-41:
County Business Patterns - South Carolina, C 3.204/3-42:
County Business Patterns - South Dakota, C 3.204/3-43:
County Business Patterns - Tennessee, C 3.204/3-44:
County Business Patterns - Texas, C 3.204/3-45:
County Business Patterns - Utah, C 3.204/3-46:
County Business Patterns - Vermont, C 3.204/3-47:
County Business Patterns - Virginia, C 3.204/3-48:
County Business Patterns - Washington, C 3.204/3-49:
County Business Patterns - West Virginia, C 3.204/3-50:
County Business Patterns - Wisconsin, C 3.204/3-51:
County Business Patterns - Wyoming, C 3.204/3-52:
County Business Patterns- New Hampshire, C 3.204/3-31:
County Business Patterns, United States, C 3.204/3-1:
Current Business Reports, Service Annual Survey, C 3.138/3-4:
Current Business Reports: Annual Survey of Communications Services, C 3.138/3-6:
Current Business Reports: Monthly Retail Trade Sales & Inventories, C 3.138/3:
Current Business Reports: Monthly Wholesale Trade, C 3.133:
Current Construction Reports: Characteristics of New Housing, C25A, C 3.215/9-3:
Current Construction Reports: Expenditures for Residential Improvements and Repairs, C50, C 3.215/8:
Current Construction Reports: Housing Starts, C20, C 3.215/2:
Current Construction Reports: New Residential Construction in Selected Metropolitan Areas, C21,
 C 3.215/15:
Current Housing Reports: Characteristics of Apartments Completed, H-131, C 3.215:H 131/
Current Housing Reports: Housing Characteristics, H-121, C 3.215:H 121/
Current Housing Reports: Housing Vacancies and Home Ownership, C 3.215:H 111/
Current Housing Reports: Market Absorption of Apartments, H-130, C 3.215:H 130/
Current Industrial Reports, C 3.158:
Current Industrial Reports, Manufacturing Profiles, C 3.158/4:
Current Population Reports, Consumer Income, C 3.186:P-60/
Current Population Reports, Household Economic Studies, C 3.186:P-70/2/
Current Population Reports, Population Characteristics, C 3.186:P-20/
Current Population Reports, Population Estimates and Projections, C 3.186:P-25/
Current Population Reports, Special Studies, C 3.186:P-23/
Federal Expenditures by State, C 3.266:
Government Finance and Employment Classification Manual, C 3.6/2:F 49/6/
Guide to Foreign Trade Statistics, C 3.6/2:F 76
Household and Family Characteristics, C 3.186/17:
Housing Vacancies and Homeownership Survey, C 3.294:
Housing Vacancy Survey, C 3.224/13-2:
International Briefs (IB) series, C 3.205/9:
Measuring America: the Decennial Censuses from 1790 to 2000, C 3.2:
Monthly Product Announcement, C 3.163/7:
Motor Freight Transportation and Warehousing Survey, C 3.138/3-5:
News Releases, C 3.295:
Public Elementary-Secondary Education Finances, C 3.191/2-10:
Quarterly Employee Retirement, C 3.242:
Quarterly Financial Report for Manufacturing, Mining and Trade Corporations, C 3.267:
Quarterly Tax Survey, C 3.145/6:
School Enrollment Social and Economic Characteristics, C 3.186/12:
State and Metropolitan Area Data Book, Statistical Abstract Supplement, C 3.134/5:
State Government Tax Collection Data by State, C 3.191/2-8:
Statistical Abstract of the U.S., C 3.134:
Supplement to the American Housing Survey For Selected Metropolitan Areas, H-171, C 3.215/16:
Supplement to the American Housing Survey, H-151, C 3.215/19-:
Survey of Minority-Owned Business Enterprises, C 3.258:
Telephone Contacts for Data Users, C 3.238/5:
The Hispanic Population in the United States, C 3.186/14-2:

U.S. Trade with Puerto Rico and U.S. Possessions, FT-895, C 3.164:895/
We, the Americans . . ., C 3.2:AM 3/
Women-Owned Businesses, C 3.250:

205. Census Bureau Regional Offices
http://www.census.gov/field/www/
Sponsor: Commerce Department — Economics and Statistics Administration (ESA) — Census Bureau
Description: This site uses a clickable image map and alternative text list to link to the Web sites of the 12 regional offices of the Census Bureau. Each office has local contact information, employment opportunities, and information on regional resources.
Subject: Census

206. Census Monitoring Board
http://govinfo.library.unt.edu/cmb/cmbp/index.htm
Alternate URL: http://govinfo.library.unt.edu/cmb/cmbc/index.htm
Sponsor: Census Monitoring Board
Description: The Census Monitoring Board was an eight-member bipartisan oversight board created in 1997 and charged "to observe and monitor all aspects of the preparation and implementation of the 2000 decennial census." Four members were appointed by the President, two by the House, and two by the Senate. The presidential and congressional appointees created separate Web sites and filed separate reports. Much of the material on the sites concerns the issue of statistical adjustment for possible undercounts. Both sites have been archived at the University of North Texas Libraries CyberCemetery Web site. The presidential appointees maintained the site that is given here as the primary URL. The alternate URL is for the congressional appointees' site.
Subject: Census Techniques

207. Census State Data Center Program
http://www.census.gov/sdc/www/
Sponsor: Commerce Department — Economics and Statistics Administration (ESA) — Census Bureau
Description: Via a clickable image map, this site provides basic contact information for the Census Data Center in each state, along with a graphical designation of services available at each center. In addition, there is a alphabetical list of those census state data centers and related Web sites and a calendar of state data center meetings. There is also a link to the State Data Center/Business-Industry Data Center Clearinghouse and Annual Report. The Clearinghouse site is geared to the needs of its Data Center members, but will be useful to others tracking census issues.

   This site has good basic directory information, including Internet contact addresses for the state data centers. Some data centers provide easier access to state level census statistics than the central Census Web site.
Subject: Census

208. ChildStats.gov
http://www.childstats.gov/
Sponsor: Federal Interagency Forum on Child and Family Statistics
Description: This site provides access to federal and state statistics and reports on children and their families, including population and family characteristics, economic security, health, behavior and social environment, and education. The Federal Interagency Forum on Child and Family Statistics offers several reports on the site, two of the most prominent being *Nurturing Fatherhood* and *America's Children: Key National Indicators of Well-Being*. The site includes the following sections: Other Forum Publications, What is the Forum, Who Are Forum Members, and International Comparisons. International Comparisons links to statistics from other sites that mirror selected indicators in the *America's Children* report. ChildStats.gov also features a list of contacts for federal statistics on children and families, and links to other Web resources on child well-being.
Subjects: Child Welfare — Statistics; Fatherhood — Statistics
Publications: *America's Children: Key National Indicators of Well-Being*, PR 43.8:
Nurturing Fatherhood, PR 42.8:

209. County and City Data Books (at Geostat)

http://fisher.lib.virginia.edu/ccdb/

Sponsor: University of Virginia. Library

Description: The Census Bureau's *County and City Data Book* series presents statistical tables for all U.S. counties, cities with 25,000 or more inhabitants, and places of 2,500 or more inhabitants. This site from the University of Virginia Library's Geospatial and Statistical Data Center offers access to data from the CD-ROM versions of the 1988 and 1994 editions of the *County and City Data Book*. Initial access is by city, state, county, or place data. The 1994 edition also includes rankings and source notes. After choosing the geographic level, the user can select which of the more than 200 variables available should be displayed. Variables cover such areas as demographics, housing, income and poverty, wholesale and retail trade, and government employment and expenditures. The results can be displayed in HTML or as a comma delimited file available via anonymous ftp.

The 2000 City and County Data Book is available online in PDF format from the Census Bureau site.

Subject: Population Statistics

Publication: *County and City Data Book*, C 3.134/2:C 83/2/

210. Directorate for Information Operations and Reports (DIOR)

http://web1.whs.osd.mil/

Sponsor: Defense Department — Directorate for Information Operations and Reports

Description: Defense procurement and personnel statistics are available from this DoD site. Procurement statistics report on the size and geographic distribution of prime contract awards and on the top companies and institutions receiving them. The Personnel section includes DoD military and civilian personnel and military casualty statistics in a variety of formats. (Statistics on Admirals and Generals formerly on the site had been removed at the time of this review.) Under the headings Military, Civilian, and Casualties, statistics are available in a mix of HTML, PDF, and spreadsheet formats. The Publications page for the Personnel section has the PDF text of the Directorate's statistical reports back to the mid-1990s. One report has historical data for military personnel back to the 1950s.

A catalog of the Directorate's reports, accessible from the main page, links to much of the available data.

Subjects: Military Forces — Statistics; Military Procurement — Statistics

Publications: *100 Companies Receiving The Largest Dollar Volume of Prime Contract Awards*, D 1.57:
100 Contractors Receiving The Largest Dollar Volume of Prime Contract Awards for RDT&E, Fiscal Year, D 1.57/2:
Atlas/State Data Abstract for the U.S. and Selected Areas, D 1.58/4:
Catalog of DIOR Reports, Department of Defense, D 1.33/4:
Civilian Manpower Statistics, D 1.61/2:
Companies Participating in the Department of Defense Subcontracting Program, D 1.57/9:
Distribution of Personnel by State and by Selected Locations, D 1.61/5:
Educational and Nonprofit Institutions Receiving Prime Contract Awards for Research, Development, Test, and Evaluation, D 1.57/8:
Prime Contract Awards, D 1.57/3:
Prime Contract Awards by Region and State, D 1.57/5:
Prime Contract Awards by Service Category and Federal Supply Classification, D 1.57/4:
Prime Contract Awards, Size Distribution, D 1.57/3-5:
Selected Manpower Statistics, Fiscal Year, D 1.61/4:
Worldwide Manpower Distribution by Geographical Area (quarterly), D 1.61/3:
Worldwide U.S. Active Duty Military Personnel Casualties, D 1.61/6:

211. Federal, State, and Local Governments (Census)

http://www.census.gov/govs/www/

Sponsor: Commerce Department — Economics and Statistics Administration (ESA) — Census Bureau

Description: This site has information and publications concerning the Census Bureau programs that cover local, state, and federal agencies and activities. These include the Census of Governments, Annual Survey of State and Local Government Finances, State Government Tax Collections Survey,

Education Finance Survey, Federal Assistance Award Data System, and Consolidated Federal Funds Reports. The site has survey forms, publications, summary reports, and press releases. Statistics are available under topical headings such as Public Employment and Payroll, Finance, Public Employment Retirement Systems, Tax Collections, and Federal Expenditures. Many of the data series are available back to 1992. There are options to view U.S. or individual state data, and reports can be downloaded in spreadsheet format or as a flat ASCII file.

Subjects: Government Employees — Statistics; Government Finance — Statistics; State Government — Statistics
Publications: *Census of Governments*, GP 3.22/2:
Consolidated Federal Funds Report, C 3.266/3:
Federal Assistance Award Data System
Public Elementary-Secondary Education Finances, C 3.191/2-10:
State Government Tax Collection Data by State, C 3.191/2-8:

212. Geospatial and Statistical Data Center: Interactive Data
http://fisher.lib.virginia.edu/active_data/
Sponsor: University of Virginia. Library
Description: While not all of its resources are from the federal government or are available to all users, this site does offer a substantial set of accessible government statistics resources. Some data sets are hosted locally by the University of Virginia Library and feature a customized search interface. Others are remote resources for which the Data Center merely provides a link and explanation. The data resources are grouped by category: demographic, economic, education, historical, international, maps and mappers, and social/health/behavioral. Federal data hosted locally includes the 1990 Census Public Use Microdata (PUMS) Files, County and City Data Books, County Business Patterns, and a United States Historical Census Data Browser.

This site is a selective gateway to social science statistics. The Data Center has done public users a service by adding simple but powerful functionality to government data sets.
Subjects: Demographics and Sociology — Statistics; Databases
Publications: *County and City Data Book*, C 3.134/2:C 83/2/
Regional Economic Information System, C 59.24:REIS:

213. GovStats
http://govinfo.library.orst.edu/
Sponsor: Oregon State University. Library
Description: Begun in 1995 as an effort to provide Web access to federal statistical information issued on CD-ROM, this site was formerly known as the Government Information Sharing Project. Many of the these federal statistical databases are now made available on the Web by the originating agency. In response, this site has been redesigned and relaunched with a pared-down set of databases: USA Counties, 1997 Census of Agriculture, U.S. Imports/Exports History, and 1992 Economic Census. The site may be adding other historical statistical databases in the future. GovStats provides a very straightforward interface to the databases it hosts. The site fills a niche in providing easy access to older federal data sets.
Subjects: Economic Statistics; Databases
Publications: *Economic Census 1992*, C 3.277:
U.S. Exports of Merchandise, C 3.278/3:
U.S. Imports of Merchandise, C 3.278/2:
USA Counties, C 3.134/6:

214. Sourcebook of Criminal Justice Statistics
http://www.albany.edu/sourcebook/
Sponsor: Justice Department — Bureau of Justice Statistics (BJS)
Description: This university site has made the *Sourcebook of Criminal Justice Statistics* available on the Web. The online version of the *Sourcebook* has tables and entire sections available in PDF format. Access is by keyword search or by browsing by section or by the contents, table and figure list, or index. Although its print counterpart is only issued annually, this Web site is regularly updated to reflect new data that will appear in the next print edition.

This is an important reference source for criminal justice statistics and can include more recent data than the printed source.

Subject: Criminal Justice — Statistics
Publication: *Sourcebook of Criminal Justice Statistics*, J 29.9/6:

215. Statistical Abstract of the United States

http://www.census.gov/statab/www/

Alternate URL: http://www.census.gov/statab/www/brief.html

Sponsor: Commerce Department — Economics and Statistics Administration (ESA) — Census Bureau

Description: The *Statistical Abstract* page at the Census Web site links to the current edition of this annual publication and to previous editions back to 1995. Published since 1878, the *Statistical Abstract of the United States* is a core reference tool with current and historical statistics on the U.S. population, health, education, workforce, government finances, elections, energy, income, prices, and more presented in a series of tables. The Web version consists of separate PDF files for each chapter of the printed book. One of these PDF files is the book's index, which can be searched with the Acrobat "find" feature. Unfortunately, the index entries are not hyperlinked to the tables in the PDF chapters.

Related resources are linked from this page, including the online version of *USA Statistics in Brief*, a pamphlet that highlights many of the statistical series of the *Abstract*. *USA Statistics in Brief* is located at the alternate URL above.

The *Statistical Abstract* has long been a research staple because of the data that it provides and the fact that each statistical table includes a citation to the source of the data—thus identifying likely sources for more information on the topic. The online version retains those attributes because it is a PDF equivalent to the print version. It does not bring many more advantages over print in terms of searching or navigation but does provide ready access to the content for those who do not have the print edition at hand.

Subjects: Social Indicators — Statistics; United States — Statistics
Publications: *Statistical Abstract of the U.S.*, C 3.134:
USA Statistics in Brief, C 3.134/2-2:

216. TIGER Page

Alternate URL: http://www.census.gov/geo/www/tiger/index.html

Sponsor: Commerce Department — Economics and Statistics Administration (ESA) — Census Bureau

Description: TIGER (Topologically Integrated Geographic Encoding and Referencing system) is the name given to the Census Bureau's digital mapping system for decennial census and other data. The central TIGER page offers TIGER-based digital geographic products, documentation and metadata, and information about TIGER. The site also links to information on LandView®, software for federal geographic data.

The TIGER/Line files are the primary public product created from the TIGER database. They are a database of geographic features, such as roads, railroads, and rivers. The files can be used with mapping or geographic information system (GIS) software that can import TIGER/Line files.

The TIGER Page is the central place to check for updates to the TIGER/Line files and related products. Explanatory material is available for both the newcomer and the experienced community of digital geographic data users.

Subjects: Census Mapping; Geographic Information Systems (GIS)

217. TranStats: the Intermodal Transportation Database

http://transtats.bts.gov

Sponsor: Transportation Department — Bureau of Transportation Statistics (BTS)

Description: TranStats offers organized access to over 100 transportation-related data bases along with the social and demographic data sets commonly used in transportation analysis. The data comes from federal agencies as well as several transportation-related organizations. The data sets are packaged with basic documentation. The site offers downloading in comma-separated value format and has some interactive mapping applications. Transportation modes covered by the data sets include aviation, highway, mass transit, rail, and others.

Subjects: Transportation — Statistics; Databases

Demographics

218. AgingStats.Gov

http://www.agingstats.gov

Sponsor: Federal Interagency Forum on Aging-Related Statistics

Description: Composed of 10 federal agencies that produce or use statistics on aging, the Federal Interagency Forum on Aging-Related Statistics maintains a Web site that serves as a finding aid for these statistics. The site links directly to aging-related statistics on its members' Web sites, including those at the Census Bureau, Veterans Affairs, National Center for Health Statistics, and the Social Security Administration. The Forum also produces its own publications, and the site currently features *Older Americans 2000: Key Indicators of Well-Being*. This publication is online in HTML and PDF formats. The site offers updated versions of some of the detailed tables in the book.

Subject: Senior Citizens — Statistics

Publication: *Older Americans 2000: Key Indicators of Well-Being*, HE 20.3852:

219. American Community Survey

http://www.census.gov/acs/www/

Sponsor: Commerce Department — Economics and Statistics Administration (ESA) — Census Bureau

Description: The Census Bureau's *American Community Survey* (ACS) is a new program that the Bureau plans to have fully implemented by 2003. The ACS will gather selected sample data annually and will eventually replace the current Census of Population and Housing long form sample data, but not the short form distributed to all U.S. households. ACS will collect demographic, housing, social, and economic information. The goal of the program is to provide governments with more timely (rather than decennial) data needed to administer federal programs, distribute funding, and plan accordingly. This site describes the ACS program's goals, methodology, data release schedule, products, and other details, and points to what ACS data is currently available. A Library section has articles, speeches, presentations and other material about the ACS.

At present, the ACS site has more information about the program than data from the program. This will change over time, and the site as it is goes a long way to answering the questions of citizens who may be surveyed.

Subject: Census Techniques

Publication: *American Community Survey*, C 3.297:

220. CensusScope

http://www.censusscope.org/

Sponsor: University of Michigan. Social Science Data Analysis Network

Description: CensusScope is a non-governmental portal to census data, with many prepared reports and maps to answer popular population questions. Sections include Charts and Trends (with trend data for the past 10, 20, or more years), Maps, Rankings, and Segregation (racial distribution).

CensusScope is a very easy-to-use Web site that can help to answer many of the most frequent Census of Population questions. For more extensive data, see the official U.S. Census site.

Subject: Census

221. Current Population Survey

http://www.bls.census.gov/cps/

Sponsors: Labor Department — Bureau of Labor Statistics (BLS); Commerce Department — Economics and Statistics Administration (ESA) — Census Bureau

Description: The Current Population Survey is the primary source of information on the labor force characteristics of the U.S. population. The survey of about 50,000 households is conducted by the

Census Bureau for the Bureau of Labor Statistics. Estimates obtained from the CPS include employment, unemployment, earnings, hours of work, and other indicators. They are available by a variety of demographic characteristics—including age, sex, race, marital status, and educational attainment—and by occupation, industry, and class of worker. The monthly CPS news release, The Employment Situation, is widely quoted for details on the current national unemployment rate.

In addition to information on the Survey, its history and methodology, the CPS site has access to the data and publications. Raw data may be accessed via FERRET, a federal electronic research and review extraction tool that takes some practice to master. Publications range from news releases to analytical reports and are organized by both topic and release date. A section called Supplements reports on the results from supplemental questions sometimes asked on the monthly survey. These include job tenure, work schedule, alternative employment and other topics. The raw data, methodology, and documentation from the supplementals are made available to interested users.

This site may be most frequently used for its monthly employment situation reports, although this information and more related statistics are available from the main Bureau of Labor Statistics site. For data users, the site provides organized access to technical documentation and information on methodology and data quality measures.

Subject: Employment — Statistics
Publication: *News, The Employment Situation*, L 2.53/2:

222. Data Extraction System
`http://www.census.gov/DES/www/welcome.html`
Sponsor: Commerce Department — Economics and Statistics Administration (ESA) — Census Bureau
Description: This site enables users to request raw data only (which must then be picked up and processed by programming or statistical analysis software elsewhere) from the following data sets: Survey of Income and Program Participation, Current Population Survey, American Housing Survey, Decennial Census Public Use Microdata Samples, and Consumer Expenditure Survey. A series of prompts allows users to specify exactly which columns and rows of data are needed. After the request has been sent, users are notified by email when the file is ready. Users then need to retrieve the file, via FTP or the Data Extraction System (DES) Web site, before it expires on the server. Instructions available on the site fully explain the data extraction process.

DES is designed for advanced users of census data. Some knowledge of database structure and the specific data elements in each of the files makes it much easier to maneuver through the prompts. Regardless, this is an important and useful tool for obtaining custom data extractions.
Subject: Census

223. Historical United States Census Data Browser
`http://fisher.lib.virginia.edu/census/`
Sponsors: Inter-University Consortium for Political and Social Research (ICPSR); University of Virginia. Library
Description: The Historical Census Data Browser has statistics from each of the decennial census reports from 1790 to 1960. The data on this site comes from data sets created by ICPSR and taken from the U.S. decennial censuses and other sources. Coverage is available for all existing counties and states during the respective time period. Subject coverage includes population and a variety of other criteria, depending on which date is chosen.

This is one of the few sites providing historical U.S. census data. The forms-based interface is easy to use and the generated HTML output is easy to browse. The tables automatically generate sums when relevant, and there are options to sort and graph the data once it is initially displayed. Those who need to do more complex manipulations of the data are referred to ICPSR for access to the original data sets.
Subjects: Census; Databases

224. Integrated Public Use Microdata Series
`http://www.ipums.umn.edu/`
Sponsor: University of Minnesota. Historical Census Projects

Description: The Integrated Public Use Microdata Series (IPUMS) Web site hosts two large data projects: IPUMS-USA and IPUMS-International. IPUMS-USA has population and household data from the U.S. decennial census from 1850 to 1990, and has added the Census 2000 Supplemental Survey data. The IPUMS-International project is building a harmonized database of census data from all countries from 1960 to 2000. Both projects are dedicated to providing free public access, though registration is required before extracting data. Users of IPUMS can download data either by extracting custom files or by downloading entire data sets.

The IPUMS tools are of use primarily to expert researchers running statistical studies using sample data. The data can not be browsed online, and extracted files are very large. Both are valuable projects to preserve and format census data, and should be of interest to social science scholars.

Subject: Census

225. International Programs Center
http://www.census.gov/ipc/www/
Sponsor: Commerce Department — Economics and Statistics Administration (ESA) — Census Bureau
Description: The International Programs Center (IPC), part of the Census Bureau's Population Division, offers a variety of international population statistics at its site. The World Population pages includes the *World Population Profile* publication; the World POPClock with a second-by-second simulation of the world's population growth; the number of births and deaths per year, month, day, hour, minute, and second for the current year; and world population estimates going back to 10,000 B.C. The IPC produces two databases, the International Data Base and the HIV/AIDS Surveillance Database. Each can be downloaded and run on a local PC, but the site also offers summary tables from each that are extensive enough to meet many reference needs. The site also describes the center and its work, and offers some software applications and a training program schedule. A Publications and Reports page lists publications from the IPC, some of which are available online in PDF format.

This is a useful site for those interested in demographics beyond the United States.
Subject: Vital Statistics — International
Publication: *World Population Profile*, C 3.205/3:WP-

226. POPClocks
http://www.census.gov/main/www/popclock.html
Sponsor: Commerce Department — Economics and Statistics Administration (ESA) — Census Bureau
Description: Two population clocks, or POPClocks, give up-to-the-minute estimates of the population. The United States POPClock estimates the resident population of the United States at the current minute and gives the criteria for how the estimate is derived, historical estimates, and documentation. The World POPClock estimates the current minute's world population, lists monthly estimates for the next year, links to other world population information and POPClocks, and provides notes on the estimates. Java and dynamic versions of the population clocks are also available.

This site is useful both as a population estimate resource and as a demonstration of the advantages of an online system that can change its data dynamically. Those citing the estimates should be sure to also read the documentation of how those estimates are reached and revised.
Subject: Population Statistics

227. Population and Household Economics Topics
http://www.census.gov/population/www/
Sponsor: Commerce Department — Economics and Statistics Administration (ESA) — Census Bureau
Description: This Census Bureau Web page presents a topical directory of more than 30 links to a variety of demographic and population statistics. Sections include Estimates, Projections, Population Profile, Age, Ancestry, Children, Disability, Income, Labor Force and many other subjects. Each of these sections leads to a substantial collection of demographic statistics. Formats for the statistical

and text publications available on this site vary between ASCII text, HTML, and PDF. The page also links to relevant bureau publications, data products, and notes on methodology and technical topics.

Subjects: Population Statistics; Finding Aids

228. State and County QuickFacts

http://quickfacts.census.gov/qfd/

Sponsor: Commerce Department — Economics and Statistics Administration (ESA) — Census Bureau

Description: State and County QuickFacts offers simple access to frequently-requested national, state, and county data from various Census Bureau programs. Choose a state from a list or from the clickable U.S. map and then select a county. Information at each geographic level is presented under three headings: people, business, and geography. At the state level, statistics are given for the state versus the country as a whole; at county level, county and state statistics are contrasted. Each state and county data table also has a link to browse more data sets for that location. The additional data sets include historical population counts, congressional district statistics, and tables from the Economic Census, County Business Patterns, and the Consolidated Federal Funds Reports, among many other resources.

This site serves as a quick reference tool as well as a resource locator. By clicking on the question mark for each data heading, users link to a page that presents the source, definition, scope, and methodology, and links to other information about that heading.

Subjects: Census; Population Statistics

Economic Statistics

229. 1997 Economic Census

http://www.census.gov/epcd/www/econ97.html

Sponsor: Commerce Department — Economics and Statistics Administration (ESA) — Census Bureau

Description: The Economic Census profiles the U.S. economy every 5 years, from the national to the local level. Variables such as number of establishments, number of employees, payroll, and measures of output (such as sales or revenue) are reported for over 15 industry sectors. The level of geography covered varies by industry sector but often goes down to the county and metropolitan area level. Detailed sector report series available at this site include: Geographic Area Series; Industry Series; Subject Series; and ZIP Code Statistics. Tables are available in HTML and PDF formats. In addition to the 1997 data, the site has a comparison with 1992 Economic Census data, and a grid identifying business data available from more current Bureau reports. The site also has the special Economic Census report on minority- and women-owned business, and background information on the 2002 Economic Census (which will begin issuing data in 2004). The site also includes information on the 2002 Economic Census. This will mark the first Economic Census that includes data for e-commerce sales across many industries.

Subjects: Economic Statistics; Industries — Statistics

Publications: *1997 Economic Census*, C 3.277:CD-EC 97

1997 Economic Census. Accommodation and Foodservices, C 3.277/2:

1997 Economic Census. Administrative and Support and Waste Management and Remediation Services, C 3.277/2:

1997 Economic Census. Arts, Entertainment, and Recreation, C 3.277/2:

1997 Economic Census. Construction, C 3.277/2:

1997 Economic Census. Educational Services, C 3.277/2:

1997 Economic Census. Finance and Insurance, C 3.277/2:

1997 Economic Census. Health Care and Social Assistance, C 3.277/2:

1997 Economic Census. Management of Companies and Enterprises, C 3.277/2:

1997 Economic Census. Manufacturing, C 3.277/2:

1997 Economic Census. Mining, C 3.277/2:

1997 Economic Census. Other Services, C 3.277/2:

1997 Economic Census. Professional, Scientific, and Technical Services, C 3.277/2:
1997 Economic Census. Real Estate and Rental and Leasing, C 3.277/2:
1997 Economic Census. Retail Trade, C 3.277/2:
1997 Economic Census. Survey of Minority-Owned Business Enterprises, C 3.277/3:
1997 Economic Census. Transportation and Warehousing, C 3.277/2:
1997 Economic Census. Utilities, C 3.277/2:
1997 Economic Census. Wholesale Trade, C 3.277/2:
Company Summary, 1997: 1997 Economic Census, C 3.277/3:
Women-Owned Businesses, 1997: 1997 Economic Census: Survey of Women-Owned Business Enterprises, C 3.277/3:

230. Bureau of Economic Analysis
http://www.bea.gov/
Sponsor: Commerce Department — Economics and Statistics Administration (ESA) — Bureau of Economic Analysis (BEA)
Description: The Commerce Department's Bureau of Economic Analysis produces the data for the U.S. national income and product accounts (NIPA's), which feature the estimates of gross domestic product (GDP) and related measures of the national economy. Close to 200 NIPA data tables are available on the site. They can be displayed in HTML and downloaded as comma delimited files. An advanced download option allows for saving in Excel format or in zipped Excel or comma delimited. A NIPA Tables page has selectable lists of frequently requested tables, a list of all tables, and an alphabetic keyword index to the tables. The list of all NIPA tables is arranged by data topic, including Personal Income and Outlays, Foreign Transactions, and Saving and Investment. The site also has interactive access to data on international transactions accounts, gross state product, and local area personal income.

A link titled Economic Overview leads to a table of quarterly figures for key economic indicators, including: GDP; personal consumption; exports and imports (in good and services); personal income; federal, state, and local government finances; and inventories. BEA's site also features special sections for GDP-related data, balance of payments, and regional data. The regional economic data includes Gross State Product and State Personal Income.The Publications section holds a collection of *Survey of Current Business* issues in PDF format going back to 1994. Selected *Survey* articles from 1987–1993 are also online. The news releases section has important periodic economic reports such as recent figures for personal income, GDP, state personal income, and U.S. international trade in goods and services. The online products catalog has sales information and an option to download many of the products as self-extracting files.

The BEA site presents important national economic statistics, usually offering multiple access points and several convenient downloading options.
Subjects: Economic Statistics; National Accounts — Statistics
Publications: *Guide to Industry and Foreign Trade Classifications for International Surveys,* C 59.8:F 76
National Income and Product Accounts, C 59.11/5-3:
Survey of Current Business, C 59.11:
User's Guide to BEA Information, C 59.8:B 89/

231. Bureau of Labor Statistics
http://www.bls.gov/
Alternate URL: http://stats.bls.gov/
Sponsor: Labor Department — Bureau of Labor Statistics (BLS)
Description: The Bureau of Labor Statistics (BLS) has made their Web site, like the bureau, a major source for employment, economic, and labor statistics. The emphasis is on access to the statistics, rather than on information about BLS. A box on the home page titled Latest Numbers presents the latest key economic indicators, so that no further clicks are needed to reach these. The featured statistics are Consumer Price Index, Unemployment Rate, Payroll Employment, Average Hourly Earnings, Producer Price Index, Employment Cost Index, Productivity, and U.S. Import Price Index. Topical sections include consistently formatted pages describing the statistical series and linking to the major tables, economic news releases, publications, and documentation. Sections called Get Detailed Statistics link to a search form for creating custom tables and also to an FTP site for those who wish to download all or large subsets of the data in a flat file. For each statistical

series, the current figures are given, with an icon of a dinosaur indicating a link to historical data.The Publications and Research Papers section includes access to the *Monthly Labor Review Online*, research papers, the *Occupational Outlook Handbook*, *The National Compensation Survey*, the BLS publications catalog, and more.

BLS tries not to hide its wealth of statistics. Many are accessible in one or two clicks. BLS assists the researcher with multiple approaches: an A to Z index, lists of most frequently requested tables, answers to current user questions, a useful data availability grid under Get Detailed Statistics, and overall consistent page layout and navigation.

Subjects: Employment — Statistics; Labor Statistics; Wages — Statistics
Publications: *Annual Pay Levels in Metropolitan Areas*, L 2.120/2-4:
BLS Handbook of Methods, L 2.3:
Career Guide to Industries, L 2.3/4-3:
Compensation and Working Conditions (quarterly), L 2.44/4:
Consumer Expenditure Survey, L 2.3/18:
Consumer Price Index, L 2.38
Employee Benefit Survey Data, L 2.46/6: to L 2.46/9:
Employee Benefits in Medium and Large Private Establishments, L 2.3/10:
Employee Benefits in State and Local Governments, L 2.3/10-2:
Employer Costs for Employee Compensation, L 2.120/2-13:
Employment Characteristics of Families, L 2.118/2:
Employment Cost Index (quarterly), L 2.117:
Extended Mass Layoffs in the ..., L 2.120/2-14:
Geographic Profile of Employment and Unemployment, L 2.3/12:
International Comparisons of Hourly Compensation Costs for Production Workers in Manufacturing, L 2.130:
Major Work Stoppages, L 2.45/3:
Metropolitan Area Employment and Unemployment, L 2.111/5:
Monthly Labor Review, L 2.6:
Monthly Series on Mass Layoffs, L 2.120/2-15:
National Compensation Survey, L 2.121
National Compensation Survey Bulletins & Summaries for all States & Divisions, L 2.121/56:
National Compensation Survey Bulletins, Summaries and Supplementary Tables for National, L 2.121/57:
National Compensation Survey, Alabama, L 2.121/1:
National Compensation Survey, Alaska, L 2.121/2:
National Compensation Survey, Arizona, L 2.121/3:
National Compensation Survey, Arkansas, L 2.121/4:
National Compensation Survey, California, L 2.121/5:
National Compensation Survey, Colorado, L 2.121/6:
National Compensation Survey, Connecticut, L 2.121/7:
National Compensation Survey, Delaware, L 2.121/8:
National Compensation Survey, District of Columbia, L 2.121/51:
National Compensation Survey, Florida, L 2.121/9:
National Compensation Survey, Georgia, L 2.121/10:
National Compensation Survey, Hawaii, L 2.121/11:
National Compensation Survey, Idaho, L 2.121/12:
National Compensation Survey, Illinois, L 2.121/13:
National Compensation Survey, Indiana, L 2.121/14:
National Compensation Survey, Iowa, L 2.121/15:
National Compensation Survey, Kansas, L 2.121/16:
National Compensation Survey, Kentucky, L 2.121/17:
National Compensation Survey, Louisiana, L 2.121/18:
National Compensation Survey, Maine, L 2.121/19:
National Compensation Survey, Maryland, L 2.121/20:
National Compensation Survey, Massachusetts, L 2.121/21:
National Compensation Survey, Michigan, L 2.121/22:
National Compensation Survey, Minnesota, L 2.121/23:
National Compensation Survey, Mississippi, L 2.121/24:

232. Census Bureau Economic Programs
http://www.census.gov/econ/www/
Sponsor: Commerce Department — Economics and Statistics Administration (ESA) — Census Bureau
Description: This page provides a central point for finding economic data from a variety of Census programs. It has quick links to the Economic Census, Statistics of U.S. Business, County Business Patterns, Annual Survey of Manufactures, Annual Capital Expenditures Data, Monthly Retail Sales and Inventories, and more. The page highlights the latest economic indicator announced, and links to an Economic Indicator Release Schedule that can be sorted by name or date.
Subject: Economic Statistics

233. Economic Statistics Briefing Room
http://www.whitehouse.gov/fsbr/esbr.html
Sponsor: White House
Description: Hosted by the White House site, Economic Statistics Briefing Room provides easy access to current federal economic indicators in eight broad categories: Employment, Income, International, Money, Output, Prices, Production, and Transportation. The site gives the most recent summary for each of the statistics. It also points to the top level of the originating Web site and has a graphic linking to a full size chart at the originating agency's site.
Subject: Economic Statistics

234. Economics and Statistics Administration
http://www.esa.doc.gov/508/esa/home.htm
Sponsor: Commerce Department — Economics and Statistics Administration (ESA)
Description: The top page of the Economics and Statistics Administration (ESA) site describes ESA offices and provides an organization chart. The ESA Links section describes this bureau's major statistical offices: the Bureau of Economic Analysis, STAT-USA, and the Census Bureau. ESA's own publications are in the U.S. Economy section, which lists and links to special reports from ESA dating back to 1995. The Press Release section has current releases from Census, BEA, and STAT-USA, and provides a calendar with the date and time of releases scheduled for this year. There is a Spanish version of the ESA site, though the publications and press releases to which it links are in English only.
Subject: Economics
Publications: *A Nation Online: How Americans Are Expanding Their Use Of The Internet*, C 60.2:
Digital Economy 2002
Falling through the Net: Toward Digital Inclusion, C 60.2:

235. Foreign Trade Statistics
http://www.census.gov/foreign-trade/www/index.html
Sponsor: Commerce Department — Economics and Statistics Administration (ESA) — Census Bureau
Description: The Foreign Trade Division (FTD) of the Census Bureau provides information from and about the division on this site. The Statistics section has the current FT900, the major monthly update of U.S. trade in goods and services. Exhibits, or data announced in the FT900 release, are available in PDF, text, or spreadsheet format. The Statistics section features reports on individual country balance of trade and products traded with the U.S., and a monthly list of the top trading partners with the U.S. The site also has State Export Data, and historic trade balance data going back to 1960.

Because this site covers the full scope of FTD's activities, sections of it may only interest researchers while other sections may only interest exporters. The site identifies the major statistical series and products offered by FTD. Researchers may also wish to investigate the U.S. International Trade Commission's Trade DataWeb.
Subject: Trade Statistics
Publications: *Imports of Steel Products*, C 3.164:900-A/
U.S. International Trade in Goods and Services, FT-900, C 3.164:900/

236. Manufacturing, Mining, and Construction Statistics
http://www.census.gov/mcd/
Sponsor: Commerce Department — Economics and Statistics Administration (ESA) — Census Bureau
Description: This Census gateway site compiles into one page all census information regarding manufacturing, mining, and construction. Data are primarily from the *Annual Survey of Manufactures*, *Current Industrial Reports* and the Economic Census, although information from other programs is available as well. Topics covered include residential construction and manufacturers' inventories. The site also carries press releases and links to new publications.
Subjects: Construction Industry — Statistics; Manufacturing — Statistics; Mining — Statistics
Publications: *1997 Economic Census*, C 3.277:CD-EC 97
Annual Survey of Manufactures, C 3.24/9
Current Industrial Reports, Manufacturing Profiles, C 3.158/4:

237. MISER Foreign Trade Database
http://www.misertrade.org
Sponsor: Massachusetts Institute for Social and Economic Research (MISER)
Description: MISER produces a quarterly state export data series and monthly exports and imports data by detailed Harmonized System commodity code. Most of its data files are only available for purchase, but the site does post some information free of charge. Free data includes the current and year-to-date figures for U.S. exports by state, and annual summary statistics for the northeastern states.
Subject: Trade Statistics

238. STAT-USA
http://www.stat-usa.gov/
Alternate URL: http://home.stat-usa.gov/
Sponsor: Commerce Department — Economics and Statistics Administration (ESA)
Description: Unlike most of the resources described in this directory, STAT-USA is a fee-based subscription service. This Commerce Department service is self-financing and does not receive regular appropriations. Free subscriptions are available for federal depository libraries, however. The goal of STAT-USA is to provide a central access point for economic, business, and international trade information produced by the U.S. Government. Its principal offerings are State of the Nation, and GLOBUS & NTDB. The State of the Nation database provides access to current and historical economic and financial releases and economic data. The GLOBUS & NTDB section has current and historical trade-related releases, international market research, trade opportunities, country analysis, and access to the files from the full National Trade Data Bank (NTDB).

STAT-USA has a huge number of databases and publications. Some of the documents are directly accessible. Others, especially within the NTDB portion, are searchable with options to limit to specific indexes such as country, product, date, and title.The STAT-USA Office of the Commerce Department maintains other for-fee subscription databases. These can be found using the alternate URL above. They include the statistical databases USA Trade Online and EuroTrade Online. Like STAT-USA, USA Trade Online is available to federal depository libraries free of charge.

This is an important, large collection of statistics and business-related full-text publications. While a significant portion of the data available here is also freely accessible from other sites, the ease of access and the unique resources available can make a STAT-USA subscription worth considering for those that would frequently use such data.
Subjects: Economic Statistics; Databases
Publications: *National Trade Data Bank*, C 1.88:
STAT-USA: The Newsletter, C 1.91/2:

239. USITC Trade Database: DataWeb

http://dataweb.usitc.gov/

Sponsor: International Trade Commission (ITC)

Description: DataWeb is a tariff and trade database designed by the U.S. International Trade Commission. The data comes from the Census Bureau, the Customs Service, and the International Trade Commission itself. The system is free of charge but requires registration. For trade data, DataWeb offers a number of options for specifying commodity level and country or country groupings. There are online sort capabilities, and report options include downloading to a spreadsheet format. The site includes complementary tools such as the Commodity Translation Wizard that translates between Harmonized Tariff Schedule codes and the SIC and NAICS classifications. The site also generates prepared summary tables for commonly requested information, such as U.S. Trade by Geographic Regions and U.S. Trade by Partner Country. A separate Tariff Database presents tariff treatment information and links to trade data. The site also has tables of scheduled and historical U.S. tariff reductions.

DataWeb is a flexible and relatively sophisticated system for U.S. trade data. Users may need to run through the search and display options several times to learn all that the system is capable of doing. For regular trade and tariff data users, DataWeb can be a very useful tool. Novices may first wish to see if the prepared trade data tables can answer their questions.

Subjects: Trade Statistics; Databases

CHAPTER 5
Congress

The United States Congress comprises 2 chambers, 535 Member offices, over 40 committees, various legislative and operational offices, and several major congressional support agencies. Most of these entities have their own Web site. In addition, many private and educational sites help to spread and interpret congressional information.

This chapter describes Web sites with legislative, electoral, or historical information from or about Congress. A list of Members' Web sites by state appears at the end. The featured sites are those of the House and Senate along with the Library of Congress THOMAS site for tracking bills and finding related congressional documents. Each of these featured Web sites is a substantive resource in itself, with numerous links to other congressional sites.

The Government Printing Office (GPO) is a legislative branch agency and produces congressional documents in print and Web formats. GPO is described in this section, but the index in the back of this book can assist in finding additional GPO resources listed in other chapters. In addition, related resources may be found in the Legal Information chapter.

Bookmarks & Favorites

U.S. Congress
- House of Representatives, http://www.house.gov
- Senate, http://www.senate.gov

Research Tools
- Legislative Publications, http://www.access.gpo.gov/su_docs/legislative.html
- THOMAS, http://thomas.loc.gov

Major Agencies
- Congressional Budget Office, http://www.cbo.gov
- Congressional Research Service, http://www.loc.gov/crsinfo/
- General Accounting Office, http://www.gao.gov

Featured Sites

240. THOMAS: Legislative Information on the Internet
http://thomas.loc.gov/
Sponsor: Library of Congress
Description: THOMAS, a service of the Library of Congress acting under the direction of the Congress, makes U.S. legislative information freely available on the Internet. The site is divided into three broad categories: Legislation, *Congressional Record*, and Committee Information. The "Bill Summary and Status" database, under the Legislation category, is the core THOMAS database; it is available for the 93rd Congress (1973) to the present. It tracks the action on each bill in Congress, provides links to the full text of the bill and related debate in the *Congressional Record*, and identifies congressional sponsors or cosponsors, amendments to the bill, and any related bills. Bills can be searched in many ways, including number, topic, and sponsor. The *Congressional Record* section includes the full text of the *Record* (from 1989 forward), its *Index* (1995 forward), and current lists of House and Senate roll call votes as provided by those chambers. The Committee Information section features the full text of committee reports (1995 forward), and links to current information provided online by the congressional committees themselves.

Toward the bottom of the front page, there are links to databases of Presidential Nominations (1987 to present) and Treaties (1967 to present). THOMAS also includes guides to the legislative process, statistics on congressional activity, links to major government Web sites, and the searchable full text of such historic documents as the Federalist Papers, the Declaration of Independence, the U.S. Constitution, and early documents from the Constitutional Convention and Continental Congress.

The many legislative databases on THOMAS can be browsed or searched using the InQuery search engine. InQuery employs a relevance-ranking algorithm for searching. Experienced searchers who wish to use Boolean searching may use native InQuery syntax to override the relevance-ranking default.

This is one of the most widely used Internet sources for legislative information. While it does not yet deliver all the committee information some might like, it does make a significant body of legislative documentation easily available to the public. Researchers will appreciate the quick links THOMAS provides, such as lists of public laws or vetoed bills as provided in "Bill Summary and Status" or the status of appropriations bills as provided on the home page. The full text of documents such as the *Congressional Record* on THOMAS are the official versions as received from the GPO Access Web service. THOMAS provides enhanced searching and puts these documents into the context of legislation introduced in the Congress.

Subjects: Legislation; Databases
Publications: *Congressional Record (Daily)*, X 1.1/A:
Congressional Record Index, X 1.1/A:
House Bills, Y 1.4/6:
House Concurrent Resolutions, Y 1.4/9:
House Joint Resolutions, Y 1.4/8:
House Resolutions, Y 1.4/7:
How Our Laws are Made, Y 1.1/7:
Senate Bills, Y 1.4/1:
Senate Concurrent Resolutions, Y 1.4/4:
Senate Joint Resolutions, Y 1.4/3:
Senate Printed Amendments, Y 1.4/5:
Senate Resolutions, Y 1.4/2:

241. United States House of Representatives

http://www.house.gov/
Sponsor: Congress — House of Representatives
Description: The U.S. House of Representatives Web service, newly redesigned for the 108th Congress, includes a wealth of current legislative and policy information. The site provides quick links to House member and committee Web sites, which vary in coverage but can provide helpful legislative information and documents. Other major sections of the site are Schedule Information, Legislative Information, General Information (the House Directory, employment and contracts information), and Search House Sites. A side bar has links to House commissions and offices, such as the Clerk of the House.

The Clerk of the House section is particularly valuable for the legislative researcher. It includes House schedules, documents, official directories, historical information, member and lobbyist financial disclosure information, and educational resources. A votes section for the current Congress lists roll call votes in reverse chronological order, indicating whether the measure passed or failed. The vote number links lead to a full report of the vote, but there is no facility to search by vote topic or to search across all votes. The House site also features a basic electronic version of the United States Code, guidance on writing to your Representative, information on visiting Capitol Hill, and links to major U.S. Government Web sites.

Current, official information on many of the operations and activities of the House is readily available from this site. Its simple home page belies the tremendous amount of information available several layers down, such as hearings transcripts provided by some committees and historical information posted by the Clerk of the House.

Subject: House of Representatives

242. United States Senate

http://www.senate.gov/
Sponsor: Congress — Senate
Description: The Senate site is a source for both current legislative news and historical Senate information. The major sections of the site are Senators, Committees, Legislation and Records, Art and History, Visitors Center, and Reference. As with the House site, the content of individual member

and committee sites varies and the committee sites typically carry their hearings schedules and testimony in some form.

The Legislation and Records section includes some legislative information unique to the Senate site and links to information on other congressional sites. The Active Legislation page identifies currently active bills and labels them by topic. The Treaties page supplements the THOMAS Treaties database with documents identifying treaties received, approved, receiving action, and reported. The Nominations page performs a similar role, and includes lists of nominations by status, nominations withdrawn, and nominations failed or returned.

Under Reference, the Senate site offers a Virtual Reference Desk with information on topics including filibusters, Senate traditions, congressional medals and honors, Senate Pages, and women and minorities in the Senate. There is also a glossary, bibliographies, information on relatively new books about the Senate, and a "Is it true..." section addressing popular rumors about Congress or legislation.
Subject: Senate

The Congressional resources in this chapter are divided into three sections, spanning the entry numbers indicated here:

General	*243–266*
Directories	*267–269*
Members	*270–809*

General

243. Architect of the Capitol
http://www.aoc.gov/
Sponsor: Congress — Architect of the Capitol
Description: The Architect of the Capitol (AOC) is responsible for maintenance, operation, development, and preservation of the United States Capitol Complex, which includes the Capitol and its grounds, the Congressional office buildings, the Library of Congress buildings, the Supreme Court building, the U.S. Botanic Garden, the Capitol Power Plant, and other facilities. The major sections of this Web site are The Capitol Complex, Visiting the Capitol, the Office of the Architect, Current and Recent Projects, The Capitol Visitor Center, and The United States Botanic Garden.

The Capitol Complex section provides extensive information on the history, art, and architecture of the Capitol Building, supplemented with many historic and contemporary photographs and illustrations. The Office of the Architect section provides information on current operations as well as a list of all Architects since 1793.

The detailed current and historical information on this site makes it a useful resource for reference or research. It may be of interest to tourists as well as students of history, government, art, architecture, historical preservation, and landscaping.
Subject: Capitol Building

244. Commission on Security and Cooperation in Europe
http://www.csce.gov/helsinki.cfm
Sponsor: Commission on Security and Cooperation in Europe (CSCE)
Description: The Commission on Security and Cooperation in Europe (CSCE), better known as the Helsinki Commission, is an independent government agency created by Congress. It monitors and encourages compliance with the Helsinki Final Act and other commitments of the countries participating in the Organization for Security and Cooperation in Europe. It is composed of nine members from the Senate and nine members from the House of Representatives, as well as one member each from the Departments of State, Defense, and Commerce. Its Web site includes information about the CSCE and OSCE, as well as the full text of the Commission's press releases, hearings, briefings, reports, statements in the *Congressional Record*, and the *CSCE Digest* newsletter. A "Select an Issue" option allows for browsing the Commission's publications by topics such as Freedom of Speech, National Minorities, Prevention of Torture, and Rule of Law. Users may also subscribe to an email service for Commission publications concerning specific topics or countries.

Subject: Human Rights
Publication: *CSCE Digest*, Y 4.SE 2/11:

245. Congressional Budget Office
http://www.cbo.gov/
Sponsor: Congressional Budget Office (CBO)
Description: The Congressional Budget Office (CBO) provides Congress with analyses needed for economic and budget decisions and with the information and estimates required for the Congressional budget process. The CBO Web site has the full text of its many publications, including economic forecasts, budget projections, analysis of the president's budget, CBO testimony before Congress, and cost estimates for bills reported by Congressional committees. CBO publications can be searched or browsed by topic. A New-Document Notification email service sends subscribers publication announcements. The site also provides information about CBO, its staffing and operations, and any current job listings.

The full text of CBO publications on this site provide a wealth of information on the federal budget and on tax and spending proposals.
Subjects: Budget of the U.S. Government; Congressional Support Agencies
Publications: *An Analysis of the President's Budgetary Proposals for Fiscal Year (annual)*, Y 10.19:
Budget and Economic Outlook: Fiscal Years 2004–2013, Y 10.13:
Budget Options, Y 10.2:B 85/3/
Final Sequestration Report for Fiscal Year 2003, Y 1.1/7:
Glossary of Budgetary and Economic Terms
Monthly Budget Review, Y 10.21/2
Social Security: A Primer
The Economic and Budget Outlook: An Update (annual), Y 10.17:
Unauthorized Appropriations and Expiring Authorizations, Y 10.22:

246. Congressional Gold Medals
http://dallaslibrary.org/CGI/goldframe.htm
Sponsor: Dallas Public Library
Description: This unofficial site provides a listing of Congressional Gold Medals given from March 25, 1776 through the present. The names are listed along with the date of receipt. For many award recipients, the site has additional information such as a photo of the medal and the text of the legislation awarding it. The list is hosted and maintained by the Dallas Public Library Government Information Center.
Subject: Congress — Awards and Honors

247. Congressional Observer Publications: U.S. Congressional Votes
http://www.proaxis.com/~cop/congvts.htm
Sponsor: Congressional Observer Publications, Inc.
Description: This commercial subscription service provides information on the roll call votes of the House and Senate from the current Congressional session back to 1996. Non-subscribers have access to a chronological list of the votes with summary information and vote totals. The subscriber version includes the full breakdown of the vote with statistics such as party and leadership votes. Subscribers also have access to special reports such as lists of close votes and missed votes.
Subject: Legislation

248. Congressional Research Service Documents from Penny Hill Press
http://pennyhill.com/
Sponsor: Penny Hill Press
Description: This commercial press offers delivery of Congressional Research Service (CRS) publications for a fee. While the site does not offer online versions of the reports, it does list CRS documents by topic and provides author, abstract, and publication date information for each item.

The site is helpful to see what CRS reports have been published and what reports are available in various subject areas.
Subject: Congressional Documents

249. Congressional Research Service Employment Opportunities

http://www.loc.gov/crsinfo/

Sponsor: Library of Congress — Congressional Research Service

Description: The Congressional Research Service is a legislative support agency located within the Library of Congress. Its mission is to provide non-partisan analysis, research and information services to the U.S. Congress. While this Web site is entitled Congressional Research Service Employment Opportunities, it also provides extensive information about the organization and activities of the CRS. The rest of the site includes information on recruitment, internships, and other employment options. Because the CRS works exclusively for Congress, this employment page is its only official public site. For actual CRS publications, see the third-party sites listed elsewhere in this work.

Subject: Congressional Support Agencies

250. Congressional Research Service Reports at the National Library for the Environment

http://www.cnie.org/NLE/CRS/

Sponsor: National Council for Science and the Environment

Description: Made available by the non-governmental National Council for Science and the Environment, this site offers access to the full text of Congressional Research Service Reports on environmental issues. The Reports are classified in broad subject listings. The most recent additions are listed first and there is a keyword search option in addition to the subject listings.

Since these reports are not directly available to the public from the Congressional Research Service, this is an important site for access to at least some of the CRS reports. While the site focuses on environmental issues, including agriculture and energy, researchers will also find some reports on general government topics such as the federal budget.

Subject: Congressional Documents

Publication: *Congressional Research Service Reports*

251. CRS Products via Congressman Christopher Shays

http://www.house.gov/shays/resources/leginfo/crs.htm

Sponsor: Congress — House of Representatives

Description: Congressman Christopher Shays has taken the initiative to offer access to Congressional Research Service reports and issue briefs from his Web site. (CRS does not make these items available directly; members of the public can request them through their representative in Congress.) CRS prepares reports on a wide range of current legislative issues. This site provides access to PDF versions divided into four categories: short reports (six pages or less); long reports; issue briefs; and appropriations reports. Users must scan each of these four lists of titles to see what is available.

Subject: Congressional Documents

252. C-SPAN.org

http://www.c-span.org/

Sponsor: C-SPAN

Description: The cable television industry created C-SPAN (Cable-Satellite Public Affairs Network) in 1979 to provide live, gavel-to-gavel coverage of the U.S. House of Representatives. U.S. Senate coverage began in 1986, when the Senate began televising its proceedings. Now C-SPAN offers audio and video of floor proceedings and some hearings over the Web. Web users can browse the schedules for C-SPAN's three cable stations and radio station and receive the public affairs and congressional programming online.

The C-Span Web site offers a number of resources for researchers and those keeping up with political developments. Under Current Events, there are links to events, broadcasts, and information for such topics as the Bush administration, the 108th Congress, and the Budget. The Resource Directory provides organized links to Web sites, C-SPAN programs, and official documents under such topical headings as Congress, White House, Judiciary, State/Local, Media Organizations, and Policy Organizations.

The Congress Guide section features a Key Votes Library with the complete vote tally for selected House and Senate votes, organized by subject. The site also includes a congressional glossary and links to congressional member, leadership, committee, caucus, and party organization sites.

Subjects: Congressional Information; Legislative Procedure

253. Federal Election Commission
http://www.fec.gov/
Sponsor: Federal Election Commission (FEC)
Description: The Federal Elections Commission (FEC) is an independent regulatory agency whose mission is to disclose campaign finance information, enforce the provisions of the law such as the limits and prohibitions on contributions, and oversee the public funding of presidential elections. The FEC Web site presents a substantial amount of useful campaign contribution and national elections information. It features three main categories on the home page: Citizens Guide, Candidate and Committee Guide, and Media Guide. These links lead to information about elections and voting and campaign finance information, reporting requirements and forms, publications and other resources, and information about campaign finance filings. Additional links lead to such sections as About FEC, FEC Services, Campaign Finance Reports and Data, Reporting Forms and Filing Information, Campaign Finance Law Resources, Elections and Voting, and News Releases. The Campaign Finance Reports and Data section provides images of the actual financial reports filed by presidential, Senate and House campaigns, political party committees, and political action committees (PACs). Throughout the site, useful information and statistics are provided on such topics as voter turnout and registration, election dates, state voter registration requirements, PACs, voting system standards, and conducting research in FEC public records. Some information is also provided in Spanish.
Subjects: Campaign Funds — Laws; Voting — Statistics
Publications: *Campaign Guide for Congressional Candidates and Committees,* Y 3.EL 2/3:13 C 76/
Combined Federal/State Disclosure Directory, Y 3.El 2/3:14-2/
FEC Reports on Financial Activity, Y 3.El 2/3:15/
Federal Election Commission Annual Report, Y 3.EL 2/3:
Independent Expenditures, Y 3.El 2/3:2 EX 7/
Record, Y 3.EL 2/3:11/
Supporting Federal Candidates: A Guide for Citizens, Y 3.El 2/3:

254. GAO Email Lists
http://www.gao.gov/subscrib.html
Sponsor: General Accounting Office (GAO)
Description: GAO provides two daily electronic mailing alert options: one for newly released GAO reports and testimony, and another for newly released Comptroller General Decisions.

Useful for those that need up-to-date information on new GAO reports and who do not want to check GPO Access or the GAO Web site on a daily basis.
Subject: Email Lists

255. General Accounting Office
http://www.gao.gov/
Sponsor: General Accounting Office (GAO)
Description: The General Accounting Office (GAO) is the investigative arm of Congress. GAO examines the use of public funds and evaluates federal programs and activities to help the Congress in oversight, policy, and funding decisions. Its Web site features the full text of GAO Reports and Testimony and recent Comptroller General Decisions and Opinions. (The full text of these Reports and Decisions is also available on GPO Access.) Email alert lists are offered to notify subscribers when new Reports or Decisions are published. The site also has the full text of special GAO reports on auditing, financial management, technology, and performance measurement for federal agencies, and the text of the Comptroller General's speeches and statements. FraudNET is a GAO service allowing anyone to report allegations of fraud, waste, abuse, or mismanagement of federal funds; the site provides an online form for reporting such allegations.
Subjects: Congressional Support Agencies; Government Administration
Publications: *Abstracts of Reports and Testimony,* GA 1.16/3-3:
Comptroller General's Annual Report, GA 1.1:
Decisions of the Comptroller General, GA 1.5:
GAO Reports, GA 1.13:
Government Auditing Standards (Yellow Book), GA 1.2:Au 2/14
Month in Review, GA 1.16/3:

256. History of the United States Capitol

http://www.access.gpo.gov/congress/senate/capitol/index.html

Sponsor: Congress — Architect of the Capitol

Description: The book *History of the United States Capitol: A Chronicle of Design, Construction, and Politics* by architectural historian William C. Allen is available full text in PDF format at this GPO Access site. Inspired by the bicentennial of the Capitol Building celebrated in 1993, the book was sponsored by the U.S. Congress and published in 2001 as Senate Document 106-29. On this GPO Access site, the book can be viewed by chapter. It includes numerous illustrations and photographs and a bibliography.

Subject: Capitol Building — History

Publication: *History of the United States Capitol: A Chronicle of Design, Construction, and Politics*

257. How Our Laws Are Made

http://thomas.loc.gov/home/lawsmade.toc.html

Sponsors: Congress — House of Representatives; Library of Congress

Description: This is an updated edition of a classic guide to the legislative process, revised and updated by Charles W. Johnson. It is available both as one long ASCII file or in HTML divided by chapter. The handbook provides a readable and nontechnical outline of the background and the numerous steps of the federal lawmaking process. It starts with the origin of an idea for a legislative proposal and follows it through its publication as a statute.

The HTML version of this classic is organized so that it is relatively easy to read the entire work or just browse relevant sections.

Subject: Legislative Procedure

Publication: *How Our Laws are Made*, Y 1.1/7:

258. John C. Stennis Center for Public Service

http://www.stennis.gov/

Sponsor: Stennis Center for Public Service

Description: The John C. Stennis Center for Public Service was created by Congress in 1988 to promote and strengthen public service in America at all levels of government. Headquartered in Starkville, Mississippi, the Center is governed by a Board of Trustees appointed by the Democratic and Republican leaders in the U.S. Senate and the U.S. House of Representatives. The Web site consists primarily of information about the Center's programs and its namesake. Programs described include the Emerging Congressional Staff Leadership Program, Congressional Staff Fellows, Stennis Student Congress, and Southern Women in Public Service. The site also includes information on the Truman Scholars program, with which it cooperates.

Subjects: Fellowships; Civics Education

259. Legislative Publications

http://www.access.gpo.gov/su_docs/legislative.html

Sponsor: Government Printing Office (GPO)

Description: This section of the GPO Access Web site provides centralized access to the legislative branch content on the site. Among the many full text congressional documents included are: congressional bills, committee hearings, committee prints, the *Congressional Directory*, *Congressional Pictorial Directory*, the *Congressional Record*, House and Senate Calendars, public and private laws, the United States Code, the pocket edition of the U.S. Constitution, and *The Constitution of the United States of America: Analysis and Interpretation: Annotations of Cases Decided*. Other sites may take these database from GPO and add better search and browse features, but the GPO site is the official original source. "The information provided on this site is the official, published version and the information retrieved from GPO Access can be used without restriction, unless specifically noted" (from the Web site, 2-26-2003).

Subjects: Congressional Documents; Databases

Publications: *Calendar of United States House of Representatives and History of Legislation*, Y 1.2/2:

Congressional Directory, Y 4.P 93/1:1

Congressional Pictorial Directory, Y 4.P 93/1:1 P/

Congressional Record (Daily), X 1.1/A:
Constitution of the United States of America: Analysis and Interpretation, Y 1.1/3:
Constitution, Jefferson's Manual, and Rules of the House of Representatives, Y 1.1/7:
Deschler's Precedents of the United States House of Representatives, Y 1.1/2:
Economic Indicators, Y 4.EC 7:EC 7/
Hinds' Precedents of the House of Representatives
House Practice: A Guide to the Rules, Precedents, and Procedures of the House (Brown), Y 1.2:
Riddick's Senate Procedure, Y 1.1/3:
Senate Calendar of Business. Daily, Y 1.3/3:
Senate Manual, Y 1.1/3:
U.S. Public Laws, AE 2.110:
United States Code, Y 1.2/5:

260. LLSDC's Legislative Source Book
`http://www.llsdc.org/sourcebook/`
Sponsor: Law Librarians' Society of Washington DC, Inc.
Description: For this online Source Book, the Legislative Interest Section of the Law Librarians' Society of Washington, DC has compiled a variety of useful legislative research tools developed by their members. Many are unique to this site. They include: GPO Congressional Publication Releases, a weekly list; a guide to Federal Legislative History Research; and instructions for finding and establishing direct links to documents online at THOMAS and GPO Access. The link to a "Table of Congressional Publication Volumes and Presidential Issuances: Part I (1873-2001)" will be of interest to legislative researchers and librarians. It is a reverse chronological correlation of Congressional session numbers; calendar year; *Congressional Record*, *Statutes at Large*, Serial Set, and *Federal Register* volume numbers; Presidential administration; and Executive Order and Presidential Proclamation numbers.

This site will be of interest to government documents librarians and serious legislative researchers, for whom the useful guides and tables may save a lot of time.
Subjects: Congressional Documents; Legislation — Research

261. Office of Technology Assessment: The OTA Legacy
`http://www.wws.princeton.edu/~ota/`
Alternate URL: `http://www.access.gpo.gov/ota/`
Sponsor: Office of Technology Assessment (OTA)
Description: After Congress terminated its Office of Technology Assessment (OTA) at the end of 1995, the official OTA site ceased. However, a number of other sites volunteered to continue to make archived OTA information available to the public. The Princeton and National Academy Press sites, whose URLs are referenced here, provide the full text of OTA publications. The GPO site gives a brief description of the former OTA site and directions on how to access documents.The Princeton site lists the reports by title, year, and topic, as they were on the official OTA site. All publications are in PDF format. Because some are very long, the site provides options to download individual sections of documents.A section titled Technology Assessment and the Work of Congress describes the history and operations of OTA, including contemporary speeches, news reports, and *Congressional Record* statements about its role.

Through the publications available at this site, OTA provided analyses of the scientific and technical policy issues for Congress. The Princeton and National Academy sites provide a valuable archive and record of this work.
Subject: Science and Technology Policy
Publication: *OTA Reports*, Y 3.T 22/2:7/

262. PoliticalMoneyLine (TM) (FECInfo)
`http://www.politicalmoneyline.com/`
Alternate URL: `http://www.fecinfo.com/`
Sponsor: TRKC Inc.
Description: This is an unofficial, commercial campaign finance information site which uses Federal Election Commission campaign contribution data and presents it in an easy-to-use format. The site

is operated by TRKC Inc., a firm that "specializes in working with data on political money moving to and from the national political arena."

Under the Search Databases Online section in the left panel, the page sets out a variety of ways for non-subscribers to retrieve contribution information. These include searching by candidate name or election cycle, donor information (name, ZIP code, employer), public action committees (PACs) and parties, IRS 527 filers, and foreign agents. Featured sections for subscribers only include information about PAC money to congressional committees, soft money, and lobbyist registrations. The rest of the main page features highlights of current election funding news.

While much of the data presented here is also available on the official FEC site, the packaging of it on PoliticalMoneyLine makes it even easier to find.

263. Project Vote Smart
http://www.vote-smart.org/
Sponsor: Project Vote Smart
Description: Project Vote Smart is an organization dedicated to voter education. Their Web site is a collection of factual information on federal, state, and local candidates for public office. Coverage includes backgrounds, issue positions, voting records, campaign finances, and the performance evaluations made by over 100 conservative to liberal special interest groups. One of the more useful sections of this site is Voting Records, which identifies the key votes of members of the House and Senate, in some cases going back to the late 1980s.
Subject: Congressional Information

264. Records of Congress
http://www.archives.gov/records_of_congress/index.html
Sponsor: National Archives and Records Administration (NARA)
Description: The Records of Congress page presents information about the Center for Legislative Archives, the repository for the historically valuable records of the U.S. Congress at the National Archives and Records Administration. The Center, located in Washington, DC holds more than 160,000 cubic feet of records dating from the First Congress to modern Congresses. The official records from the committees of the House of Representatives and the Senate—the standing, select, special, and joint committees, where Congress accomplishes the majority of its work—represent the core holdings of the Center. It also holds some collections from legislative support agencies, such as publications of the U.S. Government from the Government Printing Office. Several online guides index and describe its committee record holdings.

The "Finding Aids to Legislative Records" section of this site provides the most value to researchers unable to travel to Washington to use the Center's collections.
Subject: Congressional Documents

265. U.S. Congressional Bibliographies
http://www.lib.ncsu.edu/stacks/senatebibs/
Sponsor: North Carolina State University (NCSU)
Description: Jack McGeachy of NCSU Libraries produces monthly bibliographies of Senate hearings, prints, and publications from title page proofs received monthly from the Senate Library. Bibliographies for the 98th Congress (1983) to the present are available. The site also offers lists of House and Senate committee meetings as recorded in the *Congressional Record* Daily Digest. The files are drawn from the electronic version of the Daily Digest available from the THOMAS Web site at the Library of Congress. The committee meeting notices from a calendar year are cumulated into a single file to facilitate searches using a Web browser's "Find" feature.

These bibliographies are primarily of interest to the depository library community, but they could also be useful for Senate researchers.
Subject: Congressional Documents

266. United States Capitol Police

http://www.uscapitolpolice.gov/
Sponsor: Congress — Capitol Police
Description: The Capitol Police Web site has information on becoming a U.S. Capitol Police Officer. The site also explains the mission of the Capitol Police.
Subject: Police

Directories

267. Biographical Directory of the United States Congress

http://bioguide.congress.gov/
Sponsor: Congress
Description: For over a century, the *Biographical Directory of the United States Congress* has provided valuable information about the more than 13,000 individuals who have served in the national legislature, including the Continental Congress, the Senate, and the House of Representatives. Congress offers an online version of this invaluable historical resource. The online version goes beyond the scope of the printed *Biographical Directory* to include images and extended information on research collections relating to each Member. This database may be searched by name, position, and state.
Subjects: Members of Congress; Directories

268. Congress.Org

http://www.congress.org/
Sponsor: Capitol Advantage
Description: "Congress.org is a free, public service of Capitol Advantage" and it is set up to help citizens "identify their Congressional representatives; research Congressional voting records; learn about the issues of the day; and send e-mail directly to Congress" (from the Web site, 2-26-2003). The site provides contact information for federal, state, and local officials and government offices. A Media Guide section makes it easy to find and send email to local and national media. A MegaVote service is available for weekly email notices of congressional votes.
Subjects: Members of Congress; Directories

269. House and Senate Directories

http://clerk.house.gov/members/
Alternate URL: http://www.senate.gov/general/contact_information/senators_cfm.cfm
Sponsors: Congress — House of Representatives; Congress — Senate
Description: The House of Representatives and the Senate each feature directory pages of members and committees on their Web sites. The primary and alternate URLs above are the member directory pages for the House and Senate, respectively; each also links to the committee directory pages. Among the various free congressional directories online, these naturally tend to be the most current and authoritative. In addition to the official listings and links to members' Web sites, the House directories page includes information on current vacancies and member addresses formatted as downloadable mailing labels. The Senate features a list that can be sorted by name, state, or party. The Senate listing includes email addresses. The House offers a Write Your Representative feature for finding and emailing your House member.
Subjects: Members of Congress; Directories

Members

Alabama

270. Sen. Jeff Sessions (R)
http://www.senate.gov/~sessions/
Email: senator@sessions.senate.gov

271. Sen. Richard C. Shelby (R)
http://shelby.senate.gov/
Email: senator@shelby.senate.gov

272. Rep. Jo Bonner (R), District: 01
http://www.house.gov/bonner

273. Rep. Terry Everett (R), District: 02
http://www.hillsource.gov/everett/

274. Rep. Mike Rogers (R), District: 03
http://www.house.gov/mike-rogers/

275. Rep. Robert B. Aderholt (R), District: 04
http://www.house.gov/aderholt/

276. Rep. Bud Cramer (D), District: 05
http://www.house.gov/cramer/
Email: budmail@mail.house.gov

277. Rep. Spencer Bachus (R), District: 06
http://www.house.gov/bachus/

278. Rep. Artur Davis (D), District: 07
http://www.house.gov/arturdavis/

Alaska

279. Sen. Lisa Murkowski (R)
http://www.senate.gov/~murkowski/

280. Sen. Ted Stevens (R)
http://stevens.senate.gov/

281. Rep. Don Young (R), District: At-Large
http://www.house.gov/donyoung/

American Samoa

282. Del. Eni F. H. Faleomavaega (D), District: At-Large
http://www.house.gov/faleomavaega/
Email: faleomavaega@mail.house.gov

Arizona

283. Sen. Jon Kyl (R)
http://kyl.senate.gov/

284. Sen. John McCain (R)
http://www.senate.gov/~mccain/
Email: John_McCain@mccain.senate.gov

285. Rep. Rick Renzi (R), District: 01
http://www.house.gov/renzi/

286. Rep. Trent Franks (R), District: 02
http://www.house.gov/franks/

287. Rep. John Shadegg (R), District: 03
http://johnshadegg.house.gov/

288. Rep. Ed Pastor (D), District: 04
http://www.house.gov/pastor/

289. Rep. J. D. Hayworth (R), District: 05
http://www.house.gov/hayworth/
Email: jdhayworth@mail.house.gov

290. Rep. Jeff Flake (R), District: 06
http://www.house.gov/flake/

291. Rep. Raul Grijalva (D), District: 07
http://www.house.gov/grijalva/

292. Rep. Jim Kolbe (R), District: 08
http://www.house.gov/kolbe/

Arkansas

293. Sen. Blanche Lincoln (D)
http://lincoln.senate.gov/

294. Sen. Mark Pryor (D)
http://pryor.senate.gov/
Email: senator@pryor.senate.gov

295. Rep. Marion Berry (D), District: 01
http://www.house.gov/berry/

296. Rep. Vic Snyder (D), District: 02
http://www.house.gov/snyder/
Email: snyder.congress@mail.house.gov

297. Rep. John Boozman (R), District: 03
http://www.house.gov/boozman/

298. Rep. Mike Ross (D), District: 04
http://www.house.gov/ross/

California

299. Sen. Barbara Boxer (D)
http://boxer.senate.gov/home.html?target=home.html

300. Sen. Dianne Feinstein (D)
http://feinstein.senate.gov/

301. Rep. Mike Thompson (D), District: 01
http://www.house.gov/mthompson/

302. Rep. Wally Herger (R), District: 02
http://www.house.gov/herger/

303. Rep. Doug Ose (R), District: 03
http://www.house.gov/ose/

304. Rep. John Doolittle (R), District: 04
http://www.house.gov/doolittle/

305. Rep. Robert T. Matsui (D), District: 05
http://www.house.gov/matsui/

306. Rep. Lynn Woolsey (D), District: 06
http://woolsey.house.gov/

307. Rep. George Miller (D), District: 07
http://www.house.gov/georgemiller/
Email: George.Miller@mail.house.gov

308. Rep. Nancy Pelosi (D), District: 08
http://www.house.gov/pelosi/
Email: sf.nancy@mail.house.gov

309. Rep. Barbara Lee (D), District: 09
http://www.house.gov/lee/
Email: barbara.lee@mail.house.gov

310. Rep. Ellen Tauscher (D), District: 10
http://www.house.gov/tauscher/

311. Rep. Richard Pombo (R), District: 11
http://www.house.gov/pombo/pombo.htm
Email: rpombo@mail.house.gov

312. Rep. Tom Lantos (D), District: 12
http://www.house.gov/lantos/
Email: CA12Lantos@mail.house.gov

313. Rep. Pete Stark (D), District: 13
http://www.house.gov/stark/
Email: petemail@stark.house.gov

314. Rep. Anna Eshoo (D), District: 14
http://www-eshoo.house.gov/
Email: annagram@mail.house.gov

315. Rep. Michael Honda (D), District: 15
http://www.house.gov/honda/
Email: mike.honda@mail.house.gov

316. Rep. Zoe Lofgren (D), District: 16
http://zoelofgren.house.gov
Email: zoe@lofgren.house.gov

317. Rep. Sam Farr (D), District: 17
http://www.house.gov/farr/

318. Rep. Dennis Cardoza (D), District: 18
http://www.house.gov/cardoza/

319. Rep. George Radanovich (R), District: 19
http://www.radanovich.house.gov/

320. Rep. Cal Dooley (D), District: 20
http://dooley.house.gov/

321. Rep. Devin Nunes (R), District: 21
http://www.nunes.house.gov/

322. Rep. Bill Thomas (R), District: 22
http://billthomas.house.gov/

323. Rep. Lois Capps (D), District: 23
http://www.house.gov/capps/

324. Rep. Elton Gallegly (R), District: 24
http://www.house.gov/gallegly/

325. Rep. Buck McKeon (R), District: 25
http://www.house.gov/mckeon/

326. Rep. David Dreier (R), District: 26
http://dreier.house.gov

327. Rep. Brad Sherman (D), District: 27
http://www.house.gov/sherman/

328. Rep. Howard L. Berman (D), District: 28
http://www.house.gov/berman/
Email: Howard.Berman@mail.house.gov

329. Rep. Adam Schiff (D), District: 29
http://www.house.gov/schiff/

330. Rep. Henry Waxman (D), District: 30
http://www.house.gov/waxman/

331. Rep. Xavier Becerra (D), District: 31
http://www.house.gov/becerra/

332. Rep. Hilda Solis (D), District: 32
http://www.house.gov/solis/

333. Rep. Diane E. Watson (D), District: 33
http://www.house.gov/watson/

334. Rep. Lucille Roybal-Allard (D), District: 34
http://www.house.gov/roybal-allard/

335. Rep. Maxine Waters (D), District: 35
http://www.house.gov/waters/

336. Rep. Jane Harman (D), District: 36
http://www.house.gov/harman/
Email: jane.harman@mail.house.gov

337. Rep. Juanita Millender-McDonald (D), District: 37
http://www.house.gov/millender-mcdonald/

338. Rep. Grace Napolitano (D), District: 38
http://www.napolitano.house.gov
Email: grace@mail.house.gov

339. Rep. Linda Sanchez (D), District: 39
http://www.house.gov/lindasanchez/

340. Rep. Edward R. Royce (R), District: 40
http://www.house.gov/royce/

341. Rep. Jerry Lewis (R), District: 41
http://www.house.gov/jerrylewis/

342. Rep. Gary Miller (R), District: 42
http://www.house.gov/garymiller/
Email: PublicCA42@mail.house.gov

343. Rep. Joe Baca (D), District: 43
http://www.house.gov/baca/

344. Rep. Ken Calvert (R), District: 44
http://www.house.gov/calvert/

345. Rep. Mary Bono (R), District: 45
http://www.house.gov/bono/

346. Rep. Dana Rohrabacher (R), District: 46
http://www.house.gov/rohrabacher/
Email: dana@mail.house.gov

347. Rep. Loretta Sanchez (D), District: 47
http://www.house.gov/sanchez/
Email: loretta@mail.house.gov

348. Rep. Christopher Cox (R), District: 48
http://cox.house.gov/
Email: christopher.cox@mail.house.gov

349. Rep. Darrell Issa (R), District: 49
http://www.issa.house.gov/

350. Rep. Randy Cunningham (R), District: 50
http://www.house.gov/cunningham/

351. Rep. Bob Filner (D), District: 51
http://www.house.gov/filner/

352. Rep. Duncan Hunter (R), District: 52
http://www.house.gov/hunter/

353. Rep. Susan A. Davis (D), District: 53
http://www.house.gov/susandavis/
Email: susan.davis@mail.house.gov

Colorado

354. Sen. Wayne Allard (R)
http://allard.senate.gov/

355. Sen. Ben Nighthorse Campbell (R)
http://campbell.senate.gov/

356. Rep. Diana DeGette (D), District: 01
http://www.house.gov/degette/

357. Rep. Mark Udall (D), District: 02
http://wwwa.house.gov/markudall/

358. Rep. Scott McInnis (R), District: 03
http://www.house.gov/mcinnis/

359. Rep. Marilyn Musgrave (R), District: 04
http://wwwa.house.gov/musgrave/

360. Rep. Joel Hefley (R), District: 05
http://www.house.gov/hefley/

361. Rep. Thomas Tancredo (R), District: 06
http://www.house.gov/tancredo/

362. Rep. Bob Beauprez (R), District: 07
http://www.house.gov/beauprez/

Connecticut

363. Sen. Chris Dodd (D)
http://dodd.senate.gov/

364. Sen. Joe Lieberman (D)
http://lieberman.senate.gov/

365. Rep. John Larson (D), District: 01
http://www.house.gov/larson/

366. Rep. Rob Simmons (R), District: 02
http://www.house.gov/simmons/

367. Rep. Rosa DeLauro (D), District: 03
http://www.house.gov/delauro/

368. Rep. Christopher Shays (R), District: 04
http://www.house.gov/shays/

369. Rep. Nancy Johnson (R), District: 05
http://www.house.gov/nancyjohnson/

Delaware

370. Sen. Joseph R. Biden (D)
http://biden.senate.gov/
Email: senator@biden.senate.gov

371. Sen. Thomas R. Carper (D)
http://carper.senate.gov/

372. Rep. Michael N. Castle (R), District: At-Large
http://www.house.gov/castle/

District of Columbia

373. Del. Eleanor Holmes Norton (D), District: At-Large
http://www.norton.house.gov/

Florida

374. Sen. Bob Graham (D)
http://graham.senate.gov/

375. Sen. Bill Nelson (D)
http://billnelson.senate.gov/

376. Rep. Jeff Miller (R), District: 01
http://www.house.gov/jeffmiller/

377. Rep. Allen Boyd (D), District: 02
http://www.house.gov/boyd/

378. Rep. Corrine Brown (D), District: 03
http://www.house.gov/corrinebrown/

379. Rep. Ander Crenshaw (R), District: 04
http://www.house.gov/crenshaw-web/jsp/default.jsp

380. Rep. Virginia Brown-Waite (R), District: 05
http://www.house.gov/brown-waite/

381. Rep. Cliff Stearns (R), District: 06
http://www.house.gov/stearns/

382. Rep. John Mica (R), District: 07
http://www.house.gov/mica/

383. Rep. Ric Keller (R), District: 08
http://www.house.gov/keller/Frset.htm

384. Rep. Mike Bilirakis (R), District: 09
http://www.house.gov/bilirakis/

385. Rep. C.W. Bill Young (R), District: 10
http://www.house.gov/young/
Email: bill.young@mail.house.gov

386. Rep. Jim Davis (D), District: 11
http://www.house.gov/jimdavis/

387. Rep. Adam Putnam (R), District: 12
http://www.house.gov/putnam/

388. Rep. Katherine Harris (R), District: 13
http://www.house.gov/harris/

389. Rep. Porter J. Goss (R), District: 14
http://portergoss.house.gov/

390. Rep. Dave Weldon (R), District: 15
http://www.house.gov/weldon/

391. Rep. Mark Foley (R), District: 16
http://www.house.gov/foley/

392. Rep. Kendrick Meek (D), District: 17
http://www.house.gov/kenmeek/

393. Rep. Ileana Ros-Lehtinen (R), District: 18
http://www.house.gov/ros-lehtinen/

394. Rep. Robert Wexler (D), District: 19
http://www.wexler.house.gov/

395. Rep. Peter Deutsch (D), District: 20
http://www.house.gov/deutsch/

396. Rep. Lincoln Diaz-Balart (R), District: 21
http://www.house.gov/diaz-balart/

397. Rep. E. Clay Shaw Jr. (R), District: 22
http://www.house.gov/shaw/

398. Rep. Alcee L. Hastings (D), District: 23
http://www.house.gov/alceehastings/
Email: alcee.pubhastings@mail.house.gov

399. Rep. Tom Feeney (R), District: 24
http://www.house.gov/feeney/

400. Rep. Mario Diaz-Balart (R), District: 25
http://www.house.gov/mariodiaz-balart/

Georgia

401. Sen. Zell Miller (D)
http://miller.senate.gov/

402. Sen. Saxby Chambliss (R)
http://www.senate.gov/pagelayout/senators/one_item_and_teasers/chambliss.htm
Email: saxby_chambliss@chambliss.senate.gov

403. Rep. Jack Kingston (R), District: 01
http://www.house.gov/kingston/
Email: jack.kingston@mail.house.gov

404. Rep. Sanford D. Bishop Jr. (D), District: 02
http://www.house.gov/bishop/
Email: bishop.email@mail.house.gov

405. Rep. Jim Marshall (D), District: 03
http://www.house.gov/marshall/

406. Rep. Denise Majette (D), District: 04
http://www.house.gov/majette/

407. Rep. John Lewis (D), District: 05
http://www.house.gov/johnlewis/

408. Rep. Johnny Isakson (R), District: 06
http://isakson.house.gov/

409. Rep. John Linder (R), District: 07
http://linder.house.gov/

410. Rep. Mac Collins (R), District: 08
http://www.house.gov/maccollins/

411. Rep. Charlie Norwood (R), District: 09
http://www.house.gov/norwood/

412. Rep. Nathan Deal (R), District: 10
http://www.house.gov/deal/

413. Rep. Phil Gingrey (R), District: 11
http://www.house.gov/gingrey/

414. Rep. Max Burns (R), District: 12
http://www.house.gov/burns/

415. Rep. David Scott (D), District: 13
http://www.house.gov/davidscott/

Guam

416. Del. Madeleine Bordallo (D)
http://www.house.gov/bordallo/
Email: madeleine.bordallo@mail.house.gov

Hawaii

417. Sen. Daniel Kahikina Akaka (D)
http://akaka.senate.gov/
Email: senator@akaka.senate.gov

418. Sen. Daniel K. Inouye (D)
http://inouye.senate.gov/

419. Rep. Neil Abercrombie (D), District: 01
http://www.house.gov/abercrombie/
Email: neil.abercrombie@mail.house.gov

419a. Rep. Ed Case (D), District: 02
http://www.house.gov/case/
Email: ed.case@mail.house.gov

Idaho

420. Sen. Larry Craig (R)
http://craig.senate.gov/portal.htm

421. Sen. Mike Crapo (R)
http://crapo.senate.gov/
Email: webmail@crapo-iq.senate.gov

422. Rep. C. L. Otter (R), District: 01
http://www.house.gov/otter/

423. Rep. Mike Simpson (R), District: 02
http://www.house.gov/simpson/

Illinois

424. Sen. Dick Durbin (D)
http://durbin.senate.gov/
Email: dick@durbin.senate.gov

425. Sen. Peter G. Fitzgerald (R)
http://fitzgerald.senate.gov/
Email: senator_fitzgerald@fitzgerald.senate.gov

426. Rep. Bobby L. Rush (D), District: 01
http://www.house.gov/rush/

427. Rep. Jesse Jackson Jr. (D), District: 02
http://www.house.gov/jackson/
Email: webmaster@jessejacksonjr.org

428. Rep. Bill Lipinski (D), District: 03
http://www.house.gov/lipinski/

429. Rep. Luis V. Gutierrez (D), District: 04
http://luisgutierrez.house.gov
Email: luis.gutierrez@mail.house.gov

430. Rep. Rahm Emanuel (D), District: 05
http://www.house.gov/emanuel/

431. Rep. Henry Hyde (R), District: 06
http://www.house.gov/hyde/

432. Rep. Danny K. Davis (D), District: 07
http://www.house.gov/davis/

433. Rep. Philip M. Crane (R), District: 08
http://www.house.gov/crane/

434. Rep. Jan Schakowsky (D), District: 09
http://www.house.gov/schakowsky/
Email: jan.schakowsky@mail.house.gov

435. Rep. Mark Steven Kirk (R), District: 10
http://www.house.gov/kirk/
Email: rep.kirk@mail.house.gov

436. Rep. Jerry Weller (R), District: 11
http://www.house.gov/weller/

437. Rep. Jerry Costello (D), District: 12
http://www.house.gov/costello/

438. Rep. Judy Biggert (R), District: 13
http://judybiggert.house.gov/

439. Rep. Dennis J. Hastert (R), District: 14
http://www.house.gov/hastert/
http://speaker.house.gov/
Email: dhastert@mail.house.gov

440. Rep. Timothy Johnson (R), District: 15
http://www.house.gov/timjohnson/

441. Rep. Don Manzullo (R), District: 16
http://manzullo.house.gov/

442. Rep. Lane Evans (D), District: 17
http://www.house.gov/evans/
Email: lane.evans@mail.house.gov

443. Rep. Ray LaHood (R), District: 18
http://www.house.gov/lahood/

444. Rep. John Shimkus (R), District: 19
http://www.house.gov/shimkus/

Indiana

445. Sen. Evan Bayh (D)
http://bayh.senate.gov/index1.html
Email: senator@bayh.senate.gov

446. Sen. Richard G. Lugar (R)
http://lugar.senate.gov/
Email: senator_lugar@lugar.senate.gov

447. Rep. Pete Visclosky (D), District: 01
http://www.house.gov/visclosky/

448. Rep. Chris Chocola (R), District: 02
http://www.house.gov/chocola/

449. Rep. Mark E. Souder (R), District: 03
http://www.house.gov/souder/

450. Rep. Steve Buyer (R), District: 04
http://www.house.gov/buyer/

451. Rep. Dan Burton (R), District: 05
http://www.house.gov/burton/

452. Rep. Mike Pence (R), District: 06
http://mikepence.house.gov/

453. Rep. Julia Carson (D), District: 07
http://www.juliacarson.house.gov
Email: rep.carson@mail.house.gov

454. Rep. John Hostettler (R), District: 08
http://www.house.gov/hostettler/
Email: John.Hostettler@mail.house.gov

455. Rep. Baron Hill (D), District: 09
http://www.house.gov/baronhill/

Iowa

456. Sen. Chuck Grassley (R)
http://grassley.senate.gov/

457. Sen. Tom Harkin (D)
http://harkin.senate.gov/
Email: tom_harkin@harkin.senate.gov

458. Rep. Jim Nussle (R), District: 01
http://nussle.house.gov
Email: nussleia@mail.house.gov

459. Rep. Jim Leach (R), District: 02
http://www.house.gov/leach/
Email: talk2jim@mail.house.gov

460. Rep. Leonard Boswell (D), District: 03
http://www.house.gov/boswell/
Email: rep.boswell.ia03@mail.house.gov

461. Rep. Tom Latham (R), District: 04
http://www.house.gov/latham/
Email: tom.latham@mail.house.gov

462. Rep. Steve King (R), District: 05
http://www.house.gov/steveking/

Kansas

463. Sen. Sam Brownback (R)
http://brownback.senate.gov/

464. Sen. Pat Roberts (R)
http://roberts.senate.gov/

465. Rep. Jerry Moran (R), District: 01
http://www.house.gov/moranks01/

466. Rep. Jim Ryun (R), District: 02
http://www.ryun.house.gov/

467. Rep. Dennis Moore (D), District: 03
http://www.house.gov/moore/

468. Rep. Todd Tiahrt (R), District: 04
http://www.house.gov/tiahrt/

Kentucky

469. Sen. Jim Bunning (R)
http://bunning.senate.gov/

470. Sen. Mitch McConnell (R)
http://mcconnell.senate.gov/
Email: senator@mcconnell.senate.gov

471. Rep. Ed Whitfield (R), District: 01
http://www.house.gov/whitfield/

472. Rep. Ron Lewis (R), District: 02
http://www.house.gov/ronlewis/

473. Rep. Anne Northup (R), District: 03
http://northup.house.gov

474. Rep. Ken Lucas (D), District: 04
http://www.house.gov/kenlucas/

475. Rep. Hal Rogers (R), District: 05
http://www.house.gov/rogers/
Email: Talk2Hal@mail.house.gov

476. Rep. Ernie Fletcher (R), District: 06
http://www.house.gov/fletcher/

Louisiana

477. Sen. John Breaux (D)
http://breaux.senate.gov/
Email: senator@breaux.senate.gov

478. Sen. Mary L. Landrieu (D)
http://landrieu.senate.gov/

479. Rep. David Vitter (R), District: 01
http://vitter.house.gov

480. Rep. William J. Jefferson (D), District: 02
http://www.house.gov/jefferson/
Email: jeffersonmc@mail.house.gov

481. Rep. Billy Tauzin (R), District: 03
http://www.house.gov/tauzin/

482. Rep. Jim McCrery (R), District: 04
http://www.house.gov/mccrery/

483. Rep. Rodney Alexander (D), District: 05
http://www.house.gov/alexander/

484. Rep. Richard Baker (R), District: 06
http://www.house.gov/baker/

485. Rep. Chris John (D), District: 07
http://www.house.gov/john/

Maine

486. Sen. Susan Collins (R)
http://collins.senate.gov/
Email: senator@collins.senate.gov

487. Sen. Olympia J. Snowe (R)
http://snowe.senate.gov/
Email: Olympia@snowe.senate.gov

488. Rep. Tom Allen (D), District: 01
http://tomallen.house.gov/
Email: rep.tomallen@mail.house.gov

489. Rep. Michael Michaud (D), District: 02
http://www.house.gov/michaud/

Maryland

490. Sen. Barbara A. Mikulski (D)
http://mikulski.senate.gov/

491. Sen. Paul S. Sarbanes (D)
http://sarbanes.senate.gov/

492. Rep. Wayne Gilchrest (R), District: 01
http://gilchrest.house.gov/

493. Rep. Dutch Ruppersberger (D), District: 02
http://www.house.gov/ruppersberger/

494. Rep. Ben Cardin (D), District: 03
http://www.house.gov/cardin/

495. Rep. Albert R. Wynn (D), District: 04
http://www.wynn.house.gov/

496. Rep. Steny Hoyer (D), District: 05
http://www.hoyer.house.gov/

497. Rep. Roscoe Bartlett (R), District: 06
http://www.bartlett.house.gov

498. Rep. Elijah E. Cummings (D), District: 07
http://www.house.gov/cummings/

499. Rep. Chris Van Hollen (D), District: 08
http://www.house.gov/vanhollen/
Email: chris.vanhollen@mail.house.gov

Massachusetts

500. Sen. Ted Kennedy (D)
http://kennedy.senate.gov/
Email: senator@kennedy.senate.gov

501. Sen. John Kerry (D)
http://kerry.senate.gov/
Email: john_kerry@kerry.senate.gov

502. Rep. John Olver (D), District: 01
http://www.house.gov/olver/

503. Rep. Richard E. Neal (D), District: 02
http://www.house.gov/neal/

504. Rep. Jim McGovern (D), District: 03
http://www.house.gov/mcgovern/

505. Rep. Barney Frank (D), District: 04
http://www.house.gov/frank/

506. Rep. Martin T. Meehan (D), District: 05
http://www.house.gov/meehan/

507. Rep. John Tierney (D), District: 06
http://www.house.gov/tierney/

508. Rep. Edward Markey (D), District: 07
http://www.house.gov/markey/

509. Rep. Mike Capuano (D), District: 08
http://www.house.gov/capuano/

510. Rep. Stephen F. Lynch (D), District: 09
http://www.house.gov/lynch/
Email: Stephen.Lynch@mail.house.gov

511. Rep. Bill Delahunt (D), District: 10
http://www.house.gov/delahunt/
Email: william.delahunt@mail.house.gov

Michigan

512. Sen. Carl Levin (D)
http://levin.senate.gov/
Email: senator2@levin.senate.gov

513. Sen. Debbie Stabenow (D)
http://stabenow.senate.gov/
Email: senator@stabenow.senate.gov

514. Rep. Bart Stupak (D), District: 01
http://www.house.gov/stupak/
Email: stupak@mail.house.gov

515. Rep. Peter Hoekstra (R), District: 02
http://www.house.gov/hoekstra/

516. Rep. Vernon J. Ehlers (R), District: 03
http://www.house.gov/ehlers/

517. Rep. Dave Camp (R), District: 04
http://www.house.gov/camp/

518. Rep. Dale E. Kildee (D), District: 05
http://www.house.gov/kildee/

519. Rep. Fred Upton (R), District: 06
http://www.house.gov/upton/

520. Rep. Nick Smith (R), District: 07
http://www.house.gov/nicksmith/

521. Rep. Mike Rogers (R), District: 08
http://www.house.gov/mikerogers/

522. Rep. Joe Knollenberg (R), District: 09
http://www.house.gov/knollenberg/
Email: rep.knollenberg@mail.house.gov

523. Rep. Candice Miller (R), District: 10
http://www.house.gov/candicemiller/

524. Rep. Thaddeus McCotter (R), District: 11
http://www.house.gov/mccotter/

525. Rep. Sander Levin (D), District: 12
http://www.house.gov/levin/

526. Rep. Carolyn Kilpatrick (D), District: 13
http://www.house.gov/kilpatrick/

527. Rep. John Conyers Jr. (D), District: 14
http://www.house.gov/conyers/
Email: john.conyers@mail.house.gov

528. Rep. John D. Dingell (D), District: 15
http://www.house.gov/dingell/

Minnesota

529. Sen. Norm Coleman (R)
http://www.senate.gov/pagelayout/senators/one_item_and_teasers/coleman.htm

530. Sen. Mark Dayton (D)
http://dayton.senate.gov/

531. Rep. Gil Gutknecht (R), District: 01
http://www.gil.house.gov/
Email: gil@mail.house.gov

532. Rep. John Kline (R), District: 02
http://www.house.gov/kline/

533. Rep. Jim Ramstad (R), District: 03
http://www.house.gov/ramstad/
Email: mn03@mail.house.gov

534. Rep. Betty McCollum (D), District: 04
http://www.house.gov/mccollum/

535. Rep. Martin Olav Sabo (D), District: 05
http://www.house.gov/sabo/

536. Rep. Mark Kennedy (R), District: 06
http://markkennedy.house.gov/
Email: mark.kennedy@mail.house.gov

537. Rep. Collin C. Peterson (D), District: 07
http://collinpeterson.house.gov/

538. Rep. James L. Oberstar (D), District: 08
http://wwwa.house.gov/oberstar/

Mississippi

539. Sen. Thad Cochran (R)
http://cochran.senate.gov/

540. Sen. Trent Lott (R)
http://lott.senate.gov/
Email: senatorlott@lott.senate.gov

541. Rep. Roger Wicker (R), District: 01
http://www.house.gov/wicker/

542. Rep. Bennie G. Thompson (D), District: 02
http://www.house.gov/thompson/

543. Rep. Chris Pickering (R), District: 03
http://www.house.gov/pickering/

544. Rep. Gene Taylor (D), District: 04
http://www.house.gov/genetaylor/

Missouri

545. Sen. Kit Bond (R)
http://bond.senate.gov/

546. Sen. James Talent (R)
http://bioguide.congress.gov/scripts/biodisplay.pl?index=T000024
Email: senator_talent@talent.senate.gov

547. Rep. Lacy Clay (D), District: 01
http://www.house.gov/clay/

548. Rep. Todd Akin (R), District: 02
http://www.house.gov/akin/

549. Rep. Richard Gephardt (D), District: 03
http://dickgephardt.house.gov/

550. Rep. Ike Skelton (D), District: 04
http://www.house.gov/skelton/

551. Rep. Karen McCarthy (D), District: 05
http://mccarthy.house.gov/

552. Rep. Sam Graves (R), District: 06
http://www.house.gov/graves/
Email: sam.graves@mail.house.gov

553. Rep. Roy Blunt (R), District: 07
http://www.blunt.house.gov/

554. Rep. Jo Ann Emerson (R), District: 08
http://www.house.gov/emerson/

555. Rep. Kenny Hulshof (R), District: 09
http://www.house.gov/hulshof/

Montana

556. Sen. Max Baucus (D)
http://baucus.senate.gov/

557. Sen. Conrad Burns (R)
http://burns.senate.gov/
Email: conrad_burns@burns.senate.gov

558. Rep. Dennis Rehberg (R), District: At-Large
http://www.house.gov/rehberg/

Nebraska

559. Sen. Chuck Hagel (R)
http://hagel.senate.gov/

560. Sen. Ben Nelson (D)
http://bennelson.senate.gov/

561. Rep. Doug Bereuter (R), District: 01
http://www.house.gov/bereuter/

562. Rep. Lee Terry (R), District: 02
http://leeterry.house.gov/

563. Rep. Tom Osborne (R), District: 03
http://www.house.gov/osborne/

Nevada

564. Sen. John Ensign (R)
http://ensign.senate.gov/
Email: info@ensignfornevada.com

565. Sen. Harry Reid (D)
http://reid.senate.gov/

566. Rep. Shelley Berkley (D), District: 01
http://www.house.gov/berkley/

567. Rep. Jim Gibbons (R), District: 02
http://www.house.gov/gibbons/
Email: mail.gibbons@mail.house.gov

568. Rep. Jon Porter (R), District: 03
http://www.house.gov/porter

New Hampshire

569. Sen. Judd Gregg (R)
http://gregg.senate.gov/
Email: mailbox@gregg.senate.gov

570. Sen. John E. Sununu (R)
http://bioguide.congress.gov/scripts/biodisplay.pl?index=S001078
Email: mailbox@sununu.senate.gov

571. Rep. Jeb Bradley (R), District: 01
http://www.house.gov/bradley

572. Rep. Charlie Bass (R), District: 02
http://www.house.gov/bass/
Email: cbass@mail.house.gov

New Jersey

573. Sen. Jon Corzine (D)
http://corzine.senate.gov/

574. Sen. Frank Lautenberg (D)
http://lautenberg.senate.gov/
Email: Frank_Lautenberg@lautenberg.senate.gov

575. Rep. Robert E. Andrews (D), District: 01
http://www.house.gov/andrews/

576. Rep. Frank A. LoBiondo (R), District: 02
http://www.house.gov/lobiondo/
Email: lobiondo@mail.house.gov

577. Rep. Jim Saxton (R), District: 03
http://www.house.gov/saxton/

578. Rep. Chris Smith (R), District: 04
http://www.house.gov/chrissmith/

579. Rep. Scott Garrett (R), District: 05
http://www.house.gov/garrett/

580. Rep. Frank Pallone Jr. (D), District: 06
http://www.house.gov/pallone/
Email: frank.pallone@mail.house.gov

581. Rep. Mike Ferguson (R), District: 07
http://www.house.gov/ferguson/

582. Rep. Bill Pascrell Jr. (D), District: 08
http://www.pascrell.house.gov
Email: bill.pascrell@mail.house.gov

583. Rep. Steve Rothman (D), District: 09
http://rothman.house.gov/

584. Rep. Donald M. Payne (D), District: 10
http://www.house.gov/payne/

585. Rep. Rodney Frelinghuysen (R), District: 11
http://www.house.gov/frelinghuysen/
Email: rodney.frelinghuysen@mail.house.gov

586. Rep. Rush Holt (D), District: 12
http://holt.house.gov/display2.cfm?id=1071&type=Home
Email: rush.holt@mail.house.gov

587. Rep. Robert Menendez (D), District: 13
http://menendez.house.gov/
Email: menendez@mail.house.gov

New Mexico

588. Sen. Jeff Bingaman (D)
http://bingaman.senate.gov/
Email: senator_bingaman@bingaman.senate.gov

589. Sen. Pete V. Domenici (R)
http://domenici.senate.gov/

590. Rep. Heather Wilson (R), District: 01
http://wilson.house.gov/

591. Rep. Steve Pearce (R), District: 02
http://www.house.gov/pearce

592. Rep. Tom Udall (D), District: 03
http://www.house.gov/tomudall/

New York

593. Sen. Hillary Rodham Clinton (D)
http://clinton.senate.gov/

594. Sen. Charles E. Schumer (D)
http://schumer.senate.gov/index.html

595. Rep. Timothy Bishop (D), District: 01
http://www.house.gov/timbishop/

596. Rep. Steve Israel (D), District: 02
http://www.house.gov/israel/

597. Rep. Peter King (R), District: 03
http://www.house.gov/king/
Email: pete.king@mail.house.gov

598. Rep. Carolyn McCarthy (D), District: 04
http://www.house.gov/carolynmccarthy/

599. Rep. Gary Ackerman (D), District: 05
http://www.house.gov/ackerman/

600. Rep. Gregory W. Meeks (D), District: 06
http://www.house.gov/meeks/
Email: congmeeks@mail.house.gov

601. Rep. Joseph Crowley (D), District: 07
http://crowley.house.gov/

602. Rep. Jerrold Nadler (D), District: 08
http://www.house.gov/nadler/
Email: jerrold.nadler@mail.house.gov

603. Rep. Anthony D. Weiner (D), District: 09
http://www.house.gov/weiner/
Email: weiner@mail.house.gov

604. Rep. Edolphus Towns (D), District: 10
http://www.house.gov/towns/

605. Rep. Major Owens (D), District: 11
http://www.house.gov/owens/

606. Rep. Nydia M. Velázquez (D), District: 12
http://www.house.gov/velazquez/

607. Rep. Vito Fossella (R), District: 13
http://www.house.gov/fossella/
Email: vito.fossella@mail.house.gov

608. Rep. Carolyn Maloney (D), District: 14
http://www.house.gov/maloney/
Email: rep.carolyn.maloney@mail.house.gov

609. Rep. Charles B. Rangel (D), District: 15
http://www.house.gov/rangel/

610. Rep. José E. Serrano (D), District: 16
http://www.house.gov/serrano/
Email: jserrano@mail.house.gov

611. Rep. Eliot L. Engel (D), District: 17
http://www.house.gov/engel/

612. Rep. Nita M. Lowey (D), District: 18
http://www.house.gov/lowey/

613. Rep. Sue Kelly (R), District: 19
http://www.house.gov/suekelly/

614. Rep. John Sweeney (R), District: 20
http://www.house.gov/sweeney/

615. Rep. Michael McNulty (D), District: 21
http://www.house.gov/mcnulty/
Email: mike.mcnulty@mail.house.gov

616. Rep. Maurice Hinchey (D), District: 22
http://www.house.gov/hinchey/

617. Rep. John M. McHugh (R), District: 23
http://www.house.gov/mchugh/

618. Rep. Sherwood Boehlert (R), District: 24
http://www.house.gov/boehlert/
Email: Rep.Boehlert@mail.house.gov

619. Rep. James T. Walsh (R), District: 25
http://www.house.gov/walsh/
Email: rep.james.walsh@mail.house.gov

620. Rep. Tom Reynolds (R), District: 26
http://www.house.gov/reynolds/

621. Rep. Jack Quinn (R), District: 27
http://quinn.house.gov/

622. Rep. Louise M. Slaughter (D), District: 28
http://www.slaughter.house.gov/
Email: louiseny@mail.house.gov

623. Rep. Amo Houghton (R), District: 29
http://www.house.gov/houghton/

North Carolina

624. Sen. Elizabeth Dole (R)
http://www.senate.gov/pagelayout/senators/one_item_and_teasers/dole.htm

625. Sen. John Edwards (D)
http://edwards.senate.gov/

626. Rep. Frank Ballance Jr. (D), District: 01
http://www.house.gov/ballance/

627. Rep. Bob Etheridge (D), District: 02
http://www.house.gov/etheridge/

628. Rep. Walter B. Jones (R), District: 03
http://jones.house.gov/

629. Rep. David Price (D), District: 04
http://www.house.gov/price/

630. Rep. Richard Burr (R), District: 05
http://www.house.gov/burr/
Email: Richard.BurrNC05@mail.house.gov

631. Rep. Howard Coble (R), District: 06
http://www.house.gov/coble/
Email: howard.coble@mail.house.gov

632. Rep. Mike McIntyre (D), District: 07
http://www.house.gov/mcintyre/

633. Rep. Robin Hayes (R), District: 08
http://www.hayes.house.gov/

634. Rep. Sue Myrick (R), District: 09
http://myrick.house.gov/
Email: myrick@mail.house.gov

635. Rep. Cass Ballenger (R), District: 10
http://ballenger.house.gov

636. Rep. Charles H. Taylor (R), District: 11
http://www.house.gov/charlestaylor/

637. Rep. Melvin L. Watt (D), District: 12
http://www.house.gov/watt/

638. Rep. Brad Miller (D), District: 13
http://www.house.gov/bradmiller/

North Dakota

639. Sen. Kent Conrad (D)
http://conrad.senate.gov/
Email: senator@conrad.senate.gov

640. Sen. Byron Dorgan (D)
http://dorgan.senate.gov/
Email: senator@dorgan.senate.gov

641. Rep. Earl Pomeroy (D), District: At-Large
http://www.house.gov/pomeroy/

Ohio

642. Sen. Mike DeWine (R)
http://dewine.senate.gov/
Email: senator_dewine@dewine.senate.gov

643. Sen. George V. Voinovich (R)
http://voinovich.senate.gov/
Email: senator_voinovich@voinovich.senate.gov

644. Rep. Steve Chabot (R), District: 01
http://www.house.gov/chabot/

645. Rep. Rob Portman (R), District: 02
http://www.house.gov/portman/

646. Rep. Michael Turner (R), District: 03
http://www.house.gov/miketurner/

647. Rep. Michael G. Oxley (R), District: 04
http://oxley.house.gov/

648. Rep. Paul E. Gillmor (R), District: 05
http://gillmor.house.gov/

649. Rep. Ted Strickland (D), District: 06
http://www.house.gov/strickland/

650. Rep. Dave Hobson (R), District: 07
http://www.house.gov/hobson/

651. Rep. John Boehner (R), District: 08
http://johnboehner.house.gov

652. Rep. Marcy Kaptur (D), District: 09
http://www.house.gov/kaptur/
Email: rep.kaptur@mail.house.gov

653. Rep. Dennis J. Kucinich (D), District: 10
http://www.house.gov/kucinich/

654. Rep. Stephanie Tubbs Jones (D), District: 11
http://www.house.gov/tubbsjones/

655. Rep. Pat Tiberi (R), District: 12
http://www.house.gov/tiberi/

656. Rep. Sherrod Brown (D), District: 13
http://www.house.gov/sherrodbrown/
Email: sherrod@mail.house.gov

657. Rep. Steven C. LaTourette (R), District: 14
http://www.house.gov/latourette/

658. Rep. Deborah Pryce (R), District: 15
http://www.house.gov/pryce/
Email: pryce.oh15@mail.house.gov

659. Rep. Ralph Regula (R), District: 16
http://wwwa.house.gov/regula/

660. This entry intentionally left blank.

661. Rep. Timothy Ryan (D), District: 17
http://timryan.house.gov/

662. Rep. Bob Ney (R), District: 18
http://www.house.gov/ney/
Email: bobney@mail.house.gov

Oklahoma

663. Sen. James M. Inhofe (R)
http://inhofe.senate.gov/

664. Sen. Don Nickles (R)
http://nickles.senate.gov/

665. Rep. John Sullivan (R), District: 01
http://sullivan.house.gov/

666. Rep. Brad Carson (D), District: 02
http://carson.house.gov/

667. Rep. Frank Lucas (R), District: 03
http://www.house.gov/lucas/

668. Rep. Tom Cole (R), District: 04
http://www.house.gov/cole/

669. Rep. Ernest J. Istook (R), District: 05
http://www.house.gov/istook/
Email: istook@mail.house.gov

Oregon

670. Sen. Gordon H. Smith (R)
http://gsmith.senate.gov/

671. Sen. Ron Wyden (D)
http://wyden.senate.gov/

672. Rep. David Wu (D), District: 01
http://www.house.gov/wu/

673. Rep. Gregory Walden (R), District: 02
http://walden.house.gov/
Email: greg.walden@mail.house.gov

674. Rep. Earl Blumenauer (D), District: 03
http://www.house.gov/blumenauer/
Email: write.earl@mail.house.gov

675. Rep. Pete DeFazio (D), District: 04
http://www.house.gov/defazio/index.htm

676. Rep. Darlene Hooley (D), District: 05
http://www.house.gov/hooley/

Pennsylvania

677. Sen. Rick Santorum (R)
http://santorum.senate.gov/

678. Sen. Arlen Specter (R)
http://www.senate.gov/~specter/
Email: arlen_specter@specter.senate.gov

679. Rep. Robert A. Brady (D), District: 01
http://www.house.gov/robertbrady/

680. Rep. Chaka Fattah (D), District: 02
http://www.house.gov/fattah/

681. Rep. Phil English (R), District: 03
http://www.house.gov/english/

682. Rep. Melissa Hart (R), District: 04
http://hart.house.gov

683. Rep. John E. Peterson (R), District: 05
http://www.house.gov/johnpeterson/
Email: john.peterson@mail.house.gov

684. Rep. Jim Gerlach (R), District: 06
http://www.house.gov/gerlach/

685. Rep. Curt Weldon (R), District: 07
http://www.house.gov/curtweldon
Email: curtpa07@mail.house.gov

686. Rep. James Greenwood (R), District: 08
http://www.house.gov/greenwood/

687. Rep. Bill Shuster (R), District: 09
http://www.house.gov/shuster/

688. Rep. Don Sherwood (R), District: 10
http://www.house.gov/sherwood/

689. Rep. Paul E. Kanjorski (D), District: 11
http://www.house.gov/kanjorski/

690. Rep. John Murtha (D), District: 12
http://www.house.gov/murtha/
Email: murtha@mail.house.gov

691. Rep. Joe Hoeffel (D), District: 13
http://www.hoeffel.house.gov/

692. Rep. Mike Doyle (D), District: 14
http://www.house.gov/doyle/
Email: rep.doyle@mail.house.gov

693. Rep. Patrick Toomey (R), District: 15
http://www.house.gov/toomey/

694. Rep. Joe Pitts (R), District: 16
http://www.house.gov/pitts/

695. Rep. Tim Holden (D), District: 17
http://www.house.gov/holden/

696. Rep. Tim Murphy (R), District: 18
http://murphy.house.gov/

697. Rep. Todd Platts (R), District: 19
http://www.house.gov/platts/

Puerto Rico

698. Rep. Aníbal Acevedo Vilá (D), District: At-Large
http://www.house.gov/acevedo-vila/
Email: anibal@mail.house.gov

Rhode Island

699. Sen. Lincoln Chafee (R)
http://chafee.senate.gov/

700. Sen. Jack Reed (D)
http://reed.senate.gov/
Email: jack@reed.senate.gov

701. Rep. Patrick J. Kennedy (D), District: 01
http://www.house.gov/patrickkennedy/

702. Rep. Jim Langevin (D), District: 02
http://www.house.gov/langevin/
Email: james.langevin@mail.house.gov

South Carolina

703. Sen. Lindsey Graham (R)
http://www.senate.gov/pagelayout/senators/one_item_and_teasers/graham.htm

704. Sen. Fritz Hollings (D)
http://hollings.senate.gov/

705. Rep. Henry Brown (R), District: 01
http://www.house.gov/henrybrown/

706. Rep. Joe Wilson (R), District: 02
http://www.house.gov/joewilson/
Email: Joe.Wilson@mail.house.gov

707. Rep. J. Gresham Barrett (R), District: 03
http://www.house.gov/barrett/

708. Rep. Jim DeMint (R), District: 04
http://www.demint.house.gov/

709. Rep. John Spratt (D), District: 05
http://www.house.gov/spratt/

710. Rep. James E. Clyburn (D), District: 06
http://www.house.gov/clyburn/
Email: jclyburn@mail.house.gov

South Dakota

711. Sen. Tom Daschle (D)
http://daschle.senate.gov/

712. Sen. Tim Johnson (D)
http://johnson.senate.gov/
Email: tim@johnson.senate.gov

713. Rep. William Janklow (R), District: At-Large
http://www.house.gov/janklow

Tennessee

714. Sen. Lamar Alexander (R)
http://alexander.senate.gov/

715. Sen. Bill Frist M.D. (R)
http://frist.senate.gov/

716. Rep. Bill Jenkins (R), District: 01
http://www.house.gov/jenkins/

717. Rep. John J. Duncan Jr. (R), District: 02
http://www.house.gov/duncan/

718. Rep. Zach Wamp (R), District: 03
http://www.house.gov/wamp/

719. Rep. Lincoln Davis (D), District: 04
http://www.house.gov/lincolndavis/

720. Rep. Jim Cooper (D), District: 05
http://www.house.gov/cooper/
Email: jim.cooper@mail.house.gov

721. Rep. Bart Gordon (D), District: 06
http://gordon.house.gov/

722. Rep. Marsha Blackburn (R), District: 07
http://www.house.gov/blackburn/

723. Rep. John Tanner (D), District: 08
http://www.house.gov/tanner/index.htm

724. Rep. Harold Ford Jr. (D), District: 09
http://www.house.gov/ford/

Texas

725. Sen. John Cornyn (R)
http://cornyn.senate.gov/

726. Sen. Kay Bailey Hutchison (R)
http://hutchison.senate.gov

727. Rep. Max Sandlin (D), District: 01
http://www.house.gov/sandlin/

728. Rep. Jim Turner (D), District: 02
http://www.house.gov/turner/

729. Rep. Sam Johnson (R), District: 03
http://www.samjohnson.house.gov/

730. Rep. Ralph Hall (D), District: 04
http://www.house.gov/ralphhall/

731. Rep. Jeb Hensarling (R), District: 05
http://www.house.gov/hensarling/

732. Rep. Joe Barton (R), District: 06
http://joebarton.house.gov/

733. Rep. John Culberson (R), District: 07
http://www.culberson.house.gov/

734. Rep. Kevin Brady (R), District: 08
http://www.house.gov/brady/
Email: rep.brady@mail.house.gov

735. Rep. Nick Lampson (D), District: 09
http://www.house.gov/lampson/

736. Rep. Lloyd Doggett (D), District: 10
http://www.house.gov/doggett/
Email: lloyd.doggett@mail.house.gov

737. Rep. Chet Edwards (D), District: 11
http://www.house.gov/edwards/

738. Rep. Kay Granger (R), District: 12
http://kaygranger.house.gov/

739. Rep. Mac Thornberry (R), District: 13
http://www.house.gov/thornberry/

740. Rep. Ron Paul (R), District: 14
http://www.house.gov/paul/

741. Rep. Rubén Hinojosa (D), District: 15
http://www.house.gov/hinojosa/

742. Rep. Silvestre Reyes (D), District: 16
http://www.house.gov/reyes/

743. Rep. Charlie Stenholm (D), District: 17
http://www.house.gov/stenholm/

744. Rep. Sheila Jackson Lee (D), District: 18
http://www.house.gov/jacksonlee/

745. Rep. Larry Combest (R), District: 19
http://www.house.gov/combest/

746. Rep. Charlie A. Gonzalez (D), District: 20
http://www.house.gov/gonzalez/

747. Rep. Lamar Smith (R), District: 21
http://lamarsmith.house.gov

748. Rep. Tom DeLay (R), District: 22
http://tomdelay.house.gov/

749. Rep. Henry Bonilla (R), District: 23
http://www.house.gov/bonilla/

750. Rep. Martin Frost (D), District: 24
http://www.house.gov/frost/

751. Rep. Chris Bell (D), District: 25
http://www.house.gov/bell/

752. Rep. Michael Burgess (R), District: 26
http://www.house.gov/burgess/

753. Rep. Solomon P. Ortiz (D), District: 27
http://www.house.gov/ortiz/

754. Rep. Ciro D. Rodriguez (D), District: 28
http://www.house.gov/rodriguez/

755. Rep. Gene Green (D), District: 29
http://www.house.gov/green/

756. Rep. Eddie Bernice Johnson (D), District: 30
http://www.house.gov/ebjohnson/

757. Rep. John Carter (R), District: 31
http://www.house.gov/carter/

758. Rep. Pete Sessions (R), District: 32
http://www.house.gov/sessions/

Utah

759. Sen. Bob Bennett (R)
http://bennett.senate.gov/

760. Sen. Orrin Hatch (R)
http://www.senate.gov/~hatch/

761. Rep. Rob Bishop (R), District: 01
http://www.house.gov/robbishop/

762. Rep. Jim Matheson (D), District: 02
http://matheson.house.gov/
Email: jim@matheson2000.com

763. Rep. Chris Cannon (R), District: 03
http://chriscannon.house.gov/
Email: cannon.ut03@mail.house.gov

Vermont

764. Sen. Jim Jeffords (I)
http://jeffords.senate.gov/

765. Sen. Patrick Leahy (D)
http://leahy.senate.gov/
Email: senator_leahy@leahy.senate.gov

766. Rep. Bernie Sanders (I), District: At-Large
http://bernie.house.gov/
Email: bernie@mail.house.gov

Virgin Islands

767. Del. Donna Christian-Christensen (D), District: At-Large
http://www.house.gov/christian-christensen/

Virginia

768. Sen. George Allen (R)
http://allen.senate.gov/

769. Sen. John Warner (R)
http://warner.senate.gov/

770. Rep. Jo Ann Davis (R), District: 01
http://www.house.gov/joanndavis/

771. Rep. Ed Schrock (R), District: 02
http://schrock.house.gov/

772. Rep. Robert C. "Bobby" Scott (D), District: 03
http://www.house.gov/scott/
Email: bobby.scott@mail.house.gov

773. Rep. J. Randy Forbes (R), District: 04
http://www.house.gov/forbes/

774. Rep. Virgil H. Goode Jr. (I), District: 05
http://www.house.gov/goode/

775. Rep. Bob Goodlatte (R), District: 06
http://www.house.gov/goodlatte/

776. Rep. Eric Cantor (R), District: 07
http://cantor.house.gov/

777. Rep. Jim Moran (D), District: 08
http://www.house.gov/moran/
Email: jim.moran@mail.house.gov

778. Rep. Rick Boucher (D), District: 09
http://www.house.gov/boucher/
Email: ninthnet@mail.house.gov

779. Rep. Frank Wolf (R), District: 10
http://www.house.gov/wolf/

780. Rep. Tom Davis (R), District: 11
http://www.house.gov/tomdavis/

Washington

781. Sen. Maria Cantwell (D)
http://cantwell.senate.gov/

782. Sen. Patty Murray (D)
http://murray.senate.gov/
Email: senator_murray@murray.senate.gov

783. Rep. Jay Inslee (D), District: 01
http://www.house.gov/inslee/

784. Rep. Rick Larsen (D), District: 02
http://www.house.gov/larsen/
Email: rick.larsen@mail.house.gov

785. Rep. Brian Baird (D), District: 03
http://www.house.gov/baird/

786. Rep. Doc Hastings (R), District: 04
http://www.house.gov/hastings/

787. Rep. George R. Nethercutt Jr. (R), District: 05
http://www.house.gov/nethercutt/

788. Rep. Norm Dicks (D), District: 06
http://www.house.gov/dicks/

789. Rep. Jim McDermott (D), District: 07
http://www.house.gov/mcdermott/

790. Rep. Jennifer Dunn (R), District: 08
http://www.house.gov/dunn/

791. Rep. Adam Smith (D), District: 09
http://www.house.gov/adamsmith/

West Virginia

792. Sen. Robert C. Byrd (D)
http://byrd.senate.gov/

793. Sen. Jay Rockefeller (D)
http://rockefeller.senate.gov/
Email: senator@rockefeller.senate.gov

794. Rep. Alan B. Mollohan (D), District: 01
http://www.house.gov/mollohan/

795. Rep. Shelley Moore Capito (R), District: 02
http://www.house.gov/capito/

796. Rep. Nick Rahall (D), District: 03
http://www.house.gov/rahall/
Email: nrahall@mail.house.gov

Wisconsin

797. Sen. Russ Feingold (D)
http://feingold.senate.gov/

798. Sen. Herbert Kohl (D)
http://kohl.senate.gov/
Email: senator_kohl@kohl.senate.gov

799. Rep. Paul Ryan (R), District: 01
http://www.house.gov/ryan/

800. Rep. Tammy Baldwin (D), District: 02
http://tammybaldwin.house.gov/index.asp
Email: tammy.baldwin@mail.house.gov

801. Rep. Ron Kind (D), District: 03
http://www.house.gov/kind/

802. Rep. Jerry Kleczka (D), District: 04
http://www.house.gov/kleczka/

803. Rep. James Sensenbrenner (R), District: 05
http://www.house.gov/sensenbrenner/
Email: sensenbrenner@mail.house.gov

804. Rep. Tom Petri (R), District: 06
http://www.house.gov/petri/

805. Rep. Dave Obey (D), District: 07
http://www.house.gov/obey/

806. Rep. Mark Green (R), District: 08
http://www.house.gov/markgreen/
Email: mark.green@mail.house.gov

Wyoming

807. Sen. Mike Enzi (R)
http://enzi.senate.gov/
Email: senator@enzi.senate.gov

808. Sen. Craig Thomas (R)
http://thomas.senate.gov/

809. Rep. Barbara Cubin (R), District: At-Large
http://www.house.gov/cubin/

CHAPTER 6
Education

Educators have embraced the potential of the Internet for reaching students and for sharing professional information with each other. Federal government offices—the Department of Education, the U.S. military, NASA, and other agencies—are also using the Internet for education information and outreach. This chapter includes general resources followed by special sections for Higher Education (including financial aid), K-12, and Web Sites for Children.

Resources from the Education Department's Educational Resources Information Center (ERIC) program are listed in the Featured Sites section and described throughout this chapter. Established in 1966, the program produces the ERIC database, one of the first publicly accessible government online (mainframe) databases. Now on the Web, ERIC continues to be an important resource. A newer initiative dates from 1997, when former President Clinton issued a memorandum to the heads of executive departments and agencies on the subject of expanding access to Internet-based educational resources. Agencies responded with "Kids Pages," which have become a standard part of federal government Web sites. Today, the Bush administration continues government use of the Web for education information with the Students.gov portal site listed in this chapter's Higher Education chapter and the No Child Left Behind policy site in this chapter's K-12 section.

Bookmarks & Favorites

Education Research
- AskERIC, http://www.askeric.org
- National Center for Education Statistics, http://nces.ed.gov

Educational Materials
- FirstGov for Kids, http://www.kids.gov
- Gateway to Educational Materials, http://www.thegateway.org

Higher Education
- IPEDS College Opportunities On-Line, http://nces.ed.gov/ipeds/cool/
- Students.gov (includes financial aid), http://www.students.gov

Major Agencies
- Department of Education, http://www.ed.gov

Featured Sites

810. AskERIC
http://ericir.syr.edu/

Sponsor: Education Department — ERIC Clearinghouse on Information and Technology

Description: AskERIC combines a question-answering service with a powerful Web interface to the ERIC database. Sections of the AskERIC system are About AskERIC, the ERIC database, Ask an ERIC Expert, Question Archive, Lesson Plans, and Mailing Lists. The home page also presents a subject guide to over 3000 selected resources, including Internet sites, discussion lists, ERIC publications, and organizations. AskERIC's implementation of the ERIC database is one of the best free versions available. Updated monthly, the AskERIC version includes coverage back to 1966. It offers both simple and advanced search options. The simple search allows keywords or phrases, and may be limited to journal articles or *ERIC Digest* and my year. The advanced search interface allows for fielded searching, using Boolean logic, of the following fields: Keyword, Author, Title, ERIC Number, Journal Citation, Descriptor, Identifier, Abstract, Geographic Source, Institution Name, Publication Type, Publication Date, ISBN, ISSN, Clearinghouse Number Government, Availability, Note, and Language. Users can access the ERIC Thesaurus for proper subject headings. The Ask an ERIC Expert service allows visitors to submit questions on educational topics to experts and receive responses by email. The responses consist of ERIC database citations or digests, Internet resources, and/or referrals to other sources of information. Users may also browse the Question Archive for previous answers to relevant information. The Lesson Plans section contains a collection of more than 2,000 lesson plans submitted by teachers. Lesson plans are arranged by subject or may be searched by keyword and grade level. Teachers may use this section to submit lesson plans, according to the posted instructions and criteria. The Mailing Lists section of the site has searchable archives for a number of education-related electronic discussion lists.

The variety of education resources available through AskERIC make this site an important resource for educators. Its straight-forward interface to the ERIC database provides easy-access to this valuable warehouse of data.

Subjects: Educational Resources; Lesson Plans; Teaching; Databases

811. Department of Education
http://www.ed.gov/
Sponsor: Education Department
Description: As the obvious starting point for government information on and about education, the U.S. Department of Education (ED) site delivers substantial information resources through a variety of access points. Major sections of the site are News, Grants and Contracts, Financial Aid, Education Resources, Research and Statistics, Policy, and About ED. The site also has special pages designed for specific groups, such as students, teachers, and parents and families. An ED Priorities section offers quick access to education-related initiatives of the Bush administration, such as "No Child Left Behind" and "Ready to Read, Ready to Learn." The site also has an A-Z Index and a personalization feature called My.ED.gov.
Subjects: Education — Policy; Educational Resources; Financial Aid to Students
Publications: *American Rehabilitation*, ED 1.211:
Annual Accountability Report, ED 1.1/6:
Annual Report on School Safety, ED 1.1/7:
Annual Report to Congress on the Implementation of the Individuals with Disabilities Education Act, ED 1.32:
Early Childhood Digest, ED 1.343/2:
Early Childhood Update, ED 1.343:
ED Initiatives, ED 1.90:
ED Review
ERIC Digests, ED 1.331/2:
Federal School Code Database, ED 1.92/2:
Field Initiated Studies Program, Abstracts of Funded Projects, ED 1.337:
Grant Award Actions Database, ED 1.83:
Guide To U.S. Department of Education Programs and Resources, ED 1.10/2:
Helping Your Child, ED 1.302:C 43/
Progress of Education in the United States of America, ED 1.41:
Teacher's Guide to the U.S. Department of Education, ED 1.8:T 22/3/
The Achiever
The Link, ED 1.303/4:

812. ERIC—Educational Resources Information Center
http://www.eric.ed.gov/
Sponsor: Education Department — Educational Resources Information Center (ERIC)
Description: While AskERIC is the preferred site for accessing the ERIC database, this Web site is the place to go for information about the ERIC system of 16 subject-specific clearinghouses, associated adjunct clearinghouses, and support components. The site has links to each of the clearinghouses as well as to the ERIC Document Reproduction Service (EDRS). This central ERIC site also has publications about ERIC and a Frequently Asked Questions section.

The ERIC system was established to provide ready access to education-related literature for practitioners in all aspects of education. When used along with the core ERIC database at AskERIC, this site provides straightforward access to information on all ERIC services.
Subjects: Educational Resources; ERIC

Publications: *ERIC Digests*, ED 1.331/2:
ERIC Review, ED 1.331:
ERICNews
Getting Online: A Friendly Guide for Teachers, Students and Parents, ED 1.308:T 22/4/
Pocket Guide to ERIC, ED 1.308:ED

813. Federal Resources for Educational Excellence (FREE)
http://www.ed.gov/free/
Sponsor: Education Department
Description: Federal Resources for Educational Excellence (FREE) is a central finding aid to hundreds of Internet-based education resources supported by 50 agencies across the U.S. federal government. Users access the database by searching or browsing by subject. The Searches and Subjects page is the main access point, although the same subjects and search interface are also present on the home page. Note that the Search function actually searches the contents of the linked sites and not just titles or descriptions. Recently added materials are listed under the New Resources section. The More for Students page highlights resources particularly appropriate for K-12 students. This is one of the most comprehensive finding aids for education-related U.S. government Web sites. Its primary focus is on K-12 resources.
Subjects: Educational Resources; Finding Aids; Kids' Pages

814. The Gateway to Educational Materials
http://thegateway.org/
Sponsor: Education Department
Description: The Gateway to Educational Materials (GEM) project is a consortium effort to provide educators with quick and easy access to the substantial but uncataloged collections of educational materials found on various federal, state, university, nonprofit, and commercial Internet sites. GEM can be browsed by keyword or subject. Its search feature allows users to specify grade levels while searching in title, subject, keywords, and description fields.
Subjects: Educational Resources; Finding Aids

The educational resources in this chapter are divided into four sections, spanning the entry numbers indicated here:

General	*815–836*
Higher Education	*837–869*
K–12	*870–904*
Web Sites for Children	*905–932*

General

815. Americans Communicating Electronically (ACE)
http://www.reeusda.gov/ecs/ace.htm
Sponsor: Americans Communicating Electronically (ACE)
Description: ACE is an outreach initiative dedicated to improving technological literacy in underserved communities. The effort is co-sponsored by USDA's Cooperative State Research, Education, and Extension Service (CSREES) and the Small Business Administration (SBA) and members come from the public and private sectors. The ACE home page offers a list of links to sites that describe community and government efforts to connect schools to the Internet, recycle computers, and provide computers for schools and nonprofit organizations. Other topics include distance learning, the "digital divide," and technology assistance for small businesses.The site also features a calendar of events dealing with government and computing, youth education in technology, access for rural areas, and related topics.
Subjects: Computer Literacy; Computers in Schools

816. DANTES - Defense Activity for Non-Traditional Education Support
http://www.dantes.doded.mil/
Sponsor: Defense Department

Description: DANTES provides support for the off-duty, voluntary education programs of the Defense Department. Their Web sites has information on certification programs, counselor support, distance learning, and tuition assistance. It also has a section about the Troops-to-Teachers program that assists military personnel interested in beginning a second career in public education as a teacher.
Subject: Military Training and Education

817. Department of Labor Educational Resources
http://www.dol.gov/asp/fibre/main.htm
Sponsor: Labor Department
Description: This DOL site features pages designed for the educational community, covering topics such as the History of the DOL, Child Labor and Youth Employment Laws, "Jobs for Kids Who Like. . . ", Mine Safety, Safety and Health, Reference Materials, and "So You Are Thinking About Dropping Out of School...". Some of these links lead to the educational pages of component agencies. Most provide information geared towards children but do not necessarily provide curriculum or teacher resources. Reference Materials contains links to Women's Bureau resources. The section addressing dropping out of school presents data on employment rate and earnings by educational attainment.
Subjects: Career Information; Educational Resources

818. Directorate for Education and Human Resources — NSF
http://www.ehr.nsf.gov/
Sponsor: National Science Foundation (NSF)
Description: The Directorate for Education and Human Resources (EHR) provides leadership in the effort to improve science, mathematics, engineering, and technology education in the United States. Its Web site includes links to descriptions of the EHR divisions and the types of projects they sponsor: the Division of Graduate Education (DGE), the Division of Undergraduate Education (DUE), the Experimental Program to Stimulate Competitive Research (EPSCoR), and the Division of Elementary, Secondary and Informal Education (ESIE). The Publications category includes selected full-text documents. The Programs category has announcements of funding opportunities. This site will be of assistance to science and engineering students and educators at all levels who are interested in pursuing grants or scholarships.
Subject: Science Education — Grants

819. Economic Education from The Federal Reserve
http://www.federalreserveeducation.org/
Sponsor: Federal Reserve
Description: The resources of this site are listed under the rather long title of "When it Comes 2 Economic Education, the Federal Reserve is Where It's @." The site organizes links to the many educational resources made available by the Federal Reserve Banks. Resource categories include Web Curriculum, Newsletters and Periodicals, Interactive Web Sites, and Non-Fed Web Sites and Resources. Featured resources include a multimedia Fed 101 site and a free video, called "The Fed Today," which can be ordered online.

This Federal Reserve site does an excellent job of pulling together educational resources from a variety of sites and putting them under a helpful interface. There are many resources aimed at teachers, but the site is also helpful to anyone wanting to learn more about the Fed.
Subjects: Economics; Educational Resources

820. EDUGATE
http://web.lmi.org/edugate/
Sponsor: Defense Department
Description: This web site provides general information about science, engineering, and mathematics educational programs sponsored in whole or in part by the DoD and provides informational resources for teachers. It features sections such as DoD Employee Programs, Student Aid, Faculty and Teacher Programs, Public Education Programs, and Equipment Donation Programs. This is an excellent resource for finding educational materials and links to DoD educational resources at all educational levels.
Subject: Military Training and Education

821. Emergency Planning

http://www.ed.gov/emergencyplan/

Sponsor: Education Department — Office of Safe and Drug-Free Schools
Description: The Emergency Planning site was launched in March 2003 as a "one-stop shop that provides school leaders with information they need to plan for any emergency, including natural disasters, violent incidents and terrorist acts." (from the Web site) The site includes crisis planning resources and model emergency plans.
Subjects: Disaster Preparedness; School Buildings

822. ERIC Clearinghouse on Assessment and Evaluation

http://ericae.net/

Alternate URL: http://ericae.net/aesearch.htm

Sponsor: Education Department — ERIC Clearinghouse on Assessment and Evaluation
Description: In addition to the ERIC database and information on the ERIC system, the Assessment and Evaluation Clearinghouse site offers such sections as Library, Test Locator, Resources, and Calls for Papers. The Library provides access to full-text books and other publications; the online journal, *Practical Assessment, Research, and Evaluation*; ERIC/AE Digests; and other online journals. Substantial resources can be found under Test Locator, which connects to searchable bibliographic databases of tests from Buros, Pro-Ed, and the Educational Testing Service (ETS). The Assessment and Evaluation on the Internet section under Resources presents a pathfinder to numerous documents on such topics as alternative assessment, goals and standards, personnel evaluation, professional standards, qualitative research, test preparation, test reviews, and more. There is a substantial body of test and assessment information on this site. Anyone interested in educational assessment, testing, and measuring learning should explore this site.
Subjects: Educational Assessment; ERIC
Publication: *Practical Assessment, Research, and Evaluation (PARE)*

823. ERIC Clearinghouse on Counseling and Student Services

http://ericcass.uncg.edu/

Sponsor: Education Department — ERIC Clearinghouse on Counseling and Student Services
Description: The ERIC Clearinghouse on Counseling and Student Services (CASS) is designed for school guidance counselors and therapists. The site includes information on the clearinghouse, online publications and a collection of *ERIC/CASS Digests*, links to selected Web resources, and Submit a Document section.
Subjects: Career Information; ERIC

824. ERIC Clearinghouse on Educational Management

http://eric.uoregon.edu/

Sponsor: Education Department — ERIC Clearinghouse on Educational Management
Description: The Clearinghouse on Educational Management acquires, indexes, abstracts, and enters into the ERIC database documents, papers, and articles on the governance, leadership, administration, and organizational structure of public and private schools. Sections of this site include Trends and Issues, Hot Topics, Publications, Directory of Organizations, Search/Find, Links, and About ERIC and ERIC/CEM. Each section is full of well-organized resources on school administration.
Subjects: Elementary and Secondary Education; ERIC

825. ERIC Clearinghouse on Information and Technology

http://ericit.org/

Sponsor: Education Department — ERIC Clearinghouse on Information and Technology
Description: The ERIC Clearinghouse on Information and Technology specializes in educational technology and library and information science. The site features *ERIC/IT Digests* and various other documents and databases from the clearinghouse. Featured sections include About, ERIC Database, Publications, Discussion Groups, Lesson Plans, Projects, Research, Educational Technology, and Library and Information Science.
Subjects: Educational Technology; ERIC; Library Science

826. ERIC Clearinghouse on Languages and Linguistics
http://www.cal.org/ericcll/
Sponsor: Education Department — ERIC Clearinghouse on Languages and Linguistics
Description: This ERIC Clearinghouse focuses on providing services and materials for language educators. Among the many resources available on this site are such features as *ERIC/CLL Digests*, About ERIC/CLL, Resource Guides, Publications, ERIC/CLL Databases, and more. The home page presents the bulk of the information available, including links to the report, *What Teachers Need to Know about Language*, Publications, and ERIC/CLL Databases as well as information about ERIC/CLL. Under ERIC/CLL Databases are a variety of resources such as the *Directory of Resources for Foreign Language Programs*. The site also offers an opportunity to ask experts language-related questions.
Subjects: ERIC; Language Education

827. ERIC Clearinghouse on Teaching and Teacher Education
http://www.ericsp.org/
Sponsor: Education Department — ERIC Clearinghouse on Teaching and Teacher Education
Description: The ERIC Clearinghouse on Teaching and Teacher Education collects, abstracts, and indexes education materials in the subject areas of teaching, teacher education, health and physical education, recreation, and dance. It also produces special publications on current research, programs, and practices. Under Becoming a Teacher, the site connects to a number of full-text InfoCards on topics relevant to becoming a teacher, including information on colleges and universities for teacher education. The Resources for Teachers section links to pages on lesson plans and teaching with technology. The Digests and Publications heading features links to *ERIC/TTE Digests* from the clearinghouse and a publications list.
Subjects: ERIC; Teacher Education; Teaching

828. ERIC Clearinghouse on Urban Education
http://eric-web.tc.columbia.edu/
Sponsor: Education Department — ERIC Clearinghouse on Urban Education
Description: The ERIC Clearinghouse on Urban Education focuses on information related to the development and education of urban children and adolescents of diverse ethnic groups. Their site provides several directories to resources from ERIC and from the Internet. The site also has a link to the ERIC Adjunct Clearinghouse for Homeless Education.
Subjects: ERIC; Urban Education

829. ERIC Document Reproduction Service
http://edrs.com/
Sponsor: Education Department — Educational Resources Information Center (ERIC)
Description: The ERIC Document Reproduction Service produces and sells microfiche and electronic collections of documents abstracted by ERIC as well as individual copies. The site includes sections such as Download Center, E*Subscribe (an online subscription service to access ERIC documents), Products, and Search and Order. Users may search for documents by accession number only or by a variety of bibliographic fields. Documents are delivered as laser-printed copies of microfiche documents, PDF documents available immediately online, or microfiche. Products may be sent by mail or fax (limited to 50 pages).
Subject: ERIC

830. ERIC Processing and Reference Facility
http://ericfac.piccard.csc.com/
Sponsor: Education Department — Educational Resources Information Center (ERIC)
Description: The facility provides technical support functions and services to the ERIC system. It produces and maintains the ERIC database and its thesaurus. Its Web site includes sections on Submitting Documents to ERIC, a Reproduction Release Form, Products, and Resources. A Ready Reference section provides documentation on the ERIC database, such as an index to ERIC accession number ranges by year and a guide to ERIC document price codes. Access to the ERIC

Thesaurus is provided through the Resources section, where users can also search or browse through an index of source journals and link to online versions of *ERIC Digests*.

This site is primarily of interest to those submitting or managing ERIC documents.
Subject: ERIC
Publication: *ERIC Digests*, ED 1.331/2:

831. Federal Highway Administration Education Pages
http://www.fhwa.dot.gov/education/
Sponsor: Transportation Department — Federal Highway Administration (FHWA)
Description: The central education page from the Federal Highway Administration provides educational information and resources on the FHWA and its Garrett A. Morgan Technology and Transportation Futures Program. Featured sections include Kindergarten through Fifth Grade, Sixth Grade through Eighth Grade, Ninth Grade through Twelfth Grade, Life-Long Learning, Instructional Aids for Teachers, and Colleges, Universities, and Trade Schools.
Subjects: Transportation; Kids' Pages

832. Federal School Code Search Page
http://www.fafsa.ed.gov/fotw0203/fslookup.htm
Sponsor: Education Department — Postsecondary Education Office
Description: This site provides searchable access to the federal Title IV School Codes required on many financial aid forms. Access is by a form that offers searches by school name and state. Search results include the Title IV School Code and offer access to a school address. The database can also search for schools by their Title IV School Code.

This can be a handy source for these codes, especially when a print source is not readily available.
Subject: Financial Aid to Students

833. Learn and Serve America
http://www.learnandserve.org/
Sponsor: Corporation for National and Community Service — Learn and Serve America
Description: Learn and Serve America is a program of the Corporation for National and Community Service that makes grants to governments and organizations for service-learning projects. The projects are designed to help students learn while the students help meet community needs. The Web site has information about the program and contact lists for state education agencies, Indian Tribes, and others administering service-learning grants. The site has resources about service-learning and a link to the National Service Learning Clearinghouse.
Subjects: Education — Grants; Volunteerism

834. NASA Langley Research Center Office of Education
http://edu.larc.nasa.gov/
Sponsor: National Aeronautics and Space Administration (NASA) — Langley Research Center (LaRC)
Description: The Langley Research Center Office of Education was created to promote programs between the center and the larger education community. The Office of Education provides education programs for students from kindergarten through the postdoctoral level, for K–12 teachers, and for university faculty. It offers distance learning programs for K–12 students. Some of the resources for educators include the NASA Educator Resource Center Network and the Virginia Science Resource Network. The site also links to the NASA Education Program and to NASA/CORE, Central Operation of Resources for Educators.
Subject: Science Education

835. National Center for Education Statistics
http://nces.ed.gov/
Sponsor: Education Department — Institute of Education Sciences — National Center for Education Statistics (NCES)
Description: NCES collects and analyzes data relating to education in the United States and other nations. Their Web site is a primary source for education statistics for all educational levels and for

data on educational assessment, libraries, and other nations' educational outcomes. The site packages NCES data in different formats for different needs. For example, there are sections for ED Stats at a Glance, Quick Tables and Figures, and NCES Fast Facts. Most data on the site are drawn from major NCES statistical publications, such as *Education Statistics Quarterly, The Condition of Education*, and *The Digest of Education Statistics*. NCES Fast Facts highlights frequently requested information, such as data on the effects of reading to children and on average tuition costs at colleges and universities. The site also includes a searchable directory of private and public schools and of colleges and public libraries.

For anyone searching for statistics related to any form of education, this site should be the first place to visit. Although statistical reports are only available from the past few years (in some cases from 1996), some of the reports include time-series data. In addition, the major reports are in PDF format, which permits easy browsing and keyword searching.

Subject: Education Statistics
Publications: *Digest of Education Statistics*, ED 1.326:
Directory of Postsecondary Institutions, ED 1.111/4:
Dropout Rates in the United States, ED 1.329:
Education Statistics Quarterly, ED 1.328/13:
Federal Support for Education, ED 1.328/8:
Indicator of the Month, ED 1.341:
Indicators of School Crime and Safety, ED 1.347:
Projections of Education Statistics, ED 1.120:
Projections of Education Statistics to 2006, ED 1.302:P 94
Selected Papers in School Finance, ED 1.310/5:
SPEEDE/ExPRESS spotlight, ED 1.133:
The Condition of Education, ED 1.109:
Youth Indicators, ED 1.327:

836. Office of Educational Technology, Department of Education
http://www.ed.gov/Technology/index.html
Sponsor: Education Department — Educational Technology Office
Description: The U.S. Department of Education's Office of Educational Technology (OET) develops national educational technology policy and works with the educational community and other offices within the Department of Education to promote national goals for educational technology. OET's Web site features information on educational technology grants, federal resources, and state and regional organizations. Topical sections cover distance learning, the digital divide, and the evaluation and assessment of educational technology.
Subject: Educational Technology — Grants

Higher Education

837. Air Force Institute of Technology
http://www.afit.edu/
Sponsor: Air Force — Air Force Institute of Technology (AFIT)
Description: A component of Air University, the Air Force Institute of Technology (AFIT) is the Air Force's graduate school of engineering and management and its institution for technical professional continuing education. General information about the school can be found in the Public Affairs section.
Subjects: Air Force; Military Training and Education

838. Air University
http://www.au.af.mil/au/index.html
Sponsor: Air Force — Air University
Description: Air University, located at Maxwell Air Force Base, conducts professional military education, graduate education, and professional continuing education for officers, enlisted personnel and

civilians. This site links to each of the component schools that make up Air University, and provides information on the University's history and mission. The Other AU Links section links to the University's course catalogs and publications, Air University Press, and Air University Library.
Subjects: Air Force; Military Training and Education
Publications: *Air and Space Power Journal*
Community College of the Air Force Catalog, D 301.80:

839. Army Logistics Management College
http://www.almc.army.mil/
Sponsor: Army — Army Logistics Management College (ALMC)
Description: The Army Logistics Management College site features information on the college and its schools. It offers an online course catalog, course schedule, curriculum areas, and an online version of *Army Logistician*.
Subjects: Army; Military Training and Education
Publication: *Army Logistician (bimonthly)*, D 101.69:

840. Carlisle Barracks and the U.S. Army War College
http://carlisle-www.army.mil/
Sponsor: Army — Carlisle Barracks
Description: Carlisle Barracks is the home of the Army War College, Military History Institute, Army Physical Fitness Research Institute, the Center for Strategic Leadership, and the Strategic Studies Institute. This site features information on the Barracks and the resident institutions. In addition to the resources and descriptions under each institution, the site features an online *Carlisle Barracks News and Banner Online*, the Carlisle Barracks online newspaper.
Subjects: Army; Military Training and Education
Publications: *Banner Online*
Carlisle Barracks News
Parameters: U.S. Army War College Quarterly, D 101.72:
Strategic Studies Institute (General Publications), D 101.146:
The Army and Homeland Security: A Strategic Perspective
The Hart-Rudman Commission and the Homeland Defense

841. Command and General Staff College
http://www-cgsc.army.mil/
Sponsor: Army — Army Command and General Staff College
Description: The U.S. Army Command and General Staff College is focused on leadership development within the Army. This site offers information on the college, its training programs, and its organizations. The journal *Military Review* is available online in its English, Spanish, and Portuguese language editions.
Subjects: Army; Military Leadership; Military Training and Education
Publications: *Military Review*, D 110.7:
Military Review (Portuguese), D 110.7/3:
Military Review (Spanish), D 110.7/2:
Prairie Warrior

842. Defense Language Institute Foreign Language Center
http://dli-www.army.mil/
Sponsor: Defense Department — Defense Language Institute (DLI)
Description: The Defense Language Institute Foreign Language Center (DLIFLC) is the primary foreign language training institution within the Defense Department. Most information about the center is available by clicking on the DLIFLC link at this site. The course catalog and DLI periodicals are available online, as is information about the school's language programs.
   The site is primarily of interest to those eligible for and interested in DLI language training.
Subjects: Language Education; Military Training and Education
Publication: *Applied Language Learning*, D 1.105:

843. ERIC Clearinghouse for Community Colleges
http://www.gseis.ucla.edu/ERIC/eric.html
Sponsor: Education Department — ERIC Clearinghouse for Community Colleges
Description: ERIC Clearinghouse for Community Colleges site features a Frequently Asked Questions section about community colleges and tools for finding community colleges online. The Publications section has summaries and bibliographies of research on community college education. This clearinghouse also offers an online reference service under the heading Ask. Other sections include the ERIC database, Submit a Document, and What's New at the Clearinghouse.
Subjects: Community Colleges; ERIC

844. ERIC Clearinghouse on Adult, Career, and Vocational Education
http://www.ericacve.org/
Sponsor: Education Department — ERIC Clearinghouse on Adult, Career, and Vocational Education
Description: The ERIC Clearinghouse on Adult, Career, and Vocational Education contains a substantial number of publications online. Under the Publications heading are such sections as *ERIC Digests* from ACVE, *Trends and Issues Alerts*, *Myths and Realities*, *Practitioner File* (P-File), *Practice Application Briefs*, and Major Clearinghouse Publications. Most of these publications are available in HTML and PDF formats. Other sections include Journals on the Web, New and Noteworthy, In-Process Abstracts, and Links to Full-Text Resources.
Subjects: Adult Education; ERIC; Vocational Education

845. ERIC Clearinghouse on Higher Education
http://www.eriche.org/
Sponsor: Education Department — ERIC Clearinghouse on Higher Education
Description: This ERIC Clearinghouse presents itself as both a resource for ERIC publications as well as a gateway to higher education information on the Web. Clearinghouse information is available under the headings What's New, About ERIC, and ERIC Database, which contains a quick guide on conducting advanced searches. The Publications page presents links to *ERIC/HE Digests*, *ERIC Trends*, *CRIB Sheets*, the *ASHE-ERIC Report Series,* and *ERIC Review: Early Intervention Programs for College.* The home page also presents links to pages of resources arranged by audience, comprising Administrators, Faculty, Parents, Librarians, and Students.
Subjects: ERIC; Higher Education

846. ERIC/Professional Development Schools
http://www.aacte.org/Eric/pro_dev_schools.htm
Alternate URL: http://www.aacte.org/Eric/default.htm
Sponsor: Education Department — ERIC Adjunct Clearinghouse on Clinical Schools (ADJ/CL)
Description: The Adjunct ERIC Clearinghouse on Clinical Schools (ADJ/CL) provides sources of information on professional development schools, clinical schools, partner schools, and similar institutions proposed for teacher education. ADJ/CL acquires, abstracts, and indexes literature on professional development schools for the ERIC database; produces bibliographies, periodic papers, digests, and other material on PDS issues, collects data on PDSs. Its site includes *ERIC/PDS Digests,* announcements, a Professional Development Schools Database, and general information on PDSs.
Subjects: ERIC; Teacher Education

847. FAA Aerospace Medicine
http://www.cami.jccbi.gov/
Sponsor: Transportation Department — Federal Aviation Administration (FAA) — Office of Aerospace Medicine
Description: The Office of Aerospace Medicine has three main sections: OAM Program Information; Aeromedical Reference Material, which offers access to the *Federal Air Surgeon's Medical Bulletin;* and Aeromedical Certification Standards and Regulations, the documents of which are offered in HTML, Word, or PDF formats. The Civil Aeromedical Institute (CAMI) handles medical certification, research, and education in aviation safety. The CAMI Web site offers resources related to CAMI research areas, including Aeromedical Certification, Aeromedical Education, Human Resources Research, Aeromedical Research, and Occupational Health. Within these sections are

links to Library, Publications, Aviation Links, and CAMI Video Page. The Publications page provides access to technical report citations, the *Federal Air Surgeon's Medical Bulletin*, some brochures, and the *Aviation Medical Examiners Directory*.

This is an excellent resource for researchers in aviation medicine and aviation safety.

Subjects: Aviation Safety; Medical Schools
Publications: *Aviation Safety Brochures AM- (Series)*, TD 4.210:
Directory, Aviation Medical Examiners, TD 4.211:
Federal Air Surgeons Medical Bulletin, TD 4.215:

848. Free Application for Federal Student Aid (FAFSA)

http://www.fafsa.ed.gov/
Sponsor: Education Department — Federal Student Aid Office
Description: For college students, FAFSA on the Web makes it possible to apply online for student financial aid. The FAFSA renewal application may also be completed online. The site provides guidance on applying for aid and the application process.
Subject: Financial Aid to Students

849. Fulbright Scholar Program

http://exchanges.state.gov/education/fulbright/
Alternate URL: http://www.iie.org/fulbright/
Sponsors: State Department — Educational and Cultural Affairs Bureau; Institute of International Education (IIE)
Description: The U.S.-sponsored Fulbright Program is a scholarly exchange program providing grants for graduate students, scholars, professionals, teachers, and administrators from the U.S. and other countries. This site for U.S. and non-U.S. applicants describes the program and links to the Fulbright Commissions around the world. Much of the program is administered for the State Department by the Institute of International Education (IIE) and its Council for the International Exchange of Scholars (CIES). The alternate URL for this entry leads to the IIE and CIES pages. These pages provide detailed information for U.S. and non-U.S. applicants. For U.S. applicants, the relevant applications are online. The site also links to related Fulbright information, including the Hubert H. Humphrey Fellowships and the Fulbright Teacher Exchange Program.
Subject: International Education — Grants

850. Information for Financial Aid Professionals

http://ifap.ed.gov
Sponsor: Education Department — Federal Student Aid Office
Description: Information for Financial Aid Professionals (IFAP) is an electronic library for financial aid professionals containing publications, regulations, and guidance regarding the administration of the Title IV Federal Student Aid (FSA) Programs. This site features technical documentation, online tools, worksheets, and schedules related to the Federal Student Aid programs. Further information is available through a link to the related Schools Portal.
Subject: Financial Aid to Students
Publications: *Direct Loans Bulletins*, ED 1.40/6:
Student Financial Aid Handbook — Institutional Eligibility and Participation, ED 1.45/4:

851. LingNet—The Linguists' Network

http://www.lingnet.org/
Sponsor: Defense Department — Defense Language Institute (DLI)
Description: LingNet is dedicated to supporting the members of the foreign language community in learning and sustaining their abilities in new languages. The site includes access to discussion forums, software libraries, news, mailing lists, and reading material for LingNet members. In addition, the site offers a compendium of links to language resources on the Internet. It also provides information on how to sign up to be a member.
Subject: Foreign Languages

852. Marine Corps University
`http://www.mcu.usmc.mil/`
Sponsor: Marine Corps — Training and Education Command
Description: The Marine Corps University site provides information about the university and its programs. Featured categories include History, Organization, Schools, and Student Information.
Subject: Military Training and Education

853. Minority University Space Interdisciplinary Network
`http://muspin.gsfc.nasa.gov/`
Sponsor: National Aeronautics and Space Administration (NASA) — Goddard Space Flight Center (GSFC)
Description: Minority University Space Interdisciplinary Network (MU-SPIN) is designed for Historically Black Colleges and Universities (HBCUs), and Other Minority Universities (OMUs). The focus of the program is on the transfer of advanced computer networking technologies to HBCUs and OMUs and their use for supporting multidisciplinary research. The Web site includes sections such as About MU-SPIN, Network Resources and Training Sites (NRTS), Programs, News, Resources, and Annual Users' Conference. MU-SPIN offers services such as hands-on training to faculty and students in accessing resources available over the Internet, hands-on training to technical staff in local area and campus network installation, management and user support, technical sessions at annual conferences, and technical video lectures on network-related issues. For minority colleges and universities, this is an important resource for high technology and computer networking information and training.
Subjects: Computer Networking; Minority Groups; Science Education

854. NASA Academy
`http://www.nasa-academy.nasa.gov`
Sponsor: National Aeronautics and Space Administration (NASA) — Goddard Space Flight Center (GSFC)
Description: This is the central page for NASA Academy summer programs for college students in science, math, engineering, or computer science. The two NASA Academy programs are the NASA Academy at Goddard Space Flight Center Academy and the Ames Astrobiology Academy at Ames Research Center. The site has application forms and detailed program information. The information on these pages will be of interest to college students interested in careers or further study with NASA and to those that advise such students.
Subject: Science Education

855. National Defense University
`http://www.ndu.edu/`
Sponsor: Defense Department — National Defense University (NDU)
Description: The National Defense University site provides an online course catalog and links to the University's component colleges: Africa Center for Strategic Studies, Joint Forces Staff College, Industrial College of the Armed Forces, Institute for National Strategic Studies, Information Resources Management College, Center for Hemispheric Defense Studies, Near East-South Asia Center for Strategic Studies, and the National War College. The site also includes an online phone book and more links to the library and various programs and centers, including the International Fellows Program, the National Security Education Program, and the Center for Counterproliferation Research.
Subjects: Military Training and Education; National Defense — Research
Publications: *Defensive Information Warfare*, D 5.402:D 36/4
Dominant Battlespace Knowledge, D 5.402:B 32
Joint Force Quarterly, D 5.20:
McNair Papers, D 5.416:
Strategic Forum, Institute for National Strategic Studies, D 5.417:

856. Naval Postgraduate School
`http://www.nps.navy.mil/`
Sponsor: Navy — Naval Postgraduate School (NPS)

Description: The Naval Postgraduate School (NPS) emphasizes education and research programs that are relevant to the Navy, defense and national and international security interests. The NPS site offers information on the school, its research, and its courses. Information is presented by topic and audience, with sections on Academics, Research, and Executive Education; Students, Faculty, Administration, and Alumni and Friends; and Library, and About NPS.
Subject: Military Training and Education

857. Naval War College
http://www.nwc.navy.mil/
Sponsor: Navy — Naval War College (NWC)
Description: The Web site for the Naval War College presents information about the institute and its programs. In addition to the latest news, speeches and presentations, upcoming events, and a set of related links, the home page links to the following sections: Welcome Aboard, About NWC, Academics, Library, Research, War Gaming, NWC Press, Museum, Reserve Affairs, Alumni Affairs, and more. Publications are accessible under the NWC Press section.
Subjects: Military Training and Education; Navy
Publications: *Naval War College Review*, D 208.209:
Newport Papers, D 208.212:

858. NSF Division of Graduate Education
http://www.ehr.nsf.gov/ehr/dge/
Sponsor: National Science Foundation (NSF)
Description: The programs of the National Science Foundation's Division of Graduate Education promote the early career development of scientists and engineers by offering support at critical junctures of their careers. This Web site describes a number of the Division's programs and fellowships that offer assistance to graduate students in the sciences. The Publications sections include some program guidelines and other electronic publications. There is also a page to search Directorate for Education and Human Resources (EHR) awards.
Subjects: Fellowships; Science Education

859. NSF Division of Undergraduate Education
http://www.ehr.nsf.gov/EHR/DUE/default.asp
Sponsor: National Science Foundation (NSF)
Description: The DUE focuses on improving undergraduate education in the sciences, mathematics, and engineering. This Web site describes the agency and its programs, including staff listings, award announcements, and press releases. The primary categories are Programs and Deadlines, Publications, Awards, About DUE, Outreach Activities, and Links. On the top page, under the category DUE Programs, are two sections entitled Workforce Development and Curriculum, Laboratory, and Instructional Development that link to various programs funded by DUE.
Subject: Science Education

860. Office of Postsecondary Education, Department Of Education
http://www.ed.gov/offices/OPE/
Sponsor: Education Department — Postsecondary Education Office
Description: The OPE home page describes the 40 plus programs administered by the office. These cover such postsecondary education topics as policy, financing, international education, and minority education. OPE Web resources are accessible under such headings as Information for Students, Planning for College, and Policy and Student Aid Professionals. Current grant competitions and their deadlines are highlighted. The site also has contact information for postsecondary education accrediting agencies.

This is a very useful site, with a substantial body of information sources of interest to both students and financial aid offices.
Subjects: Financial Aid to Students; Higher Education
Publications: *Direct Loans Newsletter*, ED 1.40/5:
Fund for the Improvement of Postsecondary Education Program Book, ED 1.23:
The Student Guide: From the U.S. Department of Education, ED 1.8:ST 9/5/

861. Office of University Programs at NASA Goddard Space Flight Center

http://university.gsfc.nasa.gov/

Sponsor: National Aeronautics and Space Administration (NASA) — Goddard Space Flight Center (GSFC)

Description: The OUP site describes the mission of the office and links to pages with descriptions of its programs for institutions and individuals. It also has links to University-Related Programs, Post-Doc Programs, and Other Programs: the Goddard Senior Fellows, NASA Academy, the Graduate Student Researchers Program, the National Space Grant College and Fellowship Program, the NRC Resident Researchers Associateship Program, and the Director's Discretionary Fund among others.

Subjects: Fellowships; Science Education — Grants

Publication: *Research and Technology Report*, NAS 1.65/2:

862. Office of Vocational and Adult Education, Department Of Education

http://www.ed.gov/offices/OVAE/

Sponsor: Education Department — Vocational and Adult Education Office

Description: This site provides information about the Office of Vocational and Adult Education programs, grants, events, legislation, and resources concerning the fields of adult education and vocational education. Key sections are High Schools, Career and Technical Education, Community Colleges, and Adult Literacy and Education.

Subjects: Adult Education; Vocational Education

863. Students.gov

http://www.students.gov/

Sponsor: Education Department

Description: Students.gov is the federal student gateway to U.S. government information. This "FirstGov for students" site is a government-wide initiative to deliver electronic services from federal agencies to postsecondary students. Featured sections include Plan Your Education, Pay for Your Education, Career Development, Community Service, Military Service, Government 101, Travel and Fun, and Additional Resources. A search interface allows users to search the site's database of links, all of FirstGov, the Education Department site, and other databases. The home page also presents featured services and links to other cross-agency federal portals.

Like the other cross-agency portals that FirstGov has spawned, this site provides an excellent single access point to the myriad of government sources providing information of use to high school and college students.

Subjects: Career Information; Financial Aid to Students; Higher Education

864. Uniformed Services University of the Health Sciences

http://www.usuhs.mil/

Sponsor: Defense Department — Uniformed Services University of the Health Sciences (USUHS)

Description: The Uniformed Services University of the Health Sciences is the nation's federal health sciences university, committed to excellence in military medicine and public health during peace and war. This Web site provides basic information about the university under the following headings University Welcome, School of Medicine, Graduate School of Nursing, Graduate Education, Academics, Administration, Admissions, Affiliations, Alumni Affairs, Recruitment and Diversity Affairs, and Research. The home page also links to information on Disaster/Terrorism Care Resources and Biological, Chemical, and Nuclear Warfare and Terrorism.

Subjects: Medical Schools; Military Training and Education

865. United States Air Force Academy

http://www.usafa.af.mil/

Sponsor: Air Force — Air Force Academy

Description: The United States Air Force Academy site provides information for cadets, staff, and faculty. It includes an Academy Virtual Tour and sections on Academics, Admissions, Athletics, Cadet Life, Current Events, Information Resources, Photos, and Newcomers Information. A link to the Academy's library system is listed under the Academics section. The system includes the Academic Library, the Base Library, and the Medical Library.

Subjects: Air Force; Military Training and Education

Publications: *Airman-Scholar, A Journal of Contemporary Military Thought*, D 305.23:
INSS Occasional Paper, D 305.24:

866. United States Military Academy at West Point
http://www.usma.edu/
Sponsor: Army — United States Military Academy (USMA)
Description: The West Point site has information for prospective and current students as well as for alumni, visitors, and the West Point community. There are sections on Admissions, Cadet Life, and the Academic, Physical, and Military Programs. A brief section on USMA History includes a time-line and list of notable graduates.
Subjects: Army; Military Training and Education

867. United States Naval Academy
http://www.usna.edu
Alternate URL: http://www.usna.navy.mil/
Sponsor: Navy — United States Naval Academy (USNA)
Description: This site contains information on the Naval Academy, mainly for students, prospective students, and midshipmen. The top level listing includes such sections as About USNA, Academics, Administration, Admissions, Alumni/Foundation Information, Athletics, Library, Midshipmen Interests, Public Affairs/Events, and What's New.
Subjects: Military Training and Education; Navy

868. USDA Graduate School
http://grad.usda.gov/
Sponsor: Agriculture Department (USDA) — Graduate School, USDA
Description: The Graduate School, USDA is a continuing education institution offering career-related courses to federal workers and the public. The main sections include Course Catalog, Visitor Center, About Us, Course Information and Registration, and Programs and Services. It also has a section with information for faculty and students, and information about the Fulbright Teacher Exchange.
Subject: Adult Education

869. Woodrow Wilson International Center for Scholars
http://wwics.si.edu/
Sponsor: Woodrow Wilson International Center for Scholars
Description: The Wilson Center supports scholarship linked to public policy by offering fellowships and special opportunities for research and writing with a focus on history, political science, and international relations. As a public-private partnership, the Center receives roughly half of its oper-ating funds from a U.S. government appropriation. The Web site has information on current Wilson Center projects and publications, and audio files of its weekly radio program, Dialogue. The site also carries essays and other items from the Center's journal, *The Wilson Quarterly*. There is informa-tion on applying for a fellowship or internship with the Center, and a Media Guide has a directory of the Center's subject experts.
Subjects: Fellowships; Public Policy — Research; Social Science Research
Publications: *CWIFP (Cold War International History Project) Bulletin*, SI 1.3/2:
The Wilson Quarterly

K–12

870. Ames Educator Resource Center
Alternate URL: http://amesnews.arc.nasa.gov/erc/erchome.html
Sponsor: National Aeronautics and Space Administration (NASA) — Ames Research Center (ARC)
Description: The page is almost exclusively descriptive of the Center, which is located at the National Aeronautic and Space Administration Ames Research Center at Moffett Field, California. It serves educators in the western states (Alaska, Arizona, Northern California, Hawaii, Idaho, Montana,

Nevada, Oregon, Utah, Washington, Wyoming). This page provides contact information, hours, and a listing of the kinds of educational materials available, only a few of which are available online. The Online Resources section links to a variety of sites about space, science, and education including Cool Picks, Aeronautics, Space, Biology, Computing, and Classroom Resources. This page also links to a list of other NASA Educator Resource Centers around the country.

This site is most useful for those that want to visit or contact the center. It would be even more useful if the lessons plans, curriculum materials, or publications were available online.

Subjects: Educational Resources; Science Education

871. ArtsEdge: The National Arts and Education Information Network
http://artsedge.kennedy-center.org/

Sponsors: Kennedy Center for the Performing Arts; National Endowment for the Arts (NEA)

Description: ArtsEdge from the Kennedy Center is a major arts resource for educators and students. Featured sections include NewsBreak, Teaching Materials, Professional Resources, User Guide, and Community Center. NewsBreak presents a daily update of events in the arts and includes sections on Job Opportunities, Grants and Funding, Competitions and Calls, Fellowships and Internships, and Professional Development News. Teaching Material offers sections on Curricula, Lessons, and Activities; Curriculum WebLinks; Get Published; Idea Exchange; and Using ArtsEdge Lessons. The Curriculum WebLinks section provides annotated lists of Web sites on such topics as ESL, Foreign Language, Mathematics, Physical Education, Science, Social Science, Design Arts, Language Arts, Performing Arts, and Visual Arts. The Sites We Host link on the home page leads to related sites such as: Duke Ellington Centennial, the African Odyssey Interactive, the National Forum, and more.

Well-designed, this site should be a primary stopping point for anyone involved in arts education.

Subject: Arts Education

872. Computers for Learning
http://www.computers.fed.gov/School/user.asp

Sponsor: General Services Administration

Description: The Computers for Learning Web site is designed for public, private, parochial, or home schools serving the K–12 student population, and other nonprofit educational organizations. The service allows these groups of students and nonprofit organizations to request donations of surplus federal computer equipment. The site includes a listing of available equipment, registration, success stories, background, and a section that describes who is eligible.

Subjects: Educational Technology; Surplus Government Property

873. Cosmic and Heliospheric Learning Center
http://helios.gsfc.nasa.gov/

Sponsor: National Aeronautics and Space Administration (NASA) — Goddard Space Flight Center (GSFC)

Description: The Cosmic and Heliospheric Learning Center is designed to increase people's interest in cosmic and heliospheric science. (The site explains that "the heliosphere is the HUGE area in space affected by the Sun.") The information on the Learning Center Web site is aimed at the general public or at about a high school level of science understanding. It features sections for Astrophysics Basics, Cosmic Rays, The Sun, and Space Weather. On the top page there are a series of images taken by various spacecraft: TRACE, ASCA, and IMAGE, which lead to information about the images.

Subjects: Science Education; Sun

874. ECENET-L [email list]
http://ericeece.org/listserv/ecenet-l.html

Sponsor: Education Department — ERIC Clearinghouse on Elementary and Early Childhood Education

Description: ECENET-L is an email discussion list for people interested in early childhood education. The list invites participation from representatives of professional associations and government

agencies, faculty and researchers, students and teachers, parents, and librarians. The Web address includes access to archives of postings.
Subjects: Early Childhood Education; Email Lists

875. ECPOLICY-L [email list]
`http://ericeece.org/listserv/ecpol-l.html`
Sponsor: Education Department — ERIC Clearinghouse on Elementary and Early Childhood Education
Description: ECPOLICY-L provides a forum for discussion of policy issues related to young children. Suggested topics include providing information about the development, care, and education of young children for state, federal, and local policymakers; raising the awareness of policymakers, educators, the media, and parents about the issues important to the future of young children; and encouraging responsiveness of the early childhood community to public issues affecting children. The Web address includes an archive of postings.
Subject: Early Childhood Education — Policy

876. ECPROFDEV-L [email list]
`http://ericeece.org/listserv/ecprof-l.html`
Sponsor: Education Department — ERIC Clearinghouse on Elementary and Early Childhood Education
Description: ECPROFDEV-L is intended to foster communication among those who teach pre-service and in-service early childhood educators, train Head Start or other early childhood program staff, and consult or facilitate learning with early childhood professionals in any setting. A link to the list's archives is provided on the Web site.
Subjects: Early Childhood Education; Teacher Education; Email Lists

877. Eisenhower National Clearinghouse
`http://www.enc.org/`
Sponsor: Eisenhower National Clearinghouse
Description: The mission of the Eisenhower National Clearinghouse (ENC) is to identify effective curriculum resources, create high-quality professional development materials, and disseminate useful information and products to improve K-12 mathematics and science teaching and learning. While not a government office, ENC is funded through a contract with the Education Department. The site has curriculum resources, useful Web links, and professional development information for teachers. Some of the special topics covered include incorporating math and science into other subjects and bringing real world math and science work into the classroom. This site provides access to many documents with high-quality content in the broad fields of mathematics and science education.
Subjects: Mathematics Education; Science Education

878. ERIC Clearinghouse for Science, Mathematics, and Environmental Education
`http://www.ericse.org/`
Sponsor: Education Department — ERIC Clearinghouse on Science, Mathematics, and Environmental Education
Description: The Web server for the ERIC Clearinghouse for Science, Mathematics, and Environmental Education features Science Education Resources, Mathematics Education Resources, Environmental Education Resources, Online Publications, Web Companions, Contributing to the Database, Resources for Parents and Children, and a Conference Calendar. Each of the topical sections includes links to relevant *Digests*, bulletins, lesson plans, and information guides.
Subjects: Environmental Education; ERIC; Mathematics Education; Science Education

879. ERIC Clearinghouse for Social Studies/Social Science Education
`http://www.indiana.edu/~ssdc/eric-chess.html`
Sponsor: Education Department — ERIC Clearinghouse for Social Studies/Social Science Education

Description: ERIC/ChESS specializes in and monitors the literature and developments in the teaching and learning of social studies, social science education, music education, and art education. The ERIC/ChESS site features such sections as About ERIC and ERIC/ChESS, Publications and Services, *ERIC/ChESS Digests*, *Keeping Up* (a news bulletin), Resource Organizations Directory, Internet Resources, Indiana Social Studies Resources, What's New, and Standards and Curriculum. Standards and Curriculum contains links to national and state social studies, art, and music standards and curriculum information on the Internet.
Subjects: ERIC; Social Studies Education
Publication: *Keeping Up*

880. ERIC Clearinghouse on Disabilities and Gifted Education
http://ericec.org/
Sponsor: Education Department — ERIC Clearinghouse on Disabilities and Gifted Education
Description: This ERIC Clearinghouse site provides information on the education of individuals of all ages who have disabilities as well as those who are gifted. It features information about the clearinghouse and the ERIC system, and sections on Searching the Databases, Submitting Documents to ERIC, the ERIC/OSEP Special Project, Research Connections, Digests, Fact Sheets and Minibibliographies, Frequently Asked Questions, Email Lists, Links to the Laws, and Gifted Education/Dual Exceptionalities.
Subjects: Disabilities; ERIC; Gifted and Talented Education; Special Education

881. ERIC Clearinghouse on Elementary and Early Childhood Education
http://ericeece.org/
Sponsor: Education Department — ERIC Clearinghouse on Elementary and Early Childhood Education
Description: The ERIC Clearinghouse on Elementary and Early Childhood Education offers descriptive information on the clearinghouse, links to external education resources, connections to other components in the ERIC system, and lists of its available publications. A Popular Topics section has information on bullying, diversity, parenting, readiness for school, and other subjects. This site also lists electronic discussion groups sponsored by ERIC/EECE.

This is a useful collection of materials on elementary education, early childhood education, and parenting.
Subjects: Early Childhood Education; ERIC
Publications: *Early Childhood Research and Practice*
Parent News

882. ERIC Clearinghouse on Reading, English, and Communications
http://www.indiana.edu/~eric_rec/
Sponsor: Education Department — ERIC Clearinghouse on Reading, English, and Communication
Description: This site is dedicated to providing educational materials, services, and course work to everyone interested in the language arts. On the home page, the site lists the latest reading research and reading news and links to resources for literacy education and children's literature. Featured sections include Family Information Center, Lesson Plans, Great Web Resources, Publications, and a Question and Answer Service. The Family Information Center category features parent involvement Web resources, free phonics information, books that help, helpful tips for parents, and information on parent workshops and a senior partners pen pal program.
Subjects: ERIC; Language Education; Reading

883. ERIC Clearinghouse on Rural Education and Small Schools
http://www.ael.org/eric/
Sponsor: Education Department — ERIC Clearinghouse on Rural Education and Small Schools
Description: The Clearinghouse on Rural Education and Small Schools covers a variety of topics, including American Indian and Alaska Native Education, Mexican American Education, Migrant Education, Outdoor Education, Rural Education, and Small Schools, each of which list relevant *ERIC Digests*. Other sections include Publications, Conferences, and About Us. Under Publications is a link to a newsletter, *ERIC/CRESS Bulletin!* and information on books.
Subjects: ERIC; Rural Education

884. GLOBE Program
http://www.globe.gov/
Sponsors: Environmental Protection Agency (EPA); National Aeronautics and Space Administration (NASA); National Science Foundation (NSF); State Department
Description: Global Learning and Observations to Benefit the Environment (GLOBE) is a worldwide network of students, teachers, and scientists working together to study and understand the global environment. This site both offers information on the program and is used by participants in the program. This program involves students in taking environmental measurements. Over 10,000 schools in more than 95 countries have already submitted over hundreds of thousands of data reports based on observations by GLOBE student scientists. The data is accessible to anyone, and there is information on how new schools can register to be included in the program. The site is available in a variety of languages including Spanish, French, German, and Arabic.

With participating schools from all over the world, this kind of collaborative project demonstrates how the Internet can be used in a K-12 environment. In addition, the Web site is well-designed and makes navigation easy even for those not familiar with GLOBE.
Subjects: Environmental Protection; Science Education

885. K12ASSESS-L [email list]
http://ericae.net/k12assess/
Sponsor: Education Department — ERIC Clearinghouse on Assessment and Evaluation
Description: The goal of K12ASSESS-L is to provide educators with a fast, convenient, and topical electronic discussion forum focusing on issues related to educational assessment in grades K-12. The Web site provides subscription information, a form for subscribing, and archives back to 1998.
Subjects: Educational Testing; Email Lists

886. Learning Page of the Library of Congress
http://lcweb2.loc.gov/ammem/ndlpedu/
Sponsor: Library of Congress
Description: Designed for the educational community, this site helps students and teachers find relevant materials within the National Digital Library collection on the Library of Congress Web pages, particularly the American Memory project. This site features sections such as Lesson Plans, Features and Activities, and Professional Development.
Subjects: Educational Technology; Social Studies Education

887. Learning Web at the U.S. Geological Survey
http://www.usgs.gov/education/
Sponsor: Interior Department — U.S. Geological Survey (USGS)
Description: The Learning Web is dedicated to K–12 education, exploration, and life-long learning on topics of concern to USGS scientists. There are sections for Students (Homework Help and Project Ideas), Teachers (Lesson Plans, Paper Models), and Explorers (Research Tools, Special Topics). Topics include water, rocks, ecosystems, and maps and images. The site also has a variety of online games and printable projects for kids.

This is useful for teachers interested in finding educational resources in science and for students looking for basic earth science information.
Subjects: Science Education; Kids' Pages

888. Live from the Hubble Space Telescope
http://quest.arc.nasa.gov/hst/
Sponsor: National Aeronautics and Space Administration (NASA) — Education Division
Description: In the spring of 1996, students in grades K–12 had a chance to use the Hubble Space Telescope (HST). The Space Telescope Science Institute (which operates Hubble) contributed three HST orbits to the Passport to Knowledge educational project for this purpose. The planets Neptune and Pluto were selected as targets for original observations by students who served as Hubble Space Telescope co-investigators, working alongside astronomers. The Web site features Live Video, Project News, Featured Events, Background, Teachers' Lounge, and a Kids' Corner. This site provides news, featured events, a video broadcast schedule, and background information on the project.

This is another excellent example of how the Internet can aid in collaborative projects with students and teachers in K–12. Users should be aware that while much of the material is still useful, the site only covers the 1996 project and is no longer updated.

Subjects: Astronomy; Science Education

889. MIDDLE-L [email list]

http://ericeece.org/listserv/middle-l.html

Sponsor: Education Department — ERIC Clearinghouse on Elementary and Early Childhood Education

Description: MIDDLE-L is a forum for information related to middle school education. It is intended for middle school educators, teacher educators, and others interested in education at the middle level. The Web address includes access to archives of postings.

Subjects: Middle Schools; Email Lists

890. MUSIC-ED [email list]

http://artsedge.kennedy-center.org/user_guide/commcent/listservs.html#musiced

Sponsor: National Endowment for the Arts (NEA)

Description: The MUSIC-ED email list discussion is focused specifically on music education. The discussions range from teaching tips among educators, to reviews of music education software, and to ideas for integrating music education with other subjects in the K–12 curriculum. The Web page provides a form interface for subscribing to this and other ArtsEdge email lists.

Subjects: Music Education; Email Lists

891. NASA Classroom of the Future Program

http://www.cotf.edu/

Sponsors: National Aeronautics and Space Administration (NASA) — Education Division; Wheeling Jesuit College

Description: The NASA Classroom of the Future program at Wheeling Jesuit College aims to bridge the gap between American schools and the expertise of NASA scientists. This site features descriptive information about the program and includes a virtual tour of the Center for Educational Technologies at Wheeling. Some of the projects available from the Products section are Astronomy Village, BioBLAST, the International Space Station Challenge. This site provides information on the projects and their current stage of development. Under Products is the NASA TV service, which streams NASA TV to viewers on the Internet. Other sections include Mission, Philosophy, Research, and a link to the main Center for Educational Technologies (CET) Web site.

Subjects: Science Education; Space

892. NASA Glenn Learning Technologies Project

http://www.lerc.nasa.gov/Other_Groups/K-12/

Sponsor: National Aeronautics and Space Administration (NASA) — Glenn Research Center

Description: This Learning Technologies site from the Glenn Research Center features educational material on airplanes and aeronautics. Primary sections include Teachers' Corner, Aeronautic Educational Resources, and Math/Sciences Resources. The site also has sections for Announcements, Publications, Resources, and Awards.

Subjects: Mathematics Education; Science Education

Publication: *Mathematical Thinking in Physics*

893. NASA Quest

http://quest.arc.nasa.gov/

Sponsor: National Aeronautics and Space Administration (NASA) — Education Division

Description: The NASA Quest Web site is the agency's vehicle for interacting with educators, students, and space enthusiasts. As a way to interest students in science and the space program, this site provides resources about the national space program and the people involved. Resources on this site are divided into four topical areas, covering space, aerospace, astrobiology, and women of NASA. In

addition, the site provides detailed information about the scientists that work for NASA, information on live Web chats and webcasts, resources for teachers, and more information about NASA. The Educators and Parents section provides a discussion list, lesson plans, and lists of standards.
Subjects: Educational Resources; Space

894. NASA Spacelink—An Aeronautics and Space Resource for Education
http://spacelink.nasa.gov/
Sponsor: National Aeronautics and Space Administration (NASA) — Education Division
Description: Spacelink is a NASA resource developed specifically for educators. It provides current and historical educational information on space, NASA, and aeronautics for the educational community. The main sections include Educator Focus, The Library, Hot Topics, Cool Picks, and Spacelink Express. Within The Library, there are links to NASA educational services and products, instructional materials, NASA projects and news, and frequently asked questions. Within these links there are teacher guides, pictures, computer software, science, mathematics, engineering and technology education lesson plans, information on NASA educational programs and services, current status reports on NASA projects and events, news releases, and television broadcasts schedules for NASA Television.

By creating this site specifically for the education community and building a large collection of relevant files, this is an essential stop for anyone in the education community interested in space and aeronautical sciences.
Subjects: Educational Resources; Space

895. NASA's Learning Technologies Project
http://learn.arc.nasa.gov/
Sponsor: National Aeronautics and Space Administration (NASA) — Education Division
Description: The goal of NASA's Learning Technologies Project (LTP) is to promote the growth of a national information infrastructure using the vast amount of information the National Aeronautics and Space Administration (NASA) has acquired since its creation. Access to this knowledge will allow the public and industry to contribute to rapid and significant advances in science, engineering, and technology. The Web site includes Feature Stories, Education Resources, Movies, and Calendar of Events. Education Resources features a grants page; a topic listing of LTP projects, with information about the programs with links to related NASA educational Web sites; and LTP product guides, where one can search various programs by grade level, by research and general interest, or by national standards for geography, science, mathematics, and technology.
Subjects: Educational Technology; Science Education

896. National Child Care Information Center
http://nccic.org/
Sponsor: Health and Human Services Department — Administration for Children and Families (ACF) — Child Care Bureau
Description: NCCIC is an Adjunct ERIC Clearinghouse for Child Care. The site provides information on the center and has links to child care topics; directories of state contacts and regulatory agencies, national organizations, and state resource sheets; information on grant and funding opportunities; publications and other resources; and a searchable database. There are also links to various projects and centers, including the Tribal Child Care Technical Assistance Center and the Child Care Partnership Project. Access to the full text of NCCIC's *Child Care Bulletin* is available as well.
Subject: Child Care
Publication: *Child Care Bulletin*, HE 23.1415:

897. National Parent Information Network
http://npin.org/
Sponsors: Education Department — ERIC Clearinghouse on Elementary and Early Childhood Education; Education Department — ERIC Clearinghouse on Urban Education
Description: National Parent Information Network (NPIN) is designed and maintained by the ERIC Clearinghouse on Urban Education and the ERIC Clearinghouse on Elementary and Early Childhood Education. NPIN's mission is to provide access to research-based information about the process of parenting, and about family involvement in education. Major categories on this site

include About NPIN, Virtual Library, Questions, Parent News, and Special Initiatives. The Virtual Library page features full-text publications including *ERIC Digests,* book summaries, and other brochures, pamphlets, and newsletters. Full-text materials have been reviewed for reliability and usefulness.

While many of the resources available through NPIN are available directly from the ERIC Clearinghouses or other sources, pulling them together in a clear organization, makes the materials more readily accessible for anyone interested in parenting topics.
Subject: Parenting

898. No Child Left Behind
http://www.nochildleftbehind.gov/
Alternate URL: http://www.nclb.gov
Sponsor: Education Department
Description: This Education Department site is dedicated to information about Public Law 107-110, the No Child Left Behind Act of 2001. The law concerns educational standards and testing, teacher training and recruitment, English language instruction, school safety, and other matters. Major sections of the site are What to Know, For Parents, and News Center. Along with fact sheets and key dates, the site includes a glossary of education policy terms related to the No Child Left Behind Act. The No Child Left Behind Act site is different from many government sites in that it concerns a single piece of legislation. The focus is on the George W. Bush administration's goals in promoting the provisions of the law and the policy behind it.
Subjects: Education — Policy; Educational Testing

899. NSF Division of Elementary, Secondary, and Informal Education
http://www.ehr.nsf.gov/EHR/ESIE/
Sponsor: National Science Foundation (NSF)
Description: Part of the National Science Foundation, the Division of Elementary, Secondary, and Informal Education (ESIE) focuses on improving preK-12 science, technology, engineering, and mathematics (STEM) education in the United States. Its Web site includes descriptions of the programs and funding opportunities offered by this agency. The site is divided into pages on Program Announcements, Publications, and Deadlines. Under Program Announcements, information is available for Teacher Enhancement programs, Instructional Materials Development programs, Informal Science Education programs, and Presidential Awards for Excellence in Science and Mathematics Teaching. The Publications page presents solicitations, documents, and other publications.
Subjects: Mathematics Education — Grants; Science Education — Grants

900. Office of Special Education Programs (OSEP), Department Of Education
http://www.ed.gov/offices/OSERS/OSEP/
Sponsor: Education Department — Special Education and Rehabilitative Services Office — Office of Special Education Programs (OSEP)
Description: The Office of Special Education Programs (OSEP) has primary responsibility for administering programs and projects relating to the education of all children, youth, and adults with disabilities, from birth through age 21. Sections describe OSEP's Programs and Projects, Grants and Funding, Legislation and Policy, Publications and Products, and Research and Statistics.
Subject: Special Education — Grants

901. PARENTING-L [email list]
http://ericeece.org/listserv/parent-L.html
Description: PARENTING-L is an Internet discussion group on topics related to parenting children (including child development, education, and child care) from birth through adolescence. Discussion ranges from family leave and parental rights issues, to parents as partners in their children's education, to the changes in children as they leave high school and begin college or get their first job. The Web address includes access to archives of postings.
Subjects: Email Lists; Parenting

902. PROJECTS-L [email list]
http://ericece.org/listserv/projec-l.html
Sponsor: Education Department — ERIC Clearinghouse on Elementary and Early Childhood Education
Description: This discussion group focuses on the project approach, which is an in-depth study of a topic undertaken by a class, a group, or an individual child. The group discusses how the approach is used in early childhood, elementary, and middle school classrooms. The Web address includes access to archives of postings.
Subjects: Teaching; Email Lists

903. School District Demographics
http://nces.ed.gov/surveys/sdds/index.asp
Sponsor: Education Department — Institute of Education Sciences — National Center for Education Statistics (NCES)
Description: This site presents demographic and geographic data from the 2000 Census, 1990 Census, and from surveys and estimates made between the censuses. A School District Maps section allows for viewing state or individual district maps using the Map Viewer application. The 2000 Census section allows for selecting and downloading data tables in a comma delimited file format. The data from this special census tabulation can be helpful for studying school districts as well as for general demographics of children and families with children.
Subjects: Census; Elementary and Secondary Education — Statistics

904. United Nations Cyber School Bus
http://www.un.org/cyberschoolbus/index.html
Sponsor: United Nations
Description: This UN site, designed for the education community, promotes education about international issues and the United Nations. The site features a wide range of resources in English with Spanish, French, Russian, Chinese, and Arabic versions. It features quizzes and games, current events information, and curriculum materials on such topics as human rights, peace education, and the United Nations itself.
Subjects: Curriculum; Social Studies Education

Web Sites for Children

905. America's Story from America's Library
http://www.americaslibrary.gov/
Sponsor: Library of Congress
Description: This Library of Congress site is designed for kids and their families. It uses digitized images from the Library's collection, accompanied by text and graphics, to create educational pages about American history and culture. Sections include: Explore the States, Jump Back in Time, and Meet Amazing Americans.
Subjects: History; Kids' Pages

906. Ben's Guide to U.S. Government for Kids
http://bensguide.gpo.gov/
Sponsor: Government Printing Office (GPO) — Superintendent of Documents
Description: With Benjamin Franklin as a guide, this GPO site for children covers topics such as the U.S. Constitution, how laws are made, the branches of the federal government, and citizenship. It features sections for specific age groups, plus a special section for parents and educators. It also offers instruction on the use of the primary source materials on GPO Access. The primary links are About Ben, K–2, 3–5, 6–8, 9–12, Parents and Teachers, and About this Site.
Subjects: Kids' Pages; Civics Education

907. CIA Home Page for Kids

http://www.cia.gov/cia/ciakids/

Sponsor: Central Intelligence Agency (CIA)

Description: The CIA offers a variety of information targeted towards children. The page includes links to Who We Are and What We Do, CIA Canine Corps, CIA Seal, Aerial Photography Pigeons, Geography Trivial Quiz, Break the Code Word Puzzle, and History. It also links to the CIA's *World Factbook* with its wealth of country information.

Subjects: Intelligence Agencies; Kids' Pages

Publication: *World Factbook*

908. Department of the Interior Kids Page

http://www.doi.gov/kids/

Sponsor: Interior Department

Description: This central DOI page for the children links to more than a dozen pages from DOI agencies. These include Wildlife Species, Butterfly Site, Coloring Book, Kids Eye View, Shorebirds, Learning Web, The Great American Landmarks Adventure, Ozark Junior Ranger, Blue Ridge, Coal Mining, Alaska, BLM Resource Explorers, and Hoover Dam.

Subjects: Environmental Education; Kids' Pages

909. DOJ Kids and Youth

http://www.usdoj.gov/kidspage/

Sponsor: Justice Department

Description: The Department of Justice page for youth provides information about the department and its agencies, primarily the FBI. Information is arranged by the following main categories: Kids (K–5th), Youth (6th–12th), Teachers and Parents, and Subjects. Links from the home page lead to special subject sections, such as Inside the Courtroom, Get It Straight (the Facts about Drugs), Civil Rights, Cyberethics for Kids, and Getting Involved in Crime Prevention.

Subjects: Criminal Justice; Kids' Pages

910. Dr. E's Energy Lab: Energy Efficiency and Renewable Energy Network

http://www.eren.doe.gov/kids/

Sponsor: Energy Department — Energy Efficiency and Renewable Energy Office

Description: This page for children from the Energy Efficiency and Renewable Energy Network (EREN) features links to the following headings: Energy Efficieny Tips, Wind Energy, Solar Energy, Geothermal Energy, Alternative Fuels, General Renewable Energy, and Ask an Energy Expert.

Subjects: Renewable Energies; Kids' Pages

911. EIA Kids' Page: What is Energy?

http://www.eia.doe.gov/kids/

Sponsor: Energy Department — Energy Information Administration (EIA)

Description: The Information Administration of the Energy Department provides this educational page about energy. Sections of this general information site include What Is Energy, Kid's Corner, Online Resources, Fun Facts, Classroom Connection, and Energy Quiz.

Students and teachers seeking education resources about energy may prefer this site to the main DOE site for children.

Subjects: Energy; Kids' Pages

912. Energy.gov Kidzone

http://www.energy.gov/kidz/kidzone.html

Sponsor: Energy Department

Description: The main Energy Department site for kids presents a mix of links, most of it appropriate for the higher grade levels. Major sections include a history of the Energy Department with historical firsts in energy and links to energy glossaries at a variety of DOE sites. Teachers and parents may be interested in some of the site's Quick Links; Contests and Events links to Web sites for energy and science educational contests and Science Projects cover science fair information.

Parents and teachers will want to use this site to find useful material. However, due to the uneven nature of the materials it links to, this site may not be the best for kids to use themselves without guidance.

Subjects: Energy; Kids' Pages

913. FBI Youth
http://www.fbi.gov/kids/6th12th/6th12th.htm
Sponsor: Justice Department — Federal Bureau of Investigation (FBI)
Description: The FBI Youth site is intended for young adults, grades 6 through 12. Sections like FBI Investigates and A Day In The Life are intended to demonstrate the type of work FBI employees do. Special Agent Challenge is a quiz the user can complete by finding the answers on the FBI Web site. The History section presents an FBI history timeline with links to more information on special topics such as Al Capone and the FBI Academy.

Subjects: Crime Detection; Kids' Pages

914. FDA Kids' Homepage
http://www.fda.gov/oc/opacom/kids/
Sponsor: Health and Human Services Department — Food and Drug Administration (FDA)
Description: The FDA Web site for children and teens presents health and safety information the sections including: Food Safety Quiz, Mac and Molly Investigator, All About Vaccines, and The Teen Scene. There is also a Parents' Corner. Two additional links are Cosmetics Quiz for Teens and Powerful Girls Have Powerful Bones. The Teen Scene features *FDA Consumer* magazine articles with important health information for teenagers, ranging from nutrition and sun safety to eating disorders and attention deficit disorder.

Subjects: Adolescents; Health Promotion; Kids' Pages

915. FEMA for Kids
http://www.fema.gov/kids/
Sponsor: Federal Emergency Management Agency (FEMA)
Description: This FEMA site provides information and resources to help children prepare for and prevent disasters. Get Ready, Get Set has information and activities about preparing for a disaster and the Disaster Area describes 10 kinds of disasters, including hurricanes and tornadoes. The Disaster Connections section has children's artwork, poems, and letters with their thoughts on disasters such as tornadoes and the September 11, 2001 attacks.

FEMA has done an excellent job pulling together a Web site of resources explaining disasters to children without scaring them.

Subjects: Disaster Preparedness; Kids' Pages

916. FirstGov for Kids
http://www.kids.gov/
Sponsor: General Services Administration
Description: This FirstGov for Kids site is a portal to Web pages designed for children. Annotated Web links are arranged by topic, such as Careers, Geography, History, Homework, Money, Safety, and Space. Each topic lists U.S. government Web pages and most also have clearly-marked sections for selected sites from organizations, educational institutions, and commercial entities.

FirstGov for Kids is an easy way for kids, as well as teachers and parents, to find kid-friendy information on the Web. It is particularly helpful as an index to government Web pages for children. A few commercial sites require logging in or are more appropriate for the teacher's use, but many have appropriate content low in advertising.

Subjects: Government Information; Finding Aids; Kids' Pages

917. Garrett A. Morgan Technology and Transportation Futures Program
http://education.dot.gov/
Sponsor: Transportation Department
Description: This program aims to connect youth with the transportation community and improve education of those in the transportation workforce. The Web site features the following sections: Teen Zine, Home and School, Reading Room, DOT Kids, About Garrett A. Morgan, the Garrett A.

Morgan Technology and Transportation Futures Program, Transportation Education and Careers, Essay Contest, and College, University, and Life-Long Learning. The Garrett A. Morgan Technology and Transportation Futures Program page has links to information for pre-kindergarden to secondary school students, information about transportation education at universities and community colleges and careers and training, and links to a virtual library and a life-long learning center.
Subjects: Transportation; Kids' Pages

918. HHS Pages for Kids
http://www.hhs.gov/kids/
Sponsor: Health and Human Services Department
Description: This page offers links to information for parents and teachers, but the primary content is links to other HHS and related agencies' Web sites for children. Featured topics include child health, smoke-free kids, and food safety.
Subjects: Health Promotion; Kids' Pages

919. HUD Kids Next Door
http://www.hud.gov/kids/kids.html
Sponsor: Housing and Urban Development (HUD)
Description: HUD's page for children is subtitled "where kids can learn more about being good citizens." The page features Meet Cool People, See Neat Things, and Visit Awesome Places. Within each of these sections are activities and pages such as Help the Homeless, Kids Volunteer, Safe Places to Play, Build a Community, and Scavenger Hunt.
Subject: Kids' Pages

920. Kids' Corner, Endangered Species
http://endangered.fws.gov/kids/
Sponsor: Interior Department — Fish and Wildlife Service (FWS)
Description: This children's site provides information on endangered species, featuring a Crossword Puzzle, Creature Features, Where Can I Find It?, Risky Critters Game, How Can Kids Help?, and Hey Teachers. Links are also available to FWS endangered species resources.
Subjects: Endangered Species; Kids' Pages

921. NASAKIDS
http://kids.msfc.nasa.gov/
Sponsor: National Aeronautics and Space Administration (NASA) — Education Division
Description: This site features a colorful, graphical interface to NASA News by Kids, Space and Beyond, Rockets and Airplanes, Projects and Games, Astronauts Living in Space, Creation Station, Our Earth, NASA toons, and Teachers' Corner.
Subjects: Space; Kids' Pages

922. NCEH Kids' Page
http://www.cdc.gov/nceh/kids/99kidsday/default.htm
Sponsor: Health and Human Services Department — Centers for Disease Control and Prevention (CDC) — National Center for Environmental Health (NCEH)
Description: Designed for the young reader, the site is based on *Take Your Children to Work Day*, a booklet that NCEH created for its employees' children to describe the important work their parents do to promote health and quality of life. It offers sections on Asthma, Birth Defects, Cruise Ship, Inspection, Disabilities, Emergency Response, Global Health, Laboratory Programs, Lead Poisoning, Refugee Health, and Activities. The booklet is available in Spanish and as a PDF version that may be downloaded and printed.
Subjects: Health Promotion; Kids' Pages

923. NIEHS' Kids Pages
http://www.niehs.nih.gov/kids/home.htm
Sponsor: National Institutes of Health (NIH) — National Institute of Environmental Health Sciences (NIEHS)

Description: This Kids Page offering from the National Institute of Environmental Health Sciences has both a Spanish language version and a text version. It includes Games and Activities, Color Our World Bright and Beautiful, Science Word Scrambles, and Science Spelling Bee. There is also a section on Environmental Health and Sciences Hot Topics, Careers, and Projects which includes a section on Asthma and Allergies and one on Children's Health.
Subjects: Environmental Education; Health Promotion; Kids' Pages

924. Patent and Trademark Office Kids' Page
http://www.uspto.gov/go/kids/
Sponsor: Commerce Department — Patent and Trademark Office (PTO)
Description: The PTO site offers children's contests, games, and puzzles having to do with creativity, invention, and the operations of the PTO. The site has sections designed for students in K–6 and 6–12, and for parents, teachers, and coaches.
Subjects: Inventions; Kids' Pages

925. Peace Corps Kids' World
http://www.peacecorps.gov/kids/
Sponsor: Peace Corps
Description: The Peace Corps offers this kids' page, with sections for What is the Peace Corps?, Make a Difference, Explore the World, Tell Me a Story, and Food, Friends, and Fun. An online quiz game called "Pack Your Bags" is also available. This site mainly provides information about the Peace Corps program. Some resources on foreign countries are listed under the sections: Explore the World and Food, Friends, and Fun.
Subjects: Geography; Kids' Pages

926. Physical Oceanography from Space
http://podaac.jpl.nasa.gov/kids/
Sponsor: National Aeronautics and Space Administration (NASA) — Jet Propulsion Laboratory (JPL)
Description: This page for students covers What is Physical Oceanography?, How do Satellites Measure the Ocean?, How do Scientists use Satellite Measurements?, Oceanography History, and Oceanography News.
Subjects: Oceanography; Kids' Pages

927. Safety City
http://www.nhtsa.dot.gov/kids/
Sponsor: Transportation Department — National Highway Traffic Safety Administration (NHTSA)
Description: Vince and Larry, the NHTSA's crash test dummies, are the guides on this children's Web site, which provides information on vehicle safety. The site features sections such as Safety School, Bike Tour, Research Laboratory, and School Bus.
Subjects: Traffic Safety; Vehicle Safety; Kids' Pages

928. Space Place
http://spaceplace.jpl.nasa.gov/spacepl.htm
Sponsor: National Aeronautics and Space Administration (NASA) — Jet Propulsion Laboratory (JPL)
Description: This Web site, designed for students in grades K–6, features facts, activities, and contests related to space science. It offers such sections as Make Spacey Things, Do Spacey Things, Space Science in Action, Dr. Marc's Amazing Facts, and Friends Share. The section for teachers, Goodies for Teachers, presents classroom activity articles from the journal *The Technology Teacher*.
Subjects: Space; Kids' Pages

929. Tobacco Information and Prevention Source (TIPS) for Youth
http://www.cdc.gov/tobacco/tips4youth.htm
Sponsor: Health and Human Services Department — Centers for Disease Control and Prevention (CDC) — National Center for Chronic Disease Prevention and Health Promotion (NCCDPHP)

Description: TIPS4Youth links to an extensive list of resources providing information to young people about smoking and advertises public health events concerning tobacco use. Sections include: How to Quit, Educational Materials, Celebrities Against Smoking, Tobacco Quiz, and materials designed to make teens more savvy about cigarette and tobacco advertising. The site also features *SGR 4 Kids*, the Surgeon General's Report for Kids about Smoking.
Subjects: Smoking; Tobacco; Kids' Pages

930. USDA for Kids
http://www.usda.gov/news/usdakids/index.html
Description: This gateway site offers links to a wide variety of children's pages from USDA agencies. Linked sites include Smokey Bear, Backyard Conservation, Food Guide Pyramid, Agriculture for Kids, History of Agriculture, Team Nutrition, Woodsy Owl, George Washington Carver Coloring Book, and more.
Subjects: Environmental Education; Farms and Farming; Nutrition; Kids' Pages

931. WhiteHouseKids.Gov
http://www.whitehouse.gov/kids/whlife/index.html
Sponsor: White House
Description: The White House for Kids Web site presents information about the White House and the nation through the pets of the Bush family: the dogs Spotty and Barney; India, the cat; and Ophelia, the longhorn. Spotty gives a tour of the White House; Barney presents the ABCs with brief messages from the president; India asks an historical question; and Ophelia presents a dream team of heroes who made a significant contribution to the country. In addition, there are brief biographies of the president, the first lady, the vice president, and Mrs. Cheney. The site also includes coloring pages, games, and a video tour of the White House.
Subjects: White House (Mansion); Kids' Pages

932. Youthlink
http://www.ssa.gov/kids
Sponsor: Social Security Administration (SSA)
Description: The Social Security kids' page offers Social Security Kids' Stuff and Hot Questions for Cool Teens. Other sections provide resources for Parents and Teachers. There is also a link for information about low-cost or free health care insurance for children.
Subjects: Social Security; Kids' Pages

CHAPTER 7
Environment

Besides the Environmental Protection Agency, many federal agencies and military offices have environmental responsibilities and publish environment-related information on the Internet. This chapter describes some of the major government sites and includes special sections for those related to climate and weather, oceans, and pollution. Related sites may be found in the Science chapter under Earth Sciences and the Technology and Engineering chapter under Energy.

The two featured agency Web sites in this chapter—those of the EPA and the National Oceanic and Atmospheric Administration—provide news, policy background, research, and information resources. Many more specialized resources exist, and they are described in subsequent sections of this chapter.

Bookmarks & Favorites

Research
- Envirofacts Data Warehouse, http://www.epa.gov/enviro/
- National Service Center for Environmental Publications,http://www.epa.gov/ncepihom/

Major Agencies
- Environmental Protection Agency, http://www.epa.gov
- Interior Department, http://www.doi.gov
   - U.S. Geological Survey, http://www.usgs.gov
- National Oceanic and Atmospheric Administration, http://www.noaa.gov
   - National Weather Service, http://www.weather.gov

(Also see related topics in Chapter 13, Science)

Featured Sites

933. Environmental Protection Agency
http://www.epa.gov/
Sponsor: Environmental Protection Agency (EPA)
Description: The central EPA site provides access to information resources about the environment, pollution, hazardous substances, and water quality. Featured sections include EPA Newsroom, Browse EPA Topics, Where You Live, Educational Resources, Laws and Regulations, Programs, Information Sources, About EPA, and For Kids. The home page presents site headlines and other news stories. The Information Sources section provides access to publications, databases, email lists, and newsletters from the EPA and its offices. The Education Resources section arranges resources by users, including Kids, Students, Teachers, and Researchers. The Browse EPA Topics provides an alphabetical list of links to EPA programs and initiatives. The section entitled Where You Live allows users to search for local information by ZIP code as well as link to state environmental agencies. A link to the AIRNOW section allows users to find ozone and air quality maps by state to learn more about air quality and air pollution in one's community.
This is an excellent entry point into a vast quantity of EPA documents and data.
Subject: Environmental Protection
Publications: *Annual Report*, EP 4.1:
Catalog of Publications: Office of Science and Technology, EP 1.21:
Coastlines, EP 8.16:
Energy Star Homes Program, EP 4.29:
EPA Journal, EP 1.67:
Fact Sheets (Environmental Protection Agency), EP 4.27:
Inside the Greenhouse, EP 1.114:

Inventory of U.S. Greenhouse Gas Emissions and Sinks, EP 1.115:
Labcert Bulletin, EP 2.3/4:
Monthly Hotline Report, EP 1.111:
National Water Quality Inventory Report to Congress, EP 2.17/2:
Natural Gas Star Partner Update, EP 6.15:
Office of Pesticides Programs Annual Report, EP 5.1:P 43/
Reusable News, EP 1.17/5:
SITE (Technology Capsule & Innovative Technology Evaluation Reports), EP 1.89/4:
Summary of the Budget, EP 1.1/4:
Superfund Innovative Technology Program, Annual Report to Congress, EP 1.89/4-4:
The Benefits and Costs of the Clean Air Act, EP 4.31:
Toxic Chemical Release Inventory Reporting Form R Instructions, EP 5.22/3:
Toxic Release Inventory, EP 5.22/2:

934. National Oceanic and Atmospheric Administration
`http://www.noaa.gov/`
Sponsor: Commerce Department — National Oceanic and Atmospheric Administration (NOAA)
Description: Providing information on environmental issues such as climate, fisheries, and the ocean, the NOAA Web site is a major scientific resource for the environmental sciences. It features recent news stories, along with such sections as About NOAA, Organizations, Education, Cool NOAA Web Sites, and Media Contacts. Beyond general agency information, most of the substantive content is located on the sites of NOAA's component divisions and offices.

Subject access is provided by links to Weather, Ocean, Climate, Coasts, Fisheries, Charting and Navigation, Research, and Satellites. In addition, the Storm Watch page offers links to the latest weather forecasts to track storms through NOAA weather satellites, get the latest weather maps, and learn how to protect yourself and your community from severe weather.

Given the broad scope of environmental topics that NOAA agencies cover, this site can be used as a finding aid for all environmental information that falls under NOAA's domain.
Subjects: Atmospheric Sciences; Environmental Science; Oceanography
Publication: *NOAA Report*, C 55.53:

The environmental resources in this chapter are divided into four sections, spanning the entry numbers indicated here:

General	935–964
Climate and Weather	965–979
Oceans	980–999
Pollution	1000–1026

General

935. Bureau of Land Management
`http://www.blm.gov/nhp/index.htm`
Sponsor: Interior Department — Bureau of Land Management (BLM)
Description: As a primary public lands management agency, the BLM features information on public lands and the BLM. The main categories on the site include News, Information, What We Do, BLM Facts, and Directory. The News section includes news releases, fire news, speeches, and legislative and regulatory actions. The BLM Online Bookstore, brochures and publications, agency budget information, and other reference resources are available under Information. A Browse button at the top of the home page provides an alphabetical index of subjects and sites.

For anyone interested in the Bureau of Land Management, its management, BLM lands, recreational philosophy, and other aspects of the BLM, this site is a rich resource.
Subject: Public Lands
Publications: *Beyond the National Parks*
Bureau of Land Management Annual Report, I 53.1:
Public Land Statistics, I 53.1/2:

936. Bureau of Reclamation
http://www.usbr.gov/main/index.html
Sponsor: Interior Department — Bureau of Reclamation (USBR)
Description: Subtitled Managing Water in the American West, this site features agency information under headings including What We Do, Newsroom, Programs, DataWeb, Feature, Publications, and Water Supply. The Publications page refers people to paper copies available from the Government Printing Office and the National Technical Information Service. The Newsroom includes some online publications. The Programs page has the bulk of the substantive content with sections such as Cultural and Archeological Resources, Irrigation, Native American, Power, Recreation, and Water Conservation.
Subjects: Hydroelectric Power; Water Supply
Publications: *Bureau of Reclamation Annual Report*, I 27.1:
Bureau of Reclamation FY Annual Performance Plan, I 27.1/5:
Bureau of Reclamation Phone Book, I 27.77:
Water Operation and Maintenance Bulletins, I 27.41:

937. Defense Environmental Network and Information Exchange (DENIX)
https://www.denix.osd.mil/denix/denix.html
Sponsor: Defense Department — Office of the Under Secretary of Defense (Installations and Environment)
Description: DENIX is a centralized resource for environment, safety, and occupational health news, policy, guidance, and information for the entire Department of Defense. The publicly accessible sections of DENIX include a Subject Areas section that organizes DENIX resources by topic, such as recycling, noise abatement, military installation cleanups, and conservation. Other sections include Publications, Policy, and Laws and Regulations.
Subjects: Defense Administration; Environmental Protection — Policy

938. Department of Energy's NEPA Web Site
http://www.eh.doe.gov/nepa/
Alternate URL: http://tis-nt.eh.doe.gov/nepa/
Sponsor: Environmental Protection Agency (EPA)
Description: This site summarizes some of the DOE's activities related to the National Environmental Policy Act (NEPA). The DOE Documents section is intended to feature full text environmental impact statements; however, a notice on the site states that most impact statements are currently not available for viewing by the public due to security concerns (12-4-2002). Other sections provide environmental impact statement schedules, NEPA compliance guides, and a *Lessons Learned* quarterly report.
Subject: Environmental Law

939. Department of the Interior
http://www.doi.gov/
Sponsor: Interior Department
Description: Functioning primarily as an access point to component agencies of the Interior Department, this site features sections on DOI Officials, News, About DOI, Bureaus/Offices, and Contacts. Eight topical menus provide subject access: Collaborative Efforts, American Indians, Fish/Wildlife, National Parks, Public Lands, Energy, Science, and Water. The hot topics section points to selected reports, speeches, and other material. A Spanish language version of the site is also available.

The site is well organized, and its multiple access points to various DOI resources make it easy to use.
Subjects: Natural Resources; Public Lands
Publications: *DOI Annual Report*, I 1.1:
People Land and Water, I 1.116:

940. Endangered Species
http://endangered.fws.gov/
Sponsor: Interior Department — Fish and Wildlife Service (FWS)

Description: This FWS page provides a broad collection of news and information on endangered species and the Endangered Species Act (ESA). Links are also provided to site sections, including Species Information; List of Threatened and Endangered Species; Laws, Policies, and Federal Register Notices; ESA and What We Do; For the Media; The *Endangered Species Bulletin*; Kid's Corner; and Partners in Conservation. The ESA and What We Do section includes links to an Overview of the Endangered Species Project, publications and fact sheets, statistics, and information on tribal rights and international agreements. Under Species Information are a summary of listed wildlife and plants, state maps, state lists, and proposed and candidate species information.
Subjects: Endangered Species; Native Plants
Publication: *Endangered Species Bulletin*, I 49.77:

941. Envirofacts Data Warehouse
http://www.epa.gov/enviro/
Sponsor: Environmental Protection Agency (EPA)
Description: Envirofacts provides various levels of access to major environmental databases from the EPA. Databases include: Toxics Release Inventory (TRI); Safe Drinking Water Information System; Permit Compliance System; and Comprehensive Environmental Response, Compensation and Liability Information System (CERCLIS).

A Quick Start feature allows users to search by ZIP code or city and state. The resulting profile identifies local data on air, toxics, waste, and water. An interactive map marks such features as Superfund sites, hazardous waste handling facilities, toxic releases, and discharges to water. More advanced capabilities can be found in the Queries, Maps, and Reports section. Researchers can choose individual databases or choose the integrated Envirofacts Multisystem Query.
Subjects: Pollutants; Databases

942. EPA's National Center for Environmental Economics
http://yosemite.epa.gov/ee/epa/eed.nsf/pages/homepage
Sponsor: Environmental Protection Agency (EPA) — National Center for Environmental Economics
Description: EPA's NCEE conducts economic research and analysis related to environmental issues, such as economic incentives for protecting the environment and the benefits and costs of environmental policies and regulations. The site has information on NCEE's reports and working papers, seminars and workshops, and an extensive catalog of Web sites concerning environmental economics.
Subject: Environmental Protection — Policy

943. Fish and Wildlife Service
http://www.fws.gov/
Sponsor: Interior Department — Fish and Wildlife Service (FWS)
Description: The Fish and Wildlife Service aims to conserve, protect, and enhance fish, wildlife, plants, and their habitats. The FWS site has current news and an alphabetical list of topical links to their Web pages. Topics include birds, fisheries, fishing, grants, hunting, legislation, news, permits, refuges, species, wetlands, and FWS law enforcement. The Index link leads to another site index, this one covering national programs, recreation sites, publications, electronic reading room, and other categories.
Subjects: Birds; Conservation (Natural Resources) — Laws; Fisheries; Natural Resources Management; Wildlife
Publications: *Endangered Species Bulletin*, I 49.77:
Federal Aid in Sport Fish Restoration Program, I 49.2:SP 6/6
Fish and Wildlife News, I 49.88:
Mourning Dove Breeding Population Status, I 49.106/5:
National Survey of Fishing, Hunting, and Wildlife-Associated Recreation, I 49.98
Waterfowl 2000: The Plan's Newsletter, I 49.100/4:
Waterfowl Population Status, I 49.100/3:

944. Forest Ecosystems Dynamics

http://forest.gsfc.nasa.gov/

Sponsor: National Aeronautics and Space Administration (NASA) — Goddard Space Flight Center (GSFC)

Description: "The Forest Ecosystem Dynamics (FED) Project is concerned with modeling and monitoring ecosystem processes and patterns in response to natural and anthropogenic effects." (from Web site, 1-27-2003) The FED Web site disseminates project information, archives spatial and scientific data sets, and demonstrates the linking of ecosystem and remote sensing models. The site features some descriptive information on the project, along with a Project Abstract, Imagery Archive, a Ecosystem Modeling Interface, an Imagery Archive, an Interactive Soil Map, and Presentations and Publications.

While most of this site will only be of interest to ecological researchers in the remote sensing and geographic information systems areas, some of the image archive may be of interest to the general public.

Subject: Forests — Research

945. GeoCommunicator

http://www.geocommunicator.gov

Sponsor: Interior Department

Description: GeoCommunicator is designed for governments, organizations, and individuals interested in land-related information. According to the site GeoCommunicator, "the first module of the National Integrated Land System (NILS), is an Internet web site containing information and searchable links for users and data providers with a common interest in cadastral land records, parcel data, and land management activities." A GeoCom Explorer tool provides access to map images, map services, geographic datasets, geographic activities, spatial solutions, clearinghouses, and land references. A Land Manager tool allows you to interact with maps containing federal land boundaries.

Subjects: Land Management; Maps and Mapping

946. Great Lakes Environmental Research Laboratory

http://www.glerl.noaa.gov/

Sponsor: Commerce Department — National Oceanic and Atmospheric Administration (NOAA)

Description: The Great Lakes Lab conducts scientific research of relevance to the Great Lakes and marine coastal environments. This site describes the lab, its mission, and its programs. An extensive Data section provides a catalog of numerous data sets. Publications are available under Products and Services. Specific topics addressed on this site include water levels, aquatic nuisance species, and aquatic contaminants.

Subject: Lakes — Research

947. Great Lakes Information Network

http://www.great-lakes.net/

Description: The Great Lakes Information Network (GLIN) is a cooperative project to provide a central place for information relating to the Great Lakes region. Sponsored in part by the Environmental Protection Agency's Great Lakes National Program Office, the site includes topics such as the Economy, Environment, Great Lakes, Education, Maps and GIS, and Tourism. Many discussion lists on Great Lake topics are hosted on the email list server. Useful links are available to related Web sites, from the Great Links in the Great Lakes Region section.

Subjects: Lakes; Midwest (United States)

948. Gulf States Marine Fisheries Commission

http://www.gsmfc.org/

Sponsor: Gulf States Marine Fisheries Commission (GSMFC)

Description: The Gulf States Marine Fisheries Commission is an organization, authorized by Congress, that includes the five Gulf (of Mexico) states (Texas, Louisiana, Mississippi, Alabama, and Florida). The Web site describes its activities with categories such as Overview, Programs, Publications, Meetings, Invasive Species, Toxic Blooms, and Regulations.

Subject: Fisheries

949. National Service Center for Environmental Publications

http://www.epa.gov/ncepihom/

Sponsor: Environmental Protection Agency (EPA)

Description: The National Service Center for Environmental Publications (NSCEP) distributes the publications of the Environmental Protection Agency. The site has a searchable publications catalog, from which publications can be ordered online. New Offerings lists newly available publications with an order link or direct Web link if the publication is available online. Other sections highlight foreign language publications, out-of-print publications, and online publications.

Subjects: Environmental Protection; Publication Catalogs

950. National Wild and Scenic Rivers System

http://www.nps.gov/rivers/

Sponsor: Interior Department — National Park Service (NPS)

Description: The Wild and Scenic Rivers Act (Public Law 90-542) is intended to protect selected rivers, keeping them free-flowing and preserving the general character of a river. This site describes the Scenic Rivers program and lists protected rivers. It also features river and water facts, river lengths, a bibliography, and links to related agencies and programs.

Subject: Rivers and Streams

951. NOAA Education Resources

http://www.education.noaa.gov/index.html

Description: The NOAA Education site has materials for teachers covering weather, climate change, oceans and coasts, weather satellites, and space environments. The Specially for Students section has educational resources and other information color-coded for K-5 grades, 6-12 grades, and higher education students. The Cool Sites for Everyone section highlights NOAA Web sites covering a variety of topics.

Subject: Environmental Education

952. NOAA Fisheries

http://www.nmfs.noaa.gov/

Sponsor: Commerce Department — National Oceanic and Atmospheric Administration (NOAA) — National Marine Fisheries

Description: The National Marine Fisheries Service, which is part of the National Oceanic and Atmospheric Administration, is concerned with fisheries: economics, trade, recreational, endangered species, strandings, and aquaculture. Top-level categories comprise HQ Offices, Regional Offices and Science Centers, Legislation and Budget, Publications, Seafood Inspection Program, Search, and Kid's Corner. A list of topics provides subject access to information about the various programs of the service. The Publications page includes *Our Living Oceans Annual Report* and *Fisheries of the United States* along with some technical reports, data sets, and links to fisheries-related publications from the various centers and offices of the NOAA and the NMFS.

Subjects: Fisheries; Marine Mammals

Publications: *Alaska Fisheries Science Center, Quarterly Report*, C 55.331/2:

Fish Meal and Oil, C 55.309/2-7:

Fisheries of the United States, C 55.309/2-2:

Fishery Bulletin, C 55.313:

Fishery Market News, C 55.318:

MMPA Bulletin, C 55.313/2:

Our Living Oceans, Annual Report on the Status of U.S. Living Marine Resources, C 55.1/2:

SFA Update, C 55.344:

USDC Approved List of Fish Establishments and Products (semiannual), C 55.338:

953. NOAA Research Organizations

http://www.oar.noaa.gov/organization/allorgmap.html

Sponsor: Commerce Department — National Oceanic and Atmospheric Administration (NOAA)

Description: This page provides links to NOAA's Environmental Research Laboratories, which carry out fundamental research, technology development, and services to improve understanding of the

Earth and its oceans and inland waters, the lower and upper atmosphere, and the space environment. The links are via a location map or an alphabetical list.
Subject: Environmental Science — Research
Publication: *FSL Forum*, C 55.628:

954. Northwest Fisheries Science Center
http://www.nwfsc.noaa.gov/
Sponsor: Commerce Department — National Oceanic and Atmospheric Administration (NOAA) — National Marine Fisheries
Description: The Northwest Fisheries Science Center is one of five research centers of NOAA Fisheries. The Research section has links to information from NWFSC's research divisions: Conservation Biology, Environmental Conservation, Fish Ecology, Fishery Resource Analysis and Monitoring, and Resource Enhancement and Utilization Technologies. The Publications page offers access to a few *White Papers* and full-text reports in the NOAA Technical Memorandum series, from 1990. The Library section provides helpful information for further research, provided by the Northwest and Alaska Fisheries Science Center Library.

This site should be useful to fisheries researchers and those interested in fisheries management in the northwest.
Subject: Fisheries

955. Office of Protected Resources
http://www.nmfs.noaa.gov/prot_res/prot_res.html
Sponsor: Commerce Department — National Oceanic and Atmospheric Administration (NOAA) — National Marine Fisheries
Description: The Office of Protected Resources coordinates the protection, conservation, and restoration of marine mammals, endangered species, their habitats, and marine protected areas. This Web site provides basic informational documents about the Marine Mammals Protection Act and the Marine Mammal Program, the Endangered Species Act, and a listing of proposed, candidate, and threatened and endangered species. Major categories include Endangered Species, Marine Mammal Conservation, Permit Information, Coral Reefs and Biodiversity, International Activities, and Reports and Publications.
Subjects: Endangered Species; Marine Life; Marine Mammals

956. Office of the Federal Environmental Executive
http://www.ofee.gov/
Sponsor: White House — Office of the Federal Environmental Executive (OFEE)
Description: The OFEE promotes environmental practices, such as recycling and procurement of recycled products, in the federal government. This site describes both the Office and the efforts federal agencies can take to further their environmental stewardship. Other topics include green buildings, environmental management systems, and computer and electronics products waste.
Subject: Recycling

957. Pacific States Marine Fisheries Commission
http://www.psmfc.org/
Sponsor: Pacific States Marine Fisheries Commission (PSMFC)
Description: The Pacific States Marine Fisheries Commission, authorized by Congress in 1947, is one of three interstate commissions dedicated to resolving fishery issues. It serves as a forum for discussion, working for coastwide consensus to state and federal authorities. Their Web site offers information in categories including Overview, Projects, Personnel, and Publications. The Publications area includes Annual Reports, Workshops, a newsletter, and Habitat Hotline.
Subject: Fisheries

958. Patuxent Wildlife Research Center
http://www.pwrc.usgs.gov/
Description: This site provides reliable information on the status and trends of the nation's biota, identifies populations, species, and ecosystems at risk before they become threatened or endangered, determines the factors causing the observed trends, and provides tools for forecasting future

trends based on alternative policy and management decisions. The site offers categories for Software, Designing a Monitoring Program, Amphibians, Butterflies, and Birds.

This site will be useful for anyone getting involved with an inventory and monitoring program as well as for those interested for some of these species for which monitoring programs are available.

959. President's Council on Environmental Quality

`http://www.whitehouse.gov/ceq/`
Sponsor: Council on Environmental Quality (CEQ)
Description: The CEQ site features a basic description of the council and Bush administration statements related to the environment. The site links to presidential task forces and federal agencies related to energy or environmental issues. It also links to NEPAnet, which gathers a wide variety of NEPA-related information, including the text of statutes, executive orders, and regulations.
Subjects: Environmental Protection — Policy; National Environmental Policy Act

960. Tox Town

`http://toxtown.nlm.nih.gov/`
Sponsor: National Institutes of Health (NIH) — National Library of Medicine (NLM)
Description: Tox Town is an educational site about toxic chemicals, designed for a general audience. The site requires the Flash Web browser plug-in, but a text-only version of the site is also available. The site uses a graphical image of a town to serve as an interface to toxics information from such agencies as the National Institutes of Health and the Environmental Protection Agency.
Subject: Toxic Substances

961. Upper Midwest Environmental Sciences Center

`http://www.umesc.usgs.gov/`
Sponsor: Interior Department — U.S. Geological Survey (USGS)
Description: The UMESC is a river-related inventory, monitoring, research, spatial analysis, and information-sharing program. One of its main program areas is the Long-Term Resource Monitoring Program (LTRMP) of the Upper Mississippi River System and adjoining geographic areas. This Web site offers biological, physical, spatial, graphic, and written information. The Data Library includes a variety of environmental data sets for the Mississippi River and collections of aerial photographs. The Science Programs site is organized into sections for aquatic sciences, river inventory and monitoring, exotic species, and terrestrial sciences. The Teachers and Students section has a variety of educational material on the Mississippi River. The Reports and Publications section includes Project Status Reports, Fact Sheets, and links to LTRMP documents.

This site provides access to a substantial amount of information for researchers on fish and wildlife, vegetation, invertebrates, water quality, water levels, sediments, contaminants, and nutrients, as well as access to aerial and satellite photography, software, scientific publications, and geographic information systems maps, quadrangles, and figures.
Subject: Rivers and Streams — Research
Publication: *River Almanac*, I 73.16:

962. USGS Ground Water Information Pages

`http://water.usgs.gov/ogw/`
Sponsor: Interior Department — U.S. Geological Survey (USGS)
Description: This site provides information about the ground water resources of the United States and groundwater activities of the USGS. It includes sections on Groundwater Data, Publications, the Groundwater Resources Program, Field Techniques and Groundwater Models, and Water Resources Information by State. Among the publications is an online version of the *Ground Water Atlas of the United States*.
Subjects: Ground Water; Water Supply
Publications: *Advisory Committee on Water Information (ACWI) Summary of Meetings*, I 19.74: *Ground Water Atlas of the United States*, I 19.89:

963. Water Resources of the United States

`http://water.usgs.gov/`
Sponsor: Interior Department — U.S. Geological Survey (USGS)

Description: As one of the major subject-oriented USGS Web sites, Water Resources of the United States covers USGS materials related to water, water use, surface water, ground water, and water quality. The primary divisions include Water Data, Publications And Products, Technical Resources, Programs, and Local Information. Publications includes links to the monthly *National Water Conditions Report* (back to 1929), online fact sheets, news releases, abstracts, and online USGS reports. The *Selected Water Resources Abstracts* available via the Abstracts link below Publications is a bibliographic database with citations to USGS publications back to 1939. It uses a search form which allows fairly sophisticated searching. The page also links to the Universities Water Information Network for abstracts covering the period from 1967 to October 1993.
Subject: Water
Publications: *National Water Conditions*, I 19.42:
National Water Summary, I 19.13/3:
Selected Water Resources Abstracts, I 19.42/7:
USGS Fact Sheets, I 19.127:
Water-Supply Papers, I 19.13:

964. Western Water Policy Review Advisory Commission
http://www.den.doi.gov/wwprac/
Sponsor: Western Water Policy Review Advisory Commission
Description: The Western Water Policy Review Advisory Commission was responsible for undertaking a comprehensive review of federal activities in the nineteen western states affecting the allocation and use of water resources. This site offers Background, Research, and Reports, including the final report.
Subject: Water Supply
Publication: *Western Water Policy Review Advisory Commission Reports*, Y 3.2:2000006843

Climate and Weather

965. Arkansas-Red Basin River Forecast Center
http://www.srh.noaa.gov/abrfc/
Sponsor: Commerce Department — National Oceanic and Atmospheric Administration (NOAA) — National Weather Service
Description: This site includes detailed forecast and precipitation data for these river basins, along with pictures of the rivers. Information, charts, and maps are available on such topics as flood outlooks, water supply, flash flooding, and drought. The quarterly newsletter, *The Gage,* is available online in HTML format.
Subjects: Rivers and Streams; Weather Forecasts
Publication: *The Gage*

966. Climate Diagnostics Center
http://www.cdc.noaa.gov/
Sponsor: Commerce Department — National Oceanic and Atmospheric Administration (NOAA)
Description: The field of climate diagnostics studies the interrelationships among climate variables such as atmospheric pressure and water temperature. Major sections of the site include Climate and Weather, Research at CDC, and Data Access and Plotting. The Climate and Weather section has a Map Room and U.S. forecasts. The Research section includes citations and some full text links to journal articles by CDC scientists. Data sets, online data analysis and visualization, climate research data access are available under Data Access and Plotting. The site also covers selected topics such as El Nino and U.S. precipitation anomalies.
Subject: Climate Research

967. Climate Monitoring and Diagnostics Laboratory
http://www.cmdl.noaa.gov/
Sponsor: Commerce Department — National Oceanic and Atmospheric Administration (NOAA) — Office of Oceanic and Atmospheric Research
Description: This site describes the lab and its research projects. It provides links to information on ongoing research at the lab, including studies on Aerosols & Radiation, Carbon Cycle-Greenhouse Gases, Halocarbons and Other Atmospheric Trace Species, Observatory Operations, and Ozone and Water Vapor. There are links to the pages for observatories in Antarctica, American Samoa, California, Hawaii, and Alaska, and to information about climate, ozone, and air quality.
Subjects: Atmospheric Sciences; Climate Research

968. Climate Prediction Center
http://www.nnic.noaa.gov/cpc/
Sponsor: Commerce Department — National Oceanic and Atmospheric Administration (NOAA) — National Weather Service
Description: The Climate Prediction Center maintains a continuous watch on short-term climate fluctuations and attempts to diagnose and predict them. This Web site provides climatological information, with highlights on U.S. Threats Assessment, Drought Assessment, ENSO Diagnostic Discussion, Seasonal Outlook, and Winter Outlook. Main sections of the site include an Index of Expert Assessments, an Index of Outlooks (Forecasts), an Index of Monitoring and Data, Crosscutting Themes, and information about the center. Under Crosscutting Themes, there is a substantial section on the El Nino and La Nina weather patterns. Under Climate Highlights, there are links to the following sections: Climate Predictions in the News, Latest Publications, and New Products, where the visitor can access press releases, a drought monitor, the *Climate Diagnostics Bulletin,* and various monitoring data.
Subjects: Climatology; El Nino; Weather Forecasts
Publications: *Climate Bulletin,* C 55.129/2:
Climate Diagnostics Bulletin (monthly), C 55.194:

969. Forecast Systems Laboratory
http://www.fsl.noaa.gov/
Sponsor: Commerce Department — National Oceanic and Atmospheric Administration (NOAA)
Description: The Forecast Systems Laboratory site describes the lab and its research mission. Data products include a variety of weather data, analyses, and predictions. Featured sections include Weather, Datasets, Projects, Publications, Software, and Organization. Publications include *FSL in Review* and *FSL Forum.* There are also links to related sites.
   This site offers useful data for the meteorologic researcher.
Subject: Meteorology — Research
Publications: *FSL Forum*
FSL in Review, C 55.602:F 76/

970. Geophysical Fluid Dynamics Laboratory
http://www.gfdl.gov/
Sponsor: Commerce Department — National Oceanic and Atmospheric Administration (NOAA) — Office of Oceanic and Atmospheric Research
Description: GFDL is a research laboratory that seeks to understand and predict the earth's climate and weather, including the impact of human activities. Its site features sections for Research, References, Technical Services, Administration, and Meetings and Seminars. The Research topics are Climate Dynamics, Atmospheric Physics and Chemistry, Oceans and Climate, Climate Diagnostics, and Weather and Atmospheric Dynamics. The Reference area provides an online GFDL bibliography and a link to the GFDL Library.
Subjects: Atmospheric Sciences — Research; Climatology — Research

971. Global Hydrology and Climate Center
http://www.ghcc.msfc.nasa.gov/
Sponsor: National Aeronautics and Space Administration (NASA) — Marshall Space Flight Center (MSFC) — Global Hydrology and Climate Center

Description: The Global Hydrology and Climate Center is active in studying the global water cycle and its effect on the climate. The site's sections feature Research, Education, Climate Impacts, News, Data, Satellite Images, Weather Forecast, and About Us. The Research section includes information on the center's studies such as lightning, remote sensing, atmospheric aerosols, global water cycle, and remote archeological research.
Subjects: Climate Research; Remote Sensing

972. National Center for Atmospheric Research
http://www.ncar.ucar.edu/ncar/
Sponsor: National Science Foundation (NSF)
Description: Sponsored by the National Science Foundation, NCAR's mission is to plan, organize, and conduct atmospheric and related science programs in collaboration with universities. This Web site features information on the Center and its research areas. The home page provides links to descriptions of the center's divisional programs. Each division's home page provides detailed information and resources. *Annual Scientific Reports* are also available.
Subjects: Atmospheric Sciences — Research; Climate Research
Publication: *Annual Scientific Reports*

973. National Centers for Environmental Prediction
http://www.ncep.noaa.gov/
Description: This site links to the Web sites for the component NCEP centers: the Aviation Weather Center, the Climate Prediction Center, the Environmental Modeling Center, the Hydrometeorological Prediction Center, the Marine Prediction Center, the Space Environment Center, the Storm Prediction Center, the Tropical Prediction Center, and NCEP Central Operations.
Subjects: Climatology; Weather Forecasts

974. National Climatic Data Center
http://lwf.ncdc.noaa.gov/oa/ncdc.html
Sponsor: Commerce Department — National Oceanic and Atmospheric Administration (NOAA) — National Environmental Satellite, Data, and Information Service (NESDIS)
Description: As the world's largest active archive of weather data, NCDC produces numerous climate publications and datasets and makes information available on this site. Users may search for weather station data for a particular location and browse data by type: satellite, radar, and climate. NCDC products may be browsed by popular use, user description, category, keywords, and more. The site's In the Spotlight section highlights topics of current interest. Information about climate is available in three categories: research, monitoring, and extremes and events.
Subjects: Climatology; Data Products; Weather
Publications: *Climatological Data (various states)*, C 55.214/51:
Hourly Precipitation Data: Various States and Countries, C 55.216/45:
Local Climatological Data: Various States , C 55.286/6-54:
Monthly Climatic Data for the World, C 55.211:
Monthly State, Regional, and National Cooling Degree Days, Weighted by Population, C 55.287/60-3:
Monthly State, Regional, and National Heating Degree Days, Weighted by Population, C 55.287/60-2:
Storm Data (monthly), C 55.212:

975. National Environmental Satellite, Data, and Information Service
http://www.nesdis.noaa.gov/
Sponsor: Commerce Department — National Oceanic and Atmospheric Administration (NOAA) — National Environmental Satellite, Data, and Information Service (NESDIS)
Description: The NESDIS page links to component NESDIS agencies such as the National Climatic Data Center, the National Geophysical Data Center, and the National Oceanographic Data Center. It also features the categories: Image of the Day, GOES Satellite Imagery, NESDIS Organization Chart, and NESDIS News Releases.
Subjects: Environmental Science; Satellites

976. National Hurricane Center—Tropical Prediction Center

http://www.nhc.noaa.gov/

Sponsor: Commerce Department — National Oceanic and Atmospheric Administration (NOAA) — National Weather Service

Description: This site features data, graphs, and other information on tropical cyclones and hurricanes. It presents one-click access to a lot of information. Menu items on the home page include Active Tropical Systems, Tropical Cyclone Centers, Tropical Weather Outlooks, Current Season Summaries and Reports, Learn About Hurricanes, and Hurricane History. The latest forecasts are featured prominently. Publications are listed under Additional Resources.

Subject: Hurricanes

977. National Severe Storms Laboratory

http://www.nssl.noaa.gov/

Sponsor: Commerce Department — National Oceanic and Atmospheric Administration (NOAA) — Office of Oceanic and Atmospheric Research

Description: The National Severe Storms Laboratory is active in investigations of all aspects of severe weather. This site offers information on its research program, providing such sections as General Information, Education, Scientific Research, and Items of Interest. The Scientific Publications section, under Scientific Research, list papers, books, and articles by lab personnel and historical data on deaths, injuries, and damage due to lightning. The home page provides subject access for topics such as Radar, Satellite, Software Development, Modeling, Tornadoes, Thunderstorms, Damaging Winds, Lightning, Hail, Winter Weather, and Flooding.

Subjects: Tornadoes; Weather — Research

978. National Weather Service

http://www.nws.noaa.gov/

Sponsor: Commerce Department — National Oceanic and Atmospheric Administration (NOAA) — National Weather Service

Description: The National Weather Service collects weather data and provides forecasts for the United States and surrounding waters. While the NWS data repository is vast, their Web site makes the most popular data easily accessible. The home page features a color-coded map of current weather warnings and advisories in the United States. A city name search box gives quick access to local short and long term weather forecasts, current conditions, and radar and satellite images. A Forecasts section links to the forecasts available on NOAA Web sites, including drought, fire, marine, aviation, and even space weather. A Weather Safety section takes a similar approach, linking to information on NOAA Weather Radio and to safety information related to storms, heat, lightning, hurricanes, tornadoes, rip currents, and floods. The Careers section includes information on how to become a meteorologist. The Organization section on the top menu bar has links to the Web sites for all of the many NWS regional offices and centers, which also provide a wealth of local U.S. data.

NWS data is reformatted and used by the media and Internet sites, but the NWS site is user-friendly enough to be consulted directly for U.S. forecasts.

Subjects: Meteorology; Weather Forecasts

Publications: *Aware*, C 55.127

Mariners Weather Log, C 55.135:

979. Storm Prediction Center

http://www.spc.noaa.gov/

Sponsor: Commerce Department — National Oceanic and Atmospheric Administration (NOAA) — National Weather Service

Description: Storm Prediction Center provides forecasts for severe thunderstorms and tornadoes over the contiguous United States. The SPC also monitors heavy rain, heavy snow, and fire weather events across the United States. Their Web site links to all of the center's forecasts, information about their research, and a variety of education and outreach services. Highlights include storm reports, tornado statistics, and current convective watches. The Education section features extensive information about tornadoes.

Subjects: Tornadoes; Weather Forecasts

Oceans

980. Atlantic Oceanographic and Meteorological Laboratory
http://www.aoml.noaa.gov/
Sponsor: Commerce Department — National Oceanic and Atmospheric Administration (NOAA) — Office of Oceanic and Atmospheric Research
Description: AOML conducts research in oceanography, tropical meteorology, atmospheric and oceanic chemistry, and acoustics. The major topical sections of the lab's Web site are Ocean and Climate, Coastal and Regional, and Hurricanes. The Publications section provides a searchable catalog of AOML-authored publications dating back to 1985. The AOML Environmental Data Server provides online access to the lab's data sets.
Subjects: Coastal Ecology; Hurricanes — Research; Oceanography
Publication: *AOML Keynotes*

981. Center for Operational Oceanographic Products and Services
http://www.co-ops.nos.noaa.gov/
Sponsor: Commerce Department — National Oceanic and Atmospheric Administration (NOAA) — National Ocean Service
Description: The Center for Oceanographic Products and Services collects, analyzes, distributes historical and real-time observations and predictions of water levels, coastal currents, and other meteorological and oceanographic data. It is also responsible for products such as the Physical Oceanographic Real-Time System (PORTS) (TM) and Tides Online. The site includes information on tide predictions, water level observations, benchmarks, station locator, publications, and product information. The predictions page offers tidal differences and other constants, which can be used to calculate tidal predictions for more than 3,000 tide stations.
Subject: Oceanography

982. Coastal and Hydraulics Laboratory
http://chl.wes.army.mil/
Sponsor: Army — Army Corps of Engineers
Description: The research activities of CHL are the major focus of this page and comprise Integrated Systems Analysis, Flood/Storm Damage Reduction, Hydro-Environmental, Navigation Support, and Military Support. Under Technical Exchange, the Data link offers the Coastal Engineering Data Retrieval System, which is a database of wind, wave, and water level data for the coastline of the United States to assist the coastal engineer. Under Library, there are direct links to recent CHL technical reports. Other documents, including the *Coastal and Hydraulic Engineering Technical Notes*, are available under CHL Publications.
Subjects: Civil Engineering; Coastal Ecology
Publications: *Coastal and Hydraulic Engineering Technical Notes*
The CERCular, D 103.42/11:

983. Coastal Ocean Program
http://www.cop.noaa.gov/
Sponsor: Commerce Department — National Oceanic and Atmospheric Administration (NOAA)
Description: NOAA's Coastal Ocean Program (COP) provides information for managing coastal ecosystems through sponsorship of scientific research. The site features Funding Announcements, Current and Historical Projects, COP Publications, and Partner Institutions. The Publications section includes some COP newsletters and the *Decision Analysis Series*.
Subject: Coastal Ecology — Grants
Publications: *NOAA Coastal Ocean Program, Decisions Analysis Program*, C 55.49/3:
NOAA Coastal Ocean Program, Project News Update, C 55.49/4:

984. Coastal Program
http://www.fws.gov/cep/cepcode.html
Sponsor: Interior Department — Fish and Wildlife Service (FWS)
Description: The Coastal Ecosystems Program works to conserve fish and wildlife and their habitats through cooperative projects with state and local governments, businesses, conservation organizations, and landowners. The site has general information about the program and fact sheets on high-priority coastal areas in the United States.
Subject: Coastal Ecology

985. Coastal Services Center
http://www.csc.noaa.gov/
Sponsor: Commerce Department — National Oceanic and Atmospheric Administration (NOAA) — National Ocean Service
Description: The Center helps the nation's coastal resource management programs by providing them with services and information and by fostering the use of new or under-utilized technology. The site describes the Center's activities in management assistance, GIS and remote sensing, coastal observing systems, spatial data, and habitat characterizations. Specific resources can be found in the sections titled Library, Publications, CD-ROMs, and Data and Information Search Tools.
Subjects: Coastal Ecology; Remote Sensing

986. Environmental Technology Laboratory
http://www.etl.noaa.gov/
Sponsor: Commerce Department — National Oceanic and Atmospheric Administration (NOAA)
Description: The Environmental Technology Laboratory develops technology, such as remote sensing systems, to gather environmental information from the oceans and atmosphere. Topical links on the lab's Web site include Microwave Systems Development, Optical Remote Sensing, and Regional Weather and Climate Applications. Under Observing Systems, the site provides a list of technologies and links to a detailed description and Web bibliography for each.
Subject: Remote Sensing — Research

987. Fleet Numerical Meteorology and Oceanography Center
http://www.fnoc.navy.mil/
Sponsor: Defense Department — Fleet Numerical Meteorology and Oceanography Center (FMOC)
Description: The Fleet Numerical Meteorology and Oceanography Center provides atmospheric and oceanographic support for the Defense Department. This site has special sections for authorized users, but the public section includes unclassified information such as extensive background on the El Nino/La Nina weather pattern. The site also includes sample satellite imagery displaying characteristics like wind and rain rate around the globe.
Subjects: Weather; Satellites

988. Marine Product Dissemination Information
http://205.156.54.206/om/marine/home.htm
Sponsor: Commerce Department — National Oceanic and Atmospheric Administration (NOAA) — National Weather Service
Description: This gateway site provides links to information resources related to marine weather forecasts. Shortcuts are provided to marine forecasts in text or graphic formats. Other links are grouped by dissemination information type, including Internet, USCG (United States Coast Guard) VHF voice, amateur "ham" radio, NOAA weather radio, and many more. Links to publications, contact information, and product release schedules are also listed. For each dissemination type, the site provides a description of the service and links to related sites.
Subjects: Maritime Transportation; Weather Forecasts

989. National Data Buoy Center
http://seaboard.ndbc.noaa.gov/
Sponsor: Commerce Department — National Oceanic and Atmospheric Administration (NOAA) — National Weather Service

Description: The National Data Buoy Center site provides buoy-measured environmental data and an overview of the NDBC. Current (Real-Time) Meteorological and Oceanographic Data are available for coastal locations in North America, Great Britain, Gulf of Mexico, and the Caribbean. Historical data are also available, grouped by station ID. Other sections of the site include Observations Search, About NDBC, Science Education, the NDBC bulletin *Sea Worthy*, and information on the Dial-a-Buoy program, which provides station information over the telephone.
Subjects: Oceans; Weather Forecasts

990. National Marine Sanctuaries
http://www.sanctuaries.nos.noaa.gov/
Sponsor: Commerce Department — National Oceanic and Atmospheric Administration (NOAA) — National Weather Service
Description: The National Marine Sanctuary System provides resource protection through conservation and management of the sanctuaries, coordinates scientific research on the sanctuaries, and facilitates multiple uses of the national marine sanctuaries. Its site serves as a central starting point for finding information on each of the marine sanctuaries, as well as providing information in such sections as the National Program, Sanctuary News, Science and Education, and a Photo Gallery. The National Program section explains the history, legislation, and regulations related to marine sanctuaries.
Subject: Marine Sanctuaries

991. National Ocean Service
http://www.nos.noaa.gov/
Sponsor: Commerce Department — National Oceanic and Atmospheric Administration (NOAA) — National Ocean Service
Description: NOS is the primary civil agency within the federal government responsible for the health and safety of the nation's coastal and oceanic environment. The Web site provides access to its oceanographic resources in sections such as About NOS, News and Events, Publications and Products, Programs, Education and Outreach, and Popular NOS Web Sites. The Popular NOS Web sites section includes links to such programs as Coastal Survey/Nautical Charts, Tide and Current Information, and Oil and Chemical Releases.
Subject: Oceanography

992. National Oceanographic Data Center
http://www.nodc.noaa.gov/
Sponsor: Commerce Department — National Oceanic and Atmospheric Administration (NOAA) — National Environmental Satellite, Data, and Information Service (NESDIS)
Description: The National Oceanographic Data Center archives and provides public access to global oceanographic and coastal data, products, and information. Click on Access Data on the home page to reach Archived Data, CD-ROMs, Publications, and an Online Store. Available data sets cover ocean currents, plankton, salinity, sea level, and more. The site also has a popular Coastal Water Temperature Guide, reporting average monthly temperatures for the U.S. coastal regions, including Hawaii.
Subject: Oceanography

993. NOAA's Coral Reef Information System
http://coris.noaa.gov/
Sponsor: Commerce Department — National Oceanic and Atmospheric Administration (NOAA) — National Ocean Service
Description: This portal to NOAA coral reef information and data products has a variety of data sets, reference resources, and information on coral reef biology and environmental threats. A Professional Exchanges section offers access to NOAA's Coral Health and Monitoring Program (CHAMP) electronic discussion list. A Publications section has citations from papers and reports published as a result of NOAA or NOAA-sponsored coral reef activities.
Subject: Coral Reefs
Publication: *The State of Coral Reef Ecosystems of the United States and Pacific Freely Associated States*

994. NOS MapFinder
http://mapindex.nos.noaa.gov/

Sponsor: Commerce Department — National Oceanic and Atmospheric Administration (NOAA) — National Ocean Service

Description: MapFinder provides centralized Web access to the National Ocean Service images and data in order to make these products more widely available to the public. Products are categorized according to theme: coastal photography, coastal survey maps, Environmental Sensitivity Index maps, estuarine bathymetry, geodetic control points, historical maps and charts, hydrographic survey outlines, nautical charts, and water-level station data.

Subjects: Maps and Mapping; Oceans

995. Office of Coast Survey
http://chartmaker.ncd.noaa.gov/

Sponsor: Commerce Department — National Oceanic and Atmospheric Administration (NOAA) — National Ocean Service

Description: The Coast Survey is the official U.S. chart making agency. It manages nautical chart data collections and information programs. This site offers information on nautical charts and hydrography via links such as Historical Maps and Charts, Wrecks and Obstructions, Navigation Services, and Hydrographic Surveys. There are electronic navigational charts to download, and print-on-demand nautical charts. The site also offers a major online service called NowCOAST. This Web-based GIS tool is designed to allow rapid spatial location of real time weather, ocean, and river information for coastal areas.

Subject: Maps and Mapping

996. Office of Ocean and Coastal Resource Management
http://www.ocrm.nos.noaa.gov/welcome.html

Sponsor: Commerce Department — National Oceanic and Atmospheric Administration (NOAA) — National Ocean Service

Description: This site features the sections About OCRM, Coastal Resource and Policy Issues, Coastal Zone Management Act, What's Happening, Resources, Publications, and Outreach. It also has links to the programs it administers: the Coastal Zone Management Program and the National Estuarine Research Reserve System.

Subject: Coastal Ecology

997. Pacific Marine Environmental Laboratory
http://www.pmel.noaa.gov/

Sponsor: Commerce Department — National Oceanic and Atmospheric Administration (NOAA) — Office of Oceanic and Atmospheric Research

Description: The Pacific Marine Environmental Laboratory (PMEL) carries out interdisciplinary scientific investigations in oceanography and atmospheric sciences. The site has sections for Research, Publications, Infrastructure, Theme Pages, and Data. Special topics include El Niño and La Niña, tsunami monitoring, 3D visualization of data, and virtual reality presentations. The Publications page offers a search of PMEL publications by year, author, title, citation, abstract, division, and media type. Access to the PMEL NOAA publications with an NTIS number is available by category of publication: data report, ERL Special Reports, Technical Memoranda, and Technical Reports. A list of PMEL in-progress publications is available as well.

Subjects: Atmospheric Sciences — Research; Oceanography — Research

998. Physical Oceanography Distributed Active Archive Center
http://podaac.jpl.nasa.gov

Alternate URL: ftp://podaac.jpl.nasa.gov/pub/

Sponsor: National Aeronautics and Space Administration (NASA) — Jet Propulsion Laboratory (JPL)

Description: The Physical Oceanography Distributed Active Archive Center is a component of the NASA Earth Observing System Data Information System (EOSDIS). The center is responsible for archiving and distributing satellite data relevant to the physical state of the ocean. The site has a data catalog, information on data tools, documentation and a link to the EOS Data Gateway site.

Data is available on sea surface height, ocean wind, and sea surface temperature. Data is also available in compressed format via FTP; the site describes its FTP procedures. While most of the data is for the use of scientists, there is some educational and public outreach information available on the site.
Subject: Oceanography

999. Tides Online
http://tidesonline.nos.noaa.gov/
Sponsor: Commerce Department — National Oceanic and Atmospheric Administration (NOAA) — National Ocean Service
Description: The Tides Online page provides users with near real-time information from water-level stations located along the projected path of severe storms such as hurricanes. Access to the information is available by selecting the Storm Surge Mode data option. The State Maps and Regional List data options provide this information from any active station, not just those in the path of a storm.
Subjects: Hurricanes; Tides

Pollution

1000. Agency for Toxic Substances and Disease Registry
http://www.atsdr.cdc.gov/
Sponsor: Health and Human Services Department — Centers for Disease Control and Prevention (CDC)
Description: ATSDR's public health mission is to prevent harmful exposures and disease related to toxic substances. This Web site offers information sources on toxic substances and provides public education on hazardous substances through the following major categories: Emergency Response, Hazardous Substances, Hazardous Waste Sites, Measuring Health Effects, Education and Training, Information Sources, and Publications. Under Hazardous Substances, the ToxFAQs section summarizes information about hazardous substances. There are also fact sheets on each of the "top 20" hazardous substances, such as arsenic, lead, and benzene.

The site provides access to the HazDat database on the release of hazardous substances from Superfund sites or from emergency events. It also has sections tailored to specific audiences: parents and children, communities, and health professionals, and Spanish language materials. There is also information on ASTDR funding opportunities.

This is an excellent site for finding toxicological data and information on hazardous substances.
Subjects: Public Health; Toxic Substances
Publications: *Agency for Toxic Substances and Disease Registry Agency Profile*, HE 20.501/2:
Hazardous Substances & Public Health, HE 20.516:
Toxicological Profiles (Drafts, Updates and Finals), HE 20.518:

1001. Air and Radiation Division, EPA Region 5
http://www.epa.gov/ARD-R5/
Sponsor: Environmental Protection Agency (EPA) — Air and Radiation Office
Description: This server comes from EPA region 5, serving the Midwest. Despite being a regional server, it boasts a great deal of substantive resources related to air pollution and the Clean Air Act. Most are listed under topical headings, including Air Quality, Air Toxics, Asbestos, Indoor Air, Global Air, and Vehicle Emissions.
Subject: Air Pollution

1002. Air Pollution—U.S. EPA Office of Air and Radiation
http://www.epa.gov/oar/
Sponsor: Environmental Protection Agency (EPA) — Air and Radiation Office
Description: The Office of Air and Radiation provides information in the following sections: Air Quality Where You Live, Indoor Air Quality, Transportation/Fuels, Off-Road Equipment, Acid Rain, Ozone Depletion, Visibility, Toxic Air Pollutants, and Radiation. In addition to detailed information

on the above topics, this site offers sections on Why Be Concerned?, What You Can Do, Quick Links, Partners, Tools and Technical Info, and Recent News and Events. Under Tools, the Publications page offers access to *Air Quality Trends Reports, Emissions Trends Report*, and numerous other brochures, pamphlets, and other publications.

This site is an excellent entry point for access to the EPA's technical and educational resources on air quality, air pollution, and the Clean Air Act.

Subjects: Air Pollution; Air Quality; Radiation
Publications: *Air Quality Trends Report*
Emissions Trends Report

1003. Air Resources Laboratory
http://www.arl.noaa.gov/
Sponsor: Commerce Department — National Oceanic and Atmospheric Administration (NOAA) — Office of Oceanic and Atmospheric Research
Description: The Air Resources Laboratory conducts atmospheric research, focusing on air quality and climate. The sites describes current research and provides access to both ARL publications and their climate and meteorological data.
Subjects: Air Quality — Research; Atmospheric Sciences

1004. AIRData
http://www.epa.gov/air/data/
Sponsor: Environmental Protection Agency (EPA) — Air and Radiation Office
Description: AIRData has annual summaries of United States air pollution data, taken from EPA's air pollution databases. The data identify emissions and pollutant levels, and include all 50 states plus District of Columbia, Puerto Rico, and the U. S. Virgin Islands.
Subjects: Air Pollution; Databases

1005. American Heritage Rivers
http://www.epa.gov/rivers/
Sponsor: Environmental Protection Agency (EPA) — Water Office — Wetlands, Oceans, and Watersheds Office
Description: The American Heritage Rivers Initiative helps communities restore and revitalize waters and waterfronts. Project objectives are natural resource and environmental protection, economic revitalization, and historic and cultural preservation. The initiative's Web site offers sections on What is the American Heritage Rivers Initiative, Designated Rivers, Your River and Its Watershed, and Services for Your River. A *State of the River Report* is available for each American Heritage River.
Subject: Rivers and Streams
Publication: *State of the River Reports*

1006. Chemicals in the Environment: OPPT Chemical Fact Sheets
http://www.epa.gov/opptintr/chemfact/
Sponsor: Environmental Protection Agency (EPA) — Prevention, Pesticides and Toxic Substances Office
Description: This site offers *Fact Sheets* and *Chemical Summaries* for selected chemicals. The *Fact Sheets* cover the chemical's identity, production and use, environmental fate, and health and environmental effects. They also include a list of laws under which the chemical is regulated, phone numbers, and the names of EPA offices and other agencies one can call or contact for more information. The *Chemical Summaries* are technical support documents that provide detailed technical information on the chemical named in the fact sheet. The older files are in ASCII; the newer files in PDF.
Subjects: Chemical Information; Toxic Substances

1007. Department of Energy Hanford Site
http://www.hanford.gov/
Sponsor: Energy Department — River Protection Office

Description: Hanford, formerly a plutonium production complex, is now one of the world's largest environmental cleanup projects. The project is being managed by the DOE as it explores ways of handling Hanford's tank waste retrieval, treatment, and disposal, and restoring the Columbia River Corridor where the plant is located. The site includes sections for General Information, Business Opportunities, Contractors, Maps, Hanford History, and Public Involvement.
Subjects: Environmental Cleanup; Nuclear Waste

1008. Enforcement and Compliance History Online (ECHO)
http://www.epa.gov/echo/
Sponsor: Environmental Protection Agency (EPA)
Description: ECHO is a new EPA information system providing violation and enforcement information on roughly 800,000 facilities that are regulated under key environmental statutes. From the home page, users can search by ZIP code to find regulated facilities and display their inspection and enforcement history. More advanced search criteria include facility name, type of industry, EPA region, city, state, and county. Searches can be filtered by a number of characteristics, such as whether the facility has multiple violations, is on Indian or federal land, or has a certain percentage of minority population within a three-mile radius.
Subject: Environmental Law

1009. Enviroene—Common Sense Solutions to Environmental Problems
http://es.epa.gov/
Sponsor: Environmental Protection Agency (EPA)
Description: Enviroene provides a single repository for pollution prevention, compliance assurance, and enforcement information and databases. It compiles a number of resources on pollution prevention projects and research. The site sections feature Enviroene Cooperatives (federal, state, and international); Solvent Substitution Data Systems; Contacts, Resources, and Vendors; and Compliance and Enforcement.
Subjects: Environmental Law; Pollutants — Regulations
Publications: *EPA Sector Notebooks*, EP 1.113:

1010. Federal Remediation Technologies Roundtable
http://www.frtr.gov/
Sponsor: Federal Remediation Technologies Roundtable
Description: The Federal Remediation Technologies Roundtable is an interagency working group supporting collaboration among the federal agencies involved in hazardous waste site remediation. Their Web site features a section on Remediation System Optimization, and a variety of tools, information, and case studies to help with selecting the best technology for remediation tasks. FRTR meeting information and publications are also online.
Subject: Environmental Cleanup
Publication: *Abstracts of Remediation Case Studies*, EP 1.2:AB 8

1011. Great Lakes Environment
http://www.epa.gov/glnpo/
Sponsor: Environmental Protection Agency (EPA) — Great Lakes National Program Office (GLNPO)
Description: This site has information on the Great Lakes, the environmental problems of the lakes, and projects to restore the environment. A Policies and Strategies section has information and publications from the EPA's Great Lakes National Program Office. Other sections provide detailed assessments, data, and reports from projects concerning Monitoring and Indicators, Ecosystems, and Toxics Reduction. The site also has information on related funding opportunities.
Subjects: Lakes; Water Pollution
Publication: *Great Lakes Atlas*

1012. Green Vehicle Guide

http://www.epa.gov/greenvehicles/

Sponsor: Environmental Protection Agency (EPA) — Air and Radiation Office
Description: This online guide uses emissions and fuel economy scores to rank the environmental performance of recent car models. Users can look up the score for a specific model and make of automobile or browse by type of vehicle, such as pickup or minivan. The site includes explanations of the rankings and information on auto emissions. A related links section points to EPA and other agency sites with more information on automobile performance and air quality.
Subject: Motor Vehicles

1013. Hazardous Waste Clean-Up Information (CLU-IN)

http://clu-in.org/

Sponsor: Environmental Protection Agency (EPA)
Description: The Hazardous Waste Clean-up Information Web Site provides information about innovative treatment technologies to the hazardous waste remediation community. The site has databases on Remediation and Characterization and Monitoring, as well as technology descriptions and selection tools in these areas. Brownfields receive particular attention. Users with a professional interest in environmental technology can subscribe to email delivery of several newsletters including: *TechDirect*, *Technology Innovation News Survey*, and *Technology News and Trends*. Archives for these newsletters are also available on the site.
Subject: Environmental Cleanup
Publications: *TechDirect*
Technology Innovation News Survey
Technology News and Trends, EP 1.10/3:

1014. Nuclear Waste Technical Review Board

http://www.nwtrb.gov/

Sponsor: Nuclear Waste Technical Review Board (NWTRB)
Description: The NWTRB is an independent agency of the U.S. government that provides scientific and technical oversight of the U.S. program for management and disposal of high-level radioactive waste and spent nuclear fuel from civilian nuclear power plants. Its site features Board Mission, Board Members, Issues, Reports, Correspondence, Testimony, Plans, Press Releases, and Calendar.
Subject: Nuclear Waste

1015. Office of Environmental Management, Department of Energy

http://www.em.doe.gov/

Sponsor: Environmental Protection Agency (EPA)
Description: This office manages the cleanup of radioactive, chemical, and other hazardous waste left after years of nuclear weapons production. Their Web site's home page has a clickable map of the United States linking to information about each of the office's many remediation sites. The site also links to the office's budget, official speeches, congressional testimony, and publications. A Laws and Regulations section links to relevant legislation, compliance agreements, guidance documents, and regulations.
Subjects: Environmental Cleanup; Nuclear Waste
Publications: *EM Progress*, E 1.90/6:
EM State Fact Sheets, E 1.90/7:
Environmental Management, E 1.90/3:
Subsistence and Environmental Health, E 1.90/5:

1016. Office of Pollution Prevention and Toxics, EPA

http://www.epa.gov/opptintr/

Sponsor: Environmental Protection Agency (EPA) — Prevention, Pesticides and Toxic Substances Office

Description: OPPT has primary responsibility for administering the Toxic Substances Control Act. It offers substantial information resources related to hazardous chemicals and their environmentally preferable alternatives. A Concerned Citizens section presents consumer information on such topics as lead-based paint, consumer product labeling, and asbestos worker protection. The Information Sources section links to resources such as hotlines and clearinghouses. The Databases and Software page links to numerous electronic resources.
Subject: Toxic Substances

1017. Office of Prevention, Pesticides, and Toxic Substances, EPA
http://www.epa.gov/opptintr/oppts/
Sponsor: Environmental Protection Agency (EPA) — Prevention, Pesticides and Toxic Substances Office
Description: The EPA Office of Prevention, Pesticides, and Toxic Substances (OPPTS) is involved in protecting public health and the environment from potential risk from toxic chemicals. The office promotes pollution prevention and the public's right to know about chemical risks and evaluates pesticides and chemicals to safeguard children and other vulnerable members of the population, as well as threatened species and ecosystems. The site features top-level sections for Pollution Prevention, Pesticides, Toxic Substances, and Science Policy, along with other links for Concerned Citizens, Tribal Activities, Headlines and Deadlines, Right to Know, International Activities, Laws and Regulations, and Test Methods and Guidelines. A Kids, Students, and Teachers section offers a selection of educational material.
Subjects: Pesticides; Toxic Substances
Publications: *P2 News2*
Pesticide Reregistration Eligibility Decisions, EP 5.27:

1018. Office of Solid Waste and Emergency Response, EPA
http://www.epa.gov/swerrims/
Sponsor: Environmental Protection Agency (EPA) — Solid Waste and Emergency Response Office
Description: OSWER provides policy, guidance, and direction for the EPA solid waste and emergency response programs. The site covers such topics as Superfund and federal facility cleanups, brownfields, oil and hazardous substance spills, underground storage tanks, and safe waste management. The Laws and Regulations section has the text of related documents, with a focus on the Resource Conservation and Recovery Act (RCRA).
Subjects: Environmental Cleanup; Hazardous Waste

1019. Office of Water, EPA
http://www.epa.gov/OW/
Sponsor: Environmental Protection Agency (EPA) — Water Office
Description: As the primary EPA agency overseeing regulatory issues relating to clean water, the Office of Water's Web site features a variety of resources related to drinking water, water pollution, watersheds, wastewater management, and the security of the nation's water infrastructure. Subject access is available from the home page via a long list from the menu Water Topics. The site also includes areas such as Publications, Funding and Grants, Databases and Software, Laws and Regulations, and Education Resources.
Subjects: Drinking Water; Water Pollution

1020. Office of Wetlands, Oceans, and Watersheds, EPA
http://www.epa.gov/owow/
Sponsor: Environmental Protection Agency (EPA) — Water Office — Wetlands, Oceans, and Watersheds Office
Description: Working with partners to protect water resources, the Office of Wetlands, Oceans, and Watersheds works in a variety of water quality areas. Featured topics include Wetlands, Watersheds, Polluted Runoff, Monitoring Water Quality, Invasive Species, and Oceans, Coasts, and Estuaries. The Databases and Mapping section includes the Watershed Assessment, Tracking, and

Environmental Results (WATERS) database. Other resources include Laws and Regulations, Funding, Publications, and the Watershed Information Initiative.
Subjects: Water Pollution; Watersheds
Publication: *Coastlines*, EP 8.16

1021. Right-to-Know Network
http://www.rtk.net/
Sponsor: OMB Watch
Description: The Right-to-Know Network is sponsored by OMB Watch, a private nonprofit group focusing on the issue of government accountability. The site was launched in 1989 as a result of the Emergency Planning and Community Right to Know Act, which mandated public access to the Toxic Release Inventory. Under Databases, it provides searchable access to U.S. Government environmental data sets including the Toxic Release Inventory; Comprehensive Environmental Response, Compensation, and Liability Information System; Emergency Response Notification System; Accidental Release Information Program; Facility Index Search; Biennial Reporting System; and more. The Master Search searches all environmental databases on RTK Net.
Subjects: Toxic Substances; Databases
Publication: *Toxic Release Inventory*, EP 5.22

1022. Sector Facility Indexing Project
http://www.epa.gov/sfipmtn1/
Sponsor: Environmental Protection Agency (EPA)
Description: The Sector Facility Indexing Project (SFIP) brings together environmental information from a number of data systems that produce facility-level profiles for five industry sectors: petroleum refining, iron and steel production, primary nonferrous metal refining and smelting, pulp manufacturing, and automobile assembly. The available information relates to compliance and inspection history, chemical releases and spills, demographics of the surrounding population, and production. Featured sections include Data Access, SFIP Indicators, Acronyms, and Status and History.
Subjects: Industries — Regulations; Pollutants — Regulations

1023. Superfund Program
http://www.epa.gov/superfund/
Sponsor: Environmental Protection Agency (EPA) — Solid Waste and Emergency Response Office
Description: This EPA portal for Superfund information covers information about the program, the individual Superfund sites, law and policy documents, community involvement, regional contacts, databases, grants and funding, and even a Superfund Photo Gallery. The page also links to EPA's Record of Decision System (RODS) with the full text of the detailed documents concerning decisions and actions for individual Superfund sites.
Subject: Environmental Cleanup

1024. Toxics Release Inventory
http://www.epa.gov/tri/
Sponsor: Environmental Protection Agency (EPA)
Description: The Toxics Release Inventory (TRI) is a source of information regarding toxic chemicals that are being used, manufactured, treated, transported, or released into the environment. It contains information concerning waste management activities and the release of toxic chemicals by facilities that manufacture, process, or otherwise use such substances. The home page provides a quick ZIP Code search option for TRI data and a link to the TRI Explorer for additional search options. An section on International TRI contains background information on other nations with similar programs and on related multinational and international efforts.
Subjects: Toxic Substances; Databases
Publication: *Toxic Release Inventory*, EP 5.22

1025. TribalAIR

http://www.epa.gov/oar/tribal/

Sponsor: Environmental Protection Agency (EPA) — Air and Radiation Office

Description: This site from the EPA's Office of Air and Radiation provides information about air quality programs in Indian Country. It includes information on regional contacts, the Tribal Authority Rule concerning the Clean Air Act, relevant presidential documents, and the Tribal Air Monitoring Support Center. The quarterly *Tribal Air News* is also available in full text.

Subjects: Air Quality; American Indians

Publication: *Tribal Air News*

1026. TTNWeb Technology Transfer Network

http://www.epa.gov/ttn/

Sponsor: Environmental Protection Agency (EPA) — Air and Radiation Office

Description: TTNWeb provides centralized access to the technical information available on the Web from the EPA's Office of Air Quality Planning and Standards. These Web resources concern air pollution science, technology, regulation, measurement, and prevention. Sample resources include the Emissions Measurement Center, the Clean Air Technology Center, and the Air Quality System.

Subjects: Air Quality; Databases

CHAPTER 8
General Reference Sources

Government Web sites often include valuable reference tools—databases, catalogs, glossaries, and directories. This chapter covers general interest, ready reference, and other miscellaneous sites not included in other chapters. Most are designed for the general public and are non-technical. In addition, there are special sections for foreign affairs, museums and the arts, and recreation information. Related chapters include Finding Aids and Starting Points, and Libraries.

Bookmarks & Favorites

General
- Geographic Names Information System, http://geonames.usgs.gov
- Official U.S. Time, http://www.time.gov
- U.S. Government Manual,
     http://www.access.gpo.gov/nara/browse-gm-02.html

Foreign Affairs
- Background Notes, http://www.state.gov/r/pa/ei/bgn/
- CIA World Factbook, http://www.cia.gov/cia/publications/factbook/

Museums and the Arts
- Smithsonian Institution, http://www.si.edu
- Institute of Museum and Library Services, http://www.imls.gov

Recreation
- Parknet (National Park Service), http://www.nps.gov

Featured Site

1027. Consumer.gov
http://www.consumer.gov/
Sponsor: Federal Trade Commission (FTC)
Description: This First.gov for Consumers gateway site links to consumer information from numerous government agencies. Major topical sections include Food, Product Safety (recalls), Health, Home and Community (emergency preparedness, home heating, mortgages), Money, Transportation, Children, Careers and Education, and Technology. Consumer news headlines and popular topics (identity theft, telemarketing, and privacy information) are featured on the main page. Rumors circulate quickly around the Internet. Consumer.gov helps as an authoritative source for finding information about scams, product recalls, and reporting consumer fraud.
Subjects: Consumer Information; Finding Aids

The general reference resources in this chapter are divided into four sections, spanning the entry numbers indicated here:

General	1028–1048
Foreign Affairs	1049–1059
Museums and the Arts	1060–1081
Recreation	1082–1089

General

1028. Advisory Commission on Intergovernmental Relations

http://www.library.unt.edu/gpo/acir/acir.html

Sponsors: Advisory Commission on Intergovernmental Relations (ACIR); University of North Texas. Libraries

Description: The Advisory Commission on Intergovernmental Relations (ACIR) was established by Congress in 1959 to study the relationships between local, state, and federal government. The Commission was closed in 1996. The University of North Texas Libraries maintains this Web site to provide permanent public access to the electronic publications that were available on the ACIR's site. The site features a brief history of the ACIR, a bibliography of publications by and about the ACIR, and online versions of many ACIR publications. Editions of *Significant Features of Fiscal Federalism*, a reference tool for data on state and federal revenues and expenditures and federal spending in the states, are available in PDF format from 1976 through 1994 and Volume I of 1995.

The ACIR materials are accessible thanks to a partnership between the University of North Texas Libraries and the U.S. Government Printing Office to provide permanent public access to the electronic Web sites and publications of defunct U.S. government agencies and commissions.

Subject: Intergovernmental Relations

Publications: *Intergovernmental Perspective*, Y 3.AD 9/8:11/
Significant Features of Fiscal Federalism, Y 3.AD 9/8:18/

1029. Citizens' Stamp Advisory Committee

http://www.usps.com/communications/organization/csac.htm

Sponsor: Postal Service (USPS)

Description: The Citizens' Stamp Advisory Committee (CSAC) is the mechanism by which subjects are selected to be featured on U.S. postage stamps. CSAC receives recommendations, evaluates them, and makes recommendations to the PostMaster General. This U.S. Postal Service site has information about CSAC, a list of current members, and the formal criteria for stamp subject selection.

Subject: Postage Stamps

1030. Federal Bulletin Board

http://fedbbs.access.gpo.gov/

Alternate URLs: ftp://fedbbs.access.gpo.gov/gpo_bbs/
telnet://fedbbs.access.gpo.gov/

Sponsor: Government Printing Office (GPO)

Description: The Federal Bulletin Board (FBB) is an electronic bulletin board service (BBS) offered by the Superintendent of Documents, U.S. Government Printing Office. It enables federal agencies to provide access to information in electronic form. It requires free registration to access some of the files. Many of the files available from the FBB are also available from other Internet sources. There are over 100 different file libraries available through the FBB. Not all government agencies contribute files, but the ones that do include the Food and Drug Administration, Department of State, Department of the Treasury, Environmental Protection Agency, Merit Systems Protection Board, Federal Labor Relations Authority, Office of Government Ethics, Supreme Court, and the Federal Depository Library Program.

Although the interface, even via the Web, is not always easy to navigate, this site offers a substantial number of government publications. This source will most likely be used by those already familiar with the specific files that are available here.

Subject: Government Publications

Publication: *List of Classes of United States Government Publications Available for Selection by Depository Libraries*, GP 3.24:

1031. Geographic Names Information System

http://geonames.usgs.gov

Sponsor: Interior Department — U.S. Geological Survey (USGS)

Description: The Geographic Names Information System (GNIS) database has federally recognized names for physical and cultural geographic features in the United States and its territories. Geographic features are defined broadly and include populated places as well as airports, cemeteries, mines, lakes, rivers, streams, schools, beaches, and parks. For each feature, GNIS provides coordinates, state and county, and feature type. GNIS has similar information for Antarctica. The site includes the FIPS55 database, the Federal Information Processing Standard (FIPS) data processing codes for named populated places, primary county divisions, and other locational entities of the United States and areas under the jurisdiction of the United States.

Subjects: Geography; Reference

1032. Gov.Research_Center
http://grc.ntis.gov/

Sponsors: National Information Services Corporation (NISC); Commerce Department — Technology Administration (TA) — National Technical Information Service (NTIS)

Description: The GOV.Research_Center is a partnership between NTIS and the National Information Services Corporation that provides a single access point to a number of government databases. This is not a free service. Each individual database has its own pricing and subscription plan. Currently available databases include AGRICOLA, AgroBase, Energy Science and Technology, Nuclear Science Abstracts, Federal Research in Progress, NTIS, NIOSHTIC, and the Registry of Toxic Effects of Chemical Substances (RTECS).

Subjects: Scientific and Technical Information; Databases

1033. Information USA
http://usinfo.state.gov/usa/infousa/

Sponsor: State Department — International Information Programs Office

Description: Information USA is designed as a resource for foreign audiences seeking information about official U.S. policies, American society, culture, and political processes. It was designed as a CD-ROM that can be used with or without an Internet connection. The site features much of the information on the CD-ROM and includes sections such as About InfoUSA, Facts About the United States, Government and Politics, Economy and Trade, Laws and Treaties, Media, Information Technology, and Education in the United States, Civil Rights, Geography and Travel, and Arts and Culture.

Subject: United States

1034. NAICS—North American Industry Classification System
http://www.census.gov/pub/epcd/www/naics.html

Sponsor: Commerce Department — Economics and Statistics Administration (ESA) — Census Bureau

Description: The North American Industry Classification System (NAICS) is the official industry classification system to be used by the U.S. statistical agencies. Adopted in 1997, NAICS replaces the Standard Industrial Classification (SIC) codes used in government reports since the 1930s. This Web site is the central location for NAICS news and documentation. It includes a crosswalk of NAICS and SIC codes; information on the 1997 *NAICS Manual* and the 2002 revision; news of agencies' implementation of NAICS; and supporting documents. A NAICS Search provides for keyword and NAICS code number searching of the 1997 and 2002 *NAICS Manual* with links to display the code's hierarchy and description. A section called Ask Dr. NAICS has an email contact and answers to frequently asked NAICS questions.

   The NAICS site helps with quick code look-ups and is particularly helpful for updates on NAICS implementation.

Subject: Industries

Publication: *North American Industry Classification System*, PREX 2.6/2:

1035. National Atlas of the United States of America
http://www.nationalatlas.gov/

Alternate URL: http://memory.loc.gov/ammem/gmdhtml/census3.html

Sponsor: Interior Department — U.S. Geological Survey (USGS)

Description: The U.S. Geological Survey and partners created the online National Atlas to supersede a printed version published in 1970. Atlas options include interactive maps, multimedia maps, map layers data warehouse, printed maps, and printable maps. Themes and data are from a range of different federal agencies. Map layers cover a wide range of topics, from abandoned coal mines to wildlife mortality. The site also includes press releases on the status of the project, partner information, and a frequently asked questions page. See the alternate URL for a digitized copy of the 1970 *National Atlas of the United States of America* available from the Library of Congress American Memory collection.

This site is not geared toward producing reference maps that can be easily printed out. It does provide a simple and effective demonstration of the power of interactive mapping.

Subjects: Maps and Mapping; United States
Publication: *National Atlas of the U.S.*, I 19.111:

1036. National Capital Planning Commission
http://www.ncpc.gov/
Sponsor: National Capital Planning Commission (NCPC)
Description: The National Capital Planning Commission (NCPC) coordinates all planning activities for federal land and buildings in the National Capital Region that includes Washington, DC and the surrounding communities in Maryland and Virginia. The Web site features information on the commission in the following sections: About the NCPC, Commission Meeting Information, Planning Initiatives, Commission Actions, and Publications. The Information for Submitting Agencies section gives guidelines for submitting proposals and offers a calendar of submission deadlines.
Subjects: Public Buildings; District of Columbia
Publications: *Designing for Security in the Nation's Capital*, NC 2.2:
Extending the Legacy: Planning America's Capital for the 21st Century, NC 2.2:
General Guidelines and Submission Requirements, NC 2.2:
NCPC Quarterly (National Capital Planning Commission Newsletter), NC 2.11/2:

1037. National Endowment for the Humanities
http://www.neh.gov/
Alternate URL: http://www.neh.fed.us/
Sponsor: National Endowment for the Humanities (NEH)
Description: The National Endowment for the Humanities (NEH) is an independent grant-making agency of the United States government supporting research, education, preservation, and public programs in the humanities. The agency's Web site provides information on applying for NEH grants and background on their grants programs. The Apply for a Grant page has application forms, deadlines, and guidelines. The News and Publications section includes press releases, lists of new grants recipients, and articles from *Humanities* magazine. The Who We Are section includes a staff directory, a list of all past NEH Chairmen, and links to the State Humanities Councils.
Subjects: Culture; Grants
Publication: *Humanities*, NF 3.11:

1038. National Historical Publications and Records Commission
http://www.archives.gov/nhprc_and_other_grants/index.html
Sponsor: National Archives and Records Administration (NARA) — National Historical Publications and Records Commission (NHPRC)
Description: NHPRC is a NARA grant-making affiliate. NHPRC makes grants nationwide to help identify, preserve, and provide public access to records, photographs, and other materials that document American history. There are sections on what the commission funds, how to apply for and administer a grant, frequently asked questions, and the composition of the commission. The main page provides links to the programs of the commission, including archival grants, educational programs, fellowships, electronic records and preservation grants, and publications grants.
Subject: Archives — Grants
Publications: *Annotation, The Newsletter of the National Historical Publications and Records Commission*, AE 1.114/2:
NHPRC Annual Report, AE 1.114:

1039. National Technical Information Service
http://www.ntis.gov/
Sponsor: Commerce Department — Technology Administration (TA) — National Technical Information Service (NTIS)
Description: NTIS is one of the major government publishing arms, featuring hundreds of thousands of publications related to scientific, technical, engineering, and business information that have been produced by or for the U.S. government. However, since it is run on a cost recovery basis, many of its services require payment. Major sections of the NTIS Web site include: NTIS Products and Services, National Audiovisual Center, New Item Announcements, Hot Products, and a new Homeland Security Information Center.

The NTIS catalog can be searched via the Search Library, under NTIS Products and Services. Searches result in citations and full abstracts. Some publications may be available online free of charge, but most must be ordered for a fee. Users can also search subsets of the catalog such as the Business Collection, Health Collection, Computer Products, or Subscriptions.

The National Audiovisual Center is a searchable catalog of videos, audiocassettes, and other media products for education and training. The Homeland Security section of the NTIS site highlights selected documents, videos, and other material available through NTIS in a broad range of areas related to homeland security.
Subjects: Government Publications; Scientific and Technical Information; Publication Catalogs

1040. Official U.S. Time
http://www.time.gov/
Sponsors: Commerce Department — Technology Administration (TA) — National Institute of Standards and Technology (NIST); Navy — Naval Observatory (USNO)
Description: This Web site provides a quick way to find the current time in all U.S. time zones including the U.S. Pacific territories. Under the heading Time Exhibits, the site also links to some educational sites about time, clocks, daylight saving, and calendars. The site is a joint effort of the National Institute of Standards and Technology (NIST) and the U.S. Naval Observatory.
Subject: Time

1041. Plain English Network
http://www.plainlanguage.gov/
Description: The Plain English Network is a government-wide group working to improve communications from the federal government to the public. The idea is to use plain language, which can be understood at first reading. The intended audience is government agencies. The site has an online version of *Writing User-Friendly Documents*, available in PDF, HTML, Word, and WordPerfect formats. Site sections include How To, Example Library, and Reference Library. The Reference Library features links to government documents about Plain Language.

While intended for government writers, other writers will find this site to be a useful reference as well.
Subject: Writing — Policy
Publication: *Writing User-Friendly Documents*

1042. Plum Book
http://www.access.gpo.gov/plumbook/2000/index.html
Alternate URL: http://www.opm.gov/plumbook/
Sponsor: Congress — Senate
Description: *United States Government Policy and Supporting Positions*, commonly known as the *Plum Book*, contains data on over 8,000 federal civil service leadership and support positions in the legislative and executive branches of the federal government as well as departments, independent agencies, and government corporations that may be subject to noncompetitive appointment. It includes positions such as chairpersons, secretaries, department and agency heads and their immediate subordinates, policy executives and advisors, and aides who report to these officials. The directory is published every four years, following each Presidential election, for the Senate Committee on Governmental Affairs. The version hosted by the Government Printing Office, the primary URL cited here, is in PDF format. The Office of Personnel Management, the alternate URL cited, has the complete copy in ASCII text format as well as PDF.

Often used as a reference for individuals seeking government appointments, the *Plum Book* is also a source for finding basic directory information, general salary levels for appointed government officials, and expiration dates for some terms of service.
Subjects: Government Employees; Presidential Appointments
Publication: *United States Government Policy and Supporting Positions*, Y 4.P 84/10:P 75/

1043. Recipe of the Week, Navy Environmental Health Center
http://www-nehc.med.navy.mil/hp/nutrit/recipes/
Sponsor: Navy — Navy Environmental Health Center
Description: Despite the title, this government site offers an archive of recipes, in addition to a new recipe each week. The recipes meet dietary guidelines and contain nutritional information. The recipes are listed under the following categories: Entrees, Salads, Side Dishes, Soups and Stews, Dips and Such, Desserts, Breakfast, Appetizers, Beverages, Holiday, and Microwave.
Subject: Recipes

1044. Time Service Department
http://tycho.usno.navy.mil/
Sponsor: Navy — Naval Observatory (USNO)
Description: The Time Service Department site provides well-documented and authoritative reference information. A variety of links use the USNO Master Clock to provide an accurate up-to-the-second time reading. Under the What Time is It? heading, there is an option for the correct time in all the major U.S. time zones and a table for converting from Universal Time (UTC).

This site is useful for more than just checking the time. The section Sunrise/Set/Moon Phase provides a sophisticated interface for looking up local times for sunrise/sunset, moonrise/moonset, moon phases, and times for the beginning and end of civil twilight, a term that is defined under the FAQ link Rise, Set, and Twilight Definitions. Using a form entry, users can designate specific dates and locations within the United States to retrieve daily or yearly reports. This section also offers another option for entering longitude and latitude for non-U.S. locations for daily and yearly reports.

This is an excellent ready-reference resource for checking the time and for looking up specific sunrise, sunset, and moon phase times for specific locations.
Subjects: Sunrise and Sunset; Time

1045. TopoZone—The Web's Topographic Map
http://www.topozone.com/
Description: TopoZone is a commercial site that has scanned USGS topographic maps for the United States. The site has all USGS 1:100,000, 1:63,360, 1:25,000, and 1:24,000 scale map for the entire United States. While the scanned quality does not have the resolution of the print versions, this is still an important resource. Access to the maps is available by place name or by latitude and longitude. The interface supports zooming and moving to adjacent map sections.
Subject: Topographic Maps

1046. United States Government Manual
http://www.access.gpo.gov/nara/nara001.html
Alternate URL: http://www.access.gpo.gov/nara/browse-gm-02.html
Sponsor: National Archives and Records Administration (NARA)
Description: This page at the GPO Access Web site provides a search interface for editions of the *U.S. Government Manual* from 1997 to present. Through this page, users can conduct keyword searches of the current edition of the *Manual*, or any combination of previous editions. Search results provide access to the *Manual* in HTML/Text and PDF formats. Search terms are highlighted in the HTML/Text version of the search results. Users many also browse through the table of contents of each edition back to 1997–98; the alternate URL given here leads to the table of contents of the 2002–03 edition. Text and PDF versions of each chapter are available through the browse interface, but only the PDF version has the agency organization charts and other graphics.

This online version of a reference classic includes a section with personnel changes that occurred after the publication was printed. All the same, users will want to check more frequently-updated sources—such as agency Web sites—for current personnel information. The strength of

the *Government Manual* is in the descriptions of the agencies, how they were established, what they do, and the nature of their primary divisions, and also in the helpful appendixes.
Subjects: Federal Government; Directories
Publication: *U.S. Government Manual*, AE 2.108/2:

1047. United States Postal Service

http://www.usps.gov/
Sponsor: Postal Service (USPS)
Description: The Postal Service Web site features reference resources and services for the general public and businesses, including: Find ZIP Codes, Calculate Postage, Changes Address, Locate Post Offices, and Track/Confirm mailings. The Find ZIP Codes section includes a ZIP+4 Code Lookup form and a link to the City/State/ZIP Code Associations page and to a state abbreviation list. Under Grow Your Business, a Business Mail 101 section explains the classes of bulk mail. The Forms section has roughly 100 U.S. postal forms in PDF format, including Postal Service employment forms. Help, a small link in the upper right corner, provides quick links to reference information such as acronyms, abbreviations, glossaries, and frequently asked questions.

USPS publications and institutional information is under the heading About USPS and News. This includes employment information, contracting information, news releases, a stamp release schedule, and USPS newsletters and publications. Under Serving the Community in this section, there is a directory of postmasters and information on USPS facilities and the security of the U.S. mail.

The USPS Web site strongly emphasizes current products and services. There is less institutional information and even less of interest to stamp collectors.
Subject: Postal Service
Publications: *Annual Report of the Postmaster General*, P 1.1:
Comprehensive Statement on Postal Operations, P 1.2:P 84/
Domestic Mail Manual, P 1.12/11:
Glossary of Postal Terms
International Mail Manual, P 1.10/5:
Mail Room Companion, P 1.47/2:
Memo to Mailers, P 1.47:
Postal Bulletin, P 1.3:
Postal Facts, P 1.60:
ZIP+4 State Directory, P 1.10/9:

1048. World News Connection

http://wnc.fedworld.gov/
Sponsors: Central Intelligence Agency (CIA) — Foreign Broadcast Information Service (FBIS); Commerce Department — Technology Administration (TA) — National Technical Information Service (NTIS)
Description: This is a subscription-based service that features news and information from thousands of non-U.S. media sources. All items in this service are translated into English. Content includes newspaper articles, conference proceedings, television and radio broadcasts, periodicals, and non-classified technical reports. Some specific news sources are the Caracol Colombia Radio, Agence Haitienne de Presse, Der Spiegel, Izvestiya, Radio Nigeria, Xinhua, and Georgian TV1.

The Foreign Broadcast Information Service, a U.S. intelligence service, has been translating open-source foreign news reports for over 60 years. NTIS now secures copyright permission and pays royalty fees to originating news sources in order to make their full-text translations available online through World News Connection. Nonsubscribers are able to browse the titles of recent news items under the Review Latest Headlines section, but only subscribers have access to the full text of articles.

This is a very useful service for a number of audiences, but the cost of subscriptions keeps most of the general Internet public out. For the curious, there is an online form for requesting a one-time free trial for a seven-day period.
Subject: News Media — International

Foreign Affairs

1049. Background Notes
`http://www.state.gov/r/pa/ei/bgn/`
Sponsor: State Department
Description: This popular publication series of brief country overviews comes from the Department of State. Each country edition of *Background Notes* is consistently formatted, with facts and narrative on aspects of the geography, people, history, government, political conditions, economy, foreign relations, U.S. relations, and travel/business conditions. The site links to issues through an alphabetical list of countries showing the date of the latest revision. Most *Background Notes* have been updated within the past 2 years, but some may be older.

For this online version of *Background Notes*, the State Department has added links to additional country information from other sources. Click on the name of the country at the top of each edition to go to more information for that country. This additional information typically includes: Chiefs of State and Cabinet Members from the CIA site; the World Factbook entry, also from the CIA site; and a link to the relevant U.S. Embassy Web site. Some country pages also have links to State Department news releases or program information related to the country.

The *Background Notes* series is useful for bringing together basic historical, political, social, and economic information for each country, and the HTML format on the Web makes it easy to link to referenced resources. However, be sure to check the date of last revision for each country issue; there may have been significant changes in a country since the last update.
Subject: Foreign Countries
Publication: *Background Notes on (various countries)*, S 1.123:

1050. Bureau of Consular Affairs
`http://travel.state.gov/`
Description: The Bureau of Consular Affairs is concerned with the safety of U.S. citizens in foreign countries, and issues passports for U.S. citizens and visas for foreign citizens traveling to the United States. Their Web site has practical news, advice, and fact sheets about travel safety, applying for a passport, and U.S. visa programs. Most information is in HTML format.

Major travel warnings are posted at the top of the site. Under Services, there are full listings of any official Travel Warnings or Public Announcements regarding terrorist threats or other conditions posing significant risks to the security of American travelers. For each individual country, there is a Consular Information Sheet, a fact sheet with practical information such as the locations of the U.S. embassy or consular offices, the local crime risks, and relevant regulations for U.S. travelers. Under About Consular Affairs, there are links to the Web sites of U.S. embassies and consulates abroad.

The Travel Publications link leads to over 20 booklets or brochures converted to HTML. Other travel, passport, and visa links on the site include: tips for American students abroad; information on preparing for a crisis abroad; lists of doctors/hospitals abroad; lists of lawyers abroad; international adoption; Visa Waiver Program; Visa Reciprocity Tables; and Print Passport Application.

The Bureau of Consular Affairs site provides simple, straightforward access to essential travel information.
Publications: *Foreign Entry Requirements*, S 1.2:F 76 E/
Passports: Applying for Them the Easy Way, S 1.2:P 26/
Tips for Travelers to..., S 1.2:
Visa Bulletin, S 1.3/4:

1051. Central Intelligence Agency
`http://www.cia.gov/`
Alternate URL: `http://www.odci.gov/`
Sponsor: Central Intelligence Agency (CIA)
Description: The CIA Web site has information about the agency, its directorates and centers, employment opportunities, press releases, speeches and testimony, its FOIA Electronic Reading Room, and a CIA Homepage for Kids. There is a Virtual Tour of the CIA, Frequently Asked Questions, and a section about the CIA Museum. Full text, bibliographic, and order information for CIA maps and

publications is available under the Library and Reference section, Publications and Reports link.Two major reference publications are online in full text: *The World Factbook* and *Chiefs of State and Cabinet Members of Foreign Governments*. In addition, the *Factbook on Intelligence* has information on the history, structure, and operations of the CIA. The annual *World Factbook* has statistics and facts about the countries of the world, focusing on geography, people, government, economy, communications, transportation, military, and transnational issues. Each entry includes color graphics for the country's map and flag. Some data may be updated online between annual editions, but in general the online edition does not track elections or other changes that occurred since its last update. In contrast, the online directory *Chiefs of State and Cabinet Members of Foreign Governments* is updated weekly. Each country's entry displays the date of the last update. Both the *World Factbook* and the *Factbook on Intelligence* can be downloaded in entirety from the CIA site as zipped (compressed format) files.

The availability of *The World Factbook* and *Chiefs of State and Cabinet Members of Foreign Governments* makes the CIA site an important reference source.

Subjects: Foreign Countries; Intelligence Agencies
Publications: *Center for the Study of Intelligence (General Publications)*, PREX 3.17:
Center for the Study of Intelligence (Monographs), PREX 3.18:
Factbook on Intelligence, PREX 3.2:
Handbook of International Economic Statistics, PREX 3.16:
Reference Aid: Chiefs of State and Cabinet Members of Foreign Governments, PREX 3.11/2:
Studies in Intelligence, PREX 3.19:
The World Factbook, PREX 3.15/2:

1052. Country Studies: Area Handbook Series
`http://lcweb2.loc.gov/frd/cs/cshome.html`
Alternate URL: `http://memory.loc.gov/frd/cs/cshome.html`
Sponsor: Library of Congress
Description: These books, alternatively known as *Country Studies* or Army *Area Handbooks* are an excellent source of detailed information on other countries. Each work in the series covers a particular foreign country, describing and analyzing its political, economic, social, and national security systems and institutions, and examining the interrelationships of those systems and the ways they are shaped by cultural factors. Each study was written by a multidisciplinary team of social scientists. Intended as background material for the U.S. Army, the series includes such countries as Kuwait and Somalia, but does not cover Canada, France, or Italy. This site offers full-text search capabilities across all of the available books (currently 101) or any combination of these. The books can also be browsed by country name and then by table of contents.

With the exception of special reports on Macau and Afghanistan, the studies at this site are electronic versions of books published by the Federal Research Division of the Library of Congress between 1988 and 1998 under a program sponsored by the U.S. Department of the Army. There is no funding for further updates to the books, and the online content is not updated. Each online handbook is labeled with a "research completed" date at the beginning or a "date as of" as the end of each section of text to help the reader evaluate the reliability of its content.

Although these books have not been updated to reflect current events, they remain valuable reference tools for the cultural and historical information they provide. Each study also includes a selective bibliography for further research. The Frequently Asked Questions page should be consulted due to the unique publication history of the series.

Subject: Foreign Countries
Publications: *Area Handbook Series*, D 101.22:550-
Pamphlets: 550-nos. Country Studies, Bibliographies, etc., D 101.22:

1053. Department of State
`http://www.state.gov/`
Alternate URL: `http://dosfan.lib.uic.edu/ERC/`
Sponsor: State Department
Description: The State Department's Web site features these sections: About the State Department; Press and Public Affairs; Countries and Regions; International Topics and Issues; History, Education, and Culture; Business Center; Travel and Living Abroad; and Employment. The More

link under each section opens up to that respective section's Web page, which offers a broader array of categories. An Archives link on the top menu bar will access the Department of State's former Web site, as it existed before January 20, 2001. The alternate URL for this site leads to the DOS-FAN Electronic Research Collection at the University of Illinois at Chicago Library, which retains archived electronic documents from the U.S. State Department Web site. Reference sources on this site include a number of directories and country reports. Under About State, there are biographies of State Department officials, U.S. ambassadors abroad, and nominees for ambassadorships. Press and Public Affairs has a link to Major Publications, which includes annual reports such as the *Country Reports on Human Rights Practices, International Narcotics Control Strategy,* and *Patterns of Global Terrorism.* The Countries and Regions section has the list of foreign diplomats in the U.S., phone numbers for the State Department country offices, *Background Notes* on countries, and links to Web sites for the U.S. embassies and missions abroad. The site also includes information on the scholarly and cultural exchanges sponsored by State; travel, passport, and visa information; and information on employment opportunities and the Foreign Service Exam. The FOIA Reading Room can be accessed directly at http://foia.state.gov.

Despite the fact that the main page is set up to give quick access to popular topics, some information treasures at the State Department site are buried several layers down. There is a word search facility provided by FirstGov, but no site index. To gain an overview of what is available at the site, users may want to click on the "More..." link for each section to see an outline.

Subjects: Diplomacy; Foreign Policy
Publications: *Annual Report on International Religious Freedom,* S 1.151:
Background Notes, S 1.123
Battling International Bribery, S 1.2:B 31/
Country Commercial Guides (annual), S 1.40/7:
Country Reports on Economic Policy and Trade Practices , Y 4.IN 8/16:C 83/
Country Reports on Human Rights Practices (annual), Y 4.IN 8/16-15:
Diplomatic List, S 1.8:
Dispatch, S 1.3/5:
English Teaching Forum, S 21.15:
Environmental Diplomacy (annual), S 1.10:
Foreign Affairs Manual & Foreign Affairs Handbooks
Foreign Consular Offices in the United States, S 1.69/2:
Foreign Relations of the U.S., S 1.1:
Foreign Terrorist Organizations, S 1.2:
International Narcotics Control Strategy Reports, S 1.146:
Key Officers of Foreign Service Posts, S 1.40/5:
Patterns of Global Terrorism, S 1.138:
Standardized Regulations (Goverment Civilians, Foreign Areas), S 1.76/3:
State (monthly), S 1.118:
Telephone Directory, S 1.21:
Treaties in Force, S 9.14:
Treaty Actions, S 9.14/2:
U.S. Department of State Indexes of Living Costs Abroad, Quarters Allowances and Hardship Differentials, S 1.76/4:
U.S. Refugee Admissions Program for FY (annual), S 1.1/7-2:
Victims of Trafficking and Violence Protection Act: 2000, Trafficking in Persons Report (annual), S 1.152:
Voting Practices in the United Nations, S 1.1/8:
World Military Expenditures and Arms Transfers, S 22.116:

1054. DOSFAN Electronic Research Collection
http://dosfan.lib.uic.edu/ERC/
Description: The University of Illinois at Chicago's library, in partnership with the Federal Depository Library Program and the U.S. Department of State, offer this site, which includes archived electronic documents from the Department of State. It has also preserved the Web sites of the former U.S. Arms Control and Disarmament Agency and United States Information Agency (USIA). The

main sections of the site include Electronic Research Collections, Archived Agency Web Sites, Alphabetic Index, and Secretaries of State (biographies and pictures from Thomas Jefferson to present). The Electronic Research Collections provides topical access to the older publications, while the Alphabetic Index provides a combination of an alphabetical arrangement with some subject groupings.

Publications: *ACDA Annual Report to Congress*, AC 1.1:
Foreign Relations of the U.S., S 1.1:
United States Information Agency: A Commemoration
World Military Expenditures, AC 1.16:

1055. International Information Programs
http://usinfo.state.gov

Sponsor: State Department — International Information Programs Office

Description: The State Department's Office of International Information Programs (IIP) communicates U.S. policy and government information abroad. The leaders, citizens, and media of other countries are the principal audience for its site, which is available in English, French, Spanish, Russian, Arabic, and Chinese. The IIP site features foreign policy reports, statements from U.S. leaders, news of diplomatic developments around the world, and articles about U.S. culture. IIP also publishes a number of electronic journals: *Economic Perspectives*, *U.S. Foreign Policy Agenda*, *U.S. Society & Values*, *Global Issues*, and *Issues of Democracy*. Issues are available online back to 1996. A section on Foreign Media presents a weekly summary of editorials and commentary from foreign press and broadcast media concerning the United States. The Washington File section has daily U.S. diplomatic news, with an option to receive articles via email. An Educational and Cultural Exchanges section includes coverage of such topics as the Fulbright Program, Office of Citizen Exchanges, Requests for Grant Proposals, and International Cultural Property Protection.

   Although this site is developed for foreign audiences, U.S. readers will find some sections—such as Foreign Media on the U.S.—to be of interest.

Subjects: Foreign Policy; International Education; News Services — International

Publications: *Economic Perspectives*, S 20.16:
English Teaching Forum (quarterly), IA 1.17:
Global Issues (various languages), S 20.18:
Issues of Democracy (various language), S 20.20:
U.S. Foreign Policy Agenda (various languages), S 20.17:
U.S. Society & Values (various languages), S 20.19:

1056. National Security Archive
http://www.gwu.edu/~nsarchiv/

Sponsor: National Security Archive

Description: The National Security Archive is an independent nongovernmental research institute and library located at George Washington University. The Archive collects and publishes declassified documents acquired through the Freedom of Information Act (FOIA). Only a fraction of the Archive's holdings are online, nevertheless the online offerings are significant. Featured sections of this site include About (the National Security Archive), Publications, Freedom of Information Act, Documents, Internships, Research, and News. The Archive has an online collection called the September 11 Sourcebooks, with public and declassified documents on such topics as U.S. terrorism policy, the Soviet war in Afghanistan, and the U.S. hunt for Osama bin Laden. Other online collections are called Electronic Briefing Books and are found under the Documents heading. They cover such topics as Cold War events, CIA involvement in Latin America, nuclear history, U.S.-China relations, the Pentagon Papers case, Iran, and U.S. intelligence agencies.

   The National Security Archive provides a valuable research service offline, with its archive of declassified U.S. documents obtained through the Freedom of Information Act and its own print and microform publications. The online collections meet some popular information needs, and present documents in context with commentary identifying the people and events related to the documents.

Subjects: Declassified Documents; Foreign Policy; Freedom of Information Act

1057. Peace Corps

http://www.peacecorps.gov/

Sponsor: Peace Corps

Description: The Peace Corps sends volunteers to developing areas of the world to help people in these areas meet their basic needs and to promote mutual understanding. The Peace Corps Web site includes information about its history and management, but most of the site is dedicated to information for potential volunteers. There is a Volunteer FAQ section, and information on the nature of the work and countries served. The site has an application guide, and potential volunteers can request an application kit or apply online. The site also has information for returning volunteers and for relatives and friends of volunteers. A portion of the site is available in Spanish.

The Peace Corps Web site is well designed and full of accessible reference information for applicants and others. Under About the Peace Corps, there is a Peace Corps history and a Fast Facts page with a printable fact sheet about Peace Corps operations. There is background information on projects in each country the Peace Corps serves, and there are lists such as Notable Returned Peace Corps Volunteers and the colleges and universities with the largest number of Peace Corps Volunteers currently serving overseas.

Subjects: Foreign Assistance; Volunteerism

1058. U.S. Agency for International Development (USAID)

http://www.usaid.gov/

Sponsor: Agency for International Development (USAID)

Description: The U.S. Agency for International Development (USAID) is an independent agency that provides economic development and humanitarian assistance around the world. Their site is organized into sections called Who, What, Where, and How. To see the range of programs with which the Agency for International Development is involved, browse some of the headings on the Web site under "What." Each of the following sections, for example, gives brief descriptions of USAID projects by country: Democracy and Governance, Education and Training, Economic Growth and Agriculture, Environment, and Health.

Under the Where category, link to regions and then to Country Overviews for detailed information on USAID projects by country. The overviews include pertinent sections from the agency's submission to Congress in support of the president's budget request for their economic and humanitarian assistance activities. Additional agency information can be found under Who and How, with links to This Is USAID, USAID Reform and Reorganization, Partner Resources, and Business and Procurement.

An alphabetical list of the agency's publications appears under the What section. Most are in PDF format. One of the listed publications, The Development Experience System (DEXS), is a family of bibliographic databases with records for over 110,000 USAID technical and program documents. DEXS can be browsed by topic or country name and searched by title, document ID, and other fields.

Subject: Foreign Assistance

Publications: *African Voices*, S 18.66:
Agency Performance Report, S 18.2:P 41/
Congressional Budget Justification
FrontLines, S 18.63
SD Abstracts
SD Developments, S 18.67:
U.S. International Food Assistance Report
U.S. Overseas Loans & Grants Online (Greenbook)
USAID Yellow Book: Contracts, Grants and Cooperative Agreements

1059. Washington File

http://usinfo.state.gov/products/washfile/

Sponsor: State Department — International Information Programs Office

Description: The Washington File makes available U.S. government official texts, policy statements, interpretive material, features, and byline articles prepared daily by the International Information

Programs, U.S. Department of State. The site offers documents from the past two weeks in sections organized by topic and world region. A WF Search option leads to a searchable archive (the database formerly known as PDQ) with texts back to 1990. A WF Mobile Edition is designed to deliver headlines and summaries of major U.S. foreign policy statements, speeches, and reports to subscribers with handheld devices such as Palm Pilots, Pocket PCs, or Web-enabled cell phones.
Subject: Foreign Policy

Museums and the Arts

1060. Advisory Council on Historic Preservation (ACHP)
http://www.achp.gov/
Sponsor: Advisory Council on Historic Preservation
Description: The Advisory Council on Historic Preservation is an independent federal agency and the major policy advisor to the federal government in the field of historic preservation. Its site features the following sections: About the Council; ACHP News; the National Historic Preservation Program; Working with Section 106; Citizen's Guide to Section 106; Training and Education; Federal, State, and Tribal Programs; and Publications. The site has the full text of the Section 106 regulations, "Protection of Historic Properties," from the *Code of Federal Regulations*. An online guidebook, *Sources of Financial Assistance for Historic Preservation Projects*, has information on federal assistance and tax incentives, as well as information on local and non-profit sources of assistance. A Frequently Asked Questions section includes such questions as "How can I get my property listed on the National Register?" and "What are some sources of funding for the preservation of my historic property?"
Subject: Historic Preservation
Publications: *Federal Historic Preservation Case Law, 1966–2000*, Y 3.H 62:
Protecting Historic Properties: A Citizen's Guide to Section 106 Review, Y 3.H 62:8/
Sources of Financial Assistance for Historic Preservation Projects

1061. American Battle Monuments Commission
http://www.abmc.gov/
Description: The American Battle Monuments Commission (AMBC) is an independent federal agency responsible for commemorating the services of the American Armed Forces where they have served since 1917. The site has information on the National World War II Memorial in Washington, DC, scheduled for completion in 2004. The AMBC also administers 24 cemeteries on foreign soil and 27 memorials here and abroad. The site has photographs and descriptions of these locations, including the Korean War Memorial, Flanders Field American Cemetery, and Normandy American Cemetery. AMBC also maintains lists of those interred at the American military cemeteries overseas and those Missing in Action from World War I, World War II, Korea and Vietnam, and those who died in Korea. Some lists are online while other require contacting the AMBC.
Subjects: Monuments and Landmarks; Veterans' Cemeteries
Publications: *American Battle Monuments Commission Annual Report*, Y 3.AM 3:1/
World War II Memorial, Y 3.AM 3:2/

1062. American Folklife Center
http://lcweb.loc.gov/folklife/
Sponsor: Library of Congress — American Folklife Center
Description: The American Folklife Center in the Library of Congress is charged with preserving and presenting American folklife. The Center incorporates the Library's Archive of Folk Culture, a repository for American folk music. Its Web site offers a number of online collections. Featured projects include the September 11 Documentary Project, Veterans History Project, and the Save Our Sounds recorded sound preservation project. Many of the Center's publications are available online, and the site also features an extensive list of links to Web resources in Ethnographic Studies. The site index is particularly useful for discovering the full scope of this site's contents.

Subjects: Folklife Studies; Music
Publications: *A Teacher's Guide to Folklife Resources for K–12 Classrooms*, LC 39.9:
Folklife and Fieldwork, LC 39.9:
Folklife Resources in the Library of Congress, LC 39.9:
Folklife Sourcebook

1063. Hill Aerospace Museum

`http://www.hill.af.mil/museum/`
Sponsor: Air Force — Hill Aerospace Museum
Description: Located at Hill Air Force Base in Utah, the Hill Aerospace Museum collection currently includes a wide variety of military aircraft and missiles, assorted munitions and weapons, ground vehicles associated with aircraft/missiles, and thousands of other historical artifacts. Its site provides information on visiting, the hours of operation, and sections About the Museum, Educational Outreach, Volunteer Program, and From the Director. There are also sections that describe current exhibits and history of the base.
Subject: Aviation — History

1064. Institute of Museum and Library Services

`http://www.imls.gov/`
Sponsor: Institute of Museum and Library Services (IMLS)
Description: The Institute of Museum and Library Services is an independent federal agency that provides funding in support of all types of museums, libraries, and archives. In addition to online editions of the IMLS monthly email newsletter, *Primary Source*, the site provides access to grant information in the section Apply for Grants and Awards. There are several PDF versions of grant applications and guidelines including *General Operating Support* and *Conservation Project Grant Application Guidelines*. The Publications and Resources section includes conference papers, awards, annual reports, and other documents concerning libraries and learning opportunities as well as links to the sections Grants in Your State and IMLS Projects Online. A Closer Look section provides highlights of the month and information about what is happening in the states and online projects. In the section IMLS News, there are links to press releases and legislative updates, and to archived editions of the *Primary Source* newsletter dating back to 2000.

Those seeking funding for public museums and libraries should be sure to browse this site. The availability and type of past awards can help inform future applicants.
Subjects: Libraries — Grants; Museums — Grants
Publications: *Conservation Assessment Program, Grant Application and Information*, NF 4.2:
General Operating Support, Grant Application And Guidelines, NF 4.9:
Museum Assessment Program, Grant Application and Information, NF 4.11:
National Leadership Grants, Grant Application and Guidelines, NF 4.11/2:
Primary Source, NF 4.15/2:

1065. National Air and Space Museum

`http://www.nasm.si.edu/`
Sponsor: Smithsonian Institution
Description: The National Air and Space Museum offers information about the museum and its programs. The site features Visitor Information, About the Museum, Educational Services, Collections and Research, Membership, Exhibitions, and News, Lectures, and Events.
Subjects: Aviation; Museums

1066. National Archeological Database

`http://www.cast.uark.edu/other/nps/nadb/`
Sponsors: Interior Department — National Park Service (NPS); University of Arkansas. Center for Advanced Spatial Technologies
Description: The National Archeological Database (NADB) is a database of databases for the archeological and historic preservation community. It is sponsored by the National Parks Service and hosted at the University of Arkansas Center for Advanced Spatial Technologies. The reports section

includes references to over 240,000 reports on archeological planning and investigation. The National (Native American Grave Protection and Repatriation Act) NAGPRA Database section provides the full text of the Native American Graves Protection and Repatriation Act, up-to-date information on regulations and guidance, and summaries of inventory and repatriation activities. NADB-MAPS (Multiple Attribute Presentation System) is a graphical application that contains a variety of maps in GIS format showing national distributions of cultural and environmental resources across the U.S. by state and county levels.
Subjects: Archeology; Databases

1067. National Center for Preservation Technology and Training (NCPTT)
http://www.ncptt.nps.gov/
Sponsor: Interior Department — National Park Service (NPS)
Description: Part of the National Park Service, the NCPTT is concerned with the art and science of preservation in areas such as archeology and historic architecture. The Center's grants program focuses on the training, technology, and basic research aspects of preservation and conservation. The Web site has information on the Center and its grants program, and has the text of the Center's *NCPTT Notes* newsletter. The Components section of the site provides information on the Center's grants and activities in materials research, preservation training, and cultural resource information management projects. A Clearinghouse section has further information on the Center's grants and projects, but also features resource guides to other training, education, and funding opportunities and a database of laboratories that provide cultural heritage preservation analytical services. NCPTT provides rich information on its own programs and interests on this site, but also hosts information services of broader interest through it Clearinghouse section.
Subject: Historic Preservation
Publication: *NCPTT (National Center for Preservation Training and Technology) Notes*, I 29.136:

1068. National Endowment for the Arts
http://www.arts.gov
Alternate URL: http://arts.endow.gov
Sponsor: National Endowment for the Arts (NEA)
Description: The NEA site includes sections such as New on the Site, Learn About The NEA, Endowment News, Applications and Grant Forms, and Publications. Learn about NEA includes lists of grant recipients, NEA's appropriations history, and a Web directory of state and regional arts agencies. Topical access includes the sections Explore, Art Forms, and Cultural Funding: Federal Opportunities. The Explore page has art features and interviews and presents new work. Art Forms offers resource information, links, and archived material for a broad list of different art forms. The Publications page features various sections such as General Interest Publications, Arts Education Publications, Accessibility Publications, Research Notes, and Research Reports.
Subject: Arts — Grants
Publication: *NEA Annual Report*, NF 2.1:

1069. National Gallery of Art
http://www.nga.gov
Sponsor: National Gallery of Art (NGA)
Description: The National Gallery of Art (NGA) Web site features information about the museum along with a number of online exhibits. The Planning a Visit section includes location, hours, maps and information about how the NGA is organized and funded. A Collections section offers a search of the collections by author, title, or subject that can be limited to items for which online images are available. An Online Tour section has over 20 online tours organized by theme or artist. The Resources section covers a broad scope, with links to information on the Arts Research Library (with online catalog); the Center for Advanced Study in the Visual Arts; curatorial records; the Gallery's archives; the Slide Library; and press materials including news of current exhibitions and recent acquisitions.
Subjects: Museums; Visual Arts

1070. National Museum of African Art
http://www.nmafa.si.edu
Sponsor: Smithsonian Institution
Description: The National Museum of African Art features information about its collections and services. The site offers General Information, This Month's Calendar, Education, Exhibitions, and Museum Resources. The Exhibitions page includes online information and images of both permanent and temporary exhibitions.
Subjects: Museums; Visual Arts; Africa

1071. National Museum of American Art
http://americanart.si.edu/
Alternate URL: http://www.nmaa.si.edu/
Sponsor: Smithsonian Institution
Description: This site includes an electronic version of a number of exhibits, images of hundreds of works of art, and reports of upcoming and recent events. Featured sections include Treasures to Go, Collections and Exhibitions, Education, Study Center, Calendar, Membership, and Museum Information. The Study Center section features inventories, a section entitled Ask Joan of Art for people who have a question about American art, and an online version of the Museum's journal, *American Art*.

   With solid design, this is an informative and well-organized site.
Publication: *American Art*

1072. National Museum of American History
http://americanhistory.si.edu/
Sponsor: Smithsonian Institution
Description: The National Museum of American History provides images, online exhibits, and research information related to American history. The site features Virtual Exhibitions, The Music Room, Timeline, You and the Museum, Not Just for Kids, and Collections, Scholarship, and Research. Educational resources are available under You and the Museum section.
Subjects: Museums; United States — History

1073. National Museum of Natural History
http://www.mnh.si.edu/
Sponsor: Smithsonian Institution
Description: This Web site presents information on the National Museum of Natural History's exhibits, collections, programs, and research. The Information Desk has facts for visitors. The Research and Collections section features a collections database, bibliographies, and products of taxonomic and nomenclatural research at the Museum. Other sections include Exhibits and Educational Resources.
Subjects: Museums; Natural History
Publication: *Global Volcanism (monthly)*, SI 3.13:

1074. National Portrait Gallery
http://www.npg.si.edu/
Sponsor: Smithsonian Institution
Description: The National Portrait Gallery offers images of many of it portraits of presidents and other important figures in American history via its Web site. The online images are especially helpful since major renovations have closed the Gallery itself through late 2005. Major sections of the site are Information, Collections, Exhibitions, and Education. The publications sales catalog is under the Information section. In the Collections section, the *Catalog of American Portraits* and records of the Gallery's permanent and study collections are available for searching.
Subjects: Museums; Visual Arts
Publications: *Catalog of American Portraits*
Profile Smithsonian National Portrait Gallery News, SI 11.16:
The National Portrait Gallery Calendar Events, SI 11.15:

1075. National Postal Museum

http://www.si.edu/postal/

Sponsor: Smithsonian Institution

Description: The National Postal Museum is funded by the U.S. Postal Service, the Smithsonian's federal appropriation, and private gifts. The museum's collections include stamps, vehicles used to transport the mail, mailboxes, postage meters, and greeting cards. The Web site has information on the museum and its collections, online exhibits, historic post office photos, and postal-related games for kids. The Frequently Asked Questions section addresses questions about the museum and about stamps and philately.

Subject: Postage Stamps

1076. President's Committee on the Arts and the Humanities

http://www.pcah.gov/

Sponsor: President's Committee on the Arts and the Humanities

Description: The President's Committee on the Arts and the Humanities advises the Office of the President on issues relating to support of the arts and humanities. The committee directs research and recognition programs to demonstrate the value of the arts and humanities, and it works to stimulate increased private investment. The site has information on grants, awards, children's programs, committee publications, and committee membership.

Subject: Culture

1077. SIEM-L [email list]

http://www.lsoft.com/scripts/wl.exe?SL1=SIEM-L&H=SIVM.SI.EDU

Description: This email discussion list, sponsored and hosted by the Smithsonian, is for exchanging ideas on producing exhibitions.

Subjects: Museums; Email Lists

1078. Smithsonian Institution

http://www.si.edu/

Sponsor: Smithsonian Institution

Description: The central Smithsonian Institution Web site has links to all other Smithsonian museum sites and to information about its research facilities, archives, and other centers. The site includes information on the history of the Smithsonian, hours and locations of the Smithsonian Museums, and links to Smithsonian affiliate museums across the U.S. Some of the featured links include Museums, Research, Education, Events, Exhibitions, Publications, Visitor Information, Membership, Giving, and Shop. The Publications sections has selected items from its popular *Smithsonian Magazine* and information on its other major periodicals. Two sections that may be particularly helpful for researchers are listed in fine print at the top right corner of the site: About Smithsonian and Websites A-Z, an extensive index of Smithsonian Web sites.

The Web site provides an excellent overview of the Smithsonian's component institutes and programs.

Subject: Museums

Publications: *Smithsonian (Web Magazine)*, SI 1.45:

Smithsonian Institution Research Reports, SI 1.37:

Smithsonian Opportunities for Research and Study, SI 1.44:

Smithsonian Year, SI 1.1:

1079. Smithsonian Institution Research Information System (SIRIS)

http://www.siris.si.edu

Sponsor: Smithsonian Institution

Description: SIRIS provides quick links to specialized databases and information resources that are located on the many Smithsonian Institution Web sites. The resources are grouped by category: Smithsonian Libraries; Archival, Manuscript, and Photographic Collections; Smithsonian American Art Museum Research Databases; Specialized Research Bibliographies; and Smithsonian Institutional History.

Subjects: Museums; Databases

1080. Smithsonian Magazine: Explore Art, Science, and History
http://www.smithsonianmag.si.edu/
Description: This online version of *Smithsonian Magazine* includes the table of contents, columns, and articles and images from the print version. Each article is accompanied by links to additional sources and archived subject-related articles. The site also has an image gallery featuring photos by selected SI photographers, membership and subscription information, contests, shopping online, and an online version of the magazine *Kids' Castle*.
Subject: History
Publication: *Smithsonian Magazine*

1081. Smithsonian Office of Fellowships
http://www.si.edu/ofg/
Sponsor: Smithsonian Institution
Description: The Office of Fellowships has applications, lists of fellowship and internship opportunities, and announcements of the current recipients. The publication *Smithsonian Opportunities for Research and Study* is available online in HTML format.
Subject: Fellowships

Recreation

1082. BLM Wild Horse and Burro Internet Adoption
http://www.adoptahorse.blm.gov/
Alternate URL: http://www.wildhorseandburro.blm.gov/
Sponsor: Interior Department — Bureau of Land Management (BLM)
Description: This site provides information on excess wild horses and burros that are removed from the range to protect and maintain healthy herds and habitat of wild, free-roaming horses and burros. These excess animals are offered for adoption to qualified people through the Adopt-A-Horse or Burro Program. Potential owners can view the available animals online in the Adoption Gallery. The site has information on adoption requirements and on how to adopt in person or over the Internet. The next Internet auction time frame and bidding period are prominently displayed on the site.The alternate URL leads to the National Wild Horse and Burro Web page.
Subject: Wild Horses

1083. National Recreation Reservation Service
http://www.reserveusa.com/
Sponsors: Army — Army Corps of Engineers; Interior Department — National Park Service (NPS)
Description: The National Recreation Reservation Service offers reservation services for over 49,500 camping facilities at 1,700 different locations managed by the USDA Forest Service and the U.S. Army Corps of Engineers. Facility information typically includes reservation options, a park map, and information on services and amenities.

1084. National Scenic Byways Program
http://www.byways.org/
Sponsor: Transportation Department — Federal Highway Administration (FHWA)
Description: The Department of Transportation has designated certain roads as National Scenic Byways or All-American Roads based on their archaeological, cultural, historic, natural, recreational, and scenic qualities. This site provides information on the National Scenic Byways Program and has information on each of the designated roads or byways. It offers maps and descriptions of noteworthy sites along the routes. The Community section has material for development professionals on available grants and promotion assistance.
Subject: Highways and Roads

1085. National Zoological Park

http://natzoo.si.edu/

Sponsor: Smithsonian Institution

Description: The National Zoo's Web site features pictures of the animals on location, news, information about the Zoo, and information on animals and their natural habitats. A Giant Pandas section under the Animals heading has PandaCams, a history of giant pandas at the National Zoo, and Frequently Asked Panda Questions. Other sections include Conservation and Science, Education, Visit, and Publications. The site also links to the Smithsonian's Conservation and Research Center and Migratory Bird Center.

Subjects: Animals; Conservation Biology; Zoos

1086. ParkNet: National Park Service

http://www.nps.gov/

Sponsor: Interior Department — National Park Service (NPS)

Description: ParkNet, the official Web site of the National Park Service, is the primary source for information on America's national parks. These include national memorials, national battlefields, national seashores, national historic sites, and other designations. The Visit Your Parks section provides access to information on each of the individual NPS units by name, state, or interest (such as fossils, fishing, or battlefields). Individual parks have Web pages with printable travel guides, maps, and background information. The Links to the Past section describes significant people, places, and events associated with the national parks, and includes learning programs and information on historic preservation grants. The NatureNet link covers natural resources data and publications in the NPS. Its major sections are Air, Biology, Geology, Social Science, and Water. LearnNPS is the education and interpretation area, with a focus on teacher resources. Info Zone features general NPS information including a link to the Library Information Center, a September 11th Remembrance site, NPS regulations by topic, digital image archives, press releases, the daily NPS news sheet *Morning Report*, volunteer opportunities, and public use statistics for each of the parks. A Bookshop link on the main page leads to GPO sales information for NPS materials, and to a commercial site for purchasing the many non-government publications sold at NPS sites.

With its broad approach to the resources and heritage of the national parks system, the NPS Web site is relevant for many audiences, including travelers, scientists, history buffs, and teachers.

Subjects: Historic Preservation; National Parks and Reserves

Publications: *CRM (Cultural Resources Management)*, I 29.86/2:

National Register Information System, I 29.76/4:

National Register of Historic Places Bulletins, I 29.76/3:

Natural Resource Year in Review, I 29.1/4:

Park Science, Resource Management Bulletin (quarterly), I 29.3/4:

Preservation Briefs, I 29.84:

Yellowstone Wolf Project Annual Report, I 29.138:

1087. Recreation.Gov - Recreational Opportunities on Federal Lands

http://www.recreation.gov/

Sponsor: General Services Administration

Description: Recreation.Gov is designed to be the central source for recreation information from the federal and local land management agencies. A database of recreation locations can be searched by state, agency, or activity (boating, camping, fishing, hiking, etc.). Each record includes phone number, address, Web URL, description, and a list of recreational opportunities at that site. Additional links include Guide to Federal Recreation Passes, National Weather Service warnings, and state tourism Web sites.

Subject: Outdoor Recreation

1088. U.S. National Parks Reservation Service
http://reservations.nps.gov/
Sponsor: Interior Department — National Park Service (NPS)
Description: This is the official site for making reservations at and checking availability of National Park campgrounds and tours. Not all NPS campgrounds or tours are available via this system but for those that are, the reservation service allows online booking and reservations.
Subject: National Parks and Reserves

1089. USGS Recreation
http://recreation.usgs.gov/
Sponsor: Interior Department — U.S. Geological Survey (USGS)
Description: This site is subtitled "Your Science Gateway for Safe and Vital Enjoyment of the Outdoors." It serves as a portal to USGS and other government information relevant to outdoor activities. Sections include: Nature Watching/Exploration, Boating, Camping, Climbing, Fishing, Hiking/Biking, and Hunting. Resources include maps, weather data, bird checklists, tide predictions, safety tips, and educational information about geology.
Subject: Outdoor Recreation

CHAPTER 9
Health Sciences

Government health sciences Web sites serve everyone from research scientists to clinicians and the general public. Health science professionals have used government Web sites to expand a tradition of disseminating research information. Government information on the Web has also been a boon to the average citizen seeking authoritative medical information written in layman's terms.

Featured sites for this chapter include major agency home pages and focused consumer sites. Following a General section, other health sites are grouped into Disease and Research sections.

Bookmarks & Favorites

Consumer Information
- CDC Travelers' Health, http://www.cdc.gov/travel/
- healthfinder, http://www.healthfinder.gov
- MedlinePLUS, http://www.nlm.nih.gov/medlineplus/
- Nutrition.Gov, http://www.nutrition.gov

Databases
- CDC Wonder on the Web, http://wonder.cdc.gov
- PubMed, http://www.ncbi.nlm.nih.gov/entrez/query.fcgi

Major Agencies
- Centers for Disease Control and Prevention, http://www.cdc.gov
- Food and Drug Administration, http://www.fda.gov
- National Institutes of Health, http://www.nih.gov

Featured Sites

1090. Centers for Disease Control and Prevention
http://www.cdc.gov/

Sponsor: Health and Human Services Department — Centers for Disease Control and Prevention (CDC)

Description: This starting point for the substantial holdings on CDC Web sites contains information about the agency including links to all CDC's component centers, institutes, and offices (under About CDC). It features a Spotlights section for current topics of interest, such as bioterrorism. Other featured categories include In the News; Travelers' Health; Funding Opportunities; Health Topics A-Z; Publications, Software, and Products; Data and Statistics; Training and Employment; and Subscriptions. Other quick links from the top-level page point to the *Morbidity and Mortality Weekly Report*, the journal *Emerging Infectious Diseases*, and Health-Related Hoaxes and Rumors. This site also links to a Spanish-language CDC site

Researchers and others interested in finding information on various diseases, disease statistics, and disease prevention would be well advised to take a look at this site. The information is well organized, and the pages are easy to navigate.

Subjects: Diseases and Conditions; Epidemiology; Public Health

Publications: *Advance Data from the Vital and Health Statistics*, HE 20.6209/3:

CDC Fact Book

Chronic Disease Notes and Reports, HE 20.7009/6:

Emerging Infectious Diseases, HE 20.7817:

Fact Sheets (NCHSTP-HIV/AIDS Prevention Division), HE 20.7320/3:

Health Information for International Travelers, HE 20.7315:

MMWR Recommendation and Reports, HE 20.7009/2-2:

Morbidity and Mortality Weekly Report, HE 20.7009:

National Vital Statistics Report (monthly), HE 20.6217:

Summary of Sanitation Inspection of International Cruise Ships, HE 20.7511:

1091. healthfinder®
http://www.healthfinder.gov/
Description: healthfinder® is the government's consumer health information gateway Web site. This site is designed to assist consumers in finding government health information on the Internet. It links to selected online publications, databases, Web sites, support and self-help groups, and government health agencies. The selected links are intended to offer reliable health information sources for the public. The primary sections include Health Library, Health Care, Directory of healthfinder® Organizations, Just for You, and About healthfinder®. Health Library has links to browse health information by broad topics: prevention and wellness, diseases and conditions, alternative medicine, and featured topics. There are also links to special resources such as medical dictionaries, health and medical journals, a medical encyclopedia, and databases. Health care offers online information for the health care consumer: background on health care providers, ratings of hospitals and nursing homes, guides to health insurance, how to report fraud or make a complaint, and privacy issues. Just for You divides the offerings by age groups and special populations such as men, women, infants, teens, seniors, health professionals, and race and ethnic groups. The Directory section presents carefully selected health information Web sites from government agencies, clearinghouses, nonprofits, and universities.

This site is an excellent starting point for finding health information and information about health services at the consumer's level, rather than the more technical information available elsewhere for medical practitioners and researchers.

1092. MEDLINEplus
http://medlineplus.gov
Sponsor: National Institutes of Health (NIH) — National Library of Medicine (NLM)
Description: MEDLINEplus, the National Library of Medicine's Web site for consumer health information, presents information on more than 500 diseases and conditions and a guide to more than 9,000 prescription and over-the-counter medications. The core of the site is the Health Topics section, which provides portal pages on a wide range of health issues, and includes a medical encyclopedia. Other sections are Drug Information, Dictionaries (medical terms), Directories (doctors, dentists, and hospitals), News, and Other Resources, which includes links to MEDLINE and to a list of U.S. consumer health libraries providing services to local residents. There is also a link to a Spanish-language version of the site.
Subjects: Medical Information; Pharmaceuticals; Databases

1093. National Institutes of Health
http://www.nih.gov/
Sponsor: National Institutes of Health (NIH)
Description: The NIH site is one of the principal starting points for finding health sciences information from the government. The Web site features the following links: Health Information, Grants and Funding Opportunities, Scientific Resources, About NIH, News and Events, and Institutes, Centers, and Offices. The About NIH link includes an introduction to the NIH including an organizational chart, a downloadable video about NIH, and information about doing business with NIH. The News and Events link features an events calendar, special reports, and press releases. The Health Information link presents a variety of sections, which include Learn About Health Conditions, Participate in Research Studies, Look Up Drug Information, Call the NIH, Find Health Literature References, and Read About Special Programs, which offers information on rare diseases, women's health, and AIDS research.

The Grants and Funding Opportunities page features NIH funding opportunities and application kits, grants policy, and award data. Among other databases, the Grants page provides access to award data including the Computer Retrieval of Information on Scientific Projects (CRISP) database, a biomedical database containing basic information on current research ventures supported by the Department of Health and Human Services. CRISP contains records dating back to 1972.

The Scientific Resources category is broad and covers NIH intramural research news, research training information, a list of NIH research labs on the Web, and computer and network support for NIH scientists. The Institutes, Centers, and Offices section lists the many component NIH organizations.

The NIH is a significant research institution in health sciences and medical research. The NIH site contains important holdings of information about the NIH and its component organizations, but more importantly, the site contains an important body of sources in the health sciences for the general public, health science researchers, and health science professionals.

Subjects: Diseases and Conditions — Research; Medical Research — Grants
Publications: *Biotechnology Resources: A Research Resources Directory*, HE 20.3037/6:
CRISP Biomedical Research Information, HE 20.3013/2-4:
Diabetes Dateline, the National Diabetes Information Clearinghouse Bulletin, HE 20.3310:/3
Medical Staff Handbook, HE 20.3044:
NIH Almanac, HE 20.3016:
NIH Extramural Data and Trends, HE 20.3055/2:
NIH Guide for Grants and Contracts, HE 20.3008/2:
Summer Research Fellowship Program Catalog, HE 20.3015/2:
Telephone and Service Directory, HE 20.3037:
The NIH Record, HE 20.3007/3:

The health resources in this chapter are divided into three sections, spanning the entry numbers indicated here:

General	*1094–1176*
Diseases	*1177–1204*
Research	*1205–1232*

General

1094. Administration on Aging
http://www.aoa.dhhs.gov/
Sponsor: Health and Human Services Department — Administration on Aging (AoA)
Description: The AoA Web site features resources for the elderly, their families, researchers, students, and professionals working with the elderly. The top level highlights current news about programs, conferences, and policy initiatives. The Press Room contains press releases and fact sheets on such topics as elder abuse prevention and respite for caregivers. A Resource Room highlights major sections of the site, including: Alzheimer's, Senior Medicare Patrols, Eldercare Locator, Grants, and Statistics about Older people. The Eldercare Locator is a nationwide directory assistance service designed to help older persons and caregivers locate local support services for aging Americans. Additionally, a Resources for the Aging section contains references to program and policy-related materials relating to the Older Americans Act and the AoA.

This site includes a great deal of useful information on aging, the elderly, and health care for the elderly, including local referral to non-AoA organizations and resources.
Subject: Senior Citizens
Publications: *Administration on Aging Annual Report*, HE 1.201:
Age Pages, HE 20.3861:
AoA Update, HE 1.1017:
Information Memorandums, HE 1.1013:
Resource Directory for Older People, HE 20.3868:

1095. Air Force Medical Service
https://www.afms.mil/sg/index.htm
Sponsor: Air Force — Air Force Medical Service
Description: This site includes information about the U.S. Air Force Surgeon General and the Air Force Medical Service. Sections include Tricare, Leadership, Public Affairs, Business Tools, and SG/Air Force Doctrine on Health Service Support. There is also a link to the monthly newsletter of the Air Force Surgeon General, *Newswire*. The link Library/Knowledge Center—which requires logging in as a guest—leads to such sections as Document Archives, Policy Letters, Presentations, Video Library, and Virtual Library, where the visitor can access medical databases, book and journal list, and over 1,500 links to health sites.
Subjects: Air Force; Military Medicine

1096. Arctic Health
http://arctichealth.nlm.nih.gov/
Sponsor: National Institutes of Health (NIH) — National Library of Medicine (NLM)
Description: The National Library of Medicine's Arctic Health site is a central point for information on Arctic health and environment. Sections cover such topics as chronic diseases, behavioral issues, traditional medicine, and the environment, and point to resources available from NLM, elsewhere in the government, or other organizations. Defining the Arctic as encompassing all or portions of Alaska, Canada, Greenland/Denmark/Faroe Islands, Iceland, Norway, Sweden, Finland and Russia, this site is built on the premise that the populations of these countries are subject to a unique set of health and environmental challenges.
Subject: Arctic Regions

1097. Armed Forces Institute of Pathology
http://www.afip.org/
Sponsor: Defense Department — Armed Forces Institute of Pathology (AFIP)
Description: The Armed Forces Institute of Pathology is involved with education, consulting, and research in pathology. The Web site features information on its research and consultation services and its Department of Medical Education. Programs of the institute include research in basic science, environmental pathology and toxicology, geographic and infectious disease pathology, oncology, molecular diagnostics, and forensic science. The Publications page provides information on its print publications and online ordering. The online version of *The AFIP Letter* is located in the What's New section of the site.
Subjects: Pathology — Research; Military Medicine
Publications: *Legal Medicine Open File*, D 101.117/7:
The AFIP (Armed Forces Institute of Pathology) Letter, D 101.117:

1098. Army Center for Health Promotion and Preventive Medicine
http://chppm-www.apgea.army.mil/
Sponsor: Army — Center for Health Promotion and Preventive Medicine
Description: This site presents information about USACHPPM including its mission, products and services, training and conferences, publications, directorates, and subordinate commands. Much of the home page is dedicated to links on health risks and health promotion topics, such as flu season, biological threats, mold, and smallpox vaccination. Other topical information can be found in the fact sheets series of publications and on some of the directorate pages. Directorates include: Clinical Preventive Medicine, Epidemiology and Disease Surveillance, Environmental Health Engineering, Toxicology, Occupational Sciences, Health Promotion and Wellness, and Laboratory Sciences.

The site has a substantial amount of information on health promotion. Though targeted at a military audience, there is also useful information for the general public.
Subject: Preventive Health Care

1099. Bureau of Health Professions
http://bhpr.hrsa.gov/
Sponsor: Health and Human Services Department — Health Resources and Services Administration (HRSA) — Health Professions Bureau
Description: The mission of the Bureau of Health Professions (BHPr) is to ensure that health care professionals deliver quality services to all geographic areas and to all segments of society. It's site features the categories Opportunities (Grants and Student Assistance), Education and Training Programs, Resources, and Special Programs. The Resources category provides access to two online databases: Health Professional Shortage Areas and Medically Underserved Areas/Medically Underserved Populations. There are also links to related primary care sites: DHHS affiliated, general health reference, associations and foundations, clinician sites, medical references, and search tools. There are links to the National Health Service Corps (a program of the U.S. Public Health Service) and the National Center for Health Workforce Information and Analysis.
Subjects: Health Occupations; Medical Schools
Publication: *Health Workforce Newslink (quarterly)*, HE 20.9315:

1100. Bureau of Primary Health Care
http://www.bphc.hrsa.gov
Sponsor: Health and Human Services Department — Health Resources and Services Administration (HRSA) — Primary Health Care Bureau
Description: BPHC's mission is to increase access to comprehensive primary and preventive health care and to improve the health status of underserved and vulnerable populations. Its site features such categories as Key Program Areas, Funding, Resources, Databases, Documents, and Find a Health Center. Some of the key program areas are: Black Lung Clinics, Community Health Centers, Health Care for the Homeless, Migrant Health Centers, and Public Housing Primary Care Program. The online databases include Health Professional Shortage Areas, Models That Work, HRSA State Profiles, Mental Health, and Drug Pricing.
Subject: Hospitals and Clinics — Grants

1101. CDC Travel Information
http://www.cdc.gov/travel/index.htm
Sponsor: Health and Human Services Department — Centers for Disease Control and Prevention (CDC)
Description: This is a detailed resource providing for health information for travelers. It includes reference materials, information on diseases and disease outbreaks, geographic and country-specific health recommendations, vaccine recommendations, safe food and water, traveling with children, special needs travelers, cruise ships and air travel, and travelers' health hotline numbers. The reference materials provide access to the CDC's yellow book, *Health Information for International Travel, 2001–2002,* the Blue Sheet, *Summary of Health Information for International Travel,* and links to other international health information-related and nonmedical sites.
Subjects: Diseases and Conditions — International; Tourism

1102. CDC Wonder on the Web
http://wonder.cdc.gov/
Sponsor: Health and Human Services Department — Centers for Disease Control and Prevention (CDC)
Description: CDC Wonder on the Web provides a single point of access to a variety of CDC reports, guidelines, and even numeric public health data. The numeric databases can provide the numbers and rates of many diseases, including sexually transmitted diseases, cancer cases, and types of mortality and births in the United States. Users can request data for any disease and demographic group by submitting special queries against available datasets. CDC Wonder also provides free text search facilities and document retrieval for several important text datasets, including the *Morbidity and Mortality Weekly Report (MMWR)* from 1982 to the present, the Fatal Accident Reporting System, and the CDC Recommends: The Prevention Guidelines System.

To use the site, CDC Wonder recommends registering. There is no charge for registration, and there is also anonymous access available.
Subject: Public Health — Statistics
Publications: *MMWR CDC Surveillance Summaries (quarterly),* HE 20.7009/2:
MMWR Recommendation and Reports, HE 20.7009/2-2:
Morbidity and Mortality Weekly Report, HE 20.7009:

1103. Center for Biologics Evaluation and Research
http://www.fda.gov/cber/index.html
Sponsor: Health and Human Services Department — Food and Drug Administration (FDA) — Center for Biologics Evaluation and Research (CBER)
Description: CBER is charged to protect and enhance public health through regulation of biological and related products including blood and devices used in the collection, storage, and testing of blood and blood components, vaccines, gene therapy, allergenics, tissue, biological therapeutics, and medical devices. Its Web site features sections such as About Us, Products, Reading Room, Meetings and Workshops, Manufacturers Assistance, and Health Professionals Assistance. The Products section includes information on recalls and withdrawals, safety issues, product approvals, errors and accidents reporting, and adverse event reporting.
Subject: Medicine and Medical Devices — Regulations
Publication: *Center for Biologics Evaluation & Research Annual Report,* HE 20.4801:

1104. Center for Devices and Radiological Health

http://www.fda.gov/cdrh/

Sponsor: Health and Human Services Department — Food and Drug Administration (FDA) — Center for Devices and Radiological Health (CDRH)

Description: The FDA Center for Devices and Radiological Health is concerned with the safety and regulation of medical devices and electronic products that produce radiation. Major sections of the Web site are: Health Topics, with consumer information, recalls, and product alerts; Industry Assistance, with guidance documents and standards; Device Program Areas, with current initiatives and statutory information; and Radiological Health, including cell phone facts, mammography, and CT scans. A section on Information Resources includes databases, laws, and regulations. The databases include a listing of medical devices in commercial distribution and the searchable text of Title 21 of the *Code of Federal Regulations* covering Food and Drugs.

Subjects: Medical Devices — Regulations; Radiation — Regulations

Publications: *Office of Device Evaluation (ODE), Annual Report,* HE 20.4618/2:

Office of Science and Technology Annual Report, HE 20.4618:

1105. Center for Drug Evaluation and Research

http://www.fda.gov/cder/

Sponsor: Health and Human Services Department — Food and Drug Administration (FDA) — Center for Drug Evaluation and Research (CDER)

Description: The Center for Drug Evaluation and Research (CDER) Web site features a number of resources on pharmaceuticals. Key resources are highlighted on the top page. These include the "Orange Book" of approved drugs, a list of newly approved drugs, a list of current drug shortages, and the Inactive Ingredients Database. The Drug Information area includes these and other sources of information on drugs, including the full text of the *National Drug Code Directory.* Other sections on the top-level page include Regulatory Guidance, Specific Audiences, and CDER Archives. In Specific Audiences, there is information for the consumer on drugs and adverse reactions and warnings.

Subject: Pharmaceuticals

Publications: *CDER Report to the Nation,* HE 20.4701:

Electronic Orange Book: Approved Drug Products with Therapeutic Equivalence Evaluations, HE 20.4715:

National Drug Code Directory, HE 20.4012:

1106. Center for Food Safety and Applied Nutrition

http://www.cfsan.fda.gov/

Sponsor: Health and Human Services Department — Food and Drug Administration (FDA) — Center for Food Safety and Applied Nutrition (CFSAN)

Description: The mission of the Center for Food Safety and Applied Nutrition is to promote and protect public health and economic interest by ensuring that the food supply is safe, sanitary, wholesome, and honestly labeled and that cosmetics are safe and properly labeled. Its site features sections Overview, Program Areas, Special Interest Areas, National Food Safety Programs, and Interacting with the Center. The Program Areas section features pages for Biotechnology, Cosmetics, Dietary Supplements, Food Additives and Premarket Approval, Food Labeling and Nutrition, Pesticides and Chemical Contaminants, Seafood, and Foodborne Illness, which offers access to the *Bad Bug Book* and the section Microbiological Methods.

Subjects: Food — Regulations; Food Safety

Publications: *Food Safety Progress Report*

The Bad Bug Book: Foodborne Pathogenic Microorganisms and Natural Toxins Handbook, HE 20.4508:98020265

1107. Center for Veterinary Medicine

http://www.fda.gov/cvm/

Sponsor: Health and Human Services Department — Food and Drug Administration (FDA) — Center for Veterinary Medicine (CVM)

Description: The CVM regulates the manufacture and distribution of drugs and feed additives intended for animals. Its Web site includes sections such as Antimicrobial Resistance, About CVM, The

Green Book (the FDA Approved Animal Drug List), Food Safety Initiative, Guidance Documents, CVM Index, CVM Updates, Biotechnology at CVM, and Aquaculture. These sections link to information about the activities of CVM including surveillance and research of the food safety initiative, regulation of fish farming and biotechnology products for animal health products and feed, and developing guidance documents. In addition, the CVM Index offers such items as the *FDA Veterinarian* newsletter (in PDF format), the online booklet *FDA and the Veterinarian* (in HTML), Adverse Drug Experience Reporting summaries, and Information for Consumers pamphlets. This index and the Guidance Documents section act as a central location for public CVM documents of interest to animal drug developers and manufacturers, veterinarians, and pet owners.
Subject: Veterinary Medicine
Publications: *FDA and the Veterinarian*, HE 20.4402:F 73/
FDA Veterinarian, HE 20.4410:

1108. Chronic Disease Prevention
http://www.cdc.gov/nccdphp/index.htm
Sponsor: Health and Human Services Department — Centers for Disease Control and Prevention (CDC) — National Center for Chronic Disease Prevention and Health Promotion (NCCDPHP)
Description: National Center for Chronic Disease Prevention and Health Promotion works to reduce the incidence of such chronic diseases as diabetes, cancer, and heart disease. Other focus areas include arthritis, tobacco use, alcohol use, physical activity, and health issues for women and minorities. The agency's Web site describes it various programs, grants, research, and public health surveillance. The site has summary facts and graphs derived from its surveillance programs for behavioral risk factors, youth risk, behavior, cancer registries, and pregnancy risks. A publications section includes research and statistical reports in full text.
Subjects: Health Promotion; Preventive Health Care
Publications: *Chronic Disease Notes and Reports*, HE 20.7617:
Physical Activity and Health: A Report of the Surgeon General. Executive Summary,
HE 20.7602:P56

1109. Club Drugs
http://www.clubdrugs.org/
Sponsor: National Institutes of Health (NIH) — National Institute on Drug Abuse (NIDA)
Description: This NIDA-sponsored site offers information on club drugs, drugs being used by young adults at all-night dance parties such as raves and at dance clubs and bars. These are defined as including MDMA (Ecstasy), Rohypnol, GHB, ketamine, methamphetamine, and LSD. Much of the site concerns NIDA efforts and information on Ecstasy.
Subjects: Drug Abuse; Ecstasy (Drug)

1110. Combined Health Information Database (CHID)
http://chid.nih.gov/
Description: CHID is a bibliographic database produced by health-related agencies of the federal government. This database provides titles, abstracts, and availability information for health information and health education resources. The value of this database is that it lists a wealth of health promotion and education materials and program descriptions that are not indexed elsewhere. New records are added quarterly and current listings are checked regularly to help ensure that all entries are up to date and still available from their original sources. Some older records are retained for archival purposes. The database can be searched in two ways. Simple Search searches on a single word or topic. The Detailed Search can be used for multiple words or multiple topics.
Subjects: Health Promotion; Databases

1111. Department of Health and Human Services
http://www.hhs.gov/
Sponsor: Health and Human Services Department
Description: The Health and Human Services site is a major resource for all the areas in health and social services that the department oversees. It uses the following topics for access to more detailed information: Diseases and Conditions; Safety and Wellness; Drug and Food Information; Disasters and Emergencies; Families and Children; Aging; and Specific Populations. It also has major sections

for: Grants and Funding; Reference Collections; Resource Locators; Policies and Regulations; and About HHS. A top-page link to All HHS News leads to press releases, fact sheets, speeches, testimony, and news from HHS agencies.

Subjects: Public Health; Social Services

Publications: *National Committee on Vital and Health Statistics (NCVHS) Accomplishments in... (annual)*, HE 20.6211:

Office of Research Integrity, Annual Report, HE 20.1/3:

Quick Draw, HE 1.65:

1112. DIRLINE: Directory of Health Organizations
http://dirline.nlm.nih.gov/

Sponsor: National Institutes of Health (NIH) — National Library of Medicine (NLM)

Description: DIRLINE (Directory of Information Resources Online) is the NLM's online database containing location and descriptive information about resources, including organizations, research resources, projects, and databases concerned with health and biomedicine. The approximately 10,000 records focus primarily on health and biomedicine, although limited coverage of some other special interests is provided as well. The database can be searched by phrase and keyword, or users may browse through database records by using subject words including Medical Subject Headings or searching for the name or location of a resource.

Subjects: Medical Information; Databases

1113. DOE Openness: Human Radiation Experiments
http://www.eh.doe.gov/ohre/

Sponsor: Energy Department

Description: This Energy Department project identifies and catalogs the federal government records of human radiation experimentation from the Cold War era. This site makes some of these documents available online. For access to this database of declassified documents, the Human Radiation Experiments Information Management System (HREX) offers simple searches, fielded searching, and the ability to select particular databases. HREX also has a tutorial. The actual records have been scanned and then run through optical character recognition software.

This site presents a treasure trove of primary material for researchers. The search interface is functional and links to scanned images of the original documents.

Subject: Radiation Exposure

Publications: *Advisory Committee on Human Radiation Experiments, Final Report*, Pr 42.8:R 11/H 88/

Human Radiation Experiments: The Department of Energy Roadmap to the Story and the Records, E 1.20/3:

1114. Electronic Orange Book
http://www.fda.gov/cder/ob/default.htm

Sponsor: Health and Human Services Department — Food and Drug Administration (FDA) — Center for Drug Evaluation and Research (CDER)

Description: This online version of *Approved Drug Products with Therapeutic Equivalence Evaluations*, known as the FDA Orange Book, includes information on prescription drugs, over-the-counter drugs, and discontinued drugs. Users can search by the following categories: Active Ingredient, Applicant Holder, Proprietary Name, or Application Number. The result categories include Active Ingredient, Dosage Form and Route, Applicant Holder, Proprietary Name, Strength, Application Number, Therapeutic Equivalents, and Reference Listed Drug. This is a useful database for verifying FDA approval of a drug and for seeing how long it has been approved.

Subjects: Pharmaceuticals; Databases

Publication: *Approved Drug Product With Therapeutic Equivalence Evaluations*, HE 20.4715:

1115. Environmental Health Information Service
http://ehp.niehs.nih.gov/

Sponsor: National Institutes of Health (NIH) — National Institute of Environmental Health Sciences (NIEHS)

Description: The Environmental Health Information Service (EHIS) produces, maintains, and disseminates information on the environment. A subscription-based site, subscribers have access to

online versions of publications such as *Environmental Health Perspectives* and its supplements, *National Toxicology Program Reports,* the *9th Report on Carcinogens,* and databases such as NTP Chemical Health and Safety Database and NTP Rodent Historical Control Database. Selected articles and publications are available free to nonsubscribers.
Subject: Environmental Health
Publications: *Environmental Health Perspectives*, HE 20.3559:
National Toxicology Program, Technical Reports, HE 20.3564:
National Toxicology Program, Toxicity Report, HE 20.3564/2:
Report on Carcinogens... Summary, HE 20.3562:

1116. FDA Consumer
http://www.fda.gov/fdac/fdacindex.html
Sponsor: Health and Human Services Department — Food and Drug Administration (FDA)
Description: This site links to issues of the *FDA Consumer* dating back to 1985. Many, but not all, of these older issues are available in their entirety in ASCII text. Since the July/August 1995 issue, the full text of FDA Consumer is available in HTML along with selected graphics. This site also includes an index to the magazine from 1985 to the present, special issues of *FDA Consumer,* and subscription information. The site also notes that in many cases, the *FDA Consumer* articles on the Web site are updated as new information becomes available and thus will not be identical to the original printed version.

This is a frequently referenced title and having an electronic version available and accessible is an important public service on the part of the FDA.
Subjects: Consumer Information; Health Products
Publication: *FDA Consumer*, HE 20.4010:

1117. Federal Occupational Health
http://www.foh.dhhs.gov/
Sponsor: Health and Human Services Department — Health Resources and Services Administration (HRSA)
Description: The Federal Occupational Health (FOH) provides occupational health services to federal government managers and their employees. The site includes Who We Are, What We Do, Library, and Member Center (for certain subscription content services). The Library section links to over 75 FOH fact sheets and Web pages addressing such topics as: anthrax information, ergonomics, emergency planning, diabetes awareness, stress management, and helping others cope with grief.

Many of the items in the Library section of this site may also be useful to managers and employees outside the federal government.
Subjects: Government Employees; Health Promotion

1118. Food and Drug Administration
http://www.fda.gov/
Sponsor: Health and Human Services Department — Food and Drug Administration (FDA)
Description: The FDA regulates the quality and safety of food and drugs, and also regulates cosmetics, medical devices, animal feed, and veterinary drugs. The FDA Web site features news, safety alerts, product recalls, statutes and regulations, and a variety of paths to information on its regulated product areas. The site map organizes links under the headings: About FDA, Interacting with FDA, News, Hot Topics, Enforcement Activities, Products Regulated by the FDA, Major Initiatives, and Publications. There are links to Information for Specialized Audiences, including AIDS patients, cancer patients, health professionals, industry, and the press. The site links to the specialized offices that make up the FDA, FDA field offices, and the FDA advisory committees.
Subjects: Food — Regulations; Pharmaceuticals — Regulations
Publications: *FDA Consumer*, HE 20.4010:
FDA Enforcement Reports, HE 20.4039:
FDA Medical Bulletin, HE 20.4003/3:

1119. Food and Nutrition Information Center
http://www.nal.usda.gov/fnic/
Sponsor: Agriculture Department (USDA) — National Agricultural Library (NAL)

Description: The FNIC site provides information to the consumer on the topics of food, food safety, nutrition, food labels, and school meals. The site includes the full text of the *Nutrition and Your Health: Dietary Guidelines for Americans*, 2000, 5th Edition. Other categories include Food Composition, Dietary Supplements, Dietary Guidelines, Food Guide Pyramid, FNIC Resource Lists, and Food Safety. There are links to several resource systems: Child Care Nutrition, WIC Works, and Healthy School Meals, and also to some databases of training and educational materials.
Subject: Nutrition
Publication: *Food and Nutrition Research Briefs*, A 17.30:

1120. Food Safety and Inspection Service
http://www.fsis.usda.gov/
Sponsor: Agriculture Department (USDA) — Food Safety and Inspection Service (FSIS)
Description: FSIS is a public health regulatory agency in the Department of Agriculture responsible for ensuring that meat, poultry, and egg products are safe, wholesome, and accurately labeled. The FSIS Web site offers information concerning the agency, its activities, and food safety issues. Main categories include FSIS Mission and Activities, News and Information, Consumer Education and Information, Publications, and Organization and Program Areas. These sections contain a number of online fact sheets, newsletters, regulations, and consumer information. The site offers access to the Recall Information Center section, which includes a recall database, and a Featured Topic category that links to current topics in the news regarding food safety.

In addition the site offers campaign materials, art kit materials, and resource materials for educators, industry, and the media for Thermy,™ the messenger of a national consumer education campaign designed to promote the use of food thermometers.

For anyone concerned with food safety issues, this site offers relevant information.
Subject: Food Safety
Publications: *Food Safety Educator*, A 110.19:
Food Standards and Labeling Policy Book, A 110.18:

1121. Food Stamp Nutrition Connection
http://www.nal.usda.gov/fnic/foodstamp/
Sponsor: Agriculture Department (USDA) — National Agricultural Library (NAL)
Description: The Food Stamp Nutrition Connection site is designed for Food Stamp Program nutrition education providers, but it includes excellent resources for anyone looking for nutrition information. The Hot Topics A-Z section points to selected Web sites covering topics such as elderly nutrition, obesity, and food security. The Resource Library section has educational materials in PDF format on topics such as dietary quality, meal planning, and safe food storage. Other materials on the site, such as seminar listings and state program links, will be of most interest to the intended audience of Food Stamp Program nutrition educators.
Subject: Nutrition

1122. Green Book
http://www.fda.gov/cvm/greenbook/greenbook.html
Sponsor: Health and Human Services Department — Food and Drug Administration (FDA) — Center for Veterinary Medicine (CVM)
Description: The FDA Approved Animal Drug List, the Green Book, is available online in searchable form. This database includes records for all animal drug products approved for safety and effectiveness by the FDA. Access to the Green Book is by chapters, which include tradenames and sponsors, active ingredients, patent information, and more. Access by keyword searching is also available. The visitor can also access the FDA Approved Animal Drug Products Online Database System, which includes information about tradename(s), ingredient(s), approved species, route(s) of administration, dose forms, and indications (*Code of Federal Regulations* information).

This is a useful database for veterinarians and anyone interested in official FDA information on specific animal drugs.
Subject: Veterinary Medicine

1123. Health Resources and Services Administration

http://www.hrsa.gov/

Sponsor: Health and Human Services Department — Health Resources and Services Administration (HRSA)

Description: This site includes information in the main categories entitled Key Program Areas, Resources, Funding, Focus On, and Centers. Under these categories, there are sections entitled About HRSA, News Room, Grants, Contracts, Key Staff, Job Opportunities, Data and Statistics, and Publications. Most of the information available from the site describes the agency and its component bureaus. Under Key Program Areas, there are links to the main bureaus of the agency: Bureau of Primary Health Care, Bureau of Health Professions, Maternal and Child Health Bureau, and the HIV/AIDS Bureau. Some of the offices and centers within HRSA include Minority Health, Rural Health Policy, Advancement of Telehealth, Quality, Public Health Practice, and Health Services Financing and Managed Care.

The Information Center page offers access to publications, which include the HSRA catalog and various newsletters, and a database of resources and referral organizations. Other categories include Featured Data Sources and Selected Grant Programs. Featured Data Sources include HRSA State Profiles, Community Health Status Indicators, and State Health Worker Profiles.

Subject: Public Health

Publications: *EMSC (Emergency Medical Services for Children) News*, HE 20.9212:
HRSA Publications Catalog
HSRA (Health Resources and Services Administration) Key Staff Directory, HE 20.9015:
Preview, HE 20.9018:

1124. Health Services/Technology Assessment Text

http://text.nlm.nih.gov/

Alternate URL: ftp://nlmpubs.nlm.nih.gov/hstat/

Sponsor: National Institutes of Health (NIH) — National Library of Medicine (NLM)

Description: Health Services/Technology Assessment Text (HSTAT) is a searchable collection of clinical practice guideline documents, technology assessment reports, and other health information. Sample contents include Reports of the Surgeon General, HIV/AIDS Treatment Information Service (ATIS) federally approved treatment guidelines, and evidence reports and technology assessments from the Agency for Healthcare Research and Quality (AHRQ). The Contents section provides a complete alphabetical lists of the documents indexed in HSTAT.

HSTAT also provides links to external databases, including the National Library of Medicine's (NLM) PubMed®, the Centers for Disease Control and Prevention (CDC) Prevention Guidelines Database, and the National Guideline Clearinghouse. These databases can be searched simultaneously with the HSTAT documents.

Subject: Clinical Medicine

Publications: *Clinical Practice Guidelines*, HE 20.6520:
Guide to Clinical Preventive Services, HE 1.6/3:C 61/3
Health Technology Assessment, HE 20.6512/7:
Quick Reference Guides for Clinicians, HE 20.6520/2:

1125. HealthierUS.gov

http://www.healthierus.gov

Sponsor: Health and Human Services Department

Description: The HealthierUS site was set up to promote public health with basic information on healthy habits. The major sections are Physical Fitness, Nutrition, Prevention, and Avoiding Risky Behaviors. Each section provides a brief narrative and links to information from federal health agencies.

Subject: Health Promotion

1126. Healthy People 2010

http://www.healthypeople.gov/

Sponsor: Health and Human Services Department

Description: Healthy People 2010 is a national health promotion and disease prevention initiative. The site features the following sections: About Healthy People, Be A Healthy Person, Leading Health

Indicators, Implementation, Data, and Publications. The Publications page gives access the initiative's publications (available in PDF, RTF, HTML, or Word formats), some of which are *Healthy People 2010 Vols. I, II*, and the *Healthy People 2010 Toolkit*. The Data section has information about the data being collected, the sources of the data, progress reviews, and provides access to the DATA2010 database.

Subjects: Health and Safety — Statistics; Health Promotion

1127. HRSA Women's Health

http://www.hrsa.gov/womenshealth/

Sponsor: Health and Human Services Department — Health Resources and Services Administration (HRSA)

Description: The Office on Women's Health coordinates the programs concerning women's health issues that are conducted throughout the HHS Health Resources and Services Administration. Major sections of the site are Funding, Publications, Contacts, News and Events, and Links.

This site provides a central location for news of HRSA programs for women. It should be of interest to professionals who manage women's health care assistance programs.

Subjects: Health Care — Grants; Women

Publication: *A Guide to the Clinical Care of Women with HIV, 2001, First Edition*

1128. Indian Health Service

http://www.ihs.gov/

Sponsor: Health and Human Services Department — Indian Health Services (IHS)

Description: As the primary federal agency responsible for providing federal health care services to American Indians and Alaska Natives, the IHS site provides a variety of information resources. Features areas include About the IHS, Area Offices and Facilities, Information Technology Resources, Press and Public Relations, Jobs and Scholarships, Resources for HIS Management, Medical and Professional Programs, and Nationwide Programs and Initiatives. Press and Public Relations includes press releases, biographies, and publications and reports. Available IHS publications include the monthly *The IHS Primary Care Provider* from 1997.

Subjects: Health Care; American Indians

Publications: *Regional Differences In Indian Health*, HE 20.319:
The IHS Primary Care Provider, HE 20.320:
Trends In Indian Health, HE 20.316:

1129. Initiative to Eliminate Racial and Ethnic Disparities in Health

http://raceandhealth.hhs.gov/

Alternate URL: http://www.omhrc.gov/

Sponsor: Health and Human Services Department

Description: In February 1998, President Clinton announced a goal that by the year 2010 the government would eliminate the disparities in six areas of health status experienced by racial and ethnic minority populations while continuing the progress made in improving the overall health of the American people. The Web site included information about the initiative, meetings, grants, and descriptions of the six areas: Infant Mortality, Cancer Management, Cardiovascular Disease, Diabetes, HIV Infection, and Immunizations. The Web page for the HHS Initiative to Eliminate Racial and Ethnic Disparities has posted a notice, which has been posted for at least one year, that the site is under revision. The notice states that a new site will be launched in 2003. In the meantime, visitors are directed to the Office of Minority Health Web site (listed elsewhere), where information is available from the U.S. Department of Health and Human Services on minority health and health disparities.

Subjects: Health Care — Policy; Minority Groups

1130. Insure Kids Now

http://www.insurekidsnow.gov/

Sponsor: Health and Human Services Department — Health Resources and Services Administration (HRSA)

Description: This site provides information on the federal government's efforts to promote health insurance coverage for children. It links to information on children's health insurance programs in each state and also includes messages promoting children's health insurance and offers answers to a variety of questions about insurance for children. Sections include About Insure Kids Now, Help Us Spread the Word, and Your State's Program.

Subjects: Health Insurance; Child Health and Safety

1131. Maternal and Child Health Bureau

http://www.mchb.hrsa.gov/

Sponsor: Health and Human Services Department — Health Resources and Services Administration (HRSA) — Maternal and Child Health Bureau

Description: The Maternal and Child Health Bureau administers Title V of the Social Security Act, which provides federal support to the states for health services for mothers and children. The Programs section of this site describes Title V and the bureau's objectives and programs. The Funding section describes available grants and provides guidance and forms. The Data section reports statistical indicators of maternal and child health.

Subjects: Motherhood; Child Health and Safety

Publications: *Title V Today*, HE 20.9215:

Title V: A Snapshot of Maternal and Child Health 2000

1132. MedWatch: the FDA Safety Information and Adverse Event Reporting Program

http://www.fda.gov/medwatch/

Sponsor: Health and Human Services Department — Food and Drug Administration (FDA)

Description: MedWatch is an initiative designed to provide clinical information about safety issues involving medical products to health care professionals and the public. Also, MedWatch allows both these groups to report adverse events and problems to the FDA. The site includes sections such as About MedWatch, What's New in the Past Two Weeks, How to Report, Submit Report, Download Forms, Safety Information, and Articles and Other Publications.

Subject: Medicine and Medical Devices — Regulations

1133. Mine Safety and Health Administration

http://www.msha.gov/

Sponsor: Labor Department — Mine Safety and Health Administration (MSHA)

Description: The MSHA is charged with enforcing safety and health standards at mines with the intent to eliminate fatal accidents, to reduce the frequency and severity of nonfatal accidents, to minimize health hazards, and to promote improved safety and health conditions in U.S. mines. The site features agency information, news releases, speeches, special reports, forms, congressional testimony, statutory and regulatory information, MSHA regulations, MSHA handbooks, Program Information Bulletins, safety and health information, hazard alerts and bulletins, Fatal Alert Bulletins, and mining statistics for such areas as injuries and accidents. Publications are under the Freedom of Information Act Reading Room section. The Our Page for Kids provides some information on prospecting and dangerous mines.

Subjects: Mining; Workplace Safety — Regulations

Publications: *Fatalgrams*, L 38.15:

Holmes Safety Association Bulletin (monthly), L 38.12:

MSHA Program Information Bulletin, L 38.17/2:

1134. Morbidity and Mortality Weekly Report

http://www.cdc.gov/mmwr/

Sponsor: Health and Human Services Department — Centers for Disease Control and Prevention (CDC)

Description: The *Morbidity and Mortality Weekly Report* (MMWR) along with its associated reports is a standard and authoritative resource for detailed health statistics. The online version presents the full text of each issue of the MMWR dating back to February 1982, volume 31 issue 5. The site has a searchable index and also features sections for Disease Trends, Straight Facts on Diseases, International Bulletins, and Continuing Education.

The CDC has done a commendable job of converting this publication to an online format and organizing the Web site so that it is relatively easy to find articles by date or source as well as by keyword using the searchable index.

Subjects: Diseases and Conditions — Statistics; Vital Statistics
Publications: *MMWR CDC Surveillance Summaries (quarterly)*, HE 20.7009/2:
MMWR Recommendation and Reports, HE 20.7009/2-2:
Morbidity and Mortality Weekly Report, HE 20.7009:

1135. National Center for Complementary and Alternative Medicine
http://nccam.nih.gov/
Sponsor: National Institutes of Health (NIH) — National Center for Complementary and Alternative Medicine
Description: The National Center for Complementary and Alternative Medicine (NCCAM) is concerned with health care practices that are outside the realm of what is considered to be conventional medicine as practiced in the United States. Their site describes their research grant opportunities and priorities, and the clinical trials they conduct. The Health Information section has information for the consumer on choosing alternative medicines or treatments, along with alerts and advisories. It also has information about specific substances used as alternative medicines. A section called "10 Things To Know About Evaluating Medical Resources on the Web" will be of general interest.
Subject: Alternative Medicine

1136. National Center for Environmental Health
http://www.cdc.gov/nceh/
Sponsor: Health and Human Services Department — Centers for Disease Control and Prevention (CDC) — National Center for Environmental Health (NCEH)
Description: NCEH promotes health and quality of life by preventing and controlling disease, birth defects, disability, and death resulting from interactions between people and their environment. The Web site features a Spotlights section for current news and issues. Other primary sections of the site include About NCEH, NCEH Health Topics, Employment and Training, Publications and Products, and Programs and Activities, as well as presenting information specifically for kids and funding. The Publications and Products section includes lists of publications by NCEH authors, full-text fact sheets and brochures, books, and SABER: Statistical Analysis Battery for Epidemiological Research. The site is also available in a Spanish-language version.
Subject: Environmental Health
Publication: *Brochures*, HE 20.7513:

1137. National Center for Health Statistics
http://www.cdc.gov/nchs/
Sponsor: Health and Human Services Department — Centers for Disease Control and Prevention (CDC) — National Center for Health Statistics (NCHS)
Description: NCHS monitors and documents the health status of the population. On their Web site, the What's New section announces recently released reports, fact sheets, and data and statistics. Other fact sheets and news releases can be found under News Releases. These are divided out by year and then by topic. Published reports are found under the Publications and Information Products category. Among the available reports are *Vital and Health Statistics Series; Advance Data from Vital and Health Statistics; National Vital Statistics Reports* (formerly *Monthly Vital Statistics Reports*); *Health, United States, 2001;* and the *NCHS Catalog of University Presentations.* Information on how to order print publications and where to write for vital records is also available in the same area. The FASTATS (as in Fast Stats) section provides an alphabetical, topical index to various health and disease facts and conditions as well as the surveys. Under the Surveys and Data Collection Systems, there are links to NHANES (National Health and Nutrition Examination Series), NHIS (National Health Interview Series), and the National Vital Statistics System, where one can access Vital Statistics of the United States, National Vital Health Statistics Reports (formerly the *Monthly Vital Statistics Report*), and other selected reports. Not all of the reports in a given series are available on the NCHS site. Even so, it contains a substantial number of major sources of health statistics.
Subjects: Health and Safety — Statistics; Health Care — Statistics; Vital Statistics
Publications: *Health United States*, HE 20.7042/6:
Healthy People 2000, Statistical Notes (nos.), HE 20.6230

ICD.9.CM International Classification of Diseases, HE 22.41/2:
Joint Meeting of the Public Health Conference on Records and Statistics and the Data Users Conference, HE 20.6214:
Life Tables, HE 20.6215:
National Hospital Discharge Survey, HE 20.6209/7:
NCHS Catalog of University Presentations, HE 20.6225:
Vital and Health Statistics, HE 20.6209:
Where to Write for Vital Records, HE 20.6210/2:

1138. National Center for Injury Prevention and Control
http://www.cdc.gov/ncipc/
Sponsor: Health and Human Services Department — Centers for Disease Control and Prevention (CDC) — National Center for Injury Prevention and Control (NCIPC)
Description: NCIPC seeks to reduce morbidity, disability, mortality, and costs associated with injuries outside the workplace. Its Web site features top-level links such as News, Facts, Data, Publications, Funding and Announcements. Topical categories include Injury Care, Violence, and Unintentional Injury. The Resources category includes the subsections Publications, Calendar, About NCIPC, and Statistics and Data. The Publications section has bibliographies of NCIPC intramural research publications, descriptions of NCIPC publications, ordering information, and other publications. The site also features WISQARSTM (Web-based Injury Statistics Query and Reporting System), a database that provides customized reports of injury-related data.
Subjects: Injuries; Safety
Publications: *Injury Control Update*, HE 20.7956:
Injury Fact Book

1139. National Council on Disability
http://www.ncd.gov/
Sponsor: National Council on Disability
Description: The National Council on Disability is an independent federal agency making recommendations to the president and Congress on issues affecting Americans who have disabilities. Past reports have covered topics such as air travel and fair housing. Its site features sections entitled What's New, Newsroom, Frequently Asked Questions, Federal Agencies, and Resources. A brochure about NCD is available in PDF format in English, Spanish, Chinese, and other languages.
Subject: Disabilities — Policy

1140. National Health Information Center
http://www.health.gov/nhic/
Description: NHIC, a health information referral service, produces this Web site that features health information for the health professional and consumer. The Health Information Resource Database includes 1,800 organizations and government offices that provide health information upon request. Entries include contact information, brief descriptive abstracts, and information about the publications and services that the organizations provide. The Publications area offers a publications list, information on Healthy People 2010, the annual National Health Observances, and a list of toll-free numbers for health information.
Publications: *Federal Health Information Centers and Clearinghouses*, HE 20.34/2:IN 3/2/
National Health Observances, HE 20.2:H 34/

1141. National Health Service Corps
http://nhsc.bhpr.hrsa.gov/
Sponsor: Health and Human Services Department — Health Resources and Services Administration (HRSA) — Health Professions Bureau
Description: NHSC recruits primary care clinicians for medically underserved areas. Its Web site has sections targeted to communities, clinicians, students, and educators. They offer scholarship for medical students who will practice in underserved areas, and also offer work experiences and residencies. The site has information about NHSC programs, online applications, and information on current communities with available positions.
Subjects: Health Care; Health Occupations — Grants
Publication: *NHSC In Touch*, HE 20.9110/9:

1142. National Immunization Program
`http://www.cdc.gov/nip/`
Sponsor: Health and Human Services Department — Centers for Disease Control and Prevention (CDC) — National Immunization Program (NIP)
Description: The Web site of the National Immunization Program provides information on immunization and vaccine safety. The site carries information on Immunization Registries, Vaccines for Children Program, Clinic Assessment Program, Grantee Assessment, Advisory Committee on Immunization Practices (ACIP), Flu Vaccine, and VACMAN (Vaccine Management System). Other broad categories are Vaccines, Vaccine Safety, Diseases, Resources, and Why Immunize. The Spotlight section highlights current topics of interest such as an update about flu shots. The site also features some information in Spanish.
Subject: Immunization

1143. National Institute of Child Health and Human Development
`http://www.nichd.nih.gov/`
Sponsor: National Institutes of Health (NIH) — National Institute of Child Health and Human Development (NICHD)
Description: The National Institute of Child Health and Human Development conducts research, clinical trials, and epidemiological studies related to the health of the human growth, development, and reproductive processes. Its Web site features About NICHD, News and Events, Intramural Research, Funding by NICHD, Research Resources, Health Information and Media, and Epidemiology, Statistics, and Prevention. The News and Events section has news releases and information about conferences, new policies, new funding opportunities, and new items to the site. Health Information features publications on health topics related to NICHD research, information on the new campaigns, and news releases and media information.
Subject: Child Health and Safety — Research
Publications: *National Institute of Child Health and Human Development Intramural Research Program: Annual Report of the Scientific Director*, HE 20.3365:
NICHD News Notes, HE 20.3364/3:

1144. National Institute of Occupational Safety and Health
`http://www.cdc.gov/niosh/homepage.html`
Sponsor: Health and Human Services Department — Centers for Disease Control and Prevention (CDC) — National Institute of Occupational Safety and Health (NIOSH)
Description: NIOSH is responsible for conducting research on the full scope of occupational disease and injury ranging from lung disease in miners to carpal tunnel syndrome in computer users. Its site provides information about NIOSH and related activities. Featured sections include About NIOSH, Publications, Databases, Spotlights, Topic Index, Safety and Health Topics, Mining Safety and Health Research, and National Occupational Research Agenda (NORA). Under Publications, a number of online publications and publication lists can be found. This includes lists of *Criteria Documents, NIOSH Alerts,* and *NIOSH Current Intelligence Bulletins (CIBs)* along with some of each of these series available in full text. The Database section includes the *NIOSH Manual of Analytical Methods* (in PDF format), the *Certified Equipment List, International Chemical Safety Cards,* and *Occupational Safety and Health Guidelines for Chemical Hazards.*
Subject: Workplace Safety
Publications: *Criteria for a Recommended Standard . . .*, HE 20.7110:
Health Hazard Evaluation Summaries, HE 20.7125:
NIOSH Alerts, HE 20.7123:
NIOSH Certified Equipment List, HE 20.7124:
NIOSH Current Intelligence Bulletins, HE 20.7155:
NIOSH Manual of Analytical Methods, HE 20.7108:994/

1145. National Institute on Aging
`http://www.nia.nih.gov/`
Sponsor: National Institutes of Health (NIH) — National Institute on Aging (NIA)
Description: The NIA Web site features a range of information on aging, from research grant information and to fact sheets for the public. The News and Events section features what's new items,

appointments, upcoming events, press releases, and media advisories of significant findings from NIA-supported research. The About the NIA section gives information about strategic planning, congressional testimony and budget requests, frequently asked questions, and the history and mission of NIA. The NIA Research Programs section lists extramural aging research at other institutions throughout the country and intramural research on the NIH campus and at the Gerontology Research Center. The Funding and Training section covers available NIA grants, the application process, and research training related to aging. The Health Information section includes publications on health and aging topics and a resource directory for the public. One link under Health Information leads to the NIA's Alzheimer's Disease Education and Referral Center. The ADEAR site contains a referral service, publications on Alzheimer's, and news on current NIA research about the disease.

The NIA provides a good mix of information on this site for researchers, health professionals, and the public. The Alzheimer's Disease material may be of particular interest to those searching for Alzheimer's information.

Subjects: Medical Research — Grants; Senior Citizens
Publication: *Progress Report on Alzheimer's Disease*, HE 20.3869:

1146. National Oral Health Information Clearinghouse

http://www.nohic.nidcr.nih.gov/

Sponsor: National Institutes of Health (NIH) — National Institute of Dental and Craniofacial Research (NIDCR)
Description: The National Oral Health Information Clearinghouse (NOHIC) is sponsored by the National Institute of Dental and Craniofacial Research and is designed as a resource for patients with special needs. The site features the sections Welcome to NOHIC, What is Special Care, Special Care Publications, the Oral Health Database, Oral Complications of Cancer Treatment, and Resource Links. The bibliographic database includes a variety of health-related materials and educational resources. It has a strong patient education focus and highlights materials such as fact sheets, brochures, videocassettes, newsletter articles, catalogs, and other educational resources for patients and professionals.
Subject: Dental Health

1147. National Rehabilitation Information Center

http://www.naric.com/

Sponsor: Education Department — Special Education and Rehabilitative Services Office — National Institute on Disability and Rehabilitation Research (NIDRR)
Description: Funded by NIDRR, the NARIC collects and disseminates the results of federally funded research projects in the area of disability and rehabilitation. The Instant Disability Information Center is a collection of online databases. It includes REHABDATA, an extensive database of literature abstracts covering physical, mental, and psychiatric disabilities, independent living, vocational rehabilitation, special education, assistive technology, and other issues related to people with disabilities. NARIC current awareness services include REHABDATA Connection and Rehabwire.
Subject: Disabilities — Research
Publication: *NIDRR Program Directory*, ED 1.215:

1148. National Women's Health Information Center

http://www.4woman.gov/

Sponsor: Health and Human Services Department — Public Health and Science Office — Women's Health Office
Description: The National Women's Health Information Center (NWHIC) is designed as a gateway for women seeking health information. NWHIC is a free information and resource service for consumers, health care professionals, researchers, educators, and students. The Web site also promotes the NWHIC's Call Center, at 1-800-994-WOMAN (1-800-994-9662) or 1-888-220-5446 for the hearing impaired. The site has information and tips on topics such as pregnancy, breast cancer, and menopause, and on women's issues related to other topics such as heart disease and quitting smoking. Other sections cover funding opportunities in women's health, hot topics in Congress, women's health statistics, and information for health professionals.
Publication: *Healthy Women Today*

1149. Navy Environmental Health Center

http://www-nehc.med.navy.mil/

Sponsor: Navy — Navy Environmental Health Center

Description: The Navy Environmental Health Center aims to ensure Navy and Marine Corps readiness through leadership in prevention of disease and promotion of health. Its site includes pages for Special Interest Areas, Specialty Leaders, Technical Forum, Library, Command History, Command Mission, and NEHC Index. The Special Interest Areas section has subsections such as Immunization Information, Anthrax Information Page, Health Promotion Friday Facts, and surveillance reports and other health bulletins. The Technical Forum section features information about preventive medicine, occupational and environmental medicine, environmental health, and epidemiology. The Specialty Leaders section offers additional information on the subjects of industrial hygiene, biochemistry, and toxicology. The Library has links to NEHC journals, directives and instructions, technical manuals, and links to other outside electronic publications.

Subjects: Preventive Health Care; Military Medicine

1150. Navy Medicine

http://navymedicine.med.navy.mil/

Sponsor: Navy — Medicine and Surgery Bureau

Description: The Navy Bureau of Medicine and Surgery provides health care to active duty Navy and Marine Corps members, to retired service members, and their families. The Web site provides information on the organization, its history, news, and publications.

Subject: Military Medicine

1151. NIH LISTSERV

http://list.nih.gov/

Sponsor: National Institutes of Health (NIH)

Description: This page provides information on the many NIH email lists along with searchable Web-based archives for many of them. The list also notes how many subscribers are currently subscribed to the list. Available lists include the following:

Email Lists: BSSRIG-L—Behavioral and Social Sciences Interest Group

CALENDAR—The NIH Calendar of Events

HEALTHFINDER-L—announcements of new consumer health info

LTCARE-L—Research on Disability and Long-Term Care

MAMMOGRAPHY CDRH-L—Mammography related items from FDA/CDRH

SBIR-STTR—NIH SBIR-STTR funding opportunities

Subjects: Medical Information; Email Lists

1152. NIH Senior Health

http://nihseniorhealth.gov/

Sponsor: National Institutes of Health (NIH) — National Institute on Aging (NIA)

Description: The NIH Senior Health site is a joint project of the National Institute on Aging and the National Library of Medicine to produce Web content for seniors that is designed in an age-appropriate style. The site uses large print and breaks content into short segments. Major sections are Alzheimer's Disease, Caring for Someone with Alzheimer's, and Exercise for Older Adults. Some sections include short video clips with the option of reading the video transcript.

Subjects: Alzheimer's Disease; Senior Citizens

1153. NLM Gateway

http://gateway.nlm.nih.gov/gw/Cmd

Sponsor: National Institutes of Health (NIH) — National Library of Medicine (NLM)

Description: The NLM Gateway provides "one-stop searching" for many of the National Library of Medicine's information resources or databases. Using this site, visitors can simultaneously search multiple retrieval systems, including various types of information that do not logically belong in PubMed, LOCATOR*plus,* or other established NLM retrieval systems. In addition to the aforementioned databases, resources include OLDMEDLINE, MEDLINEplus (consumer health information), AIDS Meeting Abstracts, and HSR Meeting Abstracts.

Subjects: Medical Information; Databases

1154. Nutrition.Gov

http://www.nutrition.gov/

Sponsor: Agriculture Department (USDA)

Description: This portal "provides easy access to all online federal government information on nutrition. This national resource makes obtaining government information on nutrition, healthy eating, physical activity, and food safety, easily accessible in one place for many Americans." (from the Web site, 1-13-2003) Major sections of the site include Food Facts, Food Safety, Lifecycle Issues, Health Management, Food Assistance, Research, and Resources. Each section provides annotated links to resources from many federal agencies, rather than presenting the information directly on this site.

This resource is an example of the federal initiative to organize information across agencies. Once can locate nutrition information on the Web without first knowing the agency that posts the information.

Subject: Nutrition

1155. Occupational Safety and Health Administration

http://www.osha.gov/

Sponsor: Labor Department — Occupational Safety and Health Administration (OSHA)

Description: The OSHA Web site contains a substantial number of pages, publications, and documents providing information both on the agency and on its regulations. Major categories include Compliance Assistance, Cooperative Programs, Newsroom, Dockets, Safety and Health Topics, Statistics, and International. Another way to access the site's contents is through an alphabetical index of topics available on the home page. The News Room section provides access to such documents as news releases, speeches, and congressional testimonies. The Publications link from this section leads to an alphabetical list of OSHA publications, most of which are online in full text. The section also includes posters, forms, fact sheets, compliance guides, and information on the video loan program. The Inspection Data link from the home page brings users to a list of OSHA databases, including Frequently Cited OSHA Standards, the SIC Manual, and BLS Workplace Injury, Illness, and Fatality Statistics.

Subject: Workplace Safety — Regulations

Publications: *Fact Sheet (series)*, L 35.24:

JS&HQ (Job Safety & Health Quarterly), L 35.9/3:

News, L 1.79:

1156. Office for the Advancement of Telehealth

http://telehealth.hrsa.gov/

Sponsor: Health and Human Services Department — Health Resources and Services Administration (HRSA)

Description: This site describes telehealth as "the use of electronic information and telecommunications technologies to support long-distance clinical health care, patient and professional health-related education, public health and health administration." The site includes articles, publications, and grants information related to telehealth. A Links section identifies other federal, state, and private organizations interested in telehealth topics.

Subject: Telemedicine

1157. Office of Disability Employment Policy

http://www.dol.gov/odep/

Sponsor: Labor Department — Office of Disability Employment Policy

Description: In the FY 2001 budget, Congress approved a new Office of Disability Employment Policy (ODEP) within the Department of Labor. Programs and staff of the former President's Committee on Employment of People with Disabilities have been integrated into this new office. ODEP manages programs, policies, and grants to further its mission to increase employment opportunities for those with disabilities.

The site features the following sections: About ODEP, Programs and Initiatives, Publications, Business Focus, Job Links, and State Liaisons. The Publications section provides access to

Americans with Disability Act brochures, ODEP reports, over 50 fact sheets on disability employment topics, and other publications. The Business Focus section organizes access to ODEP programs and resources under such topics as Customers with Disabilities, Laws and Legal Rights, and Worksite Accommodations.

This site offers an excellent overview on many issues related to employment for people with disabilities.

Subjects: Disabilities — Policy; Employment Discrimination — Laws
Publication: *Getting Down to Business: A Blueprint for Creating and Supporting Entrepreneurial Opportunities for Individuals with Disabilities* , PREX 1.10/19:B 96/

1158. Office of Global Health
http://www.cdc.gov/ogh/
Sponsor: Health and Human Services Department — Centers for Disease Control and Prevention (CDC)
Description: These pages contain information related to OGH's mission of collaborating with other nations and international organizations to promote healthy lifestyles and to prevent high rates of disease, disability, and death in the global health arena. The top level page presents sections entitled CDC's Global Presence, Partnerships, Publications and Links.
Subject: Health Care — International
Publication: *Global Health Activities Report*

1159. Office of Minority Health
http://www.omhrc.gov/
Sponsor: Health and Human Services Department — Public Health and Science Office — Minority Health Office
Description: The Office of Minority Health is concerned with public health issues affecting racial and ethnic minorities in the United States. This site features a broad collection of material on minority health issues. Featured sections include What's New, Initiatives, Programs, Health Disparities, Resource Center, Data and Statistics, Publications, Conferences, and About OMH.
Subjects: Health Policy; Minority Groups
Publications: *Closing the Gap (bimonthly)*, HE 20.40:
HIV Impact Newsletter, HE 20.40/2:

1160. Office of the Assistant Secretary for Planning and Evaluation
http://aspe.os.dhhs.gov/
Sponsor: Health and Human Services Department
Description: ASPE is responsible for policy analysis and development, coordination, and advice; strategic planning; legislation development; economic analysis; and policy research and evaluation for the Department of Health and Human Services. The ASPE site features sections such as Disability, Aging, and Long-Term Care; Health Policy Issues; Human Services Policy Issues, Program Systems Issues, and Science Policy Issues. The Frequently Used section has links to *The Catalog of Federal Domestic Assistance* and HHS Poverty Guidelines.
Subjects: Health Care — Policy; Social Services — Policy
Publications: *Catalog of Federal Domestic Assistance*, PrEx 2.20:
PIC Highlights, HE 1.62:

1161. Office of the Surgeon General
http://www.surgeongeneral.gov/sgoffice.htm
Sponsor: Health and Human Services Department — Public Health and Science Office — Surgeon General
Description: The Surgeon General's Web site has current and historical information on the office, including portraits and biographies of all previous Surgeons General. A section called Being Healthy provides health tips for different demographic groups and has sections for kids, parents, and educators. The News and Public Affairs section has press releases and links to other government public health resources, such as the National Vaccine Program site and the National Women's Health Information Center.

Reports of the Surgeon General from 1994 to present are online. Order information is provided for the rest of the Surgeon General reports series going back to the first such report in 1964. The Publications section of this site also points to the National Library of Medicine's Reports of the Surgeon General site, which has PDF copies of all the Surgeon General reports (see separate entry).
Subject: Public Health — Policy
Publications: *Mental Health: A Report of the Surgeon General*, HE 20.402:
Mental Health: Culture, Race, and Ethnicity, A Supplement to Mental Health: A Report of the Surgeon General, HE 20.402:
Oral Health in America: A Report of the Surgeon General, HE 20.3402:
Reducing Tobacco Use: A Report of the Surgeon General, HE 20.7602:
Surgeon General's Call To Action to Promote Sexual Health and Responsible Sexual Behavior, HE 1.2:
The Surgeon General's Call To Action To Prevent and Decrease Overweight and Obesity, HE 20.2:
The Surgeon General's Call To Action To Prevent Suicide, HE 20.2:
Women and Smoking: A Report of the Surgeon General, HE 20.7615:
Youth Violence: A Report of the Surgeon General, HE 20.2:

1162. Organ Donation
http://www.organdonor.gov/
Sponsor: Health and Human Services Department — Health Resources and Services Administration (HRSA)
Description: This DHHS site provides general information on the process of organ and tissue donation and information on how to sign up. On the main page is a discussion on how to become an organ and tissue donor. The following sections provide additional information: Frequently Asked Questions; Grant Application Reference Center; Related Organizations; Donor/Recipient Stories; and Critical Data (current numbers on waiting list candidates, transplants, and donors). There is also a downloadable donor card and brochure.
Subject: Medical Information

1163. Over-the-Counter
http://www.fda.gov/cder/otc/
Sponsor: Health and Human Services Department — Food and Drug Administration (FDA) — Center for Drug Evaluation and Research (CDER)
Description: The Over-the-Counter (OTC) site offers information for consumers and industry about nonprescription drugs. Featured sections include New OTC Labeling Information and Warnings and Publications for Industry. There are also links to information about new labeling requirements for over-the-counter human drugs.
Subject: Over-The-Counter Drugs

1164. Prevention Online (PREVLINE): SAMHSA's National Clearinghouse for Alcohol and Drug Information
http://www.health.org/
Sponsor: Health and Human Services Department — Substance Abuse and Mental Health Services Administration (SAMHSA)
Description: The National Clearinghouse for Alcohol and Drug Information (NCADI) is the information service of the Center for Substance Abuse Prevention of the Substance Abuse and Mental Health Services Administration in the U.S. Department of Health and Human Services. NCADI is the world's largest resource for current information and materials concerning substance abuse. Its Web site, Prevention Online (PREVLINE) offers access to searchable databases and substance abuse prevention materials related to alcohol, tobacco, and drugs. The site divides content into sections for Family, Youth, School, Workplace, and Community.
Subject: Substance Abuse
Publications: *CSAP Technical Assistance Bulletins (TABS) (Center for Subst. Abuse Prevention)*
CSAT Technical Assistance Publications (TAPS) (Center for Subst. Abuse Treatment)
CSAT Treatment Improvement Protocols (TIPS)
Drug Abuse Warning Network (DAWN), HE 20.416/3:

Preliminary Estimates of Drug-Related Emergency Department Episodes, HE 20.421:
Substance Abuse Treatment Facility Locator, HE 20.410/3:
Tips for Teens about ..., HE 20.8002:T 49/

1165. PubMed
http://www.ncbi.nlm.nih.gov/PubMed/
Alternate URL: http://www.ncbi.nlm.nih.gov/entrez/query.fcgi?db=PubMed
Description: PubMed is one of two free gateways to the database offered by NLM. This Web version not only provides access to MEDLINE, it also includes links to many sites providing full text articles and other related resources. Other PubMed services include Journal Browser, MeSH (Medical Subject Heading Browser), Single Citation Matcher, Clinical Queries (for physicians), and LinkOut, which provides links to a wide variety of relevant web-accessible online resources. Boolean searching is available as well. There is also a section entitled Related Resources, with links to Consumer Health, Clinical Alerts, ClinicalTrials.gov, and the other free MEDLINE gateway, NLM Gateway. In addition, PubMed, which is part of NCBI's Entrez Retrieval System, provides access and links to the integrated molecular biology databases included in Entrez. These databases contain DNA and protein sequences, 3-D protein structure data, population study data sets, and assemblies of complete genomes in an integrated system.
Subjects: Medical Information; Medline; Databases
Publication: *Index Medicus*, HE 20.3612

1166. Reports of the Surgeon General
http://sgreports.nlm.nih.gov/NN/
Sponsor: National Institutes of Health (NIH) — National Library of Medicine (NLM)
Description: This site carries the full text of all the official Reports of the Surgeon General, back to the first report in 1964 on *Smoking and Health*. The National Library of Medicine has digitized these along with conference proceedings, pamphlets, photographs, and brochures from the Office of the Surgeon General. Documents are in PDF and photographs are in JPEG format. Within groupings by document type, links to the items can be displayed in chronological order or alphabetically by title. A search engine provides full text or fielded search options, searching for a text string in the scanned images or the metadata.
Subject: Public Health — Policy

1167. Smokefree.gov
http://www.smokefree.gov/
Sponsor: National Institutes of Health (NIH) — National Cancer Institute (NCI)
Description: The National Cancer Institute maintains this site to help smokers quit and to disseminate their free materials on the topic. The site also promotes other state and national anti-smoking campaigns.
Subject: Smoking

1168. Social Security Online–For Women
http://www.ssa.gov/women/
Sponsor: Social Security Administration (SSA)
Description: This site provides Social Security program information on retirement, survivors, disability, and Supplemental Security Income benefits relevant to women. It offers seven main categories that correspond to various life stages of women: Working Woman, Beneficiary, Bride, New Mother, Divorced Spouse, Caregiver, and Widow. There is a link to additional federal Web sites that are of interest to women, such as the Department of Health and Human Services Women's Health Web site, Health Care Financing Administration's Children's Health Insurance Program, and the Small Business Administration's Online Women's Business Center. Under the heading, What Every Woman Should Know About, there are links to Social Security, Retirement, Survivors, Disability, Supplemental Security Income, and Medicare. From the Quick Start heading, one can search for services online, the nearest field office, answers to frequently asked questions, and the top ten requested services. As on the main SSA site, women at this site can apply for social security retirement insurance benefits, calculate retirement benefits, or request a social security statement.
Subjects: Social Security; Women

1169. Substance Abuse and Mental Health Services Administration

http://www.samhsa.gov/

Sponsor: Health and Human Services Department — Substance Abuse and Mental Health Services Administration (SAMHSA)

Description: SAMHSA's mission is to assure that quality substance abuse and mental health services are available to the people who need them and to ensure that substance abuse prevention and treatment information as well as diagnosis and treatment of mental illnesses are used more effectively in the general health care system. This site features such sections as Policy Issues, Grant Opportunities, Contract Opportunities, Statistics and Data, Legislative Information, and Workplace Resources.The Statistics section offers descriptions of and reports and data from the National Household Survey on Drug Abuse (NHSDA) series, the Drug and Alcohol Services Information System (DASIS) series, and the Drug Abuse Warning Network (DAWN). The site also links to several component agencies: the Center for Mental Health Services, Center for Substance Abuse Prevention, and the Center for Substance Abuse Treatment, and clearinghouses: National Mental Health Services Knowledge Exchange Network (KEN), Prevline, Treatment Improvement Exchange (TIE), and Office of Applied Statistics.

Subjects: Mental Health; Substance Abuse

Publications: *National Household Survey on Drug Abuse*, HE 20.417/5:
National Household Survey on Drug Abuse Population Estimates, HE 20.417/2:
SAMHSA News (quarterly), HE 20.425:
Substance Abuse and Mental Health Statistics Sourcebook, HE 20.402:SO 8
Treatment Improvement Protocol (TIP), HE 20.418:

1170. The President's Council on Physical Fitness and Sports

http://www.fitness.gov/

Sponsor: President's Council on Physical Fitness and Sports

Description: Established by Executive Order in 1956, the President's Council on Physical Fitness and Sports promotes physical fitness and sports participation for Americans of all ages. The Web site has information on the history, mission, and membership of the Council under the section About PCPFS. The President's Challenge section has information on the Council's awards program, including the Presidential Physical Fitness Award. A Reading Room section has online brochures promoting fitness and health. *PCPFS Research Digests* is a quarterly summary of the latest scientific information on issues relating to physical activity. The section Other Federal Publications points to relevant pamphlets online at a variety of health and information agencies.

Subjects: Physical Fitness; Sports

1171. Title V Information System

http://www.mchdata.net/

Sponsor: Health and Human Services Department — Health Resources and Services Administration (HRSA) — Maternal and Child Health Bureau

Description: The Title V Information System (TVIS) electronically captures data from annual Title V Block Grant applications and reports. Title V of the Social Security Act covers a major federal block grant program funding health promotion efforts for mothers, infants, and children. The TVIS system provides information on key measures of maternal and child health (MCH) in the United States. The data can be searched by state, range of years, types of MCH services, levels of spending, and other categories. A State Narratives section has reports from each state, providing a written context for the data.

Subjects: Reproductive Health — Statistics; Child Health and Safety — Statistics

1172. ToxFAQs

http://www.atsdr.cdc.gov/toxfaq.html

Sponsor: Health and Human Services Department — Toxic Substances and Disease Registry Agency

Description: ToxFAQs offers informational summaries about hazardous substances. Each fact sheet includes information about exposure to hazardous substances found at hazardous waste sites and the effects of exposure on human health. The page offers an alphabetical index as well as search capabilities. There are also links to resources from ATSDR, which include toxicological profile

information sheets of substances found at national priorities list sites, public health statements, and minimal risk levels for hazardous substances.
Subjects: Hazardous Waste; Toxic Substances

1173. TOXNET
http://toxnet.nlm.nih.gov/
Sponsor: National Institutes of Health (NIH) — National Cancer Institute (NCI)
Description: TOXNET is a group of databases on toxicology, hazardous chemicals, and related areas. The site allows for searching the databases separately or all together. Hosted databases include the Hazardous Substances Data Bank, Chemical Carcinogenesis Research Information Service (CCRIS), TOXLINE's toxicology bibliographic information, and the Toxics Release Inventory (TRI).
Subjects: Chemical Information; Toxic Substances

1174. TRICARE, Military Health System
http://www.tricare.osd.mil/
Sponsor: Defense Department — TRICARE Management Activity
Description: TRICARE is the health care benefit for the military. This Web site provides information and documents for TRICARE beneficiaries and providers, including a map of TRICARE regions with their 800 numbers. The site also carries brochures and fact sheets on specific topics related to TRICARE coverage.
Subjects: Health Insurance; Military Medicine

1175. www.FoodSafety.gov: Gateway to Government Food Safety Information
http://www.foodsafety.gov/
Sponsor: Health and Human Services Department — Food and Drug Administration (FDA) — Center for Food Safety and Applied Nutrition (CFSAN)
Description: FoodSafety.gov is a gateway providing links to selected government food safety-related information. A steering committee consisting of individuals with different backgrounds reviews all potential sites for inclusion on the FoodSafety.gov Web site. It includes sections such as Consumer Advice, News and Safety Alerts, Industry Assistance, Report Illnesses and Product Complaints, Foodborne Pathogens, National Food Safety Programs, Federal and State Gov't Agencies, and Kids, Teens, and Educators.

1176. www.health.gov
http://www.health.gov/
Sponsor: Health and Human Services Department — Public Health and Science Office — Disease Prevention and Health Promotion Office
Description: This health gateway site consists entirely of links to other government metasites and special topic sites. These include Dietary Guidelines for Americans, Environmental Health Policy Committee, Office of Disease Prevention and Health Promotion, Healthy People 2010, National Health Information Center, Office of Public Health and Science, Health Section, and the Public Health Functions Project.
Subject: Health and Safety

Diseases

1177. Cancer Control and Population Sciences
http://dccps.nci.nih.gov/
Sponsor: National Institutes of Health (NIH) — National Cancer Institute (NCI)
Description: This division of the National Cancer Institute funds and coordinates cancer research and disseminates the research findings. The Web site organizes a large amount of research program information into several broad categories: applied research, behavioral research, epidemiology and genetics research, surveillance research, and survivorship research. Other sections of the site cover current research, related information and resources, funding opportunities, and research findings. Like the rest of the site, the Information and Resources section uses a simple menu to lead to a

large volume of information. It includes Cancer Control publications and compilations of resources on tobacco control, health disparities, statistics, patient information, and cancer journals.
Subject: Cancer — Research
Publication: *Researchers' Toolbox, HE 20.3186/2:*

1178. Cancer.gov Clinical Trials
`http://www.cancer.gov/clinical_trials`
Sponsor: National Institutes of Health (NIH) — National Cancer Institute (NCI)
Description: This NCI site provides information on cancer-related clinical trials. The site includes sections entitled Understanding Clinical Trials, Finding Trials, Types of Cancer, Conducting Clinical Trials, Clinical Trial Results, Recent Developments, and Educational Resources.
Subjects: Cancer; Clinical Trials

1179. CDC National Prevention Information Network
`http://www.cdcnpin.org/`
Sponsor: Health and Human Services Department — Centers for Disease Control and Prevention (CDC) — National Center for HIV, STD, and TB Prevention (NCHSTP)
Description: The CDC National Prevention Information Network (NPIN) focuses on control and prevention of HIV/AIDS, Sexually Transmitted Diseases (STDs), and Tuberculosis (TB). NPIN includes reference and referral services, educational materials, publications, clinical trial information, treatment information, and the CDC HIV/STD/TB Prevention News Update, a news clipping service to help keep up with news related to HIV/STD/TB. Other sections include Databases, Publications, and Research. The searchable databases include Resources and Services Database, Prevention News Update Database, a Funding Database, and an Educational Materials Database.
Subjects: AIDS; HIV Infections; Sexually Transmitted Diseases; Tuberculosis
Publication: *CDC HIV/STD/TB Prevention News Update, HE 20.7318:*

1180. Diabetes Public Health Resource
`http://www.cdc.gov/diabetes/`
Description: This site communicates practical information on diabetes prevention and control. It includes a diabetes fact sheet, frequently asked questions, and diabetes statistics. A map of the U.S. links to service and contact information for state-based diabetes prevention and control programs. The Publications section links to online texts and order information for publications from the CDC's Division of Diabetes Translation; it includes some Spanish-language publications. The News and Information section has CDC statements, press releases, and congressional testimony related to diabetes.
Subject: Diabetes

1181. Gulf War Veterans' Illnesses
`http://www.gwvi.ncr.gov/`
Sponsor: Presidential Advisory Committee on Gulf War Veterans' Illnesses
Description: This site comes from the President's Advisory Committee and includes information on the committee's activities. Major links include Committee Purpose, Committee Members, Meeting Schedule, Meeting Transcripts, Interim Report, Final Report, Supplemental Letter Report, and Special Report. "The Presidential Advisory Committee on Gulf War Veterans' Illnesses terminated November 1997, and its Web page now resides, unedited, in its final form on the GulfLINK server. For your convenience, the Web address remains the same." (from the Web page)

Although not updated for current developments, this is a good source for information about the committee's activities and for information on the Gulf War Veterans' Disease.
Subject: Gulf War Disease
Publications: *Final Report, Presidential Advisory Committee on Gulf War Veterans' Illnesses,*
  Pr 42.8:AD 9/FINAL
Interim Report, Presidential Advisory Committee on Gulf War Veterans' Illnesses,
  Pr 42.8:AD 9/INT.REPT

1182. GulfLINK
http://www.gulflink.osd.mil/
Description: This site contains documents related to the possible causes of the illnesses being reported by veterans of the Persian Gulf War of 1991. GulfLINK includes a substantial collection of documents, including reports, congressional testimony, and declassified documents. The declassified documents are in ASCII and are searchable by keyword and browsable by release date. Other documents on the site include press releases, fact sheets, bibliographies, and speeches. Altogether, these create a sizable database of resources on the Gulf War Veterans' Disease. This collection is of use to veterans, health care workers, and researchers.
Publication: *GulfNEWS*, D 1.95/5:

1183. HIV/AIDS Bureau
http://hab.hrsa.gov/
Sponsor: Health and Human Services Department — Health Resources and Services Administration (HRSA) — HIV/AIDS Bureau
Description: The HIV/AIDS Bureau coordinates the federal programs funded under the Ryan White Comprehensive AIDS Resources Emergency (CARE) Act. CARE Act programs are designed to help individuals with HIV disease who lack health insurance and financial resources for their care. The programs include health care and support, grants, training, and technical assistance. This site provides detailed information on the CARE Act itself, and on the related policy, programs, and funding. A Reports and Studies section has statistics on clients served by the program, and data on funds allocated by service type. Other sections include Grant Opportunities, Education and Training, and Publications.
Subjects: AIDS; HIV Infections

1184. HIV/AIDS Surveillance Report
http://www.cdc.gov/hiv/stats/hasrlink.htm
Description: These semiannual reports contain detailed statistics on the incidence of HIV and AIDS in the United States, including data by state, metropolitan statistical area, mode of exposure to HIV, sex, race/ethnicity, age group, vital status, and case definition category. The annual editions go back to 1982. From 1998 forward, the reports are available in HTML format.
Subjects: AIDS — Statistics; HIV Infections — Statistics
Publication: *HIV/AIDS Surveillance Report*, HE 20.7011/38

1185. National Cancer Institute
http://www.nci.nih.gov/
Alternate URL: http://cancer.gov/
Sponsor: National Institutes of Health (NIH) — National Cancer Institute (NCI)
Description: The National Cancer Institute has given the alternate name Cancer.gov to its main Web site. The site includes sections covering research programs, research funding, basic information explaining cancer and its treatment, clinical trials information, and statistics. A Resources section includes a Publication Locator, NCI Calendar of Scientific Meetings, and links to their Web sites.

The NCI's site is an important and substantial resource for any kind of cancer question.
Subject: Cancer
Publications: *Atlas of Cancer Mortality in the United States: 1950–94*, HE 20.3152:M 84/4
Cancer Progress Report, HE 20.3172/3:
Nation's Investment in Cancer Research, A Budget Proposal for FY..., HE 20.3190:
NCI Fact Book, HE 20.3174:
NCI Investigational Drugs, Chemical Information, HE 20.3180/2-2:
PLCO News (semi-annual), HE 20.3194:

1186. National Center for HIV, STD, and TB Prevention
http://www.cdc.gov/nchstp/od/nchstp.html
Sponsor: Health and Human Services Department — Centers for Disease Control and Prevention (CDC) — National Center for HIV, STD, and TB Prevention (NCHSTP)
Description: As the name of the agency implies, the NCHSTP Web site features three main sections that correspond to the agency's four main divisions: HIV/AIDS Prevention, STD Prevention, TB

Elimination and Global AIDS. Each of the division pages contain links to relevant MMWRs along with fact sheets and other publications. The HIV/AIDS Prevention page contains the largest amount of information sources including statistics, trials, treatment, funding, and conferences.

For information on any of the three areas covered by NCHSTP, this site is worth a visit. It offers sources for both researchers, patients, and the public.

Subjects: AIDS; HIV Infections; Sexually Transmitted Diseases
Publications: *HIV/AIDS Surveillance Report*, HE 20.7320:
Reported Tuberculosis in the United States, HE 20.7310:

1187. National Center for Infectious Diseases
http://www.cdc.gov/ncidod/
Sponsor: Health and Human Services Department — Centers for Disease Control and Prevention (CDC) — National Center for Infectious Diseases (NCID)
Description: One major resource on this site is the electronic version of the journal *Emerging Infectious Diseases* (EID). The goals of EID and the NCID Web site are to promote the recognition of new and reemerging infectious diseases and to improve the understanding of factors involved in disease emergence, prevention, and elimination. The site features resources for teachers and students along with material for health professionals. More information is available from NCID's division pages, including Global Migration and Quarantine, Vector-Borne Diseases, and Viral Hepatitis. The site also has a Infectious Disease Index, with an alphabetical list of diseases and links to information about them.

Especially within the online pages of EID, this site contains a great deal of information on the prevention and control of traditional, new, and reemerging infectious diseases both in the United States and around the world.

Subject: Diseases and Conditions
Publications: *Emerging Infectious Diseases*, HE 20.7817:
Health Information for International Travel, HE 20.7818:
Summary of Health Information for International Travel, HE 20.7818/2:

1188. National Heart, Lung, and Blood Institute
http://www.nhlbi.nih.gov/index.htm
Sponsor: National Institutes of Health (NIH) — National Heart, Lung, and Blood Institute (NHLBI)
Description: A major feature of this site is the Health Information section, with links to various categories for either the general public or the health professional on such topics as Heart and Vascular Diseases, Lung Diseases, Blood Diseases and Resources, and Sleep Disorders. There are also links to List of Publications and Information Center sections. Other main sections on this site include About the NHLBI, Scientific Resources, Research Funding, News and Press Releases, Clinical Guidelines, Studies Seeking Patients, Technology Transfer, and Committees, Meetings, and Events.
Subject: Heart Disease — Research
Publication: *HeartMemo (quarterly)*, HE 20.3225:

1189. National Institute of Allergy and Infectious Diseases
http://www.niaid.nih.gov/default.htm
Sponsor: National Institutes of Health (NIH) — National Institute of Allergy and Infectious Diseases (NIAID)
Description: NIAID supports and conducts basic research in immunology, microbiology, and infectious disease. On this site, users can explore research on AIDS, allergic and immunologic diseases, asthma, biodefense (smallpox, anthrax), bug-borne diseases, global health issues, influenza, and more. The agency information on this site includes press releases, job openings, calendars of events, publications, and clinical trials recruitment. On the research side, the site lists research activities and resources including the NIH AIDS Research and Reference Reagent Program catalog. All these offerings are available under one of the following sections: Latest News, About NIAID, Information, Research Divisions, and Opportunities.
Subjects: AIDS — Research; Allergies — Research; Diseases and Conditions — Research; Medical Research — Grants

1190. National Institute of Arthritis and Musculoskeletal and Skin Diseases
http://www.niams.nih.gov/
Sponsor: National Institutes of Health (NIH) — National Institute of Arthritis and Musculoskeletal and Skin Diseases (NIAMS)
Description: The NIAMS Web site provides basic health information, information about basic research, clinical and epidemiologic research, research databases, and grant opportunities in the fields of rheumatology, orthopedics, dermatology, metabolic bone diseases, heritable disorders of bone and cartilage, inherited and inflammatory muscle diseases, and sports medicine. Featured categories include About NIAMS, News and Events, Health Information, and Research and Training: Around the Country and at the Bethesda Campus, which offers information about grants and contracts, clinical trials, and researcher resources. The Health Information section includes pamphlets on such conditions as acne, arthritis, lupus, fibromyalgia, osteoporosis, vitiligo, knee problems, and sport injuries.
Subjects: Arthritis — Research; Diseases and Conditions — Research; Medical Research — Grants

1191. National Institute of Diabetes and Digestive and Kidney Disease
http://www.niddk.nih.gov/
Sponsor: National Institutes of Health (NIH) — National Institute of Diabetes and Digestive and Kidney Disease (NIDDK)
Description: The NIDDK site features information on disorders covered by the agency, including diabetes, digestive diseases, endocrine diseases, hematologic diseases, kidney diseases, nutrition and obesity, and urologic diseases. The site provides the following areas: Welcome to NIDDK, Health Information, Research Funding Opportunities, Clinical Research, NIDDK Laboratories, and Reports, Testimony, and Plans. Under Health Information, the page lists the various diseases that the institute covers and links to online pamphlets and other publications. Health Information also includes links to National Education Programs for diabetes and kidney disease, and to National Information Clearinghouses for diabetes, kidney and urologic diseases, digestive diseases, and weight control.
Subjects: Diabetes — Research; Medical Research — Grants; Kidney Disease — Research
Publications: *National Diabetes Information Clearing House (fact sheets)*, HE 20.3323/2:
Prevent Diabetes Problems, HE 20.3326:
Research Updates in Kidney and Urologic Health, HE 20.3324/2:

1192. National Institute of Environmental Health Sciences
http://www.niehs.nih.gov/
Sponsor: National Institutes of Health (NIH) — National Institute of Environmental Health Sciences (NIEHS)
Description: NIEHS, an institute for research on environment-related diseases, links to a wide variety of information in the environmental health area. Featured sections include Environmental Health Information, News, Intramural and Extramural Research Programs, National Toxicology Program, National Center for Toxicogenomics, and links to abstracts of articles in the *Environmental Health Perspectives* and *EHP Toxicogenomics* journals. For the education community, the site also offers two sections: Teacher Support and Kids' Pages.
Subjects: Toxicology (Medicine) — Research; Environmental Health — Research
Publication: *Brochures and Fact Sheets*, HE 20.3520:

1193. National Institute of Mental Health
http://www.nimh.nih.gov/
Sponsor: National Institutes of Health (NIH) — National Institute of Mental Health (NIMH)
Description: The NIMH sites feature areas such as News and Events, Clinical Trials, Funding Opportunities, For the Public, For the Practitioner, For Researchers, and Intramural Research. Information on the agency includes press releases, descriptions of the component offices and departments, and an NIMH events calendar. The For the Public section includes basic material on specific mental disorders such as autism, depression, eating disorders, and schizophrenia. Some Spanish-language material is also available. In the For Researchers section, a statistics page has data on mental health from several different sources.
Subjects: Brain — Research; Mental Health — Research
Publications: *Research Fact Sheets*, HE 20.8139:
Science on our Minds, HE 20.8102:

1194. National Institute of Neurological Disorders and Stroke
http://www.ninds.nih.gov/
Sponsor: National Institutes of Health (NIH) — National Institute of Neurological Disorders and Stroke (NINDS)
Description: NINDS supports biomedical research on disorders of the brain and nervous system. Primary categories on the NINDS Web include Neuroscience News, Intramural Research, Funding, and a section listing conditions for which clinical trial patients are being sought. Under the Disorders section, one can browse information about specific disorders, which are listed alphabetically. The entries include information on what research is being done and referrals to any major organizations concerned with the disorder. Disorders in this section include Alzheimer's Disease, Autism, Bell's Palsy, Carpal Tunnel Syndrome, Epilepsy, Lou Gehrig's Disease, Muscular Dystrophy, and Strokes.
Subjects: Brain — Research; Neurology — Research

1195. National Institute on Deafness and Other Communication Disorders
http://www.nidcd.nih.gov/
Sponsor: National Institutes of Health (NIH) — National Institute on Deafness and Other Communication Disorders (NIDCD)
Description: The NIDCD Web site features sections entitled About NIDCD, News and Events, Research Funding, Health Information, and Research. Along with a few full-text pamphlets, the Health Information section includes publications and a link to the fact sheet about the NIDCD Information Clearinghouse, which is a computerized database of references to brochures, books, articles, fact sheets, organizations, and hard-to-find educational materials on deafness and communication disorders. Topics covered under Health Information include hearing, ear infections, deafness, balance, smell and taste, and voice, speech, and language. Some information is also available in Spanish.
Subject: Hearing Disorders — Research
Publications: *Inside NIDCD Information Clearinghouse (newsletter) (semi-annual)*, HE 20.3666: *Resource Directory*, HE 20.3660/2:

1196. National Institute on Drug Abuse
http://www.drugabuse.gov/
Sponsor: National Institutes of Health (NIH) — National Institute on Drug Abuse (NIDA)
Description: The NIDA site includes categories of About NIDA, What's New, Information on Drugs of Abuse, Publications, In the News, and Funding. The Publications page includes the full text of *NIDA Notes* dating back to 1995 and several publications of NIDA's *Research Report Series*. Other featured areas on the top-level page include Information for Researchers and Health Professionals, Information for Parents and Teachers, and Information for Students. Some of the links available through these areas are International, Treatment Research, Clinical Trials Network, Prevention Research, Drugs of Abuse, and Marijuana Information.
Subject: Drug Abuse
Publications: *Mind Over Matter*, HE 20.3965/3:
Monitoring the Future, National Survey Results on Drug Abuse, HE 20.3968:
NIDA Research Report Series, HE 20.3965/2:
Research Monograph Series, HE 20.3965:
Science and Practice Perspectives

1197. Office of Cancer Survivorship
http://dccps.nci.nih.gov/ocs/
Sponsor: National Institutes of Health (NIH) — National Cancer Institute (NCI)
Description: This Web site is designed for researchers, health professionals, advocates, and cancer survivors and their families. It features the following sections: About Cancer, Post Treatment Resources, Funding Opportunities, Current Research, and Research Findings. The Post Treatment Resources section is the area that may be of most assistance to cancer survivors and their families.
Subject: Cancer

1198. Office of Disease Prevention (ODP)
http://odp.od.nih.gov
Sponsor: National Institutes of Health (NIH)
Description: The NIH Office of Disease Prevention coordinates preventive medicine research across NIH centers and with agencies and organization outside of NIH. The site features sections on Upcoming Workshops and Conferences, Resources for Patients, Information for Researchers, and Information for Health Workers.
Subject: Preventive Health Care — Research
Publication: *National Institutes of Health Consensus Development Conference Reports*, HE 20.3046:

1199. Office of Disease Prevention and Health Promotion
http://odphp.osophs.dhhs.gov/
Sponsor: National Institutes of Health (NIH)
Description: The Office of Disease Prevention and Health Promotion works to strengthen the disease prevention and health promotion priorities of the Department of Health and Human Services. Their Web site links to relevant publications online and to current announcements of conferences, initiatives, and news in the disease prevention community.
Subject: Preventive Health Care

1200. President's New Freedom Commission on Mental Health
http://www.mentalhealthcommission.gov/
Sponsor: White House — President's New Freedom Commission on Mental Health
Description: President's New Freedom Commission on Mental Health is charged with studying the U.S. mental health service delivery system and advising the president on methods to improve it. This site includes information on the commission, its mission, members, and meetings.
Subject: Mental Health — Policy

1201. State Cancer Legislative Database Program
http://www.scld-nci.net/
Sponsor: National Institutes of Health (NIH) — National Cancer Institute (NCI)
Description: The National Cancer Institute (NCI) has provided summaries of legislation affecting cancer prevention and control since the early 1980s. Since 1989, NCI has monitored cancer-related state legislation and maintained the State Cancer Legislative Database (SCLD) Program. This site provides facts sheets, newsletters, presentations, legislative summaries, and inquiries regarding this program.
Subject: Cancer — Legislation
Publications: *SCLD (State Cancer Legislative Database) Update*, HE 20.3182/9-2:
SCLD Fact Sheets, HE 20.3182/9-3:
SCLD Updates Index (Database), HE 20.3182/9:

1202. Surveillance, Epidemiology, and End Results (SEER) Program
http://seer.cancer.gov/
Sponsor: National Institutes of Health (NIH) — National Cancer Institute (NCI)
Description: The Surveillance, Epidemiology, and End Results (SEER) program collects and publishes cancer incidence and survival data from a number of population-based cancer registries. Its data and publications are available on this site. The site features sections: Databases; Data Collection Tools; Cancer Statistics; Recent Reports; Statistical Software; and Analysis Tools.
Subject: Cancer — Statistics
Publication: *SEER Cancer Statistics Review*, HE 20.3186:

1203. United States Renal Data System
http://www.usrds.org/
Sponsors: Health and Human Services Department — Centers for Medicare and Medicaid Services; National Institutes of Health (NIH) — National Institute of Diabetes and Digestive and Kidney Disease (NIDDK)
Description: The United States Renal Data System (USRDS) is a national data system that collects, analyzes, and distributes information about end-stage renal disease (ESRD) in the United States.

The organization's work is funded by the Health and Human Services agencies National Institute of Diabetes and Digestive and Kidney Diseases and Centers for Medicare and Medicaid Services. The site includes the Annual Data Report on end-stage renal disease in the United States and the Renal Data Extraction and Referencing (RenDER) System database.
Subject: Kidney Disease — Statistics
Publication: *United States Renal Data System, Annual Data Report*, HE 20.3325:

1204. White House Office of National AIDS Policy
http://www.whitehouse.gov/onap/aids.html
Sponsor: White House — National AIDS Policy Office
Description: The White House Office of National AIDS Policy post its information on a section of the White House Web site. Major sections are Prevention and Education, General Information, and Global Pandemic. Each section links to executive agencies with AIDS-related programs.
Subject: AIDS — Policy

Research

1205. Agency for Healthcare Research and Quality
http://www.ahrq.gov/
Sponsor: Health and Human Services Department — Healthcare Research and Quality Agency
Description: AHRQ, formerly the Agency for Health Care Policy and Research, is charged with supporting research designed to improve the quality of health care, reduce its cost, and broaden access to essential services. Its Web site features a wide range of resources in sections including Clinical Information, Consumer and Patients, Data and Surveys, Funding Opportunities, Research Findings, and Quality Assessment. There are also buttons for information on children's, women's, and minority health.
Subject: Health Policy
Publications: *AHCPR Research Activities*, HE 20.6512/5:
Clinical Classifications for Health Policy Research, HE 20.6514/3:
Evidence Report/Technology Assessment (series), HE 20.6524:
MEDTEP (Medical Treatment Effectiveness Program) Update (semi-annual), HE 20.6517/5:
MEPS (Medical Expenditure Panel Survey) Chartbooks, HE 20.6517/7:
MEPS (Medical Expenditure Panel Survey) Highlights, HE 20.6517/6:
MEPS (Medical Expenditure Panel Survey) Research Findings, HE 20.6517/9:
Methodology Report, HE 20.6517/8:

1206. ClinicalTrials.gov
http://clinicaltrials.gov/
Sponsor: National Institutes of Health (NIH) — National Library of Medicine (NLM)
Description: The National Library of Medicine has developed this site to provide patients, family members, and the public current information about clinical research studies. This site currently contains approximately 5,200 clinical studies sponsored primarily by the National Institutes of Health and other federal agencies. Users may search the database by keyword, conduct a fielded search, or browse by condition or by sponsor of the study. Results may be filtered by trials no longer recruiting patients.
Subject: Clinical Trials

1207. Comprehensive Epidemiologic Data Resource
http://cedr.lbl.gov/
Sponsor: Energy Department
Description: The Comprehensive Epidemiologic Data Resource (CEDR) is a repository of data from occupational and environmental health studies of workers at Energy Department facilities and nearby community residents. The core data comes from the Energy Department's epidemiological studies of workers at nuclear weapons facilities, beginning in the 1960s. CEDR continues to be a repository for data about the facilities workforce. This Web site catalogs and links to the data sets or information on obtaining them. In some cases, users must register with CEDR to get the data.

Subjects: Radiation Exposure — Research; Environmental Health — Research
Publication: *CEDR, Comprehensive Epidemiologic Data Resource*, E 1.20/3:0339

1208. Computational Bioscience and Engineering Laboratory
`http://cbel.dcrt.nih.gov/`
Sponsor: National Institutes of Health (NIH)
Description: CBEL's work addresses areas requiring high-performance computing with projects in areas such as image processing, structural biology, computational chemistry, biomedical imaging, searches of genetic databases, and computationally intensive statistical applications. Its Web site features links to the lab's divisions and research publications, which is a list of publications from lab staff.
Subjects: Biological Medicine — Research; Medical Computing — Research

1209. CRISP—A Database of Biomedical Research Funded by NIH
`http://crisp.cit.nih.gov/`
Alternate URL: `https://www-commons.cit.nih.gov/crisp/`
Sponsor: National Institutes of Health (NIH)
Description: CRISP (Computer Retrieval of Information on Scientific Projects) is a searchable database of federally funded biomedical research projects. The site offers two databases, one a searchable database of current awards and the other an historical awards database. The Basic Query Form has fields for searching keywords, principle investigator name, award type, activity, grant number, institution, state, and grant title. The Advanced Query Form provides some additional choices for the kind of Boolean operation to perform on the search.
Subjects: Biological Medicine — Research; Databases

1210. Fogarty International Center
`http://www.fic.nih.gov/`
Sponsor: National Institutes of Health (NIH) — John E. Fogarty International Center (FIC)
Description: The FIC aims to improve people's health through the promotion of international cooperation and advanced study in the biomedical sciences. The FIC fosters research partnerships between American scientists and foreign counterparts through grants, fellowships, exchange awards and international agreements. The FIC Web site serves as one means for sharing such information. The main categories include About the Fogarty International Center, Regional Activities, Programs and Initiatives, International Services (NIH), Multilateral Initiative on Malaria, and News, Events, and Information. Publications and a directory of grants can be found under News, Events, and Information.
Subjects: Biological Medicine — Grants; Medical Research — International

1211. GrantsNet
`http://www.hhs.gov/grantsnet/`
Sponsor: Health and Human Services Department — Grants and Acquisition Management Office
Description: GrantsNet is a tool for finding and exchanging information about federal grant programs. Under the link, Electronic Roadmap to Grants, the page is divided into four regions: Introduction to HHS Grants, Application Process, Managing Grants, and Useful Resources. The Introduction section has such links as How to Find Information and NIH Guide. Application Process offers information on how to apply and writing grant proposals and has standard forms in PDF format to download. Under Managing Grants, there are such sections as Grants Administration Manual, Grants Policy Statements, and Laws, E.O.s, and Regulations. While the focus of this gateway site is on HHS grants, it is useful for finding grant information from some other agencies as well.
Subjects: Grants; Public Health — Grants; Social Services — Grants
Publication: *Grants Administration Manual*, HE 1.6/7:

1212. Human Genome Project Information
`http://www.ornl.gov/TechResources/Human_Genome/home.html`
Sponsor: Energy Department — Science Office
Description: Human Genome Project Information page serves as a gateway information about the U.S.

Human Genome Project coordinated by the Department of Energy and the National Institutes of Health. Major sections include Research and Genome Data, Medicine and the New Genetics, Education, and Ethical/Legal/Social Issues. The Publications section links to the full text of related publications.

This site is a rich source of information for any researcher.

Subject: Genomics — Research

1213. Interagency Edison
http://www.iedison.gov/

Sponsor: National Institutes of Health (NIH)

Description: NIH grantees are required by law to report on activities involving the disposition of certain intellectual property rights that result from federally-funded research. In order to facilitate compliance for cases involving inventions, patents, and licenses that have resulted from NIH funding agreements, the Office of Policy for Extramural Research Administration developed this online Extramural Invention Information Management System (code-named Edison). Edison has been designed to streamline grantees' administrative tasks in complying with the law. The original project has been expanded to include other agencies beyond the NIH.

Subject: Grants Management

1214. Joint Genome Institute
http://www.jgi.doe.gov/

Sponsor: Energy Department — Joint Genome Institute (JGI)

Description: The JGI is a merging of LLNL's, LANL's, and LBNL's Human Genome Centers into one organization. It provides access to the information and chromosome data from the Human Genome Centers. The site includes sections for Inside JGI, Who We Are, JGI Programs, and News and Events. The JGI Programs and Inside JGI sections have access to the human chromosome sequencing and mapping data as well as a monthly summary.

Subject: Genomics — Research

1215. Lab of Neurosciences
http://www.grc.nia.nih.gov/branches/lns/index.html

Sponsor: National Institutes of Health (NIH) — National Institute on Aging (NIA)

Description: LNS conducts research using brain imaging. The goal of basic research at the LNS is to establish methods for preventing and treating age-related neurological disorders. This site offers an extensive overview of the aging nervous system and neurodegenerative disorders and features information on its project areas: neurochemistry and metabolism and molecular and cellular biology of brain aging and neurodegenerative diseases. At the bottom of the page are links to the various sections of LNS, which represent the different research areas of the lab.

Subject: Neurology — Research

1216. Lister Hill National Center for Biomedical Communications
http://www.lhncbc.nlm.nih.gov/

Sponsor: National Institutes of Health (NIH) — National Library of Medicine (NLM)

Description: This page primarily describes the activities of the center in the areas of healthcare communication, computing, and information sciences. Projects include the Visible Human Project, building archival digital collections, research in natural language systems, and work on approaches to automated indexing.

Subjects: Medical Computing — Research; Medical Information — Research

1217. National Bioethics Advisory Commission
http://bioethics.georgetown.edu/nbac/

Sponsor: National Bioethics Advisory Commission (NBAC)

Description: The charter of the National Bioethics Advisory Commission expired on October 3, 2001. This advisory committee dealt with topics of human subjects in research. The archived site includes areas such as General Information, Recent News, Meetings, Reports, and Search. The Reports section includes annual and biannual reports and reports on various ethical issues in research: human cloning, use of human biological material, the involvement of people with mental disorders, and use of human stem cells. There is also an index of NBAC reports in PDF format.

Subject: Bioethics — Policy

1218. National Center for Biotechnology Information

http://www.ncbi.nlm.nih.gov/

Sponsor: National Institutes of Health (NIH) — National Library of Medicine (NLM)

Description: NCBI conducts basic and applied research in computational molecular biology, and maintains a variety of databases related to their work. NCBI maintains the PubMed medical literature database, and this site features a link to it. This site also describes and links to many of their other software tools and databases, including: Entrez, a retrieval system for searching several of their databases; GenBank®, the NIH genetic sequence database; and Online Mendelian Inheritance in Man (OMIM), a catalog of human genes and genetic disorders. It includes taxonomy resources for organisms commonly used in molecular research projects. Other sections are About NCBI, Genomic Biology, Research at NCBI, Tools for data mining, Software Engineering, and Education.

This is an important site for genome and genetic sequence researchers. The site provides access to multiple databases with detailed help files for use in searching the databases. NCBI gives multiple means of accessing the data.

Subjects: Genomics — Research; Molecular Biology — Research; Databases

Publications: *Entrez Sequences Browser*, HE 20.3624:

NCBI Newsletter, HE 20.3624/2:

PubMed, HE 20.3627:

1219. National Center for Research Resources

http://www.ncrr.nih.gov/

Sponsor: National Institutes of Health (NIH) — National Center for Research Resources (NCRR)

Description: The NCRR site features a variety of resources for biomedical researchers. The research, grants, and publications of each NCRR division are described in their respective sections: Clinical Research, Research Infrastructure, Comparative Medicine, and Biomedical Technology. The Access Scientific Resources section links to information on NCRR-supported research resources such as the National Gene Vector Laboratories, cell cultures, and DNA materials. NCRR Publications offers directories, reports, fact sheets on their grant programs, *NCRR Reporter*, and other documents. Other sections include Research Funding Opportunities and News and Events.

Subjects: Biological Medicine — Research; Medical Research — Grants

Publication: *NCRR Reporter*, HE 20.3013/6:

1220. National Center for Toxicological Research

http://www.fda.gov/nctr/

Sponsor: Health and Human Services Department — Food and Drug Administration (FDA) — National Center for Toxicological Research (NCTR)

Description: NCTR conducts peer-reviewed scientific research in support and anticipation of the Food and Drug Administration's regulatory needs. Its Web site provide links to various sections including About Us, What's New, Initiatives, Events, Divisions and Science at NCTR. Initiatives include programs in food safety, bioterrorism, biotechnology, antimicrobial resistance, and HIV/AIDS. NCTR research divisions include Biochemical Toxicology, Microbiology, Molecular Epidemiology, and Neurotoxicology.

Subjects: Biotechnology — Research; Molecular Biology — Research; Toxicology (Medicine) — Research

1221. National Eye Institute

http://www.nei.nih.gov/

Sponsor: National Institutes of Health (NIH) — National Eye Institute (NEI)

Description: The National Eye Institute supports research to prevent and treat eye diseases and other vision disorders. The Health Information section on the NEI Web site includes fact sheets and guides written at the consumer level. These cover glaucoma, macular degeneration, diabetic eye disease, eye anatomy, and other topics. Other sections of the site include Research Funding, NEI Laboratories, and Education Programs. The site also has statistics on the most common eye diseases.

Subject: Vision Disorders — Research

Publication: *Outlook*, HE 20.3766:

1222. National Human Genome Research Institute

http://www.genome.gov/

Sponsor: National Institutes of Health (NIH) — National Human Genome Research Institute (NHGRI)

Description: NHGRI is the lead agency for the Human Genome Project, an international research effort to determine the DNA sequence of the entire human genome. This site brings together news, research reports, and educational resources related to the project. Specific sections cover the research; health, as it relates to genetics; and related policy, legislation, and legal and ethical concerns. The Grants section links to information on current opportunities, funding history, and active research.

Subject: Genomics — Research

1223. National Institute of Dental and Craniofacial Research

http://www.nidcr.nih.gov/

Sponsor: National Institutes of Health (NIH) — National Institute of Dental and Craniofacial Research (NIDCR)

Description: The NIDCR site offers a substantial collection of documents and information on dental research. Major sections include Health Information, Funding for Research and Training, Clinical Trials, Research, News and Reports, and About NIDCR. The Health Information section links to publications and resources on topics such as fluoride, gum diseases, oral cancer, smokeless tobacco, temporomandibular disorders, and tooth decay and cavity prevention.

Subject: Dental Health — Research

Publications: *NIDCR Research Digest*, HE 20.3413:

Spectrum Series, HE 20.3417:

1224. National Institute of General Medical Sciences

http://www.nigms.nih.gov/

Alternate URL: http://locus.umdnj.edu/nigms/

Sponsor: National Institutes of Health (NIH) — National Institute of General Medical Sciences (NIGMS)

Description: NIGMS supports basic biomedical research that is not targeted at specific diseases but lays the foundation for advances in disease diagnosis, treatment, and prevention. Major sections are Research Funding, Training and Careers, Minority Programs, and About NIGMS. The alternate URL hosts the NIGMS Human Genetic Mutant Cell Repository, which includes the NIGMS *Catalog of Cell Cultures and DNA Samples*.

Subject: Biological Medicine — Research

Publications: *Catalog of Cell Cultures and DNA Samples*, HE 20.3464:

NIGMS Minority Programs Update (annual), HE 20.3469:

Why Do Basic Research?, HE 20.3452:R 31/3

1225. National Institute of Nursing Research

http://www.nih.gov/ninr/

Sponsor: National Institutes of Health (NIH) — National Institute of Nursing Research (NINR)

Description: The NINR site features information on the broad range of nursing research. The site includes sections for About NINR, News and Information, and Research Funding and Programs. News and Information includes publications such as *NINR Focus Series*, Research Directions, a collection of online descriptions of selected studies, and Priority Expert Panel (PEP) Reports, representations of the original documents of the National Center for Nursing Research (now NINR) in conjunction with the National Nursing Research Agenda. The Research Funding and Programs page has grant information and program announcements.

Subject: Nursing — Research

1226. National Institute on Alcohol Abuse and Alcoholism

http://www.niaaa.nih.gov/

Sponsor: National Institutes of Health (NIH) — National Institute on Alcohol Abuse and Alcoholism (NIAAA)

Description: The NIAAA site features the sections About NIAAA, Publications, Databases, Press

Releases, Extramural Research, and Conferences and Events. The Publications include the full text of the bulletin, *Alcohol Alert,* along with pamphlets, brochures, research monographs, and other publications. The Databases section links to several databases including the Alcohol and Alcohol Problems Science Database, commonly known as ETOH.

Publications: *Alcohol Alerts*, HE 20.8322:
Alcohol Health & Research World (quarterly), HE 20.8309:
Special Report to U.S. Congress on Alcohol and Health, HE 20.8313:

1227. National Institute on Disability and Rehabilitation Research
`http://www.ed.gov/offices/OSERS/NIDRR/`
Sponsor: Education Department — Special Education and Rehabilitative Services Office — National Institute on Disability and Rehabilitation Research (NIDRR)
Description: National Institute on Disability and Rehabilitation Research (NIDRR) sponsors disability research and works with other federal agencies that conduct disability research through the Interagency Committee on Disability Research (ICDR). The Research and Statistics section of the site includes links to publications and databases including the Traumatic Brain Injury Database and the Spinal Cord Injury Database. The Programs and Projects section lists projects currently funded by NIDRR.
Subject: Disabilities — Research

1228. National Toxicology Program
`http://ntp-server.niehs.nih.gov/`
Sponsor: National Institutes of Health (NIH) — National Institute of Environmental Health Sciences (NIEHS)
Description: NTP conducts toxicity/carcinogenicity studies on agents suspected of posing hazards to human health. Chemical-related study information is submitted to NIEHS and is archived and maintained. More than 800 chemical studies are on file, and much of this information is available on the NTP Web server, including the *Annual Plan,* the annual *Report on Carcinogens,* NTP Study Databases, and information on the status of NTP studies. The NTP Study Database is searchable and includes long-term carcinogenecity studies, short-term toxicity studies, immunotoxicity studies, reproductive toxicity studies, and teratology studies. The site also features such sections as NTP Background, NTP Fact Sheets, Grants, Testing Information and Study Results, and NTP Centers for Evaluation.

This site contains a significant amount of toxicological data for researchers and those interested in the scientific basis for the regulation of toxic chemicals.
Subject: Toxicology (Medicine) — Research
Publications: *Annual Report on Carcinogens*, HE 20.23/4:
National Toxicology Program, Annual Plan, Fiscal Year, HE 20.3551/2:
NTP Technical Report on the Toxicology and Carcinogenesis Studies ..., HE 20.3564:

1229. NCI-Frederick (National Cancer Institute at Frederick)
`http://web.ncifcrf.gov/`
Sponsor: National Institutes of Health (NIH) — National Cancer Institute (NCI)
Description: NCI-Frederick is one of the main NCI cancer research centers. Its Web site features About NCI-Frederick, Research, Research Technology Program, Scientific Research Resources, Campus Resources, and Career Opportunities. There is also a News and Events section that features news about research and information about events and seminars.

This site is primarily useful for providing information on the FCRDC and its research efforts.
Subject: Cancer — Research

1230. NIH Clinical Center (Warren Grant Magnuson Clinical Center)
`http://www.cc.nih.gov/index.cgi`
Sponsor: National Institutes of Health (NIH)
Description: The Warren Grant Magnuson Clinical Center is the research hospital at the National Institutes of Health and is involved in a variety of clinical studies. The home page of its Web site features the following categories: The Hospital at NIH, This Week at the NIH Clinical Center, Research Today, Medical and Science Education, Healthy Living, and Clinical Research Studies.

The Hospital at NIH category offers general information about the clinical center and information and resources for patients. Under the Patient Education section, there is a list of many publications and resources in topics ranging from coping to self care and support. Research Today discusses current research at the center. Medical and Science Education is aimed at the research professional and offers information about training in clinical research, upcoming conferences, meetings, and special programs. Information on and patient recruitment for current clinical research studies is available under Clinical Research Studies.
Subject: Clinical Medicine
Publication: *Pharmacy Update*, HE 20.3054:

1231. NIH Human Embryonic Stem Cell Registry
http://escr.nih.gov
Sponsor: National Institutes of Health (NIH)
Description: The Stem Cell Registry lists institutions that have developed human embryonic stem cell lines meeting criteria necessary for federal funding of stem cell research. The site outlines the criteria as announced by President George W. Bush. For each institution, the site identifies the stem cell lines available and gives complete institutional contact information.
Subject: Biology — Research

1232. Visible Human Project®
http://www.nlm.nih.gov/research/visible/visible_human.html
Sponsor: National Institutes of Health (NIH) — National Library of Medicine (NLM)
Description: The National Library of Medicine's Visible Human Project® is creating complete, anatomically detailed, three-dimensional representations of the normal male and female human body. Acquisition of transverse CT (CAT scan), MR (magnetic resonance), and cryosection images of representative male and female cadavers has been completed. The long-term goal of the Visible Human Project is to produce a system of knowledge structures that will transparently link visual knowledge forms to symbolic knowledge formats such as the names of body parts. The site includes detailed information on the project and projects based on the visible human data set: applications for viewing images, sources of images and animations, and products. Other sections are the following: Mirror Sites, Tools, Media Productions, Related Projects, and Funding Sources.
Subjects: Human Anatomy and Physiology; Medical Computing

CHAPTER 10

Law and Law Enforcement

This chapter encompasses law and criminal justice, including some of the agencies that have been newly organized into the Department of Homeland Security.

The General section of this chapter includes sites relevant to civil, criminal, and administrative law, and basic resources such as the United States Code. These are followed by federal courts in the Courts section and, in the Law Enforcement section, a variety of sites for prevention, enforcement, and policy.

The Department of Homeland Security has the newest presence in this area and is one of our featured sites. For more information on homeland security legislation and reorganization, see the special section in the front of this book. Another featured site, the National Criminal Justice Reference Service, has been around much longer and serves as a vital resource for criminal justice research.

Bookmarks & Favorites

Law
- U.S. Code, http://www4.law.cornell.edu/uscode/
- U.S. Courts: The Federal Judiciary, http://www.uscourts.gov

Law Enforcement
- National Criminal Justice Reference Service, http://www.ncjrs.org

Major Agencies
- Homeland Security Department, http://www.dhs.gov
- Justice Department, http://www.usdoj.gov
  - Federal Bureau of Investigations, http://www.fbi.gov

Featured Sites

1233. Department of Homeland Security
http://www.dhs.gov
Sponsor: Homeland Security Department
Description: The Web site for the newly created Department of Homeland Security has information on both the organizational transition as well as the Department's current activities. Major substantive sections are: Emergencies and Disasters; Travel and Transportation; Immigration and Borders; Research and Technology; and Threats and Protection. The DHS Organization section includes an organization chart, transition planning, and budget information. The Press Room section includes press releases, speeches, testimony, and legislative information. Sections targeted to specific audiences include Citizens, Business, Government, and Employees. The business section covers the Department's contracting and procurement relationship with private business. The Government section includes links to state homeland security and emergency offices, information on grants available to state and local governments, and tribal governments disaster management information.
Subject: Homeland Security

1234. National Criminal Justice Reference Service
http://www.ncjrs.org/
Sponsor: Justice Department — National Criminal Justice Reference Service (NCJRS)
Description: The National Criminal Justice Reference Service (NCJRS) responds to queries from law enforcement and corrections officials, lawmakers, judges and court personnel, and researchers. The site contains a vast number of publications on a wide range of criminal justice and law enforcement topics including the reference compilation *Sourcebook of Criminal Justice Statistics*. It also provides access to the NCJRS Abstracts Database, which contains summaries of more than

160,000 criminal justice publications; federal, state, and local government reports; books; research reports; journal articles; and unpublished research.

Other topical links on the main page include Corrections, Courts, Crime Prevention, Statistics, Drugs and Crime, International, Juvenile Justice, Law Enforcement, and Victims of Crime. These topic sections include both electronic publications housed on these servers and links to external Internet resources. Access to the publications is available through the topics or via a full-text key-word search. The site also includes a catalog of NCJRS print publications, a list of federal grants available from the DOJ, and a conference calendar.

NCJRS is a collection of clearinghouses that support all bureaus of the DOJ Office of Justice Programs including the National Institute of Justice, the Office of Juvenile Justice and Delinquency Prevention, the Bureau of Justice Statistics, the Bureau of Justice Assistance, and the Office for Victims of Crime. It also supports the White House Office of National Drug Control Policy.

The vast number of publications available from the Justice Information Center make this a very useful site for criminal justice statistics and recent reports. Just a few of the publications are listed below. Many more are available.

Subject: Criminal Justice
Publications: *Capital Punishment*, J 29.11/3:
Compendium of Federal Justice Statistics, J 29.20:
Criminal Victimization in the United States, J 29.9/2:
Federal Law Enforcement Officers, J 29.11:L 41/2/
NCJRS Abstracts Database, J 28.31/2-2:
Prison and Jail Inmates at Midyear, J 29.11:P 93
Probation and Parole in the United States
Sourcebook of Criminal Justice Statistics, J 29.9/6-2:
Survey of State Procedures Related to Firearm Sales, J 29.2:F 51/2:

The legal resources in this chapter are divided into three sections, spanning the entry numbers indicated here:

General	*1235–1265*
Courts	*1266–1294*
Law Enforcement	*1295–1325*

General

1235. ADA Home Page
http://www.ada.gov
Alternate URL: http://www.usdoj.gov/crt/ada/adahom1.htm
Sponsor: Justice Department — Civil Rights Division
Description: The Americans with Disabilities Act (ADA) site features information on enforcement of the ADA, certification of building codes, and technical assistance. Under the Enforcement heading, status reports are available along with press releases and information on how to file complaints. The site also gives a toll-free number for the ADA information line, information on new or proposed regulations, and link to information about the ADA Technical Assistance Program and ADA Mediation Program.

This site will be most useful to those trying to comply with ADA.
Subject: Americans with Disabilities Act (ADA)
Publications: *Enforcing the ADA, A Status Report from the Department of Justice*, J 1.106:
Guide to Disability Rights Laws, J 1.8:D 63/2

1236. Antitrust Division
http://www.usdoj.gov/atr/
Sponsor: Justice Department — Antitrust Division
Description: The Antitrust Division uses its Internet site to provide full-text cases, information about the division and its activities, and press releases. The Public Documents section links to press releases, speeches, guidelines, the division's workload statistics, and other publications. The

Antitrust Case Filings page includes online cases arranged alphabetically going back to 1994. The site also highlights current cases on the top-level page.
Subject: Antitrust Law

1237. BusinessLaw.gov
http://www.businesslaw.gov/
Sponsor: Small Business Administration (SBA)
Description: This Small Business Administration site is subtitled "Legal and Regulatory Information for America's Small Business." Plain English Guides walk through many of the steps for starting, operating, and closing a small business, pointing out legal and regulatory responsibilities along the way. A State and Local section has similar guides for each U.S. state. A Federal Regulatory section has information on the rulemaking process and on the rights of businesses. The site also has general advice on finding and hiring a lawyer, going to court, and using alternative dispute resolution.
Subject: Small Business — Laws

1238. Civil Division
http://www.usdoj.gov/civil/home.html
Sponsor: Justice Department — Civil Division
Description: The Civil Division represents the United States, its departments and agencies, Members of Congress, Cabinet officers, and other federal employees in litigation. Special sections of the site include Radiation Exposure Compensation Program, Vaccine Injury Compensation Program, and Consumer Litigation. A Selected Cases section features documents from a handful of cases, such as the litigation against tobacco companies and health care fraud litigation.
Subject: Litigation

1239. Civil Rights Division
http://www.usdoj.gov/crt/
Sponsor: Justice Department — Civil Rights Division
Description: The Civil Rights Division of the Justice Department enforces federal statutes prohibiting discrimination. Pages for each of the division's organizational sections hold most of the content at the site. The organizational sections are Appellate; Coordination and Review; Criminal; Disability Rights; Educational Opportunities; Employment Litigation; Housing and Civil Enforcement; Special Litigation; Voting; and Office of Special Counsel for Immigration Related Unfair Employment Practices. Each section typically includes background material on the relevant area of practice, statutes enforced, and cases or briefs.
Subject: Civil Rights — Laws
Publication: *Enforcing the ADA, A Status Report from the Department of Justice*, J 1.106:

1240. Commission on Civil Rights
http://www.usccr.gov/
Sponsor: Civil Rights Commission
Description: The Web site of the United States Commission on Civil Rights (USCCR) features sections including About the Commission, Publications, Meeting Calendar, Regional Offices, Information on Filing a Complaint, and News Releases. Publications cover such topics as equal employment opportunity, voting rights, and race relations. There is a list of publications available online and a link to the complete catalog of USCCR publications.
Subject: Civil Rights
Publication: *Civil Rights Directory*, CR 1.10:15

1241. Community Relations Service
http://www.usdoj.gov/crs/
Description: The Community Relations Service (CRS) was established by the Civil Rights Act of 1964 to help communities resolve serious racial or ethnic conflicts. Major sections of the Web site include Commonly Asked Questions, Publications and Useful Handbooks, and the Map of CRS Regional and Field Offices. Publications cover such topics as hate crime, police use of force, and conflict resolution.

Subjects: Dispute Resolution; Mediation
Publication: *Annual Report of the Community Relations Service*, J 23.1:

1242. Consumer Sentinel
http://www.consumer.gov/sentinel/
Sponsor: Federal Trade Commission (FTC)
Description: Consumer Sentinel has information on consumer fraud and a facility for reporting fraud complaints. Under the Fraud Trends heading, the site has statistics on fraud and identity theft complaints.
Subject: Fraud

1243. Copyright Office
http://lcweb.loc.gov/copyright/
Sponsor: Library of Congress — Copyright Office
Description: The U.S. Copyright Web site includes information on copyright law, registering a work for copyright protection, and searching existing copyright records. It also covers emerging legal and policy issues in the realm of copyright, such as those concerning digital media. The site supplies copies of the Office's circulars, fact sheets, and forms. These cover specific aspects of registering a work for copyright, fees, licensing, deposit requirements, the duration of copyright, and other topics. *Copyright Basics*, an overview, is available online in English and Spanish. The section on How to Register a Work includes separate sections for literary works, visual arts, performing arts, sound recordings, and periodicals.

Simple in design and organization, this site does an exemplary job of providing frequently requested documents and information in an easy-to-find manner.
Subjects: Copyright Law; Intellectual Property
Publications: *Annual Report of the Register of Copyright*, LC 3.1:
Catalog of Copyright Entries, LC 3.6/6:
Copyright Basics, LC 3.4/2:1
Copyright Information Circulars, LC 3.4/2:
Forms, LC 3.14:
NewsNet, LC 3.4/3:

1244. Decisions of the Comptroller General of the United States
http://www.gao.gov/decisions/decision.htm
Sponsor: General Accounting Office (GAO) — Comptroller General
Description: The Comptroller General of GAO issues decisions regarding use of federal appropriations, government contract bid protests, and major federal regulations. This site provides access to the full text of recent decisions, in HTML and PDF formats. For older decisions going back to January 1996, there is a link to the database on GPO Access.

While the decisions are also available as one of the GPO Access databases, this version provides a good explanation of and easy access to the most recent decisions.
Subject: Government Contracts — Regulations
Publication: *Decisions of the Comptroller General*, GA 1.5:

1245. Department of Justice
http://www.usdoj.gov/
Sponsor: Justice Department
Description: The central Web site for the Justice Department provides links to the department's 50-plus component divisions and programs. The site also brings together the department's publications, press releases, budget information, and overview information. The Legal Documents section compiles links to Justice briefs, letters, and other documents under these headings: Antitrust; Civil; Civil Rights; Criminal; Environment; Office of Legal Counsel; Office of Solicitor General; Terrorism-Related Documents; U.S. Trustees; and Violence Against Women Program. A home page section titled Information for Individuals and Communities links to information on Justice Department assistance in such areas as dispute resolution, civil rights and liberties violations, domestic violence, and safe communities.The site also has extensive information relating to the Freedom of Information Act (FOIA). The FOIA section includes basic reference material explaining FOIA, a list

of principal FOIA contacts at federal agencies, links to other agencies' FOIA sites, and links to the annual FOIA reports submitted by federal departments and agencies. In addition to this government-wide material, Justice also provides links to the online FOIA reading rooms of its component divisions and offices.

Subject: Law and Law Enforcement
Publications: *Annual Report of the Attorney General of the United States*, J 1.1:
Office of Inspector General Semiannual Report to Congress, J 1.1/9:
Opinions of the Office of Legal Counsel, J 1.5/4:
Report of the Attorney General to Congress on Administration of Foreign Agents Registration, J 1.30:
United States Attorneys' Bulletin, J 31.12:
United States Attorneys' Manual, J 1.8:AT

1246. EConsumer.gov
http://www.econsumer.gov/
Sponsor: Federal Trade Commission (FTC)
Description: The Econsumer.gov site is a collaborative effort of over 30 nations, with the Federal Trade Commission taking the lead for United States participation. The site was developed in response to the international nature of Internet fraud. It provides general information about consumer protection in all countries that belong to the International Marketing Supervision Network (IMSN), contact information for consumer protection authorities in those countries, and an online complaint form. The site can be viewed in English, French, German, and Spanish.
Subject: Fraud

1247. Elaws—Employment Laws Assistance for Workers and Small Businesses
http://www.dol.gov/elaws/
Sponsor: Labor Department
Description: Elaws is an interactive system designed to help employees and employers understand their respective rights and responsibilities under the laws and regulations administered by the Department of Labor. The page links to various Elaws Advisors who are housed on the Web sites of component DOL agencies. Each Elaws Advisor provides information about a specific law or regulation. The Advisor imitates the interaction that an individual might have with a DOL employment law expert. It asks questions, provides information, and directs the user to the appropriate resolutions based on the user's responses. Featured areas of expertise of the Advisors include Workplace Safety, Employing Veterans, Wage and Hour Issues, and Drug-Free Workplace.
Subject: Labor Law

1248. Executive Office for United States Attorneys
http://www.usdoj.gov/usao/eousa/
Sponsor: Justice Department — United States Attorneys
Description: This agency serves the U.S. Attorneys. It features a directory of the U.S. Attorneys' Offices, providing attorney names, office addresses, and links to the office Web sites. The site also describes legal education programs for federal personnel provided through the National Advocacy Center.
Subject: Litigation

1249. Federal Administrative Decisions and Other Actions
http://www.law.virginia.edu/admindec
Sponsor: University of Virginia. School of Law. Library
Description: Maintained at the University of Virginia Law School Library, this page fills an important niche in finding legal information on the Web. It is a finding aid for administrative actions that fall outside the usual scope of the *Code of Federal Regulations* and the *Federal Register*. Its lengthy list includes links to items such as the advisory opinions from the Consumer Product Safety Commission, Department of Energy directives, Federal Labor Relations Authority decisions, Food and Drug Administration enforcement reports, and Postal Service administrative decisions. It links

to Electronic FOIA Reading Rooms for each agency covered, since these reading rooms often contain such administrative decisions and actions.
Subjects: Administrative Law; Finding Aids

1250. Federal Bureau of Prisons
http://www.bop.gov/
Sponsor: Justice Department — Federal Bureau of Prisons
Description: The Bureau of Prisons is responsible for the federal prison system and federal inmates. The BOP page features links to Public Information, BOP Directory, Inmate Information, Employment, Acquisition, and FOIA/Policy. The Public Information page includes: Quick Facts and Statistics, *Weekly Population Report,* Publications; Press Releases; and Documents, Articles, and BOP History. The Inmate Locator is a database of federal prisoners searchable by name or identification number.
Subject: Prisons
Publications: *State of the Bureau*, J 16.1:
Weekly Population Report, J 16.32:

1251. Federal Energy Regulatory Commission
http://www.ferc.gov
Alternate URL: http://www.ferc.fed.us/
Sponsor: Federal Energy Regulatory Commission (FERC)
Description: FERC is an independent regulatory commission, organized under the Department of Energy, with responsibility in the areas of the electricity, natural gas, oil, and hydroelectric power businesses. The Web site has information on FERC's role, particularly in market oversight and investigations and in the specific energy sectors. The site also serves as a central point for parties filing documents with FERC and for researchers seeking FERC documents. The Federal Energy Regulatory Records and Information System (FERRIS), under the heading Documents and Filing, has replaced several separate FERC databases. FERRIS provides a single point of access to over 20 years of documents submitted to and issued by FERC. Under the heading Legal Matters, the site has dockets for active cases before their Administrative Law Judges, and summaries of cases.
Subject: Energy — Regulations
Publication: *Annual Report, Federal Energy Regulatory Commission*, E 2.1:

1252. Federal Mine Safety and Health Review Commission
http://www.fmshrc.gov/
Sponsor: Federal Mine Safety and Health Review Commission (FMSHRC)
Description: The Federal Mine Safety and Health Review Commission is an independent adjudicative agency that provides administrative trial and appellate review of legal disputes arising under the Federal Mine Safety and Health Amendments Act of 1977. Sections featured at the site include About FMSHRC, Rules, Guides and Publications, Recent Decisions, Published Decisions, FOIA, and Strategic Plan, Performance Plans, and Reports. The full text of the decisions are available in ASCII and PDF formats.
Subject: Mining — Laws
Publication: *Decisions, Federal Mine Safety and Health Review Commission*, Y 3.M 66:9/

1253. GSA Board of Contract Appeals
http://www.gsbca.gsa.gov/
Sponsor: General Services Administration — Board of Contract Appeals
Description: The Board of Contract Appeals hears and decides contract disputes between government contractors and the General Services Administration, as well as other agencies such as the State Department and the Commerce Department. The board's Web site has decisions issued since October 1996, and an archive of decisions issued between October 1992 and October 1996. The site also carries the board's rules of procedure.
Subject: Government Contracts — Laws

1254. Historical Publications of the United States Commission on Civil Rights
`http://www.law.umaryland.edu/edocs/usccr/html%20files/usccrhp.asp`
Sponsor: University of Maryland. Thurgood Marshall Law Library
Description: This site provides access to PDF copies of Civil Rights Commission documents that are in the collection of the University of Maryland Thurgood Marshall Law Library. It includes a selection of documents dating back to the Civil Rights Act of 1957, which created the original Civil Rights Commission. Topics covered by the materials include the Voting Rights Act, school desegregation, police-community relations, and racial and ethnic relations. The documents can be listed by title, date, subject, or Superintendent of Documents number.
Subject: Civil Rights

1255. Identity Theft
`http://www.consumer.gov/idtheft/`
Sponsor: Federal Trade Commission (FTC)
Description: This site serves as a central point for government information on identity theft, described as when someone appropriates your personal information without your knowledge to commit fraud or theft. The site has information on preventing, responding to, and reporting identity theft. It includes sections on state and federal laws on identity theft, copies of related government reports and testimony, information on current legal cases and investigations, and news updates.
Subject: Identity Theft

1256. Legal Services Corporation
`http://www.lsc.gov/`
Description: Legal Services Corporation is a private, nonprofit corporation established by Congress to ensure equal access to justice under the law for all Americans. Its Web site has information about LSC's activities and a clickable map of the United States for finding LSC programs by state. The Press Room section includes substantive background and documents from and about LSC, including LSC statutes, regulations, and appropriations.
Subject: Legal Assistance
Publications: *Equal Justice Magazine*
Semiannual Report to the Congress, Legal Services Corporation, Y 3.L 52:1/

1257. Office for Victims of Crime
`http://www.ojp.usdoj.gov/ovc/`
Sponsor: Justice Department — Justice Programs Office
Description: The Office for Victims of Crime site features current news and resources from the agency. Major sections include: Grants and Funding; Help for Victims; Publications; OVC Resource Center; Training and Technical Assistance; and Resources for International Victims. Most of the publications are available online, either in HTML, ASCII, or PDF formats. The Help for Victims section directs users to resources, especially non-governmental organizations and their Web sites, that can assist with such areas child abuse, campus crime, elder abuse, sexual abuse, workplace violence, and terrorism and mass violence. It also includes a table of toll-free numbers for assistance. Much of the funding and technical assistance information on the OVC Web site is for professionals and organizations managing victims assistance programs. The Help for Victims section can be of direct interest to individuals.
Subject: Victims of Crime
Publications: *OVC Fact Sheets,* J 34.4:
OVC National Directory of Victim Assistance Funding Opportunities, J 34.10:
OVC's Legal Series Bulletins, J 34.3/3:
Report to Congress, Office for Victims of Crime, J 34.2:

1258. Office of the Law Revision Counsel
`http://uscode.house.gov/`
Sponsor: Congress — House of Representatives — Office of the Law Revision Counsel
Description: "The Office of the Law Revision Counsel prepares and publishes the United States Code, which is a consolidation and codification by subject matter of the general and permanent laws of the United States." (from the Web site) The Law Revision Counsel makes the U.S. Code available

online for searching, browsing, or downloading. The site also features the Office's classification tables, which show where recently enacted laws will appear in the United States Code and which sections of the Code have been amended by those laws. Also see the separate entry for the U.S. Code site sponsored by the Legal Information Institute.
Subject: Laws

1259. Office of Tribal Justice
http://www.usdoj.gov/otj/
Sponsor: Justice Department — Tribal Justice Office
Description: The Office of Tribal Justice was established in 1995 with the purpose of increasing the responsiveness of the DOJ to the concerns of the American Indian Nations, individual Indians and others interested in Indian affairs. The site has a description of the office and links that include Office of Tribal Justice Mission Statement, Department of Justice Sovereignty Policy, Attorney General Remarks, Presidential Statements, Grants and Funding, Congressional Testimony, Indian Country Law Enforcement, and Press Releases.
Subject: American Indians

1260. Postal Rate Commission
http://www.prc.gov/
Sponsor: Postal Rate Commission (PRC)
Description: The Postal Rate Commission is an independent regulatory agency that reviews Postal Service requests for changes in postal rates. Of general interest, the site lists current and historical postal rates. Most of the rest of the site is dedicated to documents from Postal Rate Commission cases. The Contents section provides the easiest access to docketed and pending cases, opinions and decisions, orders, commission rules, and the *Domestic Mail Classification Schedule*.
Subject: Postal Service — Regulations
Publication: *Domestic Mail Classification Schedule*

1261. Ready.gov
http://www.ready.gov
Sponsor: Homeland Security Department
Description: The Ready.gov Web site was set up in early 2003 by the Department of Homeland Security to inform people about how to prepare for potential terrorist attacks. Sections cover how to make a kit of emergency supplies, how to plan what you will do in an emergency, and how to detect and react to specific threats such as bomb explosions or a chemical attack.
Subjects: Disaster Preparedness; Homeland Security

1262. REGINFO.GOV
http://reginfo.gov/
Sponsor: General Services Administration
Description: The Regulatory Information Service Center established the REGINFO.GOV site to assist users who want to find information about federal, state, and local regulation. The Web site links to regulatory information from other sites such as the *Federal Register* and the *Code of Federal Regulations* at GPO Access. However, it also has its own version of the *Unified Agenda*, which is housed at the http://ciir.cs.umass.edu/ua/ site. Other links include Regulations Pending and Reviews Completed, Information Collections Under Review/Approvals Expired (OMB), Inventory of Approved Information Collections (OMB), and links to federal legislation, state and local governments, federal agencies, and federal judiciary materials.
Subjects: Regulatory Policy; Finding Aids

1263. Regulations.gov
http://www.regulations.gov
Sponsor: Environmental Protection Agency (EPA)
Description: Launched in early 2003, Regulations.gov is intended to make it easier for the general public to participate in the federal regulations review process. Users can search by agency or word to find proposed and final regulations currently open for comment. Search results include a docket ID, *Federal Register* citation and date for when the regulation was first published, and final date

for comments. The results also have links to view the *Federal Register* announcement in text or PDF formats and a link to a Web form for submitting comments. The site is an interagency effort led by the Environmental Protection Agency. Other supporting agencies are the Food and Drug Administration, the National Archives and Records Administration Office of the Federal Register, and the Government Printing Office. As noted on the site, "Every effort is made to ensure that the website includes all rule and proposed rule notices that are currently open for public comment. Users who want to verify the current status of a proposed or final rule and associated comment requirements are urged to check the official edition of the Federal Register."
Subject: Regulatory Policy

1264. U.S. Code
http://www4.law.cornell.edu/uscode/
Sponsor: Legal Information Institute (LII)
Description: Cornell's Legal Information Institute (LII) offers this popular and free interface for searching the U.S. Code. The Code can be searched by word, by title and section number, or browsed. The site also features a table of popular names of laws, such as Voting Rights Act and Railroad Retirement Act. Where these laws can easily be linked to one part of the Code, LII does so. Most popular names are not linked, however, and since these have no Public Law or other citation, they are of little reference use. Also see the separate entry for the Office of the Law Revision Counsel.
Subject: Laws

1265. U.S. Office of Special Counsel
http://www.osc.gov
Sponsor: Office of Special Counsel (OSC)
Description: The OSC is an independent federal investigative and prosecutorial agency with the mission of protecting federal employees and applicants from prohibited personnel practices, especially reprisal for whistleblowing. The agency is also concerned with adherence to the Hatch Act, which restricts political activity by federal government employees. Major sections of the site explain prohibited personnel practices, whistleblower procedures and protections, and Hatch Act rules. The site also covers the Uniformed Services Employment and Reemployment Rights Act (USERRA), which prohibits discrimination against persons because of their service in the Armed Forces Reserve, the National Guard, or other uniformed services.
Subjects: Government Employees — Laws; Hatch Act
Publication: *Annual Reports to Congress from the U.S. Office of Special Counsel*, MS 2.1:

Courts

1266. Court of Appeals. (01) First Circuit
http://www.ca1.uscourts.gov/
Alternate URL: http://www.law.emory.edu/1circuit/
Sponsor: Court of Appeals. (01) First Circuit
Description: The First Circuit covers Maine, Massachusetts, New Hampshire, Puerto Rico, and Rhode Island. The Court's official site has current opinions available in HTML or WordPerfect formats. Opinions can also be sent via email if you know the case number. The Emory University law school library site has electronic versions of the opinions from the First Circuit of the federal Court of Appeals for 1995 to the present. Access is by month of decision, first party, second party, or keyword search. The official site also includes the court calendar, rules and procedures, forms, filing instructions, and links to the Web sites of other courts in the First Circuit.
Subject: Federal Appellate Courts

1267. Court of Appeals. (02) Second Circuit
http://www.ca2.uscourts.gov/
Alternate URL: http://csmail.law.pace.edu/lawlib/legal/us-legal/judiciary/second-circuit.html
Sponsor: Court of Appeals. (02) Second Circuit

Description: The Second Circuit covers Connecticut, Vermont, and New York. The Court's official site has opinions issued within the past 30 days. Opinions can be browsed by date range or searched by case name or docket number. The alternate URL, from Pace University School of Law, has the text of opinions from 1995 to the present. They are in HTML format and can be browsed by month and year. The official site also offers a court directory, forms, the Second Circuit Handbook, and biographies of the judges.
Subject: Federal Appellate Courts

1268. Court of Appeals. (03) Third Circuit
http://www.ca3.uscourts.gov/
Alternate URL: http://vls.law.vill.edu/Locator/3/
Sponsor: Court of Appeals. (03) Third Circuit
Description: The Third Circuit covers Delaware, New Jersey, Pennsylvania, and the Virgin Islands. At its official site, the Court has the text of the recent month's opinions. These are linked from the headings for Precedential and Not Precedential Opinions on the home page. For older opinions, the Court links to the Villanova University School of Law site listed here as the alternate URL. Villanova has the full text of the decisions from the Third Circuit of the federal Court of Appeals from May 1994 to the present. Most of the opinions are available in ASCII text format, but they began using PDF format in April 2002. The Court's site also has a Death Penalty Information section, listing the appeals status and history for individuals given a death sentence in courts within the Third Circuit. The Information and Forms section includes a court calendar, phone directory, and general information on the Court.
Subject: Federal Appellate Courts

1269. Court of Appeals. (04) Fourth Circuit
http://www.ca4.uscourts.gov/
Sponsor: Court of Appeals. (04) Fourth Circuit
Description: The Fourth Circuit covers Maryland, North Carolina, South Carolina, Virginia, and West Virginia. The Court of Appeals site has their opinions online going back 1996, and the full text of the opinions can be searched. The Information section of the site includes judge biographies, filing instructions, and a map of the districts within the Fourth Circuit. Other sections include Docket, Mediation, Argument Calendar, Rules and Procedures, Forms and Notices, and Court Links.
Subject: Federal Appellate Courts

1270. Court of Appeals. (05) Fifth Circuit
http://www.ca5.uscourts.gov/
Sponsor: Court of Appeals. (05) Fifth Circuit
Description: The Fifth Circuit covers Louisiana, Mississippi, and Texas. The official Fifth Circuit Court of Appeals Web site includes full-text cases and information about the Court. Case materials are available for decisions rendered and published electronically since 1991. The cases are available in HTML format. Users can search by date, docket number, or keyword. User can also sign up to have opinions sent by email as soon as they are posted on the site. The site also includes dockets, calendars, and biographies of judges. The Court Library's section includes jury instructions, court history, general reference links, and a historical index to where justices' biographies have appeared in print.
Subject: Federal Appellate Courts

1271. Court of Appeals. (06) Sixth Circuit
http://www.ca6.uscourts.gov/
Sponsor: Court of Appeals. (06) Sixth Circuit
Description: The Sixth Circuit covers Kentucky, Michigan, Ohio, and Tennessee. The official site of the Sixth Circuit of the federal Court of Appeals offers online cases available back to 1994. From July 1999 forward, they are in HTML and PDF formats. Prior to 1999 they are in ASCII text format with an option to download a WordPerfect version. Under Court Information, this site has the oral argument calendar and status of pending cases by district. The court rules are under the heading Local Rules.
Subject: Federal Appellate Courts

1272. Court of Appeals. (07) Seventh Circuit

http://www.ca7.uscourts.gov

Sponsor: Court of Appeals. (07) Seventh Circuit

Description: The Seventh Circuit covers Illinois, Indiana, and Wisconsin. This site offers information about the Seventh Circuit and has searchable access to its opinions. The opinions may also be browsed by date range. Other sections of the site include Calendar, Rules and Guides, Annual Reports, Library, and Other 7th Circuit Links.

Subject: Federal Appellate Courts

1273. Court of Appeals. (08) Eighth Circuit

http://www.ca8.uscourts.gov/index.html

Sponsor: Court of Appeals. (08) Eighth Circuit

Description: The Eighth Circuit covers Arkansas, Iowa, Minnesota, Missouri, Nebraska, North Dakota, and South Dakota. This site features the Eighth Circuit Court of Appeal's opinions released since 1998. These electronic versions are available in ASCII format and can be searched by date range and keyword. Opinions may also be browsed by the name of the authoring judge. The site also has the court calendar, rules, publications, forms, and fee schedules. It links to the same basic information for the Bankruptcy Appellate Panel for the Eighth Circuit.

Subject: Federal Appellate Courts

1274. Court of Appeals. (09) Ninth Circuit

http://www.ca9.uscourts.gov/

Sponsor: Court of Appeals. (09) Ninth Circuit

Description: The Ninth Circuit covers Alaska, Arizona, California, Hawaii, Idaho, Montana, Nevada, Oregon, Washington, Guam, and the Northern Mariana Islands. The Ninth Circuit Court of Appeals Web site has the text of its opinions back to 1995. The electronic versions are available in ASCII text format and since September 2000, in PDF format. Opinions can be browsed by date or case number. Other sections of the site include the court calendar, rules, phone directory, and status of pending cases.

Subject: Federal Appellate Courts

1275. Court of Appeals. (10) Tenth Circuit

http://www.ck10.uscourts.gov

Alternate URLs: http://www.kscourts.org/ca10/
http://www.law.emory.edu./10circuit/

Sponsor: Court of Appeals. (10) Tenth Circuit

Description: The Tenth Circuit covers Colorado, Kansas, New Mexico, Oklahoma, Utah, and Wyoming. This official site features information on the Circuit and links to online full-text versions of the decisions from the Tenth Circuit of the federal Court of Appeals. The actual cases are at the two alternate URLs: Emory Law School from August 1995 to October 1997 and Washburn University School of Law from October 1997 to the present. All cases at the Emory site are in full text on the Web or can be downloaded in ASCII format. Cases on the Washburn site are in full text on the Web and can be downloaded in WordPerfect or RTF formats.

Subject: Federal Appellate Courts

1276. Court of Appeals. (11) Eleventh Circuit

http://www.ca11.uscourts.gov/

Alternate URL: http://www.law.emory.edu/11circuit/

Sponsor: Court of Appeals. (11) Eleventh Circuit

Description: The Eleventh Circuit covers Alabama, Florida, and Georgia. Electronic versions of the opinions from the Eleventh Circuit available from November 1994 to the present in a downloadable zipped format. For enhanced access, the Court points to a collection at Emory University's law school library site which covers the same time period but can be searched and displayed in HTML or WordPerfect formats.The site also includes a court directory, brief biographies of the justices, court rules in PDF format, and links to district and bankruptcy court sites within the Eleventh District.

Subject: Federal Appellate Courts

1277. Court of Appeals. District of Columbia Circuit
http://www.cadc.uscourts.gov/
Alternate URL: http://www.ll.georgetown.edu/federal/judicial/cadc.cfm
Description: The D.C. Circuit Court of Appeals hears appeals from the U.S. District Court for the District of Columbia, and also for many federal administrative agencies. The Court's Web site carries the ASCII text version of it opinions, going back to September 1997. Georgetown University's law library site, the alternate URL provided here, carries the opinions in HTML format going back to March 1995. The Court's official site also has sections for News and Information, Rules and Procedures, Calendar, and Court Offices. The site's home page highlights new and recently updated documents and recently released opinions.

Due to the jurisdiction of the Court, researchers will find the site useful for documents in high profile cases such as *U.S. v. Microsoft*.
Subject: Federal Appellate Courts

1278. Court of Appeals. Federal Circuit
http://www.fedcir.gov/
Alternate URL: http://www.ll.georgetown.edu/federal/judicial/cafed.cfm
Description: The U.S. Court of Appeals for the Federal Circuit has nationwide jurisdiction to hear appeals in specialized cases. The Federal Circuit Court's Web site has copies of its precedential opinions, issued within the past 90 days, in Microsoft Word format. For earlier opinions, the Federal Circuit site points to the Web site of Georgetown University's Law Library; there, the opinions are available back to August 1995. Other sections of the Court's official site include Rules and Forms, Calendar and Dispositions, and Information, Statistics, and Directions.
Subject: Federal Appellate Courts

1279. Department of Labor Office of Administrative Law Judges (OALJ)
http://www.oalj.dol.gov/
Sponsor: Labor Department — Office of Administrative Law Judges (OALJ)
Description: The Labor Department's administrative law judges preside over cases related to many of the Department's programs, such as black lung benefits cases and Fair Labor Standards Act enforcement. The office also includes the Board of Contract Appeals (BCA) and the Board of Alien Labor Certification Appeals (BALCA). Decisions and other online documents are organized in the OALJ Law Library by program area, including Davis Bacon Act, Longshore, Federal Contracts Compliance Program, Black Lung, Whistleblower, and Immigration.
Subject: Labor Law
Publications: *Guide to Case Types*, L 1.7/2:
Judges' Benchbook of the Black Lung Benefits Act, L 1.2:

1280. Federal Judicial Center
http://www.fjc.gov/
Sponsor: Federal Judicial Center (FJC)
Description: The Federal Judicial Center conducts research on federal court operations and history, and it manages training programs for federal judges and court employees. The FJC Web site has a substantial number of online publications and information on the judicial branch. Under the heading General Information about the FJC, the site includes the usual descriptive information along with the *Federal Judiciary Center Annual Report*. The Publications section has an online catalog as well as one that can be downloaded in PDF version. Many of the reports are available online in PDF format, while others must be purchased or requested from the FJC according to instructions at the site.
Subject: Federal Courts
Publications: *A Guide to the Preservation of Federal Judges' Papers*, JU 13.8:
Annual Report / Federal Judicial Center, JU 13.1:
Directory of Manuscript Collections Related to Federal Judges, 1789–1997, JU 13.14:
Federal Courts and What They Do
Guideline Sentencing Update, JU 13.8/3:

1281. FindLaw: Cases and Codes: U.S. Circuit Courts

http://www.findlaw.com/casecode/courts/

Sponsor: Findlaw, Inc.

Description: This central finding aid for legal information offers this section with online, searchable, full-text, HTML versions of cases from all the Circuit Courts. Most go back to about 1995 and are searchable by docket number, party name, or words in the full-text. The cases can also be browsed by date. FindLaw also provides a court directory for each circuit.

Like their Supreme Court database, FindLaw's Circuit Court site is an easy-to-use tool for searching for recent opinions. In addition, the site functions as a metasite for the other Web sites about the courts and that also provide full-text cases online.

Subjects: Federal Courts; Finding Aids

1282. FindLaw: Supreme Court Opinions

http://www.findlaw.com/casecode/supreme.html

Sponsor: Findlaw, Inc.

Description: FindLaw, a major finding aid for Internet law sources, features Supreme Court opinions in HTML format back to 1893, volume 150 of the *U.S. Reports*. Browsable by year and volume number, cases are searchable by citation, case title, and full text. The opinions have hypertext links from references to other cases available through FindLaw. In addition, at the top of each case is a link to a search for other cases in this database that cite the displayed case.

This is an excellent, free source for Supreme Court opinions on the Web.

Subject: Supreme Court

1283. FLITE Supreme Court Decisions

http://www.fedworld.gov/supcourt/

Alternate URL: http://www.access.gpo.gov/su_docs/supcrt/

Sponsors: Commerce Department — Technology Administration (TA) — National Technical Information Service (NTIS); Government Printing Office (GPO) — Superintendent of Documents

Description: The Federal Legal Information Through Electronics (FLITE) database of Supreme Court opinions provides public access to a formerly limited access database. The file consists of 7,407 Supreme Court opinions dating from 1937 through 1975, from volumes 300 through 422 of *U.S. Reports*. Access is by case name or a keyword search on the full text. This database is available through NTIS Fedworld and, at the alternate URL, GPO Access.

Access to FLITE only occurred after a long battle with the U. S. Air Force using Freedom of Information Act requests. Its availability adds a significant amount of case law material to the other case law sites that are freely available on the Internet. However, FindLaw provides even greater access to Supreme Court cases.

Subject: Supreme Court

1284. History of the Federal Judiciary

http://www.fjc.gov/history/home.nsf

Sponsor: Federal Judicial Center (FJC)

Description: The History of the Federal Judiciary Web site presents basic reference information about the history of the federal courts and the judges who have served on the federal courts since 1789. Major sections on this site include: Judges of the United States Courts, which allows users to search for judges by name or by alphabetical listing; Courts of the Federal Judiciary, which contains a legislative history for every court in the system; and Landmark Judicial Legislation, presenting the text of 21 statutes related to the organization and jurisdiction of the federal judiciary. A section called Judicial Administration and Organization has brief descriptions and histories for court offices and staff positions, such as law clerks, court criers, U.S. Marshals, and librarians; each entry contains references for further reading. Other sections include a Historic Courthouse Photographic Exhibit, Judicial History News, and a featured section on the *Amistad* slavery case.

Subjects: Federal Courts — History; Judges

1285. LII Supreme Court Collection

http://supct.law.cornell.edu/supct/

Sponsor: Legal Information Institute (LII)

Description: The Legal Information Institute at Cornell University has the full text of Supreme Court decisions back to 1990, in HTML and PDF formats. LII also offers a Historic Collection with approximately 300 selected historic decisions dating back to 1793. All decisions can be searched by keyword or browsed by topic, decision author, or party name. Each current opinion at LII consists of a syllabus, the opinion, and optionally concurring and dissenting opinions. A syllabus is associated with most of the opinions and summarizes the ruling. When the Court is in session, the site also has current Court orders and case update documents such as the calendar and list of pending oral arguments.

LII also offers an email current awareness service, called liibulletin, which includes syllabi of U.S. Supreme Court decisions in bulletin format within hours after their release. In addition, the site has links to a legal glossary, biographies of the current justices, the *Rules of the Supreme Court*, and other online sources for Supreme Court materials including the Court's official site. The LII Supreme Court Collection is not the most comprehensive collection online, but it provides one of the best interfaces and does a good job in documenting the content and context of its collection.

Subject: Supreme Court

1286. Occupational Safety and Health Review Commission

http://www.oshrc.gov/

Sponsor: Occupational Safety and Health Review Commission (OSHRC)

Description: OSHRC is an independent federal agency created to decide contests of citations or penalties resulting from OSHA inspections. The Review Commission functions as an administrative court, with established procedures for conducting hearings, receiving evidence, and rendering decisions by its administrative law judges (ALJ). Its site features full-text versions of recent decisions by the commission and administrative law judges under the section entitled Decisions. Other sections are Procedural Rules, Publications, Press Releases, OSH Act, Budget, and About OSHRC.

Subject: Workplace Safety — Laws

Publications: *Biennial Report of the U.S. Occupational Safety and Health Review Commission*
Commission Decisions, Y 3.OC 1:10-6/
Guide to E-Z Trial Procedures, Y 3.OC 1:2
Guide to Review Commission Procedures, Y 3.OC 1:8 P

1287. PACER Service Center

http://pacer.psc.uscourts.gov/

Sponsor: Administrative Office of the U.S. Courts

Description: "Public Access to Court Electronic Records (PACER) is an electronic public access service that allows users to obtain case and docket information from Federal Appellate, District and Bankruptcy courts, and from the U.S. Party/Case Index." (from the Web site, 01-06-03) The service is fee-based and is financed through the collection of these user fees. The type of information available through case dockets on PACER includes listing of all parties and participants in the case, a chronology of case events, appellate court opinions, and judgments or case status. The main sections include PACER Overview, Register for PACER, U.S. Party/Case Index, PACER Documents, and PACER Announcements. U.S. Party/Case Index is a national index for U.S. district, bankruptcy, and appellate courts. One may conduct nationwide searches to determine whether or not a party is involved in federal litigation. PACER Documents includes access to the *PACER Service Center User Manual* in PDF format and the *U.S. Party/Case Index User Manual* in WordPerfect or ASCII text formats. Other documents such as guides, user manuals, or guidelines are also available in PDF, WordPerfect, or ASCII.

Subjects: Federal Courts; Databases

1288. Supreme Court of the United States

http://www.supremecourtus.gov/

Sponsor: Supreme Court of the United States

Description: The Supreme Court's official Web site has the full text of its opinions from the present term and going back to the Court's 2000 term (for which all decisions were issued in 2001). Opinions can be browsed by term and are in reverse date order. The Opinions section of the site also contains an excellent explanation of the differences between various print and electronic versions in the section Information About Opinions, reminding researchers that "only the bound volumes of the *United States Reports* contain the final, official text of the opinions of the Supreme Court." Having said that, the Opinions section also carries PDF versions of the bound volumes of *United States Reports*. These include all of the opinions, orders, and other materials issued each term and are online for the 1991 term forward. Other helpful material in the Opinions section includes a directory of the many print and electronic versions of Supreme Court opinions available from other sources, and a Case Citation Finder with the official citation for published opinions from 1790 forward.

Other sections of the site include About the Supreme Court, Docket, Oral Arguments, Bar Admissions, Court Rules, Case Handling Guides, Orders and Journal, Visiting the Court, and Public Information. The Public Information section includes Press Releases, Media Advisories, and the justices' speeches. The section About The Court has PDF copies of factsheets on the Court's operations and history, including a list of justices from 1789 to present and biographies of the current members.

The official Supreme Court site does not have the best searchable interface to its opinions, but it is useful for current documents and news from the Court. The site is also valuable for information about the history of the Court and the documents it generates.

Subject: Supreme Court

Publications: *Rules of the Supreme Court of the United States*, JU 6.9:
Slip Opinion, JU 6.8/B:
United States Reports, JU 6.8:

1289. The Oyez Project: A U.S. Supreme Court Multimedia Database

http://oyez.org/

Sponsor: Northwestern University

Description: The Oyez Project Web site is an educational site being developed at Northwestern University. The site is collecting summary information on major constitutional law cases decided by the Supreme Court. For these, it attempts to obtain and attach a sound recording (in RealPlayer format) of the oral arguments heard by the Court. The site also features a virtual tour of the Supreme Court Building.

Subject: Supreme Court — History

1290. U.S. Court of Appeals for the Armed Forces

http://www.armfor.uscourts.gov/

Sponsor: Court of Appeals for the Armed Forces

Description: This site provides information about the Court of Appeals for the Armed Forces with access to online opinions. These are available back to 1997 and are available in HTML format. Access is by date. The site also has information on court history, jurisdiction, judges, rules, and scheduled hearings.

Subject: Military Justice

1291. U.S. Courts: The Federal Judiciary

http://www.uscourts.gov/

Sponsor: Administrative Office of the U.S. Courts

Description: The Administrative Office of the U.S. Courts maintains this site, which features sections describing the U.S. Supreme Court, Courts of Appeals, District Courts, and Bankruptcy Courts. These sections explain the operations of the court, provide caseload statistics and other material, and link to the online site for each court. An Educational Outreach section of the site has lesson plans and classroom resources. Electronic Access covers about court information systems. For the legal professional, Federal Rulemaking covers federal rules of practice, procedure, and evidence. The Newsroom section has press releases, featured publications, federal judgeship vacancies, and data on judicial salaries. The Library section has a list of publications and statistical reports, with links to the full text. Finally, a Court Links page has links to federal court Web sites. The U.S. Courts site provides clear explanations of the workings of the federal judiciary. The site itself is an excellent reference tool, addressing popular topics in a succinct manner. Finally, the court links pages are conveniently arranged for quickly locating the proper court or for bookmarking for future reference.

Publications: *Federal Probation Journal*, JU 10.8:
Judicial Business of the United States Courts, JU 10.1/4:
The Third Branch, Bulletin of the Federal Courts, JU 10.3/2:
Understanding the Federal Courts, JU 10.2:
Wiretap Report, JU 10.19:

1292. United States Court of Federal Claims
http://www.uscfc.uscourts.gov/
Sponsor: Court of Federal Claims
Description: The Court of Federal Claims is authorized to hear primarily money claims founded upon the Constitution, federal statutes, executive regulations, or contracts, with the United States. In addition, "(t)he Court has been given new equitable jurisdiction in the area of bid protests, as well as jurisdiction in vaccine compensation, civil liberties, product liability, oil spills, and various other areas of the law over the last sixteen years." (from the Web site, January 6, 2003) Court opinions are available from July 1997 to the present. The online versions are available in PDF format, and access is by date. The site also includes court rules, judicial biographies, forms, general orders of the court, and information from its Office of Special Masters.
Subject: Federal Courts

1293. United States Court of International Trade
http://www.cit.uscourts.gov/
Sponsor: Court of International Trade
Description: The United States Court of International Trade handles litigation rising out of international trade disputes. Its Web site has sections for the court calendar, court staff directory, rules and forms, and biographies of the judges. Slip opinions are online for 1999 forward, in PDF format.
Subjects: Federal Courts; International Trade — Laws

1294. United States Tax Court
http://www.ustaxcourt.gov/
Sponsor: Tax Court
Description: The U.S. Tax Court, a federal court established by Congress under Article I of the Constitution, provides a judicial forum for affected persons to dispute "tax deficiencies" as determined by the Commissioner of Internal Revenue, prior to payment of the disputed amounts. The site has such sections as Today's Opinions, Historical Opinions, Forms, Rules, Press Releases, and general information about contacts, fees and charges, and FAQs. The Historical Opinions sections offers a search of past opinions by release date, petitioner's name, judge, opinion type, and sorted by case name or release date. Forms has applications for admission to practice before the court for lawyers and nonlawyers with instructions. Under Rules of Practice and Procedure, there is a list of interim Rules (pending publication in the *Reports of the Court* by GPO), which include amendments to existing Rules and new Titles.
Subjects: Federal Courts; Taxation — Laws
Publication: *Rules of Practice and Procedure, U.S. Tax Court*, JU 11.8:

Law Enforcement

1295. ATF Online - Bureau of Alcohol, Tobacco, and Firearms
http://www.atf.gov/
Sponsor: Justice Department — Bureau of Alcohol, Tobacco, Firearms, and Explosives
Description: As part of the Homeland Security Act of 2002, the Bureau of Alcohol, Tobacco, Firearms, and Explosives (ATF) was transferred from the Treasury Department to the Justice Department in early 2003. (Certain functions of the ATF remain with Treasury in the newly created Alcohol and Tobacco Tax and Trade Bureau or TTB. See separate entry for the TTB Web site.) ATF is a law enforcement organization charged with enforcing federal laws and regulations relating to alcohol, tobacco, firearms, explosives and arson. As of this writing, the ATF Web site features news, organizational information, and major sections for Firearms, Arson and Explosives, and Laboratories. A section on Explosives, Bomb Threat, and Detection Resources includes a bomb threat checklist, suspect letter and package indicator, and other security guides. The Regulations section has current notices of proposed rulemaking in the areas of alcohol, tobacco, and firearms/explosives. The Publications section, as of this writing, includes publications relevant to both the law enforcement mission transferred to Justice and the revenue mission that has remained at Treasury.
Subjects: Law Enforcement; Wanted People
Publications: *Alcohol and Tobacco Newsletter*, T 70.18/2:
Alcohol, Tobacco and Firearms Bulletin, T 70.7:
ATF Annual Report, T 70.1:
ATF Explosives Industry Newsletter
ATF Industry Circulars, T 70.10:
Federal Firearms Licensee Newsletter, T 70.18:
Firearms Curios or Relics List, T 70.15:
Firearms State Laws and Published Ordinances, T 70.14:
Monthly Statistical Release—Beer, T 70.9/4:
Monthly Statistical Release—Wine, T 70.9/5:

1296. Attorney General
http://www.usdoj.gov/ag/index.html
Sponsor: Justice Department — Attorney General
Description: The United States Attorney General is head of the Justice Department and chief law enforcement officer of the federal government. This site describes the office and has some biographical information on the current Attorney General. It also provides links to speeches, testimony, *Annual Reports*, and FOIA.
Subject: Law Enforcement
Publication: *Annual Report of the Attorney General of the United States*, J 1.1:

1297. Bureau of Justice Assistance
http://www.ojp.usdoj.gov/BJA/
Sponsor: Justice Department — Justice Programs Office
Description: The Bureau of Justice Assistance (BJA) supports local criminal justice agencies throughout the United States, offering grants, training, and technical assistance. The BJA Web site includes information on a number of grant programs including the Local Law Enforcement Block Grant Program and the Byrne Formula Grant Program. All major BJA assistance is described in the Programs section. In the Justice Topics section, major areas of BJA focus are described, and there are links to related publications, related Web sites, and any relevant BJA training. The Publications section has a list of publications available either in ASCII or PDF formats. A wider search on criminal justice or related documents is possible via a link to the National Criminal Justice Reference Service Abstract Database.
Subject: Law Enforcement — Grants
Publication: *Local Law Enforcement Block Grants Program*, J 26.33:

1298. Counterterrorism Office
http://www.state.gov/s/ct/
Sponsor: State Department — Counterterrorism Office
Description: The State Department's Counterterrorism Office develops U.S. counterterrorism policy and coordinates U.S. efforts to improve counterterrorism cooperation with foreign governments. This site includes statements on U.S. policy and describes the programs of the Office, both in the U.S. and internationally. It links to counterterrorist-related Executive Orders and to the annual publication *Patterns of Global Terrorism*. The Office maintains the immigration Terrorist Exclusion List, as well as a list of organizations and individuals linked to terrorism to the extent that their assets may be blocked.
Subject: Terrorism — Policy
Publication: *Patterns of Global Terrorism*, S 1.138:

1299. Diplomatic Security Service
http://ds.state.gov/
Sponsor: State Department — Diplomatic Security Bureau
Description: The Bureau of Diplomatic Security (DS) is the security and law enforcement arm of the Department of State. Overseas, DS manages the security programs that protect U.S. diplomatic personnel who work in U.S. diplomatic missions around the world. DS also assists foreign embassies and consulates in the United States with the security for their missions and personnel. The home page has main sections entitled: About Diplomatic Security (overview, history, speeches, publications), Diplomatic Immunities, Investigations, Protection, Countering Terrorism, and Career Opportunities. The Diplomatic Immunities section includes a downloadable PDF copy of *Diplomatic Immunity from Criminal Jurisdiction: Summary of Law Enforcement Aspects*. The Counterterrorism section describes the activities of the Intelligence and Threat Analysis office and links to its publications *Political Violence Against Americans* and *Issues in Global Crime*. While this site focuses mainly on the protection of the diplomatic corps, some of the material may also be of interest to U.S. law enforcement personnel.
Subject: Terrorism
Publications: *Issues in Global Crime*, S 1.149:
Political Violence Against Americans, S 1.138/2:

1300. Drug Enforcement Administration
http://www.usdoj.gov/dea/
Sponsor: Justice Department — Drug Enforcement Administration (DEA)
Description: The DEA Web site focuses on information about current illegal drug threats and recent DEA enforcement actions. A Briefs and Background section organizes DEA reports, news releases, fact sheets and other material under the categories of Drug Trafficking and Abuse (includes drug descriptions), Law Enforcement, Drug Policy, and DEA Resources for specific audiences (parents, teachers, students, legislators, physicians, etc.). The Inside the DEA section has alphabetized links to major DEA programs, such as Forensic Sciences, Intelligence, Marijuana Eradication, Money Laundering, and the DEA Museum in Arlington, VA. The Local News section links to a page for each of DEA's field divisions, with news, phone numbers, and information on local fugitives.
Subjects: Drug Control; Law Enforcement
Publications: *Drugs of Abuse*, J 24.2:D 84/
Get It Straight: The Facts about Drugs, J 24.2:D 84/21
Speaking Out Against Drug Legalization, J 24.2:D 84/20

1301. Equal Employment Opportunity Commission
http://www.eeoc.gov/
Sponsor: Equal Employment Opportunity Commission (EEOC)
Description: The EEOC coordinates federal equal employment opportunity regulations and investigates charges of employment discrimination. The site offers introductory information on the laws for employees and employers. The Laws, Regulations, and Policy Guidance section provides more technical information, with the text of EEOC regulations and laws enforced by the EEOC. The Publications section includes an order form and direct links to those publications available online.

Employment rights fact sheets can be ordered in English and other language versions (Arabic, Chinese Haitian Creole, Korean, Russian, Spanish, Vietnamese, etc.)

The EEOC provides a straightforward Web site with information for multiple audiences such as employees, employers, small businesses, attorneys, and employment rights policy workers.

Subject: Employment Discrimination — Laws

Publications: *Annual Performance Plan*, Y 3.Eq 2:1/
Enforcement Guidances, Y 3.EQ 2:2

1302. FCC Enforcement Bureau

http://www.fcc.gov/eb/

Sponsor: Federal Communications Commission (FCC) — Enforcement Bureau

Description: The FCC's regulatory enforcement arm offers this site with links to its divisions and field offices, and the main categories: What We Do, How To File a Complaint, Headlines, Key People, and Documents. The links under What We Do include Broadcast Issues, Consumer Telephone-Related Issues, Emergency Alert System Information, and Local Telephone Competition Enforcement. The Documents section includes news releases, notices, orders, reports and other material from the Enforcement Bureau.

Subjects: Broadcasting — Laws; Telecommunications — Laws

1303. Federal Bureau of Investigation

http://www.fbi.gov/

Sponsor: Justice Department — Federal Bureau of Investigation (FBI)

Description: Most of the FBI's public Web information about its activities can be found in the About Us section, under the Headquarters and Programs topic. This includes links to substantial information on specific programs, such as the FBI Academy, Laboratories, National Instant Criminal Background Check, Financial Crimes Section, Civil Rights Section, Organized Crime Section, Evidence Response Team, and *Uniform Crime Reports.*Other sections of the site focus on Terrorism, FBI's Most Wanted, Interagency Programs, Employment Opportunities, information for the press, and information for parents and children. The Library and Reference section features a Publications area with links to selected publications available online. Reference material in this section includes biographies of all FBI Directors over time, a history of the FBI, and profiles of famous cases.

Because information is spread throughout the many sections of this site, first time users may want to consult the site map along with the About Us section.

Subjects: Crime Detection; Law Enforcement; Wanted People

Publications: *Cybernotes*, J 1.14/23-2:
FBI Law Enforcement Bulletin, J 1.14/8:
Forensic Science Communications, J 1.14/18-2:
Handbook of Forensic Services
Hate Crime Statistics, J 1.14/2:C 86/17/
Highlights (National Infrastructure Protection Center), J 1.14/23-3:
Law Enforcement Officers Killed and Assaulted, Uniform Crime Report, J 1.14/7-6:
Terrorism in the United States, J 1.14/22:
Uniform Crime Reports, J 1.14/7:

1304. Federal Law Enforcement Training Center

http://63.117.243.216/

Sponsor: Treasury Department — Federal Law Enforcement Training Center (FLETC)

Description: FLETC, the federal government's centralized law enforcement training facility, is scheduled to move to the newly created Department of Homeland Security. Its current site includes the Catalog of Training Programs and profiles of its programs in such areas as financial fraud investigations, enforcement techniques, driver training, and security specialties. Publications available on the site include the *Annual Report*, FLETC Directives, and FLETC Orders. The best way to access information on this site is through the Contents link, under About the FLETC. The Contents page is a detailed site map listing contents that might otherwise be missed.

These pages will be of interest primarily to those considering FLETC training.

Subjects: Homeland Security; Law Enforcement

1305. Financial Crimes Enforcement Network (FinCEN)

http://www.fincen.gov/

Sponsor: Treasury Department
Description: FinCEN implements the Department of the Treasury's policies to prevent and detect money laundering. The agency works with the law enforcement (local, national, and international), financial, and regulatory communities. Major topical sections of the site are Law Enforcement, International, and Regulatory. Other sections are About FinCEN and Publications.

Much of the information on this site will be of primary interest to regulated financial institutions
Subjects: Financial Crimes; Money Laundering — Laws
Publication: *FinCEN Strategic Plan 2000–2005*, T 1.2:C 86

1306. Fugitives and Missing Persons

http://www.usdoj.gov/09fugitives/

Sponsor: Justice Department
Description: This site includes links to lists of wanted fugitives from the FBI, the DEA, the U.S. Marshals Service, and the InterAgency International Fugitive Lookout. The FBI's Web site also contains information about kidnapping and missing persons investigations, as well as parental kidnappings. These pages include pictures, descriptions of the crimes, and information on contacting the appropriate law enforcement agency.
Subjects: Criminals; Wanted People

1307. Gang Resistance Education and Training Program

http://www.atf.treas.gov/great/index.htm

Sponsor: Treasury Department — Bureau of Alcohol, Tobacco, and Firearms (ATF)
Description: The Gang Resistance Education And Training Program (G.R.E.A.T.) site includes a variety of topics including Resource Guide, Curriculum, Philosophy and History of GREAT, Agencies, Partnerships, Focus on Youth, Guidelines, Management Training, National Training Program, and Statistics. The curriculum is designed to be taught by uniformed police officers and Federal agents to elementary, junior high, and middle school students.
Subject: Juvenile Delinquency

1308. IGnet—Federal Inspectors General

http://www.ignet.gov/

Description: IGnet is a gateway site that serves the IG community, consisting of the offices of Inspectors General who conduct audits, investigations, and inspections in more than 60 federal agencies. There are two IG councils: the President's Council on Integrity and Efficiency (PCIE), and the Executive Council on Integrity and Efficiency (ECIE). The IGnet Web site features the sections The Inspectors General, Reports and Periodicals, PCIE and ECIE, Related Sites, and What's New. There is also a link to PCIE/ECIE related organizations. The IG Directory/Homepages link under The Inspectors General section offers contact information for Presidentially Appointed Inspectors General and Designated Federal Entity Inspectors General. From the PCIE and ECIE section, one can access quality standards for inspections and investigations as well as an HTML version of the Yellow Book, known officially as *Government Accounting Standards*.

IGnet provides a broad range of materials for both IG employees and for whistleblowers interested in contacting one of the IG offices.
Subject: Inspectors General
Publications: *A Progress Report to the President*, PREX 2.36/2:
Government Auditing Standards (Yellow Book), GA 1.2:Au 2/14
Journal of Public Inquiry, Pr 42.8/4:

1309. Immigration and Naturalization Service

http://www.ins.gov/

Sponsor: Justice Department — Immigration and Naturalization Service (INS)
Description: The Immigration and Naturalization Service is scheduled to be dismantled under the Homeland Security Act of 2002 (PL 107-296). The functions of INS are to be carried over to two separate organizations within the new Department of Homeland Security: one for border security

and the other for immigration services. The current INS Web site features a large About INS section, covering the agency's mission, accomplishments, budget, statistics, and a section on the expected transition and restructuring. Reference sections include a glossary and extensive list of Frequently Asked Questions. Other sections cover Immigration Services and Benefits; Law Enforcement and Border Management; Field Offices; and Laws, Regulations, and Guides.
Subjects: Homeland Security; Immigration Law
Publications: *Forms*, J 21.19:
INS Communique (monthly), J 21.25:
Interim Administrative Decisions under Immigration and Nationality Laws, J 21.11/2:
Statistical Yearbook of the Immigration and Naturalization Service, J 21.2/10:
Triennial Comprehensive Report on Immigration, J 21.21:

1310. JUSTNET—Justice Technology Information Network
http://www.nlectc.org/
Sponsor: Justice Department — National Institute of Justice (NIJ) — National Law Enforcement and Corrections Technology Center (NLECTC)
Description: JUSTNET is the home page for the National Law Enforcement and Corrections Technology Center (NLECTC), which assists state and local law enforcement and corrections personnel with technology, equipment, and information systems. The Web site describes NLECTC programs in technology assistance, equipment testing and evaluation, and training assistance. It also provides a directory of grants for law enforcement from government and non-government sources. A Criminal Justice Links section has an extensive annotated directory of Web resources organized by topic.
Subject: Law Enforcement — Grants
Publication: *TechBeat*, J 28.37:

1311. National Drug Intelligence Center
http://www.usdoj.gov/ndic/
Sponsor: Justice Department — National Drug Intelligence Center (NDIC)
Description: The NDIC produces strategic domestic drug intelligence for the counter drug community, focusing on drugs, gangs, and violence. The site features the following sections: About the National Drug Intelligence Center, Meet Our Directors, NDIC Reports, Employment Opportunities, NDIC Locations, and Freedom of Information Act. The NDIC Reports page has publications about national and state drug threat assessments, drug type threat assessments, and information bulletins. Most of these publications are in HTML or PDF formats.
Subjects: Drug Control; Intelligence Agencies
Publication: *National Drug Threat Assessment*, J 1.2:D

1312. National Institute of Justice (NIJ)
http://www.ojp.usdoj.gov/nij/
Sponsor: Justice Department — National Institute of Justice (NIJ)
Description: The NIJ supports research, evaluation, and demonstration programs, development of technology, and both national and international information dissemination in the area of criminal justice. The Web site has information on the Institute, its programs, funding opportunities and fellowships, and publications.
Subject: Criminal Justice — Research
Publications: *National Institute of Justice Annual Report to Congress*, J 28.1:
National Institute of Justice Journal, J 28.14/2-2:

1313. National Youth Violence Prevention Center
http://www.safeyouth.org/home.htm
Sponsor: Health and Human Services Department — Centers for Disease Control and Prevention (CDC)
Description: National Youth Violence Prevention Center is a clearinghouse for prevention information, publications, research, and statistics on violence committed by and against children and teens. The site is sponsored by the Centers for Disease Control and Prevention in collaboration with a number of other federal agencies including the FBI and the Bureau of Alcohol, Tobacco, and

Firearms. The Publications section provides subject access to youth violence-related publications from a variety of federal agencies. The Funding section pulls together information on a number of relevant grants. There are also special sections written for Parents and Guardians, Professionals, and Teens.
Subject: Juvenile Delinquency

1314. Office of Information and Privacy
http://www.usdoj.gov/oip/oip.html
Sponsor: Justice Department
Description: The Office of Information and Privacy (OIP) manages the Department of Justices' responsibilities related to the Freedom of Information Act (FOIA) and the Privacy Act. These responsibilities include coordinating and implementing policy development and compliance government-wide for the FOIA and compliance by the DOJ for the Privacy Act and deciding all appeals from denials of access to information under those acts by any DOJ component. Its site includes online access to a number of documents including the *DOJ Annual FOIA Report*.
Subject: Freedom of Information Act
Publications: *DOJ Annual FOIA Report*, J 1.1/11:
FOIA Post, J 1.58/1:

1315. Office of Justice Programs
http://www.ojp.usdoj.gov/
Sponsor: Justice Department — Justice Programs Office
Description: The Office of Justice Programs provides federal leadership, coordination and assistance to the nation's justice system. OJP and its program bureaus are responsible for collecting statistical data and conducting analyses, identifying emerging criminal justice issues, providing technical assistance and training in areas of need, developing and testing promising approaches to address these issues, evaluating program results, and disseminating these findings and other information to state and local governments. The Web site features About OJP, OJP Press Releases, OJP Publications—A to Z, Grants and Funding, and Technical Assistance Guide. It also has links to the Web sites of the component OJP Program Offices, Support Offices, and Bureaus under four main headings: The Justice System, Crime Victims, Fighting Crime, and Hot Topics.
Subjects: Criminal Justice — Research; Law Enforcement — Grants
Publications: *The NIJ Research Review*, J 28.24/10:
Weed & Seed In-Sites, J 1.110:

1316. Office of Juvenile Justice and Delinquency Prevention
http://ojjdp.ncjrs.org/
Sponsor: Justice Department — Justice Programs Office
Description: This site offers information on the Office and its activities. Featured sections include About OJJDP, Juvenile Justice Facts and Figures, Highlights, Resources, Programs, Publications, and Grants and Funding. The Highlights area provides information on conferences, funding opportunities, press releases, and new publications. The Publications section includes information about OJJDP publications and access to full text publications on the NCJRS site. Publications cover the juvenile justice aspects of such topics as courts, corrections, gangs, substance abuse, violence, and victimization.
Subjects: Juvenile Delinquency; Juvenile Justice
Publications: *OJJDP Annual Report*, J 32.1:
OJJDP Fact Sheets, J 32.21:

1317. Office of National Drug Control Policy
http://www.whitehousedrugpolicy.gov/
Sponsor: White House — National Drug Control Policy Office
Description: This White House Office provides a wide variety of information on drug control policy. The site features pages for About ONDCP, News, Drug Facts, Publications, Policy, Funding, Prevention, Treatment, Enforcement, State and Local, International, and Science and Technology. Specific programs, such as Drug-Free Communities and Drug-Free Workplace, are described. The Publications page includes reports and fact sheets from both the ONDCP and other federal agencies.

Subject: Drug Policy
Publications: *National Drug Control Policy*, PREX 26.1/2:
Pulse Check (semiannual), PrEx 26.10:

1318. Office of the Associate Attorney General
http://www.usdoj.gov/aag/index.htm
Sponsor: Justice Department
Description: This page offers a brief description of the office of the Associate Attorney General along with FOIA, speeches, and testimony by the Associate Attorney General.
Subject: Law Enforcement Policy

1319. Office of the Deputy Attorney General
http://www.usdoj.gov/dag/index.html
Sponsor: Justice Department
Description: This page provides information on the office of the Deputy Attorney General. It features the Deputy Attorney General's speeches, testimony, FOIA, and to a link to publications and documents which include *Health Care Fraud and Abuse Control Program* and a *Survey of the Federal Death Penalty System*.
Subject: Law Enforcement Policy
Publications: *Health Care Fraud and Abuse Control Program Annual Report*
The Federal Death Penalty System: A Statistical Survey, J 1.2:

1320. Rewards for Justice
http://www.rewardsforjustice.net/
Sponsor: State Department — Diplomatic Security Bureau
Description: This Web site promotes awareness of the State Department's monetary awards program for information that assists in countering acts of international terrorism against United States. The site includes photos and information on the most wanted terrorists. An Act of Terror section catalogs international terrorist incidents where crimes have been committed against U.S. citizens or property. The Recent Campaigns section describes significant current awards offered. Information about the rewards program is also available in over 10 non-English languages, including Spanish, French, Arabic, Russian, German, Farsi, and Pashtu.
Subject: Terrorism

1321. U.S. Border Patrol
http://www.ins.usdoj.gov/graphics/lawenfor/bpatrol/
Sponsor: Justice Department — Immigration and Naturalization Service (INS) — Border Patrol
Description: The INS Border Patrol is scheduled to become part of the newly created Department of Homeland Security. Their current home page features information on the mission, operations, and national strategies of the Border Patrol. Featured sections include Overview, Border Patrol Strategy, Border Patrol Sector Map, List of Border Patrol Sectors, and What's New.
Subjects: Homeland Security; International Borders

1322. U.S. Marshals Service
http://www.usdoj.gov/marshals/
Sponsor: Justice Department — Marshals Service
Description: The U.S. Marshals' site contains information on the agency, employment opportunities, and lists of auctions and wanted fugitives. Featured sections include Want To Be a Deputy?, Top 15 Wanted Fugitives, Major Fugitive Cases, Sales of Seized Assets, History, Roll Call of Honor, Marshals Service Missions, District Offices, News Releases, Publications, FOIA Reading Room, and Speeches and Testimonies. The Publications page has online fact sheets and the official newsletter, *The Marshals Monitor*.
Subjects: Law Enforcement; Wanted People
Publications: *The Marshals Monitor*
U.S. Marshals Service: Fact Sheets, J 25:15:

1323. United States Park Police

http://www.nps.gov/uspp/findex.htm

Sponsor: Interior Department — National Park Service (NPS)

Description: This site describes the role and activities of the U.S. Park Police, law enforcement officers with jurisdiction in National Park Service areas and certain government properties. The site includes press releases and the U.S. Park Police Most Wanted List.

Subjects: National Parks and Reserves; Police

1324. United States Parole Commission

http://www.usdoj.gov/uspc/

Sponsor: Justice Department — Parole Commission

Description: This page describes the commission and its works. There are links to such sections as Mission, The Victim/Witness Program, Our History, FOIA and Online Reading Room, and Standard Conditions of Release. Questions such as "how does the Commission decide if someone is eligible for parole?" and "what happens at a parole hearing?" are addressed in a section called Answering Your Questions.

Subject: Prisoners

1325. United States Sentencing Commission

http://www.ussc.gov/

Sponsor: Sentencing Commission

Description: The U.S. Sentencing Commission offers a site where users can browse and download commission documents and materials. In addition to sentencing guidelines manuals and federal sentencing statistics, the site includes numerous other publications, reports to Congress, documents about guideline training and education, and commission meeting information. A side bar links to related information, such as state sentencing commissions and the Probation Officers Advisory Group.

Subject: Sentencing

Publications: *Annual Report*, Y 3.SE 5:1

Guidelines Manual, Y 3.SE 5:8 G 94/

Sourcebook of Federal Sentencing Statistics, Y 3.SE 5:1/996

CHAPTER 11
Libraries

Federal government-sponsored libraries often have publicly available Web sites that describe their collections and policies, offer online access to their catalog, or present guides for further research in specialized areas. Some libraries are focused on serving internal clients or in-person researchers, and they may have little more than contact information online. Others are charged with reaching a broader audience, and their Web sites can be valuable starting points for Internet research.

The featured site for this chapter is the Library of Congress, a pioneer on the Web with a growing site and resources relevant to multiple audiences. A section for national libraries has entries for the National Agricultural Library, National Education Library, and National Library of Medicine. That section is preceded by one for Federal Depository Libraries. It includes many of the resources developed by the Government Printing Office and depository libraries to support the Federal Depository Library program.

Bookmarks & Favorites

National Libraries
- Library of Congress, http://www.loc.gov
- National Agricultural Library, http://www.nal.usda.gov
- National Library of Education, http://www.ed.gov/NLE/
- National Library of Medicine, http://www.nlm.nih.gov

Related Programs and Agencies
- GPO Library Services, http://www.access.gpo.gov/su_docs/fdlp/libpro.html
- National Archives and Records Administration, http://www.archives.gov
  - Presidential Libraries, http://www.archives.gov/presidential_libraries/
- National Commission on Libraries and Information Science, http://www.nclis.gov

Featured Site

1326. Library of Congress
http://www.loc.gov/
Sponsor: Library of Congress
Description: As the largest library in the world, it is only fitting that the Library of Congress Web site should be one of the most extensive and information-packed governmental library Web sites. Its American Memory section, with scanned images, movies, audio files, and other reproductions of historic documents, is an example of the great potential that the Internet has for making rare collections available to the public. The site's Exhibitions section has digital versions of major exhibitions at the Library dating back to 1993. Another major section, the Global Gateway, emphasizes the international nature of the Library's collection and staff expertise. The Wise Guide and America's Library sections provide interactive, educational introductions to the Library and its collections. A section called Especially For organizes information by audience, including researchers, librarians, archivists, teachers, publishers, blind persons, and kids and families. The Find It section includes links to the site map and site search tools, but also to the Library of Congress catalogs, research centers descriptions, and Ask a Librarian online reference service. The Library site also links to the legislative information service THOMAS. This and other specialized sections are described in more detail elsewhere in this directory.

While the Web site offers only a very small fraction of the material available in the Library itself, it does provide a significant collection of free online material as well as detailed information about LC's collections and services. This is a large, growing site offering substantial resources of interest to librarians, historical researchers, publishers, lawyers, Congress, and the general public.

Subjects: Digital Libraries; Libraries; United States — History
Publications: *Area Handbook Series*, D 101.22:550-
Bibliographic Products and Services, LC 30.27/2:
CONSER LINE, LC 30.22/2:
FEDLINK (Federal Library and Information Network) Technical Notes, LC 1.32/5:
FLICC Newsletter, LC 1.32:
LC Cataloging Newsline, LC 9.16:
LC Science Tracer Bullet, LC 33.10:
Library of Congress Information Bulletin, LC 1.18:
NewsNet, LC 3.4/3:
Thomas: Legislative Information on the Internet, LC 1.54/2:

The library resources in this chapter are divided into three sections, spanning the entry numbers indicated here:

General	1327–1371
Depository	1372–1392
National	1393–1399

General

1327. Access to Archival Databases (AAD)
http://www.archives.gov/aad/
Sponsor: National Archives and Records Administration (NARA)
Description: The National Archives launched the Access to Archival Databases (AAD) System in early 2003. The purpose of AAD is to provide the public with access to historic databases and other electronic records held by the Archives. As of this writing, AAD includes 30 archival series of electronic records. They vary widely in subject matter but have in common the fact that they identify specific persons, geographic areas, organizations, or dates—making them useful as finding aids. The databases can be browsed by selecting Search and clicking on All Series. They include several Korean Conflict casualty and prisoner of war files, the Japanese-American Internee File from 1942-1946, the Work Stoppages Historical File from 1953-1981, and a Civil War Sites database compiled a decade ago.
    AAD is an important step in making electronic archives accessible.
Subjects: Archives; Databases

1328. AFIT Academic Library
http://library.afit.edu/?p=6
Sponsor: Air Force — Air Force Institute of Technology (AFIT)
Description: The Air Force Institute of Technology Library site includes section on About the Library, Electronic Journals, Research Databases, Online Library Catalogs, and Library Tutorials. Another section, Subject Guides to Web Resources, offers subject category searches to find relevant electronic indexing/abstracting databases and other major Web links.
Subject: Scientific and Technical Information

1329. Air Force Research Laboratory Technical Library
http://www.wrs.afrl.af.mil/library/
Sponsor: Air Force — Air Force Research Laboratory
Description: The main page of the Air Force Resource Laboratory (AFRL) Web site has three main headings: Library Catalogs, Electronics Resources, and Information. This Web site features a journals holdings list, an electric materials request form, a division newsletter, and more. Under STINFO, the Scientific and Technical Information Office, the library provides information on publishing a technical report. Under the Electronic Resources heading, other sections include Standards/Technical Orders, Patents, Technical Reports, and Subject Guides.
Subject: Scientific and Technical Information

1330. Air University Library and Press
http://www.au.af.mil/au/aul/aulv2.htm
Sponsor: Air Force — Air University
Description: The Air University Library Web site provides information on the library and its services. The site also includes the library's catalog, list of periodicals, bibliographic databases, and bibliographies. The library compiles bibliographies, under the Locate Books section, on topics ranging from Asymmetric Warfare to Weapons of Mass Destruction. The library also offers excellent compilations of links to defense-related journals and news services online.

Although many sections of the site are open only to authorized users, other researchers will find the publicly accessible bibliographies, electronic journals and news links, and periodical index to be of benefit.
Subjects: Military Information; Bibliographies
Publication: *Air University Library Index to Military Periodicals*, D 301.26/2:

1331. Aiso Library and Learning Center
http://160.133.228.85/aisoweb/aisolib.htm
Sponsor: Defense Department — Defense Language Institute (DLI)
Description: Aiso Library is the academic library for the Defense Language Institute Foreign Language Center. For those not studying at the Institute, the most helpful section may be Reference Links. This includes Language Links, which links to key Web sites for 19 languages. The sites typically include links for foreign language newspapers, search engines, cultural resources, alphabets, and other language information.
Subjects: Foreign Languages; Language Education

1332. Center for Electronic Records
http://www.nara.gov/nara/electronic/homensx.html
Sponsor: National Archives and Records Administration (NARA)
Description: As part of the National Archives, the Center for Electronic Records preserves and provides access to federal government electronic records of continuing value. This site features sections including Frequently Asked Questions; Information for Researchers; Title List and Description of Center for Electronic Records' Holdings; Information about Electronic Records for Archivists, Federal Records Managers, and IRM Personnel; and Staff Bibliography, which includes a brief bibliography of staff publications relating to electronic records. The subsequent pages describe the holdings of data files, services available to federal agencies, how to request files, and technical specifications of the data files. The site also links to two of the Center's frequently requested collections, the records of U.S. military casualties from the Korean and Vietnam conflicts.
Subjects: Archives; Government Information

1333. Corps of Engineers Library Information Online
http://libweb.wes.army.mil/usace/coelis.htm
Sponsor: Army — Army Corps of Engineers
Description: The Corps of Engineers Library Information Online (CELIO) is an online union list for the Corps of Engineers Library Network. The site has a Web-based searchable interface to the union list and a directory of participating libraries including their points of contact, email addresses, and telephone numbers.
Subject: Civil Engineering — Research

1334. CRREL Virtual Library
http://www.crrel.usace.army.mil/library/crrel_library.html
Sponsor: Army — Army Corps of Engineers — Engineer Research and Development Center (ERDC)
Description: The Cold Regions Research & Engineering Laboratory Library site offers basic information about the library, including a list of library staff, periodical holdings, and CRREL publications lists. Featured sections include Cold Regions Bibliography, Online catalog, and Technical Publications. The Bibliography section links to the Bibliography on Cold Regions Science and Technology and the Antarctic Bibliography.

Subjects: Climate Research; Antarctica — Research
Publications: *Antarctic Bibliography*
Bibliography on Cold Regions Science and Technology
Current Antarctic Literature

1335. Department of the Interior Library
http://library.doi.gov/
Sponsor: Interior Department
Description: The DOI Library's site features sections Online Catalog, Training Sessions, Collections, Services, Law Library, and Periodicals Online. Its online catalog includes over 100,000 items, while the collection section offers bibliographies, a periodical list, and new titles.
Subject: Public Lands — Research

1336. Digital Preservation
http://www.digitalpreservation.gov/ndiipp/
Sponsor: Library of Congress
Description: Digital Preservation is the Web site for the National Digital Information Infrastructure and Preservation Program (NDIIPP), a collaborative effort led by the Library of Congress and including the National Archives, the National Library of Medicine, and other agencies and organizations. The site has information about the program, its strategic planning, report and papers, and press releases.
Publication: *Preserving Our Digital Heritage: Plan for the National Digital Information Infrastructure and Preservation Program*

1337. Engineer Research and Development Center Research Library
http://libweb.wes.army.mil/
Sponsor: Army — Army Corps of Engineers — Engineer Research and Development Center (ERDC)
Description: The Waterways Experiment Station Library site features information about the library's services and provides access to its online catalog and Quick Reference Links.
Subject: Civil Engineering — Research

1338. EPA National Library Network
http://www.epa.gov/natlibra/
Sponsor: Environmental Protection Agency (EPA)
Description: This site provides information about the EPA National Library Network Program, links to EPA libraries, and provides access to the Online Library System (OLS) union catalog. A Publications section includes an online version of *Core List for An Environmental Reference Collection*, an extensive bibliography and resource guide.The OLS includes access to several special collections: National Service Center for Environmental Publications, Environmental Financing Information Network, National Enforcement Training Institute, Subsurface Remediation Information Center, and Air Pollution Technical Info Center.
Subject: Environmental Protection — Research

1339. Federal Bureau of Prisons Library
http://bop.library.net/
Sponsor: Justice Department — Federal Bureau of Prisons
Description: This library Web site is primarily a Web interface to the library catalog. The site also includes a description of the library, a periodical list, and a video list.
Subject: Prisons — Research

1340. Federal Library and Information Center Committee
http://www.loc.gov/flicc/
Sponsor: Library of Congress — Federal Library and Information Center Committee (FLICC)
Description: FLICC and FEDLINK provide service and guidance to federal libraries and information centers. This Web site features the sections Education and Training, Federal Library Resources,

Account Management, Information for Vendors, and Contracting/Vendor Products and Services. Separate links to FLICC and FEDLINK provide more information from each of these offices.
Subject: Libraries
Publications: *Annual Forum, Federal Information Policies*, LC 1.47:
FEDLINK (Federal Library and Information Network) Technical Notes, LC 1.32/5:
FLICC Newsletter, LC 1.32:

1341. Fermilab Information Resources Department
http://fnalpubs.fnal.gov/
Sponsor: Energy Department — Fermi National Accelerator Laboratory
Description: The Fermilab Library Web site features access to a Web interface to its catalog, a list of journal holdings, and a bibliography of Fermilab preprints. While not all of the preprints are available in full text, those that are available online (in Postscript or PDF formats) have direct links to their location in a preprint archive.
Subject: Preprints

1342. General Services Administration Library Catalog
http://gsa.library.net/
Sponsor: General Services Administration
Description: This page provides some basic information on the GSA library collection, borrowing information, and contact information. However, the primary function of the page is to offer a Web interface to its library catalog.
Subject: Government Administration — Research

1343. Glenn Technical Library
http://grctechlib.grc.nasa.gov/
Sponsor: National Aeronautics and Space Administration (NASA) — Glenn Research Center
Description: The NASA Glenn Research Center's Technical Library site features such sections as Who We Are, What We Do, and Collections We Have. It also has a list of their journal holdings and a section called Where You Can Go, which lists Internet sites on science, aviation, and engineering topics that have been evaluated by the Glenn Research Center Library.
Subject: Aerospace Engineering — Research

1344. Goddard Space Flight Center Library
http://library.gsfc.nasa.gov/
Sponsor: National Aeronautics and Space Administration (NASA) — Goddard Space Flight Center (GSFC)
Description: This Web site provides information about two libraries: the Goddard Space Flight Center Library and the Wallops Library. The Resources category features links to article/paper search engines, standards and technical reports, journals, and books. The Standards and Technical Reports section has various technical report databases including the NASA Technical Report Server, the Goddard Technical Report Server (GTRS), and a NASA acronyms database. It also links to the Balloon Technology Database at the Wallops Library, which has bibliographic references to literature on balloons. The Reference section has several useful compilations, including a Virtual Reference Shelf, Subject Channels, and Subject Guides.
Subject: Scientific and Technical Information

1345. INTL-DOC [email list]
http://gateway.library.uiuc.edu/doc/idtf/intl-doc.htm
Sponsor: Government Documents Round Table (GODORT)
Description: INTL-DOC features discussions by international document librarians and users and publishers of International Governmental Organizations (IGO) materials. The list is intended primarily for those working with IGO documentation. However, it also welcomes items related to the literature of foreign national governments and of international affairs in general.
   This is an essential list for government documents librarians that work with IGO publications.
Subjects: Government Publications — International; Email Lists

1346. LLNL Library

http://www.llnl.gov/library/index.html

Sponsor: Energy Department — Lawrence Livermore National Laboratory (LLNL)

Description: This LLNL Library site features Web-based online catalogs and descriptions of its services and collections. LLNL-authored, unclassified technical reports are available under the section Documents Online. The site also features links to major LLNL online publications.

Subjects: Scientific and Technical Information; Weapons Research

Publication: *Science Technology Review*, E 1.53:

1347. Los Alamos National Laboratory Research Library

http://lib-www.lanl.gov/

Sponsor: Energy Department — Los Alamos National Laboratory (LANL)

Description: While many of the resources at this site are restricted to authorized LANL users, the general public can search the online catalog, view journal holdings, and browse the collections of links to public Web sites. The Reports page also provides a service to outside users by gathering links to online reports collections from the Energy Department and other sources.

Subject: Scientific and Technical Information

1348. Lunar and Planetary Institute Library

http://cass.jsc.nasa.gov/library/library.html

Sponsor: Lunar and Planetary Institute (LPI)

Description: Also known as the Center for Information and Research Services (CIRS), this library organizes and maintains a collection of space-science-related materials in a variety of media, including books, journals, documents, maps, and images. The library portion features two Web interfaces to its online catalog—easy and expert. Under the Regional Planetary Image Facilities category, other sections include Image Collection, Map Collection, and Journal Collection. The site also offers access to the following Internet resources: Planetary Imagery Sites, Planetary Information Sites, Planetary Science WWW Sites, Planetary Mission Sites, and Planetary Journal Sites.

Subject: Planetary Science — Research

1349. MERLN (Military Educational Research Library Network)

http://merln.ndu.edu/

Sponsor: Defense Department — National Defense University (NDU)

Description: MERLN (The Military Educational Research Library Network) is a Web site of military education libraries cooperating in collecting, organizing and sharing educational resources. The site is organized geographically based on the location and mission of its members: MERLN North America, Asia- Pacific, Caribbean-Latin America, Europe, International Fellows, and Near East-South Asia. MERLN (North America), for example, represents the senior military education institutions in the U.S., Canada, and the U.S. military academies and provides links to the libraries' home page. In addition, the site features several military bibliographic catalogs, several digitized collections previously unavailable to the public, and other electronic resources.

Subject: Military Information

1350. NASA Langley Research Center Technical Library

http://library.larc.nasa.gov/Public/index.htm

Sponsor: National Aeronautics and Space Administration (NASA) — Langley Research Center (LaRC)

Description: The Langley Technical Library has created this page for public use, excluding material that is only available to staff and authorized users. The site has background information, a description of its services for visitors, a Virtual Reference Desk, and a Technical Reports section. Technical Reports links to the Aeronautics and Space Access Page Technical Report Server, the Langley Technical Report Server, and the NASA Technical Report Server.

Subject: Scientific and Technical Information

1351. National Commission on Libraries and Information Science
http://www.nclis.gov/
Sponsor: National Commission on Libraries and Information Science (NCLIS)
Description: The National Commission on Libraries and Information Science is an independent agency of the federal government charged with advising the executive and legislative branches on national library and information policies and plans. NCLIS reports, testimony, and other works are organized under these categories: Government Information Policy, National Information Policy, and International Information Policy. NCLIS's reports on public library statistics are available in the Statistics and Surveys section.
Subjects: Information Policy; Libraries — Policy
Publications: *Comprehensive Assessment of Public Information Dissemination*, Y 3.L 61:2 D 63/
NCLIS Annual Report, Y 3.L 61:1/

1352. National Defense University Library
http://www.ndu.edu/library/library.html
Sponsor: Defense Department — National Defense University (NDU)
Description: The NDU Library site has a variety of resources that are accessible to the general public. These include a Web-based catalog and such sections as eResources and Digitized Collections. The Publications section has *Current Journal Articles*, the library's in-house current awareness system, as well as staff-prepared bibliographies that cover a number of defense topics and provide thorough coverage of NATO.
Subject: Military Information

1353. National LINCS
http://www.nifl.gov/lincs/index.html
Sponsor: National Institute for Literacy (NIFL)
Description: The National Institute for Literacy and its partners sponsor this site as a gateway to adult education and literacy resources on the Internet. Featured sections on the LINCS home page include About Literacy (facts, statistics, policy, and legislation), Literacy Resources, News and Events, and About NIFL and LINCS. The site also features links to U.S. regional programs.
Subject: Literacy
Publications: *EEF HOT (Highlights on Teaching) Topics Newsletter*, Y 3.L 71:20/
Policy Updates, Y 3.L 71:18/
State Policy Updates, Y 3.L 71:17/

1354. National Radio Astronomy Observatory Library
http://www.nrao.edu/library/
Sponsor: National Science Foundation (NSF) — National Radio Astronomy Observatory (NRAO)
Description: This site features the Library's catalog and many external resources, particularly preprint sites. The NRAO RAPs database includes records for published papers and preprints for staff and visitor works, from 1957 forward. The site also includes a collection of links to astronomy resources and libraries on the Web.
Subjects: Astronomy — Research; Preprints

1355. Navy Department Library
http://www.history.navy.mil/library/
Sponsor: Navy — Department of the Navy
Description: The Navy Department Library traces it beginnings to a request from President John Adams in 1800. The library's current Web site provides online access to its catalog of resources on the U.S. Navy and has online copies of its bibliographies on naval history. The Special Collections section includes selected full text and images. The site also has research guides on Navy Cruise Books, Military History and National Security, and Terrorism.
Subject: Navy — History

1356. NCAR Library
http://www.ucar.edu/library/
Sponsor: National Science Foundation (NSF)
Description: The National Center for Atmospheric Research Library site includes information on the library and its services. Featured sections include Catalog, Ejournals, Information Resources, Services, Collection, and NCAR Archives.
Subject: Atmospheric Sciences — Research

1357. NIEHS Library
http://library.niehs.nih.gov/
Sponsor: National Institutes of Health (NIH) — National Institute of Environmental Health Sciences (NIEHS)
Description: The NIEHS Library serves the scientific and administrative staff of NIEHS, but it also provides limited services to the public. Publicly accessible resources on the site include Book Catalog, Web Starting Points, Reference Resources, and NIEHS Publications.
Subject: Health and Safety — Research

1358. NIH Library Online
http://nihlibrary.nih.gov/
Sponsor: National Institutes of Health (NIH)
Description: The NIH Library Online site features information about the library and services. While most information is restricted to authorized users, the Internet Sites section provides an extensive catalog of public Web sites covering science and medicine topics.
Subject: Medical Information

1359. Nimitz Library
http://www.nadn.navy.mil/Library/
Sponsor: Navy — United States Naval Academy (USNA)
Description: The Nimitz Library Web site features information about the library and its services, including interlibrary loan request forms, reserves forms, online searching requests, library hours, and a newsletter. The sections on the top page include Starting Your Research, Library Catalog, Electronic Journals, Subject Gateways, Databases, and Electronic Reference Books. Information is provided for faculty, midshipmen, staff, alumni and visitors, and USNA family members.
Subject: Engineering Research

1360. NIST Virtual Library
http://nvl.nist.gov/
Sponsor: Commerce Department — Technology Administration (TA) — National Institute of Standards and Technology (NIST)
Description: Beyond general information about the library and its services, the NIST Library site offers its online catalog, standards information, subject guides, and links to NIST publications. The site links to an online version of the *Journal of Research*. It also features a list of other NIST sites with online publications, which can be a very useful finding aid when searching for a specific NIST document. The Databases page includes access to NIST's Fire Research Information Service (FRIS), an online bibliographic database on fire research-related topics.
Subject: Scientific and Technical Information
Publication: *Journal of Research of the National Institute of Standards and Technology*, C 13.22:

1361. NOAA Central Library
http://www.lib.noaa.gov/
Sponsor: Commerce Department — National Oceanic and Atmospheric Administration (NOAA)
Description: The central NOAA library site describes the library services, gives library hours and policies, lists links to other NOAA libraries, and includes the ability to submit electronic reference questions. It includes the NOAA Library Catalog or NOAALINC, a Web-based online catalog using Sirsi software. The section NOAA Library and Information Network provides links to NOAA libraries by state. A NOAA Browser section provides direct links to over 500 NOAA science, policy, and administrative sites. NOAA Browser is organized in a hierarchical manner that reflects NOAA's

organization. Another section, WINDandSEA: The Oceanic and Atmospheric Sciences Internet Locator, has over 1,000 selected links to science and policy sites organized by topic and alphabetically within topic. All of these sites have been reviewed and annotated by a technical information specialist of the NOAA Central Library staff

Subjects: Atmospheric Sciences — Research; Oceanography — Research

1362. NOAA Seattle Regional Library
http://www.wrclib.noaa.gov/lib/
Sponsor: Commerce Department — National Oceanic and Atmospheric Administration (NOAA)
Description: This regional NOAA library serves NOAA agencies in the western region. Basic library information, such as hours, policies, and services, are provided, along with access to the online catalog, charts and maps, and environmental data and databases.
Subject: Atmospheric Sciences — Research

1363. Northwest and Alaska Fisheries Science Centers' Library
http://lib.nwfsc.noaa.gov/
Sponsor: Commerce Department — National Oceanic and Atmospheric Administration (NOAA) — National Marine Fisheries
Description: Aside from information on its library services, this site offers links to a number of online resources under the headings: Library Catalogs; Fisheries Resources; Maps, Charts, Tides, and Weather; Government and University Links; and General Online Tools. The site also describes the collections of the Fisheries Center Archives.
Subject: Fisheries — Research

1364. Presidential Libraries
http://www.archives.gov/presidential_libraries/index.html
Sponsor: National Archives and Records Administration (NARA) — Presidential Libraries Office
Description: This National Archives Web page provides general information about the presidential libraries system and contact information hours for each presidential library. Links to each of the Web sites of the presidential libraries are listed as well. The libraries in the system are the Bush Library, Carter Library, Clinton Presidential Materials Project, Eisenhower Library, Ford Library, Ford Museum, Hoover Library, Johnson Library, Kennedy Library, Nixon Presidential Materials Staff, Reagan Library, Roosevelt Library, and Truman Library. The site also compiles information on private foundations associated with NARA's Presidential Libraries which provide grants-in-aid for researchers studying Presidential Library holdings.
Subject: Presidential Documents

1365. Ralph J. Bunche Library
http://www.state.gov/m/a/ls/
Sponsor: State Department
Description: This page offers a description of the main State Department library. The Library's mission is to support the research needs of State Department personnel, and it offers few services to the public. The site describes the library's collection and offers information on interlibrary loan.
Subject: Foreign Policy — Research

1366. Ruth H. Hooker Research Library InfoWeb
http://infoweb.nrl.navy.mil/
Sponsor: Navy — Naval Research Laboratory (NRL)
Description: This is the Naval Research Laboratory library Web site. The online catalog includes the library's books, journals, and unclassified reports. A Technical Reports section provides selected, annotated links to Web resources for technical reports. The Government Info section focuses on government links of interest to NRL researchers, particularly those in the engineering, science, and military subject areas.
Subject: Engineering Research

1367. Scientific Library, National Cancer Institute-Frederick
http://www-library.ncifcrf.gov/
Sponsor: National Institutes of Health (NIH) — National Cancer Institute (NCI)
Description: The Scientific Library's site offers public access to its online catalog and selected list of links to Web resources. Topics covered by the links collections include biomedical, clinical medicine, bioterrorism, chemistry, veterinary science, and patents.
Subject: Medical Information

1368. SILIBS-L [email list]
http://www.lsoft.com/scripts/wl.exe?SL1=SILIBS-L&H=SIVM.SI.EDU
Sponsor: Smithsonian Institution
Description: This email list, sponsored and hosted by the Smithsonian, is maintained for the purpose of disseminating announcements and information from Smithsonian Institution libraries.
Subjects: Libraries; Email Lists

1369. Smithsonian Institution Libraries
http://www.sil.si.edu/
Sponsor: Smithsonian Institution
Description: This principal starting point for information about the various Smithsonian Institution Libraries includes the sections Digital Library, Exhibitions, Branch Libraries, Special Collections, Research and Internships, and Give to the Libraries. The Digital Library section is a gateway to everything from annual reports and fact sheets to the library catalog and bibliographies. Many of the online resources are included in the library's Galaxy of Knowledge sections, highlighting collections in science, industry, art, and American history. The current edition of the newsletter *Information* is available in PDF format with access to back issues.
Subject: Libraries
Publication: *Bulletin / Smithsonian Institution. Bureau of American Ethnology*, SI 2.3:

1370. The Marine Corps University Libraries
http://www.mcu.usmc.mil/MCRCweb/library.htm
Sponsor: Marine Corps
Description: This library site features links to sections Catalog Searches, Bibliographies, CDs and Databases, Family Library, Journals and Magazines, Maps, Microforms, News Sources, Online Publications, and Reference Materials. The Catalog is only available from within the firewall, but the site also links to the Military Educational Research Library Network (MERLN), which includes records from this library as well.

1371. United States Naval Observatory Library
http://www.usno.navy.mil/library/
Sponsor: Navy — Naval Observatory (USNO)
Description: This site provides access to the USNO Library's online catalog and collection of historical photos. It also has historical photos of the library, dating back to the 1890's. The Astronomical Resources section provides selected Web links.
Subject: Astronomy — Research

Depository

1372. American Library Association Government Documents Roundtable
http://sunsite.berkeley.edu/GODORT/
Sponsor: Government Documents Round Table (GODORT)
Description: The central site for the American Library Association Government Documents Roundtable group has links to government documents resources and news about government information issues. Topics covered by GODORT committees include the digitization of government information and legislation affecting access to government information. The Resources section has fact sheets about the Federal Depository Library Program and selected links to Government

Printing Office and FDLP Web pages. A Professional Resources section links to relevant e-journals, discussion lists, professional associations, and state and regional documents groups.

The GODORT site is an excellent tool for government documents librarians, but also has resources of use to other librarians and anyone interested in government information issues.

Subjects: Federal Depository Library Program; Government Publications

1373. Basic Depository Library Documents—The Unauthorized HTML Editions
`http://www.du.edu/bdld/`
Sponsor: University of Denver Library
Description: Thomas Tyler at the University of Denver Library has collected key administrative documents for federal depository libraries and put them into HTML format. The Basic Depository Library Documents (BDLD) collection includes Depository Library Program Laws, Item Lists, the Superseded List, and more.

This is an essential collection of documents for those who manage federal depository libraries.

Subject: Federal Depository Library Program
Publications: *Collection Development Guidelines for Selective Depository Libraries*, GP 3.29:D 44/
Depository Library Directory, GP 3.36:L 61
Designation Handbook for Federal Depository Libraries, GP 3.29:D 44/3
Explanation of the Superintendent of Documents Classification System, GP 3.2:C 56/8/
Federal Depository Library Manual, GP 3.29:D 44/993
GPO Classification Manual, GP 3.29:P 88/993
GPO Depository Union List of Item Selections, GP 3.32/2:
Guidelines for the Federal Depository Library Program, GP 3.29:D 44/993/supp.2
List of Classes of United States Government Publications Available for Selection by Depository Libraries, GP 3.24:
Superseded List, GP 3.2:Su 7

1374. Brochures and Pamphlets (Government Documents)
`http://ublib.buffalo.edu/libraries/units/cts/acq/doctab.html`
Sponsor: University of Buffalo. Library
Description: This site includes links to online government works as well as ones that have been digitized at the University of Buffalo Libraries. Many of these sources are online pamphlets, and this site can function both as a finding aid for online government books as well as an original source. Access to the list is alphabetical by subject area. There is also a section of Spanish-language pamphlets. Each listing includes the title and SuDoc number as well as links to the document. The publications are in HTML unless they are identified as being in PDF.

Subjects: Government Publications; Finding Aids

1375. Catalog of U.S. Government Publications
`http://www.gpo.gov/catalog`
Alternate URL: `http://www.access.gpo.gov/su_docs/locators/cgp/`
Sponsor: Government Printing Office (GPO) — Superintendent of Documents
Description: The online *Catalog of U.S. Government Publication* searches government publications cataloged since January 1994 up to the present. It can be used to find government publications available at federal depository libraries and on the Web. It is not, however, a sales catalog. Search results include a link to the online version of the publication if one is available. They also include a link to find federal depository libraries in your area that may have the item. The print counterpart of this database is the *Monthly Catalog of United States Government Publications*, which dates from 1895 and is available in most depository libraries.

The database currently uses the WAIS search engine, which is not as sophisticated as many commercial search engines available today. Users should follow the search examples and Helpful Hints sections provided. In particular, the use of quotations marks to find exact phrases and the use of the boolean AND will help to narrow your search.

Subjects: Government Publications; Databases

1376. Depository Library Council
http://www.access.gpo.gov/su_docs/fdlp/council/index.html
Sponsor: Government Printing Office (GPO) — Depository Library Council (DLC)
Description: The Depository Library Council advises the Public Printer on policy matters dealing with the Federal Depository Library Program. This site includes information in the following categories: About the Council, Congressional Testimony, Council Meeting Sites, Members of Council, Reports and Publications, Recommendations and Responses, and Minutes of Meetings. The lists of members go back to 1973 and the minutes back to 1994.
Subject: Federal Depository Library Program

1377. DocTech-L [email list]
http://library.usu.edu/Govdocs/doctech2.html
Sponsor: Utah State University. Government Documents Department
Description: DocTech-L is for any type of question regarding the technical processing of government documents in library collection. Topics cover processing of federal, state, or United Nations documents that are in the format of paper, fiche, or electronic.
Subjects: Government Publications; Email Lists

1378. Documents Data Miner
http://govdoc.wichita.edu/ddm/GdocFrames.asp
Sponsor: Wichita State University. Library
Description: The Documents Data Miner (DDM) is a collection management tool for federal depository libraries. Hosted at Wichita State University in conjunction with the Federal Depository Library Program, DDM is designed to support management of federal depository library collections. It includes a search engine that searches files from the latest *List of Classes* by agency, item number, SuDoc stem, title search, format, and status. DDM features a number of other resources and tools allowing for collection data gathering.

This is a very useful tool for government documents librarians at the depository libraries.
Subject: Federal Depository Library Program
Publication: *List of Classes of United States Government Publications Available for Selection by Depository Libraries*, GP 3.24:

1379. Enhanced Shipping List Service
http://ublib.buffalo.edu/libraries/units/cts/acq/gpo/
Sponsor: University of Buffalo. Library
Description: Paper, separate, electronic, and microfiche GPO shipping lists are available on this site in ASCII text format. It offers a Shipping List Inclusion/Label Program that is designed to help check the shipping lists against a library's selection profile and get the SuDoc numbers on the documents. Using scanned shipping lists that are available on this site soon after their release, the program matches a specific library's profile and prints out the labels needed.

This site is of significant assistance to those who process federal documents for depository libraries.
Subject: Federal Depository Library Program

1380. FDLP Desktop
http://www.access.gpo.gov/su_docs/fdlp/
Sponsor: Government Printing Office (GPO) — Superintendent of Documents
Description: This site was established by GPO to provide news, information, and communication for and about the Federal Depository Library Program (FDLP) and its Library Program Service (LPS). On the home page, featured sections include About the FDLP, Depository Management, Electronic Collections, Locator Tools and Services, Processing Tools, and askLPS. The Publications page includes online full-text versions of *Administrative Notes, Administrative Notes Technical Supplement*, and various FDLP instructions, manuals, and guides. *Administrative Notes* is available back to August 1996, and *Administrative Notes Technical Supplement* is available back to July 1996. The FDLP site also features an option to Locate Regional Depository Libraries by any combination of city, state, congressional district, library type, or various other characteristics.

Subject: Federal Depository Library Program
Publications: *Administrative Notes Technical Supplement*, GP 3.16/3-3:
Federal Depository Library Directory, GP 3.36:L 61/

1381. GODORT Cataloging Committee

http://www2.lib.udel.edu/godort/cataloging/
Sponsor: Government Documents Round Table (GODORT)
Description: This page contains some information on the committee including minutes, membership, and bylaws. For non-committee members some sections of interest include Cataloging Pre-1976 U.S. Government Publications; Government Documents Retrospective Conversion Projects; Cataloging Government Internet Resources and the Implementation of PURL Technology; and the Toolbox for Processing and Cataloging Federal Government Documents.
Subject: Federal Depository Library Program

1382. GOVDOC-L [email list]

http://docs.lib.duke.edu/federal/govdoc-l/
Sponsor: Duke University. Perkins Library
Description: This is the oldest, and still the primary, email list for documents librarians. While it is neither hosted nor sponsored by the federal government, the discussions, questions, and announcements relate directly to the practice of government documents librarianship. The list includes needs and offers notices, job announcements, and discussions of government Internet sites. The Web site provides instructions on using this listserv, and forms for managing subscriptions. Access to the GovDoc-L Archives is also available.

Previously, the Government Printing Office used GOVDOC-L for its official announcements to depository libraries. GPO now has its own announcements list, called GPO-FDLP-L.
Subjects: Federal Depository Library Program; Email Lists

1383. Government Information and Depository Management Clearinghouse

http://sunsite.berkeley.edu/GODORT/education/clearinghouse/index.html
Sponsor: Government Documents Round Table (GODORT)
Description: The goal of the clearinghouse is to gather in one place the many tools available to government information librarians to facilitate management of electronic government information. Major sections of the site are: Clearinghouse Topics Web Page, Tutorials for Using Government Information, and Tutorials for Training Government Documents staff. Topics pages include: User Access for Electronic Government Information, Library Administration Advocacy, and Providing an Instruction Section on Government Information.
Subject: Federal Depository Library Program

1384. Government Information Technology Committee

http://sunsite.berkeley.edu/GODORT/gitco/
Sponsor: Government Documents Round Table (GODORT)
Description: The Government Information Technology Committee (GITCO) Web site includes such sections as Meetings, Membership, Projects, CD-ROM Doc: GODORT CD-ROM Documentation Service, Bylaws, and GITCO's Government Information Web Page Template.
Subject: Federal Depository Library Program

1385. Government Printing Office

http://www.gpoaccess.gov/
Alternate URL: http://www.gpo.gov/
Sponsor: Government Printing Office (GPO)
Description: The Government Printing Office produces and disseminates government information in print and electronic formats. Their Web site provides catalogs and sales information for print and other physical formats. It also carries a number of significant government documents in Web database form. The GPO home page includes information about the agency, various access points for government information products, business opportunities for contracting printers and others, and information for federal agencies wishing to use the services of GPO. Under Access to Government Information Products, there are links to the Online Bookstore, to an introduction to the nationwide

Federal Depository Library Program, and to the major government information database collection of *GPO Access.*

The GPO site includes a vast amount of government information, particularly in its *GPO Access* databases. Specific sections of the GPO site are described separately in this directory.

Subjects: Government Information; Printing
Publications: *Annual Report,* GP 1.1:
Ben's Guide to U.S. Government for Kids, GP 3.39:
Biennial Report to Congress on the Status of GPO Access, GP 1.1/2:
Biennial Survey of Depository Libraries: Results, GP 3.33/4:
Catalog of U.S. Government Publications, GP 3.8/8-9:
Daily Depository Shipping List, GP 3.16/3:
ePUB Illustrated, GP 1.40:
Federal Depository Library Directory, GP 3.36/2:
List of Classes of United States Government Publications Available for Selection by Depository Libraries,
  GP 3.24:
NET (New Electronic Titles), GP 3.40:
Proceedings of the Annual Federal Depository Library Conference, GP 3.30/3:
Style Manual, GP 1.23/4:

1386. GPO Congressional Publications Releases
http://www.llsdc.org/gpo/
Sponsor: Law Librarians' Society of Washington DC, Inc.
Description: Members of LLSDC's Legislative Research Special Interest Section transcribe, from twice-daily GPO telephone recordings, the week-by-week listing of newly issued congressional documents for sale by the GPO. These listings are then archived on this site and sent to the LLSDC and GOVDOC-L listservs.
Subject: Congressional Documents

1387. GPO Online Bookstore
http://bookstore.gpo.gov/index.html
Sponsor: Government Printing Office (GPO)
Description: The GPO Sales Product Catalog is searchable by keyword or browsable by topic on this site. Documents can be ordered online. The site also features the sections What's New, Best Sellers, Ordering Information, and Bookstore Locations, as well as a sign-up form for the New Titles email alert service.
Subjects: Government Publications; Publication Catalogs
Publication: *Sales Product Catalog,* GP 3.22/7:

1388. GPOLISTSERV
http://listserv.access.gpo.gov/
Sponsor: Government Printing Office (GPO)
Description: The Government Printing Office offers over 15 email announcement lists. This page describes how the lists work. Click on 'online mailing list archives' to view the individual lists. For each list there are instructions on how to subscribe, and users can view past announcements. Lists include a weekly mailing of the *Federal Register* table of contents, new public and private laws available on *GPO Acces,* and announcements of new sales publications that are not distributed in print to federal depository libraries.
Subjects: Government Publications; Email Lists

1389. Locate a Federal Depository Library
http://www.access.gpo.gov/su_docs/locators/findlibs/index.html
Sponsor: Government Printing Office (GPO) — Superintendent of Documents
Description: Use a clickable map of the United States and U.S. Commonwealths and Territories to find federal depository libraries by location. Users can also search by state, area code, or congressional district, or view a list of all depositories. The site also links to information about the Federal Depository Library Program.

This site is designed to be used by researchers and the general public. The FDLP Desktop site includes a directory with more sophisticated search features that is intended for use by librarians.
Publication: *A Directory of U.S. Government Depository Libraries*, Y 4.P93/1-10:

1390. Needs and Offers List
http://www.und.edu/fdlp/
Sponsor: University of North Dakota. Library
Description: This electronic edition of the Needs and Offers List enables government documents librarians in the Federal Depository Library Program to trade government publications. Some depository libraries receive duplicate copies while others fail to receive specific publications. The Needs and Offers List facilitates communication between libraries to fill those needs.
Subject: Federal Depository Library Program
Publication: *Needs and Offers List*, GP 3.31:

1391. New Electronic Titles on GPO Access
http://www.access.gpo.gov/su_docs/locators/net/
Sponsor: Government Printing Office (GPO) — Superintendent of Documents
Description: The New Electronic Titles page from GPO's Superintendent of Documents site highlights new Web resources added to the *Catalog of U.S. Government Publications* each month. Each Web button for a given month displays publications newly available on the Web. The lists are available for the current month back to January 2001.

As federal agencies publish more and more of their documents online, the New Electronic Titles list helps researchers track this government information migration.
Subject: Government Publications

1392. New Titles by Topic
http://bookstore.gpo.gov/alertservice.html
Sponsor: Government Printing Office (GPO)
Description: New Titles by Topic is a Government Printing Office email alert service. Subscribers are alerted when the Superintendent of Documents makes new products available for sale on a selected topic. At present, the service consists of separate email lists for notices of publications within these subject area: Business; Defense and Security; Elementary and Secondary Education; Employment and Occupations; Federal Statistics; Health Care; Military History; and Travel and Tourism.
Subjects: Government Publications; Email Lists

National

1393. Library of Congress Listservs
http://lcweb.loc.gov/flicc/listsrvs.html
Alternate URLs: http://lcweb.loc.gov/acq/conser/consrlin.html
http://lcweb.loc.gov/catdir/lccn/
Sponsor: Library of Congress
Description: The Library of Congress hosts a number of email lists on its site. The primary URL provides information on several lists including FEDLIB: Federal Librarians Discussion List; FEDCAT-L: FEDLINK Cataloging Peer Council; FEDLIBIT: Federal Librarians Information Technology Discussion; FEDREF-L: Federal Reference Librarians' Discussion List; and OCLCFED: FEDLINK OCLC Members List. Most of these lists are primarily of interest to federal government librarians, but FEDREF-L will be of interest to the entire government documents librarian community.The lists at the alternate URLs are distribution lists and not discussion lists. For example, the CONSER (Cooperative ONline SERials) Program sends out in paper its newsletter *CONSER* or its electronic version *CONSERline*, which is also archived on the Web site. The *LC Cataloging Newsline* is available at the second alternate URL and via an email list.

Subjects: Libraries; Email Lists
Publications: *CONSERline*
LC Cataloging Newsline, LC 9.16:

1394. Library of Congress Online Catalog
http://catalog.loc.gov/
Sponsor: Library of Congress
Description: The Library of Congress Online Catalog is a database of approximately 12 million records representing books, serials, computer files, manuscripts, cartographic materials, music, sound recordings, and visual materials in LC's collections. The Online Catalog also provides cross-references, notes, and circulation status as well as information about materials still in the acquisitions stage. Additional information on the catalog is provided in Search Help and Frequently Asked Questions sections. The Online Catalog page also links to online catalogs maintained for the Library of Congress Prints and Photographs Division and the Recorded Sound Reference Center.
Subject: Library Catalogs

1395. National Agricultural Library
http://www.nal.usda.gov/
Sponsor: Agriculture Department (USDA) — National Agricultural Library (NAL)
Description: As a major source for national and international agricultural information, the NAL Web site links to some of NAL's many resources and acts as a gateway to its associated institutions. Primary categories include About NAL, AGRICOLA, Search NAL Web Site, AgNIC, Services and Programs, Publications and Databases, News, and Ag Events Calendar.

About NAL describes NAL's collections, products, and services. It also includes a mission statement, visitor information, and a staff locator. Publications and Databases lists online documents and links to many databases. Publications include support material for AGRICOLA and online indexes to USDA serial publications such as the *Agricultural Economic Reports* and *USDA Agriculture Handbooks*. The databases include AGRICOLA, Journals Indexed in AGRICOLA, USDA Nutrient Database for Standard Reference, several databases of educational and nutrition materials, and technical databases maintained by USDA and by other agencies.

On the AGRICOLA page, two options are available: NAL Online Catalog (books, reports, maps, journals/periodicals, CD-ROMs) and Journal Article Citation Database (articles, reprints, book chapters). The latter contains records from AGRICOLA from 1984 to the present and is updated daily. The search software has search and browse, keyword search, and advanced keyword search.

This site can be used as an excellent starting point for finding agricultural information. With the availability of Agricola and NAL's catalog, it is a central resource for all kinds of agricultural information.
Subjects: Agriculture Information; Libraries
Publications: *Agriculture Libraries Information Notes*, A 17.23:
Animal Welfare Information Center Bulletin, A 17.27/2:
Land Grant Libraries and Other Cooperating Institutions
List of Journals Indexed in Agricola, A 17.18/5:
NAL Agricultural Thesaurus
National Agriculture Library Annual Report, A 17.1:

1396. National Archives and Records Administration
http://www.archives.gov
Sponsor: National Archives and Records Administration (NARA)
Description: The National Archives and Records Administration (NARA) oversees the archival records of the executive, congressional, and judicial branches of the federal government. Its Web site includes information about their holdings and online access to a few digitized collections. The Research Room section provides an introduction to what the Archives has and how to find it. There are special sections on how to do research related to genealogy and veterans' service records, two popular research areas. A Research Topics section provides similar information for over 20 additional topics, from African American History to the Watergate Tapes. The Research Room section also links to NARA's Archival Research Catalog (ARC), formerly known as NARA Archival Information Locator database (NAIL). ARC currently includes records for less than 15 percent of

NARA's nationwide holdings. The site also features information on the National Historical Publications and Records Commission, which awards grants and conducts training to assist documents preservation efforts. The Digital Classroom section of the site provides initial ideas and methods for teaching with primary sources and sample lesson plans. The Online Exhibit Hall section features selected exhibits from NARA and reproductions of documents like the Magna Carta. For the archivist, the Records Management section offers news and information pertaining to federal records management policy. The site also has a section describing its Records of Congress.

NARA's Web site explains the agency's varied responsibilities and includes materials that might not be expected to originate from the agency. For example, NARA oversees the Presidential Libraries. It also houses the Office of the Federal Register, which is responsible for the *Federal Register* publication but also for coordinating the Electoral College.

This site is unusual in the scope of materials available. While very little actual archival material is online, NARA has put selected high-interest items on the site.

Subject: Archives

Publications: *Citing Records in the National Archives of the United States*, AE 1.113:17/
Guide to Federal Records in the National Archives of the United States, AE 1.108:G 94/
ISOO (Information Security Oversight Office) Annual Reports, AE 1.101/3:
NARA Bulletin, AE 1.103:
National Archives and Records Administration Annual Report, AE 1.101:
Prologue
Quarterly Compilation of Periodical Literature Reflecting the Use of Records in the National Archives,
   AE 1.128:

1397. National Library of Education

http://www.ed.gov/NLE/

Sponsor: Education Department — National Library of Education (NLE)
Description: The National Library of Education collects information primarily in the area of education with special emphasis on theory, policy, and research. Its site features descriptive information about the library, its services, visitor information, and links to external resources. Featured sections include About Us, ERIC, Gateway to Educational Materials (GEM), Virtual Reference Desk (VRD), United States Network for Education Information (USNEI), National Clearinghouse for Educational Facilities (NCEF), and Resources. The Education Publications section provides online ordering of the Department of Education's publications, posters, videos, and other products. The FAQ section has quick links to the sources needed to answer questions on topics such as the dropout rate, expenditure per pupil, literacy rates, financial aid, and statistics on degrees conferred.
Subject: Education Research

1398. National Library of Medicine

http://www.nlm.nih.gov/

Sponsor: National Institutes of Health (NIH) — National Library of Medicine (NLM)
Description: As a major resource for information on health sciences literature, the National Library of Medicine (NLM) offers many resources through these pages. The main sections of NLM's site are Health Information, Library Services, Research Programs, New and Noteworthy, and General Information. It also has a direct link to its free MEDLNE*plus* service which provides consumer health information.The General Information section covers library hours, services, job openings, and location. Press releases and announcements can be found under the New and Noteworthy heading. Library Services includes links to databases, publications, training, grants, and the catalog. The Databases subsection lists NLM's searchable databases, such as MEDLINE, TOXNET, and ClinicalTrials.gov. The NLM Publications subsection includes the full text of *NLM Fact Sheets*, *NLM Technical Bulletin*, and other NLM publications. The Extramural Grants and Contracts section includes a variety of descriptions and announcements of extramural funding opportunities. The NLM Web site serves as a gateway to the programs and information produced by the library. It will be of use to the general public, researchers, and medical librarians.

Subjects: Libraries; Medical Information
Publications: *Current Bibliographies in Medicine*, HE 20.3615/2:
Gratefully Yours, HE 20.3625:
List of Journals Indexed in Index Medicus, HE 20.3612/4:
List of Serials Indexed for Online Users (annual), HE 20.3618/2:
National Library of Medicine Fact Sheet, HE 20.3621:
NLM LOCATORplus, HE 20.3626:
NLM Newsline, HE 20.3619:
NLM Programs and Services Annual Report
NLM Technical Bulletin (monthly), HE 20.3603/2:

1399. National Library Services for the Blind and Physically Handicapped (NLS)
http://www.loc.gov/nls
Sponsor: Library of Congress — National Library Services for the Blind and Physically Handicapped (NLS)
Description: NLS administers a free library program circulating Braille and recorded materials to eligible borrowers through a network of cooperating libraries. The Learn section of the site has information on how NLS works. The next section, Find Books and Magazines in Braille or Audio, includes the online catalog of Braille and audio books, *Braille Book Review* and other bibliographies. The NLS Publications section include NLS fact sheets, bibliographies, circulars, and directories of libraries and resources related to reading material for the blind and physically handicapped. The Publications section also includes information on Digital Talking Books and Web-Braille. The NLS site is designed for text-based browsers, such as Lynx, frequently used by blind readers. Under About This Site, users can find more references that may be helpful in designing accessible Web sites.
Subjects: Libraries; Vision Disorders
Publications: *Braille Book Review*, LC 19.9:
For Younger Readers, Braille and Talking Books, LC 19.11/2:
Magazines in Special Media, LC 19.11/2-2:
News, LC 19.13:
Overseas Outlook
Talking Book Topics, LC 19.10:
Update, LC 19.13/2:

CHAPTER 12
Military

Occupying the .mil Internet domain, the U.S. military has long maintained numerous publicly accessible Web sites. After the September 11, 2001 terrorist attacks, the military began a security review of their Internet content. Sections of some sites have been removed. Other sites have been added to the list of those that are open only to military personnel or contractors. This chapter includes publicly accessible sites and notes if access to portions of these sites is restricted.

Web sites operated by the military and service branches range from recruiting sites and Pentagon news services to sites representing individual bases, research facilities, and personnel services. They may include news of current military operations, U.S. military history, information on contracting opportunities or technology transfer, or basic science research summaries. This chapter has sections for the Air Force, Army, and Navy, and for sites for military families. The featured Web sites listed below are finding aids for the massive amount of military information still available online. The DefenseLink site is also a good source for current military news headlines.

Bookmarks & Favorites

Defense Department
- DefenseLink, http://www.defenselink.mil

Armed Services
- Air Force, http://www.af.mil
- Army, http://www.army.mil
- Coast Guard, http://www.uscg.mil
- Marine Corps, http://www.usmc.mil
- National Guard Bureau, http://www.ngb.army.mil
- Navy, http://www.navy.mil

Featured Sites

1400. AJAX: U.S. and International Government Military, Intelligence, and Law Enforcement Agency Access
http://www.sagal.com/ajax/
Sponsor: Sagal Computer Systems
Description: The AJAX site is a central finding aid for Web sites of U.S. and international government military and intelligence agencies. It lists entries for other sites by the following categories and then alphabetically by acronym: U.S. Government Intelligence Agencies, U.S. Government Law Enforcement Agencies, U.S. Government Defense Agencies, U.S. Government Defense Laboratories, U.S. Military Branches, U.S. Government Regulatory Agencies, U.S. Government Regulatory Agencies, International Intelligence Agencies, International Law Enforcement Agencies, International Military and Defense Agencies, NATO Military and Defense Agencies, and Private Intelligence and Law Enforcement Agencies. Under each of these headings is a list of single line entries which include acronyms and full names of the linked agencies.

This is a very basic finding aid, but easy to use. While the total number of sites included is not large, AJAX does link to the important top level agency servers from the military, intelligence, law enforcement, and other government agencies.
Subjects: Defense and Intelligence; Finding Aids

1401. DefenseLINK: U.S. Department of Defense

http://www.defenselink.mil/

Sponsor: Defense Department

Description: DefenseLINK is the official Department of Defense Web site. The home page is divided into four categories: DoD News, DoD Internal News, DoD Sites, and Special Reports. At the bottom of the page there are links to popular military sites such as Introduction to the Department of Defense ("DoD 101"), Today's Military, U.S. Reserve Forces ("Reserves 101"), the Quadrennial Defense Review, and Defense Almanac.

DoD News includes press releases, press briefings, contract announcements, speeches, and interview transcripts. One can subscribe to receive any (such as contracts announcements) or all news from this section delivered by email. DoD Internal News has articles from the American Forces Press Service, and audio and video files from the American Forces Radio and Television Service. The news is produced internally but is freely available to the public at this site. DoD Sites has quick links to sections of Defense Web sites, indexed to be accessible to the public. Sample topics are Budget, Business Opportunities, Facts and Statistics, and Recruiting. DoD Special Reports are timely articles or Web pages such as those recognizing holidays or commemorating historical events.

A Publications link is at the top of the DefenseLINK home page. It leads to a page of links to popular resources, some published by DoD and some not. The links cover a variety of guides, regulations, forms, and reports including a dictionary of military terms, personnel statistics, Directives and Instructions, and the full text of the current *Annual Report to the President and the Congress*. The Directives and Instructions link leads to a Washington Headquarters Services page with DoD Directives in ASCII, PDF, and SGML format.

With its clear organization and frequent updates, DefenseLINK is an excellent starting point when looking for U.S. military Web sites, news, or information.

Subjects: Military Information; Finding Aids

Publications: *Defense Almanac*, D 2.15/3:

Defense Issues, D 2.15/4:

Department of Defense Annual Report, D 1.1:

DISAM (Defense Institute of Security Assistance Management) Journal of International Security Assistance Management, D 1.86:

DoD Directives, D 1.6/8-2:

General/Flag Officer Worldwide Roster (quarterly), D 1.61/8:

Report on Biological Warfare Defense Vaccine Research & Development Programs, D 1.2:

1402. SearchMil.com

http://www.searchmil.com/

Sponsor: MaxBot.com

Description: SearchMil.com is a search engine that specializes in indexing pages in the ".mil" domains. With more than one million military Web pages indexed, SearchMil.com also provides access to cached versions of the pages in case the live version may be unavailable. It uses popularity techniques to rank its results and displays excerpts from the page with search terms highlighted. Searchers can use quotation marks for phrase searching and the + and - symbols to require or exclude terms. SearchMil.com is case sensitive when upper case letters are used. It defaults to searching with a Boolean "AND," but Boolean searching is not otherwise supported. With its focus on public pages within the .mil domain, SearchMil.com is an excellent starting point for any search for military Web pages. Some general search engines, such as AllTheWeb.com advanced search, offer the ability to limit search results to the .mil domain and can be used in conjunction with SearchMil.com.

Subjects: Military Information; Search Engines

The military resources in this chapter are divided into five sections, spanning the entry numbers indicated here:

General

1403. ACQWeb

http://www.acq.osd.mil/

Sponsor: Defense Department — Office of the Under Secretary of Defense for Acquisition, Technology, and Logistics

Description: ACQWeb is the official Web site for the Office of the Under Secretary of Defense for Acquisition, Technology, and Logistics (AT & L). The Office advises the Secretary of Defense on "on all matters pertaining to the Department of Defense's acquisition process, research and development; advanced technology; test and evaluation; production; logistics; military construction; procurement; economic security; and atomic energy" (from the Web site, 2/7/2003). An AT & L Documents section posts the full text of the Under Secretary's press releases, speeches, and testimony before Congress. The Office Navigator page presents a large menu of the component offices including Acquisition Resources, Interoperability, Small and Disadvantaged Business Utilization, and Defense Procurement. A Heavy Hitters section links to key acquisitions documents and guides, including the Defense Federal Acquisition Regulations Supplement (DFARS), a Web-based Acquisition Deskbook, Acquisition Guidebooks in PDF format, and tools for the OMB Circular A-76 cost comparison process for commercial activities.

ACQWeb is a central Web site for Defense Department personnel involved in acquisitions work. It will also be relevant to those contracting with the Defense Department or needing online access to defense acquisitions regulations and guides.

Subjects: Defense Administration; Military Procurement

Publications: *AR Today*, D 1.6/11-3:

Defense Federal Acquisition Regulations Supplement, D 1.6:AC 7/998

Small Business Innovation Research (SBIR) Program, D 1.48/3:

Small Business Specialists, D 1.6/17:

Subcontracting Directory, D 1.6/16:

1404. American Forces Information Service

http://www.defenselink.mil/afis/

Sponsor: Defense Department — American Forces Information Service (AFIS)

Description: The American Forces Information Service (AFIS) is the principal internal information organization within the Department of Defense, providing news, information, and entertainment for the U.S. military worldwide. Its Web site links to the text, audio, and video from various Defense news services; schedule information for Armed Forces Radio and Television Service; articles from the *Stars and Stripes* newspaper; and the *Early Bird* daily current awareness service. There are also links to the primary Web news sites for each of the armed services and for the Joint Chiefs. An Imagery section has current and archival photographs and videos of U.S. defense operations.

In addition to disseminating news, AFIS trains Defense Department personnel in media communications and provides technical support for communications. The site links to information about the AFIS Defense Information School for training in media relations, broadcasting, journalism, video production, and related media skills.

Because this site is intended primarily for Defense Department use, some sections may be restricted to internal, authorized users. For those outside the military seeking quick access to current defense news, DefenseLINK is the more accessible site. However, the AFIS site is helpful in presenting the full span of armed forces news services.

Subjects: Military Information; News Services

Publications: *AFPS News*, D 2.21:

Stars and Stripes

The Early Bird, D 2.19:

1405. Anthrax Vaccine Immunization Program

http://www.anthrax.osd.mil/

Sponsor: Defense Department

Description: This site features fact sheets on anthrax, the Department of Defense vaccination program, the safety of the vaccine, and possible adverse reactions. Online educational toolkits have slide presentations, brochures, and other instructional materials and are tailored for use by individuals, clinicians, and military commanders. The Resource Center section has a bibliography on the anthrax vaccine, documentation of released vaccine lots, and a compilation of related policies.

In 1998, The Secretary of Defense called for vaccination of all military service members against anthrax. This site was set up to inform the military about the new vaccination program and to help military commanders inform their units. The site has grown to cover related developments, but its focus remains the military's Anthrax Vaccination Immunization Program.

Subject: Anthrax

1406. Arlington National Cemetery

http://www.arlingtoncemetery.org

Sponsor: Arlington National Cemetery

Description: The official Web site for Arlington National Cemetery contains information on all aspects of this historic cemetery. The site is organized into these sections: Maps, Visitor Information, Funeral Information, Ceremonies, Historical Information, and Photo Gallery. It also features links to related sites, a site map, and contact information. The site is rich in historical information covering topics such as famous memorials, lists of famous individuals buried at Arlington, the origins of "Taps" and the 21-gun salute, and the history of the Tomb of the Unknowns. The Photo Gallery includes photographs of military burial ceremonies. The Funeral Information section includes information on eligibility for internment or inurnment at Arlington.

While it may not be obvious from the simple and uncluttered home page, this site is information-rich. Researchers looking for historic information are advised to look under both the Visitor Information and Ceremonies sections as well as under Historic Information. There is a site map to aid in exploration, but no search engine.

Subjects: Military History; Veterans' Cemeteries

1407. Army and Air Force Exchange Service

http://www.aafes.com/

Sponsor: Defense Department — Army and Air Force Exchange Service (AAFES)

Description: The AAFES serves active duty military members, retirees, reservists, and their dependents by providing goods and services as a corporation and central store, selling a wide range of consumer products. While AAFES physical facilities are located on military bases, its online presence provides access to its services from anywhere with Web access. This Web site includes online shopping, returns, catalogs, military locations, job openings, and information on AAFES, with most sections open only to authorized users.

This site caters foremost to the active and retired military community authorized to shop at Army and Air Force Exchanges. Others may find useful information in the About AAFES section, which explains the history and operations of the military base exchanges and provides information for suppliers or manufacturers wanting to do business with AAFES.

Subject: Military Morale and Welfare

1408. Bureau of Arms Control

http://www.state.gov/t/ac/

Alternate URL: http://dosfan.lib.uic.edu/acda/

Sponsor: State Department — Arms Control Bureau

Description: The State Department's Bureau of Arms Control is responsible for international agreements on conventional, chemical/biological, and strategic forces, treaty verification and compliance. Official remarks, fact sheets and press releases are available by topic: Biological Weapons Convention, Chemical Weapons Convention, and Missile Defense. Under Treaties, the site has the full text of such documents as the Geneva Protocol and the Strategic Arms Reduction Treaty (START I). An Archive section links to a previous version of the Bureau's Web pages. A sidebar highlights recent major treaty actions and statements with links to the relevant documents.

The Bureau handles many of the functions of the old Arms Control and Disarmament Agency (ACDA). ACDA was merged with the State Department in 1999 and is now no longer in operation. The alternate URL leads to the archived Web site of the old ACDA site, which is now maintained as part of the Electronic Research Collection of historic State Department materials by the federal depository library at the University of Illinois at Chicago.

The current Bureau site provides quick access to frequently requested treaties and documents related to arms control, and to news of current Administration activities in this realm.
Subjects: Arms Control; International Agreements
Publication: *World Military Expenditures*, AC 1.16:

1409. Bureau of Nonproliferation
http://www.state.gov/t/np/
Sponsor: State Department — Nonproliferation Bureau
Description: The Bureau of Nonproliferation site is divided into sections covering nuclear nonproliferation, Nuclear Weapons Free Zones, biological weapons, chemical weapons, export controls, advanced conventional weapons, the Nonproliferation and Disarmament Fund, and relevant treaties and agreements. A Highlights section links to information on current developments.
Subject: Nonproliferation

1410. Central Command
http://www.centcom.mil/
Sponsor: Defense Department — Central Command
Description: The United States Central Command (USCENTCOM) is one of nine Unified Combatant Commands assigned operational control of U.S. combat forces. Its area of responsibility includes the Horn of Africa, South and Central Asia, and Northern Red Sea regions, as well as the Arabian Peninsula and Iraq. The Web site has information about the Central Command, its leadership, news releases, and a list of its operations and exercises with links for more information.
Subject: Unified Combatant Commands

1411. Chemical and Biological Defense Information Analysis Center
http://www.cbiac.apgea.army.mil/
Sponsor: Defense Department — Chemical and Biological Defense Information Analysis Center (CBIAC)
Description: CBIAC is a Defense Information Analysis Center established to be the Defense Department's focal point for information related to Chemical and Biological Defense (CBD) technology. It covers topics such as biological warfare, chemical identification, disaster preparedness, and medical effect and treatment. Access to some sections of the site, such as the CBIAC Bibliographic Database, is limited to authorized users. The site offers the following sections: About Us, CBIAC Bibliographic Database, Products, Inquiries, Current Awareness, CBD Resources, and Technical Area Tasks. Under CBD Resources, a Key Documents section has several reports, field manuals, and briefings in PDF format. A Current Headlines section pulls together news stories from various commercial news sources on the topic of chemical and biological weapons. Under Current Awareness, the quarterly *CBIAC Newsletter* reports on awarded contracts, new publications, and upcoming symposia. Under Products, there is a PDF copy of the current CBIAC reports catalog and an online order form.

Public users of this site may find the most value in the Products and CBD Resources sections.
Subjects: Biological Warfare; Chemical Warfare; Information Analysis Centers
Publication: *CBIAC Newsletter*

1412. CIA Electronic Reading Room
http://www.foia.cia.gov/
Sponsor: Central Intelligence Agency (CIA)
Description: This is the CIA's public, online gateway for those investigating access to agency documents through the Freedom of Information Act and the Electronic Freedom of Information Act. The Your Rights section identifies the laws governing the release of documents. The Search section is a searchable database of records created since 1940 and released or declassified under the Freedom of Information Act since November 1996. The documents have been scanned in and one can search their full text. A Frequently Requested Records section has the full text of a small set of frequently requested documents such as UFOs Fact or Fiction?, Atomic Spies: Ethel and Julius Rosenburg, POW MIA, Francis Gary Powers: U2 Pilot Shot Down by the Soviets, the Bay of Pigs Report, and

Human Rights in Latin America. Under Special Collections, the site identifies declassified documents collections at Princeton ad the National Archives, and describes the CIA's Historical Review Program to review and declassify historically significant information.

The CIA Electronic Reading Room will answer the basic questions a researcher may have about FOIA and other access to declassified documents from the CIA. Researchers may also wish to check the Web site of the private National Security Archive group, which maintains a repository of declassified documents obtained through FOIA.

Subjects: Declassified Documents; Freedom of Information Act; Intelligence

1413. DefendAMERICA
http://www.defendamerica.mil/
Sponsor: Defense Department
Description: The DefendAMERICA Web site was set up after the September 11, 2001 terrorist attacks to carry news of the U.S. military's efforts to fight global terrorism. Using a news format, the site features current articles and photos as well as audio and video files. It also enables citizens to send email or thank you's to the military services and has descriptions of military equipment used in the war against terrorism. A side panel has links to related government and military Web sites. A Backgrounder section links to Web pages concerning such topics as actions in Afghanistan, Al Qaeda, and smallpox vaccination.
Subjects: Military Operations; Terrorism

1414. Defense Energy Support Center
http://www.desc.dla.mil/main/deschome.htm
Sponsor: Defense Department — Defense Energy Support Center
Description: The Defense Energy Support Center, formerly known as the Defense Fuel Supply Center Entry Point, provides energy support to the military. It acquires, stores, and distributes fuel. The DESC site includes an introduction to DESC, its locations, and employment information. A section on Doing Business With DESC includes information on contracts, Small Business Office support, and Freedom of Information Act filings. DESC publications are linked under the Customer Service section. The Publications page includes an PDF version of the *DESC Fact Book,* with detailed statistical information on the business operations of DESC. A Photo Library section has uncaptioned historical photographs of military fuel operations.
Subject: Military Logistics
Publications: *DESC Fact Book*, D 7.1/6-2:
Fuel Line, D 7.24:

1415. Defense Finance and Accounting Service
http://www.dfas.mil/
Sponsor: Defense Department — Defense Finance and Accounting Service (DFAS)
Description: The DFAS site features information on accounting and related areas within the DoD. Under Money Matters, the site includes information about military pay, civilian pay, retired and annuitant pay, vendor pay, travel pay, transportation pay, and garnishment and involuntary allotments. DFAS News features press releases and information about new additions to the Web site. The site also includes sections for Electronic Commerce, Careers, Legislative Affairs, and a Reference Library. The Reference Library contains briefings, regulations, guides, and financial statements as well as some archived documents.

The pay scales section will be of most interest to non-Defense users. For Defense users, the site of most interest may be the myPay area under Money Matters, which allows one to make certain changes to one's pay information and submit questions about pay.
Subject: Defense Administration

1416. Defense Information Systems Agency
http://www.disa.mil/
Sponsor: Defense Department — Defense Information Systems Agency (DISA)
Description: The Defense Information Systems Agency develops information technology systems for the military. The DISA Web site provides basic information about the agency, its major mission areas, and its programs and field commands. Links to core mission areas include: Information Assurance, Defense

Message System, Global Combat Support System, Global Command and Control System, and Electronic Business. The Publications section includes circulars, notices, and policy letters.
Subjects: Military Computing; Communications Technology
Publication: *Circulars*, D 5.104:

1417. Defense Intelligence Agency
http://www.dia.mil/
Sponsor: Defense Department — Defense Intelligence Agency (DIA)
Description: The DIA provides military intelligence to warfighters, defense policymakers and force planners, in the Department of Defense and the Intelligence Community, and in support of U.S. military planning and operations and weapon systems acquisition. Its Web site includes agency information under the following sections: Agency Overview, History, Careers, Business/Contracting, and Public Affairs. The Public Affairs section has press releases, Frequently Asked Questions about DIA, information on the Freedom of Information Act, and a FOIA Archive with records on such topics as Pan Am Flight 103, poisonous snakes, and UFOs.
Subjects: Intelligence Agencies; Military Intelligence

1418. Defense Logistics Agency
http://www.dla.mil/
Sponsor: Defense Department — Defense Logistics Agency (DLA)
Description: The Defense Logistics Agency is the central supply and distribution agency for the military, providing goods such as weapons parts, fuel, uniforms, food rations, and medical supplies. The DLA site is a central access point to subsidiary DLA agencies and some of their publications. Key topic areas are Business Opportunities, Information Technology, and Corporate Headquarters. Other sections are About DLA, News, Library, and Employment. The Library section includes links to previous congressional testimony from DLA, Electronic Freedom of Information Act information, and *Dimensions,* DLA's news magazine in PDF format.
Subject: Military Logistics
Publications: *Defense Standardization Program Journal*, D 1.88:
DLAPS Publications, D 7.41:
Form Flow, D 7.41/2:
Fuel Line, D 7.24:
Log Lines, DLA News Customers can use, D 7.43:

1419. Defense Prisoner of War/Missing Personnel Office
http://www.dtic.mil/dpmo/
Sponsor: Defense Department — Defense Prisoner of War/Missing Personnel Office (DPMO)
Description: The DPMO Web site declares its mission to explain the federal government's efforts to account for missing personnel from all wars. News releases on the site, from 1996 to present, document activities, agreements, and major events, as well as announcements when a soldier's remains are identified. The site documents policies, archival research results, and DNA identification procedures. It features lists reported from missing personnel databases from the Cold War, Vietnam, and Korea. It also has information on family support and National POW/MIA Recognition Day.
Subject: Prisoners of War

1420. Department of Defense Single Stock Point for Specifications, Standards, and Related Publications
http://www.dodssp.daps.mil/
Sponsor: Defense Department — Defense Automated Printing Service (DAPS)
Description: This site provides access to information about military specifications and standards. It includes access to PDF versions of the DoD Index of Specifications and Standards (DoDISS). Authorized users can link to the Acquisition Streamlining and Standardization Information System (ASSIST) database, a management and research tool which includes DoDISS and other military specifications and standards documents. Other sections include a Procurement GATEWAY, the Technical Manual Publish-On-Demand System (TMPODS), the Navy Electronic Directives System (NEDS), and Navy Forms Online.

This site is useful for locating specific military standards.
Subjects: Military Publishing; Standards and Specifications
Publication: *Index of Specifications and Standards*, D 1.76:

1421. DISA Information Assurance Program Management Office
http://www.disa.mil/infosec/iaweb/default.html
Sponsor: Defense Department — Defense Information Systems Agency (DISA)
Description: The Defense Information Security Agency (DISA) Information Assurance Program
Management Office is concerned with all aspects of computer security for the Defense Information
Infrastructure. The Office's Web site has practical information on such topics as computer viruses
and vulnerability alerts; however, many sections are not accessible by non-military users.
Subject: Computer Security

1422. Document Automation and Production Service
http://www.daps.dla.mil/
Sponsor: Defense Department — Defense Logistics Agency (DLA)
Description: The Defense Logistic Agency's Document Automation and Production Service provides
professional printing, copying, duplicating, scanning, imaging, document conversion, CD-ROM, and
Web services to the Defense Department and the Federal Executive Branch. Its site features sections such as Corporate Information, Customer Information, Frequently Asked Questions,
Products, Locations, News, and Events. The Locations link offers a search for locations by state or
country and has links to regional offices and its headquarters. A Links section features a list of Web
sites concerning the practice of "knowledge management" from both the military and outside
organizations.
 Primarily useful to the Defense community for locating nearby offices, this site will also be of
interest to other organizations investigating automated printing and document conversion options.
Subjects: Military Publishing; Printing

1423. DoD 101: Introduction to the United States Department of Defense
http://www.defenselink.mil/pubs/dod101/
Sponsor: Defense Department
Description: The U.S. military service branches are older than the nation, but the Department of
Defense was not established in its current form until 1949. This DoD public relations site explains
the Department's history, structure, and operations with a minimum of technical language. Sections
include: How We Evolved; Who We Work For; and How We're Organized. The site is set up like a
slide presentation and can be viewed in a number of formats, including graphical HTML, outline
HTML, and PDF.
Subject: Military Forces

1424. DoD Dictionary of Military Terms
http://www.dtic.mil/doctrine/jel/doddict/
Sponsor: Defense Department — Joint Chiefs of Staff
Description: This is the online version of the *DOD Dictionary of Military and Associated Terms*. It
provides very brief explanations of such terms as "prearranged fire" and "reserved obstacles." The
site also links to the Joint Acronyms and Abbreviations list, which links from acronym to full name.
Subjects: Military Information; Reference
Publication: *Department of Defense Dictionary of Military and Associated Terms* , D 5.12:

1425. DoD Resource Locator (GILS)
http://sites.defenselink.mil/
Sponsor: Defense Department
Description: The DOD Resource Locator is a catalog of publicly available DOD information sources,
including Web sites, Web publications, and Freedom Of Information Act (FOIA) electronic reading
room documents. The records are in GILS (Government Information Locator Service) format and
link to the resource described. Users may search the database or browse records by military
branch.
Subjects: Military Information; Finding Aids

1426. DoD-CERT Online
http://www.cert.mil/
Sponsor: Defense Department
Description: The Department of Defense Computer Emergency Reponse Team (DoD-CERT) manages military computer security. The site carries alerts, bulletins, and technical advisories, but these and many other sections may be accessed only by authorized users. The site also links to vendors' operating system security bulletins and other armed forces computer security Web sites.
Subject: Computer Security

1427. European Command
http://www.eucom.mil/
Sponsor: Defense Department — European Command
Description: The territory covered by the U.S. European Command extends from the North Cape of Norway, through the waters of the Baltic and Mediterranean seas, most of Europe, parts of the Middle East, and to the Cape of Good Hope in South Africa. The Command's Web site has news releases, information on major operations, a chronological list of exercises, the Command's *Posture Statement* that is submitted to congressional oversight committees, and other publications.
Subject: Unified Combatant Commands

1428. General Dennis J. Reimer Training and Doctrine Digital Library
http://155.217.58.58/atdls.htm
Sponsor: Army
Description: The Army Training and Doctrine Digital Library is the single repository of approved Army training and doctrine information. For access to distribution-restricted documents and information, users need to register. Registration is limited to active duty and reserve component military personnel, U.S. government employees, and government contractors with a documented "need to know." The site features the following sections: The Library, Documents, What's Hot, Register, Search, and Joint/Multiservice.
Subject: Military Doctrine

1429. Hazardous Technical Information Services
http://www.dscr.dla.mil/htis/htis.htm
Sponsor: Defense Department — Defense Logistics Agency (DLA)
Description: This site serves the DoD community with questions concerning the compliant management of hazardous materials and wastes. Several HTIS publications are available in full text, including the *HTIS Bulletin* and the *Storage and Handling of Hazardous Materials Manual*, and there is a long list of links to DoD and other Web sites relating to hazardous materials.
Subject: Hazardous Waste
Publications: *HTIS (Hazardous Technical Information Services) Bulletin*, D 7.2/3: *Storage and Handling of Hazardous Materials Manual*

1430. Headquarters, Marine Corps
http://www.hqmc.usmc.mil/
Sponsor: Marine Corps
Description: This site offers links to the Marine Corps Headquarters offices, including the Commandant of the Marine Corps, Chaplain of the Marine Corps, Public Affairs, Manpower and Reserve Affairs, Historical Division, Legislative Affairs Office, and Marine Corps Uniform Board.
Subject: Marine Corps

1431. Home for Heroes: The Armed Forces Retirement Home
http://www.defenselink.mil/specials/heroes/
Sponsor: Defense Department — Armed Forces Retirement Home
Description: The Armed Forces Retirement Home consists of the U.S. Soldiers' and Airmen Home in Washington, DC and the U.S. Naval Home in Gulfport, MS. This Web site describes the facilities and gives a photographic tour of each. It also profiles selected veterans living there.
Subject: Veterans

1432. Information Assurance Technology Analysis Center

http://iac.dtic.mil/iatac/

Sponsor: Defense Department — Information Assurance Technology Analysis Center (IATAC)
Description: This Information Analysis Center has been charged with gathering information on information assurance technologies, system vulnerabilities, research and development, and models and providing analyses to support the development and implementation of effective defenses against information warfare attacks. The Web site features sections such as About IATAC, Products/Services, Resources, and News and Events. The Resources section links to publications and Web sites on the topic of information security and intelligence.
Subjects: Computer Security; Electronic Warfare; Information Analysis Centers

1433. Infrared Information Analysis Center

http://iac.dtic.mil/iria/

Sponsor: Defense Department — Infrared Information Analysis Center (IRIA)
Description: The Infrared Information Analysis (IRIA) Center Web site offers descriptive information about this Information Analysis Center and its area of research. IRIA's focus is on military sensing science and technology. Major sections include General Information, Available Resources, Military Sensing Symposia, and IRIA Services. An Information Links and Resources section has selected links to other Web resources on remote sensing and electo-optics.
Subjects: Imaging Technology; Remote Sensing

1434. JCS Link

http://www.dtic.mil/jcs/

Sponsor: Defense Department — Joint Chiefs of Staff
Description: JCS Link offers information on the Joint Chiefs of Staff, the Joint Staff, and the combatant commands. Featured links are Organization, People, Hot Topics, Library, News and Events, and Related Sites. Organization explains the office of the Joint Chiefs and has links to the directorates. People has biographies of the Joint Chief, Service Chiefs, and Combatant Commanders. The Library includes: Joint Doctrine information; JCS speeches; a link to the Joint Electronic Library; history of the Joint Staff with a list of all former Joint Chiefs; and a Publications and Reports section. News and Events links to DefenseLink for the text of press releases and the transcripts of DoD briefings.
Subject: Military Leadership
Publication: *Joint Force Quarterly*, D 5.20:

1435. Joint Forces Command

http://www.jfcom.mil/

Sponsor: Defense Department — Joint Forces Command
Description: The Joint Forces Command has responsibility for strategic issues, training of joint forces, and integration of U.S. military capabilities. Headquartered in Norfolk, Virginia, they are one of nine unified commands in the Department of Defense. Their Web site provides information on their mission, operations, goals, and component forces.
Subject: Unified Combatant Commands

1436. Logistics Operations

http://www.supply.dla.mil/

Sponsor: Defense Department — Defense Logistics Agency (DLA)
Description: Logistics Operations includes supply centers, service centers, and a distribution center. Their site includes the *Customer Assistance Handbook*, a guide to military logistics terminology, and information for customers and vendors.
Subjects: Military Procurement; Military Supplies
Publication: *Customer Assistance Handbook*, D 7.6/20:

1437. Marine Corps Intelligence Department

http://hqinet001.hqmc.usmc.mil/DirInt/

Sponsor: Marine Corps

Description: Marine Corps Intelligence is part of the U.S. Intelligence Community. The department's Web site has information on their mission, functions, and organization.
Subject: Military Intelligence

1438. Marine Forces Reserves
http://www.marforres.usmc.mil/
Sponsor: Marine Corps — Marine Forces Reserves (MFR)
Description: The Marine Forces Reserves site provides practical information for those currently in the Reserves, including information on reserve duty opportunities, mobilization, Tricare health insurance, and current news. In addition, there is information for the media, information on the Toys for Tots program, and a link to the site for the Marine Forces Reserve Band.
Subject: Marine Corps
Publications: *Continental Marine*, D 214.23:
Marine Forces Reserve News, D 214.36:

1439. Marines
http://www.marines.com/
Sponsor: Marine Corps
Description: This is the Marine Corps recruiting site. It offers a Flash presentation (and HTML alternative) geared towards specific audiences. It also has a form for requesting additional information. For a general information site about the Marines see http://www.usmc.mil, the Official Marine Corps Website.
Subjects: Marine Corps; Military Recruiting

1440. MDA Link
http://www.acq.osd.mil/bmdo/
Sponsor: Defense Department — Missile Defense Agency (MDA)
Description: The Defense Department's Missile Defense Agency (MDA) is charged with developing an integrated missile defense system. In 2002, Secretary of Defense Donald H. Rumsfeld redesignated the Ballistic Missile Defense Organization (BMDO) as the Missile Defense Agency (MDA), elevating the organization to agency status. MDA Link is the agency's Web site.MDA Link explains the Basics of Missile Defense and the Ballistic Missile Defense System. Other resources include public statements from the agency, program fact sheets, a Ballistic Missile Defense Glossary, a history of U.S. missile defense efforts, and the program's recent budget history. Under Resources, the Other Reports section includes the "Welch Report" documents from the National Missile Defense Review Committee.
Subject: Missile Defense
Publication: *Ballistic Missile Defense Organization, Report to Congress*, D 1.1/6:

1441. Military Career Guide Online
http://www.militarycareers.com
Sponsor: Defense Department
Description: This online guide from the Defense Department is a central information resource about careers and specializations in the U.S. armed forces, for both enlisted and officer personnel. A career database has details on more than 150 occupations. The database can be searched by keyword or browsed by career area, such as Health Care, Transportation, or Construction. Each entry has information on job duties, training, and entry requirements, and identifies the civilian counterpart occupation for comparison purposes. A section titled Introduction to the Armed Services has information specific to the Army, Navy, Air Force, and Marines.
Subject: Military Recruiting
Publication: *Military Careers: A Guide to Military Occupations and Selected Military Career Paths*, D 1.6/15:

1442. MilitaryCity.com
http://www.militarycity.com/
Sponsor: Army Times Publishing Company
Description: MilitaryCity.com is the central access point for the online versions of the commercially published newspapers *Army Times*, *Navy Times*, *Air Force Times*, and *Marine Corps Times*. News from the publications is limited to subscribers, as are many other features of this site. Free news content for non-subscribers consists of Associated Press wire stories concerning the military.
Subjects: Military Forces; News Services

1443. Modeling and Simulation Information Analysis Center
http://www.msiac.dmso.mil/
Sponsor: Defense Department — Modeling and Simulation Information Analysis Center (MSIAC)
Description: Featuring information on the Modeling and Simulation Information Analysis Center's services and products, this site offers sections such as Modeling and Simulation (M&S) FAQs, M&S Calendar, M&S News, *M&S Journal Online*, and links to other modeling and simulation Internet sites.
Subjects: Information Analysis Centers; Military Computing
Publication: *M&S Journal Online*

1444. National Cemetery Administration
http://www.cem.va.gov
Sponsor: Veterans Affairs Department
Description: Designed to meet the information needs of U.S. military veterans, this site explains burial and memorial benefits available through the VA's National Cemetery Administration. Featured sections include: Cemeteries, Burial Benefits, Headstones and Markers, Presidential Memorial Certificates, Military Funeral Honors, State Cemetery Grants Program, Locating Veterans, and obtaining Military Records and Medals. The Cemeteries section lists information on the VA's National Cemeteries as well as State Veterans Cemeteries, Arlington National Cemetery, Department of the Interior National Cemeteries, and American Battle Monuments Commission Cemeteries. An FAQ section covers facts on burial benefits, eligibility, and related topics.
Subject: Veterans' Cemeteries

1445. National Nuclear Security Administration
http://www.nnsa.doe.gov/
Sponsor: Energy Department — National Nuclear Security Administration
Description: The National Nuclear Security Administration (NNSA) within the Department of Energy officially began operations on March 1, 2000. Its mission is to carry out the national security responsibilities of the Department of Energy, including maintenance of nuclear weapons, promotion of international nuclear safety and nonproliferation, and management of the naval nuclear propulsion program. The NNSA Web site includes press releases and links to field offices and facilities. A Documents section has speeches and testimony from the NNSA Administrator, information on the NNSA Advisory Committee, budget information, and leadership biographies.
Subject: Nuclear Weapons

1446. National Reconnaissance Office
http://www.nro.gov/
Sponsor: Defense Department — National Reconnaissance Office (NRO)
Description: Part of the U.S. government intelligence community, the National Reconnaissance Office (NRO) designs, builds, and operates the nation's reconnaissance satellites. The NRO site has sections for Who We Are, What's New, NRO News (current year), Archives (news from previous years), Corona, FOIA, Community Outreach, and Doing Business with the NRO. Corona was the first photo reconnaissance satellite system that operated until 1972. The images have been declassified, and some are available here.
Subject: Intelligence Agencies

1447. National Security Agency

http://www.nsa.gov/

Sponsor: Defense Department — National Security Agency (NSA)

Description: Specializing in cryptology, the National Security Agency (NSA) works to protect U.S. information systems security and to produce foreign intelligence. The NSA Web site features non-sensitive information about this sometimes secretive agency. The About NSA section includes biographies of the agency heads and answers to frequently asked questions. Another section is dedicated to the National Cryptologic Museum and NSA's Cryptologic History, including the 1940s VENONA project to decipher Soviet government messages. The INFOSEC (information systems security) section describes NSA's government computer security efforts and education programs. It includes a list of universities NSA has designated as "Centers of Academic Excellence in Information Assurance Education." A separate section details NSA's mathematics education outreach program. Acquisitions, Small Business, and Technology Transfer sections have information for companies and other organizations seeking opportunities to work with NSA. An Employment Opportunities section has detailed information on NSA career paths and student training programs. NSA's Public Information Release Programs include four types of documents: press releases, selected public speeches and briefings given by the agency's leadership, Freedom of Information Act (FOIA) releases, and declassified documents. Press releases and selected briefing are available from the site. The FOIA section has some frequently requested documents such as those relating to UFO's and the John F. Kennedy Assassination. Declassified documents have been turned over to the National Archives; this site explains the documents project and how to access the collection at the Archives.

Subjects: Cryptography and Encryption; Intelligence Agencies

1448. Nonproliferation and International Security Division

http://www.lanl.gov/orgs/nis/

Sponsor: Energy Department — Los Alamos National Laboratory (LANL)

Description: This division of Los Alamos National Lab is charged with developing and applying pre-eminent science and technology to the problem of proliferation of weapons of mass destruction. Program areas within the division include Nonproliferation, Research and Development, and International Technology. A Research section links to background on specific projects. The Publications section gives access to annual reports and several other documents. Other sections feature an organization chart and news releases.

Subject: Nonproliferation — Research

1449. Northern Command

http://www.northcom.mil/

Sponsor: Defense Department — Northern Command

Description: The Northern Command (USNORTHCOM) was established in 2002 to counter threats and aggression aimed at the United States and its territories. It also provides military assistance to civilian authorities in support of homeland defense. The Command's geographic area of responsibility includes North America, Puerto Rico, the U.S. Virgin Islands, and air, land, and sea approaches. The Command's Web site has information on its leadership and mission, and on its support of local, state, and federal authorities and "first responders" to emergencies.

Subject: Unified Combatant Commands

1450. Pacific Command

http://www.pacom.mil/

Sponsor: Defense Department — Pacific Command

Description: The U.S. Pacific Command (PACCOM) is one of nine Unified Combatant Commands assigned operational control of U.S. combat forces. Headquartered in Hawaii, the Command's geographic area of responsibility is the Asia-Pacific region including China, Russia, Japan, India, the Philippines, and North and South Korea. The Command's site includes news releases and links to Asia-Pacific news media on the Web. It also has information on the Command's exercises and operations, leadership, and leadership speeches.

Subject: Unified Combatant Commands

1451. Pentagon Renovation Program

http://renovation.pentagon.mil/

Sponsor: Defense Department

Description: Even before the September 11, 2001 terrorist attack on the Pentagon, a massive renovation program for the building was underway. This site is a central point for information about the renovation. It features news, photos, and a Press Clippings section with links to media coverage of the project. Each phase of the rebuilding project is described, and there is information on contractor opportunities related to the project. The site includes the *PENREN this Week* newsletter reporting on construction progress.

Subject: Military Bases and Installations

1452. Profile—Life in the Armed Forces

http://www.spear.navy.mil/profile/

Sponsor: Defense Department

Description: This site offers an HTML version of *Profile* magazine, published by the DoD High School News Service. *Profile* is designed to inform high school students and career guidance counselors about the benefits, opportunities, and programs available in the military services. The site highlights *Profile's* "Basic Facts" issue with enlistment, training, and education opportunities for each branch of the armed services. A Related Links section links to the recruiting Web sites for each of the services.

Subject: Military Recruiting

Publication: *Profile: Life in the Armed Forces*, D 1.41:

1453. Selective Service System

http://www.sss.gov/

Sponsor: Selective Service System (SSS)

Description: The Selective Service site features information about the agency and the military draft, and can be used to register online or check a registration. The site includes topics such as About the Agency, News and Public Affairs, History/Records, Publications, Registration Information, What Happens in a Draft, Fast Facts, and Frequently Asked Questions. History/Records includes historical draft statistics, a guide to requesting archival records of draft registrants, and general history of the draft in the United States. The Publications section contains current and past editions of the agency's *Annual Report to Congress* and newsletter, *The Register*.

Subject: Military Draft

Publications: *Annual Report to Congress*, Y 3.SE 4:1

The Register, Y 3.SE 4:27/

1454. Southern Command

http://www.southcom.mil/home/

Sponsor: Defense Department — Southern Command

Description: The United States Southern Command (USSOUTHCOM) is headquartered in Miami and is one of nine unified commands. Their area of responsibility includes Latin America south of Mexico, the waters adjacent to Central and South America, the Caribbean Sea and Caribbean nations and territories, the Gulf of Mexico, and a portion of the Atlantic Ocean. The Command's Web site includes information on their mission, activities, and components.

Subject: Unified Combatant Commands

1455. Special Operations Command

http://www.socom.mil/

Sponsor: Defense Department

Description: The U.S. Special Operations Command (USSOCOM) provides little information for the public through its Web site. What publicly accessible information there is concerns the Command's acquisitions office and is directed to businesses wishing to market to USSOCOM. Special Operations is one of nine unified combatant commands.

Subject: Unified Combatant Commands

1456. SportsLink

http://dod.mil/armedforcessports/

Description: This is a central site for sports activities in the military. It features a calendar of armed forces championship competitions and sections on each of the included sports.

Subjects: Military Morale and Welfare; Sports

1457. State-Level Casualty Lists from Vietnam and Korean Conflict

http://www.archives.gov/research_room/research_topics/korea_and_vietnam_casualties.html

Sponsor: National Archives and Records Administration (NARA)

Description: The National Archives Center for Electronic Records has indexed the records for U.S. military casualties from Korea and Vietnam by the state "home of record" for the service member. In addition to providing free online access to these lists, the page describes how to order copies of these databases. For Korea, the database includes records for persons who died as a result of hostilities in Korea from 1950-57, including those who died while missing or captured. For Vietnam, the database includes records for persons who died 1956-1998, as a result of either a hostile or non-hostile occurrence in the Southeast Asian Combat Area, including those who died while missing or captured.

Subjects: Korean War; Vietnam War

1458. Strategic Command

http://www.stratcom.af.mil/

Sponsor: Defense Department — Strategic Command

Description: United States Strategic Command (USSTRATCOM) is one of the nine Unified Combatant Commands of the Defense Department. USSTRATCOM has responsibility for command and control, military space operations, computer and information operations, and early warning of and defense against nuclear or conventional attack. The Web site has information on the Command's organization, history, and leadership. Major sections include Ballistic Missile Submarines, Bombers, Intercontinental Ballistic Missiles, Manned Space Flight Support, and Military Space Forces.

Subject: Unified Combatant Commands

1459. Survivability/Vulnerability Information Analysis Center

http://iac.dtic.mil/surviac/

Sponsor: Defense Department — Survivability/Vulnerability Information Analysis Center (SURVIAC)

Description: SURVIAC is a DoD information analysis center covering nonnuclear survivability/vulnerability data, information, methodologies, models, and analysis relating to U.S. and foreign aeronautical and surface systems. Its Web site features sections entitled Mission & Information, Products & Services, and Links. The latter includes information on a variety of databases, models, services, and products, much of it dealing with aircraft damage in conventional combat. A need-to-know and proper security clearance are the requirements to access much of the information described, but the descriptions give a helpful overview of the combat survivability research field.

Subjects: Information Analysis Centers; Weapons Systems — Research

1460. Task Force Eagle

http://www.tfeagle.army.mil/

Sponsor: Army — Task Force Eagle

Description: This is the official Web site for Task Force Eagle's Stabilization Force (SFOR) peacekeeping mission in Bosnia-Herzegovina. The site includes history about the conflict and individual troop units, task force sites, and images. The full text of the *Talon*, a newsletter for the troops in Bosnia-Herzegovina, is available from 1995 in PDF format. A second news service on the site, the *Tuzla Night Owl*, is a compilation of articles translated from local open source periodicals, TV, and radio broadcasts. There is also a link to the NATO publication *SFOR Informer*.

Subjects: Army; Bosnian Conflict

Publication: *Talon*, D 101.144:

1461. The National Guard
http://www.ngb.army.mil/
Sponsor: National Guard Bureau
Description: The Guard Web site provides information about the National Guard Bureau, the Army National Guard, and the Air National Guard. The site includes information on National Guard leadership and the organization. A News and Reference section reports on Guard activities and includes fact sheets and Guard publications.
Subject: National Guard

1462. Transportation Command
http://www.transcom.mil/
Sponsor: Defense Department — Transportation Command
Description: The mission of the United State Transportation Command (TRANSCOM) is "to provide air, land, and sea transportation for the Department of Defense in time of peace and time of war." (from the Web site) Most general information about the Command is under the Newcomers Info and History sections. A Publications section has news releases, speeches, pamphlets, reports, and other documents. The Flight Info section has information about airlifts of personnel, government cargo, and non-governmental humanitarian assistance.
Subjects: Airlifts; Military Logistics; Unified Combatant Commands

1463. U.S. Chemical Weapons Convention Web Site
http://www.cwc.gov/
Sponsor: Commerce Department — Bureau of Industry and Security (BIS)
Description: This site brings together background information, regulations, documents, and reports related to U.S. compliance with the Chemical Weapons Convention. The treaty affects U.S. private industries that produce, process, consume, import or export dual-use chemicals that could be used to produce chemical weapons. The site includes handbooks and forms to assist companies with compliance.
Subject: Chemical Warfare

1464. U.S. Commission on National Security/21st Century
http://www.nssg.gov/
Sponsor: Commission on National Security/21st Century (USCNS/21)
Description: The U.S. Commission on National Security/21st Century, also known as the Hart-Rudman Commission, was a bipartisan, independent advisory commission charged with thinking comprehensively and creatively about how the United States should provide for its national security in the first quarter of the 21st century. This site featured three debate forums: Institutional Redesign, Securing the National Homeland, and Recapitalizing America's Science and Education. Other sections included About Us, Reports, and News. Its final report is available in PDF format.

The debate forums are no longer functioning, and no new reports have been added to the site since early 2001. However, in light of the tragic events of September 11, 2001, the final report is an important document of reference regarding security issues in the United States against terrorism.
Subject: National Security — Policy
Publication: *Road Map for National Security: Imperative for Change: The Phase III Report of the U.S. Commission on National Security/21st Century*, PR 43.2:SE 1/R 53/FINAL

1465. United States Coast Guard
http://www.uscg.mil/USCG.shtm
Sponsor: Transportation Department — Coast Guard
Description: The Coast Guard is scheduled to be transferred in its entirety to the newly created Department of Homeland Security. Prior to the transfer, the Coast Guard operated under the Transportation Department during peacetime and under the Secretary of the Navy in wartime or when directed by the president. The breadth of information on the Coast Guard's Web site reflects its multiple missions. Its mission includes national defense and homeland security, but also maritime search and rescue, International Ice Patrol operations, polar and domestic waterway ice-breaking, bridge administration, aids to navigation, recreational boating safety, vessel traffic management, at-sea enforcement of living marine resource laws and treaty obligations, at-sea drug and illegal migrant interdiction, and port security and safety. All of these topics are covered by the Web site.

Major sections are The USCG, Our People, and Our Missions. Under The USCG, the Facts File leads to a wealth of reference information, such as budget and personnel statistics, annual reports, and past commandants of the Coast Guard. The History section, also under The USCG has information on lighthouses, Coast Guard flags, the Coast Guard Museum, historic photographs, and much more.

Subjects: Coast Guard; Homeland Security
Publications: *Coast Guard Magazine*, TD 5.3/11:
Marine Safety Manual, TD 5.8:SA 1/2/
Marine Safety Newsletter, TD 5.66:
Navigation and Vessel Inspection Circulars, TD 5.4/2:
Navigation Rules: International-Inland, TD 5.6:IN 8/
Proceedings of the Marine Safety Council United States (monthly), TD 5.13:
Ship Structure Committee, TD 5.63:
Systems Times, TD 5.68:
The Reservist (bimonthly), TD 5.14:

1466. United States Institute of Peace

http://www.usip.org/
Sponsor: United States Institute of Peace (USIP)
Description: The United States Institute of Peace is an independent, nonpartisan federal institution created and funded by Congress to strengthen the nation's capacity to promote the peaceful resolution of international conflict. Its site features sections such as Highlights (current Institute news), Publications, Research Areas, Library and Links, Education and Training, Grants, Fellowships, and About the Institute (with a directory of experts). The Publications section includes a list of books available from USIP and an online, full-text version of *Peace Watch*, the Institute's magazine. The Library has digital collections concerning peace agreements and truth commissions, annotated links on selected countries and topics, and a list of links to Ministries of Foreign Affairs on the Web.

For research into peace and the U.S. involvement in peace processes, this can be a very useful site. Researchers will find the Library and Links section maintained by the USIP Jeannette Rankin Library to be well organized and maintained. For those needing a speaker or an expert to consult, the directory of specialists is accessible by name or topic, and is easy to use.

Subjects: International Relations; Peace
Publications: *Peace Watch*, Y 3.P 31:15-2/
Special Reports, Y 3.P 31:20/

1467. United States Marine Corps

http://www.usmc.mil/
Sponsor: Marine Corps
Description: The official Web site for the U.S. Marine Corps focuses on current news, featuring articles written by Marines and accompanied by photographs. A Newslinks section points to articles about Marines that have appeared in commercial newspapers and wire services. The site has a Marine Corps Equipment Fact File, and information on doing business with the Marine Corps. There are also links to sites about the United States Marine Band, Marine Corps Museum, Marines history, and publications from the Marines.

This site has a substantial amount of information on the Marines and appears to be updated frequently.

Subject: Marine Corps
Publications: *Concepts and Issues*, D 214.27:
Marine Corps Doctrine Manuals (MCRP, MCWP, MCRP series), D 214.9/9:
Marines (monthly), D 214.24:

1468. USCG Navigation Center

http://www.navcen.uscg.gov/
Sponsor: Transportation Department — Coast Guard
Description: The U.S. Coast Guard Navigation Center provides navigation services that promote safe transportation and support the commerce of the United States. The site features News, Almanacs, Global Positioning System (GPS), Differential Global Positioning System (DGPS), Electronic

Navigation, and LORAN-C. Note that the Coast Guard is scheduled to be transferred in entirety to the newly created Department of Homeland Security.
Subject: Maritime Transportation
Publications: *Federal Radionavigation Plan*, D 1.84:
Radionavigation Bulletin, TD 5.3/10:

1469. Vietnam-Era Prisoner of War Missing in Action Database
http://lcweb2.loc.gov/pow/powhome.html
Sponsor: Library of Congress
Description: This database has been established to assist researchers interested in investigating U.S. Government documents pertaining to U.S. military personnel listed as unaccounted for in Southeast Asia during Vietnam. The title of this collection is "Correlated and Uncorrelated Information Relating to Missing Americans in Southeast Asia." The database does not contain full-text documents, but the site explains how the actual documents can be obtained. The site also provides access to documents from U.S.-Russia Joint Commission on POW/MIAs, an attempt to locate Americans thought to have been held in the former Soviet Union.
Subjects: Prisoners of War; Databases

1470. Weapons Systems Technology Information Analysis Center (WSTIAC)
http://wstiac.alionscience.com/
Sponsor: Defense Department — Weapons Systems Technology Information Analysis Center (WSTIAC)
Description: WSTIAC is the central information service for the Defense community covering research and development in advanced technologies relevant to weapons systems. Site sections include About WSTIAC, Products and Services, Information Resources, User Help Desk, and News and Events.
Subjects: Information Analysis Centers; Weapons Research

Air Force

1471. Air and Space Power Chronicles
http://www.airpower.maxwell.af.mil/
Description: *Air and Space Power Chronicles* is a DoD online magazine intended to promote professional dialogue and development for military airmen. The site carries the full text of *Air and Space Power Journal* (formerly *Airpower Journal*, 1987–1999, and *Aerospace Power Journal*, 2000–Summer 2002), supplemented by book reviews, a discussion forum, and contributed articles not published in the *Journal*. Current issues of *Aerospace Power Journal* can be downloaded in PDF format, or viewed in HTML or Word format. Archival issues back to 1987 are in HTML format. Archival issues of *Air University Review*, which preceded the journals, are indexed and available online for 1977–1987. A Contrails section links to Web sites of interest to *Air and Space Power Journal* readers, such the Air War College and Airpower Research Institute Research Reports.

Spanish and Portuguese versions of *Air and Space Power Journal* are also online, with archival issues back to 1994 and 1996, respectively.
Subject: Air Force
Publications: *Air University Review*, D 301.26:
Airpower Journal, D 301.26/24:
Airpower Journal (Portuguese), D 301.26/24-2:
Airpower Journal (Spanish), D 301.26/24-3:

1472. Air Combat Command
http://www2.acc.af.mil/
Sponsor: Air Force — Air Combat Command (ACC)
Description: The Air Force's Air Combat Command, headquartered at Langley Air Force Base in Virginia, provides air combat forces for the Unified Combatant Commands. A Sites section has a U.S. map with ACC locations, and a Multimedia Gallery has images and videos of ACC aircraft and

bases. Most information on the ACC Web site is under the Library category. The Library section links to ACC Mission and Responsibilities; Air Demonstration Team Schedules; ACC Unit and Base information; and related Web sites and publications. The Library also links to the ACC online magazine *Combat Edge*, going back to 2000.
Subject: Military Aircraft
Publication: *Combat Edge*, D 301.44/2:

1473. Air Education and Training Command
http://www.aetc.randolph.af.mil/
Description: The Air Education and Training Command is responsible for the Air Force programs in military, technical, and flight training, and education at many levels including security assistance, medical and dental, and officer development. The site provides information on Air Force career opportunities, tuition assistance, the GI Bill, basic military training, technical training, and flying training. It also links to the Air Force Academy, Air Force ROTC, and Community College of the Air Force.
Subject: Military Training and Education

1474. Air Force Bands Program
http://www.af.mil/band/index.shtml
Sponsor: Air Force — Air Force Bands
Description: Part of the Air Force Link site, this page provides an overview of the Air Force and Air National Guard bands. Click the Navigate button to go to sections titled About Bands, Audition Information, Band Locations, Contact Information, Official Fact Sheet, Performance Schedule, Requesting Bands, and Sound Files.
Subject: Military Bands

1475. Air Force Inspection Agency
http://afia.kirtland.af.mil/
Alternate URL: http://www.af.mil/news/factsheets/Air_Force_Inspection_Agency.html
Sponsor: Air Force — Air Force Inspection Agency (AFIA)
Description: The Air Force Inspection Agency's mission is to provide Air Force senior leaders with independent assessments of mission capability, health care, and resource management. The agency conducts management reviews and health inspections, and provides guidance and information for Air Force commanders, inspectors general, and inspectors. Most of the content on this sparse site concerns the health inspections and medical readiness operations. The site also features the full text of the Air Force Inspector General's magazine, *TIG Brief*, back to 1997.
Subjects: Defense Administration; Inspectors General
Publication: *TIG Brief*, D 301.119:

1476. Air Force Link—Official Web Site of the U.S. Air Force
http://www.af.mil/
Sponsor: Air Force
Description: This central Air Force site divides its wealth of information into categories such USAF Sites, FAQs, News, Photos, Library, Careers, and History. USAF Sites provides organizational and alphabetical access to numerous official Air Force sites available to the public without restrictions. Frequently Asked Questions covers topics such as aircraft, weapons, bases, the Air Force Song, military memorabilia, and contacting military personnel. The Library section has links to Air Force publications, leadership biographies, and speeches. The Library also has links to over 50 base newspapers online and over a dozen Air Force magazines. Air Force Link has print, radio, and TV news produced by the Air Force. An Air Force Link Plus service provides a daily Internet broadcast in RealPlayer format.

For Air Force information, this is the first place to look. The site is well organized, offers substantial information content, and is easy to navigate.
Subject: Air Force
Publications: *Air Force News*, D 301.122:
Airman, D 301.60:
Citizen Airman, D 301.8:

Flying Safety, D 301.44:
Report of Air Force Research Regarding the 'Roswell Incident', D 301.2:R 73/2/
The Nation's Air Force, D 301.1/3:
U.S. Air Force Policy Digest, D 301.120:

1477. Air Force Office of Scientific Research (AFOSR)
http://www.afosr.af.mil/
Description: AFOSR directs the Air Force's basic research program, with research directorates in the fields of mathematics, space sciences, physics, electronics, aerospace, and materials sciences. This site features sections covering the agency's background and biographies of leadership; Doing Business with AFOSR (grants, contracts, and research opportunities); Research Products and Publications; Education and Researcher Assistance Programs; and a list of Nobel Prize winners sponsored by AFOSR.
Subject: Military Research Laboratories

1478. Air Force Rescue Coordination Center (AFRCC)
http://www2.acc.af.mil/afrcc/
Sponsor: Air Force — Air Combat Command (ACC)
Description: The AFRCC is the single federal agency responsible for coordinating search and rescue activities in the continental United States. AFRCC also coordinates search and rescue agreements, plans, and policy. This Web site describes their history, mission, operations, and work with the Civil Air Patrol. A Links section includes Web links to other federal and private search and rescue organizations.
Subject: Search and Rescue

1479. Air Force Research Laboratory
http://www.afrl.af.mil/
Sponsor: Air Force — Air Force Research Laboratory
Description: The Air Force Research Laboratory conducts basic and applied research aimed towards improving the Air Force fighting capabilities. Its directorates include Air Vehicles, Directed Energy, Human Effectiveness, Information, Materials and Manufacturing, Munitions, Propulsion, Sensors, and Space Vehicles. Most of the nonclassified content available is on the respective directorates' pages. Click on the large graphics in the center of the page to go to the AFRL HQ page. The Headquarters page includes The Reading Room, Corporate Strategy, Organization, Where We Are, and Symposiums, Seminars, and Conferences.
Subject: Military Research Laboratories

1480. Air Force Reserve Command
http://www.afrc.af.mil/
Sponsor: Air Force — Air Force Reserve (AFRES)
Description: The Air Force Reserve Command Web site features News, AFRC Units, Publications and Forms, Directorates, and Information for Reservists and Families. The home page also links to the Air Force Reserve Advisory Board and to information on the Air Force Reserve Band.
Subject: Military Reserves

1481. Air Intelligence Agency
http://aia.lackland.af.mil/
Sponsor: Air Force — Air Intelligence Agency (AIA)
Description: The AIA Web site provides information on the Air Force's Air Intelligence Agency, headquartered at Lackland Air Force Base in San Antonio, Texas. It includes such sections as About AIA, Organization, Products and Services, and Careers (with military, civilian, and reserve job information). About AIA features the following sections: Mission/Vision, History of AIA, Executives, and Fact Sheet. The Products and Services page features AIA Publications and Forms, FOIA Information, and the online edition of the *Spokesman* magazine.
Subjects: Intelligence Agencies; Military Intelligence
Publication: *Spokesman*, D 301.124:

1482. Air Mobility Command
`https://amcpublic.scott.af.mil/`
Sponsor: Air Force — Air Mobility Command (AMC)
Description: The Air Mobility Command (AMC) mission is to provide airlift, air refueling, special air mission, and aeromedical evacuation for U.S. forces. The AMC public information site has information about AMC including fact sheets and an organization chart. A Business Links section has contracting information. The Library section features a Photo Gallery, information on donations for humanitarian airlifts, a list of sources for Air Force insignia and patches, and links to news and related information available elsewhere.
Subjects: Airlifts; Military Logistics

1483. Airforce.com
`http://www.airforce.com/index_fr.htm`
Sponsor: Air Force
Description: This Air Force recruitment site offers information for prospective recruits, with an emphasis on the variety of career tracks available. An Education section includes links to the Air Force Academy and Reserve Office Training Corps sites. The site also features an Air Force advisor locator and a link to the Air Force Thunderbirds site.
Subject: Military Recruiting

1484. Assistant Secretary of the Air Force (Financial Management and Comptroller) SAF/FM
`http://www.saffm.hq.af.mil/`
Sponsor: Air Force
Description: SAF/FM manages the financial operations of the U.S. Air Force. Its site features Air Force budget documentation for fiscal year 1999 to present, organizational chart, and publications. The periodical publication *The Air Force Comptroller* provides further detail on the current budget and finance matters. The annual publication *USAF Statistical Digest* has historical data on Defense and Air Force appropriations, and Air Force personnel, bases, and aircraft inventory. Much of the rest of the site is intended for Air Force military and civilian personnel and their finance managers.
Subject: Defense Administration
Publications: *The Air Force Comptroller*, D 301.73:
USAF Statistical Digest, D 301.83/3:

1485. Aviano Air Base
`http://www.aviano.af.mil/`
Description: This site features the home page of the Aviano Air Base in Italy, which includes sections such as Wing Leadership, Wing Information, History and Heraldry, Newcomer's Information, Photo Gallery, Public Affairs, and the base newspaper *Vigileer*.
Subject: Air Force Bases
Publication: *Aviano Vigileer*, D 301.123:

1486. Brooks City-Base
`http://www.brooks.af.mil/`
Sponsor: Air Force — Brooks Air Force Base
Description: Brooks Air Force Base in Texas is home of the 311th Human Systems Wing and the USAF School of Aerospace Medicine. Major sections of the Brooks Web site include base and community information and sections for Organizations and Associate Units, Environmental, Research, Medical, and Business Opportunities. Most information about activities at Brooks can be found in the Organizations and Associate Units section. The Business Opportunities section has information for contractors about acquisitions.

For basic information on Brooks AFB and its divisions, especially with regards to aerospace medicine, the site is well worth visiting.
Subject: Air Force Bases
Publication: *Discovery / Brooks Air Force Base*

1487. Eglin Air Force Base
http://www.eglin.af.mil/
Sponsor: Air Force — Eglin Air Force Base
Description: The Eglin public site offers information about this Florida Air Force base and its programs. Main areas on the Web site include Frequently Asked Questions, Jobs, Business Opportunities, Organizations, Base Services, and History.
Subject: Air Force Bases

1488. Eielson Air Force Base
http://www.eielson.af.mil/
Sponsor: Air Force — Eielson Air Force Base
Description: Eielson Air Force Base in Alaska, home of the 354th Fighter Wing, features information about it units, employment opportunities, and business opportunities on its public Web site. There are fact sheets on the base, its units, and its aircraft, including historical information. The site also has a photo archive and information from the 354th Fighter Wing Historian Office.
Subject: Air Force Bases

1489. Headquarters Air Force Materiel Command
http://www.afmc.wpafb.af.mil/
Sponsor: Air Force — Air Force Materiel Command (AFMC)
Description: Headquartered at Wright-Patterson Air Force Base, the Air Force Materiel Command (AFMC) equips and supplies the Air Force through supply management, depot maintenance, systems testing and evaluation, information services, and combat support. The AFMC site features the following sections: Organizations, Programs, Library, FOIA, and News. Library includes AFMC electronic forms and links to other Air Force or DoD forms as well as a few online publications. The Organizations section is a hypertext-linked directory that provides access to AFMC departments, field operating agencies, air logistics centers, product centers, test centers, laboratories, and more. The News section links to AFMC periodicals *Leading Edge* and *Ecotone*.
Subjects: Military Logistics; Military Supplies
Publications: *Ecotone*, D 301.126:
Leading Edge, D 301.125:

1490. Headquarters Air Force—HAF DASH 1
http://www.hafdas.hq.af.mil/
Sponsor: Air Force — Air Force Headquarters
Description: The Headquarters Air Force (HAF) site consists of information about the organization and its supporting offices. The HAF Organizations section has an organization chart and listing of office Web sites and any office overview briefings in the Web. The site also has the full text of the HAF *Information Bulletin*.

Largely targeted to the information needs of Air Force military and civilian personnel, this site includes sections limited to the .mil Internet domain.
Subject: Defense Administration

1491. Headquarters Air Reserve Personnel Center
http://arpc.afrc.af.mil/
Sponsor: Air Force — Air Force Reserve (AFRES)
Description: The Air Reserve Personnel Center site has information about pay, promotions, awards, decorations, mobilization, assignments, career paths, retirement, and benefits for reservists. The Main Subjects section and A-Z site map provide easy access to the site's contents.
Subject: Military Reserves
Publication: *The Publicist*

1492. Hickam Air Force Base
http://www.hickam.af.mil/
Sponsor: Air Force — Hickam Air Force Base
Description: Hickam Air Force Base on Oahu, Hawaii is home to the 15th Air Base Wing and the Headquarters Pacific Air Forces (PACAF). Web site sections include News, Leaders, Facts,

Contracting, and Publications and Forms. News features the base newsletter, the *Hickam Kukini*. The Hickam Web site also serves as site for Headquarters PACAF. The PACAF site links to the Web sites of other Pacific air bases, including Andersen, Eielson, Elmendorf, Kadena, Kunsan, Misawa, Osan, and Yokota.
Subject: Air Force Bases

1493. Hill Air Force Base

http://www.hill.af.mil/
Sponsor: Air Force — Hill Air Force Base
Description: This site features information on this Utah Air Force base and the Ogden Air Logistics Center. It features the sections Newcomers Information, Business and Employment Opportunities, Publications and Forms, Organizations, and base news in the *Hilltop Times*. It has some subject links for the F-16 Fighting Falcon, the C-130 Hercules Aircraft, and the Peacekeeper intercontinental ballistic missiles.
Subjects: Air Force Bases; Military Logistics

1494. Kunsan Air Base

http://www.kunsan.af.mil/
Sponsor: Air Force — Kunsan Air Force Base
Description: The Kunsan Air Force Base in Korea is the home of the 8th Fighter Wing, the Wolf Pack. The base Web site categories About Kunsan, News and Links, and Photo Gallery.
Subject: Air Force Bases

1495. National Headquarters Civil Air Patrol

http://www.capnhq.gov/
Sponsor: Air Force — Civil Air Patrol (CAP)
Description: The Civil Air Patrol (CAP) flies U.S. inland search and rescue missions and supports disaster relief, humanitarian assistance efforts, drug interdiction, and the U.S. Air Force homeland defense. The site features sections such as Publications, CAP Forms, Homeland Security, Airfield Photos, Cadet Programs, Aerospace Education and Training, and Join CAP. The Publications section features some regulations, publications catalogs, and a variety of online documents in PDF format. The Join CAP section includes background information on this nonprofit civilian organization, an official auxiliary to the Air Force. The Airfield Photos section has a list of all FAA-registered airports in each state, each with the airfield code and with airfield photos for many of them. Some site sections are restricted to CAP members.

Useful for CAP members and those interested in joining, this site also provide useful background information on the CAP and its activities.
Subject: Civil Air Patrol

1496. Scott Air Force Base

https://public.scott.af.mil/
Sponsor: Air Force — Scott Air Force Base
Description: This public Web site features links to information on organizations at Scott, including the 375th Airlift Wing Public Information, HQ Air Mobility Command Public Information, Air Force Communications Agency, and U.S. Transportation Command. It also links to base information, such as Scott Links of Interest and Scott Newcomers Guide.
Subject: Air Force Bases

1497. Space and Missile Systems Center—SMC Link, Los Angeles Air Force Base

http://www.losangeles.af.mil/
Sponsor: Air Force — Air Force Space and Missile Systems Center
Description: Part of the Air Force Space Command, the Los Angeles-based Space and Missile Systems Center (SMC) manages the acquisitions programs for military satellites and space systems. The 61st Air Base Group is also at the base and described at this site. The SMC Public Affairs section of the Web site has links to news releases, leadership biographies, speakers bureau information, and

the Center newsletter *Astro News*. The home page also has a link to "Air Force Over Hollywood," with information on the Air Force liaison to the entertainment industry.
Subject: Air Force Bases

1498. U.S. Air Forces in Europe (USAFE)
http://www.usafe.af.mil/home.html
Sponsor: Air Force — Air Forces in Europe Command (USAFE)
Description: U.S. Air Forces in Europe is the air component of the U.S. European Command. Headquartered at Ramstein Air Base, Germany, it includes air bases in England, Italy, and Germany. The USAFE Web site features some basic information on the Air Forces in Europe with sections for About Us, USAFE News Service, Library, and Related Links. The Related Links section links to Web sites for the individual Air Force bases. The Library category includes aircraft fact sheets, biographies of leadership, and frequently asked questions. The site also links to a USAFE Anthrax Information site.
Subject: Air Force Bases

1499. Wright-Patterson Air Force Base
http://www.wpafb.af.mil/
Alternate URL: http://ascpa.public.wpafb.af.mil/
Sponsor: Air Force — Wright-Patterson Air Force Base
Description: This is the main public Web site for Wright-Patterson, home of the Aeronautical Systems Center (ASC). Missions at Wright-Patterson include logistics management, research and development, and flight operations. The site features Facts and History, the USAF Museum, WPAFB Organizations, and Acquisition. The Acquisition section includes links to ASC Contracting Business Opportunities, ASC Public Affairs, ASC Small Business Office, and ASC Helping Industry Do Business with Government. The alternate URL is for the Aeronautical Systems Center Public Affairs Web site, which has further information on Wright-Patterson operations, particularly for media and community relations.
Subject: Air Force Bases

Army

1500. Army and Army Reserves Recruiting
http://www.goarmy.com/
Sponsors: Army; Army — Army Reserves (USAR)
Description: Established as a recruitment site for both the Army and the Army Reserves, this site features information likely to be of interest to prospective members. It includes the following sections: Army 101, Basic Training, Jobs, Soldier Profiles, Contact/Recruiter Locator, Reserve/Part-Time, and ROTC/Officer Training. Basic Training presents profiles of recruits and videos from their nine-week basic training and includes some information in Spanish.
Subject: Military Recruiting

1501. Army Civilian Personnel On Line
http://cpol.army.mil/
Sponsor: Army
Description: Army Civilian Personnel On Line provides employment, training, and career information for civilian personnel professionals, managers, and employees. The site features such sections as Army's Vacancy Announcements, Resume Builder, Army Employment Opportunities in Europe, Army Benefits Center, and Position Description Library. A Policy and Guidance Library, under the heading Reference, includes Army personnel bulletins and newsletters.
Subjects: Civilian Defense Employees; Job Openings
Publications: *Civilian Personnel Bulletins*, D 101.138:
Employee Relations Bulletin, D 101.136:
SES Bulletins, D 101.140:
TAPES Newsletter, D 101.137:

1502. Army Financial Management
http://www.asafm.army.mil/
Sponsor: Army
Description: This site features a variety of information on Army accounting and financial management practice. Sections include Army Budget, Financial Operations, and Cost and Economic Analysis Center. The Budget section has detailed materials on the current fiscal year and a table providing organized access to budget documents from previous years.
Subjects: Army; Defense Administration
Publications: *Department of the Army Fiscal Year Annual Financial Report*, D 101.1/17:
Department of the Army Justification of Estimates, D 101.121/2:
Resource Management (quarterly), D 101.89:
The Army Budget, D 101.121:
The Economic Bulletin, D 101.143:

1503. Army Intelligence Center and Fort Huachuca
http://usaic.hua.army.mil/
Sponsor: Army — Fort Huachuca Garrison
Description: This Web site serves the students and soldiers from the Army Intelligence Center and Fort Huachuca in Arizona. The sections include Units and Organizations, Current Events, For Students, Military Intelligence (MI) Heritage, Training/MI Professionals, and Fort Huachuca. The MI Heritage section covers Army and Military Intelligence history, with links related to military museums, and the Fort Huachuca section has information on the Fort's history. The Units and Organizations section has an interactive organizational chart for Military Intelligence.

This site is designed for military intelligence professionals and students, not the general public. The Web design and heavy use of graphics and acronyms may make it difficult to navigate.
Subjects: Army Bases; Military Intelligence
Publication: *Military Intelligence*, D 101.84:

1504. Army Publishing Directorate
http://www.usapa.army.mil/
Alternate URL: http://www.army.mil/usapa/index.html
Sponsor: Army — Army Publishing Agency (USAPA)
Description: The Publishing Directorate is the Army's agency for publishing and distributing information products. The site features electronic forms and publications, ordering information, and administrative news. It also links to Official Army Publications Web Sites. The alternate site has publications and forms, and is recommended by Army Publishing as a backup should their own site be down.
Subject: Military Publishing

1505. Army Research Laboratory
http://www.arl.army.mil/
Sponsor: Army — Army Materiel Command
Description: The main directorates of the Army Research Laboratory (ARL) reflect their research focus: Computational and Information Science, Sensors and Electron Devices, Survivability and Lethality Analysis, Weapons and Materials Research, Human Research and Engineering, and Vehicle Technology. A Research Opportunities section on the site links to information on Collaborative Technology Alliances, Contracting Opportunities, the ARL Technology Transfer Office, and other funding opportunities. The Organization section has an interactive organization chart with links to leadership biographies and the Web sites for each of the research directorates.
Subjects: Military Research Laboratories; Weapons Research

1506. Army Team C4IEWS
http://www.monmouth.army.mil/
Sponsor: Army — Fort Monmouth
Description: The C4IEWS headquartered at Fort Monmouth is the Command, Control, Communications, Computers, Intelligence, Electronic Warfare, and Sensors division of the Army. Its Web site features an Administrative Offices Directory, Business Opportunities, Acquisition

Initiatives, Garrison Support, and links to the various commands within C4IEWS. The Business Opportunities section has procurement information and a link to the Small and Disadvantaged Utilization Office.

Subjects: Military Computing; Military Technology

1507. ArmyLINK
http://www.dtic.mil/armylink/
Sponsor: Army
Description: ArmyLINK is designed to provide a link between the Army and the public. Major categories are News Room, Community Relations, and Links for Public Affairs Professionals. The News Room has Army News Service stories, photos from current operations, links to over one hundred Army newspapers online, and speeches from the Secretary of the Army, Army Chief of Staff, and Sergeant Major of the Army. Community Relations explains how to request Army assets for special events, such as airshows, and has a calendar of the upcoming airshows involving the Army. While the Links for Public Affairs Professional section is directed to Army staff, links of broader interest include Soldiers Radio and Television, Army Broadcasting Service, and the Golden Knights Army Parachute Team. An extensive Frequently Asked Questions section linked at the top of the ArmyLINK home page covers such topics as obtaining one's military records, locating former soldiers, Army ranks and insignia, military history, and military retirement.

This site is most useful for quick links to current Army news from a wide variety of Army sources. The Frequently Asked Questions section is particularly helpful because it also provides links to relevant military Web sites with more information on the topic.

Subject: Army

1508. Center for Army Lessons Learned (CALL)
http://call.army.mil/
Sponsor: Army — Center for Army Lessons Learned (CALL)
Description: "The Center for Army Lessons Learned (CALL) exists to collect and analyze data from a variety of current and historical sources, including Army operations and training events, and produce information serving as lessons for military commanders, staff, and students. CALL disseminates these lessons and other research materials via a variety of print and electronic media, including this Web site" (from the Web site, January 30, 2002). A Products section includes links to newsletters, handbooks, training techniques and vignettes, and a training video library. The materials cover situations such as night-time combat, checkpoint operations, and "winning in the desert." The CALL Web site also makes the CALL thesaurus of U.S. military terminology available for browsing. A Search button on the CALL home page leads to their own search engine for the .mil domain and links to other favorite Internet search engines. CALL has a reciprocal link with the Foreign Military Studies Office which, like CALL, is based at Fort Leavenworth, Kansas. Some information on the CALL site, particularly many of the databases, is available only to authorized users.

Subject: Military Information
Publications: *BCTP/BCBST Perceptions*, D 101.22/29:
Center for Army Learned Lessons, D 101.22/25:
CMTC Trends, D 101.22/26:
CTC Quarterly Bulletin, D 101.22/30:
News from the Front, D 101.22/25-2:
NTC Trends, D 101.22/27:
Red Thrust Star, D 101.147:

1509. Defense Language Institute Foreign Language Center and Presidio of Monterey, California
http://pom-www.army.mil/
Sponsors: Defense Department — Defense Language Institute (DLI); Army — Presidio of Monterey
Description: The Defense Language Institute Foreign Language Center (DLIFLC), a joint service installation for training military linguists, is based at the Presidio of Monterey Army Garrison. The most detailed information about the Center can be found in its General Catalog, in the DLIFLC section of the site under the link Academic Administration. Aside from organizational information

about the Center, full text course materials on world religions and culture can also be found in the DLIFLC section. The Presidio section of the site includes brief information on the garrison and information on contracting. On the home page, About the Installation gives a brief account of the location's last 200 years of history. The DLIFLC/Presidio site also links to *Applied Language Learning*, a journal about foreign language instruction.
Subjects: Army Bases; Language Education
Publication: *Applied Language Learning*, D 1.105:

1510. Redstone Arsenal
http://www.redstone.army.mil/
Sponsor: Army — Redstone Arsenal
Description: The Redstone Arsenal in Alabama is the home of the U.S. Army Aviation and Missile Command (AMCOM). Redstone played an early role in U.S. rocket research and the site has a wealth of historical information on that era including videos of early rockets and a biography of Wernher Von Braun, who worked at Redstone in the 1950's. A section on Doing Business with Team Redstone has extensive information for contractors. Other sections of this otherwise public site may be closed for security reasons, according to information posted at the site.
Subjects: Army Bases; Missile Defense; Rockets — History

1511. SBCCOM Online—U.S. Army Soldier and Biological Chemical Command
http://www.sbccom.army.mil/
Alternate URL: http://hld.sbccom.army.mil/
Sponsor: Army — Army Materiel Command
Description: The Army's Soldier and Biological Chemical Command (SBCCOM) performs research, development and acquisition of protective equipment; manages America's chemical weapons stockpile; and trains for and responds to biological and chemical emergencies. Under Products and Programs, the site has numerous fact sheets on items such as body armor, camouflage paint, air-drop delivery systems, and Meal Ready-to-Eat (MRE) rations. Other sections describe the research, materials testing, and chemicals analysis projects at SBCCOM. A Publications section under About SBCCOM offers access to the Command's online newsletter, *e-Catalyst*, some historical information, and annual reports. A Business section includes information on contracting and technology transfer.The alternate URL above refers to a separate Web site for SBCCOM's Homeland Defense Business Unit, whose mission is to "enhance the response capabilities of military, federal, state and local emergency responders to terrorist incidents involving weapons of mass destruction" (from the site, 2-9-2003). The site describes SBCCOM's homeland defense services in enhancing emergency preparedness and response.
Subjects: Chemical Warfare; Military Supplies
Publication: *Catalyst*, D 101.145:

1512. Soldiers Online
http://www.army.mil/soldiers/
Sponsor: Army — Army Publishing Agency (USAPA)
Description: This is the online version of the well-known print publication, *Soldiers,* the official magazine of the Army. It is not intended to be a simple reproduction of the paper version, but rather an "electronic sister" to the print version. The site features the most recent version, but it also maintains archives back to July 1994, with a keyword search capability. Other available sections include the Soldiers Almanac, Transforming America, Hot Topics, Soldiers Staff, and Briefings.

Well designed and arranged, this site offers substantial content. It gives a view of what is available in the print publication along with an archive of older issues.
Subject: Army
Publication: *Soldiers*, D 101.12:

1513. U.S. Army
http://www.army.mil/
Sponsor: Army
Description: This is the central Web site for the Army. The left sidebar has links to Army news services, such as Army Pentagon Newsbreak Radio in RealPlayer format and Army Newswatch

Television in Quicktime format from Soldiers Radio and Television. It also links to photos, speeches, and Army Symbols and History. The side bar on the right has quick links to an alphabetical index of information on Army Web sites, a directory of Army leadership, and Web pages on recruitment, retirement, reserves, veterans, and more. Current headlines and photos are featured in the center of the home page.The site has a Career Management section and another on Well-Being with sections on pay and benefits, health care, education, housing, family programs, and recreation. An Installations section is actually an extensive Web directory to Headquarters, the Secretariat, and Commands, as well as installations and the Army Reserve and National Guard; it features maps and organization charts. A Reference section has links to publications, forms, and libraries of interest. Well designed and well organized, the Army's site should be one of the first stopping points for anyone seeking information about the U.S. Army, its bases, or current news. It is also a good resource for those in active service, the reserves, or retired from the Army. As a supplement, check the ArmyLINK site for information about the Army's participation in community events or other questions frequently asked by the public.
Subject: Army

1514. U.S. Army Center of Military History
http://www.army.mil/cmh-pg/
Sponsor: Army — Center of Military History (CMH)
Description: The Center of Military History site offers many full-text military history books and documents and a museum display of Army art. The majority of the collection can be found under the Online Bookshelves section, arranged by time period and collection. A Force Structure and Unit History section includes links to unit lineage and honors information and a partial list of unit special designations or nicknames. The site has a Medal of Honor citations list, a directory of Army museums, Army Nurse Corps history, and defense acquisitions history. A Frequently Asked Questions section addresses questions such as finding official unit records, and provides brief background on "frequently researched topics" such as the integration of the U.S. Army and the origin of the 21-gun salute. The site also features a series of guides to researching military history, including oral history techniques, and a separate section on the history of military history.
Subject: Military History
Publication: *Publications of the United States Army Center of Military History*, D 114.10:

1515. U.S. Army Safety Program
http://safety.army.mil/home.html
Sponsor: Army — Army Safety Center
Description: The Army Safety Program provides a source of technical support to assist commanders in hazard identification, risk management, and accident investigation and reporting. The site features links including Safety Program, Risk Management, Safety Messages, and Accident Overview. The Quick View area provides subject access to the site. Top-page sections include CP-12 (Career Program-12, Army Safety Professionals), RMIS (Risk Management Information System), Guidance, Training, Tools, Links, and Media, under which the online journal *Countermeasure* is available in PDF format back to early 1996.
Subjects: Military Operations; Safety
Publication: *Countermeasure*, D 101.125:

1516. U.S. Army Signal Center and Fort Gordon
http://www.gordon.army.mil/
Sponsor: Army — Army Signal Command
Description: This site describes the mission and organization of the Army Signal Center in Fort Gordon, Georgia. The Center is the home base of the Signal Regiment, which manages Army information and communications technology and systems worldwide. Along with information specific to the Center, the site has general information relating to careers in the Signal Regiment and the history of the Signal Corps. Under the heading Regiment, the latest online edition of the *Army Communicator* is available in HTML format.
Subject: Military Technology
Publication: *Army Communicator, Voice of the Signal Corps*, D 111.14:

1517. United States Army Band
http://www.army.mil/armyband/
Sponsor: Army — Army Bands
Description: The Army Band's site provides general information on the band and its concerts. Featured sections include Leaders and Directors, Events, Vacancies, and Ensembles. The site has a brief history of the Army Band. A Listening Room section offers performances such as "The Stars and Stripes Forever" and "Battle Hymn of the Republic" in Real Audio format.
Subjects: Military Bands; Music

1518. United States Army Reserve
http://www.army.mil/usar/
Sponsor: Army — Army Reserves (USAR)
Description: The Army Reserve Web site features current news and organizational information on the Reserve. A Resources section links to information on reservist training and benefits. The News and Reference Section has online publications, including *Army Reserve Magazine* and several Reserve unit magazines.
Subject: Military Reserves
Publication: *Army Reserve Magazine (bimonthly)*, D 101.43:

Navy

1519. Bureau of Naval Personnel
http://www.bupers.navy.mil/
Sponsor: Navy — Naval Personnel Bureau
Description: The Bureau of Naval Personnel's site serves current personnel with information on career development, promotion selection boards, quality of life services, and the personnel pay assistance center. The News Stand page includes access to online versions of the publications *Link-Perspective* for Navy professionals and *Shift Colors* for retirees.

The site will primarily be of interest to those in the Navy. Some sections are only open to authorized, registered users.
Subject: Defense Administration
Publications: *Link-Perspective*, D 208.19/2:
Shift Colors, The Newsletter for Navy Retirees, D 208.12/3-2:

1520. Naval Medical Logistics Command
http://www-nmlc.med.navy.mil/
Sponsor: Navy — Naval Medical Logistics Command
Description: The Naval Medical Logistics Command provides medical and dental materiel management and logistical support to the operating forces, U.S. Marine Corps, and shore activities. Much of the Command's Web site is now restricted to government or military users. A Public Access section has information for prospective contractors.
Subject: Military Medicine

1521. Naval Sea Systems Command—NAVSEA
http://www.navsea.navy.mil/
Sponsor: Navy — Naval Sea Systems Command (NAVSEA)
Description: The Naval Sea Systems Command develops, acquires, modernizes, and maintains affordable ships, ordnance, and systems for the Navy. The NAVSEA site features organizational and technical information along with a video and image gallery and a link to contractor information. Major sections include News, Programs, Innovations, About NAVSEA, and the Web directory of NAVSEA Commands.
Subjects: Military Ships; Military Technology
Publication: *Financial Policy and Procedures Update*, D 211.30:

1522. Naval Undersea Warfare Center
http://www.nuwc.navy.mil/
Sponsor: Navy
Description: Naval Undersea Warfare Center (NUWC) is the Navy's research, development, testing, engineering, and fleet support center for submarines, weapons associated with undersea warfare, and other underwater systems. Its Web site features information on its divisions in Keyport, WA and Newport, RI. Other sections include Leadership, History, Strategy, Events, and a Library page pointing to external Web resources. The History section discusses the history of the Navy in Rhode Island.
Subjects: Submarines; Underwater Warfare

1523. NavResOnLine
http://www.navres.navy.mil/
Sponsor: Navy — Naval Reserve Forces
Description: NavResOnLine is the gateway for Naval Reserve Force information on the Web. The site features links such as Naval Reserve Force, Naval Air Force Reserve, *Naval Reservist News*, Navy Jobs, Reserve Recruiting, and alphabetical and category lists of Naval Reserve Web sites.
Subject: Military Reserves
Publication: *Naval Reservist News*, D 207.309:

1524. Navy Blue Angels
http://www.blueangels.navy.mil/
Sponsor: Navy
Description: This site offers information on the choreographed flying of the Navy's Blue Angels squadron, including biographies of the Blue Angels Officers and Enlisted Team. The site features the Show Schedule, Practice Schedule, information on how to apply, and a long list of Frequently Asked Questions. The Gallery section includes photos, videos, and computer wallpaper and screen-savers.
Subject: Military Aircraft

1525. Navy History
http://www.history.navy.mil/
Sponsor: Navy — Naval Historical Center
Description: With a broad collection of online historical information, the Naval Historical Center's site breaks down its numerous links into two main categories: Naval Historical Center Overview and Branches. Under the latter, featured sections include Contemporary History, Photographic Section, Early History, Naval Aviation History, Naval Aviation News, Navy Art Gallery, the Navy Museum, Ships History, and Underwater Archaeology. Under Overview, the site offers Introduction to the Center, Wars and Conflicts of the U.S. Navy, The NHC News Room, Navy Birthday Information, USS Constitution, *Professional Readings in U.S. Naval History,* Publications, Events at the Naval Historical Center, Visiting the Naval Historical Center, and Fellowships, Grants, and Internships.Under the FOIA/Electronic Reading Room, there is access to the Naval History Bibliography Series page, which offers a broad collection of references for further reference.

While there is not a great depth of online historical material here, the broad scope of the collection and the reference to print resources makes this an excellent starting point for historical information about the Navy.
Subject: Military History
Publications: *Cruise Books of the United States Navy in World War II: A Bibliography*, D 221.17:2
Historical Manuscripts in the Navy Department Library: A Catalog, D 221.17:3
Naval Aviation News, D 202.9:
The Reestablishment of the Navy, 1787-1801 Historical Overview and Select Bibliography,
    D 221.17:4
The Spanish-American War: Historical Overview and Select Bibliography, D 221.17:5
United States Naval History: A Bibliography, D 221.17:1

1526. Navy Online
http://www.navy.mil/nol/
Sponsor: Navy
Description: Navy Online is the technical gateway to the United States Department of the Navy online resources. It provides access to Naval Web sites by alphabetical or category listings and via a search interface.
Subject: Navy

1527. Navy.com
http://www.navy.com/
Alternate URL: http://www.elnavy.com/
Sponsor: Navy
Description: This is the primary Navy recruiting site. A Careers section provides information on the many fields of specialty for officers or the enlisted. Explore the Navy has information on educational programs, travel benefits, and other aspects of a naval career. The alternate URL points to a similar site designed for Hispanic Americans; it has English and Spanish versions.

The Careers section in particular should be helpful for anyone interested in joining the Navy or armed services.
Subject: Military Recruiting

1528. Office of Naval Intelligence
http://www.nmic.navy.mil/
Sponsor: Navy — Naval Intelligence Office
Description: The Office Of Naval Intelligence (ONI) Web site includes overview information about the office, employment opportunities, location, and FOIA instructions. Under About ONI, the Welcome and Mission sections include information on the office. The History section provides an illustrated history of ONI since its founding in 1882.
Subjects: Intelligence Agencies; Military Intelligence

1529. Space and Naval Warfare Systems Center
http://enterprise.spawar.navy.mil/spawarpublicsite/
Sponsor: Navy — Space and Naval Warfare Systems Command (SPAWAR)
Description: SPAWAR's mission is to develop and maintain integrated command, control, communications, computer, intelligence, and surveillance systems. Its Web site features sections on advanced technology and space systems along with such sections as About SPAWAR, Products and Services, Business Opportunities, Fact Sheets, and SPAWAR in the News. A Reference Library section includes official instructions, manuals, handbooks, and technical papers.
Subject: Military Technology

1530. U.S. Navy: Welcome Aboard
http://www.navy.mil/
Sponsor: Navy
Description: This official Web site of the Navy features sections including Navy Leadership, Navy Organization, Status of the Navy, Navy News Stand, Navy Careers, Our Ships, and an online version of *All Hands* magazine. A Fact File links to fact sheets on Navy aircraft, weapons, submarines, surface ships, and various Navy forces. The Site Index provides topical and organizational access to sections of the site. It also links to some of the Navy publications online.
Subject: Navy
Publications: *All Hands (monthly)*, D 207.17:
Approach, D 202.13:
Budget of the Department of the Navy, D 201.1/1:
Fathom, D 201.32:
Forward . . . From the Sea, D 201.2:SID 12
Highlights of the Department of the Navy FY ... Budget, D 201.1/1-2:
Naval Reservist News, D 207.309:

1531. United States Navy Band
http://www.navyband.navy.mil/
Sponsor: Navy — Navy Band
Description: The Navy Band's site features Band History, Education Resources, Upcoming Performances, Press Information, Performing Units, Career Opportunities, and links to the other military bands. A Sights and Sounds section includes performance sound files in mp3 format. Also, there is a link to the bimonthly Navy band newsletter, *fanfare*, which can be viewed online or received as an email subscription.
Subjects: Military Bands; Music

Sites for Families

1532. Air Force Crossroads
http://www.afcrossroads.com/
Sponsor: Air Force
Description: Air Force Crossroads is the official community Web site of U.S. Air Force. Designed for Air Force family members, the site offers a multitude of links that offer information important to families. Some of the links include the following: Casualty and Loss, DoD Installations, Education, Eldercare, Employment, Family Separation and Readiness, Medical and Dental, Parenting, Relocation, Spouse Network, and Teens and Youth. It also links to known Department of Defense sites that contain information for military family members.
Subject: Military Morale and Welfare

1533. Assistant Chief of Staff for Installation Management
http://www.hqda.army.mil/acsimweb/homepage.shtml
Sponsor: Air Force
Description: The Assistant Chief of Staff for Installation Management (ACSIM) is the Army's proponent for military bases and the soldiers, civilians, and families that live on them. The site includes sections such as Installations, Regulations, Functional Links and Organizational Links. The Installations section has an alphabetical index that links to installation and facility Web sites. Functional links includes sections on Army Real Property and on Congressional Actions (tracking military spending bills and related legislation). Organizational Links include BRAC (Base Realignment and Closure), CFSC (Community and Family Support Center), Army Environmental Center, and Facilities and Housing.
Subject: Military Bases and Installations
Publications: *Army Families Quarterly*, D 101.123:
INSTALLATIONS: News for and about Basops, D 101.142:

1534. Department of Defense Education Activity (DoDEA)
http://www.odedodea.edu/
Sponsor: Defense Department — Department of Defense Education Activity
Description: This site is the official Web presence of the K-12 schools operated by the Department of Defense, both overseas and in the United States. The site features sections including Schools, Students, Calendars, Alumni, and Publications. The site has a great deal of information including school directories and profiles, distance education programs, school performance measures and standardized achievement test scores, and *Teacher to Teacher,* the newsletter of the DoDEA Teachers of the Year.
Subjects: Elementary and Secondary Education; Military Morale and Welfare
Publication: *Teacher to Teacher*

1535. Federal Voting Assistance Program
http://www.fvap.gov/
Sponsor: Defense Department — Federal Voting Assistance Program (FVAP)
Description: The FVAP provides U.S. citizens worldwide a broad range of nonpartisan information and assistance to facilitate their participation in the voting process regardless of where they work or

live. Located within the Department of Defense, FVAP is responsible for serving military personnel, their families, and other U.S. citizens residing outside the United States. The Web site features sections including Absentee Voting Topics, State by State Instructions, FVAP Publications, Information for Armed Forces Recruitment Offices, Information for Local Elections Officials, and Communicating with Your Elected Officials. There is also an online version of the federal postcard application for voter registration and absentee ballots.
Subject: Voting
Publications: *Voting Assistance Guide*, D 2.14:VAG
Voting Information News, D 1.96:

1536. LIFELines
Alternate URL: http://lifelines2000.org/
Sponsor: Navy
Description: The Navy has partnered with the Naval Reserve, Marine Corps, and Coast Guard to build this portal to quality of life information for military personnel. The site links to information on chaplains, education, family life, financial management, legal assistance, relocation, and veteran and retiree support services, among many topics. The site also features print and broadcast military news and links to organizations such as the Marine Corps Key Volunteer Network and the Navy Family Ombudsman.
Subject: Military Morale and Welfare

1537. MAPsite: Military Assistance Program
http://dod.mil/mapsite/
Sponsor: Defense Department — Military Assistance Program
Description: MAPsite, the central site for the DoD's Military Assistance Program, informs military personnel and their families about relocation, employment, and money management. The home page highlights new DoD news and publications of assistance to military families and links to related sites such as Military Teens on the Move, Military Children and Youth, and Special Needs Network.
Subject: Military Morale and Welfare

1538. Military Children and Youth
http://military-childrenandyouth.calib.com/index.htm
Sponsor: Defense Department — Military Family Resource Center
Description: Sponsored by the Department of Defense, the National Clearinghouse for the Military Child Development Program operates this site to share information on military child development models with the civilian community, and to support the military community with information on available resources. The site gives an overview of programs for youth from birth through age 18, as well as parenting programs, and posts research based on these efforts. The site also has the full text of related laws, policies, and guidelines, and documents on such topics as the demographics of military families and preventing child abuse. A Networking and Partnerships section includes PDF copies of the Military Child Development Center Directory and the Military Youth Program Directory. An Online Databases section links to the Military Child Care Database and the Military Family Resource Center Database.
Subject: Child Care

1539. Military Family Resource Center
http://mfrc.calib.com/
Sponsor: Defense Department — Military Family Resource Center
Description: This site is designed as a resource for policy makers and those providing services to active duty service members, reservists, and their families. It includes access to quality of life policies, research initiatives, and resource referrals. Featured sections include Statistics, Program Manager Resources, and Policy Information. The Statistics section includes the *Profile of the Military Community* demographic report. Other relevant documents and publications are listed in the Program Manager Resources section.
Subject: Military Morale and Welfare

1540. Military Sentinel
http://www.consumer.gov/military/
Sponsors: Defense Department; Federal Trade Commission (FTC)
Description: Military Sentinel is a cooperative project of the Federal Trade Commission and the Department of Defense for members of the armed services and their families. To file a consumer complaint, users click on the seal representing their service branch. The site also links to a selection of relevant military and civilian consumer Web sites.
Subjects: Consumer Information; Military Morale and Welfare

1541. Military Teens On the Move (MTOM)
http://dticaw.dtic.mil/mtom/
Sponsor: Defense Department — Military Assistance Program
Description: Military Teens On the Move gives military adolescents tips on dealing with a parent's military career and relocations, and other issues such as getting a driver's license or preparing for college.
Subjects: Adolescents; Military Morale and Welfare

CHAPTER 13
Science

The federal government is involved in basic and applied science, in helping to disseminate scientific information, and in encouraging scientific research in academia and other research centers. This chapter includes government Web sites concerned with biology, earth and atmospheric sciences, physics, and space exploration, and those addressing multiple science topics. Other chapters in this book also include science-related sites. The Technology and Engineering chapter includes applied science topics, computer science, and energy research sites. The Agriculture and Health Science chapters also includes sites reporting on scientific research.

The featured Web site for this chapter, science.gov, was launched in late 2002. It is a collaborative effort from the federal government's major science agencies and is labeled the "FirstGov for Science."

Bookmarks & Favorites

Science Research
- PrePrint Network, http://www.osti.gov/preprint/
- Science.gov, http://www.science.gov

Specific Topics
- Global Change Master Directory, http://gcmd.gsfc.nasa.gov
- NASA Human Spaceflight, http://spaceflight.nasa.gov

Major Agencies
- Energy Department, http://www.energy.gov
- National Aeronautics and Space Administration, http://www.nasa.gov
- National Institutes of Health, http://www.nih.gov
- National Science Foundation, http://www.nsf.gov
- U.S. Geological Survey, http://www.usgs.gov

(Also see Chapter 15, Technology and Engineering.)

Featured Site

1542. science.gov
`http://www.science.gov/`
Sponsor: Energy Department — Scientific and Technical Information Office
Description: The science.gov site represents a collaborative effort by a group of government agencies to select and share the best of their online science information. It was developed by an interagency working group of fourteen scientific and technical information organizations. The Energy Department's Office of Scientific and Technical Information (OSTI), listed here as the sponsor, hosts the site. The science Web resources can be browsed by topic or searched by word. The search feature allows users to select a combination of government science Web sites and databases to search. Specific results can be marked for saving, allowing users to build a custom list of relevant Web sites. Indexed resources in science.gov include: AGRICOLA, National Biological Information Infrastructure, STINET Report Collection, DOE Energy Citations Database, PubMed, ERIC, and National Science Foundation publications.

Science.gov is an example of the current effort to build agency-independent access to government information through subject-oriented portals. It allows for easy discovery of science and technical information distributed through government Web sites.
Subjects: Scientific and Technical Information; Finding Aids

The science resources in this chapter are divided into five sections, spanning the entry numbers indicated here:

General

1543. Argonne National Laboratory
http://www.anl.gov/
Sponsor: Energy Department — Argonne National Laboratory (ANL)
Description: The Energy Department's Argonne National Laboratory maintains a Web site with a mix of information on research, technology transfer, and educational opportunities. Major sections include About Argonne, Research and Facilities, Tech Transfer, News and Publications, Educational Programs, Postdoc Fellowships, and Export Control. The site identifies five key research and facilities areas: basic science, energy resources, environmental management, nuclear reactor safety and technology, and facilities including the Advanced Photon Source and the Argonne Tandem-Linear Accelerator System. Basic science at Argonne includes work in materials science, physics, chemistry, biology, high-energy physics, and mathematics and computer science, including high-performance computing. Educational opportunities include undergraduate, graduate, and K-12 teacher internships and fellowships.

The extensive Technology Transfer section identifies commercialization and licensing opportunities, explains partnering with Argonne, and includes a Technology Tour of the Lab's work with specific technologies. Argonne also sponsors a number of technology transfer awards, described at this site. The News and Publications section includes scientific papers, resources for science journalists, the quarterly magazine *logos*, the annual *Frontiers*, *Tech Transfer Highlights* newsletter, and information on a science-writing internship. A "Gee Whiz!" section for the general public features an Ask-A-Scientist service, a downloadable arithmetic game, a link to the Lab's International Nuclear Safety Center site, and information on the Rube Goldberg Machine Contest for high school students.

With a wealth of thoughtfully organized information, the Argonne site is equipped to serve audiences ranging from DOE and university scientists to technology companies, educators, students, and the general public.
Subjects: Nuclear Energy — Research; Research Laboratories; Scientific Research
Publications: *Argonne News*, E 1.86/2:
Frontiers, Argonne National Laboratory, Research Highlights, E 1.86/4:
Future Drive, E 1.86/8:
logos, E 1.86/3:
Tech Transfer Highlights, E 1.86/90:

1544. BIOCIS-L Biology Curriculum Innovation Study [email list]
http://www.lsoft.com/scripts/wl.exe?SL1=BIOCIS-L&H=SIVM.SI.EDU
Sponsor: Smithsonian Institution
Description: This is an email discussion list sponsored and hosted by the Smithsonian. Topics of discussion focus on innovative curriculum design in biology.
Subjects: Science Education; Email Lists

1545. Brookhaven National Laboratory
http://www.bnl.gov/world/
Sponsor: Energy Department — Brookhaven National Laboratory (BNL)
Description: BNL is a nondefense research institution that conducts basic and applied investigations in a multitude of scientific disciplines including experimental and theoretical physics, materials sciences, energy sciences, chemistry, biology, environmental research, and more. Its Web site serves as a gateway to its many research projects and divisional sites. Sections include Research Facilities

(where the accelerator facilities are described), Research Departments and Divisions, and Research Centers and Databases. A Technology Transfer section lists licensing opportunities, cooperative research, and research and development assistance for U.S. businesses. The News and Info section, listed along the top navigational bar, has press releases, fact sheets, and publications. Because the BNL site includes so much information on so many projects and fields of science, the Site Index can be a very helpful approach to discovering information on the site.

Subjects: Particle Accelerators; Research Laboratories
Publications: *Brookhaven Bulletin*
Discover Brookhaven

1546. Chemical Emergency Preparedness and Prevention Office

`http://yosemite.epa.gov/oswer/ceppoweb.nsf/content/index.html`
Sponsor: Environmental Protection Agency (EPA) — Chemical Emergency Preparedness and Prevention Office (CEPPO)
Description: This EPA office provides leadership, advocacy, and assistance to prevent and prepare for chemical emergencies, to respond to environmental crises, and to inform the public about chemical hazards in their community. Its site features sections on Risk Management Plans, Emergency Planning and Community Right-to-Know, Laws and Regulations, Preventing Chemical Accidents, and CEPPO's Role in Homeland Security. A section called Chemicals In Your Community includes a link to the Toxic Release Inventory database. The Tools and Resources section includes publications and links to EPA and non-EPA databases and software.
Subjects: Disaster Preparedness; Toxic Substances
Publications: *CEPPO Alerts*, EP 9.16:
Chemicals In Your Community, EP 1.2:C 42/
Fact Sheets and Technical Assistance Bulletins, EP 9.17:

1547. Chemical Safety And Hazard Investigation Board

`http://www.chemsafety.gov/`
Sponsor: Chemical Safety And Hazard Investigation Board
Description: Chemical Safety and Hazard Investigation Board (CSB) is an independent, scientific investigatory board with the mission of promoting the prevention of major chemical accidents. The CSB Web site features a variety of information on chemical spills and other accidents. Featured sections include About the CSB, Investigations (with news releases), Chemical Incident Reports Center, Chemlinks, and Reporting Chemical Incidents. The front page features headlines of news items and reports. There is also a side bar of Publications of Note.
Subjects: Chemical Industry; Industrial Accidents
Publication: *Investigations and News*, Y 3.C 42/2:16

1548. Cold Regions Bibliography Project

`http://www.coldregions.org/`
Sponsor: American Geological Institute (AGI)
Description: This site hosts two government-sponsored databases: *Bibliography on Cold Regions Science and Technology* and the *Antarctic Bibliography*. The *Bibliography on Cold Regions Science and Technolog* covers science and engineering research related to material and operations in a winter battlefield, the nature and impact of cold on facilities and activities, cold-related environmental problems, and the impact of human activity on cold environments. It is funded in part by the U.S. Army Cold Regions Research and Engineering Laboratory (CRREL) and the National Science Foundation (NSF). The *Antarctic Bibliography* covers literature related to the Antarctic region from disciplines including biology, geological sciences, medical sciences, meteorology, oceanography, atmospheric and terrestrial physics. It is funded in part by NSF. Both databases have been available for searching free of charge in the past, but may be subject to subscription charges now or in the future. The Cold Regions Bibliography was previously compiled at the Library of Congress. In 2000, the American Geological Institute was awarded a 5-year contract to maintain the two databases.
Subjects: Databases; Antarctica — Research
Publications: *Antarctic Bibliography*
Bibliography on Cold Regions Science and Technology

1549. DOE Information Bridge
http://www.osti.gov/bridge/
Sponsor: Energy Department — Scientific and Technical Information Office
Description: The DOE Information Bridge provides free access to full-text DOE research and development reports in physics, chemistry, materials, biology, environmental sciences, energy technologies, engineering, computer and information science, renewable energy, and other topics. The database begins January 1995, and the reports are available in GIF, TIFF, and PDF format. The easy search provides author, title, bibliographic, or full-text and bibliographic searching while the advanced search adds additional field searching and Boolean capabilities.
Subjects: Scientific and Technical Information; Databases
Publication: *DOE Information Bridge*, E 1.137:

1550. Eclipse Home Page
http://sunearth.gsfc.nasa.gov/eclipse/eclipse.html
Sponsor: National Aeronautics and Space Administration (NASA) — Goddard Space Flight Center (GSFC)
Description: This site provides details on total and partial solar and lunar eclipses around the world. It includes eclipse maps, listings, path coordinates, explanations, and predication information. With the greatest details for recent times, the site also has sections entitled Five Thousand Year Catalog of Solar Eclipses, Seven Thousand Year Catalog of Very Long Solar Eclipses, and Five Thousand Year Catalog of Lunar Eclipses. The site also offers a variety of publications, bulletins, data, educational material, and other sources. Eclipse predictions are by Fred Espenak of GSFC.

The clear organization of this site makes it an excellent reference source on the topic.
Subjects: Eclipses; Sun

1551. Federal Laboratory Consortium for Technology Transfer
http://www.federallabs.org/
Sponsor: Federal Laboratory Consortium (FLC)
Description: The Federal Laboratory Consortium for Technology Transfer (FLC) works to help move the federal laboratories' research and development into the U.S. private sector. Its site features links to the labs and technology transfer sites, patent and licensing searchable databases, and lab locator services. The FLC Laboratory Locator is a service to enable a user to request technical assistance and be partnered with the appropriate laboratory.
Subject: Technology Transfer

1552. Lawrence Berkeley National Laboratory
http://www.lbl.gov/
Sponsor: Energy Department — Lawrence Berkeley National Laboratory (LBL)
Description: The Berkeley Lab conducts basic research in a wide range of fields including physical biosciences, earth sciences, materials sciences, computing sciences, nuclear science, life science, chemical science, energy, information technology, and environmental sciences. Its Web site features many categories, including About the Lab, Scientific Programs, News, Publications/Pictures, Educational Sites, and Organization. For an overview of the many programs and projects at the lab, see the Scientific Programs page where its numerous divisions are listed by subject. The Search option is available for searching either the main Berkeley Lab Web server or all the lab Web servers, and there is also an index and directory for access to the lab's pages and personnel. Both the News and the Publications pages provide access to publications from the Berkeley Lab. These include the Berkeley Lab *Research Review*, news releases, annual reports, and a catalog of scientific reports. The LBL site is well-organized and provides a substantial set of scientific information. The large number of subsidiary sites accessible from the top level LBL page make this an important site to search for scientists from many fields.
Subjects: Physics — Research; Research Laboratories
Publication: *Berkeley Lab Research Review*, E 1.53/2:

1553. Lawrence Livermore National Laboratory

http://www.llnl.gov/

Sponsor: Energy Department — Lawrence Livermore National Laboratory (LLNL)

Description: The research areas of LLNL range from nuclear weapons, clean and affordable energy, and bioscience research to robotics, lasers and optics, and astronomy, to name a few. The Science and Technology section provides a keyword search of Lawrence Livermore (LL) Web pages, via its Science and Technology Catalog, which are catalogued and cross-referenced by research areas and technologies. The Research Areas section links to projects by topic. In addition, a search link will enable the visitor to do a general search of all LLNL Web servers as well. For online versions of the lab's published research papers, reports, and periodical, look under the Publications section. This includes full-text HTML and PDF format issues of *Science and Technology Review* as far back as 1994 (where it appears under its previous title of *Energy and Technology Review*). The site also provides a LLNL phone directory and information about job opportunities and educational programs.

The LLNL provides a substantial amount of online full-text documents of interest to researchers. The site should be the starting point for anyone seeking more information about the lab's programs or its areas of expertise.

Subjects: Nuclear Weapons — Research; Research Laboratories

Publication: *Science and Technology Review: Lawrence Livermore Laboratory*, E 1.53:

1554. Los Alamos National Laboratory

http://www.lanl.gov/worldview/

Sponsor: Energy Department — Los Alamos National Laboratory (LANL)

Description: Created to help in the development of nuclear weapons, the Los Alamos National Laboratory's major areas of research now include bioscience, chemistry, computer and computational sciences, earth and environmental sciences, and the nonproliferation of weapons of mass destruction. The Organization page provides a hierarchical list of LANL organizations and offices. The Education page lists LANL programs that support education from K-12 through postdoctorate level. For information on LANL itself, see the Working with LANL, Community, News, and Life at LANL sections. The site carries the Lab's new magazine, *Los Alamos Research Quarterly*, which focuses on the Lab's contributions to national and global security. The site also features an extensive section on the history of Los Alamos and the development of the atomic bomb, with links to the Bradbury Science Museum and Los Alamos Historical Society.

Subjects: Nuclear Weapons; Physics — Research; Research Laboratories

Publication: *Los Alamos Research Quarterly*

1555. NASA Dryden Flight Research Center

http://www.dfrc.nasa.gov/

Sponsor: National Aeronautics and Space Administration (NASA) — Dryden Flight Research Center (DFRC)

Description: Dryden is responsible for flight research and flight testing. Its Web site features About Dryden, Education, History, News Room, Research, and Organizations. The Research section includes Research Programs, Research Projects, Research Facilities, and Technical Reports. The News Room includes news releases, biographies, and fact sheets.

Subjects: Aerospace Engineering — Research; Aircraft — Research

1556. NASA Education Program

http://education.nasa.gov/index.html

Sponsor: National Aeronautics and Space Administration (NASA) — Education Division

Description: The NASA Education Program Web site provides information about the education programs that NASA offers to K–12 educators and students as well as to undergraduate and graduate students and faculty at universities. The main categories at this site include Guide to NASA's Education Programs, NASA Education and Information Services, and NASA Education Contacts. There are links to the education offices at the dozen NASA centers and facilities across the country. The site also links to the education resources for each of the strategic parts of NASA: Aerospace Technology, Biological and Physical Research, Earth Science, Human Exploration and Development

of Space, and Space Science. A Resources for Educators section has links to information on teacher workshops and fellowships, curriculum support materials, multimedia resources, and more.
Subject: Science Education

1557. NASA Subject Index
http://www.nasa.gov/nasaorgs/subject_index.html
Description: The NASA Subject Index provides a topical approach to the wealth of material NASA has made available on the Web. Under broad topics such as Aeronautics, Geosciences, Life Sciences, and Space Sciences, this site links to programs and divisions throughout NASA. With the exception of adding the term "microgravity," the topic categories follow those used by NASA's Scientific and Technical Information Program.

While this site if far from comprehensive, it makes an excellent starting point for finding scientific information from NASA by broad topics.
Subjects: Space; Finding Aids

1558. National Science Foundation
http://www.nsf.gov/
Sponsor: National Science Foundation (NSF)
Description: As one of the government's major scientific agencies, the NSF promotes science and engineering research and education. Its site features a topical breakdown of NSF program areas into broad subjects such as biology, education, computer information sciences, engineering, geosciences, math and physical sciences, polar research, and social, behavioral, and economic sciences. Other sections include Funding, Publications, and News and Media. A Science Statistics section includes a wealth of publications and data from NSF, particularly on science and engineering education and funding. There is a NSF staff and organizations directory available, and one can search the NSF Web site by directorate, the subject areas of which parallel the program areas. One can also conduct a search for specialized information by type of searcher: for example, student, principal investigator, sponsored research office, or educators.

The NSF site is a major source for information on NSF grants. The Grants and Awards section features award data, deadlines, and a listing of funding opportunities. The data section offers information about research projects that NSF has funded since 1989 including abstracts and the names of principal investigators and their institutions. A Publications button provides keyword search and browse access to the many NSF publications that are available online.

For all those involved with NSF grants or interested in applying for one, this is an essential site to visit. It provides very useful information on grants in the sciences. The NSF provides useful statistics and publications on science and engineering education. It also offers a substantial number of documents online.
Subjects: Science Education; Scientific Research — Grants
Publications: *Antarctic Journal of the United States (quarterly)*, NS 1.26:
Arctic Research of the United States (semiannual), NS 1.51/2:
E-Bullet, NS 1.3:
Frontiers, Newsletter of the National Science Foundation, NS 1.57:
Graduate Students and Postdoctorates in Science and Engineering, NS 1.22/11:
Grant Policy Manual, NS 1.20:G76/2/
National Patterns of R&D Resources, NS 1.22/2:
NSF Engineering Online News, NS 1.22/10:
Science and Engineering Doctorate Awards, NS 1.44:
Science and Engineering Indicators, NS 1.28/2:
Science Engineering Research Facilities at Universities and Colleges, NS 1.53:
SRS Data Brief, NS 1.11/3:
Tipsheet: NSF News Media Tips, NS 1.59:
Women, Minorities, Persons with Disabilities in Science and Engineering, NS 1.49:

1559. Naval Research Laboratory
http://www.nrl.navy.mil/
Sponsor: Navy — Naval Research Laboratory (NRL)

Description: This is the top-level site for the many directorates and divisions of the NRL. The research focus is broad, covering scientific areas within the realm of the Navy's concern with sea, sky, and space. Major research areas include oceanography and atmospheric science, ocean acoustics, marine meteorology and geosciences, remote oceanic and atmospheric sensing, and space technology. The site offers access to its material under the following sections: About NRL, Accomplishments, Research, Doing Business with NRL, News Room, and Field Sites. A search section has both a word search feature and links to all of NRL's component Web sites. Publications information is in the News Room section.

This site can serve as a starting point to a very rich collection of scientific research.

Subjects: Navy — Research; Research Laboratories
Publications: *NRL Fact Book*, D 201.17/3:
NRL Review, D 210.17/2:

1560. Oak Ridge National Laboratory

http://www.ornl.gov/
Sponsor: Energy Department — Oak Ridge National Laboratory (ORNL)
Description: Oak Ridge National Laboratory is a multiprogram science and technology laboratory. ORNL research areas include neutron sciences, carbon management, high performance computing, complex biological systems, materials science, and energy, and environmental systems. The Science and Technology section of this Web site describes these and other areas of research and links to the Lab's Publications page. A searchable publications database, the Comprehensive Publications and Presentations Registry (CPPR), has bibliographic information for ORNL reports from 1985 and the full-text of many reports from the late 1990s on. Online magazines and newsletters include: *ORNL Review*, *Fossil Report*, *Human Genome News*, and the *ORNL Reporter*. The Publications page also links to a history of ORNL and each of its research divisions.

An Education section describes a variety of opportunities available through the Lab for pre-college up to postdoctorate and faculty levels. A Business section explains its R&D partnerships and lists contacts in technology and patent areas. Further information on technology transfer is available in the Science and Technology section.

Subjects: Research Laboratories; Scientific Research
Publications: *Fossil Report*
Human Genome News, E 1.99/3:
Materials and Components in Fossil Energy Application, E 1.23:
Oak Ridge National Laboratory Review, E 1.28/17:
ORNL Reporter

1561. Pacific Northwest National Laboratory

http://www.pnl.gov/
Sponsor: Energy Department — Pacific Northwest National Laboratory (PNNL)
Description: PNNL conducts research in nearly every field of basic science with the goal of solving problems in the environment, energy, health, and national security. Its Web site features information on the lab and its research projects in sections such as About Us, Outreach, News and Publications, Science and Technology, and Business Opportunities and Partnerships. Under Science and Technology, topical access is available for Energy, Environment, Health and Safety, Information Technology, National Security, and Nuclear Technology and information about licensing technology capabilities from the lab. The News and Publications link includes news releases, tipsheets, and some newsletters as well as a list of scientific publications, which offer citations and references for all entries and links to some documents.

Subject: Research Laboratories
Publications: *Breakthroughs*
Energy Science News, E 1.19/4:

1562. PrePRINT Network

http://www.osti.gov/preprint/
Sponsor: Energy Department — Scientific and Technical Information Office
Description: The PrePRINT Network is a Web gateway to full text preprints, manuscripts intended for future publication, which are stored on distributed preprint servers. The preprints are in the areas

of physics, materials, chemistry, mathematics, biology, environmental sciences and other areas related to the Energy Department's research interests. They are made available by a variety of sources, including academic institutions, government research laboratories, scientific societies, and individual scientists.

Researchers can search all preprints or choose individual preprint sites to search. A Browse option lists all of the included preprint servers and has direct links to those sites. Subject Pathways allows for browsing by topic. Through a service called PrePRINT Alerts, users can save a subject interest profile and receive email notification when new preprints are added to their selected categories.

Subjects: Preprints; Scientific and Technical Information

1563. Sandia National Laboratories

http://www.sandia.gov/

Sponsor: Energy Department — Sandia National Laboratories

Description: Sandia focuses on research and development related to national security goals. The Programs section of the Sandia site discusses activities in the areas of nuclear weapons, nonproliferation and materials control, energy and critical infrastructure, and emerging threats such as chemical and biological agents. The Capabilities section describes Sandia's work in homeland security. The News section has links to news releases, congressional testimony, and Sandia publications.

Subjects: Research Laboratories; Weapons Research

Publication: *Sandia Technology*, E 1.20/5:

1564. The National Academies

http://www.nas.edu/

Description: Chartered by Congress to advise the federal government on matters of science, technology, and medicine, the National Academies are private, nonprofit societies of distinguished scholars. The National Academy of Sciences, along with the National Academy of Engineering and the Institute of Medicine, are supervised by the National Research Council. All four provide scientific advice to Congress on a variety of topics. The Web site features sections on all four organizations and a topical list of subject areas. These include Agriculture, Behavioral and Social Sciences, Computer Sciences and Technology, Education, Engineering, Environmental Issues, Earth Sciences, Health and Medicine, Policy and Research Issues, Space, Mathematics and Physics, and Transportation. The Publications section via the National Academy Press Web site provides full-text access to over 2,500 reports. Browse abstracts from the latest research papers or view full-text articles from selected back issues of *The Proceedings of the National Academy of Sciences* for free online; the current edition is available by subscription, while *NewsReport* is available for free online.

This site should be of broad interest to the scientific and science policy community. The topical lists provide summaries and in some cases full-text reports from these distinguished bodies. It is also useful for the availability of the prestigious *Proceedings of the National Academy of Sciences*.

Publications: *NewsReport*

Proceedings of the National Academy of Sciences

1565. U.S. Army Cold Regions Research and Engineering Laboratory

http://www.crrel.usace.army.mil/

Sponsor: Army — Army Corps of Engineers — Engineer Research and Development Center (ERDC)

Description: This Army Corps of Engineers laboratory conducts scientific and engineering research on cold temperature environments. The CRREL site features the following sections: About CRREL, News and Events, Research and Engineering, Reports and Products, Library, and Partnering and Business Opportunities. It is under the Reports and Products section that the site offers access to lists of CRREL technical reports (from 1996, in PDF format), fact sheets, the Cold Regions Bibliography Database, and an Ice Jam Database.

Subjects: Engineering Research; Research Laboratories

Publications: *CRREL Report*, D 103.33.12:

CRREL Special Reports, D 103.33/2:

1566. United States Naval Observatory
http://www.usno.navy.mil/
Sponsor: Navy — Naval Observatory (USNO)
Description: The Naval Observatory is responsible for measuring the positions and motions of the Earth, Sun, Moon, planets, stars and other celestial objects; providing astronomical data; determining precise time; measuring the Earth's rotation; and maintaining the Master Clock for the United States. The Web site provides access to the divisions of the USNO, including its departments under the headings of Astrometry, Astronomical Applications, Earth Orientation, Time Service, and the Flagstaff Station. It also offers such popular links as Sky This Week, Star Catalogs, Sun Rise/Set, and the official time.

This site is useful for information on the official current time and general information on the Naval Observatory and its programs.
Subjects: Astronomy; Observatories

1567. Wallops Flight Facility
http://www.wff.nasa.gov/
Sponsor: National Aeronautics and Space Administration (NASA) — Wallops Flight Facility
Description: Wallops is responsible for the management and implementation of suborbital research programs, including sounding rockets, scientific balloons, and scientific aircraft. It also provides facilities and expertise to launch and operate suborbital and small orbital payloads. Wallops is also a key facility for operational testing, integration, and certification of NASA and commercial next-generation, low-cost orbital launch technologies. Available categories include Welcome, Vision and Mission, Doing Business with Wallops, Technical Capabilities, Programs and Projects, Public and Educational Outreach, Viewing Launches at Wallops, and Wallops Schedules.
Subject: Rockets

1568. William R. Wiley Environmental Molecular Sciences Laboratory
http://www.emsl.pnl.gov/
Sponsor: Energy Department — Environmental Molecular Sciences Laboratory (EMSL)
Description: The EMSL national research lab conducts fundamental research in molecular and computational sciences, particularly in relation to energy technologies. Its Web site includes sections on Research, Resources, News, Products, Visitor Information, and People. Products includes some workshop proceedings and technical reports and links to hardware, data, and software and basis sets. News has awards, achievements, and announcements. Resources together with People highlight the equipment, facilities, and expertise that this lab has to offer.
Subjects: Research Laboratories; Scientific Research

Biology

1569. Astrobiology at NASA
http://astrobiology.arc.nasa.gov/
Sponsor: National Aeronautics and Space Administration (NASA) — Ames Research Center (ARC)
Description: Astrobiology is the study of the origin, evolution, distribution, and destiny of life in the universe. It uses multiple scientific disciplines and space technologies. The site features a wealth of NASA information on this topic, including Latest News, Roadmap, Science Goals, Technologies, Missions, Workshops, Education, Public Engagement, Astrobiology Institute, Media Center, Related Links, and References.
Subject: Astrobiology

1570. Berkeley Drosophila Genome Project
http://www.fruitfly.org/
Sponsor: University of California
Description: The Berkeley Drosophila Genome Project (BDGP) is a consortium of the Drosophila Genome Centers and is funded by the National Human Genome Research Institute, the National

Cancer Institute, the Department of Energy, and the Howard Hughes Medical Institute. The site features the following search options: Berkeley Fly Database, Map Viewers, Analysis Tools, and FlyBase All Searches. Projects include Genomic Sequencing, Transposon Insertions, cDNAs and ESTs, and SNPs. Resources at the site include publications, materials, downloadable data sets, and methods.
Subject: Genomics — Research

1571. Biological Resources Division at USGS
http://biology.usgs.gov/
Sponsor: Interior Department — U.S. Geological Survey (USGS)
Description: Rich with graphic images of birds, plants, and insects, this site features information on a broad range of biological topics. The Biological Resources Division has offices across the United States and works to augment the scientific knowledge needed to support the nations' biological resources. The National Activities section links to information on numerous projects, such as the Bird Banding Laboratory, National Biological Information Infrastructure (NBII), and the Nonindigenous Aquatic Species Program. The Division's Expertise Database provides contact information for expertise in everything from American Elk to Zooplankton. The Features area of the home page has links to a photo gallery, Learning Room, and related links for non-scientists.

With information for children, the general public, and researchers, this site offers one of the best government starting points for general biological information.
Subject: Natural Resources — Research

1572. Biology and Biotechnology Research Program
http://www-bio.llnl.gov/
Sponsor: Energy Department — Lawrence Livermore National Laboratory (LLNL)
Description: The LLNL biology research program focuses on genomics, molecular and structural biology, and bioengineering research. Offering basic descriptive information on the Program and its research areas, this site features the following categories: Quick Program Overview, Research in Progress, Program Accomplishments, Abstracts, Program Management and Funding Sources, BBRP Staff, and Educational Opportunities. The Abstracts section includes a list of publications by members of the Program.

Consisting primarily of brief descriptions of research conducted by the Program, past and present, this site will be primarily of interest to other researchers in biotechnology.
Subject: Biology — Research

1573. Integrated Taxonomic Information System
http://www.itis.usda.gov/
Sponsor: Agriculture Department (USDA)
Description: The Integrated Taxonomic Information System (ITIS) is an excellent tool for looking up taxonomic names and common names of the biota of North America (the biota refers to all the plant and animal life in an area). ITIS is a partnership of United States, Canadian, and Mexican agencies, other organizations, and taxonomic specialists cooperating on the development of an online, scientifically credible list of biological names. The Web site features What's New, About ITIS, Data Access, and TRED—Taxonomic Resources and Experts Directory. The Data Access page includes the sections Query the ITIS Database, User Defined Report, Taxonomic Classification, Scientific Name Search with Common Names, Publications and Services, and links to download data. The ITIS database can be searched by scientific name, vernacular name, or taxonomic serial number. The records in the database include scientific name, vernacular name, taxonomic serial number, author, rank, credibility rating, and synonym name and synonym TSN.
Subject: Biological Names

1574. Laboratory of Structural Biology
http://dir.niehs.nih.gov/dirlsb/
Sponsor: National Institutes of Health (NIH) — National Institute of Environmental Health Sciences (NIEHS)

Description: The lab's mission is to provide insights into the biological processes that impact human environmental health. The site has information on the lab's facilities, principal investigators, and research groups. The research groups specialize in such areas as biomolecular crystallography and DNA repair and nucleic acid enzymology.
Subject: Molecular Biology — Research

1575. MAMMAL-L Mammalian Biology [email list]
http://www.lsoft.com/scripts/wl.exe?SL1=MAMMAL-L&H=SIVM.SI.EDU
Sponsor: Smithsonian Institution
Description: This is an email discussion list, sponsored and hosted by the Smithsonian, on the biology of mammals.
Subjects: Mammals; Email Lists

1576. National Biological Information Infrastructure (NBII)
http://www.nbii.gov/
Sponsor: Interior Department — U.S. Geological Survey (USGS)
Description: The goal of the National Biological Information Infrastructure (NBII) is to improve access to data and information on biological resources. NBII is a collaborative program involving federal and state government agencies, international organizations, and non-government, academic, and private industry partners. Its Web site is maintained by the U.S. Geological Survey Center for Biological Informatics. The site includes information developed by the NBII program, but also links to other government and non-government sites for coverage of many topics. The sections titled Current Biological Issues, Biological Disciplines, and Geographic Perspectives serve as extensive topical portals. A Teacher Resources section links to educational resources on botany, aquatic biology, reptiles, insects, and other topics. The Data and Information section has a variety of links to online glossaries, textbooks, journals, museums, organizations, and associations.

Earth and Atmospheric Sciences

1577. Aeronomy Laboratory at NOAA
http://www.al.noaa.gov/
Sponsor: Commerce Department — National Oceanic and Atmospheric Administration (NOAA)
Description: The Aeronomy Laboratory conducts basic research on the chemical and physical processes of the Earth's atmosphere. This research concentrates on the lower two layers of the atmosphere, the troposphere and stratosphere. The Web site offers information on the Lab's research projects in both technical and nontechnical descriptions. Featured links include The Environmental Issues, Current and Recent Field Campaigns, Bulletin Board, Accomplishments and Plans, Our People and Our Facilities, Contributions at Many Levels, and Why We Do What We Do.
Subject: Atmospheric Sciences — Research

1578. Alaska Volcano Observatory
http://www.avo.alaska.edu/
Sponsor: Interior Department — U.S. Geological Survey (USGS)
Description: The AVO site has sections entitled Updates, Products, About Us, What's New, and Atlas of Alaskan and Kamchatkan Volcanoes. It provides weekly updates and periodic information releases describing the current state of volcanic activity along the Aleutian arc. The Updates section contains weekly updates within the last two months with later ones accessible from the archives. The site also offers weekly Kamchatkan volcanic activity reports.

The AVO site is of interest to scientists and the general public in the vicinity of these volcanoes.
Subject: Volcanoes

1579. Cascades Volcano Observatory

http://vulcan.wr.usgs.gov/

Sponsor: Interior Department — U.S. Geological Survey (USGS)

Description: The CVO watches volcanoes and other natural hazards including earthquakes, landslides, and debris flows in the western United States. Its goal is to provide accurate and timely information pertinent to the assessment, warning, and mitigation of natural hazards. Toward this end, its Web site offers Volcanoes and Menu of Interest categories, with information on hazards, monitoring, volcanic features, and individual volcanoes. The site includes a collection of pictures; a glossary of hazards, volcanic features, and terminology; a link to the USGS Volcano Hazards Program, and general information about volcanoes. There are also sections entitled Living With Volcanoes, Visit a Volcano, and Educational Outreach.

This site is of interest to volcanologists and the general public living near or visiting the areas of volcanic activity in the Cascades. In addition, the basic, available information makes the site useful to anyone searching for background information on volcanoes.

Subject: Volcanoes

1580. Coastal and Marine Geology Program

http://marine.usgs.gov/

Sponsor: Interior Department — U.S. Geological Survey (USGS)

Description: This program is involved with geologic issues of coastal and marine areas related to environmental quality and preservation, natural hazards and public safety, natural resources, and earth sciences information and technology. This site features Topics of Study, Regions of Study, About Us, and News and Events. Topics of Study include beaches, erosion, corals, wetlands, tsunamis, sonar mapping, and sea-level change. News and Events includes the monthly newsletter *Sound Waves*.

Subjects: Coastal Ecology; Geology

Publication: *Sound Waves*

1581. Destination: Earth

http://www.earth.nasa.gov/

Sponsor: National Aeronautics and Space Administration (NASA) — Earth Science Office

Description: Destination: Earth is the public outreach Web site for NASA's Earth Science Enterprise (ESE). ESE is concerned with applying space-based capabilities to studying the effects of natural and human-induced changes on Earth and the global environment. The Science section of the site describes research projects in such areas as solar radiation, the global carbon cycle, and Earth system modeling research. Other sections describe spaceborne earth science missions, research opportunites, research applications, and NASA's history of earth science research. The site also has sections for teachers and for kids.

Students, teachers, and researchers can find a broad collection of useful climatological and earth science material on this site.

Subject: Global Change — Research

1582. Earth Observing System

http://eospso.gsfc.nasa.gov/

Sponsor: National Aeronautics and Space Administration (NASA) — Goddard Space Flight Center (GSFC) — Earth Observing System (EOS) Project Science Office

Description: EOS consists of a science component and a data system supporting a coordinated series of polar-orbiting and low-inclination satellites for long-term global observations of the land surface, biosphere, solid Earth, atmosphere, and oceans. The main categories of this Web site are What's New, For Educators, For News Media, For Scientists, Data Services, and Mission Profiles. Under For Scientists, the Science Publications and Reports section offers access to data products and reference handbooks, brochures, fact books, reports from EOS, and an online bimonthly publication, *The Earth Observer.* Under For Educators, the Educational Publications section offers posters, lithographs, fact sheets and fact books, and CD-ROMs for educators.

Subject: Planetary Science

Publication: *NASA Facts*, NAS 1.20

1583. Earth Resources Observation Systems
http://edc.usgs.gov/
Sponsor: Interior Department — U.S. Geological Survey (USGS)
Description: The EROS Data Center is a data management, systems development, and research center for the USGS National Mapping Division. Categories include About EROS, Products, Science, Satellite Missions, and National Satellite Land Remote Sensing Data Archive. The Products section has links or availability information on: aerial photographs, topographic maps, digital raster elevation data, imagery collected from satellites, and land use data sets. The Publications section is under About EROS and includes citations for scientific and technical materials authored or co-authored by the professional staff at the EROS Data Center.
Subjects: Maps and Mapping; Remote Sensing

1584. EarthExplorer
http://edcsns17.cr.usgs.gov/EarthExplorer/
Sponsor: Interior Department — U.S. Geological Survey (USGS)
Description: EarthExplorer is a system for querying and ordering satellite images, aerial photographs, and cartographic products through the U.S. Geological Survey. EarthExplorer is JAVA based and provides cross inventory search capabilities, multiple browse viewing, standing request functionality, and secured e-commerce support for product orders. Users may log in as guests or as registered users, who have access to more features than guests do. Users who plan to access EarthExplorer frequently may wish to register. With this service, scientists can evaluate data sets of satellite images, aerial photos, and cartographic products to determine their availability and place online requests for products.
Subject: Maps and Mapping

1585. Earthquake Hazards Program
http://earthquake.usgs.gov/
Sponsor: Interior Department — U.S. Geological Survey (USGS)
Description: The mission of the Earthquake Hazards Program is to understand the characteristics and effects of earthquakes and to provide and apply this information and knowledge to reduce deaths, injuries, and property damage from earthquakes. This site features the following sections: Latest Quakes, EQ Facts and Lists, Hazards and Preparedness, Science and Technology, EQ Glossary, For Teachers, For Kids, and Products and Services. The Products section has information on maps, CD-ROMs and videos, and global and national databases. Hazards and Preparedness offers maps of probable hazards, fact sheets, information about predicting earthquakes, and links to sites about earthquake preparedness. The Frequently Asked Questions section is quite extensive, presenting much information about earthquakes, prediction, myths, preparedness, historical quakes, and measurement.
Subject: Earthquakes

1586. Earthquake Hazards Program-Northern California
http://quake.wr.usgs.gov/
Sponsor: Interior Department — U.S. Geological Survey (USGS)
Description: This USGS site focuses specifically on earthquake activity in Northern California. Several types of maps are available: Real-Time Earthquake Maps for California-Nevada, the United States, and the World and Real-Time Shaking Maps (for California). There is a section about earthquake probabilities for the San Francisco Bay Area as well. The site still features a broad range of information about earthquakes. Major sections include Latest Quake Information, General Quake Information, Earthquake Research, Hazards and Preparedness, and Special Features. The Latest Quake Information page provides geographic summaries for California, the United States, and for regions all over the globe. For USGS Hazard Reduction fact sheets and seismic hazard maps, the Hazards and Preparedness link provides a large collection.
   This site provides excellent detail on Northern California seismic conditions.
Subject: Earthquakes

1587. Federal Geographic Data Committee
http://www.fgdc.gov/

Description: The Federal Geographic Data Committee coordinates the National Spatial Data Infrastructure (NSDI), which encompasses policies, standards, and procedures for organizations to cooperatively produce and share geospatial data. Its Web site offers information on the FGCD and the NSDI in sections such as Metadata, Clearinghouse, Standards, Framework, Stakeholders, FGDC Organization, NSDI, Publications and Special Reports, Cooperative Agreements Program/Funding, and Data. The Clearinghouse section can be used to help organizations make their collections searchable and accessible on the Internet. The Standards section features some of the FGDC standards, including those out for review, along with standards documents by sponsoring organizations, and standards directives.

Subject: Geography
Publication: *FGDC Newsletter*, I 19.115/4:

1588. Geology Discipline Home Page
http://geology.usgs.gov/index.shtml

Sponsor: Interior Department — U.S. Geological Survey (USGS)

Description: U.S. Geological Survey Geology Discipline studies natural hazards, earth resources, and geologic processes. The site provides a central point for geology-related publications and for links to all related USGS programs. The programs are grouped into three categories: Resources includes Energy and Minerals programs; Hazards includes Earthquakes, Landslides, and Volcanoes; and Landscapes has Astrogeology, Earth Surface Dynamics, and Coastal and Marine Geology. Each section leads to detailed information about the program and the science involved.

This site is a useful starting point for finding geology information from the USGS. However, many other geology sources are available on the main USGS server, so it may require looking on both.

Subject: Geology

1589. Global Change Master Directory
http://gcmd.gsfc.nasa.gov/

Sponsor: National Aeronautics and Space Administration (NASA)

Description: NASA's Global Change Master Directory (GCMD) is a catalog of Earth science data sets and services pertaining to global change research. The GCMD database includes data sets covering such topics as snow and ice, agriculture, atmosphere, biosphere, hydrosphere, oceans, land surface, and human dimensions of global change. The GCMD offers data set descriptions in a standard format, the Directory Interchange Format (DIF). Through any one of the search interfaces, the user may freely search the GCMD database. The resulting metadata records provide information on the nature of the data (e.g., parameters measured, geographic location, time range) and where the data are stored. In addition, the GCMD site has categories such as Describe Your Data, First Time Here, User Connection, and What's New. Under First Time is access to Software and Documentation, Collaborations, and Metadata Standards and Protocols. On the home page, one can conduct a search by key word or by data center, location, instrument, platform, or project.

This well constructed directory can assist researchers in finding data sets and serve as a model for similar Web projects.

Subjects: Data Products; Global Change

1590. Goddard Distributed Active Archive Center
http://xtreme.gsfc.nasa.gov/

Sponsor: National Aeronautics and Space Administration (NASA) — Goddard Space Flight Center (GSFC)

Description: The Goddard Distributed Active Archive Center (DAAC) provides data and related services for global change research and education, especially upper atmosphere, atmospheric dynamics, and the global biosphere. These Internet sites provide access to information on the various data sets available from DAAC such as the Tropical Rainfall Measuring Mission data and Sea-viewing Wide Field-of-view Sensor Project data. Featured sections include Atmospheric Chemistry, Atmospheric Dynamics, Field Experiments, Hydrology, Land Biosphere, Interdisciplinary Data and Resources, and Ocean Color. There is also a link to the MODIS (Moderate-resolution Imaging Spectroradiometer) Data Support Web site.

Subjects: Atmospheric Sciences; Global Change

1591. Hawaiian Volcano Observatory

`http://wwwhvo.wr.usgs.gov/`

Sponsor: Interior Department — U.S. Geological Survey (USGS)

Description: HVO conducts research on the volcanoes of Hawai`i and works with emergency-response officials to protect people and property from earthquakes and volcano-related hazards. The site has information on current activity, history, and hazards for Mauna Loa and Kilauea volcanoes as well as links for such sections as About HVO, Earthquakes, Other Volcanoes, Volcanic Hazards, Products, and Photo Gallery. This site provides online access to *Volcano Watch*, a weekly newsletter for the general public, written by scientists at the USGS Hawaiian Volcano Observatory. The newsletter is in HTML, and the site offers archives back to 1994.

This site will be of great interest to anyone living on the Big Island of Hawai`i and provides educational information for anyone else interested in volcanoes and volcanology.

Subject: Volcanoes

Publication: *Volcano Watch*

1592. HazardMaps.gov

`http://www.hazardmaps.gov`

Description: HazardMaps.gov is an interactive atlas of hazards data and map services. The site is designed to assist in the mapping of multiple hazards to show areas of hazard overlap. A Multi-Hazard Atlas can display multiple natural hazards data by state, congressional district, or FEMA Region. It can be used to access, modify, and display datasets. The site also features a Hazards Data Exchange, an archive of spatial data.

1593. Mineral Resources Program—USGS

`http://minerals.usgs.gov/`

Sponsor: Interior Department — U.S. Geological Survey (USGS)

Description: This USGS site offers access to minerals information formerly supplied by the now-defunct Bureau of Mines. The site features statistics and information on the worldwide occurrence, quantity, quality, and availability of mineral resources and offers online access to numerous publications such as the *Mineral Industry Surveys* and the *Minerals Yearbook*. Access to information in the yearbook is by commodity, country, or state. The site also features the following sections: Issues; Mineral Resources Teams; Featured Pages, which has a Commodity Statistics and Information section; and What's New. The Contacts section lists mineral specialists by commodity, country, and resource.

This is a very useful site for tracking down statistical information on minerals as commodities.

Subject: Minerals

Publications: *Metal Industry Indicators*, I 19.129:
Mineral Commodity Summaries (annual), I 19.166:
Mineral Industry Surveys (annual), I 19.161:
Mineral Industry Surveys (quarterly), I 19.160:
Mineral Industry Surveys, Aluminum in . . ., I 19:130
Mineral Industry Surveys, Antimony in . . ., I 19:131
Mineral Industry Surveys, Bauxite and Alumina in . . , I 19:132
Mineral Industry Surveys, Bismuth in . . ., I 19:133
Mineral Industry Surveys, Cement in . . ., I 19:134
Mineral Industry Surveys, Chromium in . . ., I 19:135
Mineral Industry Surveys, Cobalt in . . ., I 19:136
Mineral Industry Surveys, Copper in . . ., I 19:137
Mineral Industry Surveys, Crushed Stone and Sand and Gravel in . . , I 19:138
Mineral Industry Surveys, Fluorspar in . . ., I 19:139
Mineral Industry Surveys, Gypsum in . . , I 19:140
Mineral Industry Surveys, Iron and Steel Scrap in . . ., I 19:141
Mineral Industry Surveys, Irone Ore in . . , I 19:142
Mineral Industry Surveys, Lead in . . ., I 19:143
Mineral Industry Surveys, Lime in . . , I 19:144
Mineral Industry Surveys, Magnesium in . . ., I 19:145
Mineral Industry Surveys, Manganese in . . , I 19:158

Mineral Industry Surveys, Mineral Industry of (Country) Minerals (annual), I 19.163:
Mineral Industry Surveys, Mineral Industry of (State) Minerals (annual, I 19.162:
Mineral Industry Surveys, Molybdenum in . . ., I 19:159
Mineral Industry Surveys, Nickel in . . , I 19:148
Mineral Industry Surveys, Phosphate Rock in . . ., I 19:147
Mineral Industry Surveys, Precious Metals in . . ., I 19:149
Mineral Industry Surveys, Silicon in . . ., I 19:150
Mineral Industry Surveys, Soda Ash and Sodium Sulfate in . . ., I 19:151
Mineral Industry Surveys, Sulfur in . . ., I 19:152
Mineral Industry Surveys, Tin in . . ., I 19:153
Mineral Industry Surveys, Titanium in . . , I 19:154
Mineral Industry Surveys, Tungsten in . . ., I 19:155
Mineral Industry Surveys, Vanadium in . . ., I 19:156
Mineral Industry Surveys, Zinc in . . ., I 19:157
Minerals Yearbook, I 19.165:
Statistical Compendium, I 19.120/4:

1594. Minerals Management Service
`http://www.mms.gov/`
Sponsor: Interior Department — Minerals Management Service (MMS)
Description: The MMS is charged with managing the nation's natural gas, oil, and other mineral resources of the outer continental shelf and to collect, verify, and distribute mineral revenues from federal offshore mineral leases and from leases from federal and Indian lands. The MMS site includes information on these tasks. Some of the links available include Mineral Revenue, Offshore Program, Newsroom, Advisory Committees, Newsroom, Congressional Affairs, and Library. A variety of publications are available in the Library under such categories as congressional, legal, environmental, scientific and technical, royalties and revenues, and statistics and facts.
Subjects: Minerals; Offshore Drilling; Public Lands
Publications: *Annual Financial Report*, I 72.2:F 49/
Federal Offshore Statistics, I 72.10:
MMS Today, I 72.17:
Offshore Stats, I 72.18:
Royalty Management Program Mineral Yearbook, I 72.13:

1595. NASA Goddard Institute for Space Studies
`http://www.giss.nasa.gov/`
Sponsor: National Aeronautics and Space Administration (NASA) — Goddard Space Flight Center (GSFC) — Goddard Institute for Space Studies (GISS)
Description: GISS is a GSFC research institute that emphasizes a broad study of global environmental change. A key objective of its research is the prediction of atmospheric and climate changes in the 21st century. Its Web site includes links for About GISS, Education, Publications, Datasets and Images, and Research. The Publications section is primarily a bibliographic listing of publications, accessed by a list of staff, some of which are available in compressed Postscript or PDF formats. The Spotlight section highlights recent research, newly released data sets, interesting news stories, or education materials.

Most of the site is geared toward the research scientist or graduate and postdoctoral student.
Subject: Global Change

1596. NASA Langley Research Center
`http://www.larc.nasa.gov/`
Sponsor: National Aeronautics and Space Administration (NASA) — Langley Research Center (LaRC)
Description: As a major center for aeronautics, atmospheric sciences, and space technology, LaRC offers a Web site featuring information about itself and its research areas. News and Events includes news releases, fact sheets and publications, and video and animation products. The Business with Us section covers procurement information and technology transfer. Other sections include Images, Research, Reports and Publications, About Us, and Education, which has a Kid's Corner.

For subject access, there are direct links to these research areas: aeronautics, Earth science, space technology, and structures and materials.

With a wide collection of aeronautical information, this site is an important resource for researchers in aeronautics.

Subject: Aerospace Engineering — Research

1597. National Earthquake Information Center

http://neic.usgs.gov/

Alternate URL: ftp://ghtftp.cr.usgs.gov

Sponsor: Interior Department — U.S. Geological Survey (USGS)

Description: As the national data center for earthquakes, the NEIC has three main goals: to determine the size and location of all destructive earthquakes in the world, to maintain a seismic database, and to improve its ability to locate earthquakes and to understand the mechanism of earthquakes. Featured sections of this site include Current Earthquake Information, Near Real Time Earthquake List, General Earthquake Information, Earthquake Search, National Seismic Hazard Mapping Project, U.S. National Seismograph Network, Today in Earthquake History, and Large Earthquakes in 2003. The site also has an Earthquake Email Notification Service. Additional links are About Us, Products and Services, and Report an Earthquake. The section Current Earthquake Information has current earthquake maps, a list of recent earthquakes, a link to the page for data available through ftp (the alternate URL). From this Web page, one can link to the other USGS earthquake Web sites.

Subject: Earthquakes

Publication: *Preliminary Determination of Epicenters,* I 19.66:

1598. National Geodetic Survey

http://www.ngs.noaa.gov/

Alternate URL: ftp://ftp.ngs.noaa.gov/pub/

Sponsor: Commerce Department — National Oceanic and Atmospheric Administration (NOAA) — National Ocean Service

Description: The NGS develops and maintains the National Spatial Reference System (NSRS) using geodetic, photogrammetric, and remote sensing techniques. The NSRS is a national coordinate system that defines latitude, longitude, height, scale, gravity, and orientation throughout the United States, including how these values change with time. The NGS Web site's featured categories include What's New, Who We Are, Products and Services, and State Advisors. Project and Division pages include remote sensing, Geoid, and Geosciences Research. Its substantial Products and Services page includes access to a variety of sections including Aerial Photos, Aeronautical Data, Calibration Base Lines, Global Positioning System Orbital Data, and Geodetic Software Programs. The technical nature of the material available on this site means that it will be of interest primarily to geodesy and remote sensing professionals.

Subjects: Geodesy; Maps and Mapping

1599. National Geophysical Data Center

http://www.ngdc.noaa.gov/

Sponsor: Commerce Department — National Oceanic and Atmospheric Administration (NOAA) — National Environmental Satellite, Data, and Information Service (NESDIS)

Description: The mission of NGDC is data management, to prepare and provide reliable data sets that are in the public domain to a wide group of users. Data groups include bathymetry and topography, geomagnetism, ocean geosciences, paleoclimate, snow and ice, solar and upper atmosphere, and space weather. There is a link to data and images from a variety of satellites as well. Other sections include About NGDC, What's New, Products, World Data Centers, and International Programs. The site contains numerous data products of use to research professionals in the relevant disciplines.

Subjects: Data Products; Environmental Science

1600. National Imagery and Mapping Agency

http://www.nima.mil/

Sponsor: Defense Department — National Imagery and Mapping Agency (NIMA)
Description: Formed from the combination of the offices of the Defense Mapping Agency, the Central Imaging Office, and the Defense Dissemination Program Office with the functions and mission of the CIA's National Photographic Interpretation Center, NIMA offers a Web site that provides access to imagery, imagery intelligence, and geospatial information. NIMA describes its mission as providing geospatial intelligence in support of national security. The Geospatial Intelligence section of the site links to a number of servers from NIMA and other sources; these include: the Geospatial Engine, Earth-Info site, and the Digital Nautical Chart(R) Home Page. The Public Affairs section has news releases and fact sheets. The publications section has the text of *Geodesy for the Layman* as well as standards and specifications publications.
Subjects: Maps and Mapping; Military Intelligence
Publications: *Fact Sheets*, D 5.361:
Geodesy for the Layman, D 5.302:G 29
Notice to Mariners, D 5.315:

1601. National Mapping Information—USGS

http://mapping.usgs.gov/

Sponsor: Interior Department — U.S. Geological Survey (USGS)
Description: As the central site for USGS map-related products and information, this site offers substantial information content on maps, geographic features, and geographic data products. It includes access to the Geographic Names Information System (GNIS), a large database of physical and cultural geographic features in the United States. Major categories for the site include: Mapping News; Mapping Products, Programs, and Services; For Parents, Teachers, and Students; and Regional Mapping Centers. The site links to several USGS map indexes and catalogs, including MapFinder, PhotoFinder, and Maps on Demand.

This National Mapping Information page pulls together so many links to data archives, product finders, and map-related products, it can be the first stop for finding United States maps and geographic data.
Subject: Maps and Mapping
Publication: *Geographic Names Information System: Digital Gazeteer*, I 19.120:G 25/ GNIS:

1602. Ocean Surface Topography from Space

http://topex-www.jpl.nasa.gov/

Sponsor: National Aeronautics and Space Administration (NASA) — Jet Propulsion Laboratory (JPL)
Description: This site describes NASA research and missions related to ocean topography, and provides related educational materials. It has information on the TOPEX/Poseidon Mission, a partnership between the United States and France to monitor global ocean topography, discover the links between the oceans and atmosphere, and improve global climate predictions. The follow-on mission, called Jason-1 is also described in detail.
Subject: Oceans — Research

1603. Office of Surface Mining

http://www.osmre.gov/

Sponsor: Interior Department — Surface Mining Office
Description: OSM has the responsibility of protecting the environment and people during coal mining and reclamation and of reclaiming abandoned mines. Featured sections include Announcements, News Releases, Abandoned Mine Reclamation, Regulation of Active Mines, Information, Statistics, and Finance and Administration. Look under Information for annual reports, photo library, directives, fact sheets, and reports, articles, and speeches.
Subject: Mining Reclamation
Publication: *Office of Surface Mining Annual Report*, I 71.1:

1604. Perry-Castañeda Library Map Collection

http://www.lib.utexas.edu/maps/index.html

Alternate URL: http://sunsite.informatik.rwth-aachen.de/Maps/

Sponsor: University of Texas at Austin. Library

Description: This site offers access to scanned versions of government maps. While only a small part of the library's printed map collection has been scanned and made available on the Web, this site has more than 5,000 map images. The maps are in JPEG and GIF image formats, and those available are all in the public domain. The online collection primarily consists of maps from the CIA, the U.S. Bureau of the Census, and the National Atlas of the United States. Anyone looking for an online version of a government map should be sure to check this site.

Subject: Maps and Mapping

Publication: *CIA Maps*, PrEx 3.10/4:

1605. Rapid Service/Prediction Center for Earth Orientation Parameters

http://maia.usno.navy.mil/

Sponsor: Navy — Naval Observatory (USNO)

Description: IERS coordinates, collects, archives, and distributes data from the various operational U.S. programs that monitor variations in the orientation of the Earth and its subsequent relation to time. Its Web site features a variety of publications and products including *IERS Bulletins: A, B, C, D*; the *IERS Annual Report*; and the *NEOS Annual Report* and offers access to a variety of standard data files available by anonymous ftp (updated twice weekly) and daily data files (updated daily). Because of the very technical nature of most of this information, the site is primarily of interest to navigators, geodesists, and those involved in timekeeping.

Publications: *IERS Bulletin*
NEOS Annual Report

1606. Total Ozone Mapping Spectrometer

http://jwocky.gsfc.nasa.gov/

Sponsor: National Aeronautics and Space Administration (NASA) — Goddard Space Flight Center (GSFC)

Description: This site features information, data, and images from the Total Ozone Mapping Spectrometer (TOMS) instruments and offer the following product areas: ozone, aerosols, reflectivity, and erythemal ultraviolet exposure. NASA's TOMS instruments provide global measurements of total column ozone on a daily basis. The Multimedia section includes animated images and video files that show ozone and aerosols and ozone features via the Northern Hemisphere, the Antarctic Ozone Hole, and UV-Absorbing Aerosols and UV Radiation files. Search by specific TOMS satellite for access to the most current images and data available along with access to archives of images and data. The Today's Ozone link has maps and data for current ozone levels at the poles and for the whole globe. The Today's Aerosols link shows the current conditions of aerosols in the world.

While geared toward researchers, the Multimedia section, Today's Ozone, Today's Aerosols, and some of the images present the data in a manner that is easily grasped by the layman as well.

Subjects: Atmospheric Sciences; Ozone

1607. U.S. Geological Survey

http://www.usgs.gov/

Description: As one of the government's primary scientific agencies, the USGS offers a broad range of scientific material on its Web site, with four broad subject categories: biology, geology, water, and mapping. Its main content is under the Browse Our Topics section, which includes topic categories such as Biological Resources, Earthquakes, Floods, Maps, Minerals, and Volcanoes. These subject categories point to separate USGS sites, which are described separately in this directory. Under Education, the site links to The Learning Web as well as to education pages for earth hazards, plants and animals, maps and images, and water. The USGS site also presents information by audience tracts: Congress, news agencies, teachers and students, and scientists. The Products section links to "locators, catalogs, and collections" by science topic and by media type. A separate section links to online products and another to USGS libraries online.

The USGS home page provides multiple access points to its rich collection of scientific resources and publications.

Publications: *Contaminant Hazard Reviews*, I 19.167:
Geographic Names Information System, I 19.16/2:
Manual of Federal Geographic Data Products, PrEx 2.6/2:G 29
National Land Cover Dataset, I 19.168:
National Water Quality Laboratory Newsletter, I 19.125:
New Publications of the USGS, I 19.14/4-2:
Open-File Reports, I 19.76:
Professional Papers, I 19.16:
Publications of the Geological Survey (annual), I 19.14:
Selected Water Resources Abstracts, I 1.94/2:
U.S. Geological Survey, Fiscal Year Yearbook (annual), I 19.1/2:
USGS Bulletins, I 19.3:
USGS Circulars, I 19.4/2:
USGS Yearbooks, I 19.1:
Water-Resources Investigations Reports, I 19.42/4:

1608. US Global Change Research Program
http://www.usgcrp.gov/
Description: The US Global Change Research Program (USGCRP) is an interagency effort focused on studying changes in the Earth's global environmental system. It was established by the U.S. Global Change Research Act of 1990. The site describes research areas and accomplishments, and highlights current research grant proposals. Specific research areas discussed include atmospheric composition, climate change, ecosystems, and land use change. A Library section has links to online documents from the participating agencies and about the USGCRP.
Subject: Global Change — Research

1609. Volcano Hazards Program
http://volcanoes.usgs.gov/
Sponsor: Interior Department — U.S. Geological Survey (USGS)
Description: This central page from the USGS Volcano Hazards Program features the headings Volcano Hazards, Worldwide and U.S. Volcano Updates, What's New on USGS Volcano Web Sites, Reducing Volcanic Risk, and Resources. For checking either current activity or historical eruptions, this is a great starting point for finding information on U.S. volcanoes.
Subject: Volcanoes

Physics

1610. Advanced Spaceborne Thermal Emission Reflectance Radiometer (ASTER)
http://asterweb.jpl.nasa.gov/
Sponsor: National Aeronautics and Space Administration (NASA) — Jet Propulsion Laboratory (JPL)
Description: ASTER (Advanced Spaceborne Thermal Emission and Reflection Radiometer) is an imaging instrument that flies on the NASA Terra satellite, launched in 1999. ASTER can obtain detailed maps of surface temperature, emissivity, reflectance, and elevation. The Web site features sections Images, Instrument, Data Products, Obtaining Data, and News.
Subject: Satellites

1611. Fermi National Accelerator Laboratory
http://www.fnal.gov/
Sponsor: Energy Department — Fermi National Accelerator Laboratory
Description: Fermilab is a research lab with a focus on the fundamental nature of matter and energy. It provides resources to conduct basic research in high-energy physics and related disciplines. It is best known for the world's highest-energy particle accelerator, the Tevatron. Available sections include About Fermilab, Inquiring Minds, Visiting Fermilab, For Physicists, Education, Public Events, and Fermilab At Work.

This site is useful for both researchers and the general public. The Education, About Fermilab with its virtual tour, Public Events with streaming video lectures, and Inquiring Minds sections all provide information for the general public, while other sections can provide contact and technical information for researchers.

Subjects: Particle Accelerators; Physics — Research; Research Laboratories
Publication: *FermiNews*

1612. Harvard-Smithsonian Center for Astrophysics

http://cfa-www.harvard.edu/

Sponsor: Harvard-Smithsonian Center for Astrophysics
Description: The Center for Astrophysics combines the resources and research facilities of the Smithsonian Astrophysical Observatory and the Harvard College Observatory under a single Director to pursue studies of basic physical processes that determine the nature and evolution of the universe. The Web site features About the Center for Astrophysics (CfA), Research, Events, Opportunities, Facilities, and Directories. The Research section includes access to the *CfA Preprint Series*, the astronomic photographic plate collection, and press releases from the Center for Astrophysics.
Subject: Astrophysics — Research

1613. High Energy Astrophysics Science Archive Research Center

http://heasarc.gsfc.nasa.gov/

Sponsor: National Aeronautics and Space Administration (NASA) — Goddard Space Flight Center (GSFC)
Description: The purpose of the High Energy Astrophysics Science Archive Research Center (HEASARC) is to support a multimission archive facility in high-energy astrophysics for scientists all over the world. Its site is part of NASA's Structure and Evolution of the Universe theme. Data from space-borne instruments on spacecraft are provided, along with a knowledgeable science-user support staff and tools to analyze multiple datasets. Featured sections include Observatories, Data Archive, Software, Utilities, Education and Outreach, HEASARC Information, and Helpdesk and FAQ. The Data Archive section provides access to the data from high-energy astrophysics satellites. The site's drop-down menu, HEASARC Resources/Education, links to a variety of images and information for K–12 students, educators, and college students.

Primarily useful for the professional astronomer and astrophysicist, this site does offer some information for the general public. The Education and Outreach section links to learning centers, with some educational material on high-energy astrophysics for various age levels.
Subject: Astrophysics — Research

1614. Jefferson Lab

http://www.jlab.org/

Sponsor: Energy Department — Thomas Jefferson National Accelerator Facility
Description: The Jefferson Lab is a nuclear physics research laboratory built to probe the nucleus of the atom to learn more about the quark structure of matter. In addition to the exploration of the nucleus, the lab has programs in education and some partnerships with industry. Its Web site features sections Scientific Program, under which are research highlights, links for higher education, and links to information about nuclear physics and experiment research; Public Connections, with links for K–12 education and an image gallery; and JLab at Work, with subsections Technology Transfer, Publications, and Doing Business.
Subjects: Nuclear Physics — Research; Particle Accelerators; Research Laboratories

1615. NASA Astrophysics Data System

http://adswww.harvard.edu/index.html

Sponsors: Harvard-Smithsonian Center for Astrophysics; National Aeronautics and Space Administration (NASA)
Description: The Astrophysics Data System (ADS) is a NASA-funded project whose main resource is an Abstract Service. It includes four sets of bibliographic databases: Astronomy and Astrophysics, Instrumentation, Physics and Geophysics, and preprints in Astronomy. In addition to the ADS

Abstracts Database, the site also provides a Scanned Journal and Proceedings Service with the full copies of these astronomy and astrophysics resources available online.

This is an important site for anyone searching for information in the astrophysics field.

Subject: Astrophysics

1616. National Radio Astronomy Observatory
http://www.nrao.edu/
Sponsor: National Science Foundation (NSF) — National Radio Astronomy Observatory (NRAO)
Description: The NRAO is a research facility that provides state-of-the-art radio telescope facilities for use by the scientific community. The instruments are used to study planets, comets, quasars, galaxies, and black holes. The NRAO site groups its links under headings such as About NRAO, Administration, Astronomer Resources, Careers, Education, Engineering, Library, Image Gallery, and Sites and Telescopes. The Library section provides access to citations to NRAO visitor and staff preprints and published articles, some of which are available in full-text Postscript format.
Subjects: Astronomy; Observatories

1617. NIST Physics Laboratory
http://physics.nist.gov/
Sponsor: Commerce Department — Technology Administration (TA) — National Institute of Standards and Technology (NIST)
Description: The Physics Laboratory supports industry by providing measurement services and research for electronic, optical, and radiation technologies. Main categories on the Web site include About the Physics Laboratory, Product and Services, Selected Projects. The Product and Services heading features the following sections: Physical Reference Data, Publications, General Interest, Measurement and Calibration, and Constants, Units, and Uncertainty. The main page has subject links to the lab's six main divisions and research areas: electron and optical physics, atomic physics, optical technology, ionizing radiation, time and frequency, and quantum physics.
Subjects: Physics — Research; Standards and Specifications

1618. Princeton Plasma Physics Laboratory
http://www.pppl.gov/
Sponsor: Energy Department — Princeton Plasma Physics Laboratory (PPPL)
Description: Princeton Plasma Physics Laboratory (PPPL) is concerned with fusion energy and plasma physics research. PPPL is managed by Princeton University for the Energy Department. The site features information about the lab, its research, and its equipment. Categories include News at PPPL, Fusion Basics, Research Projects, Education Programs, Publications, and Technology Transfer. The Publications section provides access to abstracts and preprints of technical reports.
Subject: Plasma Physics — Research

1619. SOHO: The Solar and Heliospheric Observatory
http://sohowww.nascom.nasa.gov/
Sponsor: National Aeronautics and Space Administration (NASA)
Description: The SOHO Internet sites provide information and status and goals of the SOHO mission to the general public, as well as to the international solar physics and solar-terrestrial physics communities. The Web site offers a broad range of information on the project in the headings: The Mission, Resources, Science, Data, and Community. The Resources section includes a section that offers "free stuff," such as a screen saver of almost real-time images of the Sun, and sections for teachers and the news media. The Publications page, under Community, features a SOHO bibliography and publications database, SOHO documentation, and links to online journals. The Data section has a photo gallery and offers access to a variety of databases.
Subjects: Solar-Terrestrial Physics; Sun

1620. Space Environment Center
http://www.sel.noaa.gov/
Sponsor: Commerce Department — National Oceanic and Atmospheric Administration (NOAA) — Office of Oceanic and Atmospheric Research

Description: The site includes many different solar images and descriptions of the space between the Sun and the Earth. The center provides real-time monitoring and forecasting of solar and geophysical events, conducts research in solar-terrestrial physics, and develops techniques for forecasting solar and geophysical disturbances. Featured sections include Space Weather Now, Online Data, Education, SEC Projects, and About SEC. Under Space Weather Now, there is a quick overview of the space environment between the Sun and Earth. Included are the most recent full-disk image of the Sun, X-ray plots from the satellites, auroral maps, real-time solar wind pages, last space weather bulletin, and the latest alert, warning, and watch.

This site presents a wealth of data for researchers in solar-terrestrial physics and for anyone interested in images and reports on the Sun and its effects on Earth.

Subjects: Space Environment; Sun

1621. Stanford Linear Accelerator Center

http://www.slac.stanford.edu/

Sponsor: Energy Department — Stanford Linear Accelerator Center (SLAC)

Description: The Stanford Linear Accelerator Center (SLAC), operated by Stanford University for the Energy Department, conducts high energy physics research. This site provides an introduction to SLAC and its programs. Featured links include About SLAC, Mission, Education, and Tours of SLAC. The SPIRES section is the home of the Stanford Public Information REtrieval System databases of high energy physics literature and research. The site also provides access to *Beam Line*, a quarterly journal of particle physics and databases of scientific preprints by SLAC authors and others in the high-energy physics community.

SLAC claims to have established the first U.S. government Web site and provides documentation of it at this site.

Subjects: Particle Accelerators; Physics — Research; Research Laboratories

Publication: *Beam Line*, E 1.113:

1622. T-2 Nuclear Information Service

http://t2.lanl.gov/

Sponsor: Energy Department — Los Alamos National Laboratory (LANL)

Description: Run by the Nuclear Physics Group of the Theoretical Division of Los Alamos National Lab, this site covers nuclear modeling, nuclear data, cross sections, nuclear masses, nuclear astrophysics, radioactivity, radiation shielding, data for medical radiotherapy, data for high-energy accelerator applications, and data and codes for fission and fusion systems. Available categories include Tour (educational material, orientation to the site), Data (sets of nuclear data), Codes (for preparing nuclear data tables for various applications), and Publications.

The very technical nature of this data means that the site will be of interest primarily to nuclear physicists.

Subject: Nuclear Physics

1623. Wind Tunnels—NASA Ames Research Center

http://windtunnels.arc.nasa.gov/WindTunnels/index.html

Sponsor: National Aeronautics and Space Administration (NASA) — Ames Research Center (ARC)

Description: This site is designed primarily for users of the NASA Ames aerodymanic testing wind tunnels. In addition to a description of the facilities, the Web site features sections: Wind Tunnel Gallery, Test Planning, Ames Research Center, and Facilities, which includes the Unitary Wind Tunnels, the 12-Foot Pressure Wind Tunnel, and the National Full-Scale Aerodynamics Complex.

Subject: Aerospace Engineering

Space Exploration

1624. Ames Research Center
http://www.arc.nasa.gov/
Sponsor: National Aeronautics and Space Administration (NASA) — Ames Research Center (ARC)
Description: The Ames Research Center site features sections related to its research mission in the aerospace, space, and computing areas, as well as an About Ames section. Under the general headings of aerospace, space, and computing, information is organized by Ames division names. Each section also has a list of Frequently Asked Questions, outlining Ames activities in that area. Other sections cover astrobiology, Center news, and educational resources for kids and teachers.
Subjects: Space Sciences — Research; Space Technology — Research

1625. Asteroid and Comet Impact Hazard
http://impact.arc.nasa.gov/
Description: The site provides access to congressional documents and NASA studies related to impact hazards along with a complete listing of all known Earth-crossing asteroids and predicted close approaches to the Earth in the near future. It offers a bibliography of key scientific papers on the impact hazard. In addition, there is a link to NASA's Near Earth Asteroid Mission that provides information about the landing of a spacecraft on the asteroid Eros. The site also presents the Torino Impact Hazard Scale, which is used to classify potential impact threats.

    With popular media exploring the concept of the earth being struck by a comet or asteroid, this site should prove interesting to the general public as well as scientists taking a more scholarly interest in the phenomena.
Subject: Planets

1626. Center for Mars Exploration
http://cmex.arc.nasa.gov/
Alternate URL: http://cmex-www.arc.nasa.gov/
Sponsor: National Aeronautics and Space Administration (NASA) — Ames Research Center (ARC)
Description: The Center for Mars Exploration (CMEX) site features a wide range of materials on Mars. These include historical references to Mars, previous Mars mission information, tools to analyze Mars, current Mars news, and papers related to the possibility of life on Mars. This site features sections including Mars News and Information, Mars Atlas/Map/Images, and Educational Resources. This large collection of Mars-related information is an excellent resource for anyone from students to professionals who are interested in researching the planet.
Subject: Mars

1627. Columbia Accident Investigation Board
http://www.caib.us/
Sponsor: Columbia Accident Investigation Board
Description: The Columbia Accident Investigation Board was established to determine actual or probable causes of the failure of NASA's Columbia space shuttle on February 1, 2003. The CAIB Web site includes information on board members, the board charter, press releases, transcripts of press briefings, and minutes of any public meetings. The site also has a Web form to use to contact the CAIB.
Subject: Space Shuttle

1628. Crustal Dynamics Data Information System (CDDIS)
http://cddisa.gsfc.nasa.gov/cddis.html
Sponsor: National Aeronautics and Space Administration (NASA) — Goddard Space Flight Center (GSFC)
Description: The Crustal Dynamics Data Information System (CDDIS) supports data archiving and distribution activities for the space geodesy and geodynamics community. This site offers access to CDDIS data sets, documents, programs, and reports.

    This site is primarily of interest to researchers in this field.
Subject: Geodesy

1629. Glenn Research Center
http://www.grc.nasa.gov/
Sponsor: National Aeronautics and Space Administration (NASA) — Glenn Research Center
Description: Formerly known as the Lewis Research Center, the Glenn Research Center was renamed after John H. Glenn. Researching aeronautics and aeropropulsion technologies is the center's main focus, but its research areas also include space applications involving power and on-board propulsion, commercial communications and launch vehicles, and microgravity research. Its Web site presents basic information about GRC and then makes the bulk of its content available under headings Subject, Organization, Project, General Information, Education, News, Visitor Center, Resources, and People. Under the Subject section, the Online Publications and Library Resources section provides access to technical reports, images, and a guide to technical report writings.
Subjects: Aerospace Engineering — Research; Space Technology — Research

1630. Goddard Space Flight Center
http://www.gsfc.nasa.gov/
Sponsor: National Aeronautics and Space Administration (NASA) — Goddard Space Flight Center (GSFC)
Description: Goddard's overall mission deals with Space Science, Technology, and Earth Science, with a focus on observations from space. This NASA field center is a major U.S. laboratory for developing and operating unmanned scientific spacecraft. The Center manages many of NASA's Earth Observation, Astronomy, and Space Physics missions and the Web site has information on each of its space missions. The site also links to detailed information on educational and University programs sponsored by NASA and Goddard. The Goddard Library, part of the site, provides information including their online catalog, links to sources for standards and technical reports, and the Goddard Projects Directory.
Subjects: Space Sciences; Space Technology

1631. Human Space Flight—International Space Station
http://spaceflight.nasa.gov/station/
Sponsor: National Aeronautics and Space Administration (NASA) — Spaceflight Office
Description: This site has extensive information about the International Space Station. It includes current news on the activities of the International Space Station crew, background information on the science being performed on the station, the status of the ongoing construction of the space station, and information on the work of past crews. It also features space station images and information on how to track the station's location in the sky.
Subjects: Space Sciences; Space Stations

1632. Jet Propulsion Laboratory
http://www.jpl.nasa.gov/
Sponsor: National Aeronautics and Space Administration (NASA) — Jet Propulsion Laboratory (JPL)
Description: JPL is the lead U.S. center for robotic exploration of the solar system. JPL spacecraft have visited all the planets except Pluto. Its Web site features information on earth and the other planets, along with the universe and space technology. The Missions page gives information on specific robotic spacecraft and the accomplishments of their missions. Major subject links on the main page include Solar System, Earth, Stars and Galaxies, and Technology. For multimedia information on the planets or the universe, see the Images and Videos page. The News section includes press releases, fact sheets, status reports, and historical releases.
Subjects: Space Technology; Spacecraft

1633. John C. Stennis Space Center
http://www.ssc.nasa.gov/
Sponsor: National Aeronautics and Space Administration (NASA) — Stennis Space Center (SSC)
Description: SSC is NASA's primary center for testing large rocket propulsion systems for the space shuttle and future generation space vehicles. The main subject links include rocket propulsion testing, commercial remote sensing, and Earth science applications. The Web site also offers information about the SSC, Stennis services, doing business with the center, and public programs.
Subjects: Propulsion Technology; Rockets

1634. Johnson Space Center
http://www.jsc.nasa.gov/
Sponsor: National Aeronautics and Space Administration (NASA) — Johnson Space Center (JSC)
Description: With a primary focus on manned space flights and the selection and training of astronauts, the Johnson Space Center (JSC) Web site features sections for Space Shuttle, Space Station, and Astronauts. The Space Shuttle and Space Station sections include information about the mission control rooms for each of those spacecraft. The Astronauts section has astronaut biographies in addition to information about astronaut selection and training. Research and Technology sections link to a number of NASA projects and include information on research opportunities and technology transfer. The site's news section includes press releases, fact sheets, a catalog of current and historical space images, the daily *Cyberspace Roundup*, and the biweekly *Space News Roundup*. The Information section has an overview and history of JSC and information about visiting the center. In addition, see the bottom half of the site map page for links to over 25 special-focus JSC Web sites.

Most of the material on this site is geared toward the public, the press, and business users. It is an excellent site for students and teachers to find material for education related to humans in space, manned space flights, and basic astronomy. It also answers popular questions about how to become an astronaut.
Subjects: Astronauts; Human Space Exploration; Spacecraft
Publications: *Astronaut Fact Book*, NAS 1.74:
Johnson Space Center Annual Reports

1635. Kennedy Space Center
http://www.ksc.nasa.gov/
Sponsor: National Aeronautics and Space Administration (NASA) — Kennedy Space Center (KSC)
Description: KSC has primary responsibility for ground turnaround and support operations, prelaunch checkout, and launch of the space shuttle and its payloads, including elements for the International Space Station (ISS). The site features information on the center, detailed space shuttle information, payload information, and links to information on other launch vehicles. Primary sections include Visit KSC, Expendable Launch Vehicles, Space Shuttle, Space Station, Online Video Coverage, Business Opportunities, Spaceport Technology Center, and Education Resources.
Subjects: Space Shuttle; Space Stations; Rockets

1636. Kennedy Space Center Visitor Complex
http://www.kennedyspacecenter.com/
Sponsor: National Aeronautics and Space Administration (NASA) — Kennedy Space Center (KSC)
Description: This site offers an overview of the nation's only launch base for manned spacecraft. Designed for visitors and the general public, this site includes such sections as Tours and Exhibits, General Information, The Space Shop, Launch Control! Educator's Zone, Just for Kids, Press Room, and Space Links.
Subjects: Space Shuttle; Rockets

1637. Liftoff to Space Exploration
http://liftoff.msfc.nasa.gov/
Sponsor: National Aeronautics and Space Administration (NASA) — Marshall Space Flight Center (MSFC)
Description: With daily updates, NASA headlines, space history, and astronaut information, the Liftoff site provides an excellent overview of U.S. space program news and current missions, as well as the science behind it and space exploration history. The site offers the following sections: NASA Update, Spacecraft, Human Journey, The Universe, Fundamentals, and Tracking. Tracking offers an application for tracking current positions of the Hubble Telescope, the International Space Station, satellites, and the space shuttles. By entering one's zip code, it is possible to see on a map of the globe the position of these space vehicles.

Geared toward teenagers and adults, this site offers a substantial amount of news and background information for anyone interested in the space program and space sciences. NASA recommends NASA Kids for those who are younger than 13 years of age.
Subjects: Science Education; Space

1638. Lunar and Planetary Institute
http://www.lpi.usra.edu/
Sponsor: Lunar and Planetary Institute (LPI)
Description: Funded by NASA, the LPI is research institute that focuses on the current state, evolution, and formation of the solar system. The Web site features the links Education, Library, Publications, Research, and Workshops and Conferences. The Research page includes access to some detailed sources such as the 3-D Tour of the Solar System, Clementine Images of the Moon, Viking stereo images of Mars, and crater databases for Ganymede and Venus. The Publications page features slide sets, an online version of the *Lunar and Planetary Information Bulletin* and *Mercury Messenger*, and some educational products, abstracts, and reports. The Education section has a wealth of information on LPI public outreach, seminars, intern programs, curriculum materials, space science educational products and instruments, and imagery for exhibits.
Subjects: Educational Resources; Planetary Science
Publication: *Lunar and Planetary Information Bulletin*

1639. Mars Exploration
http://mars.jpl.nasa.gov/
Sponsor: National Aeronautics and Space Administration (NASA) — Jet Propulsion Laboratory (JPL)
Description: With detailed information on the various exploratory missions on Mars, this site features several main categories: Overview, Science, Technology, Missions, Newsroom, Classroom, Events, Gallery, and FunZone. It links to specific missions including 2001 Mars Odyssey, Mars Global Surveyor, and past missions, which include Mariner, Viking, Mars Observer, Mars Pathfinder, and Mars Polar Lander.

Written for the student or non-technical adult, this site offers a substantial collection of current information and imagery related to Mars as well as fun things to do for kids.
Subject: Mars

1640. Marshall Space Flight Center
http://www.msfc.nasa.gov/
Sponsor: National Aeronautics and Space Administration (NASA) — Marshall Space Flight Center (MSFC)
Description: Marshall's goals are to develop and maintain space transportation and propulsion systems, conduct microgravity research, and develop space optics manufacturing technology. Its Web site provides a broad range of technical and background information on the many projects, scientific disciplines, and specific space flight missions with which the center is involved. The Science and Space Projects pages give information on specific flights and ongoing research. Science also has a Spanish-language section, called Ciencia @ NASA. Other featured sections include Highway to Space, About Us, News Center, What We Do For You, and Education.
Subjects: Microgravity; Propulsion Technology; Space Technology

1641. Microgravity Research Program
http://microgravity.msfc.nasa.gov/
Sponsor: National Aeronautics and Space Administration (NASA) — Marshall Space Flight Center (MSFC)
Description: This site describes the Microgravity Research Program at NASA's Marshall Space Flight Center. The program studies the effects of low gravity (microgravity) on biological, chemical, and physical processes. The site explains current goals and activities in microgravity specialty areas such as biotechnology, combustion science, fluid physics, and materials science. A Space Product Development section focuses on practical applications in agribusiness, biotechnology, and materials development. For the novice, there is a section explaining microgravity. Other sections include Data Archives, Research Results, Missions, and Conferences.
Subject: Microgravity — Research

1642. NASA History
http://www.hq.nasa.gov/office/pao/History/index.html
Sponsor: National Aeronautics and Space Administration (NASA) — History Office

Description: The NASA History Program, dating back to 1959, documents and preserves the agency's history. The site includes a brief history of NASA—including that of its predecessor, NACA—and an extensive topical index to historical information distributed on the many NASA Web sites. Information on the program's print and online publications is located under About the NASA History Office. The What's New section highlights new print and online materials. The Topical Index this site provides is very helpful for tracking down historical information on NASA's many Web sites. The online publications provide direct access to some historical reference works otherwise not readily available.

Subjects: Space — History; Spacecraft — History
Publications: *Apollo by the Numbers: A Statistical Review*, NAS 1.21:
Skylab: A Chronology
The Apollo Spacecraft Chronology, Vol. I - IV
The Problem of Space Travel: The Rocket Motor, NAS 1.21:

1643. NASA Human Spaceflight
http://spaceflight.nasa.gov/
Sponsor: National Aeronautics and Space Administration (NASA)
Description: This is NASA's central site for information on the Space Shuttle, the Space Station, and other manned space flights. Featured sections include Space Shuttle, Space Station, Space News, Behind the Scenes, Realtime Data, Beyond, Gallery, History, and Outreach. The main page of the Beyond section features information about the exploration of Mars and the possibility of life on Mars as well as links to other sections that include Missions, Human Crew, Technology, Why Explore? and Science. The Realtime Data page offers SkyWatch, a program that allows the user to track the path of the space station for sightings in one's locale. The Outreach section leads to education-related information, from the high school level up to teacher or faculty programs. This site has a weath of information for anyone interested in human spaceflight.
Subjects: Space Shuttle; Space Stations; Spacecraft

1644. NASA Shuttle
http://spaceflight.nasa.gov/shuttle/
Sponsor: National Aeronautics and Space Administration (NASA) — Spaceflight Office
Description: The NASA shuttle site has information on all U.S. space shuttle flights from 1981 to the present. As of this writing, current information focuses on the catastrophic loss of the Space Shuttle Columbia and its crew.
   This site is well organized and the information content is current and available in various multimedia formats.
Subject: Space Shuttle

1645. NASA Tech Briefs
http://www.nasatech.com/
Sponsor: Associated Business Publications
Description: *NASA Tech Briefs* publishes information on any commercially significant technologies developed in the course of NASA research and development. The publication is a joint publishing venture of NASA and Associated Business Publications (ABP); this Web site is run by ABP. The site offers free downloadable Technical Support Packages, which provide in-depth information on the innovations described in the *NASA Tech Briefs*. Qualified individuals are eligible for a free U.S. subscription to *NASA Tech Briefs*. The site offers subscription request forms and renewal forms.
Subjects: Space Technology; Technology Transfer
Publication: *NAS 1.29/3-2: NASA Tech Briefs*

1646. National Aeronautics and Space Administration (NASA)
http://www.nasa.gov/
Sponsor: National Aeronautics and Space Administration (NASA)
Description: The central NASA Web server provides access to hundreds of NASA Web sites and general information on the agency itself. General categories on the front page include About NASA, News, Events, Multimedia, Missions, NASA Careers, and NASA TV. Feature stories on representative NASA projects are divided into sections titled Improve Life Here, Extend Life to There, and

Find Life Beyond. The site also has pointers to information for target audiences: kids, students, educators, and media. Major public reports can be found in the Media section. A drop-down menu at the bottom of the page provides links to NASA's divisions (strategic enterprises) and field centers. Strategic Enterprises include: Aerospace Technology, Biological and Physical Research; Earth Science; Human Exploration and Development of Space; and Space Science. A link at the top of the page leads to information on NASA Web sites that are available in Spanish language versions.
Subject: Space
Publications: *NASA Facts*, NAS 1.20:
NASA Strategic Plan, NAS 1.15:

1647. National Space Science Data Center
http://nssdc.gsfc.nasa.gov/
Sponsor: National Aeronautics and Space Administration (NASA) — Goddard Space Flight Center (GSFC)
Description: National Space Science Data Center serves as the permanent archive for data from NASA spaceflight missions. The data are intended for use by the professional scientific community. The General Public Page guides others to popular resources such as the Photo Gallery and Image Catalog.The data are related to the fields of astronomy and astrophysics, solar and space plasma physics, and planetary and lunar science. The site has an online Master Catalog of available data and resources. Some resources are available online; others must be ordered.
Subject: Space Sciences

1648. Office of Space Commercialization
http://www.ta.doc.gov/space/index.shtml
Sponsor: Commerce Department — Technology Administration (TA)
Description: The Commerce Department's Office of Space Commercialization promotes the competitiveness of the U.S. commercial space industry. OSC conducts policy development, market analysis, and outreach and education. The site features special sections on satellite navigation, satellite imaging, space transportation, satellite communications, and space transportation. Publications can be found in the Library section.
Subject: Space Technology

1649. Planetary Sciences at the NSSDC
http://nssdc.gsfc.nasa.gov/planetary/
Sponsor: National Aeronautics and Space Administration (NASA) — Goddard Space Flight Center (GSFC)
Description: The NSSDC is responsible for the collection and storage and distribution of planetary images and other data to scientists, educators, and the general public. This site offers a separate page for each planet as well as for the moon, asteroids, and comets. Each of these separate pages features fact sheets, images, a Frequently Asked Questions file, other resources, and information on spacecraft missions to that specific astral body. Other links connect to a variety of NSSDC data resources.

This site offers a substantial body of textual and pictorial information for all the planets in our solar system. Information is available at many levels, from the child to the research scientist. It is definitely worth a visit by anyone looking for basic information or images of the planets, the moon, asteroids, or comets.
Subjects: Planetary Science; Planets

1650. Project Galileo: Journey to Jupiter
http://galileo.jpl.nasa.gov/
Alternate URL: http://www.jpl.nasa.gov/galileo/indexold.html
Sponsor: National Aeronautics and Space Administration (NASA) — Jet Propulsion Laboratory (JPL)
Description: The Galileo site provides an extensive collection of information on the Galileo spacecraft and the planet Jupiter. The site includes current images and data from Jupiter, a brief introduction to the mission, and an online guide to Galileo's exploration of Jupiter. Available sections of the page include Jupiter, Moons, Images, Mission, Explorations, Education, and News. The About This Site link leads to the former Web page (see alternate URL above), which will serve as the Official Galileo Archives.

Much of the material is obviously aimed at students and teachers, although the site is equally useful for the general public.

Subjects: Jupiter; Spacecraft

1651. Radiometric Calibration and Development Facility

http://ssbuv.gsfc.nasa.gov/

Sponsor: National Aeronautics and Space Administration (NASA) — Goddard Space Flight Center (GSFC)

Description: This site describes the NASA facility for calibration, characterization, and development of new remote sensing instrumentation. A major section of the site is dedicated to the Shuttle Solar Backscatter Ultraviolet Project. Each specific shuttle mission that has had an ozone measurement component has a link to that project. The site also offers solar spectral irradiance plots. The flight results appear in its Publications section. Other sections include Ongoing Research, Planned Research, and Accomplishments.

Subject: Remote Sensing

1652. Space Calendar

http://www.jpl.nasa.gov/calendar/

Sponsor: National Aeronautics and Space Administration (NASA) — Jet Propulsion Laboratory (JPL)

Description: JPL's Space Calendar covers space-related activities and anniversaries for the coming year. Included are over 1,400 links to related Web pages. The Calendar includes historical events such as the launching of various spacecraft, conferences, current launch dates, and celestial events such as an eclipse or an asteroid near-Earth flyby. The site also offers calendar archives for 2000 through 2002.

This is an excellent resource for amateur astronomers and those interested in the history of space exploration.

Subject: Space — History

1653. Space Science

http://spacescience.nasa.gov/

Sponsor: National Aeronautics and Space Administration (NASA) — Space Science Office

Description: NASA's Space Science Enterprise is responsible for all of NASA's programs relating to astronomy, the solar system, the sun, and its interaction with Earth. Its site offers access to information via sections Images, Missions, Education, Administration, Committees, and Research Solicitations. The Administration section links to home pages for the themes under which the programs of the Office of Space Science are organized: Origins, Structure and Evolution of the Universe, Solar System Exploration, and Sun-Earth Connection. The Research Solicitations page includes access to the Space Science Research Announcement Email List, open solicitations, the Status of OSS Research Grants page, Online Space Science Mission Data, and a guidebook for proposal writing. The Publications link, under Administration, leads to the *NASA Strategic Plan*, *Space Science Enterprise Strategic Plan*, and other science policy documents. The Space Science Missions page has quick links to the home pages of roughly one hundred missions under four categories: Under Study, In Development, Operating, and Past Missions.

Subject: Space Sciences

Publications: *Announcement of Opportunities for Participation in . . . (series)*, NAS 1.53:
NASA Strategic Plan, NAS 1.15:

1654. Space Station Biological Research Project

http://brp.arc.nasa.gov/

Sponsor: National Aeronautics and Space Administration (NASA) — Ames Research Center (ARC)

Description: The Space Station Biological Research Project (SSBRP) is responsible for the facilities that will be used to conduct nonhuman life sciences research on board the International Space Station. The Web site describes the gravitational biology laboratory that is being planned for the space station and provides links to more information on some of the instrumentation and habitats planned for the SSBRP facilities.

Subjects: Biology — Research; Space Stations

1655. Space Telescope Science Institute

http://www.stsci.edu/resources/

Sponsor: Space Telescope Science Institute

Description: The Space Telescope Science Institute (STScI) is one of the astronomy centers operated by the Association of Universities for Research in Astronomy, Inc. (AURA) for NASA. It is responsible for the scientific operation of the Hubble Space Telescope and will also be supporting the Next Generation Space Telescope (NGST) for NASA. The site includes pictures, press releases, educational activities, HST observations, HST instrumentation, and a data archives. The main categories include Science Initiatives, Catalogs and Surveys, Publications, Software, Hardware, Picture Gallery, and Educational Acitivites. Home page links under Astronomy Resources include the Digitized Sky Survey and Visual Target Turner.

Subjects: Astronomy; Telescopes

1656. Welcome to the Planets

http://pds.jpl.nasa.gov/planets/

Sponsor: National Aeronautics and Space Administration (NASA) — Jet Propulsion Laboratory (JPL)

Description: This is a collection of many of the best images from NASA's planetary exploration program. The collection has been extracted from the interactive CD-ROM *Welcome to the Planets*. The basic organization of the site presents links to each of the planets and several small bodies in our solar system and to each of the explorers or instruments (satellites, Hubble Space Telescope, or shuttle) that took the pictures. Each link leads to a series of photos of the planet, spatial body, or explorer. Each photo of the planet leads to an explanation of the photo, including a Real Audio caption, as well as linking to a profile of the planet. Similarly, each photo of the explorer has an explanation of the explorer with a Real Audio caption. There are links to information about ordering the CD-ROM and a glossary as well.

This is an excellent site for anyone seeking background information and images of the planets. (The site notes that this collection of images replaces the former online version of Welcome to the Planets.)

Subject: Planets

Publication: *Welcome to the Planets*, NAS 1.86:P 69/CD

CHAPTER 14
Social Services

The federal government sometimes uses the Web to reach its consumers—citizens, businesses, and state and local government—directly. Sites like DisasterHelp and GovBenefits, both described in this chapter, demonstrate that approach. Other sites in this chapter take the traditional approach of describing their agency and its activities. Those activities include developing programs and policies in areas such as housing, community development, volunteer services, welfare, and employment for recipients such as veterans, children, and the elderly.

Bookmarks & Favorites

Sites for Service Consumers
- DisasterHelp, http://www.disasterhelp.gov
- GovBenefits.gov, http://www.govbenefits.gov
- Medicare, http://www.medicare.gov

Federal Assistance
- Catalog of Federal Domestic Assistance, http://www.cfda.gov

Major Agencies
- Health and Human Services Department, http://www.hhs.gov
  - Administration for Children and Families, http://www.acf.dhhs.gov
  - Centers for Medicare and Medicaid Services, http://cms.hhs.gov
- Housing and Urban Development Department, http://www.hud.gov
- Social Security Agency, http://www.ssa.gov
- USA Freedom Corps, http://www.usafreedomcorps.gov
- USDA Food and Nutrition Service, http://www.fns.usda.gov/fns/
- USDA Rural Development, http://www.rurdev.usda.gov
- Veterans Affairs Department, http://www.va.gov

Featured Site

1657. Catalog of Federal Domestic Assistance (CFDA)
http://www.cfda.gov/

Sponsor: General Services Administration — Office of Governmentwide Policy (OGP)

Description: The Web version of the classic print document, *Catalog of Federal Domestic Assistance* (CFDA), is a searchable version of the catalog with additional information and links. The CFDA describes a broad range of federal assistance programs, including formula-based grants, guaranteed loans, insurance, counseling, training, information services, and donation of goods. Most of the programs are not for direct assistance to individuals, but rather for state and local governments or other organizations who administer distribution of the aid. Catalog entries include a program identifier number, description, eligibility requirements, program contact information, and details on the application and awards process.Searching is available by program number and by keyword. Browse capabilities are available by the following categories: Functional Area, Agency, Sub-Agency, Program Title, Applicant Eligibility, Beneficiary, Program Deadline, and Type of Assistance. The full text of the CFDA can be browsed by chapter. The CFDA Web site also has information on using the catalog, applying for assistance, and writing grant proposals.

This resource is highly recommended for governments and others researching federal assistance programs. The online CFDA has content and features for both new and advanced users. (New users in particular should study the sections explaining what is and is not included in the CFDA.) The

site takes advantage of Web technology by providing value-added features such as a list of the top ten catalog programs as measured by number of hits received on those catalog entries.
Subjects: Government Loans; Grants
Publication: *Catalog of Federal Domestic Assistance*, PrEx 2.20:

The social services resources in this chapter are divided into four sections, spanning the entry numbers indicated here:

General	*1658–1685*
Housing and Community Development	*1686–1699*
Welfare and Benefits	*1700–1713*
Workers	*1714–1721*

General

1658. Access Board: A Federal Agency Committed to Accessible Design
http://www.access-board.gov/
Sponsor: Access Board
Description: The U.S. Access Board, also known as the Architectural and Transportation Barriers Compliance Board, is an independent federal agency whose mission is to promote accessibility for people with disabilities. Its Web site features the sections About the Board, Accessibility Guidelines and Standards, Enforcement, Publications, and Technical Assistance, Training, and Research. The Guidelines section includes online versions of *ADA Accessibility Guidelines (ADAAG) for Buildings and Facilities* as well as *Electronic and Information Technology Accessibility Standards (Section 508)* and other guidelines. The About the Board section includes the newsletter *Access Currents* and information on relevant laws and policies. The Publications section has the full text of publications organized under topics including facilities, public rights-of-way, transportation, and communication.
Subject: Americans with Disabilities Act (ADA)
Publications: *Access Currents*, Y 3.B 27:16
ADA Accessibility Guidelines for Buildings and Facilities (ADAAG), Y 3.B 27:8 AM

1659. Afterschool.gov
http://www.afterschool.gov/
Sponsor: General Services Administration
Description: This site is designed to connect visitors to federal resources in support of children and youth during after-school hours. Major sections include Running a Program, Planning Activities, Keeping Current, Community Links, and Sites for Kids and Teens. Running a Program covers how to get funding, safety issues, special needs, and state regulations, among other topics. The Keeping Current section includes collections of links to clearinghouses, newsletters, and research reports. Many of the Web resources to which the site refers are sponsored by non-governmental organization.
Subject: Child Care

1660. AmeriCorps
http://www.americorps.org/
Sponsor: Corporation for National and Community Service — Americorps
Description: Americorps, a program of the Corporation for National and Community Service, maintains this site with information about their projects and available resources. Under Who We Are, the site describes AmeriCorps*VISTA (Volunteers in Service to America) and AmeriCorps*NCCC (National Civilian Community Corps). The site also has news of funding opportunities and Americorps grant applications. A link to Join Americorps, the program's recruiting site, leads to information for prospective volunteers.
Subject: Volunteerism

1661. Bureau of Indian Affairs
http://www.doi.gov/bureau-indian-affairs.html
Sponsor: Interior Department — Bureau of Indian Affairs (BIA)
Description: The BIA site features a variety of descriptive information on the agency and its functions and services. A Hot Issues section lists current issues, major reports, and topics of interest. Other featured sections include Budget, News, Tribal Leaders Directory, List of Federally Recognized Tribes, History, Self-Governance, Tribal Services, Statistics, Tracing Your Indian Ancestry, and Indian Education Programs.
Subject: American Indians

1662. Center for Nutrition Policy and Promotion
http://www.usda.gov/cnpp/
Sponsor: Agriculture Department (USDA) — Center for Nutrition Policy and Promotion (CNPP)
Description: The Center for Nutrition Policy and Promotion is the focal point within USDA for scientific research linked with the nutritional needs of the public. Its site offers About CNPP, How to Get Information from CNPP, *Nutrition Insights*, *Dietary Guidelines for Americans*, Food Guide Pyramid, *Nutrient Content of the U.S. Food Supply*, and *Cost of Food at Home*.
Subjects: Dietary Guidelines; Nutrition
Publications: *Cost of Food at Home Estimated for Food Plans at Four Cost Levels*, A 98.19/2:
Expenditures on Children by Families: Annual Report, A 1.38:
Family Economics and Nutrition Review, A 98.20:
Nutrition and Your Health: Dietary Guidelines for Americans, A 1.77:232/

1663. Citizen Corps
http://www.citizencorps.gov
Sponsor: USA Freedom Corps
Description: A part of the USA Freedom Corps, Citizen Corps was announced by President Bush in January 2002 with the goal of supporting community efforts to counter crime, terrorism, or other threats. This Web site describes the major programs it supports: Neighborhood Watch; CERT (Community Emergency Response Teams); and VIPs (Volunteers in Police Service); and Medical Reserve Corps. There is also a PDF copy of *The Citizens' Preparedness Guidebook*, produced by the National Crime Prevention Council with support from the Department of Justice.
Subject: Volunteerism
Publication: *United for a Stronger America: Citizens' Preparedness Guide*, J 26.8:

1664. Code Talk
http://www.codetalk.fed.us/
Sponsor: Housing and Urban Development (HUD) — Office of Native American Programs (ONAP)
Description: Code Talk was established to deliver electronic information from government agencies and other organizations to Native American communities. The name is based on the Native American Code Talkers, heroes of the two World Wars. It has links to such sections as Current Issues, Key Topic Areas, Resources and Tools, About Code Talk, American Indian/Alaskan Native Links, and Federal Offices.
Subject: American Indians

1665. Consumer Product Safety Commission
http://cpsc.gov/
Sponsor: Consumer Product Safety Commission (CPSC)
Description: The Consumer Product Safety Commission develops and enforces standards to reduce the risk of injury or death from consumer products. The CPSC Web site includes the sections About Us/Vacancies, Business, Consumer and Spanish-language materials, 4 Kids, Recalls/News, Library/FOIA, What's New/Calendar, and Pressroom. The Report Unsafe Products area allows users to make their own reports of problem products. The Recall section has product recall announcements organized by date, category, and company. The Library section includes access to full-text publications including, in PDF format, the *Consumer Product Safety Review* and the *Annual Report to Congress*, dating from 1990.

This is a useful site for consumers, both for reporting defective consumer products, and for seeing what products have been recalled.
Subjects: Product Recalls; Product Safety
Publications: *Annual Report*, Y 3.C 76/3:1
Consumer Product Safety Review (quarterly), Y 3.C 76/3:28
CPSC Public Calendar, Y 3.C 76/3:26

1666. Corporation for National and Community Service
http://www.cns.gov/
Sponsor: Corporation for National and Community Service
Description: The Corporation for National and Community Service manages three major programs: AmeriCorps, Learn and Serve America, and the National Senior Service Corps. (These entities are described separately in this directory.) It is a federal corporation governed by a Board of Directors. The CNCS Web site has prominent links to the Web sites for its programs and how to volunteer. The About Us section has information on staff and organizational structure, a narrative of the organization's legislative history, its annual report to Congress, a historical timeline of U.S. national service efforts, fact sheets, and the newsletter *National Service News*. Other sections cover grants and funding, jobs and internships, and profiles of service efforts in each state.
Subject: Volunteerism
Publications: *National Service News*, Y 3.N 21/29:16
Senior Corps Update, Y 3.N 21/29:15

1667. CYFERNet: Child, Youth, and Families Education and Research Network
http://www.cyfernet.org/
Sponsor: Agriculture Department (USDA) — Cooperative State Research, Education, and Extension Service (CSREES)
Description: The Child, Youth, and Family Education and Research Network (CYFERNet) is a resource directory for community-based education programs for children, youth, parents, and family. The site offers sections divided by research subject: Early Childhood, School Age, Teens, Parents and Family, and Community. The site also offers sections based on tools: Community Project Profiles, Professionals Database, Evaluation, Program Support, and Technology.
Subjects: Children — Research; Families — Research

1668. Department of Veterans Affairs
http://www.va.gov/
Sponsor: Veterans Affairs Department
Description: The VA Web site features a variety of sections useful to veterans and those helping veterans claim benefits. The principal categories include Health Benefits and Service, Education Benefits, Compensation and Pension Benefits, Vocational Rehabilitation and Employment Services, Burial and Memorial Benefits, and Life Insurance Program. Each leads to detailed program and resource information, and many of the sections include online application or service forms. Other sections include Hot Topics, About VA, and Veteran Data.

This should prove useful to veterans and anyone involved in assisting veterans. Using the site map should help to uncover all information available here.
Subject: Veterans
Publications: *Annual Report, Veterans Health Administration, Office of Research and Development*, VA 1.1/6:
Board of Veterans' Appeals Decisions, VA 1.95/2:
CIO Information In The News, VA 1.103:
Geographic Distribution of VA Expenditures, State County, and Congressional District, VA 1.2/11:
Gulf War Review, VA 1.104:
Journal of Rehabilitation Research and Development, VA 1.23/3:
Rehabilitation R&D Progress Reports, VA 1.23/3-2:
Summary of Medical Programs, VA 1.43/5:
VA Handbooks, VA 1.18:
VHA Highlights, VA 1.101:

1669. DisabilityInfo.gov

http://www.disabilityinfo.gov/

Sponsor: White House

Description: Launched by the Bush administration in 2002, DisabilityInfo.gov is designed to be a portal to federal Web sites and programs of concern to persons with disabilities. The site is divided into topical sections: Employment, Education, Housing, Transportation, Health, Income Support, Technology, Community Life, and Civil Rights.

Subject: Disabilities

1670. DisasterHelp

http://www.disasterhelp.gov

Sponsor: Federal Emergency Management Agency (FEMA)

Description: DisasterHelp is an interagency portal to federal government and other information about responding to disasters and emergencies. It is meant to help both the general public and first responders such as local police, fire, and rescue squads. Disaster subject channels include: Hurricane, Fire, Hazmat, Earthquake, Flood, Tornado, Anti-Terror, and Disease. Other sections link to information arranged by Federal Emergency Management Agency region and by first responder community, such as emergency managers or emergency medical technicians.

Subject: Disaster Assistance

1671. Family and Youth Services Bureau (FYSB)

http://www.acf.dhhs.gov/programs/fysb/

Sponsor: Health and Human Services Department — Administration for Children and Families (ACF) — Family and Youth Services Bureau (FYSB)

Description: The Family and Youth Services Bureau (FYSB) provides runaway and homeless youth service grants to local communities, and funds research and demonstration projects. FYSB disseminates information for parents, young people and students, youth service professionals, and policymakers through its National Clearinghouse on Families & Youth and National Runaway Switchboard, which are accessible from this site. Featured sections include Grant Programs, Funding Announcements, Research and Demonstration Projects, and Network of Support.

Subjects: Adolescents; Social Services — Grants

Publication: *Toward a Blueprint for Youth: Making Positive Youth Development a National Priority*

1672. Famine Early Warning System Network (FEWS NET)

http://www.fews.net/

Alternate URL: http://www.fews.org/

Sponsor: Agency for International Development (USAID)

Description: FEWS Net offers monthly and special reports on crops, food prices, and country updates related to possible famines in Africa. FEWS Net is funded by the U.S. Agency for International Development, but is implemented through a partnership with other federal agencies and regional organizations in Africa. The home page features timely status reports on famine emergencies and links to drought information by region and country. Other sections offer more in-depth analysis regarding markets, risks, and specific natural hazards and health threats.

In July 2000, FEWS became FEWS NET (Famine Early Warning System Network). Although no new material after June 2000 is posted at the alternate URL listed above, the site will be maintained to provide access to historical information. Additional reports produced by the predecessor program are available in English and French at the archived site.

Subjects: Famine; Africa

Publications: *FEWS (Famine Early Warning System) Bulletin*, S 18.68:
FEWS (Famine Early Warning System) Special Report, S 18.68/2:

1673. FirstGov for Seniors

http://www.seniors.gov/

Sponsor: Social Security Administration (SSA)

Description: The mission of FirstGov for Seniors is to provide one comprehensive Web site where seniors can go to find health and security information and services. This site features current news items alongside four main categories: Departments, Federal Portals, Federal Agencies, and State

Web sites. Under Departments, there is topical access to such sections as Health, Consumer Protection, Education and Training, Work and Volunteer, Services, Tax Assistance, Travel and Leisure, Legislation, and Seniors and Computers. Under each section, there are further links to subject-related information and links to other federal and state government Web sites related to the subject.
Subject: Senior Citizens

1674. Food and Nutrition Service
http://www.fns.usda.gov/fns/
Description: This FNS site features information on its services such as the Women, Infants, and Children (WIC) and food stamps programs. Its main sections include Food Stamps, Food Distribution, Child Nutrition (including school lunch programs), WIC Program/Farmers' Market, Team Nutrition, and Food Distribution. Each section provides basic information on the program including information on applying, hotline numbers, links to other relevant USDA sites, and basic fact sheets. A Program Data section has statistics on the major FNS programs, such as the number of meals served in the National School Lunch Program or the average monthly benefit per person in the Food Stamp Program. The Public and Media Information includes press releases, publications, speeches, and other documents.
Subjects: Food Stamps; Nutrition; School Meal Programs
Publication: *WIC Program and Participants Characteristics*, A 98.17:

1675. GovBenefits
http://www.govbenefits.gov
Sponsor: Labor Department
Description: Through a series of screening questions, the GovBenefits site helps citizens find information on government benefits programs for which the may be eligible. The site provides descriptions and contact information for programs matching the criteria established through the screening questions. The site does not ask for the user's name, Social Security Number, or other identifiers. Individuals should use the provided contacts to determine their eligibility for specific benefits. GovBenefits is maintained through a partnership of many federal agencies, though the Labor Department has been the lead partner.
Subject: Social Welfare

1676. Inter-American Foundation
http://www.iaf.gov/
Description: The Inter-American Foundation is an independent agency providing assistance to Latin America and the Caribbean by awarding grants directly to local organizations throughout the region. Its Web site features the sections About IAF, News and Events, Grants, Fellowships, and Publications. The Publications page links to some annual reports and *Grassroots Development*, the journal of the IAF. The site also offers links to Spanish and Portuguese versions of its Web pages.
Subjects: Foreign Assistance; South America
Publications: *Grassroots Development*, Y 3.IN 8/25:15
Inter-American Foundation (annual), Y 3.IN 8/25:
Inter-American Foundation, In Review, Y 3.IN 8/25:1

1677. National Network for Child Care
http://www.nncc.org/
Sponsor: Agriculture Department (USDA) — Cooperative State Research, Education, and Extension Service (CSREES)
Description: The National Network for Child Care is an Internet resource developed through the Cooperative Extension Service and landgrant universities. It includes links to articles, report, and Web sites on the topic of child care and development. The site also hosts an email forum, KIDCARE; users can subscribe via the Web form on the site. A series of *Connections* newsletters is online, including *Family Child Care Connections*, *Child Care Center Connections*, and *School-Age Connections*.
Subject: Child Care

1678. Office of Community Development
http://www.rurdev.usda.gov/ocd/
Sponsor: Agriculture Department (USDA) — Rural Development
Description: The Office of Community Development is a part of the U.S. Department of Agriculture's Rural Development program. OCD operates special community development initiatives and provides technical support to USDA-Rural Development's community development staff in offices throughout the United States.

  Although this site is of most interest to USDA employees, for the public it serves as a gateway to other rural development initiatives, including the Rural Economic Area Partnership.
Subject: Rural Development

1679. Office of Population Affairs
http://opa.osophs.dhhs.gov/
Sponsor: Health and Human Services Department — Public Health and Science Office — Population Affairs Office
Description: The Office of Population Affairs operates programs concerned with reproductive health, family planning, and adolescent pregnancy. Their Web site offers the following sections: Grants, Office of Family Planning, Office of Adolescent Pregnancy Programs, Publications, Data and Statistics, and Legislation. The Data and Statistics page provides convenient access to relevant statistics from various federal agencies. The Legislation section has the full text of the statutes and regulations under which OPA operates.
Subjects: Family Planning; Reproductive Health

1680. Partnerships Against Violence Network—PAVNET Online
http://www.pavnet.org/
Sponsor: Agriculture Department (USDA) — National Agricultural Library (NAL)
Description: The Partnerships Against Violence Network (PAVNET) Online brings together information on violence prevention programs, funding sources, and technical assistance from seven different federal agencies. The Web site features sections entitled Research Database, Programs, Funding, Pavnet Mailgroup, and Other Resources. Research Database has records describing federally-funded research on violence. The Programs section includes links to violence prevention programs, and also to curricula and teaching materials, and available technical assistance. Interested users can subscribe to the Pavnet anti-violence email forum using a Web form on the site.
Subjects: Crime; Victims of Crime

1681. Senior Corps
http://www.seniorcorps.org/
Sponsor: Corporation for National and Community Service — Senior Corps
Description: Senior Corps is a program of the Corporation for National and Community Service involving volunteers ages 55 and older. The Web site describes its major projects: Foster Grandparents, Retired and Senior Volunteer Program (RSVP), and Senior Companion Volunteer Program. The Senior Corps in Your State section describes Corps activities in each state. The site includes a grant application, history of the Senior Corps program, and information for prospective volunteers.
Subjects: Senior Citizens; Volunteerism

1682. Social Security Death Index
http://www.ancestry.com/search/rectype/vital/ssdi/main.htm
Alternate URL: http://www.ntis.gov/products/pages/ssa-death-master.asp
Sponsors: Ancestry.com; Commerce Department — Technology Administration (TA) — National Technical Information Service (NTIS)
Description: Made available by a commercial genealogical publishing company, the Social Security Death Index is searchable by name, Social Security number, birth, death, and last residence information. Records include the individual's birth date, death date, Social Security number, and last residence. The database contains the records of deceased persons who possessed Social Security numbers and whose death had been reported to the Social Security Administration.

  The alternate URL from the federal government's National Technical Information Service

describes the file, its contents, and its uses in more detail. It also offers a for-fee subscription version of the database, with weekly or monthly updates.
Subjects: Genealogy; Social Security; Databases

1683. USA Freedom Corps
http://www.usafreedomcorps.gov
Sponsor: USA Freedom Corps
Description: The USA Freedom Corps is a presidential initiative proposed in the wake of the September 11, 2001, terrorist attacks. Its goal is to encourage and support volunteerism and national service. The For Volunteers section of the site has information on finding volunteer opportunities, creating a record of service, and available scholarships, awards, and fellowships. The For Organizations section has information tailored to schools and educators, non-profits, and businesses. Interested users can also sign up to receive a monthly email newsletter called *Network of Service*.
Subject: Volunteerism

1684. Violence Against Women Office
http://www.ojp.usdoj.gov/vawo/
Sponsor: Justice Department — Justice Programs Office
Description: Established as a source for assistance to women victims of violence, this site includes a variety of sections such as State-by-State Grant Activities, Information About Sexual Assault, What Communities Can Do, and Federal Violence-Against-Women Laws and Regulations. The site brings together links to Justice Department publications and statistics on the topic, and also links to each state agency that administers the office's formula grants.
Subject: Victims of Crime
Publications: *Laws*, J 35.5:
Press Releases, J 35.7:
Violence Against Women Act News, J 35.20:

1685. Women's Bureau
http://www.dol.gov/wb/welcome.html
Sponsor: Labor Department — Women's Bureau
Description: The Labor Department's Women's Bureau features news of its initiatives on its Web site. Current programs include Women in High Tech Jobs, Women in Apprenticeship and Nontraditional Occupations Act, and On-line Distance Learning. Its Publication section has fact sheets and reports, and the Statistics section has data on the leading occupations of employed women with comparisons to men's employment and pay in those occupations.
Subjects: Occupations — Statistics; Women — Policy
Publication: *Facts on Working Women*, L 36.114/3:

Housing and Community Development

1686. Appalachian Regional Commission
http://www.arc.gov/
Sponsor: Appalachian Regional Commission (ARC)
Description: The Appalachian Regional Commission supports economic and social development in the Appalachian region. The site features About ARC, Appalachian Regions, News and Events, *Appalachia Magazine*, and Online Resource Center sections. Appalachia is defined as the region following the spine of the Appalachian Mountains from southern New York to northern Mississippi, including all of West Virginia and parts of 12 other states: Alabama, Georgia, Kentucky, Maryland, Mississippi, New York, North Carolina, Ohio, Pennsylvania, South Carolina, Tennessee, and Virginia. The site's On-line Resource Center highlights resources for community planning, funding, and regional data and research.
Subject: Rural Development

Publications: *Annual Report, Appalachian Regional Commission*, Y 3.AP 4/2:1/
Appalachia Magazine, Y 3.AP 4/2:9-2/

1687. Community Connections Information Center
http://www.comcon.org/
Sponsor: Housing and Urban Development (HUD) — Community Planning and Development Office
Description: The Community Connections clearinghouse is the information center for HUD's Office of Community Planning and Development (CPD). This site serves state and local agencies, nonprofit organizations, public interest groups, and others interested in housing and community development. The site features sections such as About Community Connections, What's New, Publications, CPD/HUD Programs and Initiatives, and Resources (Funding and Assistance). The Publications section includes a list of publications that can be requested, and an archive of weekly fax broadcasts.
Subject: Community Development

1688. Federal Housing Finance Board
http://www.fhfb.gov/
Sponsor: Federal Housing Finance Board
Description: The Federal Housing Finance Board regulates the 12 Federal Home Loan Banks that improve the supply of funds to local lenders that finance loans for home mortgages. This site features background information on the Federal Housing Finance Board, the system and its programs, and it links to each of the regional Federal Home Loan Banks. Major programs include the Affordable Housing Program and the Community Investment Program. The Monthly Interest Rate Survey press release is online along with summary tables downloadable in the Excel spreadsheet format. The same information is available for the Adjustable Rate Mortgage Index. In the Press and Reading Room section, there is an index to articles in the Finance Board's publication, *Building Blocks*.
Subject: Home Mortgages
Publication: *Monthly Interest Rate Survey and Annual Summary*, FHF 1.15:

1689. Ginnie Mae
http://www.ginniemae.gov/
Sponsor: Housing and Urban Development (HUD) — Government National Mortgage Association (Ginnie Mae)
Description: Ginnie Mae, a wholly owned government corporation within HUD, aims to help provide affordable, government-insured mortgages to American families. Its Web site includes sections for investors, homeowners, mortgage-backed securities, issuers, and information about Ginnie Mae. Full-text issues of *All Participants Memoranda* and its annual reports are available online.
Subject: Housing Finance
Publications: *All Participants Memoranda (Ginnie Mae)*, HH 1.37/4:
Annual Report, Government National Mortgage Association, HH 1.37:
Mortgage-Backed Securities Handbook, HH 1.6/6:

1690. Housing and Urban Development — Homes and Community
http://www.hud.gov/
Sponsor: Housing and Urban Development (HUD)
Description: The HUD Web site describes the agency's programs in housing and community development. The site offers the following sections among others: HUD News; Homes: Buying, Selling, Renting, Improvements, Foreclosure, Homeless, Fair Housing, HUD Homes, FHA Refund, and Foreclosures; Communities; Working with HUD; Resources; and Tools. The Working With HUD page has sections for funding, contracting opportunities with HUD, links to local information, and information about HUD. Under Resources, an online library has a directory of HUD directives and policies and is organized into bookshelves on subjects such as Freedom of Information Act, fair housing, congressional activity, legal information, and funding. The Tools section lists over 25 HUD email lists for interested users. These cover general and very specific topics, such as news from the Office of Affordable Housing, public and Indian housing, U.S. border issues, and state-based news. The site also offers information by audience type under the Section Just for You. The long list includes first-time Homebuyers, Senior Citizens, Veterans, People With Disabilities,

Farmworkers/colonias, Native Americans, Students, Researchers, Lenders, Brokers, Appraisers, Small Businesses, and Grantees/Nonprofits.

Well designed, this site offers a great deal of information useful for consumers and for businesses. Multiple access points are provided, making it an easy site to navigate. See also the HUD User site for additional HUD documents.

Subjects: Community Development; Housing
Publications: *HOMEfires: Policy Newsletter of the HOME Investment Partnerships Program*, HH 1.114/3:
Legal Opinions of the Office of General Counsel (annual), HH 1.86:
News Releases, HH 1.99/6:

1691. HUD User
`http://www.huduser.org/`
Sponsor: Housing and Urban Development (HUD) — Policy Development and Research Office
Description: HUD User is the primary source for Federal Government reports and information on housing policy and programs, building technology, economic development, urban planning, and other housing-related topics. The main sections include About HUD User, Publications, Periodicals, Data Sets, Bibliographic Database, Order Online, Ongoing Research, and Community Builders. There are several online full text publications available under Publications. The HUD User Bibliographic Database offers access to bibliographic information on thousands of reports, articles, case studies, and other research literature on topics related to housing and community development. The Data section includes the original electronic data sets for *American Housing Survey* and from other housing research initiatives.
Subjects: Community Development — Research; Housing — Research; Databases
Publications: *Annual Adjustment Factors*, HH 1.34:
Cityscape—A Journal of Policy Development and Research, HH 1.75/2:
FieldWorks: Ideas Housing and Community Development, HH 1.75/3:
Guide to PD&R Data Sets
Income Limits and Section 8 Fair Market Rents, HH 1.126:
Recent Research Results, HH 1.84:
State of the Cities, HH 1.2:C 49/13/
U.S. Housing Market Conditions (quarterly), HH 1.120/2:
Urban Research Monitor, HH 1.23/8:

1692. HUD's Client Information and Policy System
`http://www.hudclips.org/`
Sponsor: Housing and Urban Development (HUD)
Description: HUDCLIPS (HUD Client Information and Policy System) is a searchable online database containing the entire inventory of official HUD policies, procedures, announcements, forms, and other materials. The Short Cuts section provides links to frequently requested documents. The Forms area features official forms in PDF and Microsoft Excel and Word template formats. The Library provides searchable and browsable access to the following databases: Federal Register, Codes, Laws, Congressional Record, Guidebooks, Handbooks and Notices, Letters, Inspector General, Veterans Affairs, Travel Regulations, Housing Waivers, and Legal Opinions.
Subjects: Housing; Publication Catalogs

1693. National Rural Development Partnership
`http://www.rurdev.usda.gov/nrdp/`
Sponsor: Agriculture Department (USDA) — Rural Business-Cooperative Service (RBS)
Description: The National Rural Development Partnership promotes rural development though partnerships with local, state, tribal, and federal governments, as well as for-profit and non-profit organizations. This site features information about the NRDP and its accomplishments. It also has links to state and national partners, information on conferences, NRDP News, and connections to other rural development sites. The site also provides information on a number of email discussion lists concerning aspects of rural development.
Subject: Rural Development

1694. Neighborhood Networks

http://www.hud.gov/nnw/nnwindex.html

Sponsor: Housing and Urban Development (HUD)

Description: Neighborhood Networks works to enhance the self-sufficiency, employability, and economic self-reliance of low-income families and the elderly living in HUD properties by providing residents with onsite access to computer and training resources at Community Technology Centers. Major sections of the site include About Neighborhood Networks, Find A Center, Start a New Center, Resources for Centers, News Room, Residents' Corner, and Success Stories. Under the Resources for Centers page, the Publications area includes fact sheets, guides, *Neighborhood Networks Newsline*, technical information, partnership reports, all in PDF format, and other multimedia materials. The site also includes a call for volunteers to participate in the Neighborhood Networks program.

Subject: Computer Literacy

Publications: *Neighborhood Networks Fact Sheet*, HH 13.16/5:

Neighborhood Networks Newsline, HH 13.16/2:

1695. Office of Housing

http://www.hud.gov/fha/fhahome.html

Sponsor: Housing and Urban Development (HUD)

Description: HUD's Office of Housing (formerly FHA) Web site features the About Housing, Single Family, Hospitals, Multifamily, Online Forums, and Reading Room. The Reading Room includes homebuying publications in Spanish, new HUD mortgagee letters, HUD handbooks, housing and mortgage glossaries, and a selection of other reports and data.

Subjects: Home Mortgages; Housing Finance

Publications: *FHA Outlook*

Housing Today, HH 1.128:

Mortgagee Letters, HH 2.6/4:

1696. Office of University Partnerships

http://www.oup.org/

Sponsor: Housing and Urban Development (HUD)

Description: This Office functions as a national clearinghouse for disseminating information about HUD's Community Outreach Partnership Centers Program. HUD established the Office of University Partnerships in 1994 to encourage university-community partnerships. Its Web site features sections About OUP, Funding, Research and Publications, Technical Assistance, and Outreach. The About OUP and Funding sections describe the eight grant programs run by OUP. The Research and Publications area includes grantee reports, literature on university-community partnerships, and OUP Publications and Research.

Subject: Community Development — Grants

1697. Rural Business-Cooperative Service

http://www.rurdev.usda.gov/rbs/

Sponsor: Agriculture Department (USDA) — Rural Business-Cooperative Service (RBS)

Description: The Rural Business-Cooperative Service (RBS) supports businesses and cooperatives in rural areas through funding and technical assistance. The site offers links to information on the service under headings such as Discover RBS, Business Programs, and Cooperative Programs. Publications are available under Library of Publications, which includes links to the magazine, *Rural Cooperatives,* and various report series: *Cooperative Information Reports*, Research Reports, Service Reports, and other miscellaneous reports.

The site provides an excellent starting point for finding information on the service and its programs. It will be of most interest to businesses and rural community leaders.

Subject: Rural Development

Publication: *Rural Cooperatives*, A 109.11:

1698. Rural Development Online
http://www.rurdev.usda.gov/
Sponsor: Agriculture Department (USDA)
Description: Rural Development is within the U.S. Department of Agriculture and administers Rural Business-Cooperative Service, Rural Housing Service, Rural Utilities Service, and Office of Community Development programs. The agency's Web site provides access to the USDA's rural development agencies. The site features sections such as About Us, Business and Cooperative, Housing and Community Facilities, Utilities, Community Development/Empowerment. The Publications section includes full-text documents in PDF, HTML, or Word formats for rural development fact sheets, regulations, strategic plans, and publications in the major categories listed above and includes a section highlighting Spanish-language publications.
Subject: Rural Development

1699. Rural Housing Service
http://www.rurdev.usda.gov/rhs/
Sponsor: Agriculture Department (USDA) — Rural Housing Service
Description: This site provides information about the agency and provides links to some of its programs areas. Featured sections include Administrator's Corner, Nonprofit Opportunities, Public Bodies Opportunities, Lender Opportunities, Developer Opportunities, Individual and Family Opportunities, Regulations, and Information for Existing Borrowers.
Subjects: Housing; Rural Development

Welfare and Benefits

1700. Administration for Children and Families
http://www.acf.dhhs.gov/
Sponsor: Health and Human Services Department — Administration for Children and Families (ACF)
Description: "The Administration for Children and Families (ACF) is a federal agency funding state, local, and tribal organizations to provide family assistance (welfare), child support, child care, Head Start, child welfare, and other programs relating to children and families." (from the Web site, 1-14-2003) Major sections of the ACF Web site are About ACF, Programs, Contacts, Grants and Contracts, State and Local, Research and Publications, and Budget and Policy. ACF oversees more than 60 programs; the Programs page provides links to these by topic, such as adoption, foster care, child support, health, and welfare and low-income assistance. The Research and Publications section includes topical ACF publications as well as statistics on ACF programs. The Budget and Policy section links to legislative and budget offices at ACF, and to policy documents from individual ACF programs.
Subjects: Child Welfare; Early Childhood Education; Families; Welfare
Publications: *ACF Directory of Program Services*
ACF News
Annual Report, HE 24.1:
Child Maltreatment: Reports from the States to the National Child Abuse and Neglect Data System, HE 23.1018:
Child Support Report, HE 24.9:
OSCE-AT (series), HE 24.14:
OSCE-IM (series), HE 24.15:

1701. Centers for Medicare and Medicaid Services
http://cms.hhs.gov/
Description: The Centers for Medicare & Medicaid Services (CMS) runs the Medicare and Medicare programs and, in cooperation with the Health Resources and Services Administration, also runs the State Children's Health Insurance Program (SCHIP). CMS was formerly known as the Health Care Financing Administration (HCFA). The CMS Web site has information on the programs it administers, which also include the Health Insurance Portability and Accountability Act (portions) and the Clinical Laboratory Improvement Amendments. The site features a section for information tailored

to consumers, and another tailored to the health professionals and state and tribal governments dealing with CMS programs. The Public Affairs section has press releases, fact sheets, and CMS congressional testimony. A resources section has a CMS glossary and acronym dictionary, the Quarterly Provider Update, program manuals, and forms.

Subjects: Health Care Finance; Medicaid; Medicare

Publications: *CMS Quarterly Provider Update*

Skilled Nursing Facility Manual

State Medicaid Manual

State Operations Manual

1702. Federal Retirement Thrift Investment Board
`http://www.frtib.gov/`

Sponsor: Federal Retirement Thrift Investment Board

Description: The Federal Retirement Thrift Investment Board administers the Thrift Savings Plan (TSP) for federal employees. Its Web site features sections Electronic Reading Room, Procurement, and Employment. The Electronic Reading Room includes an annual FOIA report and annual audit report. It also links to TSP forms and publications.

Subject: Government Employees

1703. Head Start Bureau
`http://www2.acf.dhhs.gov/programs/hsb/index.htm?/`

Sponsor: Health and Human Services Department — Administration for Children and Families (ACF) — Head Start Bureau

Description: Head Start is a child development program that serves low-income children and their families. Its Web site features Announcements, Legislation/Regulations/Policies, Head Start Grantees, Research/Statistics, and Head Start Partners. The Research/Statistics section includes fact sheets and some recent reports. The site also features sections on finding Head Start programs near you, getting your child into Head Start, and how to start a Head Start program.

This site provides basic information on Head Start programs for the general public and offers some services specific to those involved with Head Start programs.

Subject: Early Childhood Education

1704. House Committee on Ways and Means
`http://www.access.gpo.gov/congress/house/house19.html`

Alternate URL: `http://waysandmeans.house.gov/Documents.asp?section=10`

Sponsor: Congress — House Committee on Ways and Means

Description: Because the House Committee on Ways and Means has jurisdiction over most of the programs authorized by the Social Security Act, its special publications can be useful sources of information on entitlement and benefits programs. Of particular use for reference and research is the committee print *Background Material and Data on Programs Within the Jurisdiction of the Committee on Ways and Means*, popularly known as the Green Book. This document is a unique collection of program descriptions and historical data on a wide variety of social and economic topics, including Social Security, employment, earnings, welfare, child support, health insurance, the elderly, families with children, poverty and taxation. At the primary URL above, the GPO Access system hosts the Ways and Means Committee's publications. To access the Green Book, users must go the Search Page for Committee Prints, a link at the bottom of the page; the Green Book is omitted from the browse lists of Committee Prints available in text and PDF formats. The alternate URL is the Publications page on the Ways and Means Committee's own Web site; its links are primarily to the source documents on GPO Access.Another Ways and Means Committee print of interest for reference and research is the *Medicare and Health Care Chart Book*, a statistical guide to issues including Medicare, health insurance, and health care spending. This chart book is available at GPO Access in text and PDF formats.

While the Green Book and Medicare Chart Book prints are often updated, they are not issued every year or even every Congress. Browse the Ways and Means Committee site to determine the most recent edition available.

Subjects: Health Insurance — Statistics; Social Security — Statistics; Welfare — Statistics

Publications: *Green Book*, Y 4.W 36:
Medicare and Health Care Chartbook , Y 4.W 36:

1705. Medicare Payment Advisory Commission
http://www.medpac.gov/
Sponsor: Congress — Medicare Payment Advisory Commission (MedPAC)
Description: Created by merging the Physician Payment Review Commission (PPRC) with the Prospective Payment Assessment Commission (ProPAC), MedPAC is a nonpartisan congressional advisory body charged with providing policy advice and technical assistance concerning Medicare payment policies. Major sections of the Web site are About MedPAC, Public Meetings, Publications, and Mailing List.
Subject: Medicare — Policy
Publication: *MedPAC Report to Congress*, Y 3.M 46/3:1/

1706. Medicare: The Official U.S. Government Site for People with Medicare
http://www.medicare.gov/
Sponsor: Health and Human Services Department — Centers for Medicare and Medicaid Services
Description: This official Medicare site for consumers features Medicare pamphlets and publications, news, and basic explanations of various aspects of Medicare. Online publications include *Medicare and You, Guide to Health Insurance for People with Medicare, Guide to Choosing a Nursing Home*, and *Choosing Long-Term Care*. The site offers Web tools to help consumers find, compare, or evaluate services. These include Nursing Home Compare, Personal Medicare Plan Finder, Medigap Compare, and Participating Physician Directory.
Subjects: Medicare; Nursing Homes
Publications: *Choosing Long-term Care*, HE 22.8:
Guide to Choosing a Nursing Home, HE 22.8:N 93/
Guide To Health Insurance For People With Medicare, HE 22.8/17:
Medicare and You, HE 22.8/16:
Medicare Hospice Benefits, HE 22.21/5:

1707. Pension Benefit Guaranty Corporation
http://www.pbgc.gov/
Sponsor: Pension Benefit Guaranty Corporation (PBGC)
Description: PBGC is a federal agency that insures and protects pension benefits in certain pension plans. Major sections include About PBGC, Legal Information and FOIA, Forms, News, Contact Information, Retirement Planning, and Publications. The Publications area includes a full-text version of the PBGC *Annual Report*, the *Pension Insurance Data Book*, fact sheets, technical updates, and newsletters. The Legal Information section includes a database of PBGC Opinion Letters. The site's Pension Search is a directory of people known to be entitled to a pension from a company that went out of business or ended its defined benefit pension plan, but who have not yet claimed their pension.

    The site offers a fair amount of content and should prove useful to anyone seeking information on one of the PBGC insured pension plans.
Subjects: Pensions; Retirement
Publications: *Annual Report / Pension Benefit Guaranty Corporation*, Y 3.P 43:1/
Fact Sheets (Pension Benefit Guaranty Corporation), Y 3.P 38/2:14/
Finding a Lost Pension, Y 3.P 38/2:
Pension Insurance Data Book, Y 3.P 38/2:2 P 38/7
Your Guaranteed Pension, Y 3.P 38/2:2 P 38/5/

1708. Poverty Guidelines, Research, and Measurement
http://aspe.os.dhhs.gov/poverty/poverty.shtml
Sponsor: Health and Human Services Department
Description: This site includes both a reprint of the HHS poverty guidelines as published annually in the *Federal Register*, from the present back to 1996, and descriptive information about the guidelines and defining poverty thresholds or poverty lines. It includes papers and articles about how poverty can be measured and how it has been measured over time.

This is a useful site for checking the current poverty guidelines, especially since it includes additional explanatory information.

Subject: Poverty

1709. Railroad Retirement Board

http://www.rrb.gov/

Sponsor: Railroad Retirement Board (RRB)

Description: The Railroad Retirement Board (RRB) is an independent agency that administers retirement-survivor and unemployment-sickness benefit programs for railroad workers and their families. Featuring a broad range of information and publications, this site includes categories such as Benefit Programs, News and Publications, Contacting the RRB, and About the RRB. Under News and Publications, the site offers statistical information, press releases, and a list of publications, which include forms, tax information, and some online general publications. The Benefit Programs includes Retirement Annuities, Survivor Benefits, Unemployment and Sickness Benefits, Social Security Benefits, and Medicare.

This site will be of most interest to those involved in the Railroad Retirement program, for whom it offers a considerable amount of useful information on their benefits.

Subjects: Railroads; Retirement

Publications: *Annual Report / Railroad Retirement Board*, RR 1.1:

Quarterly Benefit Statistics Report, RR 1.16:

Railroad Retirement and Unemployment Insurance Systems Handbook, RR 1.6/2:R 31/

RRB News

1710. Social Security Advisory Board

http://www.ssab.gov/

Sponsor: Social Security Advisory Board

Description: The Social Security Advisory Board is an independent, bipartisan board whose purpose is to advise the President, Congress, and Commissioner of Social Security on the Social Security and Supplemental Security Income programs. The site has information on the Board's authority and operations and has brief biographies of its members. The Board's reports are online in full text back to 1997.

Subject: Social Security

1711. Social Security Online

http://www.ssa.gov/

Sponsor: Social Security Administration (SSA)

Description: The central Web site of the Social Security Administration leads to a tremendous amount of information and online services from the agency. The home page offers current news and a side bar indexing Web site information in these categories: Benefits Information; Benefit Payments; Special Gateways (Spanish-language, American Indians, Women, etc.); About SSA; Online Direct Services; Services for Business; Research and Data; Financing, Planning, and Budgeting; SSA Program Rules; and Reporting Fraud. There is also a link to the "Top 10" services requested from users of the site; these include: applying for Social Security benefits online; requesting a replacement Medicare card online; cost of living data; replacing or changing your Social Security card; and requesting a statement of your lifetime earnings and estimate of your Social Security benefits.Many of the consumer-oriented publications can be found through the Benefits Information group of links on the home page. Other SSA publications listing can be found under the Research and Data grouping. These links lead to the SSA Office of Policy and the Office of the Chief Actuary, each of which its own publications section. The Press Office has press releases, frequently requested statistics, and fact sheets.The site also features online transaction and information services. These include a service for getting your personal Social Security Statement, a retirement planner, benefits applications, a field office locator, and a platform for businesses to file W-2 wage reports online.

Subject: Social Security

Publications: *Actuarial Notes*, SSA 1.25:
Actuarial Studies, SSA 1.25/2:
Annual Report of the Board of Trustees of the OASDI Trust Funds, SSA 1.1/4:
Annual Statistical Supplement to the Social Security Bulletin, HE 3.3/3:
Compilation of Social Security Laws, Y 4.W 36:10-3/
Disability Notes, SSA 1.31:
Earnings and Employment Data for Wage and Salary Workers Covered by Social Security, by State and County, SSA 1.17/3:
Fast Facts and Figures About Social Security, SSA 1.26:
Income of the Aged Chartbook, SSA 1.2:IN 2/
Income of the Population 55 or Older, SSA 1.30:
OASDI Beneficiaries by State and County, SSA 1.17/4:
Program Operations Manual System (POMS)
Seguro Social, hechos sobre cupones de alimentos, SSA 1.2:F 73/2/
Social Security Agreements (various countries), SSA 1.29:
Social Security Bulletin, SSA 1.22:
Social Security Handbook, SSA 1.8/3:
Social Security Programs Throughout the World (annual), SSA 1.24:
Social Security Rulings, HE 3.44/2:
Social Security: Basic Facts, SSA 1.2:F 11/
SSA's Accountability Report for FY..., SSA 1.1/2:
SSI Recipients by State and County, SSA 1.17:
What You Need to Know When You Get Retirement or Survivors Benefits..., SSA 1.20:

1712. Thrift Savings Plan
http://www.tsp.gov/
Sponsor: Federal Retirement Thrift Investment Board
Description: The Thrift Savings Plan (TSP) is a retirement savings plan for federal civilian employees and for uniformed services members. This site offers basic information on the TSP. Major sections of the site include TSP Features, Rates of Return, Current Information, Forms and Publications, Calculators, Account Access, and Lost Participants.
Subject: Government Employees

1713. Welfare to Work Highlights
http://wtw.doleta.gov/
Sponsor: Labor Department — Employment and Training Administration (ETA)
Description: The Labor Department's page on the Welfare to Work program features current announcements, publications, workshops, and guides. Major sections include Formula Grants (data for each state), Competitive Grants, Policy, and Resources. There are also sections for business, researchers, and the workforce community. A drop-down menu includes selections for laws and regulations, rural information, reports and publications, fact sheets, and directives.

This site will be of interest to state governments and others receiving or applying for Welfare to Work grants, and to individuals with a professional interest in the related policies and program performance.
Subject: Welfare
Publication: *Ideas That Work*, L 37.26:

Workers

1714. Catherwood Library Electronic Archive
http://www.ilr.cornell.edu/library/e_archive/default.html?page=home
Sponsor: Cornell University. Catherwood Library
Description: The Catherwood Library offers this online archive of government reports, statistics, and public policy papers from various commissions and task forces. The subject focus is on the workforce and the employer-employee relationship. Reports include those from the Glass Ceiling Commission, Commission on Family and Medical Leave, and the 21st Century Workforce Commission, among others.

This collection is small but focused, and it provides an excellent service in maintaining access to government reports that might not otherwise be available on the Web.
Subjects: Child Labor; Labor-Management Relations — Policy; Workforce — Policy
Publications: *A Workable Balance*, Y 3.2:F 21/W 89
Commission on the Future of Worker-Management Relations. Final Report, L 1.2:F 11/4
Forced Labor: The Prostitution of Children, L 29.2:C 43
Good for Business: Making Full Use of the Nation's Human Capital, L 1.2:B 96
Working Together for Public Service, L 1.2:W 89/36

1715. Federal Labor Relations Authority
http://www.flra.gov/
Sponsor: Federal Labor Relations Authority (FLRA)
Description: The Federal Labor Relations Authority is an independent agency responsible for administering the labor-management relations program for Federal employees. Its Web site includes information on the FLRA, news, decisions, policies, guidelines, and announcements. Major sections include Filing a Case, Court Opinions, News and Publications, and Alternative Dispute Resolution.
Subjects: Government Employees; Labor-Management Relations
Publications: *Annual Report, Federal Labor Relations Authority*, Y 3.F 31/21-3:
Decisions of the Federal Labor Relations Authority, Y 3.F 31/21-3:10-4/
FLRA Bulletin, Y 3.F 31/21-3:15/
FLRA News, Y 3.F 31/21-3:14-14

1716. Federal Mediation and Conciliation Service
http://www.fmcs.gov/internet/
Sponsor: Federal Mediation and Conciliation Service (FMCS)
Description: FMCS is an independent agency set up by Congress to promote sound and stable labor-management relations. Its Web site has sections on Who We Are, What We Do, Learning, and Resources. The What We Do section covers collective bargaining, workplace mediation, negotiated rulemaking, preventive mediation, arbitration, the FMCS grants program, and best practices. The site also describes the FMCS e-service, called Technology Assisted Group Solutions (TAGS), that includes capabilities for online meetings, online voting, and other services. The Resources section has articles by and about FMCS.
Subjects: Labor-Management Relations; Mediation

1717. Merit Systems Protection Board
http://www.mspb.gov/
Sponsor: Merit Systems Protection Board (MSPB)
Description: The Board serves as guardian of the federal government's merit-based system of employment, principally by hearing and deciding appeals from federal employees of removals and other major personnel actions. The board also hears and decides other types of civil service cases, reviews significant actions and regulations of the Office of Personnel Management, and conducts studies of the merit systems. Its Web site includes additional descriptive information on the board along with links to such sections as Decisions, Studies, Offices, Support, and FOIA. The Studies section includes access to its newsletter, *Issues of Merit*. The *Merit Systems Protection Board Decisions* are available by year or by keyword search. The decisions are available for browsing online.

Subjects: Government Employees; Labor-Management Relations
Publications: *Decisions of U.S. Merit Systems Protection Board*, MS 1.10:
Issues of Merit, MS 1.17:

1718. National Longitudinal Surveys (NLS) Annotated Bibliography
http://www.nlsbibliography.org/
Sponsor: Labor Department — Bureau of Labor Statistics (BLS)
Description: The NLS Annotated Bibliography is an on-going effort to provide the public with an up-to-date searchable record of research based on data from all cohorts of the National Longitudinal Surveys (NLS). The NLS gather detailed information about the labor market experiences and other aspects of the lives of a sample of men and women. The NLS Bibliography contains citations and abstracts of NLS-based journal articles, working papers, conference presentations, and dissertations. The last printed version of the bibliography was published in 1995, and this site is a continuation of that effort to provide an online bibliography of research based on data from the NLS.
Subject: Workforce — Research

1719. Office of Compliance
http://www.compliance.gov/
Sponsor: Office of Compliance
Description: The Office of Compliance is responsible for implementing the law that extends the rights and protections of 11 employment and labor laws to covered employees in the legislative branch of the federal government. Its Web site has general information on the office and sections such as Organization, Agency Publications, Safety and Health, Disability Access, Unfair Labor Practices, Studies, and Decisions of the Board of Directors. The Publications section includes links to relevant procedural rules as well as a brochure about employee rights and the dispute resolution procedure, a manual, and a poster from the Office of Compliance.

Although the Office of Compliance works only with legislative branch employees, this site can be of general use to others interested in employee rights.
Subjects: Labor Law; Legislative Branch — Regulations

1720. Office of Worker and Community Transition
http://www.wct.doe.gov/
Sponsor: Energy Department — Worker and Community Transition Office
Description: OWCT's goal is to minimize social and economic impacts on workers and communities affected by the downsizing of DOE's defense-related facilities and to encourage the disposition of DOE's unneeded assets. This Web site includes a variety of documentation including press releases, workshop summaries, secretarial memorandums, contact lists, and general information related to OWCT. Major categories include Program Documentation, Program Metrics, Key Accomplishments, What's New, and Links and Contacts.
Subject: Community Development

1721. Planning Your Future—A Federal Employee's Survival Guide
http://safetynet.doleta.gov/
Sponsor: Labor Department — Employment and Training Administration (ETA)
Description: This site is aimed at U.S. federal employees who have been downsized, are retiring, or are otherwise making career changes. The site features sections Starting a New Career, Your Federal Retirement, RIFs and Buyouts, and Resources for Career Transition Professionals.
Subjects: Career Information; Government Employees; Retirement

CHAPTER 15

Technology and Engineering

This chapter includes a variety of technology and engineering sites, and has sections for communications, computer science, energy, and transportation. Resources described in the Military and the Science chapters may also be of interest.

Many of the resources described in this chapter reflect the federal government's interest in technology and engineering advancements to promote military superiority. Other sites are concerned with the technology and engineering services required for operations of the federal government itself. Still others, such as the FCC and National Institute of Standards and Technology sites, concern the government's close relationship with supporting or regulating U.S. businesses. As with the military research sites, many of these include information on technology transfer or licensing opportunities.

Bookmarks & Favorites

Research Resources
- DOE Information Bridge, http://www.osti.gov/bridge/
- NASA Scientific and Technical Information, http://www.sti.nasa.gov
- Scientific and Technical Information Network, http://stinet.dtic.mil
- SciTechResources.gov, http://www.scitechresources.gov

Major Agencies
- Army Corps of Engineers, http://www.usace.army.mil
- Energy Department, http://www.energy.gov
- Federal Communications Commission, http://www.fcc.gov
- National Aeronautics and Space Administration, http://www.nasa.gov
- National Institute of Standards and Technology, http://www.nist.gov
- Transportation Department, http://www.dot.gov

Featured Sites

1722. NASA Scientific and Technical Information (STI)
http://www.sti.nasa.gov/
Alternate URLs: ftp://ftp.sti.nasa.gov/
gopher://gopher.sti.nasa.gov/
telnet://nris1.casi.sti.nasa.gov
Sponsors: National Advisory Committee for Aeronautics (NACA); National Aeronautics and Space Administration (NASA)
Description: NASA defines STI as basic and applied research results from the work of scientists, engineers, and others. The NASA Scientific and Technical Information Program is charged with disseminating STI both from NASA research and aerospace research worldwide. The main body of its citation database is the CASI Technical Report Server (also known as RECONselect), which contains bibliographic citations for *Scientific and Technical Aerospace Reports* (STAR file series), journal articles, conference proceedings, and citations from the National Advisory Committee for Aeronautics (NACA) collection, NASA's predecessor organization. The site also features the NASA Video Catalog and the NASA STI Catalog, which includes links to the *NASA Thesaurus* materials. Issues of *Spinoff*, the annual publication reporting on commercialized NASA technology, are on the site going back to 1996. The site also links to the *Spinoff* database of every technology reported in the publication since its inception in 1976.

This site provides a major bibliographic database of broad interest to the engineering and scientific communities. The CASI Technical Report Server, with its field search options, is fairly easy to use for a beginning searcher, and the availability of more detailed help information makes it a functional tool for the information professional as well. Anyone searching for technical report citations should visit this site.

Subjects: Scientific and Technical Information; Databases
Publications: *Aeronautical Engineering*, NAS 1.21:7037
Aerospace Medicine and Biology, NAS 1.21:7011
Gridpoints, NAS 1.97:
NASA Patent Abstracts Bibliography, NAS 1.21:7039
NASA STI Directory, NAS 1.24/4:
NASA Thesaurus, NAS 1.21:
Scientific and Aerospace Technical Reports, NAS 1.9/4:
Spinoff, Annual Report, NAS 1.1/4:
STI Bulletin, NAS 1.76:

1723. SciTechResources.gov
`http://www.scitechresources.gov/`
Sponsor: Commerce Department — Technology Administration (TA) — National Technical Information Service (NTIS)
Description: For SciTechResources.gov, the National Technical Information Service (NTIS) reviews government scientific and technical Web sites and selects sites with contacts and information deemed relevant to its audience. The audience is identified as scientists, engineers, technologists, and science aware citizens. The main feature of the site is a searchable catalog of the selected Web sites. Each record has a brief description of the Web site and link to the source. One can also search the "Science for Citizens" database of just those sites selected by database editors as being of general interest. The site includes Featured Lists extracted from its database. These include lists of portals, popular general interest sites, and sources of articles and R&D publications.

Researchers may also wish to check the Science.gov site, to which SciTechResources.gov is a contributor.
Subjects: Scientific and Technical Information; Finding Aids

The technology and engineering resources in this chapter are divided into five sections, spanning the entry numbers indicated here:

General	*1724–1752*
Communications and Media	*1753–1763*
Computer Science	*1764–1787*
Energy	*1788–1808*
Transportation	*1809–1836*

General

1724. Advanced Materials and Processes Technology Information Analysis Center
`http://amptiac.iitri.org/`
Sponsor: Defense Department — Advanced Materials and Processes Technology Information Analysis Center (AMPTIAC)
Description: The Advanced Materials and Processes Technology Information Analysis Center, a DTIC-sponsored Information Analysis Center, is concerned with materials technology information. The site offers resources under sections entitled About AMPTIAC, Products and Services, Information Resources, User Help Desk, and News and Events. Its searchable bibliographic database includes citations to books, standards, journal articles, and symposium papers covering materials-related topics from AMPTIAC and two other IACs: The Reliability Analysis Center (RAC) and the Manufacturing Technology Information Analysis Center (MTIAC). The site also offers the MatPro database, which cites Web sites, companies, reference books and other resources relating to advanced materials.
Subjects: Information Analysis Centers; Materials Science; Databases

1725. Advanced Technology Program
http://www.atp.nist.gov/
Sponsor: Commerce Department — Technology Administration (TA) — National Institute of Standards and Technology (NIST)
Description: Through cost-sharing with industry and non-profit research institutions, the Advanced Technology Program (ATP) at the National Institute of Standards and Technology works to accelerate the development of innovative technologies that can benefit the national economy. Main sections of the Web site include About ATP, ATP Partnerships, Products and Services, Resources for ATP Recipients, and High-Risk R&D Areas. Separate sections also highlight the contributions of the four ATP Offices: Chemistry and Life Sciences, Information Technology and Electronics, and Economic Assessment.
Subjects: Research and Development — Grants; Technology — Research

1726. Army Corps of Engineers
http://www.usace.army.mil/
Sponsor: Army — Army Corps of Engineers
Description: The Army Corps of Engineers provides engineering services for military construction and for civil works projects in the areas of flood control, waterway navigation and emergency response, among others. Major sections of the Corps site are Who We Are, Where We Are, Environmental Principles, Services for the Military, Services for the Public, Doing Business With Us, Working for Us, News and Information, and Search and Reference. Under Who We Are, the section How the Corps is Organized has organization information as well as links to the Corps of Engineers component Web sites. The News and Information section offers access to news releases, brochures, technical reports, and the monthly command newspaper Engineer Update (available in HTML back to April 1996).

This site offers a substantial number of links and information about the Corps of Engineers' activities.
Subjects: Civil Engineering; Waterways
Publications: *Circulars (EC Series)*, D 103.4:
Engineer Regulations (ER Series), D 103.6/4:
Engineer Update, D 103.69:
Manuals (EM Series), D 103.6/3:
Monthly Bulletin of Lake Levels for the Great Lakes, D 103.116:
Public Works Digest, D 103.122/3:
The Red Book: Annual Summary of Operations, D 101.1/13:

1727. Cold Regions Science and Technology Information Analysis Center
http://www.crrel.usace.army.mil/library/crstiac/crstiac.html
Sponsor: Army — Army Corps of Engineers — Engineer Research and Development Center (ERDC)
Description: The Cold Regions Science and Technology Information Analysis Center (CRSTIAC) manages information generated by the Army's Cold Regions Research and Engineering Laboratory (CRREL). This area of science and engineering covers knowledge of the winter battlefield, of the environment, of basic physical processes, and of engineering technology that works in the cold. However, its Web site consists primarily of information about the lab and the center's activities and information services.
Subjects: Engineering Research; Information Analysis Centers

1728. Construction Engineering Research Laboratory
http://www.cecer.army.mil/td/tips/index.cfm
Alternate URL: http://www.cecer.army.mil/
Sponsor: Army — Army Corps of Engineers — Engineer Research and Development Center (ERDC)
Description: The Construction Engineering Research Laboratory (CERL) conducts research in civil engineering and environmental quality to support sustainable military installations for the Army. The Web site has information about CERL, contracting and employment opportunities, and technology transfer and partnerships. For each area of research, the site presents a background report

with contacts for additional information. Research themes include land management, land restoration, energy systems, and seismic engineering. The Publications section includes technical reports and other documents produced by CERL.

Subject: Civil Engineering — Research
Publication: *Construction Engineering Research Laboratory: Technical Reports*, D 103.53:

1729. Defense Nuclear Facilities Safety Board

http://www.dnfsb.gov/

Sponsor: Defense Nuclear Facilities Safety Board
Description: The Defense Nuclear Facilities Safety Board is responsible for independent, external safety oversight of the Energy Department (DOE) nuclear weapons complex. Its site offers information on the Board's members, organizational structure, and enabling legislation. The Public Documents section includes DNFSB *Annual Report to Congress, Recommendations,* Technical Documents Log, *Technical Reports, Staff Issue Reports,* and *Site Representatives Weekly Activities Reports.* An interactive map on the site's home page provides access to these documents by DOE nuclear site name. The Publications section also includes the text of congressional testimonies, speeches, correspondence, press releases, and other documents.

Subject: Nuclear Weapons
Publications: *Annual Report,* Y 3.D 36/3:1
Annual Report to Congress [Defense Nuclear Facilities Safety Board], Y 3.D 36/3:1/
DNFSB Site Representatives Weekly Activities Report, Y 3.D 36/3:11
DNFSB Staff Issue Reports, Y 3.D 36/3:12
DNFSB Technical Reports, Y 3.D 36/3:9
Recommendations of the DNFSB, Y 3.D 36/3:10

1730. Defense Sciences Engineering Division

http://www-eng.llnl.gov/documents/eng/dsed/

Sponsor: Energy Department — Lawrence Livermore National Laboratory (LLNL)
Description: The Division provides electronics engineering solutions for partners in industry and government in support of defense and non-defense activities, particularly in the areas of electromagnetics and power conversion. Its site includes information on the Division's core areas of specialization: Electromagnetics, Power and Pulser Technologies, Chemistry and Material Science, Instrumentation and Data Acquisition, and Visualization. The site also features information on special areas of research such as pulsed plasma processing of effluent gases and toxic chemicals, plasma heated waste remediation methods, and ground penetrating imaging radar systems.

Subject: Military Technology — Research

1731. Defense Technical Information Center

http://www.dtic.mil/

Sponsor: Defense Department — Defense Technical Information Center (DTIC)
Description: The Defense Technical Information Center is the Department of Defense's central distribution point for technical defense-related information. The DTIC offers the Defense community, including contractors, a broad range of services for locating and delivering technical reports, research summaries, summaries of independent research and development, and other relevant publications. Access to many services on this site are restricted to registered users. However, a significant portion of DTIC-held information is available to the general public from the National Technical Information Service.

The primary area for locating DTIC-accessible information is the Products and Services page. This includes information on DTIC databases, current awareness products, customer service, and other products and services. Other major sections are Registration, Find A Document, and Ordering. A section called DTIC From A to Z provides a quick index of links to DTIC offices and Web products.

For defense contractors and defense personnel, this should be the first site to visit when searching for defense technical material. Even for the general public, the site offers some sections that may be of use in verifying citations to defense technical reports. Registered users can search the

site for specific information, but the site also explains how to contact DTIC to have DTIC personnel conduct the search. For authorized users that do not know how to gain access, the site provides information on registering with DTIC and ordering from DTIC.
Subject: Scientific and Technical Information
Publications: *Air University Library Index to Military Periodicals*, D 301.26/2:
Department of Defense Dictionary of Military and Associated Terms, D 5.12/3:
DTIC Digest, D 10.11:
DTIC Review, D 10.11/2:1/1
Joint Federal Travel Regulations, D 1.6/4-5:
MTC: Militarily Critical Technologies, D 10.13:
Products and Services Catalog, D 10.12:P 94/

1732. HTECH-L [email list]
Alternate URL: `http://www.lsoft.com/scripts/wl.exe?SL1=HTECH-L&H=SIVM.SI.EDU`
Sponsor: Smithsonian Institution
Description: This is an Email discussion list, sponsored and hosted by the Smithsonian, on the history of technology. It is archived and searchable for subscribers, using the listserv database commands.
Subject: Technology — History

1733. Idaho National Engineering and Environmental Laboratory
`http://www.inel.gov/`
Sponsor: Energy Department — Idaho National Engineering and Environmental Laboratory (INEEL)
Description: The Idaho National Engineering and Environmental Laboratory (INEEL) supports the U.S. Department of Energy's missions in environment, energy, science and national defense, including managing radioactive and hazardous waste. The INEEL site hosts information about INEEL research breakthroughs, the history and background of the lab and its staff, and data on the national programs it manages. Scientific research at the lab includes biotechnology, surface chemistry, nuclear and radiological sciences, materials processing, and sensors. The INEEL Publications and Public Documents sections on the site may be found quickly by using the Site Index. An Education section describes the pre-college and college-level programs, internships, and fellowships available through INEEL.
Subjects: Engineering Research; Nuclear Waste; Research Laboratories

1734. Information Analysis Center Hub
`http://iac.dtic.mil/`
Sponsor: Defense Department — Defense Technical Information Center (DTIC)
Description: This site provides a central directory for home pages of the DoD Information Analysis Centers (IACs). The IACs establish databases of historical, technical, scientific, and other data and information on a variety of technical topics. Information collections include unclassified, limited distribution, and classified information. The IACs also collect, maintain, and develop analytical tools and techniques including databases, models, and simulations. Most of the home pages of the IACs describe the databases that they maintain, although they rarely provide public access.

The IACs include the Advanced Materials Technology Information Analysis Center, the Chemical Warfare/Chemical and Biological Defense IAC, the Chemical Propulsion Information Agency, the Data and Analysis Center for Software, the Human Systems Information Analysis Center, the Information Assurance Technology Analysis Center, the Infrared Information Analysis Center, the Manufacturing Technology Information Analysis Center, the Modeling and Simulation Information Analysis Center, the Nondestructive Testing Information Analysis Center, the Reliability Analysis Center, the Survivability/Vulnerability Information Analysis Center, the Weapon Systems Technology Information Analysis Center, the Airfields, Pavements, and Mobility Information Analysis Center, the Coastal Engineering Information Analysis, the Cold Regions Science and Technology Information Analysis Center, the Concrete Technology Information Analysis Center, the DoD Nuclear Information and Analysis Center, the Environment Information

Analysis Center, the Hydraulic Engineering Information Analysis Center, the U.S. Army Shock and Vibration Information Analysis Center, and the Soil Mechanics Information and Analysis Center. Most of the resources from the IACs will only be of interest to the defense community because of the access restrictions. However, there are a few databases of unclassified material available.

Subjects: Information Analysis Centers; Military Information; Scientific and Technical Information

1735. Manufacturing Engineering Laboratory

http://www.mel.nist.gov/

Sponsor: Commerce Department — Technology Administration (TA) — National Institute of Standards and Technology (NIST)

Description: The National Institute of Standards and Technology Manufacturing Engineering Laboratory (MEL) focuses on measurements and standards issues in parts manufacturing. The MEL Web site features an interactive organizational chart with profiles of the respective divisions: Precision Engineering, Manufacturing Metrology, Intelligent Systems, Manufacturing Systems Integration, and Fabrication Technology. Background pages on MEL research projects report staffing, funding, goals, and accomplishments. Research areas include Calibration, Material Removal Processes, Laser and Optics, Surface and Nanometer-Scale Manufacturing, and Simulation and Visualization. The Products and Services section of the site includes a MEL Publications database and information on calibrations and Standards Reference Materials supported by MEL.

Subject: Manufacturing Technology

1736. Manufacturing Extension Partnership—Hands On Help for Manufacturers

http://www.mep.nist.gov/

Sponsor: Commerce Department — Technology Administration (TA) — National Institute of Standards and Technology (NIST)

Description: MEP is a network of extension centers and experts offering technical and business assistance to smaller manufacturers. This site describes the program and offers a directory of the extension centers.

Subject: Manufacturing

1737. Manufacturing Technology Information Analysis Center

http://iac.dtic.mil/mtiac/

Sponsor: Defense Department — Defense Technical Information Center (DTIC)

Description: MTIAC aims to promote the exchange of manufacturing technology information. The center will serve any U.S. manufacturing interest, although some of its services are limited to authorized users. The Products and Services section features information on its special reports, how to request customized research, and MTIAC publications, including a few full-text reports. The Data and Information section describes MTIAC databases and online services, which are available to authorized users through DTIC or MTIAC.

Subject: Manufacturing Technology

1738. Manufacturing Technology Program (ManTech)

https://www.dodmantech.com/

Sponsor: Defense Department

Description: The ManTech Web site offers information on the DoD Manufacturing Technology Program, which focuses on improved processes in the production of weapons systems. The site describes the program activities in such areas as metals, composites, and electronics research. The Publications and Links section offers access to full text strategy and planning documents, papers, presentations, and proceedings of the Defense Manufacturing Conference. The site also includes information on the program's funding, relevant legislation, business opportunities, and technology transfer.

Subject: Manufacturing Technology

1739. NACA Technical Report Server

http://naca.larc.nasa.gov/

Sponsors: National Advisory Committee for Aeronautics (NACA); National Aeronautics and Space Administration (NASA)

Description: The National Advisory Committee for Aeronautics was NASA's predecessor and was operational from 1917–1958. This site provides date and keyword searching of the titles and abstracts of NACA technical reports published in that 41-year period. Many reports are available in full as PDF images of the originals. Under the heading Other NACA Information, there are sections about related publications and software and links to airfoil studies maintained elsewhere.
Subjects: Aviation — Research; Databases

1740. NASA TechFinder
http://technology.nasa.gov/
Sponsor: National Aeronautics and Space Administration (NASA)
Description: NASA TechFinder is labeled as the "NASA Commercialization Portal." TechFinder highlights NASA technologies which have commercial potential. Two searchable databases focus on licensing opportunities and software tools. Technology Opportunity Sheets from the NASA Field Centers describe the benefits, applications, and commercialization status of technologies developed at each Center. A Success Stories section documents NASA spinoffs into the commercial sector.
Subjects: Space Technology; Technology Transfer

1741. NASA Technology Portal
http://nasatechnology.nasa.gov/
Sponsor: National Aeronautics and Space Administration (NASA)
Description: The NASA Technology Portal is divided into tabbed sections: Highlights (news, events, featured content); Enterprises; NASA Technology; Commercial Technology; Educational Technology; and Technology Development Process (focusing on NASA's strategic plan for technology). The Enterprises section highlights technology projects in each of the agency's strategic enterprise areas: space science, earth science, aerospace technology, human exploration and development of space, and biological and physical research. The NASA Technology section links to NASA sites related to technology and spotlights new technology. The Commercial Technology and Educational Technology sections gather links to resources in those areas.

NASA maintains so many Web sites that this portal is a useful starting point for exploring the NASA Web universe relating to research, commercialization, and educational resources in space technology.
Subject: Space Technology
Publications: *Aerospace Technology Innovation*, NAS 1.95:
Spinoff, Annual Report, NAS 1.1/4:

1742. National Institute of Standards and Technology
http://www.nist.gov/
Sponsor: Commerce Department — Technology Administration (TA) — National Institute of Standards and Technology (NIST)
Description: NIST, within the Department of Commerce, seeks to promote economic growth by working with industry to develop and apply technology, measurements, and standards. In addition to general information about NIST (overview, budget, interactive organization chart, fact sheets, speeches, and testimony), the site hosts extensive information on individual programs. The home page links to sites for each of the eight NIST Laboratories: Building and Fire Research; Chemical Science and Technology; Electronics and Electrical Engineering; Information Technology; Manufacturing Engineering; Materials Science and Engineering; Physics; and Technology Services. Other featured topics include standards, assistance to small manufacturers, calibrations, laboratory accreditations, R&D funding, Standard Reference Materials (SRMs), and weights and measures.

One section of the home page presents relevant information by user type: industry, researchers, news media, general public, and kids. Information for researchers includes descriptions of grants available from NIST, links to free databases and software, and NIST research and reference resources. The news media section leads to press releases and the newsletters *NIST Update* and *Technology at a Glance*. The general public section includes educational material about NIST history, everyday applications of NIST's work, the metric system, and time measurement. A Virtual Library has the NIST Library's online catalog and Web guides on such topics as biotechnology, engineering, physics, and materials science. A Publications section centralizes access to NIST online publications and ordering information. Finally, the site features a NIST Clock and NIST software you can download to use the Internet to automatically set your computer clock to the correct time.

The NIST Web site does an excellent job of communicating information to multiple audiences, from scientific and technical researchers to the manufacturing and trade businesses and the general public and education communities. For any topic covered by NIST, the user will find a wealth of accessible information within several clicks.

Subjects: Research and Development; Research Laboratories; Standards and Specifications
Publications: *Federal Information Processing Standards Publications (FIPS Pubs) Index*,
   C 13.52:58/INDEX
Journal of Research of the National Institute of Standards and Technology, C 13.22:
NIST Conference Calendar, C 13.10/3-2:
NIST Standard Reference Materials Price List, C 13.48/4-2:
NIST Tech Beat
NIST Update, C 13.36/7:
*Specifications, Tolerances, and Other Technical Requirements for Weighing and Measuring
   Devices (Handbook 44)*, C 13.11/2:
SRM (Standard Reference Materials), C 13.48/4-3:
Technology at a Glance, C 13.75:
*Uniform Laws and Regulations in the Areas of Legal Metrology and Engine Fuel Quality
   (Handbook 130)*, C 13.11:130/

1743. National Technology Transfer Center
http://www.nttc.edu/default.asp
Sponsors: National Technology Transfer Center (NTTC); Wheeling Jesuit College
Description: Established by Congress in 1989, the Robert C. Byrd National Technology Transfer Center (NTTC) works to help American businesses to find technologies, facilities and researchers within the federal labs and agencies with which they can partner. NTTC also trains entrepreneurs in the areas of e-commerce, technology commercialization, and licensing and negotiation, and runs a technology management training and apprenticeship (ETAP) program for minority students. The Web site features such sections as About NTTC, Technology Brokerage, Products, Services, Events, Opportunities, and Resources. These sections include announcements of new federal technologies available for licensing; technology transfer opportunities; Small Business Innovative Research (SBIR) and Small Business Technology Transfer Research (STTR) grant solicitations; resources and current research activities; and access to NTTC's collection of databases. The NTTC databases, which require a subscription for access, include a directory of federal lab resources, SBIR solicitations and awards, and federal licensable technologies and patents.

This site collects numerous excellent resources for technology transfer and makes them easily accessible.

Subjects: Commercialization; Technology Transfer

1744. Naval Facilities Engineering Command
http://www.navfac.navy.mil/
Sponsor: Navy — Naval Facilities Engineering Command
Description: Naval Facilities Engineering Command (NAVFAC) manages the planning, design and construction of shore facilities for U.S. Navy activities around the world. This site features links to such sections as Acquisitions Online, Base Realignment and Closure, Navy Housing Program, Navy Public Works, and Publications, which includes *NAVFAC Instructions* and *Navy Civil Engineer* magazine.

The Base Realignment and Closure section has detailed information of interest to those living near the affected areas. Other information available on this site will primarily be of use to those working with Navy engineers or involved with some of these facilities.

Subject: Military Bases and Installations
Publication: *Navy Civil Engineer*, D 209.13:

1745. Naval Observatory GPS Operations
http://tycho.usno.navy.mil/gps.html
Sponsor: Navy — Naval Observatory (USNO)

Description: This central Global Positioning System (GPS) site features the categories USNO GPS Data and Information Files, Global Positioning System Overview, Current GPS Constellation, GPS Time Transfer Operations, GPS Interactive Satellite Visibility, and GPS Information. There is also a link to a running clock set at universal time (UTC) with conversions to other time zones.

1746. Nondestructive Testing Information Analysis Center

http://www.ntiac.com/

Sponsor: Defense Department — Nondestructive Testing Information Analysis Center (NTIAC)

Description: This DoD Information Analysis Center's Web site features information on nondestructive testing. Primary sections include NTIAC Current Interests, Nondestructive Evaluation (NDE) Current Awareness, *NTIAC Newsletter*, and NDE Links. Some of the current topics of interest include nondestructive testing of aluminum gas cylinders and detection of corrosion under paint. Under SBIR Information, the site provides abstracts of Small Business Innovation Research awards granted for projects related to nondestructive evaluation. Few publications are available online; there is an online price list and order information for other publications.

Subjects: Information Analysis Centers; Nondestructive Testing — Research

Publication: *NTIAC Newsletter*

1747. Reliability Analysis Center

http://iac.dtic.mil/rac/

Sponsor: Defense Department — Reliability Analysis Center (RAC)

Description: The Reliability Analysis Center (RAC) mission is to collect, analyze, and disseminate data and information on reliability, maintainability, and quality of manufactured components and systems. The primary sections of its Web site are About RAC, Products and Services, Information Resources, and News and Events. The Information Resources section includes R&M Library, a searchable bibliographic database on RAC topics. Information Resources also has a directory of Web resources on maintainability, reliability, and structural integrity.

Subjects: Information Analysis Centers; Reliability Engineering

Publication: *Journal of the Reliability Analysis Center*

1748. Scientific and Technical Information Network (STINET)

http://stinet.dtic.mil/

Sponsor: Defense Department — Defense Technical Information Center (DTIC)

Description: The scope of the Scientific and Technical Information Network (STINET) database includes defense research topics, the basic sciences, and specific documents such as conference papers and patent applications. There are two versions of STINET: a public one and a secure, limited-access version. Public STINET is free of charge and only requires registration upon document ordering. It provides access to citations to unclassified unlimited documents that have been entered into DTIC's Technical Reports Collection since December 1974 as well as some full text reports for those citations. The Secure STINET is available only to registered DTIC users. It provides access to the same unclassified information contained in Public STINET plus the last five years of active full-text reports, Interagency Gray Literature Working Group information, limited special collections and resources, and other services such as commercial databases.

STINET is an important resource because of its unique scope and inclusion of gray literature. Non-military users should be aware that some of the publications may have access restrictions on them and thus be difficult to obtain.

Subjects: Scientific and Technical Information; Databases

1749. Technology Administration

http://www.ta.doc.gov/

Sponsor: Commerce Department — Technology Administration (TA)

Description: The Technology Administration (TA) works to maximize technology's contribution to America's economic growth. The site links to the three agencies that the TA manages: the Office of Technology Policy (OTP), the National Institute of Standards and Technology (NIST), and the National Technical Information Service (NTIS). It provides details on several TA activities, including the Interagency GPS Executive Board (IGEB) and the Advanced Technology Program (ATP). The Publications section includes PDF copies of Technology Administration reports.

Subjects: Commercialization; Technology Transfer
Publications: *Pacesetter*, C 1.94:
Technology in the National Interest, PrEx 23.2:T 22/2
The Dynamics of Technology-based Economic Development: State Science & Technology Indicators (Second Edition), C 1.202:
U.S. Corporate R&D Investment, 1994–2000 Final Estimates, C 1.202:

1750. Technology Transfer Information Center
http://www.nal.usda.gov/ttic/
Sponsor: Agriculture Department (USDA) — National Agricultural Library (NAL)
Description: Part of the USDA National Agricultural Library, the Technology Transfer Information Center (TTIC) aims to assist in the transfer of federal agricultural research results to commercial products. The Web site includes the categories Tools for Practitioners and Policy Makers, New Technologies and Partnerships, and Resources for Inventors, along with sections for publications and information about TTIC. The New Technologies and Partnerships category includes access to Tektran, a database of Agricultural Research Service prepublication notices. The TTIC Publications section offers bibliographies on technology transfer and agricultural research, technology transfer reports, and several other documents. Other resources on the site include sample university technology transfer processes, daily news on patent cases, and coverage of hot topics such as biofuels and invasive species.

Aside from news of agricultural research developments, this site is helpful for information on technology transfer, government research partnerships, patents, funding sources for small business, and other resources of interest to entrepreneurs in many fields.
Subjects: Agricultural Research; Technology Transfer

1751. U.S. Fire Administration
http://www.usfa.fema.gov/
Sponsor: Federal Emergency Management Agency (FEMA)
Description: As part of Federal Emergency Management Agency, the Fire Administration seeks to reduce life and economic losses due to fire, arson, and related emergencies. Its Web site provides resources and information for both firefighting professionals and the general public. There are fact-sheets on home fire prevention and safety in English and Spanish. Under the heading Fatality Notices, the site has statistics on firefighter fatalities and access to the National Fallen Firefighters Memorial Database. Another section describes The Administration's National Fire Academy and its residential and distance education programs. Detailed information is provided on the Assistance to Fire Fighters (also known as F.I.R.E.) Grant Program for assisting fire departments in training, equipment purchases, and other areas. The Data Center has statistics on U.S. fires from the National Fire Incident Reporting System. The Hotel-Motel List offers a searchable database of hotels and motels that meet fire and life federal safety requirements.
Subjects: Fire Prevention; Firefighting — Grants
Publications: *Fire in the United States*, FEM 1.117:
Firefighter Fatalities, FEM 1.116:
Hazardous Materials Guide for First Responders, FEM 1.108:H 32
Technical Report Series, FEM 1.115:
Uses of NFIRS: The Many Uses of the National Fire Incident Reporting System, FEM 1.102:F 51/15

1752. Waterways Experiment Station
http://www.wes.army.mil/
Sponsor: Army — Army Corps of Engineers — Engineer Research and Development Center (ERDC)
Description: A U.S. Army Corps of Engineers facility in Mississippi, the Waterways Experiment Station (WES) houses the headquarters of the Engineer Research and Development Center (ERDC) and four of its seven laboratories. The site links to pages for each of the labs: Coastal and Hydraulics Laboratory, Geotechnical and Structures Laboratory, Environmental Laboratory, and Information

Technology Laboratory. A Services section describes several unique research centers: Centrifuge Research Center, Materials Testing Center, and CADD/GIS Technology Center.
Subjects: Civil Engineering; Engineering Research
Publication: *Waterways Experiment Station: WIS (Wave Information Study) Reports,* D 103.24/14:

Communications and Media

1753. Corporation for Public Broadcasting (CPB)
http://www.cpb.org/
Sponsor: Corporation for Public Broadcasting (CPB)
Description: The Corporation for Public Broadcasting is a private, nonprofit corporation created by Congress in 1967. The CPB receives partial funding through annual congressional appropriations, and in turn funds public television and radio programming. The Web site describes CPB with an FAQ, appropriations history, chart of all CPB funding sources, annual report, press releases, and history of public broadcasting in the U.S.

The site describes and links to CPB partners, including the Public Broadcasting Service (PBS), National Public Radio (NPR), Public Radio International (PRI), and the Annenberg Foundation. Sections titled Television and Radio highlight CPB-funded programs and provide guidelines for grants and contract applicants. An Education section describes services for educators, educational programming, and available grants. The site also describes CPB programming for digital TV and radio, and projects for content delivery via the Web.
Subject: Broadcasting

1754. FCC Consumer and Governmental Affairs Bureau
http://www.fcc.gov/cgb/
Sponsor: Federal Communications Commission (FCC) — Consumer and Governmental Affairs Bureau
Description: The FCC's Consumer and Governmental Affairs Bureau (CGB) informs consumers on telecommunications issues and works with other government agencies at all levels of government in formulating telecommunications policy. The CGB Web site organizes information for various audiences: consumers; consumers with disabilities; tribal, state, and local governments; industry; the military; and the news media. The site includes consumer alerts and fact sheets on such topics as phone bill charges, the Federal Universal Service Fund, telemarketers, the Emergency Alert System, and television closed captioning. The site also links to the ECFS Express online comment system for filing a public complaint about telecommunications services.

The Consumer Information Directory and other services on this site provide clear, current, and authoritative explanations of common consumer questions and alert users to telephone, broadcast, and Internet scams. The site also helps to explain the consumer side of a wide range of technologies such as cell phones, CB radio, the V-Chip, and the Emergency Alert System.
Subjects: Consumer Information; Telecommunications; Telephone Service

1755. FCC International Bureau
http://www.fcc.gov/ib/
Alternate URL: ftp://ftp.fcc.gov/pub/Bureaus/International/
Sponsor: Federal Communications Commission (FCC) — International Bureau
Description: The International Bureau administers the Federal Communications Commission's international telecommunications policies and obligations. In addition to basic agency information, this site features current headlines and a hot topics section. The Application section includes Earth Station Licensing information, fee filing guides, and a link to the International Bureau electronic filing system. An Industry Information section includes Commission decisions on submarine cable landing licenses, headlines and rulemakings related to the World Trade Organization Basic Telecommunications Agreement, and other information.
Subject: Telecommunications — International

1756. FCC Media Bureau
`http://www.fcc.gov/mb/`
Sponsor: Federal Communications Commission (FCC) — Media Bureau
Description: The Media Bureau manages policy and licensing programs relating to electronic media, including cable television, broadcast television, and radio. The site carries news on regulatory and licensing developments and links to each of the Bureau's divisions. Media Bureau fact sheets offered on the site cover such topics as cable TV regulation, children's television, digital television, and applying for a radio or TV broadcast station. The Official Documents section includes documents from the Media Bureau and from its recent predecessors, the Mass Media Bureau and Cable Services Bureau. The front page has quick links to pages on major media company mergers and to statistics on the number of broadcast stations.
Subject: Broadcasting — Regulations

1757. FCC Office of Engineering and Technology
`http://www.fcc.gov/oet/`
Alternate URL: `ftp://ftp.fcc.gov/pub/Bureaus/Engineering_Technology/`
Sponsor: Federal Communications Commission (FCC) — Office of Engineering and Technology
Description: The Office of Engineering and Technology is concerned with frequency allocation, spectrum usage, advanced communications technologies, and other matters related to communications engineering. The site has information on the Office's function, its organization, public documents, and engineering resources. The Online Information section provides access to public documents including press releases, public notices, orders, and proposed rules, as well as engineering resources including software, databases, technical documents, and geographic mapping resources. This Web site also includes information on radio frequency safety, V-chip technical requirements, digital television channel allotment, and other issues in its Project and Initiatives and Online Resources sections.
Subject: Communications Technology — Regulations

1758. FCC Wireless Telecommunications Bureau
`http://wireless.fcc.gov/`
Sponsor: Federal Communications Commission (FCC) — Wireless Telecommunications Bureau
Description: The Wireless Telecommunications Bureau handles FCC domestic wireless telecommunications programs and policies for such services as cellular, paging, mobile marine, and other wireless communications. In addition to basic agency information, this site features press releases, public notices, commission decisions, open proceedings, and orders. Other sections on the site include Auctions, Universal Licensing System, Public Safety, Antenna Structure Registration, Wireless Communication Services, and Licensee Information, which includes links to other consumer information sites. The Auctions page includes schedules, general information, auction data, and definitions related to in-progress, completed, and future auctions of broadcast frequencies.
Subject: Wireless Communications — Regulations

1759. Federal Communications Commission
`http://www.fcc.gov/`
Sponsor: Federal Communications Commission (FCC)
Description: The Federal Communications Commission (FCC) site provides centralized access to information about the Commission and its work, along with biographies of the commissioners and links to the FCC bureaus and offices. The top-level page features current FCC headlines and a link to the Web version of *FCC Daily Digest*, which is also available via email delivery. The *Daily Digest* is a synopsis of Commission orders, news releases, speeches, public notices and all other FCC documents released each business day, with links to the full text of the documents. Issues are online back to 1994, but only issues from late 1996 forward have the document links. Other top-level links include Auctions, Commission Registration System, Fees, FOIA, Forms, and Consumer Fact Sheets.

The Search page includes several finding aids in addition to the simple box for searching words on the Web site, such as an alphabetical subject index. Another, EDOCS, is a database of *Daily Digest* entries for FCC documents posted to the FCC Web site since March 1996. Search results can be displayed in Citator format, with citations to the FCC Record Index, FCC Reports 2nd Series, and the *Federal Register*. A General Menu Reports database allows for searching of all FCC licensing databases through a single interface.

For anyone following the telecommunications industry, the FCC site can function as a primary information and current awareness source. The availability of the *Daily Digest* is especially useful for librarians as this item is not distributed to depository libraries.
Subject: Telecommunications — Regulations
Publications: *Annual Report*, CC 1.1:
FCC Forms, CC 1.55/2:
Federal Communications Commission Daily Digest, CC 1.56:
Statistics of Communications Common Carriers, CC 1.35:
Telephone Directory, CC 1.53:

1760. Institute for Telecommunication Sciences (ITS)
http://www.its.bldrdoc.gov/
Sponsor: Commerce Department — National Telecommunications and Information Administration (NTIA)
Description: The Institute for Telecommunications Sciences is the research and engineering branch of the National Telecommunications and Information Administration (NTIA). This site includes sections entitled About ITS, News and Events, Programs and Projects, Publications, and Resources. The Programs and Projects page links to information on such projects as Audio Quality Research, Video Quality Research, Radio Frequency Interference Monitoring System, and Radio Channel Impulse Response Measurement Systems. It also has a link to information about cooperative research and development agreements (CRADAs) with ITS. The Publications page offers access to a variety of NTIA reports and a glossary of telecommunications terms.
Subject: Communications Technology — Research

1761. International Broadcasting Bureau
http://www.ibb.gov/
Sponsor: International Broadcasting Bureau
Description: This site explains the international broadcasting operations of the federal government, which had been part of the former U.S. Information Agency (USIA). The International Broadcasting Bureau (IBB) is supervised by the Broadcasting Board of Governors, established as an independent federal entity in 1999. The IBB is comprised of the Voice of America (VOA), Radio Sawa, WORLD-NET Television and Film Service, and the Office of Cuba Broadcasting (Radio and TV Marti). The IBB Web site features program schedules and text, sound, and video content from its news and cultural reporting, including VOA *News Now* broadcasts and *On The Line*, WORLDNET TV, and Radio/TV Marti. Other features include an International Crime Alert list of wanted criminals, and an Engineering section that discusses such topics as signal interference, jamming, and monitoring reception of shortwave broadcasts.
Subject: Broadcasting — International

1762. National Telecommunications and Information Administration
http://www.ntia.doc.gov/
Sponsor: Commerce Department — National Telecommunications and Information Administration (NTIA)
Description: The National Telecommunications and Information Administration (NTIA), within the Commerce Department, is the Executive Branch agency with principal responsibility for domestic and international telecommunications and information policy issues. The NTIA Web site has information about the Administration, its publications, and press releases. Much of the information on the site is found on the pages for the NTIA's component offices, such as International Affairs and Spectrum Management. The Grants Programs section of the site links to pages for its major programs, the Technology Opportunities Program (TOP) and the Public Telecommunications Facilities Program (PTFP).

Since much information is filed under NTIA office names, the site map greatly facilitates information-finding.
Subject: Telecommunications — Policy

Publications: *A Nation Online: How Americans Are Expanding Their Use Of The Internet*, C 60.2:N 19
Institute for Telecommunications Sciences: Annual Technical Progress Report, C 60.14:
Manual of Regulations & Procedures for Federal Radio Frequency Management (Redbook), C 60.8:R 11/
United States Frequency Allocations: the Radio Spectrum (wall chart), C 60.16:R 11

1763. Voice of America
http://www.voa.gov/
Sponsor: International Broadcasting Bureau
Description: The Voice of America (VOA) is an international broadcasting service funded by the U.S. Government. VOA programs—covering U.S. news, information, and culture—are produced and broadcast in English and over 50 other languages through radio, satellite, and the Internet. The VOA Web site highlights daily VOA News wire stories and broadcasts. Current and past VOA programs are available, usually in RealAudio formats, as are the VOA times and frequencies for broadcast.
Subject: Broadcasting — International
Publications: *VOA Guide*, IA 1.6/3:
VOA History, B 1.2:2001039297
Voice of America Broadcast Schedules, IA 1.6/4:

Computer Science

1764. Aeronautical Systems Center Major Shared Resource Center
http://www.asc.hpc.mil/
Sponsor: Defense Department — High Performance Computing Modernization Program (HPCMP)
Description: The Aeronautical Systems Center Major Shared Resource Center (ASC MSRC) is a facility for scientific high-performance computing research and visualization, located at Wright Patterson AFB. This DOD high-performance computing site provides information on the center, its services, and its hardware and software resources. The site hosts the full PDF version of *ASC MSRC Journal* back to the Spring 1999 issue. An Education area includes information on training and degree programs.
 Primarily of interest to authorized users of the Center's resources, this site may also be interesting to anyone else active in high performance computing.
Subjects: High Performance Computing; Military Computing
Publication: *ASC MSRC Journal*, D 301.121:

1765. Army High Performance Computing Research Center
http://www.arc.umn.edu/
Sponsor: Army — Army High Performance Computing Research Center (AHPCRC)
Description: The Army High Performance Computing Research Center (AHPCRC) mission is to conduct research into the development and application of computational science tools to defense technology. This High Performance Computing (AHPCC) Center works to establish joint programs between academia and the Army for collaborative research into the use of AHPCC for solving Army and defense challenges. It also aims to develop educational programs and curricula in AHPCC and its application. The Web site offers information about the Center's Educational Programs, Computing System Resources, Organization, Conferences, Publications, and Research. Publications include the *AHPCRC Bulletin* and the *AHPCRC Technical Report* series.
 Although access to AHPCRC computing resources is limited to approved applicants from partner universities, this site can be useful for those interested in AHPCRC training or publications.
Subjects: High Performance Computing; Military Computing
Publications: *AHPCRC Bulletin*
AHPCRC Technical Report Series

1766. DACS and Defense Software Collaborators
http://www.dacs.dtic.mil/
Sponsor: Defense Department — Data and Analysis Center for Software (DACS)

Description: Two Defense Department Web sites, those of the Data and Analysis Center for Software (DACS) and the Defense Software Collaborators (DSC), merged to form this single site. DACS is a DoD Information Analysis Center providing software information and technical support to the DoD software community. The Collaborators Web site was set up to share information on DoD-sponsored software resources. Topics addressed include Cleanroom Software Engineering, Data Mining, Programming Languages, and XML. The site also includes sections for Technical Reports, Bibliographic Services, Education and Training, Software-related Sites, and Calendar of Events. Technical reports are available online and cover such areas as formal methods, interoperability, software quality, and technology transfer. The DACS newsletter, *Software Tech News*, is online in both HTML and PDF formats.
Subjects: Military Computing; Software

1767. Defense Advanced Research Projects Agency
http://www.darpa.mil/
Sponsor: Defense Department — Defense Advanced Research Projects Agency (DARPA)
Description: DARPA, founded in 1958 as the Advanced Research Projects Agency (ARPA), manages research and development to promote the technological superiority of the U.S. military. The DARPA Web site features an overview and history of the agency, with links to the Web sites of its component Offices. The Doing Business with DARPA and Solicitations sections provide information on contracts and grants processes. A special Web section called DARPA Legacy highlights DARPA-sponsored technologies that have transitioned to successful products. The site also includes DARPA budget information and news releases.
Subject: Military Technology — Research
Publication: *Defense Advanced Research Projects Agency: Technology Transition*, D 1.2:T 22/8

1768. Department of Defense Network Information Center
http://www.nic.mil/
Sponsor: Defense Department — Defense Information Systems Agency (DISA)
Description: The Department of Defense NIC is responsible for operating the ".MIL generic Top Level Domain Registry" (assigning DoD Internet hosts and domains), the DoD Assigned Numbers Registry (assigning IP network numbers and Autonomous System Numbers for DoD entities), and the DoD Internet Routing Registry. The site includes a link to the DoD Computer Emergency Response Team page and an index to the full text of Internet Engineering Task Force documents such as Internet Drafts and Request for Comments.

The DoD NIC is an essential point of contact for any U.S. military organization that desires to establish or expand its Internet presence. For public users, information is restricted and users must consent to monitoring in order to use the site.
Subject: Military Computing

1769. Distributed Systems Department
http://george.lbl.gov/
Sponsor: Energy Department — Lawrence Berkeley National Laboratory (LBL)
Description: Berkeley Lab's Distributed Systems Department develops software components that will work in a distributed computing environment to help scientists address large-scale computing problems and collaborate in real-time from geographically distant points. The site's Groups and Research Areas section describes much of the Department's work. The groups are Collaborative Technologies, Distributed Security, Data Intensive Distributed Computing, Grid Technology, and Networking. The site also links to some of the Department's previous work with imaging technologies, including the educational Whole Frog Project.
Subject: Computer Networking — Research

1770. DoD High Performance Computing Modernization Program
http://www.hpcmo.hpc.mil/
Sponsor: Defense Department — High Performance Computing Modernization Program (HPCMP)

Description: The Defense Department's High Performance Computing Modernization Program (HPCMP) provides supercomputer services, high-speed network communications, and computational science expertise for the research, development, and test activities of the Defense laboratories and test centers. These pages provide information on the program, its goals, and its activities. The Community section has a list of links to non-defense High Performance Computing Sites. Two online publications are featured: the *High Performance Computing Modernization Plan* and the *High Performance Computing Contributions to DoD Mission Success*.

While focusing on military HPC, this site will be of interest to others in the HPC community.

Subjects: High Performance Computing; Military Computing
Publications: *High Performance Computing Contributions to DoD Mission Success*
HPC (High Performance Computing) Modernization Plan, D 1.106:

1771. Energy Sciences Network
http://www.es.net/
Sponsor: Energy Department — Lawrence Berkeley National Laboratory (LBL)
Description: The Energy Sciences Network, or ESnet, is a high-speed network funded by the Department of Energy to provide network and collaboration services in support of the agency's research missions. ESnet is used by researchers at national laboratories, universities and other institutions and provides direct connections to all major DOE sites with high performance speeds. Major sections of the Web site are Tools, Conferencing, Network Research, Committees, External Publications, and About ESnet. The About ESnet section includes ESnet brochures, program plans, a staff directory, and network maps.

This Web site is aimed at existing and potential ESnet customers. It is useful for finding descriptive information on the network and its services, along with some general information on next generation Internet research and development.

Subject: Computer Networking

1772. eStrategy - eGov Strategies
http://www.estrategy.gov/
Sponsor: General Services Administration
Description: The GSA Office of Electronic Government and Technology operates the eStrategy site as its home page. The site has information about electronic government policy and initiatives. The E-Gov Policy Documents identifies and describes key laws, executive orders, OMB circulars, congressional reports, and other documents. The main part of the page groups government Web links into three subject areas: Delivery of Government Services and Information; Emerging Technology and Standards; and Securely Doing Business with the Government (covering encryption and authentication).

The eStrategy site is useful for locating major government information policy documents and for assessing federal government work in this area.

Subject: Government Information — Policy

1773. FedCIRC
http://www.fedcirc.gov/
Sponsor: Homeland Security Department
Description: FedCIRC, the Federal Computer Incident Response Center, is becoming part of the newly created Department of Homeland Security. FedCIRC is the central point for reporting, analyzing, and assisting with computer security threats in the federal government. The site includes advisories about computer viruses and Internet worms, and about software and system vulnerabilities. It links to information on viruses and on detecting intrusions.FedCIRC Web content is migrating to the new Homeland Security Department Web site, but the independent site may be maintained for some time into 2003.

Subject: Computer Security

1774. Federal Technology Service
http://www.fts.gsa.gov/
Sponsor: General Services Administration — Federal Technology Service (FTS)

Description: The General Services Administration's Federal Technology Service (FTS) supplies federal agencies with telecommunications, information technology systems, hardware and software, consulting services, information security services and products, and integrated technology solutions. Its Web site describes its services and features links to FTS programs and regional offices.
Subjects: Information Technology; Telephone Service

1775. Government Domain and Registration Service
http://www.nic.gov
Alternate URL: http://www.gov-registration.gov
Sponsor: General Services Administration
Description: This site, run by the GSA, is the registry for the .gov and .fed.us top-level domains. It offers a Whois lookup of sites registered in those domains as well as providing authorized users the ability to register new or modify existing domains. The site also offers an Online Reference and Contact Information sections, as well as online and downloadable forms through the Online Registration section.
Subject: Internet

1776. Information Sciences and Technology Directorate
http://infotech.arc.nasa.gov/
Sponsor: National Aeronautics and Space Administration (NASA) — Ames Research Center (ARC) — Advanced Supercomputing Division (NAS)
Description: This site is the home page for the NASA Ames Research Center Information Sciences and Technology Directorate. Major divisions are Supercomputing, Human Factors, and Computational Sciences. For each division, the site features job openings, research focus, organizational structure, and a link to the division's homepage. Special links highlight division research in artificial intelligence for robotic spacecraft, aviation human factors research, and high performance distributed computing.
Subjects: High Performance Computing; Human Factors — Research; Space Technology — Research

1777. Information Technology Laboratory
http://www.itl.nist.gov/
Sponsor: Commerce Department — Technology Administration (TA) — National Institute of Standards and Technology (NIST)
Description: This NIST lab develops the tests and test methods used by researchers and scientists to measure, compare, and improve information technology systems. This site provides extensive information in such program areas as Security; Information Access; Networking Research; Software Testing; Convergent Information Systems; Pervasive Computing; and Mathematics, Statistics and Computational Science. Other sections include About ITL, Products and Publications, ITL News, and Upcoming Events.
Subject: Information Technology — Research
Publication: *ITL Bulletin*, C 13.76:

1778. In-Q-Tel
http://in-q-tel.com/
Sponsor: In-Q-Tel
Description: In-Q-Tel is a private, non-profit enterprise funded by the Central Intelligence Agency (CIA). It was established to help the U.S. intelligence community apply new commercial information technologies to intelligence and analysis. The In-Q-Tel Web site has information about the organization including history, mission, leadership biographies, and press releases. The Technologies section gives an overview of their efforts in the areas of knowledge management, search and discovery, security and privacy, distributed data collection, and geospatial technology.
Subjects: Information Technology; Intelligence

1779. IT Policy Home Page
http://www.itpolicy.gsa.gov/
Description: The Information Technology (IT) Home Page is provided by the General Services Administration as a central government location for IT-related topics, pages, and sites. Of the many

available sections on this page, it includes Accessibility (Section 508), Federal Webmasters, Legislation and Regulation, IT Policy Documents, Records Management, and Center for IT Accommodation (CITA).

1780. NASA Advanced Supercomputing Division
http://www.nas.nasa.gov/
Sponsor: National Aeronautics and Space Administration (NASA) — Ames Research Center (ARC) — Advanced Supercomputing Division (NAS)
Description: The NASA Advanced Supercomputing Division (NAS) provides research, development, and delivery of high-end computing services and technologies, such as applications and algorithms, tools, system software, and hardware to facilitate NASA mission success. The Web site describes NAS activities and identifies opportunities for research partnerships and grants. The About NAS section features a description of the NAS Information Power Grid project, and links to the Division's quarterly *Gridpoints* magazine. The Media Resources and Education Resources pages are targeted to journalists and educators, respectively. The Research and Technology section describes current focus areas, including problem-solving environments, networks, high-performance computing, and mass storage. It also links to NAS technical reports, grant reports, conference papers, available software, and sample datasets.
Subject: High Performance Computing
Publication: *Gridpoints*, NAS 1.97:

1781. National Coordination Office for Information Technology Research and Development
http://www.itrd.gov/
Sponsor: National Coordination Office for Information Technology Research and Development (ITRD)
Description: The National Coordination Office for Information Technology Research and Development coordinates planning, budget, and assessment activities for the federal IT R&D program. The NCO/IT R&D reports to the White House Office of Science and Technology Policy (OSTP) and the National Science and Technology Council (NSTC). The Web site is intended to provide information about multi-agency information technology research and development. The site hosts information from the Interagency Working Group on Information Technology R&D and the President's Information Technology Advisory Committee, as well as information about the NCO. The full text of the Interagency Working Group's annual *Supplement to the President's Budget* (commonly referred to as the Blue Book) is available going back to 1994.
Subject: Information Technology — Research
Publications: *Digital Libraries: Universal Access to Human Knowledge*
Supplement to the President's Budget (Blue Book)
Transforming Health Care Through Information Technology
Using Information Technology to Transform the Way We Learn

1782. National Energy Research Scientific Computing
http://www.nersc.gov/
Sponsor: Energy Department — Lawrence Berkeley National Laboratory (LBL)
Description: The National Energy Research Scientific Computing Center (NERSC) provides high-performance computing services to scientists supported by the DOE Office of Science. This site describes the Center's computing resources, and the evolution and current activities of NERSC. The Research section links to information on the projects and publications of the NERSC research groups: Applied Numerical Algorithms; Center for Bioinformatics and Computational Genomics (CBCG); Center for Computational Sciences and Engineering (CCSE); Future Technologies/Software Tools; Imaging and Collaborative Computing; Scientific Computing; Scientific Data Management Research and Development; and Visualization.

Although the computing resources of NERSC are limited to authorized scientists, the NERSC site provides some information for the larger population of those interested in computational sciences and high-performance computing.
Subjects: High Performance Computing; Scientific Research

1783. Next Generation Internet Initiative (NGI)

http://www.ngi.gov/

Sponsor: National Coordination Office for Information Technology Research and Development (ITRD)

Description: Since the Next Generation Internet (NGI) Program has been completed, this site is no longer being updated. For ongoing work in related areas, the site now refers to the Interagency Working Group's Large Scale Networking (LSN) Coordinating Group. A simple menu on the site still links to previous pages on NGI publications, endorsements, legislation and testimony, grants, awards, projects, and researchers.

Subject: Computer Networking

1784. NIST Computer Security Resource Clearinghouse

http://csrc.ncsl.nist.gov/

Sponsor: Commerce Department — Technology Administration (TA) — National Institute of Standards and Technology (NIST)

Description: The Computer Security Resource Clearinghouse (CSRC) is designed to collect and disseminate computer security information and resources to help users, systems administrators, managers, and security professionals better protect their data and systems. The site highlights NIST work in current areas of focus: Cryptographic Standards and Applications; Security Testing; Security Research and Emerging Technologies; Security Management and Guidance; and Outreach, Awareness and Education. The site also highlights NIST work on Public Key Infrastructure and Encryption technologies. A Links section includes lists of links to academic, government, and professional Web sites concerning computer security.

Subject: Computer Security

1785. Section 508

http://www.section508.gov/

Sponsor: General Services Administration

Description: Section 508 of the Rehabilitation Act requires federal agencies to make their electronic and information technology accessible to people with disabilities. This GSA site is intended to help both agencies and vendors comply with the law. A summary of technical standards covers software, Web-based systems, multimedia products, desktop computers, and more. The Communications/Media section links to articles on section 508, and the Resources and Links section points to government and non-government information on assistive and accessible technology.

Subject: World Wide Web — Laws

1786. SHOTHC-L [email list]

http://www.lsoft.com/scripts/wl.exe?SL1=SHOTHC-L&H=SIVM.SI.EDU

Sponsor: Smithsonian Institution

Description: This Email discussion list, sponsored and hosted by the Smithsonian, features discussion on issues related to the history of computing.

Subject: Computer Science — History

1787. Very High Speed Backbone Network Service (vBNS+)

http://www.vbns.net/

Sponsor: National Science Foundation (NSF)

Description: The very high speed Backbone Network Service (vBNS+) is the product of a cooperative venture between WorldCom and the National Science Foundation. It is a nationwide network supporting high-performance, high-bandwidth research applications. The major substantive sections of this site are About vBNS+ and Library. The About section includes descriptions of Advanced Services, NSF's High Performance Network Connections program for higher education, Multicast Services, and Prices. The Library includes presentations and published papers regarding vBNS.

Subject: Computer Networking

Energy

1788. Alternative Fuels Data Center
http://www.afdc.doe.gov/
Sponsor: Energy Department — Energy Efficiency and Renewable Energy Office
Description: Alternative fuels for vehicles is the single theme of this DOE Office of Transportation Technology Web site. The site describes fuels such as biodiesel, ethanol, propane, compressed natural gas (CNG), and the P-Series fuel blend. An Alternative Fuel Vehicles section includes buying guides, evaluations, statistics, and federal and state buying incentives and laws. There is an alternative fuel station locator for finding CNG, E85, LPG, BioDiesel, LNG, and Electric refueling stations. A Periodicals page provides a long list of government and commercial, free and subscription newsletters and magazines on alternative fuel topics.
Subject: Fuels
Publications: *Alternative Fuel News*, E 1.114/4:
Alternative Fuel Price Report
Biofuels News

1789. Bioenergy Information Network
http://bioenergy.ornl.gov/
Sponsor: Energy Department — Oak Ridge National Laboratory (ORNL)
Description: This page gathers links to various research programs investigating liquid and gaseous fuels produced from dedicated energy crops such as grasses and fast-growing short-rotation trees. The projects focus on the domestic production, recovery, and conversion of these feedstocks to economically priced, environmentally beneficial fuels such as ethanol, methanol and biodiesel. The major components are the Department of Energy's National Biofuels Program, ORNL's Bioenergy Feedstock Development Program, and NREL's Biofuels Program. The site provides this information through links such as DOE's National Biofuels Program, DOE BioPower Program, DOE Regional Biomass Energy Programs, ORNL Bioenergy Feedstock Development, and Publications and FAQs. Most sections offer numerous full-text reports, white papers, and program descriptions. Another site offering, BioBib and Other Databases, is a small bibliographic database of articles, conference proceedings, and other reports of research in the biofuels area.

For anyone interested in renewable energy and biofuels, this is an information-rich resource.
Subject: Renewable Energies

1790. Bonneville Power Administration
http://www.bpa.gov/
Sponsor: Energy Department — Bonneville Power Administration (BPA)
Description: The Bonneville Power Administration is a self-financing federal power marketing agency that sells the power generated by 31 federally-owned dams and one nuclear power plant in the Pacific Northwest. Information on BPA is under the At A Glance section of the site. The Environment, Fish, and Wildlife section describes BPA programs and policies in those areas. The Doing Business section leads to extensive information for both energy businesses and consumers on topics such as Power Business, Transmission Business, Energy Efficiency, and How to Sell to BPA. The Power of Learning page includes teacher resources and kids pages. News and Events has rate case information and BPA publications such as BPA *Annual Reports*, *Quarterly Financial Reports*, and a PDF version of BPA's *Journal* magazine.
Subject: Hydroelectric Power
Publications: *Annual Report*, E 5.1:
BPA Facts
Journal, Bonneville Power Administration, E 5.23:
Keeping Current
Quarterly Report, E 5.1/2:

1791. Directives, Regulations, Policies, and Standards Portal
http://www.directives.doe.gov/
Sponsor: Energy Department

Description: The site centralizes access to DOE management and operations documents, organized under index tabs: Directives, Technical Standards, Forms, and Secretarial Delegations of Authority. A fifth tab labeled Electronic Library leads to an interface for searching one or more of the following: Title 10 of the *Code of Federal Regulations*; DOE Directives; Federal Acquisition Regulations; Executive Orders published in the *Federal Register*; Rules and Proposed Rules published in the *Federal Register*; Technical Standards; and the *U.S. Code*.
Subject: Energy — Regulations

1792. Energy Citations Database
http://www.osti.gov/energycitations/
Sponsor: Energy Department — Scientific and Technical Information Office
Description: Energy Citations Database indexes energy and energy-related scientific and technical information from the Department of Energy (DOE) and its predecessor agencies, for material published from 1948 to the present. The citations include bibliographic information and abstracts. For some of the newer works cited, there are direct links to the full text on Web pages or in PDF format. The indexed articles, books, papers, dissertations and patents cover such topics as chemistry, climatology, engineering, geology, oceanography, and physics. An advanced search page allows searching by title, subject, identifier numbers, and other bibliographic fields. An advanced sort feature allows sorting of search results by relevance, publication date, system entry date, resource/document type, title, research organization, sponsoring organization, or the unique OSTI identifier number.
Subjects: Scientific and Technical Information; Databases

1793. Energy Efficiency and Renewable Energy Network (EREN)
http://www.eren.doe.gov/
Sponsor: Energy Department — Energy Efficiency and Renewable Energy Office
Description: The Energy Efficiency and Renewable Energy Network (EREN) Web site consolidates DOE information on energy efficiency and renewable energy. The site is divided into three sections: an Energy Information Portal; DOE Offices and Programs related to renewable energies and energy efficiency; and related press releases. The portal section covers such topics as bioenergy, hydropower, and energy efficiency in buildings. The links to DOE offices provide alternate access points, including the Biomass Program, Industrial Technologies Program, and Weatherization.
Subjects: Energy Conservation; Renewable Energies

1794. Energy Information Administration
http://www.eia.doe.gov/
Sponsor: Energy Department — Energy Information Administration (EIA)
Description: The Energy Department's Energy Information Administration provides data, forecasts, and analyses regarding energy and its interaction with the economy and the environment. EIA's Web Site presents this information by geography, fuel type, economic sector, available price data, and subject area such as imports, production, climate change, utilities, and financial analyses. The site also has an A-Z Index and a special section for historical data, some of it back to 1949. The About Us section explains EIA's data processes, forecasting methods, analysis activities, and the policy-independent nature of its work.

EIA has an extensive line of statistical publications and datasets, many of which are available on this site. The Publications section includes both current and archival editions. The site also has a section that centralizes all of the email update services available for regular notification of new data releases on petroleum, coal, natural gas, consumption, forecasts, U.S. state and international data, and other topics.

For highly specialized information beyond what is available on the site, EIA provides a directory of it subject experts on a wide range of topics such as natural gas pipeline capacity, energy taxation, greenhouse gases, and crude oil supply forecasts. The site also includes an energy glossary, energy-related web links, and a calendar of energy conferences.

With its broad scope and multiple access points, the EIA Web site is the place to start when looking for energy-related data. Value is added by presenting the data in a variety of ways; for example, an Energy Data Ranking section features lists such as Leading Gas Suppliers, Top Petroleum Net

Exporters, and 100 Largest Utility Plants. Much of the data is at the U.S. national level, but state, regional, and international data is also available.

Subjects: Energy — Statistics; Energy Policy

Publications: *Annual Energy Outlook*, E 3.1/4:

Annual Energy Review, E 3.1/2:

Coal Data: A Reference, E 3.11/7-7:

Coal Industry Annual, E 3.11/7-3:

Country Analysis Briefs

Crude Oil Watch, E 3.34/3:

Distillate Watch, E 3.13/5:

EIA Publications Directory, E 3.27:

Electric Power Annual (Volume 1), E 3.11/17-10:

Electric Power Monthly, E 3.11/17-8:

Emissions of Greenhouse Gases in the United States, E 3.59:

Energy Education Resources, Kindergarten through 12th Grade, E 3.27/6:

Energy INFOcard, E 3.2:IN 3

Energy Information Directory, E 3.33:

Financial Statistics of Major Investor Owned Electric Utilities, E 3.18/4-2:

Financial Statistics of Major Publicly Owned Electric Utilities, E 3.18/4-3:

Fuel Oil and Kerosene Sales, E 3.11/11-3:

Greenhouse Gas Volunteer, E 3.59/3:

Historical Natural Gas Annual, E 3.11/2-2:

International Energy Annual, E 3.11/20:

International Energy Outlook, E 3.11/20

International Energy Outlook, With Projections to..., E 3.11/20-3:

International Petroleum Statistics Report, E 3.11/5-6:

Inventory of Electric Utility Power Plants in the United States, E 3.29:

Inventory of Nonutility Electric Power Plants in the United States, E 3.29/2:

Monthly Energy Review, E 3.9:

Motor Gasoline Watch, E 3.13/6:

Natural Gas Monthly, E 3.11:

Natural Gas Weekly Market Update, E 3.11/2-12:

Oil and Gas Field Code Master List, E 3.34/2:

Oil and Gas Lease Equipment and Operating Costs, E 3.44/2:

On-Highway Diesel Prices, E 3.13/8:

Performance Profiles of Major Energy Producers, E 3.37:

Petroleum Marketing Annual, E 3.13/4-2:

Petroleum Marketing Monthly, E 3.13/4:

Petroleum Supply Annual, E 3.11/5-5:(year)/V.1

Petroleum Supply Annual, E 3.11/5-5:(year)/V.2

Petroleum Supply Monthly, E 3.11/5:

Propane Watch, E 3.13/7:

Quarterly Coal Report, E 3.11/9:

Renewable Energy Annual, E 3.19/2:

Renewable Energy: Issues and Trends, E 3.19/2-2:

Retail Gasoline Prices, E 3.13/9:

Short Term Energy Outlook, E 3.31:

State Electricity Profiles, E 3.2:ST 2/5

State Energy Data Reports, E 3.42:

State Energy Price and Expenditure Reports, E 3.42/3:

U.S. Crude Oil, Natural Gas, and Natural Gas Liquids Reserves, E 3.34:

Uranium Industry Annual, E 3.46/5:

Voluntary Reporting of Greenhouse Gases, E 3.2:V 88/

Voluntary Reporting of Greenhouses Gases Annual Report, E 3.59/2:

Weekly Petroleum Status Report, E 3.32:

Winter Fuels Report, E 3.32/3:

1795. Energy Resources Program
http://energy.usgs.gov/
Sponsor: Interior Department — U.S. Geological Survey (USGS)
Description: The USGS Energy Resources Program studies the natural occurrence of energy resources in the United States and the world and develops models and methodologies for this work. The Web site features a World Petroleum Assessment, National Oil and Gas Assessment, and National Coal Resource Assessment. It includes a wealth of information concerning Alaskan resources. Major sections include Coal, Oil and Gas, Other Energy Sources, Environmental and Human Health, Publications, and Energy Links. The Energy Links sections includes the Web sites for relevant associations and organizations in addition to government agencies and congressional committees.
Subject: Fossil Fuels

1796. Energy, Science, and Technical Information
http://www.osti.gov/
Sponsor: Energy Department — Scientific and Technical Information Office
Description: This site is a gateway to databases and other information resources for scientific and technical topics relevant to the Energy Department. It links to the Energy Citations, Information Bridge, PrePRINT Network, and EnergyFiles sites described elsewhere in this chapter. Under Search Options, the site adds value to its linked databases by allowing users to search across all or a custom selection of the databases. Other linked resources include federal research and development announcement sites. This site formerly hosted PubScience, a database of peer-reviewed journal literature that was discontinued in November of 2002. In its place there are links to several free database services that emphasize citations to a wide range of medical literature.

The OSTI page provides centralized access to a major federal databases in the sciences although the selection is weaker with the loss of PubScience. To direct researchers to this resource, libraries and schools may wish to reproduce the one-page "OSTI Flyer" under About OSTI.
Subjects: Preprints; Scientific and Technical Information; Databases
Publications: *DOE Information Bridge*, E 1.137:
DOE Reports Bibliographic Database, E 1.17/2:
E-PhySCI News
Federal R&D Project Summaries, E 1.142:
GrayLit Network, E 1.137/3:

1797. Energy.gov - U.S. Department of Energy
http://www.energy.gov/
Sponsor: Energy Department
Description: The central Department of Energy Web site provides a great deal of information about the agency and energy topics along with links to the many DOE laboratories, offices, and programs. A graphical "Energy and your..." menu leads to the "kidzone" and to consumer-focused information on energy issues related to health, home, transportation, school, business, community, the world, and the future. A side panel menu called "Energy and..." leads to pages with extensive information and links on: Data and Prices; Efficiency; Environmental Quality; National Security; Science and Technology; and Sources and Production. The Press Room section has press releases, testimony, speeches, events information, and a selection of newspaper editorials on energy topics. A National Library section has links to databases, an energy glossary, and the online publications center. An A-Z Index offers alternative access points to the entire DOE site.

This is a well organized site, and it is easy to navigate. It is makes an excellent starting point for searching for any level of energy-related information, although the Energy Information Administration site is also highly recommended.
Subject: Energy Policy
Publications: *DOE This Month*, E 1.54:
Energy Matters, E 1.140/3:
FEMP Focus, E 1.89/4:
Fuel Economy Guide: EPA Fuel Economy Statistics, E 1.8/5:
National Telephone Directory, E 1.12/3:
OIT Times, E 1.140/2:
The Manhattan Project: Making the Atomic Bomb, E 1.35/2:0001/2

1798. EnergyFiles – Energy Science and Technology Virtual Library
http://www.osti.gov/EnergyFiles/
Sponsor: Energy Department — Scientific and Technical Information Office
Description: EnergyFiles is a portal to energy-related scientific and technical information from a wide array of sources. The site uses subject pathfinders to guide users to the diverse databases and tools available. Pathfinder topics include: Biology and Medicine; Chemistry; Fission and Nuclear Technologies; Fossil Fuels; Geosciences; Physics; Power Transmission; and Renewable Energy. The pathfinders lead to searchable databases, Web sites, and relevant organizations, among other resources. The site includes a list of all information sources used, with Web links to the source.
Subjects: Scientific and Technical Information; Finding Aids

1799. Fossil Energy
http://fossil.energy.gov
Alternate URL: http://www.fe.doe.gov
Sponsor: Energy Department — Fossil Energy Office
Description: Functioning as a gateway to information on the Department of Energy's coal, oil, natural gas, and petroleum reserves programs, this site features a broad range of resources. Topical sections include: Electric Power R&D; Oil and Gas R&D; Fuels R&D; Oil Reserves; Electricity Regulation; and Gas Regulation. A side panel links to "in-depth profiles" of such issues as the Strategic Petroleum Reserve and Clean Coal Technology. A section for students includes primers on coal, oil, and natural gas; a fossil fuels glossary; and an explanation of how an oil well works. The site also describes the Energy Department's Office of Fossil Energy, it activities, budget, business opportunities, congressional testimony, and publications. The R&D Projects section includes searchable online fact sheets about active and past research and development projects.
Subject: Fossil Fuels
Publications: *Clean Coal Technology: The Investment Pays Off*
Project Fact Sheets, E 1.90/8:
Strategic Petroleum Reserve, Annual Report for Calendar Year, E 1.90/2:

1800. Fuel Economy
http://www.fueleconomy.gov/
Description: The Department of Energy and Environmental Protection Agency cosponsor this site which is also referred to by its Web address, www.fueleconomy.gov. A database is available to find and compare gas mileage, greenhouse gas emissions, and air pollution ratings for various car and truck models. The Gasoline Prices section of the site links to gas price data from other sources and has information on related topics such as gasoline taxes and regional variations in retail price. An Advanced Technologies section explains the inefficiencies of the modern internal combustion engine and describes current and future technologies to improve efficiency. The annual *Fuel Economy Guide*, online in PDF format, compiles fuel economy values for the model year for gasoline and alternative fuel cars and light trucks, minivans, and sport utility vehicles.
Subjects: Gasoline; Motor Vehicles — Statistics
Publication: *Fuel Economy Guide*, E 1.8/5:

1801. National Renewable Energy Laboratory
http://www.nrel.gov/
Sponsor: Energy Department — National Renewable Energy Laboratory (NREL)
Description: The National Renewable Energy Laboratory was originally established as a national center for federally sponsored solar energy research and development, but it has since expanded into areas of energy efficiency, photovoltaics, wind energy, advanced vehicle technologies, biofuels, biomass electric, fuels utilization, and other renewable energy fields. The NREL Web site sections include Research and Technology, Technology Transfer, Data and Documents, Clean Energy Basics, and Educational Programs. The Research and Technology page provides subject access to the NREL areas of research, with descriptive information on the topics and more detailed information on related NREL programs. The Data and Documents section links to a variety of research resources: Alternative Fuels Data Center; Photo Library; Publications; Renewable Electric Plant Information System; and Renewable Resource Data Center.

The availability of many full text documents and detailed project descriptions makes this an excellent site for finding information on solar, wind, and other renewable energy topics.
Subjects: Renewable Energies — Research; Research Laboratories
Publication: *State Renewable Energy News*, E 1.141:

1802. Nuclear Regulatory Commission
http://www.nrc.gov/
Sponsor: Nuclear Regulatory Commission (NRC)
Description: The Nuclear Regulatory Commission is an independent agency charged with regulating civilian use of nuclear materials. Its Web site organizes information into three topical sections: Nuclear Reactors, Nuclear Materials (uranium, plutonium), and Radioactive Wastes. Each of these sections has a "quick links" option so that all related, hierarchical links can be seen on one page. This reveals information that would otherwise be several links down, such as maps and lists of reactors and spent fuel storage locations. A section for students and teachers includes pictures and very basic information on nuclear reactors, emergency planning and radiation, and a glossary of nuclear terminology.

The home page has a "What's Happening" list linking to news releases, a public meeting schedule, webcasts of NRC meetings, and the text of current rulemakings. The rulemakings page also features draft rule text for comment and summaries of NRC published rules going back to 1985. The most complete information on obtaining NRC documents is in the Electronic Reading Room section. Here, the Collections of Documents by Type link leads to Commission meeting transcripts and speeches, NRC Formal Publications (the NUREG series), forms, and regulations. The Electronic Reading Room also includes information on the online document database called ADAMS (for Agencywide Documents Access and Management System). ADAMS has the full text of regulatory and technical documents and reports written by NRC, NRC contractors, or NRC licensees, and made public since November 1, 1999. ADAMS requires special client software, which can be downloaded from the site.

The NRC site does an excellent job of arranging access to current information and major public documents. Access to NRC documents would be improved if the ADAMS documents and legacy information were moved to a Web-based interface.
Subject: Nuclear Energy — Regulations
Publications: *Brochure Reports (NUREG-BR) Series*, Y 3.N 88:31/
Forms, Y 3.N 88:59/
Interagency Steering Committee on Radiation Standards (annual), Y 3.N 88:10/
NMSS Licensee Newsletter (quarterly), Y 3.N 88:57/
NRC Brochures (NUREG/BRs), Y 3.N 88:31
NRC News Releases, Y 3.N 88:7
NRC Staff Reports (NUREGs), Y 3.N 88:10
Rules & Regulations (Title 10 Chapter 1 CFR), Y 3.N 88:6/
Sealed Source and Device Newsletter (SS&D), Y 3.N 88:57-2/
Telephone Directory, Y 3.N 88:14
Weekly Information Report, Y 3.N 88:50/

1803. Office of Civilian Radioactive Waste Management
http://www.ocrwm.doe.gov/
Sponsor: Energy Department — Civilian Radioactive Waste Management Office
Description: Charged with building a system for spent nuclear fuel and high-level radioactive waste disposal, the Office of Civilian Radioactive Waste Management offers its Web site as a means of providing current information on its activities. Primary headings include Overview, Program Management, Yucca Mountain Project, and Waste Acceptance and Transportation. The Yucca Mountain section has a set of its own pages about the topic, including a catalog of technical documents. The Program Management page has Quality Assurance information and background on the budget and funding. The Waste Acceptance and Transportation page features information about the Office's activities related to the storage and transportation of spent nuclear fuel. A separate section, OCRWM In The News, has a continually updated list of links to Nevada newspaper articles about the Yucca Mountain project.

Since the Senate approved development of the Yucca Mountain Project in July 2002, content on the OCRWM site has become focused on that large, central project.
Subjects: Nuclear Waste; Yucca Mountain Project

1804. Savannah River Site
http://www.srs.gov/
Alternate URL: http://sro.srs.gov/index.html
Sponsor: Energy Department
Description: A former production site for weapons-grade nuclear materials, the Savannah River Site (SRS) is now focused on management of the nuclear stockpile and nuclear materials, and on related environmental issues. The Web site features information under the sections About SRS, Business Opportunities, Outreach Programs, Science and Technology, Environment, and Publications. The Savannah River Operations Office oversees the management and operations contractors of the Savannah River Site. The office's link from the SRS site (the alternate URL listed here) provides information about the Office's mission, budget, news releases, employment opportunities, and business opportunities.
Subject: Nuclear Weapons

1805. Smart Communities Network
http://www.sustainable.doe.gov/
Sponsor: Energy Department — Energy Efficiency and Renewable Energy Office
Description: This Energy Department site was formerly titled Center of Excellence for Sustainable Development. The intention of the site is to provide communities with information on sustainable development. It includes pages on Land Use Planning, Transportation, Green Buildings, Community Energy, Sustainable Business, Disaster Planning, and Rural Issues. The site also offers a monthly newsletter available via email.

For urban and rural planners, the resources on this site should prove useful in finding how other communities solve similar problems. For the general public, this site can be an excellent starting point for information on community development.
Subjects: Community Development; Sustainable Development

1806. Subject Portals (Energy)
http://www.osti.gov/subjectportals/
Sponsor: Energy Department — Scientific and Technical Information Office
Description: The Subject Portals page links to subject-focused sites on the following topics: photovoltaics, geothermal energy, superconductivity, wind energy, biopower, environmental management, biofuels, FreedomCAR and vehicle technologies, and hydropower. Each specific subject site identifies the relevant Energy Department offices, news releases, and related links. A Distributed Search feature on the subject pages provides for searching across several Energy Department databases but does not offer resources unique to the topic area.
Subject: Energy — Research

1807. Tennessee Valley Authority
http://www.tva.gov/
Sponsor: Tennessee Valley Authority (TVA)
Description: The Tennessee Valley Authority is a federal corporation and public power company. It operates fossil fuel and nuclear power plants, and manages a system of 49 dams. The major sections of the TVA Web site are: About TVA, Power System, Environmental Stewardship, River System, Economic Development, Investor Resources, and News and Media. The Power System section includes information on how power is generated at fossil fuel, hydroelectric, and nuclear plants. The River System section includes information on flood control, Tennessee River navigation, water quality, and the regional public recreation areas operated by TVA. The Environmental Stewardship section features TVA's *Annual Environmental Report*, environmental impact statements, and environmental assessments. The News and Media section features the online newsletter *Inside TVA* and *TVA Today*, a news service for employees. A helpful alphabetical site index can be found under the "site help" link.
Subjects: Electricity; Utilities (Energy)

Publications: *Annual Report of the Tennessee Valley Authority*, Y 3.T 25:1
Inside TVA
TVA Today, Y 3.T 25:74

1808. Western Area Power Administration
http://www.wapa.gov/
Sponsor: Energy Department — Western Area Power Administration (WAPA)
Description: The Western Area Power Administration markets and delivers hydroelectric power in the central and western United States. Its site includes categories such as Doing Business with Western, Power Marketing, Power Operations, Energy Services, Electric Power Training Center (EPTC), and General Information (fact sheets, speeches, publications).
Subjects: Hydroelectric Power; West (United States)
Publication: *Annual Report*, E 6.1:

Transportation

1809. Amtrak
http://www.amtrak.com/
Sponsor: Amtrak (National Railroad Passenger Corporation)
Description: With train schedules and reservations available from the Amtrak site, passengers can use this site to plan rail excursions, book trips, and check on train schedules. Main sections include Reservations, Plan Your Trip, Trains and Destinations, and Amtrak Services. The site provides online booking through a secure server as well as timetables in PDF format and information on special promotional fares.

Amtrak, officially the National Passenger Railroad Corporation, is a federally chartered for-profit public corporation. For information on its operations and finances, see the Press Room and About Amtrak sections of the site.
Subjects: Amtrak; Railroads
Publication: *Amtrak Annual Report*

1810. Aviation Consumer Protection Division
http://airconsumer.ost.dot.gov/
Sponsor: Transportation Department
Description: The Aviation Consumer Protection Division of the Transportation Department receives the public's complaints about airline consumer issues and works with the aviation industry to improve compliance with consumer protection requirements. The Air Problems and Complaints section explains how to file a complaint and includes an email address and other filing options. The Air Travel Consumer Report section has monthly statistics on flight delays, mishandled baggage, and other complaint areas. The Service Cessations section has a chronology and detailed information on airlines that have ceased flight operations. The Travel Tips and Publications section has consumer information on such topics as travel with animals and charter flights. It includes an HTML version of the publication *Fly Rights: A Consumer Guide to Air Travel*.
Subjects: Airlines; Consumer Information

1811. Centennial of Flight
http://ww.centennialofflight.gov
Alternate URL: http://www.centennialofflight.af.mil
Sponsors: Air Force; U.S. Centennial of Flight Commission
Description: Established by law in 1998, the U.S. Centennial of Flight Commission is charged with leading the commemoration of 100 years of powered flight. The start of powered flight is designated as the Wright brothers' flight on December 17, 1903. The commission's Web site includes a section on the history of flight, a section on the Wright Brothers, and information on the events marking the centennial celebration.The alternate URL above points to a similar commemorative site

hosted by the Air Force. The Air Force will also host events and will publicize the aviation history of Wright-Patterson Air Force Base in Ohio.
Subject: Aviation — History

1812. Central Federal Lands Highway Division
http://www.cflhd.gov/
Sponsor: Transportation Department — Federal Highway Administration (FHWA)
Description: The Federal Lands Highway Program administers highway programs in cooperation with other federal agencies and provides transportation engineering services for the planning, design, construction, and rehabilitation of the highways and bridges on or providing access to federally owned lands. The Central Federal Lands Highway Division has responsibility for most states west of the Mississippi River. This site contains information on projects, procurement, design resources, and technology development. The Projects section lists the projects by state with links to construction documents.
Subjects: Highways and Roads; West (United States)

1813. Chemical Propulsion Information Agency
http://www.cpia.jhu.edu/
Sponsor: Defense Department — Chemical Propulsion Information Agency (CPIA)
Description: This DoD Information Analysis Center is a clearinghouse for information on chemical, electrical and nuclear propulsion for missile, space, and gun propulsion systems. The site features such sections as Propulsion News, CPIA Publications, CPIA Bulletin, Propulsion Database, Technology Reviews, Propulsion Homepages, Propulsion Acronyms and Trade Names, and Meeting Announcements. Technology Reviews are brief summaries of technologies of current or historical interest to the propulsion community. The Propulsion Database contains over 20,000 citations to nonclassified technical reports and conference papers covering 25 years of propulsion technology. This Web version is a less powerful version of the full database (Propulsion Information Retrieval System), which is sold on CD-ROM.

This is an excellent site for research into propulsion technology and for keeping current with such research. It has fewer restricted sections than many other military sites.
Subjects: Information Analysis Centers; Propulsion Technology; Rockets

1814. Department of Transportation
http://www.dot.gov/
Sponsor: Transportation Department
Description: The central Department of Transportation Web site offers an excellent starting point for tracking down a wide variety of transportation resources. The About DOT section provides easy access to component DOT offices, bureaus, and administrations as well as initiatives, plans, library resources, reports, and publications. Other featured sections include DOT News, Doing Business with DOT, Safety, Dockets/Regulations, Jobs and Education, and DOT Access (policy on equal access to transportation). The FAQ section covers questions about aviation, boating and child/vehicle safety, and links to the National Transportation Library for more information.Many documents are easily accessible from the publications area under About DOT, but not all. For example, to find the *SPE News* online (formerly *The DOTted Line*), a user has to go under the Doing Business with DOT link and then successively under the sections DOT Acquisitions and Grants, Electronic Acquisition Reference Library. When in doubt, try the internal search engine or go directly to the specific branch, if known.
Subject: Transportation
Publications: *Air Travel Consumer Report*, TD 1.54:
Aviation Economic Orders, TD 1.6/2:
DOT Telephone Directory, TD 1.9:
FOCUS, TD 2.30/13-2:
Office of the Inspector General: Semiannual Report to Congress, TD 1.1/3:
Public Roads, TD 2.19:
Red Light Reporter, TD 2.74:
Research & Technology Transporter, TD 2.70:

SPE News, TD 1.59:
Transportation Acquisition Circular (TAC), TD 1.6/3:
Transportation Acquisition Manual, TD 1.8:
Transportation Link, TD 1.25/4:
TranspoTopics, TD 1.25/2:
U.S. Department of Transportation FY ... Procurement Forecast, TD 1.62:
Volpe Transportation Journal, TD 10.15:

1815. Eastern Federal Highway Lands Division
`http://www.efl.fhwa.dot.gov/`
Sponsor: Transportation Department — Federal Highway Administration (FHWA)
Description: The Federal Lands Highway Program administers highway programs in cooperation with other federal agencies and provides transportation engineering services for the planning, design, construction, and rehabilitation of the highways and bridges on or providing access to federally owned lands. The Eastern Division serves 31 states east of the Mississippi River, Puerto Rico, and the Virgin Islands. The site has sections on Projects, Procurement, Design Resources, and Technology Development. A Planning and Public Involvement section includes National Environmental Policy Act documents and public notices. The site also has traffic advisories related to current projects.
Subject: Highways and Roads

1816. Fatality Analysis Reporting System (FARS) Web-Based Encyclopedia
`http://www-fars.nhtsa.dot.gov/`
Sponsor: Transportation Department — National Highway Traffic Safety Administration (NHTSA)
Description: The Fatality Analysis Reporting System (FARS) presents data from motor vehicle crashes in the United States that result in the death of an occupant of a vehicle or a nonmotorist within 30 days of the crash. This site is designed to make the FARS data easily accessible through the Web. Fact sheets reporting trends in the data are listed towards the bottom of the site's home page and include fatal crash statistics relating to alcohol, school buses, speeding, pedestrians, children, and other topics.Users can create their own queries and simple maps of the data as well. The query system allows for choosing multiple variables concerning the crashes and characteristics of the persons, vehicles, or drivers involved. Data can be reported in text, spreadsheet, or chart formats.
Subject: Accidents (Motor Vehicles) — Statistics

1817. Federal Aviation Administration
`http://www.faa.gov/`
Description: The FAA offers an extensive Web presence with information on air traffic accidents, aviation safety, airport security, and system efficiency. The site's major sections are Aviation Safety, Regulatory/Advisory, Space Transportation, Traveler Briefing (on-time statistics, complaint procedures, security tips), Certification, Air Traffic, and Newsroom. The Newsroom has press releases, fact sheets, testimony, speeches, reports, and other documents. The Safety section provides detailed information on airline and aircraft safety along with aviation safety press releases and public information. The site also has extensive information on careers in aviation, including how to become a pilot, mechanic, air traffic control specialist, or security screener. An Aviation Education page includes curriculum guides and links to information about aviation scholarships.
Publications: *Air Traffic Publications Library*, TD 4.78:
Aviation Capacity Enhancement Plan, TD 4.77:
Aviation System Indicators, TD 4.75:
FAA Aviation News, TD 4.9:
FAA Intercom, TD 4.5/2:
Federal Aviation Regulations, TD 4.6:
National Plan Integrated Airport Systems, TD 4.33/3:
Notices to Airmen, TD 4.12/2:

1818. Federal Highway Administration
http://www.fhwa.dot.gov/
Sponsor: Transportation Department — Federal Highway Administration (FHWA)
Description: The FHWA site offers access to a wide range of textual and statistical information related to the nation's highways and roads. The FHWA Program section serves as an index to many of the Administration's activities and offices, such as bridge technology, Intelligent Transportation Systems, the Highway Safety Program, and the National Highway Institute's fellowships, grants, and coursework. The Electronic Reading Room links to FOIA information and lists of publications online. Other sections include What's New, Legislation and Regulations, About FHWA, Employee Phone Directories, and Doing Business with FHWA. The site also links to Web sites for Scenic Byways and for National Traffic and Road Closure Information.
Subject: Highways and Roads
Publications: *Financing Federal-Aid Highways*, TD 2.30/5:
Greener Roadsides, TD 2.30/16-2:
Highway Information Quarterly, TD 2.23/4:
Highway Information Updates, TD 2.23/5:
Highway Statistics (annual), TD 2.23:
Highway Traffic Noise in the United States: Problem and Response, TD 2.23/7:
Innovative Finance, TD 2.75/2:
Innovative Finance Quarterly, TD 2.75:
Our Nation's Highways: Selected Facts & Figures, TD 2.23/6:
Traffic Volume Trends, TD 2.50:
Women in Transportation, TD 2.30/5

1819. Federal Maritime Commission
http://www.fmc.gov/
Sponsor: Federal Maritime Commission (FMC)
Description: The Federal Maritime Commission is responsible for the regulation of shipping in the foreign trades of the United States. Its Web site is designed for consumers and providers of international shipping services who want to know how to contact the FMC. The site includes press releases, regulations, public information, information on FMC bureaus and offices, and commonly used forms.
Subject: Shipping — Regulations
Publications: *Formal Docket Decisions*, FMC 1.10:
Freedom of Information Act Annual Report, FMC 1.1/2:
News Releases, FMC 1.7:
Speeches and Remarks (Federal Maritime Commission), FMC 1.9/3:

1820. Federal Railroad Administration
http://www.fra.dot.gov/
Sponsor: Transportation Department — Federal Railroad Administration (FRA)
Description: The Federal Railroad Administration consolidates government support of railroad activities and provides regulation and research for improved railroad safety. The site includes sections on Safety, Railroad Development, Passenger Rail, Regulations and Legislation, Business with FRA (acquisitions and grants), Public Affairs, and Data Central (safety statistics). The Passenger Rail section covers Alaska Railroad, Amtrak, High Speed Rail, and Maglev. The FRA Team section identifies the component offices of the Administration.
Subjects: Railroad Safety; Railroads — Regulations

1821. Federal Transit Administration
http://www.fta.dot.gov/
Sponsor: Transportation Department — Federal Transit Administration (FTA)
Description: The Federal Transit Administration assists in the planning, development and financing of public transportation. A side bar on the Web site links to its major sections, including: The Transportation Equity Act for the 21st Century (TEA-21); Surface Transportation Reauthorization; National Transit Library; National Transit Database; Post 9/11 Security; Offices; New Starts (new systems and major extensions of existing systems); Bus Rapid Transit; Metropolitan Capacity

Building Program; and Welfare-to-Work (Job Access and Reverse Commute Program Grants). The National Transit Library section provides an alphabetical guide to FTA publications online.FTA grant program information is all linked from one page. It includes the *Grants Management Workbook* and FTA Program Fact Sheets identifying the appropriation, eligible purposes, allocation of funding, office contact, and more. Other grants information is organized into eligibility sections, such as grants for rural areas and grants for transportation for elderly persons and persons with disabilities.

Subjects: Mass Transit; Transportation — Grants
Publications: *Annual Report on New Starts: Proposed Allocations of Funds for FY...*, TD 7.1/2:
Grants Management Workbook
Innovative Financing Handbook, TD 7.8:
National Transit Database, TD 7.11/2-2:
Report on Funding Levels and Allocations of Funds for Transit New Starts/Major Capital Investments, TD 7.20:
Transit Planning and Research Programs Fiscal Year Project Directory, TD 7.19:T 68/

1822. Flight Standards Service
`http://www.mmac.jccbi.gov/afs/`
Sponsor: Transportation Department — Federal Aviation Administration (FAA)
Description: The FAA's Flight Standards Service aims to provide the public with accident-free aircraft operations. Its site offers links to their Regulatory Support Division, the Civil Aviation Registry, and the Flight Procedure Standards Branch. The Regulatory Support Division provides access to several publications including the *Aviation Maintenance Alerts*.
Subject: Aircraft — Regulations
Publication: *Aviation Maintenance Alerts*, TD 4.414:

1823. Hazmat Safety
`http://hazmat.dot.gov/`
Sponsor: Transportation Department
Description: This site offers extensive information resources on issues concerning the transportation of hazardous materials. The site includes the sections Who and Where We Are, Rules and Regulations, Exemptions and Approvals, Training Information, OHM Publications and Reports, News and Discussion, Available Files and Documents, Spills, Emergency Response Guidebook, Risk Management, International Standards, FOIA, and Hazmat Enforcement.
Subjects: Toxic Substances — Regulations; Transportation Security
Publications: *Biennial Report on Hazardous Materials Transportation*, TD 10.2:M 41/
Emergency Response Guidebook, TD 9.8:
Penalty Actions Taken by the Department of Transportation for Violations of the Hazardous Materials Transportation Regulations, TD 10.2:H 33/

1824. Maritime Administration
`http://marad.dot.gov/`
Sponsor: Transportation Department — Maritime Administration (MARAD)
Description: The Transportation Department's Maritime Administration (MARAD) promotes the United States merchant marine for both waterborne commerce and as a naval and military auxiliary in time of war or national emergency. The Web site features information in sections such as About MARAD, News, Education, Programs and Initiatives, and Publications and Statistics. The Education section has information about the U.S. Merchant Marine Academy, a page for kids, and maritime history links. Programs and Initiatives describes the Maritime Security Program, cargo preference laws, shipbuilding funds, maritime academies, environmental activities, the Port Economic Impact Kit, and more. Publications include *Glossary of Shipping Terms* and *Compilation of Maritime Law*. Statistics cover fleet inventory, waterborne traffic, shipbuilding, and related topics.
Subjects: Merchant Marine; Shipping

Publications: *Introducing the Maritime Administration*, TD 11.2:M 33/3
Maritime Labor-Management Affiliations, TD 11.8/2:
Maritime Publications Index, TD 11.9:97004760
Merchant Fleets of the World, Sea-Going Steam and Motor Ships of 1,000 Gross Tons and Over, TD 11.14:
Report on U.S. Shipbuilding and Repair Facilities, TD 11.25:
U.S. Foreign Waterborne Transportation Statistics, TD 11.35:
U.S. Maritime Administration Annual Report, TD 11.1:
Vessel Inventory Report, TD 11.11:

1825. Mike Monroney Aeronautical Center

http://www.mmac.jccbi.gov/

Sponsor: Transportation Department — Federal Aviation Administration (FAA)

Description: The Mike Monroney Aeronautical Center is a training and logistics center for the FAA. Major DOT training organizations at the Center are the FAA Academy, the Transportation Safety Institute, and the Civil Aeromedical Institute. The Center's staff also works in engineering, research, safety, and aviation systems standards areas. The Center's Web site features the following sections: Certification, Logistics, Services, Engineering, Research, Standards, and Training. Additional categories include About MMAC, Aircraft/Airmen, Aviation Education, History, News Releases, and Offices.

Subject: Aviation

Publication: *FAA Intercom*, TD 4.5/2:

1826. National Aeronautical Charting Office: NACO Online

http://www.naco.faa.gov/

Sponsor: Transportation Department — Federal Aviation Administration (FAA) — National Aeronautical Charting Office (NACO)

Description: National Aeronautical Charting Office (NACO) is charged with the compilation, reproduction, and distribution of aeronautical navigation products and digital databases for the U.S., its territories and possessions. The NACO Online site describes the office and provides information on how to order its products. It also includes sections for Catalog, Online Products, Agent Listing, and Special Notices. Online Products includes airport diagrams and Visual Flight Rule (VFR) Chart Bulletins.

Subjects: Aviation; Maps and Mapping

1827. National Highway Traffic Safety Administration

http://www.nhtsa.dot.gov/

Sponsor: Transportation Department — National Highway Traffic Safety Administration (NHTSA)

Description: NHTSA sets and enforces safety performance standards for motor vehicles and assists state and local governments with grants for local highway safety programs. The NHTSA Web site has databases of product recalls, consumer complaints, technical service bulletins and defects investigations for cars, child seats, tires, and auto equipment. There are car and tire safety tips, as well as regulatory information on such topics as fuel economy, child seats, safety standards, and air bags. A section on Traffic Safety and Occupant Protection covers topics such as aggressive driving, alcohol, child passengers, school buses, and pedestrian and bicycle safety. It also includes state legislative fact sheets on open container laws, motorcycle helmet use, driver's blood alcohol level, and related topics. Popular links on the site's side panel include Docket Management System, Grants, Publications Catalog, and Safety Materials Catalog.

This site offers a substantial collection of information on the government's testing of vehicles and its auto safety ratings and makes it accessible for consumers. The site also brings together grants, regulatory, and state and national legislative information concerning motor vehicle standards and traffic safety.

Subjects: Motor Vehicles — Regulations; Traffic Safety; Vehicle Safety

Publications: *Automotive Fuel Economy Program*, TD 8.26:
Buying a Safer Car for Child Passengers, TD 8.66:
Crashworthiness Research News, TD 8.61:
NHTSA Now
State Legislative Fact Sheets, TD 8.65:
Traffic Safety Digest, TD 8.40:
Traffic Safety Facts, TD 8.2:T 67/13/
Traffic Techs, TD 8.63:

1828. National Transportation Safety Board

http://www.ntsb.gov/

Sponsor: National Transportation Safety Board (NTSB)

Description: The National Transportation Safety Board site provides information on its programs and the primary areas of safety with which the NTSB works. These programs include Aviation, Highway, Marine, Railroad, and Pipeline and Hazardous Material. Each of these pages includes a listing of recent accidents and a publications list of accident reports and studies. Information about the NTSB includes biographies of the current Board members and an organization chart. The NTSB Most Wanted section links to information on safety improvements recommended by the Board. Other major sections are News and Events, Data and Information Products, and Information Sources and Contacts. New and Events includes documents from recent major investigations and information on board meetings and public hearings. Data and Information Products includes accident statistics, legal documents, and Safety Recommendation Letters. The Information Sources and Contacts section provides not only phone numbers but helpful instructions on how to obtain different types of information from the NTSB.

Subjects: Safety; Transportation

Publications: *Aircraft Accident Reports*, TD 1.112:
Hazardous Materials Accident Reports, TD 1.129:
Highway Accident Reports, TD 1.117:
Marine Accident Reports, TD 1.116:
Pipeline Accident Reports, TD 1.118:
Railroad Accident Reports, TD 1.112/3:

1829. Saint Lawrence Seaway Development Corporation

http://www.seaway.dot.gov/

Alternate URL: http://www.greatlakes-seaway.com/

Sponsor: Transportation Department — Saint Lawrence Seaway Development Corporation (SLSDC)

Description: The Saint Lawrence Seaway Development Corporation (SLSDC) works to ensure the safe transit of vessels through the two U.S. locks and navigation channels of the Saint Lawrence Seaway System. SLSDC works cooperatively with the Canadian Saint Lawrence Seaway Management Corporation, and many of the links on this site lead to a binational Web site run by both corporations (see alternate URL). The Briefing Room section includes press releases, toll schedule and radio messages, while annual reports are available from 1994 under a separate heading. Other sections include Port Profiles, Seaway Pacesetter Awards, Regulations, and the Seaway Handbook.

Subject: Shipping

1830. Share the Road Safely

http://www.nozone.org/

Sponsor: Transportation Department — Federal Motor Carrier Safety Administration

Description: This site is part of a national public outreach highway safety campaign to educate people about how to share the road safely with large trucks and buses. There are safety tips for car drivers, motorcyclists, and pedestrians as well as for truck and bus drivers. Most of the site describes the resources and partners that are part of the education campaign.

Subject: Traffic Safety

1831. Surface Transportation Board
http://www.stb.dot.gov/
Sponsor: Transportation Department — Surface Transportation Board (STB)
Description: The Surface Transportation Board is an independent adjudicatory body administratively housed within the Department of Transportation. The Board is responsible for the economic regulation of interstate surface transportation, primarily railroads. Its Web site features sections: Economics and Environment, Publications, Electronic Reading Room, Mergers and Acquisitions, and People and Functions. The Economics section has railroad financial data, employment data, rate studies, and wage statistics. Other available sections include Decisions and Notices, Filings, Recordations, Rail Consumer Assistance Program, and Public Info/Media.
Subject: Railroads
Publication: *Surface Transportation Board Reports: Decisions of the Surface Transportation Board*, TD 13.6/2:

1832. Transportation Security Administration (TSA)
http://www.tsa.gov/
Sponsor: Transportation Department — Transportation Security Administration (TSA)
Description: The Transportation Security Administration was established within the Department of Transportation in response to the terrorist attacks of September 11, 2001. TSA has responsibility for transportation security nationwide, with an initial focus on airport security. The TSA Web site has information on its mission, history, and budget. Along with the front page of the site, the Travelers and Consumers section provides information on how security regulations affect the individual and includes information on what items are prohibited from carry-on luggage. A Law and Policy section has information on the statutory authority of the TSA, security regulations, and communications with Congress. Sections on Industry Partners and on Security and Law Enforcement are intended for professionals or entities in the transportation business. The Briefing Room section has press releases, publications, speeches, testimony, and a tally of TSA progress.
Subjects: Aviation Safety; Transportation Security
Publication: *Criminal Acts Against Civil Aviation*, TD 4.811:

1833. Turner Fairbank Highway Research Center
http://www.tfhrc.gov/
Sponsor: Transportation Department — Federal Highway Administration (FHWA)
Description: TFHRC is the applied research facility of the Federal Highway Administration charged with research into preservation and improvement of national highways, especially in areas such as safety, intelligent transportation systems, pavements, and materials and structural technologies. Its Web site has other sections such as Human–Centered Systems, Research, Products, and links to other lab and research Web sites. Online versions of three periodicals are available: *Transporter*, *Focus*, and *Public Roads*.
Subjects: Highways and Roads — Research; Pavements — Research
Publications: *FOCUS*, TD 2.30/13-2:
Public Roads, TD 2.19:
Research & Technology Transporter, TD 2.70:

1834. U.S. Merchant Marine Academy
http://www.usmma.edu/
Description: The Merchant Marine Academy site has information on the Academy's admissions, academics, and other activities. The site includes a section for the American Merchant Marine Museum, on the grounds of the Academy. The Academy is operated by the Transportation Department's Maritime Administration.

1835. Western Federal Lands Highway Division
http://www.wfl.fhwa.dot.gov/
Description: The Federal Lands Highway Program administers highway programs in cooperation with other federal agencies and provides transportation engineering services for the planning, design, construction, and rehabilitation of the highways and bridges on or providing access to federally owned lands. The Western Federal Lands Highway Division serves Oregon, Washington, Idaho, Montana, Wyoming and Alaska. This site has information on projects, procurement, and design resources. It also has information on the Forest Highway Program and links to information on any road construction or closures for the states the division serves.
Subjects: Highways and Roads; West (United States)

1836. William J. Hughes Technical Center
http://www.tc.faa.gov/
Sponsor: Transportation Department — Federal Aviation Administration (FAA)
Description: The William J. Hughes Technical Center is an aviation research, development, engineering, test, and evaluation facility. Center activities involve test and evaluation in air traffic control, communications, navigation, airports, and aircraft safety and security, as well as long-range R&D projects. Information on the work of the Center is under the Technical Program Areas and Technical Support Organizations headings on the Center's Web site. The General Information section includes news releases, a glossary of aviation acronyms, Technical Center Overview, and the newsletter *Intercom*.
Subject: Aviation Safety — Research
Publication: *FAA Intercom*, TD 4.5/2:

CHAPTER 16

White House Information

As the second presidential administration on the Web, the Bush administration continues the practice of posting press releases, radio addresses, and other presidential communications online. Offices directly supporting the White House have Web pages on the White House site and closely integrated with it.

This chapter includes Web sites sponsored by the current presidential administration as well as finding aids for presidential documents from this and other administrations. Several agencies closely related to the White House—the Secret Service and the Federal Emergency Management Agency—are joining the new Department of Homeland Security but are currently still listed here. Archival sites from the previous administration are described at the end of this chapter.

Bookmarks & Favorites

Presidential Documents
- Budget, http://www.gpo.gov/usbudget
- Federal Register and Presidential Documents,
    http://www.archives.gov/federal_register/
- Presidential Directives, http://www.fas.org/irp/offdocs/direct.htm
- Presidential Directives and Where to Find Them,
    http://lcweb.loc.gov/rr/news/directives.html
- Public Papers of the President,
    http://www.access.gpo.gov/nara/pubpaps/srchpaps.html
- Weekly Compilation of Presidential Documents,
    http://www.access.gpo.gov/nara/nara003.html
- White House News, http://www.whitehouse.gov/news/

Featured Site

1837. White House
http://www.whitehouse.gov
Sponsor: White House
Description: The White House Web site combines current news and policy statements from the administration with historical information relating to both the building and the Executive Office of the Presidency. Organized with the White House as a metaphor for the site, principle sections are: President/Oval Office; News and Policies/West Wing; Vice President/VP Office; History and Tours/Blue Room; First Lady/East Wing; and Search/Library.

The President section includes current information, speeches, and photos, along with biographies and portraits or photos for all previous Presidents. News and Policies has the full text of the Press Secretary's press briefings and White House press releases, the President's weekly radio addresses, the President's speeches, proclamations, and executive orders, and a list of nominations made by the President. Users may sign up to receive emailed news from the White House on such themes as Weekly Review, Homeland Security, Health Care, and Education. Under Offices in the President section, there is a link to the President's Cabinet with photos of the Cabinet members and links to their home departments and offices. Also of note, History and Tours features an online tour of the White House, and the First Lady section has current speeches and photos as well as biographical information on past First Ladies. A Spanish version and a text-only version of the site are also available.

The White House site should be the first online stop for those seeking current presidential news, statements, and documents; for biographies of elected and appointed White House officials; for the speeches of the Vice President and First Lady; and for a wealth of historical information about the White House and its occupants.

Subjects: First Lady; Presidency; White House (Mansion)
Publications: *National Security Strategy of the United States of America*, PR 43.2:
National Strategy for Homeland Security, PR 43.14:
Reliable, Affordable, and Environmentally Sound Energy for America's Future: Report of the National Energy Policy Development Group, PR 43.2:EN 2

The White House resources in this chapter are divided into two sections, spanning the entry numbers indicated here:

General	*1838–1868*
Clinton Administration Archives	*1869–1872*

General

1838. Budget of the United States Government
http://www.whitehouse.gov/omb/budget/
Alternate URL: http://www.gpo.gov/usbudget/
Sponsor: Office of Management and Budget (OMB)
Description: The Office of Management and Budget provides the full text of the current U.S. budget and supporting documents online. This site includes brief summaries of each budget document with a link to the PDF version. The GPO site, at the alternate URL, hosts the budget documents for this and prior years. Most of the files are in PDF with some tables available in spreadsheet format. Using the GPO site, one can also search the budget documents by word(s) and display the retrieved sections in PDF or text format. The site provides access to the budget documents back to fiscal year 1996 and the *Economic Report of the President* back to 1995.
Subjects: Budget of the U.S. Government; Government Finance
Publications: *Analytical Perspectives*, PREX 2.8/5:
Budget of the United States Government, PrEx 2.8:
Budget of the United States Government, Appendix, Y 1.1/7:(NOS.)/V.2
Budget System and Concepts of the United States Government, PREX 2.8/12:
Economic Report of the President, Pr 42.9:
Historical Tables, Budget of the United States Government, Y 1.1/7:(NOS.)/V.4

1839. Citizens' Handbook—Your Guide to the U.S. Government
http://www.whitehouse.gov/government/handbook/
Sponsor: White House
Description: Intended to help citizens find government information online, the White House's Citizen's Handbook presents links to selected U.S. Government Web sites including FirstGov, the Government Information Locator Service (GILS), the Federal Citizen Information Center (FCIC) National Contact Center, and the United States Information Service [sic]. This online handbook also links the visitor to various government sites to search about topics ranging from safety; employment; housing; health; learning, education, and training; art, museums, and libraries within the Smithsonian network, the Kennedy Center, and the Library of Congress; and travel. Unfortunately, the Citizens' Handbook site does not appear to be receiving the attention that other government Web portals have received. As of this writing, the site still refers to USIS, which has not been in existence since it merged with the State Department in 1999. (The linked resource is still maintained, though by State's Office of International Information Programs.) In addition, the GILS link does not match the other linked resources in its usefulness to the average citizen.
Subjects: Federal Government; Finding Aids

1840. Codification of Presidential Proclamations and Executive Orders
http://www.archives.gov/federal_register/codification/codification.html
Sponsor: National Archives and Records Administration (NARA) — Federal Register Office

Description: The Office of the Federal Register presents this online version of the *Codification of Presidential Proclamations and Executive Orders*, which covers proclamations and executive orders issued by the president from April 13, 1945, through January 20, 1989. Documents that had no legal effect on January 20, 1989 are excluded. The Disposition Tables section lists all the documents back to 1945, noting if the document has been revoked, superseded, or is otherwise obsolete. Earlier proclamations and executive orders are included if they were amended or otherwise affected by documents issued during the 1945-1989 period. This site also links to an Executive Orders Disposition Tables page for documents from January 24, 1953 to the present, including title, signature date, *Federal Register* citation, and detailed history of amendments and revocations.
Subjects: Executive Orders; Presidential Documents
Publication: *Codification of Presidential Proclamations and Executive Orders*, AE 2.113:

1841. Council of Economic Advisers
http://whitehouse.gov/cea/
Sponsor: Council of Economic Advisers (CEA)
Description: The Council of Economic Advisers (CEA), consisting of one Chairman and two members, advises the President of the United States on domestic and international economic policy and assists in the preparation of the *Economic Report of the President*. The CEA site describes the mission and operations of the Council, links to current CEA publications and the text of the Chairman's speeches, and provides a list of all previous Chairmen back to the Council's establishment in 1946.
Subjects: Economic Statistics; Economic Policy; Presidential Advisors
Publications: *Economic Indicators*, Y 4.EC 7:EC 7/
Economic Report of the President, Pr 42.9:

1842. Electoral College
http://www.archives.gov/federal_register/electoral_college/electoral_college.html
Sponsor: National Archives and Records Administration (NARA) — Electoral College
Description: NARA oversees the Electoral College, and this part of its Web site includes statistics and summaries of the votes in the Electoral College for every presidential election since George Washington. It features such sections as Procedural Guide to the Electoral College, Electoral College Calculator, Relevant Provisions of the U.S. Constitution and Federal Law, and Allocation of Electoral Votes, Based on the 2000 Census. The site also links to Web sites for the individual state electoral colleges; the information presented on these state sites varies widely.
Subject: Electoral College

1843. Faith-Based and Community Initiatives
http://www.whitehouse.gov/government/fbci/
Sponsor: White House — Faith-Based and Community Initiatives Office
Description: The White House Office of Faith-Based and Community Initiatives was created by Executive Order in January 2001 to facilitate the involvement of religious and community institutions in federal social services programs. The Office's site, hosted at the White House Web site, features reports, speeches, and other documents related to the initiative. It links to the Centers for Faith-Based and Community Initiatives in other federal agencies and provides information on conferences and grants.
Subjects: Charities; Social Services — Policy
Publication: *Guidance to Faith-Based and Community Organizations on Partnering with the Federal Government*

1844. Federal Emergency Management Agency
http://www.fema.gov/
Sponsor: Federal Emergency Management Agency (FEMA)
Description: The Federal Emergency Management Administration has been an independent federal agency but is now joining the new Department of Homeland Security. FEMA's current Web site features news and victim assistance information for any current disasters in the United States. The site provides emergency preparedness advice for hurricanes, tornadoes, floods, earthquakes and other risks, and seasonal warnings in its Storm Watch section. Special FEMA programs described

include the U.S. Fire Administration, fire prevention and safety grants, the National Flood Insurance Program, and the National Urban Search and Rescue Response System. The Library link on the bottom connects to publications, archives, press releases, and publications. There are also separate pages for the media and kids. Some information is provided in Spanish.

FEMA attempts to provide clear, factual information for those preparing for risks or recovering from a disaster. While the home page focuses on current events, an alphabetical site index helps users locate information that otherwise might be missed. Lists cataloging past disasters and other information in the Library section can be useful for reference and research.

Subject: Disaster Assistance
Publications: *Are You Ready? A Guide to Citizen Preparedness*, FEM 1.8/3:34/
CONPLAN : United States Government Interagency Domestic Terrorism Concept of Operations Plan, FEM 1.2:2002000140
Emergency Management Institute, Course Listings and Descriptions, FEM 1.17/2:
FEMA News Releases, FEM 1.28:
FEMA Staff Online Phone Directory, FEM 1.14:
Flood Insurance Manual, FEM 1.8:
National Flood Insurance Program Community Status Book, FEM 1.210
Recovery Times, FEM 1.26:

1845. First Ladies' Gallery
http://www.whitehouse.gov/history/firstladies/
Sponsor: White House
Description: The First Ladies' Gallery presents brief biographies for all First Ladies from Martha Washington to the current day. For many, a portrait is available. The biographies are taken from the book *The First Ladies* written by Margaret Brown Klapthor and Allida Black (contributing author), published by the White House Historical Association with the cooperation of the National Geographic Society.
Subject: First Lady

1846. First Lady Laura Bush
http://www.whitehouse.gov/firstlady/
Sponsor: White House — First Lady's Office
Description: The First Lady's Web page links to her biography, the full text of her speeches and statements, and press releases from the Office of the First Lady. One section focuses on her education initiatives. The site links to historical information on past First Ladies and on the East Wing, which is used by First Lady Laura Bush and her staff.
Subject: First Lady

1847. National Economic Council
http://www.whitehouse.gov/nec/
Sponsor: National Economic Council
Description: The National Economic Council coordinates the economic policy-making process with respect to domestic and international economic issues. NEC coordinates the economic policy advice for the president and ensures that economic policy decisions and programs are consistent with the president's stated goals. The site provides only a brief overview of the council and names the current director.
Subjects: Economic Policy; Presidential Advisors

1848. National Security Council
http://www.whitehouse.gov/nsc/
Sponsor: National Security Council (NSC)
Description: The National Security Council is the president's forum for considering national security and foreign policy matters with his senior national security advisors and Cabinet officials. The NSC Web site provides only basic information about the Council, describing its establishment, membership, and function. There is a link to a section entitled The History of the NSC: 1947–1997,

which gives historical information about the council from Truman to Clinton with an appendix of the assistants to the president for national security affairs during these years.
Subjects: National Security — Policy; Presidential Advisors

1849. Office of Administration
http://www.whitehouse.gov/oa/
Sponsor: White House — White House Office of Administration
Description: The Office of Administration provides administrative support services to all units within the Executive Office of the President. These services include information, personnel, and financial management; data processing; library services; records maintenance; and general office operations, such as mail, messenger, printing, procurement, and supply services. The site features sections on competitive vacancies within the Executive Office of the President, the Freedom of Information Act, and the Preservation Office. The Preservation Office page presents the mission and history of the Office of Administration, an historical timeline of the Executive Office, information on tours of the Executive Building, and links to historical Web sites.
Subject: White House (Mansion)

1850. Office of Faith-Based and Community Initiatives
http://www.whitehouse.gov/government/fbci/
Sponsor: White House — Faith-Based and Community Initiatives Office
Description: The White House Office of Faith-Based and Community Initiatives was created by President George W. Bush. This site gathers links to policy, documents, speeches, and new releases related to the Office. Featured reports include *Rallying the Armies of Compassion*, which was also reprinted with a Presidential transmittal as House Document 107-36. A site section called Grants Catalog identifies federal grant opportunities that may be of interest to small, faith-based and community groups.
Subject: Social Services — Grants
Publications: *Guidance to Faith-Based and Community Organizations on Partnering with the Federal Government*
Rallying the Armies of Compassion, Y 1.1/7:107-36

1851. Office of Management and Budget
http://www.whitehouse.gov/omb/
Sponsor: Office of Management and Budget (OMB)
Description: The Office of Management and Budget (OMB) assists the president in overseeing the preparation of the Federal budget and supervises budget administration in Executive Branch agencies. In addition, OMB oversees the administration's procurement, financial management, information, and regulatory policies. OMB's Web site covers each of these areas of responsibility.
 Primary sections of the site include: President's Budget, Federal Management, Office of Information and Regulatory Affairs (OIRA), Communications and Media, Legislative Information, and Information for Agencies. This last section includes OMB Circulars, Memoranda, and Bulletins. Documents in the President's Budget section include budget supplementals and amendments, and *A Citizen's Guide to the Federal Budget*. The OIRA section includes information on federal statistical programs and standards, information policy, and e-government.
 This well organized site is most useful for the availability of the *OMB Circulars*, such as OMB Circular A-130 establishing administration policy for the management of federal information resources. As explained at the site, *OMB Circulars* are a major tool used by the Executive Office of the President to exercise managerial and policy direction over federal agencies when the nature of the subject matter is of continuing effect.
Subjects: Budget of the U.S. Government; Government Administration
Publications: *Budget of the Unites States Government*, PREX 2.8/8:
OMB Bulletin, PREX 2.3:
OMB Circulars, PREX 2.4:
The Statistical Program of the United States Government, PREX 2.10/3:

1852. Office of Science and Technology Policy
http://www.ostp.gov/
Sponsor: White House — Office of Science and Technology Policy (OSTP)
Description: Established in 1976, the Office of Science and Technology Policy (OSTP) serves as a source of scientific and technological analysis and judgment for the president with respect to major policies, plans, and programs of the federal government. OSTP has assumed a role in advancing fundamental science, education and scientific literacy, investment in applied research, and international cooperation. The Web site offers general information on the organization and activities of OSTP. The What's New section has press releases, speeches, and testimony dating back to 2001.

OSTP works with the National Science and Technology Council (NSTC) and President's Committee of Advisors on Science and Technology (PCAST). The OSTP Web site hosts information about the membership and activities of these two organizations.
Subject: Science and Technology Policy

1853. President's Commission on the United States Postal Service
http://www.treas.gov/offices/domestic-finance/usps/
Sponsor: President's Commission on the United States Postal Service
Description: Created in late 2002, the President's Commission on the Postal Service is charged with making recommendations for the USPS by the end of July 2003. The commission's Web site is hosted on the Treasury Department's site. It includes commission documents, press releases, and meeting information.
Subject: Postal Service — Policy

1854. Presidential Directives and Executive Orders
http://www.fas.org/irp/offdocs/direct.htm
Sponsor: Federation of American Scientists (FAS)
Description: This site focuses on intelligence-related Presidential Directives and Executive Orders, dating from the Truman administration. It lists them, for example, under the sections of National Security Study or NS Decision Directives from the Reagan administration, National Security Reviews or NS Decisions from the (George H.W.) Bush administration, and Presidential Review Directives or Presidential Decision Directives from the Clinton administration. Copies of the documents that are not still classified are available online here.The site also directs users to related resources, such as the National Security Archive organization and its repository of presidential directives on national security topics.
Subjects: Intelligence; Presidential Documents

1855. Presidential Directives and Where to Find Them
http://www.loc.gov/rr/news/directives.html
Sponsor: Library of Congress
Description: Although not a source for the directives themselves, this page presents a concise guide to finding presidential directives, documents issued by the National Security Council that are signed or authorized by the president. The guide lists print and online sources. It is intended for researchers using the Library of Congress, but will be of use to others as well.
Subject: Presidential Documents

1856. Presidential Job Performance
http://www.ropercenter.uconn.edu/
Sponsor: Roper Center for Public Opinion Research
Description: The Roper Center Web site reports job approval ratings for presidents from Franklin Roosevelt to the current administration. Prior to the current administration, the ratings are from the Gallup Organization. For the current administration, polling organizations include ABC News/Washington Post, NBC News/Wall Street Journal, and Gallup/CNN. Find the approval rating section by selecting Online Access to Data from the site's main menu, and then selecting Presidential Approval Rating.
Subject: Presidency

1857. Presidential Pardons
http://jurist.law.pitt.edu/pardons.htm
Sponsor: University of Pittsburgh School of Law
Description: Part of the University of Pittsburgh School of Law JURIST Web site, Presidential Pardons has a wealth of information on relevant law, history, and statistics. Sections include Constitutional Basis, Administration/Regulations, Cases, Clemency Statistics, Notable Pardons, Glossary, and Bibliography.

  The content and organization of Presidential Pardons lends itself both to ready reference and as a starting point for more extensive legal or historical research.
Subject: Pardons

1858. President's Foreign Intelligence Advisory Board
http://www.whitehouse.gov/pfiab/
Sponsor: White House — President's Foreign Intelligence Advisory Board
Description: The President's Foreign Intelligence Advisory Board provides advice to the president concerning the quality and adequacy of intelligence collection, analysis and estimates, counterintelligence, and other intelligence activities. The Board, through its Intelligence Oversight Board, also advises the president on the legality of foreign intelligence activities. The site includes basic information on the role and history of the board and list of past chairpersons.
Subjects: Intelligence; Presidential Advisors

1859. President's National Medal of Science
http://www.nsf.gov/nsb/awards/nms/medal.htm
Sponsor: National Science Foundation (NSF)
Description: The National Medal of Science was established by Congress in 1959 as a Presidential Award to be given to individuals "deserving of special recognition by reason of their outstanding contributions to knowledge in the physical, biological, mathematical, or engineering sciences." In 1980, Congress expanded this recognition to include the social and behavioral sciences. This site features information on nomination procedures, former Medalists, and members of the President's Committee. To see what information is available, move your computer mouse over the Medal of Science heading.
Subject: Science — Awards and Honors

1860. Presidents of the United States (POTUS)
http://www.potus.com
Alternate URL: http://www.ipl.org/div/potus/
Sponsor: Internet Public Library
Description: The Presidents of the United States (POTUS) Web site is created by Robert Summers and hosted by the Internet Public Library, a University of Michigan School of Information project. For the current and all former presidents, the POTUS site provides background information, election results, Cabinet members, notable events, and some points of biographical interest. Each president's page features links to other Web sites for more information when available. For example, some Cabinet member names may link to an Internet-accessible biography. There are two versions of the site: one at the primary URL above and one at the alternate. At the time of this writing, the material at the primary URL had been updated most recently.

  IPL's POTUS can be a convenient starting point, but researchers must remember to evaluate each of the linked Internet sources for quality.
Subjects: Presidency; President's Cabinet

1861. Public Papers of the Presidents of the United States
http://www.gpo.gov/nara/pubpaps/srchpaps.html
Sponsors: National Archives and Records Administration (NARA) — Federal Register Office; Government Printing Office (GPO)
Description: This GPO database makes available material that was compiled and published in the series entitled *The Public Papers of the Presidents of the United States*. Although the series covers presidents back to Hoover, only the papers of the Clinton administration and one volume for

George H. W. Bush are available online at this time. The site states that "volumes covering years prior and subsequent to the ones that are currently available will be added on an incremental basis." Each volume in the series contains the papers and speeches of the President of the United States that were issued by the Office of the Press Secretary during the specified time period.

This site allows users to search each annual edition alone or in combination with other editions. Results are in HTML and PDF formats. Users may also browse the database by type of material, including Photographic Portfolio, Presidential Documents Published in the *Federal Register*, Subject, Name, and Table of Contents.

Publication: *Public Papers of the President*, AE 2.114:

1862. Results.gov: Resources for the President's Team
http://www.results.gov
Sponsor: White House — Executive Office of the President
Description: This site is designed for federal employees and "members of the President's team." A section on the President's Management Agenda features information on the agenda, quarterly scorecards rating departments' progress on the agenda, and updates from the individual departments. A section on the President and his Management Team has a directory of Bush administration appointees with photographs and brief biographies. The Tools for Success section has information on ethics, records management, the legislative process, and government oversight.
Subject: Government Administration — Policy

1863. Secret Service
http://www.treas.gov/usss/
Sponsor: Treasury Department — Secret Service
Description: The U.S. Secret Service is being transferred in whole from the Department of the Treasury, where it was founded in 1865, to the new Department of Homeland Security. The current Secret Service Web site describes the agency and its work in such sections as History, Strategic Plan, Director, and FAQ. Topical sections include Protection, Investigations (covering counterfeit and fraud), Employment, and Partnerships. The Press Room includes press releases and information on fugitives wanted by the Secret Service.

Although the Secret Service does not discuss details of its security operations, its Web site is designed to give clear answers to many of the questions the public may have. The FAQ answers questions such as "Who is the Secret Service authorized to protect?" and "How long do former presidents receive Secret Service protection after they leave office?"
Subjects: Counterfeiting; Homeland Security; Law Enforcement
Publication: *Know Your Money*, T 34.2:

1864. The President's Council on Bioethics
http://www.bioethics.gov/
Description: Established in 2001, the Council is charged with advising the president on bioethical issues that may emerge as a consequence of advances in biomedical science and technology. The Web site includes a Council meeting schedule, meeting transcripts, and brief biographies of its members. Council working papers (under Background Materials) are available in HTML. The Bookshelf section consists of a selection of readings in history, fiction, philosophy, and poetry that concern bioethical dilemmas. A short list of related sites includes a link to the archived site of the National Bioethics Advisory Commission, whose charter expired in 2001.
Subjects: Bioethics — Policy; Presidential Advisors

1865. Vice President Richard Cheney
http://www.whitehouse.gov/vicepresident/
Sponsor: White House — Vice President's Office
Description: Vice President Cheney's Web page includes links to his biography, speeches and statements, and a biography of Mrs. Cheney. Links to the full text of the speeches and statements are listed in reverse chronological order. There is also historical information on the Ceremonial Office of the Vice President, located in the Eisenhower Executive Office Building.
Subject: Vice President

1866. Weekly Compilation of Presidential Documents

http://www.access.gpo.gov/nara/nara003.html

Sponsor: National Archives and Records Administration (NARA) — Federal Register Office

Description: *The Weekly Compilation of Presidential Documents*, published every Monday, contains the text of the president's speeches, bill signing statements, Executive Orders, Proclamations, communications to Congress, and other presidential materials released by the White House during the preceding week. *Weekly Compilation* documents from 1993 to the present can be searched by keyword separately or by combining years. Beginning with the 2001 edition, users can also browse the documents by clicking on a weekly table of contents.

Subject: Presidential Documents

Publication: *Weekly Compilation of Presidential Documents*, AE 2.109:

1867. White House Fellows Program

http://www.whitehousefellows.gov/

Sponsor: White House

Description: The non-partisan White House Fellows Program was established by President Lyndon B. Johnson in 1964 to provide professionals first-hand experience in governing the nation early in their careers. Each Fellow works full time for one year as a special assistant to a Cabinet member or senior presidential advisor. The site has information on the program, selection criteria, application process, current class of Fellows, and prominent alumni.

Subject: Fellowships

1868. White House Military Office

http://www.whitehouse.gov/whmo/

Sponsor: White House

Description: This site explains the role and responsibilities of the White House Military Office. There are links to pages describing each of the Office's units: the White House Communications Agency, Presidential Airlift Group (Air Force One), White House Medical Unit, Camp David, Marine Helicopter Squadron One, Presidential Food Service, and the White House Transportation Agency.

Subject: President

Clinton Administration Archives

1869. Al Gore, Vice President of the United States

http://clinton4.nara.gov/WH/EOP/OVP/VP.html

Alternate URLs: http://clinton2.nara.gov/WH/EOP/OVP/index.html
http://clinton3.nara.gov/WH/EOP/OVP/
http://clinton1.nara.gov/White_House/EOP/OVP/html/GORE_Home.html

Sponsor: National Archives and Records Administration (NARA)

Description: The former vice president's Web site has been moved to and archived at the National Archives and Records Administration site. Four different versions or windows of this site are accessible (via the primary and alternate URLs), representing the four different "snap shots" preserved of the Clinton White House Web site as it evolved during the president's stay in office. Thus, the vice president's Web site looks as it did at these four different times. The most recent Web site, the primary URL, (July 2000–January 2001) features sections entitled News Releases, Speeches, Initiatives, and Biography and links to other sections of the Clinton White House Web site. Links to other sites outside the White House Web page will no longer work.

Subject: Vice President

1870. Clinton Presidential Materials Project

Alternate URL: http://clinton.archives.gov/

Sponsor: National Archives and Records Administration (NARA)

Description: In addition to the material that appears in the *Public Papers of the Presidents* series, administrations create numerous records, personal and donated papers, and memorabilia. Under federal law, this material is maintained by the National Archives and Records Administration.

Although much of this material will not be available to researchers and the public for a few years, this site presents one important resource from the Clinton administration: its Web sites. In addition to information about the Clinton Presidential Materials Project, this site links to archived White House Web sites.In 1994, the Clinton administration created the first Web site for the White House. The initial design was revised several times during Clinton's two terms. The White House staff took a "snap shot" of each of these versions of the White House Web site, and each one is preserved by NARA. Users may browse and search each "frozen" Web site, or perform a search across all versions. These Web sites are considered historical materials, and are not updated or changed. Links to outside resources no longer work, and some images have been omitted due to rights issues. While many electronic documents preservation issues are yet to be resolved, the National Archives and Records Administration has provided a valuable public service by answering the question: Where do Web sites of previous administrations go?
Subject: Presidential Documents

1871. Hillary Rodham Clinton, First Lady of the United States
`http://clinton4.nara.gov/WH/EOP/First_Lady/html/HILLARY_Home.html`
Alternate URLs: `http://clinton3.nara.gov/WH/EOP/First_Lady/html/HILLARY_Home.html`
`http://clinton2.nara.gov/WH/EOP/First_Lady/html/HILLARY_Home.html`
Sponsor: National Archives and Records Administration (NARA)
Description: The Web site of the former first lady, Mrs. Hillary Rodham Clinton, is now archived by NARA at the Clinton Presidential Materials Project Web site. At the section entitled White House Web Sites, search the three different versions of the Clinton White House Web site to access the different Web pages of the former first lady. The primary URL leads to the last and latest version of her Web site as the first lady. Her previous two Web pages can be accessed via the alternate URLs.The former first lady's Web site includes biographical information, her speeches, the text of her weekly column, "Talking It Over," recipes, discussion of life in the White House, and biographies and portraits of former first ladies.

The speeches and column of a first lady are not typically available in other government publication outlets. This page provides access to material that might not otherwise be readily accessible.
Subject: First Lady

1872. National Partnership for Reinventing Government (NPR)
`http://govinfo.library.unt.edu/npr/`
Description: The National Partnership for Reinventing Government has ended, but its Web site has been archived—exactly as it appeared on January 19, 2001—by the Government Printing Office's Federal Depository Library Program and its partner, the University of North Texas Libraries Government Documents Department. The archived Web site includes such sections as Who We Are; Hammer Awards; Accomplishments; Initiatives; High Impact Agencies; REGO E-Zine; Speeches; and Library, with HTML and PDF versions of many of the NPR publications. Vice President Gore's National Partnership for Reinventing Government (formerly known as the National Performance Review) made extensive use of its Web site. The archived site continues to provide access to an enormous amount of information about this initiative and accomplishments.
Publications: *National Performance Review Regulatory Sector Reports*, PrVp 42.18:
Reinvention Roundtable, PrVp 42.15:

CHAPTER 17

State and Local

The last two chapters of this book move beyond the resources of the U.S. federal government. This chapter focuses on U.S. state and local governments, while the next covers international and foreign government sites.

Many state and local governments have made tremendous strides in using the Internet to share information and facilitate services. State executive, judicial, and legislative information is available on the Web just as it is at the federal level. But, just as these governments are geographically dispersed, their Web sites also are decentralized. In the General section, this chapter highlights several Web resources that bring the links together in one site or serve as central information resources for the state and local governments themselves.

Following the General section, sites sponsored by state and local governments are listed in alphabetic order by state name. Each state's entry describes several major state government sites and is followed by a brief listing of city and county sites. While the emphasis of this book is clearly on resources at the federal level, this abbreviated listing of state and local government resources will provide an entry to more non-federal government information.

Bookmarks & Favorites

State and Local Government
- Cities Online,
  http://www.usmayors.org/uscm/meet_mayors/cities_online/
- State and Local Government on the Net,
  http://www.statelocalgov.net/index.cfm
- State Legislatures, State Laws, and State Regulations
  http://www.llsdc.org/sourcebook/state-leg.htm

Featured Sites

1873. State and Local Government on the Net
http://www.statelocalgov.net/index.cfm
Alternate URL: http://www.piperinfo.com/state/index.cfm
Sponsor: Piper Resources
Description: The core of this site is a directory of state and local government Web sites, organized alphabetically by state name. For each state or territory, resources are categorized by State Home Page, State Directory, Statewide Offices, Legislative Branch, Judicial Branch, Executive Branch, Boards and Commissions, Regional, Counties, Cities, and Libraries. In addition to the state and local listings, the site features links to several federal resources of special interest to communities, multi-state sites, and national organizations relevant to state and local government. This is an excellent finding aid for state and local government resources. Categorizations within each state's listing make it easy to quickly identify the pertinent Web site. The site has a selective policy for inclusion of links, clearly explained in an FAQ.
Subjects: State Government; Finding Aids

1874. State Legislatures, State Laws, and State Regulations
http://www.llsdc.org/sourcebook/state-leg.htm
Sponsor: Law Librarians' Society of Washington DC, Inc.
Description: This site provides a compact list of Web links and phone numbers. For each state, there are links to the legislature, code, and regulations, where available. These are followed by phone numbers for the state legislative information service and state library or state law library. Links to other Web sites relevant to state law or policy research are provided at the very bottom of the page.

This concise and useful list is compiled and maintained by Rick McKinney for the Law Librarians Society of Washington, DC.
Subject: State Legislatures

The state and local government resources in this chapter are divided into two sections, spanning the entry numbers indicated here:

General	1875–1885
Individual States	1886–4524

General

1875. Association of State and Territorial Health Officials
http://www.astho.org/
Sponsor: Association of State and Territorial Health Officials (ASTHO)
Description: The Association of State and Territorial Health Officials (ASTHO) is a nonprofit public health organization that represents the leaders of state and territorial health agencies. The site features news and policy on such topics as bioterrorism, environmental health, infectious diseases, and access to health care. The State and Territorial Links section has a map for access to the Web sites of the state and territorial health agencies.
Subject: Public Health

1876. Cities Online
http://www.usmayors.org/uscm/meet_mayors/cities_online/
Sponsor: U.S. Conference of Mayors
Description: The U.S. Conference of Mayors provides this directory of city government Web sites. A clickable map of the U.S. and its territories leads to the available city sites for the state or area selected.
Subjects: Local Government; Directories

1877. FirstGov for State Workers
http://www.statelocal.gov/
Sponsor: General Services Administration
Description: Formerly called the U.S. State and Local Gateway, this portal is a federal interagency project that has been developed to give state and local government officials and employees easy access to federal information. It organizes links to federal Web resources on topics such as Health, Education, Grants, Financial Management, and Public Safety.
Subject: State Government

1878. Municipal Codes
http://www.spl.org/selectedsites/municode.html
Sponsor: Seattle Public Library
Description: This page links to U.S. city and county codes that are freely available on the Web. The site also links to several code publishers that offer commercial access.
Subject: Local Government — Laws

1879. National Association of Counties
http://www.naco.org/
Sponsor: National Association of Counties
Description: The National Association of Counties represents county governments in federal policy and legislative matters. Under About Counties, their Web site links to an extensive directory of county governments and officials. This section also links to a selection of county codes and county administrative policies online.
Subject: Local Government

1880. National Center for State Courts
http://www.ncsconline.org/
Sponsor: National Center for State Courts
Description: The National Center for State Courts (NCSC) is an independent, nonprofit organization concerned with the administration of state courts. The site features links to Web sites for similar court and justice administration associations. The Library section includes a Court Information Database and a directory of links to state, federal, and international court Web sites.
Subject: State Courts

1881. National Conference of State Legislatures
http://www.ncsl.org/
Sponsor: National Conference of State Legislatures (NCSL)
Description: NCSL is a bipartisan organization serving state legislators and legislative staff. While many valuable sections of the site are available only to NCSL members or subscribers, the site does freely offer some policy and reference information. NCSL policy news and positions are organized by topics such as State Budgets, State-Federal Relations, and Tax and Revenue. The State Legislatures section includes an index to state legislative Web sites. Reference information in the About State Legislatures section includes 50-state compilations of legislature session dates, legislator compensation, leadership positions in state legislatures, and other information. The Press Room section has links to the state capitals' newspapers online, as well as to editorial cartoons. This site should be of broad interest to state legislators and to officials, managers, and administrators of state legislative bodies. Others can benefit from the reference information and background on policies of interest to state governments.
Subject: State Legislatures

1882. National Governors Association (NGA) Online
http://www.nga.org/
Sponsor: National Governors' Association (NGA)
Description: The NGA site features state government news and policy background along with reference information about the current U.S. state governors. NGA policy positions and summaries of current legislative issues are organized by topics such as federalism, homeland security, and Superfund and brownfields. The Governors section has lists of the current governors, their Web sites, postal addresses, staff, speeches, media contacts, and terms of office.
Subject: Governors

1883. State Law: State Government and Legislative Information
http://www.washlaw.edu/uslaw/statelaw.html
Sponsor: Washburn University. School of Law
Description: With an emphasis on state law, this site has sections for each state which include links to sites for Attorneys General, legislatures, courts, statutes, constitutions, and local legal resources. The state sections also have search forms for state judicial opinions and state statutes when those are available.

Since the developers take a broad view of what constitutes legal resources, State Law is useful for those interested in judicial and legislative information as well as general state and local government information. Weak points include a search function that searches the site's Archive but is poorly documented, and links that are not uniformly kept up to date.
Subject: State Courts

1884. State Legislative History Research Guides
http://www.law.indiana.edu/lib/netres/govt/stateurlslist.html
Sponsor: Indiana University School of Law
Description: This site lists links to legislative research guides for most, but not all, states in the U.S. The online guides are listed in alphabetical order by state. Each state's name links directly to its legislature.
Subject: State Legislatures

1885. State Search
https://www.nascio.org/stateSearch/
Sponsor: National Association of State Chief Information Officers (NASCIO)
Description: State Search is a functional index to state government agency Web sites. Links to state agencies are organized under categories such as Disabilities Agencies, Employment Services, Police, and Treasurers.
   The functional approach and uncluttered style of this site make it a serviceable finding aid.
Subjects: State Government; Finding Aids

Alabama

1886. Alabama Legislature
http://www.legislature.state.al.us/
Description: The Legislature site has information on legislators and committees, current activities, and the state legislative process. Bill status and legislative documents are on the site's ALISON system, along with the state code and constitution.

1887. Alabama.gov
http://www.alabama.gov/
Sponsor: Alabama State Government
Description: Alabama.gov links to state agencies and organizations, as well as to the Web sites for Alabama cities and counties. It includes a government services section and travel and state facts section.
Subject: Alabama

1888. State of Alabama Judicial System Online
http://www.judicial.state.al.us/
Sponsor: Alabama. Supreme Court
Description: This site links to Alabama state courts information, including judicial biographies and support information from the Administrative Office of Courts.
Subject: Alabama

Local Governments

1889. Andalusia
http://www.andalusianet.com

1890. Athens
http://www.ci.athens.al.us

1891. Auburn
http://www.auburnalabama.org

1892. Baldwin County
http://www.co.baldwin.al.us

1893. Birmingham
http://www.ci.bham.al.us

1894. Blount County
http://www.blounthome.com/Main.htm

1895. Cullman County
http://www.co.cullman.al.us

1896. Daphne
http://www.daphneal.com

1897. Dothan
http://www.dothan.org

1898. Enterprise
http://www.entercomp.com/users/city/

1899. Etowah County
http://www.etowahcounty.org

1900. Fairhope
http://www.cofairhope.com

1901. Florence
http://www.ci.florence.al.us

1902. Gadsden
http://www.ci.gadsden.al.us

1903. Goodwater
http://www.goodwater.org

1904. Gulf Shores
http://www.ci.gulf-shores.al.us

1905. Heflin
http://www.cityofheflin.org

1906. Hoover
http://www.hooveral.org

1907. Houston County
http://www.houstoncounty.org

1908. Hueytown
http://www.hueytown.org

1909. Huntsville
http://www.ci.huntsville.al.us

1910. Irondale
http://www.cityofirondale.org

1911. Jasper
http://www.jaspercity.com

1912. Jefferson County
http://www.jeffcointouch.com/ieindex.asp

1913. Limestone County
http://www.co.limestone.al.us

1914. Lincoln
http://www.lincolnalabama.com

1915. Madison County
http://www.co.madison.al.us

1916. Mobile
http://www.ci.mobile.al.us

1917. Montgomery
http://www.montgomery.al.us

1918. Opelika
http://www.ci.opelika.al.us

1919. Oxford
http://www.oxfordalabama.org

1920. Pelham
http://www.pelhamonline.com/PelhamOnlineMain.asp?ID=2

1921. Pell City
http://www.cityofpellcity.com

1922. Prattville
http://www.prattville.com

1923. Russellville
http://www.russellvillegov.com

1924. Tuscaloosa
http://www.ci.tuscaloosa.al.us

1925. Tuscaloosa County
http://www.co.tuscaloosa.al.us

1926. Valley
http://www.cityofvalley.com/

1927. Walker County
http://www.walkercounty.com

1928. Wetumpka
http://www.wetumpka.al.us

Alaska

1929. Alaska Court System
http://www.state.ak.us/courts/
Alternate URL: http://www.touchngo.com/sp/sp.htm
Sponsor: Alaska. Court System
Description: This site includes Alaska Supreme Court and Court of Appeals slip opinions. Access is by date. Unfortunately, opinions are removed from this site once they are printed. However, the alternate URL includes the full text of the Supreme Court opinions from 1991 through the present.
Subject: Alaska

1930. Alaska State Legislature
http://www.legis.state.ak.us/
Sponsor: Alaska. Legislature

Description: This site features the Alaska statutes back to 1993, a current bill tracking system, and the text of bills back to 1983. The Information Documents section has reference material on the state legislators and legislative process.
Subject: Alaska

1931. State of Alaska Online
http://www.state.ak.us/
Sponsor: Alaska State Government
Description: State of Alaska Online has information from state agencies and on state government services. Other sections include information on finding jobs and on doing business in Alaska.
Subject: Alaska

Local Governments

1932. Anchorage
http://www.muni.org/homepage/

1933. Bristol Bay Borough
http://www.theborough.com

1934. Delta Junction
http://www.delta-junction.org/

1935. Dillingham
http://www.ci.dillingham.ak.us

1936. Fairbanks
http://www.ci.fairbanks.ak.us/

1937. Fairbanks North Star Borough
http://www.co.fairbanks.ak.us

1938. Juneau
http://www.juneau.lib.ak.us

1939. Kenai
http://www.ci.kenai.ak.us

1940. Kenai Peninsula Borough
http://www.borough.kenai.ak.us

1941. Kodiak Island Borough
http://www.kib.co.kodiak.ak.us

1942. Lake and Peninsula Borough
http://www.bristolbay.com/~lpboro/

1943. Matanuska-Susitna Borough
http://www.co.mat-su.ak.us

1944. Petersburg
http://ci.petersburg.ak.us/

1945. Sitka
http://www.cityofsitka.com

1946. Soldotna
http://www.ci.soldotna.ak.us

1947. Valdez
http://www.ci.valdez.ak.us

1948. Wrangell
http://www.wrangell.com

Arizona

1949. Arizona @ Your Service ™
http://www.az.gov/webapp/portal/
Sponsor: Arizona State Government
Description: The Arizona state site is designed as a portal to state agencies and services as well as to cities, counties, and travel and leisure information.

This site is well-designed, with information arranged by broad topic and with quick links to frequently requested information.
Subject: Arizona

1950. Arizona Judicial Branch
http://www.supreme.state.az.us/
Sponsor: Arizona. Supreme Court
Description: This site includes both Arizona Supreme Court and Court of Appeals opinions. They are available in PDF format. The state supreme court opinions go back to 1998 and the court of appeals opinions to 2000.
Subject: Arizona

1951. Arizona State Legislature
http://www.azleg.state.az.us/
Sponsor: Arizona. Legislature
Description: This site features an online version of the *Arizona Revised Statutes*, current legislation status, committee agendas, and a members directory. The full text of bills is available along with current status and subsequent versions of the bills as well as live webcasts of the state senate and house of representatives. Archival coverage goes back to the 1995 legislative session.

This is a well-designed site with a great deal of full-text legislative material available.
Subject: Arizona

Local Governments

1952. Apache County
http://www.co.apache.az.us

1953. Apache Junction
http://www.ci.apache-jct.az.us

1954. Avondale
http://www.ci.avondale.az.us

1955. Benson
http://www.cityofbenson.com

1956. Bullhead City
http://www.bullheadcity.com

1957. Camp Verde
http://www.cvaz.org/

1958. Casa Grande
http://www.ci.casa-grande.az.us

1959. Chandler
http://www.chandleraz.org

1960. Chino Valley
http://www.ci.chino-valley.az.us

1961. Clarkdale
http://www.clarkdale.az.us

1962. Cochise County
http://www.co.cochise.az.us

1963. Coconino County
http://co.coconino.az.us

1964. Douglas
http://www.ci.douglas.az.us

1965. Eagar
http://www.eagar.com

1966. Fountain Hills
http://www.ci.fountain-hills.az.us

1967. Gilbert
http://www.ci.gilbert.az.us

1968. Glendale
http://www.ci.glendale.az.us

1969. Goodyear
http://www.ci.goodyear.az.us

1970. Holbrook
http://www.ci.holbrook.az.us

1971. La Paz County
htto://www.co.la-paz.az.us

1972. Lake Havasu City
http://www.ci.lake-havasu-city.az.us

1973. Maran
http://www.marana.com

1974. Maricopa County
http://www.maricopa.gov

1975. Mesa
http://www.ci.mesa.az.us

1976. Mojave County
http://www.co.mohave.az.us

1977. Navajo Count
http://www.co.navajo.az.us

1978. Oro Valley
http://www.ci.oro-valley.az.us

1979. Page
http://www.ci.page.az.us

1980. Paradise Valley
http://www.ci.paradise-valley.az.us/townhall/

1981. Payson
http://www.ci.payson.az.us

1982. Peoria
http://www.peoriaaz.com

1983. Phoenix
http://www.ci.phoenix.az.us

1984. Pima County
http://www.co.pima.az.us

1985. Pinal County
http://www.co.pinal.az.us

1986. Prescott
http://www.cityofprescott.net/

1987. Prescott Valley
http://www.ci.prescott-valley.az.us

1988. Queen Creek
http://www.queencreek.org

1989. Safford
http://www.ci.safford.az.us

1990. Saint Johns
http://www.stjohnsaz.com

1991. Scottsdale
http://www.scottsdaleaz.gov/

1992. Sedona
http://www.city.sedona.net

1993. Show Low
http://www.ci.show-low.az.us

1994. Sierra Vista
http://www.ci.sierra-vista.az.us

1995. Springerville
http://www.springerville.com

1996. Surprise
http://www.surpriseaz.com

1997. Tempe
http://www.tempe.gov

1998. Tombstone
http://www.cityoftombstone.com

1999. Tucson
http://www.ci.tucson.az.us

2000. Yavapai County
http://www.co.yavapai.az.us

2001. Yuma
http://www.ci.yuma.az.us

2002. Yuma County
http://www.co.yuma.az.us

Arkansas

2003. access Arkansas.org
http://www.state.ar.us/
Sponsor: Arkansas State Government
Description: This Arkansas government site highlights the state's e-government services and online directories of Arkansas state offices, counties, and cities. Other sections include business, tourism, community, and education information.
Subject: Arkansas

2004. Arkansas General Assembly
http://www.arkleg.state.ar.us/
Sponsor: Arkansas. Legislature
Description: This site features sections on Legislators and Committees, Meetings and Events, Research Resources, Bills and Resolutions, and Acts. The session bills and acts are accessible by number or via the keyword search option and are available in HTML format. Another option gives current bill status information. The Arkansas Code is available under Research Resources in an HTML and Java version.
Subject: Arkansas

2005. Arkansas Judiciary
http://courts.state.ar.us/
Sponsor: Arkansas. Supreme Court
Description: This site provides access to opinions of the Arkansas Supreme Court and the Court of Appeals back to 1994. Access is by date and the opinions are available in HTML and WordPerfect 5.1 formats. The site also features information on state judges, the Arkansas court system, bar exam, and judiciary-related government bodies.
Subject: Arkansas

Local Governments

2006. Barling
http://www.barlingar.com

2007. Benton County
http://www.co.benton.ar.us

2008. Cherokee Village
http://www.cherokeevillage.org

2009. Conway
http://www.cityofconway.org

2010. Eureka Springs
http://www.cityofeurekasprings.org

2011. Fayetteville
http://www.uark.edu/ALADDIN/cityinfo/cityweb/

2012. Fort Smith
http://www.fsark.com

2013. Hot Springs
http://www.ci.hot-springs.ar.us

2014. Jonesboro
http://www.jonesboro.org

2015. Little Rock
http://www.littlerock.org

2016. Maumelle
http://maumelle.dina.org/

2017. Melbourne
http://www.melbournear.com

2018. North Little Rock
http://www.northlr.org

2019. Pine Bluff
http://cityofpinebluff.com

2020. Pulaski County
http://www.co.pulaski.ar.us

2021. Rogers
http://www.rogersarkansas.com

2022. Siloam Springs
http://www.siloamsprings.com

2023. Springdale
http://www.springdaleark.org

2024. Texarkana
http://www.txkusa.org/arkansas/

2025. Washington County
http://www.co.washington.ar.us

2026. West Memphis
http://www.ci.west-memphis.ar.us

California

2027. California Court
http://www.courtinfo.ca.gov/
Sponsor: California. Judicial System
Description: Linking to many of the different California court and judiciary sites, this page is a central starting point for judicial information from California. The site has links to the Opinions, Forms, Rules, Programs, and Reference. The Opinions area contains the slip opinions of the Supreme Court and Courts of Appeal issued in the last 60 days.
Subject: California

2028. California Online Services
http://www.ca.gov/state/portal/myca_homepage.jsp
Sponsor: California State Government
Description: This main California Web site offers a wealth of information, including details on travel, transportation, and California history and culture. Choose the Government section for links to all three branches of government.
Subject: California

2029. Official California Legislative Information
http://www.leginfo.ca.gov/
Sponsor: California. Legislature
Description: This public site for the California Legislature features five main categories: Bill Information, California Law, Legislative Publications, Today's Events, and Your Legislature. It includes daily updates of both Assembly and Senate bills and the full text of the California Codes. The bills are available back to the 1993–94 session and are searchable by bill number, keyword, or author.
Subject: California

Local Governments

2030. Adelanto
http://www.ci.adelanto.ca.us

2031. Agoura Hills
http://www.ci.agoura-hills.ca.us

2032. Alameda
http://www.ci.alameda.ca.us/home/index.html

2033. Alpine County
http://www.alpinecountyca.com/

2034. American Canyon
http://www.ci.american-canyon.ca.us

2035. Anaheim
http://www.anaheim.net

2036. Anderson
http://www.ci.anderson.ca.us

2037. Angels Camp
http://www.angelscamp.gov/

2038. Antioch
http://www.ci.antioch.ca.us

2039. Apple Valley
http://www.applevalley.org

2040. Arcadia
http://www.ci.arcadia.ca.us

2041. Arroyo Grand
http://www.arroyogrande.org

2042. Atwater
http://www.ci.atwater.ca.us

2043. Azusa
http://www.ci.azusa.ca.us/

2044. Bakersfield
http://www.ci.bakersfield.ca.us

2045. Baldwin Park
http://www.baldwinpark.com

2046. Banning
http://www.ci.banning.ca.us

2047. Beaumont
http://www.ci.beaumont.ca.us

2048. Bell Gardens
http://www.ci.bell-gardens.ca.us

2049. Bellflower
http://www.bellflower.org

2050. Belmont
http://www.belmont.gov

2051. Benecia
http://www.ci.benicia.ca.us

2052. Berkeley
http://www.ci.berkeley.ca.us

2053. Beverly Hill
http://www.ci.beverly-hills.ca.us

2054. Big Bear Lake
http://www.citybigbearlake.com

2055. Bradbury
http://www.cityofbradbury.org

2056. Brea
http://www.ci.brea.ca.us

2057. Brentwood
http://www.ci.brentwood.ca.us

2058. Brisbane
http://www.ci.brisbane.ca.us

2059. Buena Park
http://www.buenapark.com

2060. Burbank
http://www.ci.burbank.ca.us

2061. Burlingame
http://www.burlingame.org/

2062. Calabasas
http://www.ci.calabasas.ca.us

2063. Calaveras County
http://www.co.calaveras.ca.us

2064. California City
http://www.city.california-city.ca.us

2065. Calistoga
http://www.ci.calistoga.ca.us

2066. Camarillo
http://www.ci.camarillo.ca.us

2067. Campbell
http://www.ci.campbell.ca.us

2068. Canyon Lake
http://www.ci.canyon-lake.ca.us

2069. Capitola
http://www.ci.capitola.ca.us

2070. Carlsbad
http://www.ci.carlsbad.ca.us

2071. Carpinteria
http://www.ci.carpinteria.ca.us

2072. Cathedral City
http://www.cathedralcity.gov/

2073. Ceres
http://www.ci.ceres.ca.us

2074. Cerritos
http://www.ci.cerritos.ca.us

2075. Chico
http://www.ci.chico.ca.us

2076. Chula Vista
http://www.ci.chula-vista.ca.us

2077. Citrus Heights
http://www.ci.citrus-heights.ca.us

2078. Claremont
http://www.ci.claremont.ca.us

2079. Clayton
http://www.ci.clayton.ca.us

2080. Cloverdale
http://www.cloverdale.net

2081. Clovis
http://www.ci.clovis.ca.us/

2082. Colton
http://www.ci.colton.ca.us/

2083. Commerce
http://www.ci.commerce.ca.us/

2084. Concord
http://www.cityofconcord.org/

2085. Contra Costa County
http://www.co.contra-costa.ca.us

2086. Corona
http://www.ci.corona.ca.us

2087. Coronado
http://www.coronado.ca.us

2088. Corte Madera
http://www.ci.corte-madera.ca.us

2089. Costa Mesa
http://www.cityofcostamesa.com

2090. Cotati
http://www.ci.cotati.ca.us

2091. Covina
http://www.ci.covina.ca.us

2092. Crescent City
http://www.crescentcity.org

2093. Culver City
http://www.culvercity.org

2094. Cupertino
http://www.cupertino.org

2095. Cypress
http://www.ci.cypress.ca.us

2096. Daly City
http://www.ci.daly-city.ca.us

2097. Danville
http://www.ci.danville.ca.us

2098. Davis
http://www.city.davis.ca.us

2099. Del Mar
http://www.delmar.ca.us

2100. Del Norte County
http://www.dnco.org/

2101. Delano
http://www.delano-ca.org/

2102. Diamond Bar
http://www.ci.diamond-bar.ca.us

2103. Dixon
http://www.ci.dixon.ca.us

2104. Downey
http://www.downeyca.org

2105. Dublin
http://www.ci.dublin.ca.us/

2106. East Palo Alto
http://www.ci.east-palo-alto.ca.us

2107. El Cajon
http://www.ci.el-cajon.ca.us

2108. El Cerrito
http://www.el-cerrito.org/home/

2109. El Dorado County
http://www.co.el-dorado.ca.us

2110. El Monte
http://www.elmonte.org

2111. El Segundo
http://www.elsegundo.org

2112. Emeryville
http://www.ci.emeryville.ca.us

2113. Encinitas
http://www.ci.encinitas.ca.us

2114. Escondido
http://www.ci.escondido.ca.us

2115. Fillmore
http://www.fillmoreca.com

2116. Folsom
http://www.folsom.ca.us

2117. Fontana
http://www.fontana.org

2118. Fort Bragg
http://www.fortbragg.com

2119. Foster City
http://www.fostercity.org

2120. Fountain Valley
http://www.fountainvalley.org

2121. Fremont
http://www.ci.fremont.ca.us

2122. Fresno
http://www.ci.fresno.ca.us

2123. Fresno County
http://www.fresno.ca.gov/

2124. Fullerton
http://www.ci.fullerton.ca.us

2125. Garden Grove
http://www.ci.garden-grove.ca.us

2126. Gardena
http://www.ci.gardena.ca.us

2127. Gilroy
http://www.ci.gilroy.ca.us

2128. Glendale
http://www.ci.glendale.ca.us/

2129. Glendora
http://www.ci.glendora.ca.us

2130. Gonzales
http://www.gonzales-ca.com

2131. Grand Terrace
http://www.ci.grand-terrace.ca.us

2132. Greenfield
http://www.greenfield-ca.com

2133. Grover Beach
http://www.grover.org

2134. Hawthorne
http://www.cityofhawthorne.com

2135. Hayward
http://www.ci.hayward.ca.us

2136. Healdsburg
http://www.ci.healdsburg.ca.us

2137. Hemet
http://www.ci.hemet.ca.us

2138. Hercules
http://www.ci.hercules.ca.us

2139. Hermosa Beach
http://www.hermosabch.org

2140. Hesperia
http://www.ci.hesperia.ca.us/city.html

2141. Highland
http://www.ci.highland.ca.us

2142. Hollister
http://hollister.ca.gov

2143. Humboldt County
http://www.co.humboldt.ca.us

2144. Imperial Beach
http://www.cityofib.com//

2145. Imperial County
http://www.co.imperial.ca.us

2146. Indio
http://www.indio.org

2147. Industry
http://www.cityofindustry.org

2148. Inglewood
http://www.cityofinglewood.org

2149. Irvine
http://www.ci.irvine.ca.us

2150. Kern County
http://www.co.kern.ca.us

2151. Kings County
http://www.countyofkings.com/

2152. La Habra
http://www.ci.la-habra.ca.us

2153. La Quinta
http://www.la-quinta.org

2154. La Verne
http://www.ci.la-verne.ca.us

2155. Lafayette
http://www.ci.lafayette.ca.us

2156. Laguna Beach
http://www.lagunabeachcity.org

2157. Laguna Niguel
http://www.ci.laguna-niguel.ca.us

2158. Lake County
http://www.co.lake.ca.us

2159. Lake Elsinore
http://www.lake-elsinore.org/

2160. Lakewood
http://www.lakewoodcity.org

2161. Lancaster
http://www.cityoflancasterca.org/

2162. Larkspur
http://www.ci.larkspur.ca.us

2163. Lassen County
http://www.co.lassen.ca.us

2164. Lemoore
http://www.lemoore.com

2165. Lindsay
http://www.lindsay.ca.us

2166. Livermore
http://www.ci.livermore.ca.us

2167. Lodi
http://www.lodi.gov

2168. Loma Linda
http://www.ci.loma-linda.ca.us

2169. Lompoc
http://www.ci.lompoc.ca.us

2170. Long Beach
http://www.ci.long-beach.ca.us

2171. Los Alamitos
http://www.ci.los-alamitos.ca.us

2172. Los Altos
http://www.ci.los-altos.ca.us

2173. Los Angeles
http://www.ci.la.ca.us

2174. Los Angeles County
http://www.co.la.ca.us

2175. Los Banos
http://www.losbanos.org

2176. Lynwood
http://www.lynwood.ca.us

2177. Malibu
http://www.ci.malibu.ca.us

2178. Manhattan Beach
http://www.ci.manhattan-beach.ca.us

2179. Manteca
http://www.ci.manteca.ca.us

2180. Marin County
http://www.marin.org/

2181. Marina
http://www.ci.marina.ca.us

2182. Mariposa County
http://www.mariposacounty.org/

2183. Martinez
http://www.cityofmartinez.org

2184. Maywood
http://www.cityofmaywood.com

2185. Mendocino County
http://www.co.mendocino.ca.us

2186. Menlo Park
http://www.ci.menlo-park.ca.us

2187. Merced
http://www.ci.merced.ca.us

2188. Merced County
http://www.co.merced.ca.us

2189. Milbrae
http://www.ci.millbrae.ca.us

2190. Mill Valley
http://www.cityofmillvalley.org

2191. Milpitas
http://www.ci.milpitas.ca.gov/

2192. Mission Viejo
http://www.ci.mission-viejo.ca.us/

2193. Modesto
http://www.ci.modesto.ca.us

2194. Monrovia
http://www.ci.monrovia.ca.us

2195. Montclair
http://www.ci.montclair.ca.us

2196. Monte Sereno
http://www.montesereno.org

2197. Monterey
http://www.monterey.org

2198. Monterey County
http://www.co.monterey.ca.us

2199. Monterey Park
http://www.ci.monterey-park.ca.us

2200. Moorpark
http://www.ci.moorpark.ca.us

2201. Moraga
http://www.ci.moraga.ca.us

2202. Moreno Valley
http://www.ci.moreno-valley.ca.us

2203. Morgan Hill
http://www.morgan-hill.ca.gov

2204. Mountain View
http://www.ci.mtnview.ca.us

2205. Murrieta
http://www.ci.murrieta.ca.us

2206. Napa
http://www.cityofnapa.org/

2207. Napa County
http://www.co.napa.ca.us

2208. Nevada County
http://www.mynevadacounty.com/

2209. Newark
http://www.newark.org

2210. Newman
http://www.cityofnewman.com

2211. Newport Beach
http://www.ci.newport-beach.ca.us

2212. Norco
http://www.ci.norco.ca.us

2213. Novato
http://www.ci.novato.ca.us

2214. Oakland
http://www.oaklandnet.com

2215. Oceanside
http://www.ci.oceanside.ca.us

2216. Ontario
http://www.ci.ontario.ca.us

2217. Orange
http://www.cityoforange.org

2218. Orange County
http://www.oc.ca.gov

2219. Orinda
http://www.ci.orinda.ca.us

2220. Oxnard
http://www.ci.oxnard.ca.us

2221. Pacifica
http://www.ci.pacifica.ca.us

2222. Palm Desert
http://www.palm-desert.org

2223. Palm Springs
http://www.ci.palm-springs.ca.us

2224. Palmdale
http://www.cityofpalmdale.org

2225. Palo Alto
http://www.city.palo-alto.ca.us

2226. Pasadena
http://www.ci.pasadena.ca.us

2227. Petaluma
http://www.ci.petaluma.ca.us

2228. Pico Rivera
http://www.ci.pico-rivera.ca.us

2229. Pinole
http://www.ci.pinole.ca.us

2230. Pismo Beach
http://www.pismobeach.org

2231. Pittsburg
http://www.ci.pittsburg.ca.us

2232. Placentia
http://www.placentia.org

2233. Placer County
http://www.placer.ca.gov

2234. Placerville
http://www.ci.placerville.ca.us

2235. Pleasant Hill
http://www.ci.pleasant-hill.ca.us

2236. Pleasanton
http://www.ci.pleasanton.ca.us/pleasanton.html

2237. Pomona
http://www.ci.pomona.ca.us

2238. Poway
http://www.ci.poway.ca.us

2239. Rancho Cucamonga
http://www.ci.rancho-cucamonga.ca.us

2240. Red Bluff
http://www.ci.red-bluff.ca.us

2241. Redding
http://www.ci.redding.ca.us

2242. Redlands
http://www.ci.redlands.ca.us

2243. Redondo Beach
http://www.redondo.org

2244. Redwood City
http://www.ci.redwood-city.ca.us

2245. Reedley
http://www.reedley.com

2246. Rialto
http://www.ci.rialto.ca.us

2247. Richmond
http://www.ci.richmond.ca.us

2248. Ridgecrest
http://www.ci.ridgecrest.ca.us/

2249. Ripon
http://www.cityofripon.org/

2250. Riverside
http://www.ci.riverside.ca.us

2251. Riverside County
http://www.co.riverside.ca.us

2252. Rocklin
http://www.rocklin.ca.gov

2253. Roseville
http://www.roseville.ca.us

2254. Sacramento
http://www.sacto.org

2255. Sacramento County
http://www.co.sacramento.ca.us

2256. Saint Helena
http://www.ci.st-helena.ca.us

2257. Salinas
http://www.ci.salinas.ca.us/

2258. San Anselmo
http://www.townofsananselmo.org

2259. San Bernardino
http://www.ci.san-bernardino.ca.us

2260. San Bernardino County
http://www.co.san-bernardino.ca.us

2261. San Bruno
http://www.ci.sanbruno.ca.us

2262. San Carlos
http://www.ci.san-carlos.ca.us/frontdoor/

2263. San Diego
http://www.ci.san-diego.ca.us

2264. San Diego County
http://www.co.san-diego.ca.us

2265. San Dimas
http://www.cityofsandimas.com/html/index.html

2266. San Francisco
http://www.ci.sf.ca.us

2267. San Jacinto
http://www.ci.san-jacinto.ca.us

2268. San Jose
http://www.ci.san-jose.ca.us

2269. San Juaquin County
http://www.co.san-joaquin.ca.us

2270. San Leandro
http://www.ci.san-leandro.ca.us

2271. San Luis Obispo
http://www.ci.san-luis-obispo.ca.us

2272. San Luis Obispo County
http://www.co.slo.ca.us/

2273. San Marcos
http://www.ci.san-marcos.ca.us

2274. San Marino
http://www.ci.san-marino.ca.us

2275. San Mateo
http://www.ci.sanmateo.ca.us

2276. San Mateo County
http://www.co.sanmateo.ca.us

2277. San Pablo
http://www.ci.san-pablo.ca.us

2278. San Rafael
http://www.cityofsanrafael.org

2279. San Ramon
http://www.ci.san-ramon.ca.us

2280. Santa Ana
http://www.ci.santa-ana.ca.us/

2281. Santa Barbara
http://www.ci.santa-barbara.ca.us

2282. Santa Barbara County
http://www.countyofsb.org/index.asp

2283. Santa Clara
http://www.ci.santa-clara.ca.us

2284. Santa Clara County
http://www.santaclaracounty.org

2285. Santa Clarita
http://www.ci.santa-clarita.ca.us

2286. Santa Cruz
http://www.ci.santa-cruz.ca.us

2287. Santa Cruz County
http://www.co.santa-cruz.ca.us

2288. Santa Fe Springs
http://www.santafesprings.org

2289. Santa Maria
http://www.ci.santa-maria.ca.us

2290. Santa Monica
http://pen.ci.santa-monica.ca.us/cm/

2291. Santa Rosa
http://www.ci.santa-rosa.ca.us/

2292. Sausalito
http://www.ci.sausalito.ca.us

2293. Scotts Valley
http://www.scottsvalley.org

2294. Seaside
http://www.ci.seaside.ca.us

2295. Shasta County
http://www.co.shasta.ca.us/

2296. Signal Hill
http://www.ci.signal-hill.ca.us/

2297. Simi Valley
http://www.ci.simi-valley.ca.us

2298. Siskiyou County
http://www.co.siskiyou.ca.us

2299. Solano County
http://www.co.solano.ca.us

2300. Sonoma
http://www.sonomacity.org/

2301. Sonoma County
http://www.sonoma-county.org

2302. South El Monte
http://www.ci.south-el-monte.ca.us

2303. South Gate
http://www.cityofsouthgate.org

2304. South Lake Tahoe
http://www.ci.south-lake-tahoe.ca.us

2305. South Pasadena
http://www.ci.south-pasadena.ca.us

2306. South San Francisco
http://www.ci.ssf.ca.us

2307. Stanislaus County
http://www.co.stanislaus.ca.us

2308. Stanton
http://www.ci.stanton.ca.us

2309. Stockton
http://www.ci.stockton.ca.us

2310. Suisun City
http://www.suisun.com

2311. Sunnyvale
http://www.ci.sunnyvale.ca.us

2312. Sutter County
http://www.co.sutter.ca.us

2313. Temecula
http://www.ci.temecula.ca.us

2314. Temple City
http://www.ci.temple-city.ca.us

2315. Thousand Oaks
http://www.ci.thousand-oaks.ca.us

2316. Tiburon
http://www.tiburon.org

2317. Torrance
http://www.ci.torrance.ca.us

2318. Tracy
http://www.ci.tracy.ca.us

2319. Trinity County
http://www.trinitycounty.org

2320. Tulare
http://www.ci.tulare.ca.us

2321. Tulare County
http://www.co.tulare.ca.us

2322. Turlock
http://www.ci.turlock.ca.us

2323. Twentynine Palms
http://www.29palms.com

2324. Union City
http://www.ci.union-city.ca.us

2325. Upland
http://www.ci.upland.ca.us

2326. Vacaville
http://www.cityofvacaville.com/

2327. Vallejo
http://www.ci.vallejo.ca.us

2328. Ventura
http://www.ci.ventura.ca.us

2329. Ventura County
http://www.countyofventura.org/

2330. Victorville
http://www.ci.victorville.ca.us

2331. Visalia
http://www.ci.visalia.ca.us

2332. Vista
http://www.ci.vista.ca.us

2333. Walnut
http://www.ci.walnut.ca.us

2334. Walnut Creek
http://www.ci.walnut-creek.ca.us

2335. Watsonville
http://www.ci.watsonville.ca.us

2336. West Hollywood
http://www.ci.west-hollywood.ca.us

2337. West Sacramento
http://www.ci.west-sacramento.ca.us

2338. Windsor
http://www.ci.windsor.ca.us

2339. Woodland
http://www.ci.woodland.ca.us

2340. Woodside
http://www.woodsidetown.org/

2341. Yolo County
http://www.yolocounty.org

2342. Yucaipa
http://www.yucaipa.org

Colorado

2343. Colorado General Assembly
http://www.state.co.us/gov_dir/stateleg.html
Sponsor: Colorado. Legislature
Description: The Colorado legislative site has the text and status of bills from the current session of the House and Senate, prior bill texts back to 1997, and a link to the state statutes online. The site also includes member and staff directories for the legislature and links to legislative support agencies.
Subject: Colorado

2344. Colorado Judicial Branch
http://www.courts.state.co.us/
Sponsor: Colorado. Supreme Court
Description: The Colorado Courts Web site links to the state's Supreme Court, Court of Appeals, Trial Courts, Water Court, and Denver Probate Court. It also links to searchable copies of the Supreme Court and Court of Appeals opinions. The site reports on the courts' operating statistics and profiles members of the state judiciary.
Subject: Colorado

2345. Colorado.gov
http://www.colorado.gov
Sponsor: Colorado State Government
Description: This official state Web site includes sections on education, employment, law enforcement, taxes, and tourism. The government section includes links to resources from the executive, judicial, and legislative branches including the state constitution, statutes, ballot issues, state agency links, and information on permits and licenses.
Subject: Colorado

Local Governments

2346. Adams County
http://www.co.adams.co.us

2347. Arapahoe County
http://www.co.arapahoe.co.us

2348. Aspen
http://www.aspengov.com

2349. Aurora
http://www.ci.aurora.co.us

2350. Boulder
http://www.ci.boulder.co.us

2351. Boulder County
http://www.co.boulder.co.us

2352. Broomfield
http://www.ci.broomfield.co.us

2353. Brush
http://www.brushcolo.com

2354. Clear Creek County
http://www.co.clear-creek.co.us

2355. Colorado Springs
http://www.springsgov.com/

2356. Craig
http://www.ci.craig.co.us

2357. Denver
http://www.denvergov.org

2358. Douglas County
http://www.douglas.co.us

2359. Durango
http://www.durangogov.org/

2360. Eagle County
http://www.eagle-county.com

2361. Edgewater
http://www.edgewaterco.com

2362. El Paso County
http://www.co.el-paso.co.us

2363. Englewood
http://www.ci.englewood.co.us

2364. Erie
http://www.ci.erie.co.us

2365. Fort Collins
http://www.ci.fort-collins.co.us

2366. Fountain
http://www.ci.fountain.co.us

2367. Frisco
http://www.townoffrisco.com

2368. Gilpin County
http://www.co.gilpin.co.us/

2369. Glenwood Springs
http://www.ci.glenwood-springs.co.us

2370. Golden
http://ci.golden.co.us/

2371. Grand County
http://www.co.grand.co.us

2372. Greeley
http://www.ci.greeley.co.us

2373. Greenwood Village
http://www.greenwoodvillage.com

2374. Gunnison
http://www.ci.gunnison.co.us

2375. Gunnison County
http://www.co.gunnison.co.us

2376. Idaho Springs
http://www.idahospringsco.com

2377. Jefferson County
http://206.247.49.21/ext/index.htm

2378. La Plata County
http://co.laplata.co.us

2379. Lafayette
http://www.cityoflafayette.com

2380. Lakewood
http://www.ci.lakewood.co.us/index.cfm?&include=/home.cfm

2381. Larimer County
http://www.co.larimer.co.us

2382. Littleton
http://www.littletongov.org

2383. Logan County
http://www.loganco.gov/

2384. Lone Tree
http://www.lone-tree.org

2385. Longmont
http://www.ci.longmont.co.us

2386. Loveland
http://www.ci.loveland.co.us

2387. Mesa County
http://www.co.mesa.co.us

2388. Minturn
http://www.minturn.org/

2389. Montrose County
http://www.co.montrose.co.us/

2390. Morrison
http://www.town.morrison.co.us

2391. Northglenn
http://www.northglenn.org

2392. Ouray County
http://www.co.ouray.co.us

2393. Pitkin County
http://www.pitkingov.com

2394. Pueblo
http://www.ci.pueblo.co.us

2395. Pueblo County
http://www.co.pueblo.co.us

2396. Routt County
http://www.co.routt.co.us

2397. San Miguel County
http://www.co.san-miguel.co.us

2398. Steamboat Springs
http://www.ci.steamboat.co.us

2399. Summit County
http://www.co.summit.co.us

2400. Superior
http://www.townofsuperior.com

2401. Vail
http://www.ci.vail.co.us/

2402. Westminster
http://www.ci.westminster.co.us

2403. Wheat Ridge
http://www.ci.wheatridge.co.us

Connecticut

2404. Connecticut General Assembly
http://www.cga.state.ct.us/
Sponsor: Connecticut. Legislature
Description: Connecticut's legislative site has the full text of bills back to 1988 and the text of the state statutes. A Legislative Info section offers search options, links to legislative schedules and rules, and

numerous options for downloading documents and reference material. Other major sections are House, Senate, Committees, and Offices.
Subject: Connecticut

2405. Connecticut Judicial Branch
http://www.jud.state.ct.us/
Sponsor: Connecticut. Courts
Description: The site features a variety of information on the courts and court schedules. Featured sections include Civil/ Family Case Look-Ups, Juror Information, Connecticut Courts, and Other Information. From this site, access is available to advanced release of full-text opinions from the supreme and appellate courts. Archived opinions from the past 2 years are also available.
Subject: Connecticut

2406. ConneCT—State of Connecticut
http://www.state.ct.us/
Sponsor: California State Government
Description: The official Connecticut home page links to the state's Executive, Judicial, and Legislative branch information as well as to sections on Licenses/Permits, Towns/Cities, and Agencies/Organizations, Tourism, Commerce, and Education.
Subject: Connecticut

Local Governments

2407. Bethlehem
http://www.ci.bethlehem.ct.us

2408. Bristol
http://www.ci.bristol.ct.us

2409. Danbury
http://www.ci.danbury.ct.us/

2410. East Hartford
http://www.ci.east-hartford.ct.us

2411. Groton
http://www.town.groton.ct.us/

2412. Hamden
http://www.hamden.com/

2413. Hartford
http://www.ci.hartford.ct.us

2414. Lebanon
http://www.lebanonct.org

2415. Manchester
http://www.ci.manchester.ct.us

2416. Meriden
http://www.cityofmeriden.org

2417. New Haven
http://www.cityofnewhaven.com

2418. New Milford
http://www.newmilford.org

2419. Newington
http://www.ci.newington.ct.us

2420. Norwich
http://www.norwichct.org

2421. Ridgefield
http://www.ridgefieldct.org

2422. Somers
http://www.town.somers.ct.us

2423. South Windsor
http://www.southwindsor.org

2424. Southbury
http://www.ci.southbury.ct.us

2425. Stamford
http://www.ci.stamford.ct.us

2426. West Hartford
http://www.west-hartford.com

2427. Westport
http://www.ci.westport.ct.us

2428. Windsor
http://www.townofwindsorct.com

2429. Woodstock
http://www.townofwoodstock.com

Delaware

2430. Delaware Courts
http://courts.state.de.us/
Sponsor: Delaware. Courts
Description: This site provides basic information on the Delaware courts. On the Supreme Court site, the Court Opinions and Orders link provides access on the top page to the current opinions and final orders (current month) in PDF format and links to past opinions and orders of 2001 in boxes below. Opinions back to November 1998 are available in zipped files in WordPerfect and Word formats.
Subject: Delaware

2431. Delaware General Assembly
http://www.legis.state.de.us/
Sponsor: Delaware. Legislature
Description: This page includes links to such sections as the State Senate, House of Representatives, Bill Tracking, Legislative Divisions, and Contact Information. Under Bill Tracking, there is access to the full text of bills and their status by bill number, bill type, or full-text search.
Subject: Delaware

2432. Delaware.gov
http://www.delaware.gov/
Sponsor: Delaware State Government
Description: The Delaware state government portal has sections designed for residents, businesses, state employees, other governments, and visitors. An eGovernment section includes a directory of online government services. The site also links to the Governor's page and sites for each of the state agencies.
Subject: Delaware

Local Governments

2433. Bethany Beach
http://www.townofbethanybeach.com

2434. Dover
http://www.cityofdover.com

2435. Kent County
http://www.co.kent.de.us

2436. Milford
http://www.cityofmilford.com

2437. New Castle County
http://www.co.new-castle.de.us

2438. Newark
http://newark.de.us

2439. Seaford
http://www.seafordde.com/

2440. Sussex County
http://www.sussexcounty.net/

2441. Wilmington
http://www.ci.wilmington.de.us

District of Columbia

2442. Washington, D.C.
http://www.dc.gov/
Sponsor: District of Columbia. Government
Description: The District of Columbia's Web site links to information from the mayor, city council, and city agencies. The city council section has information on current legislation and the text of the D.C. code. Other sections focus on citizen services, business services, and visitor information.
Subject: District of Columbia

Local Governments

2443. Washington, D.C.
http://www.dc.gov/

Florida

2444. Florida State Courts
http://www.flcourts.org/
Sponsor: Florida. Courts
Description: The Florida State Courts site links to Web sites for the state's supreme court, courts of appeals, circuit courts, and county courts. The Opinions and Rules section links to the full text of opinions from the Florida Supreme Court and the courts of appeals and to rules of procedure. It also provides links to other sites offering the text of opinions.
Subject: Florida

2445. MyFlorida.com
http://www.state.fl.us/
Sponsor: Florida State Government
Description: The major sections of this extensive state government portal are Visitor, Floridian, Business, Government, and a personalization feature called My Page. A section called 411 has searchable directories for finding phone numbers of state agencies, city and county governments, colleges, and public schools; it can be browsed or searched by topic or employee name.
Subject: Florida

2446. Online Sunshine—The Florida Legislature
http://www.leg.state.fl.us/
Sponsor: Florida. Legislature
Description: The Florida legislative site includes the text of bills from 1998 up to the current session and the text of the state statutes and constitution. Bills and other legislative documents are in the Session section, where a pull-down menu can be used to select the appropriate session year. The site also has a directory of registered legislative lobbyists indexed by name and legislative interest.
Subject: Florida

Local Governments

2447. Alachua County
http://www.co.alachua.fl.us

2448. Altamonte Springs
http://www.ci.altamonte-springs.fl.us

2449. Aventura
http://www.cityofaventura.com

2450. Bal Harbour
http://www.village.bal-harbour.fl.us

2451. Bay County
http://www.co.bay.fl.us

2452 Boca Raton
http://www.ci.boca-raton.fl.us

2453. Brevard County
http://countygovt.brevard.fl.us/

2454. Brooksville
http://www.ci.brooksville.fl.us

2455. Broward County
http://www.co.broward.fl.us/

2456. Cape Coral
http://www.capecoral.net

2457. Charlotte County
http://www.co.charlotte.fl.us

2458. Clay County
http://www.claycountygov.com

2459. Clearwater
http://www.clearwater-fl.com/

2460. Cocoa
http://www.cocoafl.org

2461. Cocoa Beach
http://www.ci.cocoa-beach.fl.us

2462. Coconut Creek
http://www.creekgov.net/

2463. Collier County
http://www.co.collier.fl.us

2464. Coral Springs
http://www.ci.coral-springs.fl.us

2465. Crystal River
http://www.crystalriverfl.org/

2466. Dania Beach
http://www.ci.dania-beach.fl.us

2467. Davie
http://www.davie-fl.gov/

2468. Daytona Beach
http://www.ci.daytona-beach.fl.us

2469. Deerfield Beach
http://www.deerfieldbch.com

2470. Deltona
http://www.ci.deltona.fl.us

2471. Dunedin
http://www.ci.dunedin.fl.us

2472. Edgewater
http://www.cityofedgewater.org/

2473. Edgewood
http://www.edgewood.cc/

2474. Escambia County
http://www.co.escambia.fl.us

2475. Eustis
http://www.eustis.org

2476. Fort Lauderdale
http://www.ci.ftlaud.fl.us

2477. Fort Myers
http://www.ci.fort-myers.fl.us/

2478. Fort Myers Beach
http://www.fmbeach.org

2479. Fort Walton Beach
http://www.fwb.org

2480. Gainesville
http://www.state.fl.us/gvl/

2481. Gilchrist County
http://www.co.gilchrist.fl.us

2482. Green Cove Springs
http://www.greencovesprings.com

2483. Greenacres
http://www.ci.greenacres.fl.us

2484. Gulfport
http://www.ci.gulfport.fl.us

2485. Hallandale Beach
http://www.ci.hallandale.fl.us

2486. Hernando County
http://www.co.hernando.fl.us

2487. Hialeah
http://www.ci.hialeah.fl.us

2488. Hialeah Gardens
http://www.cityofhialeahgardens.org

2489. Highland Beach
http://www.ci.highland-beach.fl.us

2490. Hillsborough County
http://www.hillsboroughcounty.org

2491. Hollywood
http://www.hollywoodfl.org

2492. Homestead
http://www.ci.homestead.fl.us

2493. Indialantic
http://www.indialantic.com

2494. Jacksonville
http://www.ci.jax.fl.us

2495. Jefferson County
http://www.co.jefferson.fl.us

2496. Jupiter
http://www.jupiter.fl.us

2497. Key Biscayne
http://www.vkb.key-biscayne.fl.us

2498. Kissimmee
http://www.kissimmee.org

2499. LaBelle
http://www.cityoflabelle.com

2500. Lake County
http://www.lakegovernment.com

2501. Lake Park
http://www.lakeparkflorida.net

2502. Lake Wales
http://www.cityoflakewales.com

2503. Lake Worth
http://169.139.15.187/

2504. Lakeland
http://www.lakelandgov.net/

2505. Lantana
http://www.lantana.org

2506. Largo
http://www.largo.com

2507. Lauderhill
http://www.lauderhill.net

2508. Lee County
http://lee-county.com/

2509. Leesburg
http://www.ci.leesburg.fl.us

2510. Leon County
http://www.co.leon.fl.us

2511. Lighthouse Point
http://www.lighthousepoint.com

2512. Live Oak
http://www.cityofliveoak.org

2513. Longwood
http://www.ci.longwood.fl.us

2514. Maitland
http://www.ci.maitland.fl.us

2515. Manatee County
http://www.co.manatee.fl.us

2516. Marco Island
http://www.cityofmarcoisland.com/

2517. Margate
http://www.margatefl.com

2518. Marion County
http://www.marioncountyfl.org

2519. Martin County
http://www.martin.fl.us

2520. Melbourne
http://www.melbourneflorida.org

2521. Miami
http://www.ci.miami.fl.us

2522. Miami Beach
http://www.ci.miami-beach.fl.us

2523. Miami-Dade County
http://miamidade.gov/

2524. Miramar
http://www.ci.miramar.fl.us/

2525. Monroe County
http://www.co.monroe.fl.us

2526. Mount Dora
http://www.ci.mount-dora.fl.us

2527. Naples
http://www.naplesgov.com/

2528. North Miami Beach
http://www.ci.north-miami-beach.fl.us

2529. North Port
http://www.ci.north-port.fl.us

2530. Ocala
http://www.ocalafl.org

2531. Ocoee
http://www.ci.ocoee.fl.us

2532. Okaloosa County
http://www.co.okaloosa.fl.us

2533. Orange County
http://www.orangecountyfl.net/

2534. Orlando
http://www.ci.orlando.fl.us

2535. Ormond Beach
http://www.ormondbeach.org

2536. Osceola County
http://www.osceola.org

2537. Palm Bay
http://www.palmbayflorida.org/

2538. Palm Beach County
http://www.co.palm-beach.fl.us

2539. Pensacola
http://www.ci.pensacola.fl.us

2540. Pinellas County
http://www.co.pinellas.fl.us

2541. Plant City
http://www.ci.plant-city.fl.us

2542. Plantation
http://www.plantation.org/

2543. Polk County
http://www.polk-county.net

2544. Pompano Beach
http://www.ci.pompano-beach.fl.us

2545. Port Orange
http://www.port-orange.org/

2546. Port Saint Lucie
http://www.cityofpsl.com

2547. Punta Gorda
http://www.ci.punta-gorda.fl.us

2548. Putnam County
http://www.putnam-fl.com/

2549. Royal Palm Beach
http://www.royalpalmbeach.com

2550. Safety Harbor
http://www.cityofsafetyharbor.com

2551. Saint Augustine
http://www.ci.st-augustine.fl.us

2552. Saint Cloud
http://www.stcloud.org

2553. Saint Johns County
http://www.co.st-johns.fl.us

2554. Saint Lucie County
http://www.stlucieco.gov

2555. Saint Petersburg
http://www.ci.saint-petersburg.fl.us

2556. Sanibel
http://www.ci.sanibel.fl.us

2557. Santa Rosa County
http://www.co.santa-rosa.fl.us

2558. Sarasota
http://www.sarasotagov.com/

2559. Sarasota County
http://www.co.sarasota.fl.us

2560. Satellite Beach
http://www.satellitebeach.org

2561. Sebastian
http://www.cityofsebastian.org

2562. Seminole County
http://www.co.seminole.fl.us

2563. Sewall's Point
http://www.sewallspoint.org

2564. Shalimar
http://www.shalimarflorida.org

2565. Stuart
http://www.cityofstuart.com

2566. Sumter
http://bocc.co.sumter.fl.us

2567. Surfside
http://www.town.surfside.fl.us

2568. Tallahassee
http://talgov.com/

2569. Tamarac
http://www.tamarac.org

2570. Tampa
http://www.tampagov.net/

2571. Tarpon Springs
http://www.ci.tarpon-springs.fl.us

2572. Tavares
http://www.tavares.org

2573. Temple Terrace
http://www.templeterrace.com

2574. Titusville
http://www.titusville.com

2575. Treasure Island
http://www.ci.treasure-island.fl.us

2576. Volusia County
http://www.volusia.org

2577. West Melbourne
http://www.westmelbourne.org

2578. West Palm Beach
http://www.cityofwpb.com/

2579. Wilton Manors
http://www.wiltonmanors.com

2580. Winter Park
http://www.ci.winter-park.fl.us

Georgia

2581. Georgia Judicial Branch
http://www.georgiacourts.org/
Sponsor: Georgia. Supreme Court
Description: This site links to all Georgia court sites as well as to judicial agencies and related information. The opinions of the Supreme Court and Courts of Appeals can be searched back to 1997.
Subject: Georgia

2582. Georgia Legislature
http://www.legis.state.ga.us/
Alternate URL: http://www.ganet.org/services/newleg/
Sponsor: Georgia. Legislature
Description: The Georgia General Assembly Web site has links for the House, Senate, and Legislation. The Legislative Search section includes both bills going back to 1995 and the *Georgia Code* (unannotated). The alternate URL is for the legislative section of the state government site.
Subject: Georgia

2583. Georgia.Gov
http://www.georgia.gov/
Sponsor: Georgia State Government
Description: Georgia.Gov organizes state government information by topic, such as Transportation, Family and Health, and Business Services and Employment. The Government section has a directory of links to state, municipal, and county government sites.
Subject: Georgia

Local Governments

2584. Albany
http://www.albany.ga.us/exec/site/

2585. Alpharetta
http://www.alpharetta.ga.us

2586. Atlanta
http://www.ci.atlanta.ga.us

2587. Augusta
http://augusta.co.richmond.ga.us

2588. Austell
http://www.austell.org

2589. Berkeley Lake
http://www.ci.berkeley-lake.ga.us

2590. Catoosa County
http://www.catoosa.com

2591. Chatham County
http://www.chathamcounty.org/

2592. Clarke County
http://www.athensclarkecounty.com

2593. Clayton County
http://www.co.clayton.ga.us

2594. Cobb County
http://www.cobb-net.com

2595. College Park
http://www.collegeparkga.com

2596. Columbia County
http://www.co.columbia.ga.us

2597. Columbus
http://www.columbusga.org

2598. Commerce
http://www.commercega.org

2599. Cordele
http://www.cityofcordele.com

2600. Coweta County
http://www.coweta.ga.us

2601. Dahlonega
http://www.cityofdahlonega.com

2602. Decatur
http://www.decatur-ga.com

2603. DeKalb County
http://www.co.dekalb.ga.us

2604. Dougherty County
http://www.albany.ga.us/site/

2605. Douglas County
http://www.co.douglas.ga.us

2606. Douglasville
http://www.ci.douglasville.ga.us

2607. East Point
http://www.eastpointcity.org/

2608. Fayette County
http://www.admin.co.fayette.ga.us

2609. Fitzgerald
http://www.fitzgeraldga.org

2610. Forsyth County
http://www.co.forsyth.ga.us

2611. Fulton County
http://www.co.fulton.ga.us

2612. Gainesville
http://www.gainesville.org

2613. Glynn County
http://www.glynncounty.org

2614. Griffin
http://www.cityofgriffin.com

2615. Gwinnett County
http://www.co.gwinnett.ga.us

2616. Habersham County
http://www.co.habersham.ga.us

2617. Hahira
http://www.hahira.ga.us

2618. Hall County
http://www.hallcounty.org

2619. Kingsland
http://www.kingslandgeorgia.com

2620. LaGrange
http://www.lagrange-ga.org/homepage.cfm

2621. Lee County
http://www.lee.ga.us

2622. Marietta
http://www.city.marietta.ga.us

2623. McDuffie County
http://www.co.mcduffie.ga.us

2624. Newton County
http://www.co.newton.ga.us

2625. Oconee County
http://www.oconeecounty.com

2626. Peachtree City
http://www.peachtree-city.org

2627. Richmond County
http://www.co.richmond.ga.us

2628. Riverdale
http://www.cityofriverdale.com

2629. Roswell
http://www.ci.roswell.ga.us

2630. Savannah
http://www.ci.savannah.ga.us/cityweb/webdatabase.nsf

2631. Smyrna
http://www.ci.smyrna.ga.us

2632. Snellville
http://www.snellville.org

2633. Spalding County
http://www.spaldingcounty.com

2634. Springfield
http://www.cityofspringfield.com

2635. Stockbridge
http://www.cityofstockbridge.com

2636. Sumter County
http://www.sumter-ga.com

2637. Suwanee
http://www.suwanee.com

2638. Thomson
http://www.ci.thomson.ga.us

2639. Troup County
http://www.troupcountyga.org

2640. Tyrone
http://www.tyrone.org

2641. Vidalia
http://www.vidaliaga.com

2642. Walker County
http://www.co.walker.ga.us/

2643. Warner Robins
http://www.warner-robins.org

2644. Wilkinson County
http://www.accucomm.net/~wilcoboc/

Guam

2645. Guam Justice Web Site
http://www.justice.gov.gu/
Sponsor: Guam. Courts
Description: This site includes the Superior Court, Supreme Court, Department of Law, Guam Code Annotated, and the Guam Bar Association among other legal resources. Supreme Court opinions are available in HTML back to 1996.
Subject: Guam

2646. Guam Legislature
http://www.legislature.guam.net/
Alternate URL: http://www.guam.net/com/senben/
Sponsor: Guam. Legislature
Description: The Speaker of Guam's unicameral legislature posts some general legislative information on his office Web site, including a legislative directory. The alternate URL above is for the site maintained by the Minority Leader; it features more detailed legislative information, such as bill status and current budget laws.
Subject: Guam

2647. Official Guam Web Site
http://ns.gov.gu/
Sponsor: Guam. Government
Description: The official Guam site provides general information on Guam, but also has links to government department and office Web sites and contact information.
Subject: Guam

Hawaii

2648. eHawaiigov
http://www.hawaii.gov/
Sponsor: Hawaii State Government
Description: This site offers an extensive directory of information on Hawaii and links to online government services. Sections include Government in Hawaii, Working in Hawaii, and Education in Hawaii. The Government in Hawaii section links to the sites for the governor's office and executive agencies, and the legislative and judicial branches.
Subject: Hawaii

2649. Hawaii State Judiciary
http://www.courts.state.hi.us/
Sponsor: Hawaii. Courts
Description: This judicial branch portal leads to the state court sites, directories of attorneys, legal self-help tips, court records and rules, and other information. Supreme Court opinions are online in full text back to 2000.
Subject: Hawaii

2650. Hawaii State Legislature
http://www.capitol.hawaii.gov/
Sponsor: Hawaii. Legislature
Description: Current bills, committee reports, and state statutes are available in full text in the Status and Documents section of this site. The Archives section has copies going back to 1999. The site also has directories for the House and Senate, links to legislative support agencies, and a guide to the state legislative process.
Subject: Hawaii

Local Governments

2651. Hawaii County
http://www.hawaii-county.com

2652. Honolulu
http://www.co.honolulu.hi.us

2653. Maui County
http://www.co.maui.hi.us

Idaho

2654. Access Idaho
http://www.accessidaho.org/
Sponsor: Idaho State Government
Description: Access Idaho is the official state Web site. It includes links to the state government agencies, online government services, and the state legislative and judicial branches. The Government section features an agency index, a state government telephone directory, and links to Idaho political parties.
Subject: Idaho

2655. Idaho Legislature
http://www2.state.id.us/legislat/
Sponsor: Idaho. Legislature
Description: The Idaho legislative site has the full text of bills for the current and previous session, the state statutes, and the state constitution. There are also lists of bills passed and bills vetoed for the session. The site includes directory information for the House and Senate, a map of the legislative districts, and a guide to the state legislative process.
Subject: Idaho

2656. Idaho State Judiciary
http://www2.state.id.us/judicial/
Sponsor: Idaho. Courts
Description: This site provides access to Idaho Supreme Court and Court of Appeals opinions for the current year. The site also offers court rules, forms, judicial rosters, and related information.
Subject: Idaho

Local Governments

2657. Ada County
http://www.adaweb.net

2658. Bannock County
http://www.co.bannock.id.us

2659. Blaine County
http://www.co.blaine.id.us

2660. Boise
http://www.co.boise.id.us/

2661. Bonner County
http://www.co.bonner.id.us

2662. Bonneville County
http://www.co.bonneville.id.us/

2663. Eagle
http://www.cityofeagle.com

2664. Fremont County
http://www.co.fremont.id.us

2665. Idaho Falls
http://www.ci.idaho-falls.id.us

2666. Jefferson County
http://www.co.jefferson.id.us

2667. Ketchum
http://www.ci.ketchum.id.us

2668. Kootenai County
http://www.co.kootenai.id.us

2669. Lewiston
http://www.cityoflewiston.org

2670. Madison County
http://www.co.madison.id.us

2671. McCall
http://www.mccall.id.us

2672. Moscow
http://www.moscow.id.us

2673. Nampa
http://www.ci.nampa.id.us/

2674. Pocatello
http://www.ci.pocatello.id.us

2675. Post Falls
http://www.postfallsidaho.org

Illinois

2676. Illinois General Assembly
http://www.legis.state.il.us/
Sponsor: Illinois. Legislature
Description: This site provides sections on Members, Schedules, Committees, Rules, Transcripts, and Votes for both chambers of the state legislature. The site also has the text of bills back to 1997, the state statues, and the state constitution.
Subject: Illinois

2677. State of Illinois
http://www.state.il.us/
Sponsor: Illinois State Government
Description: The Illinois Web site has sections on living, working, visiting, learning, and doing business in Illinois. The Government section links to state agencies, the executive and legislative branches, and counties and municipalities.
Subject: Illinois

2678. Supreme Court of Illinois
http://www.state.il.us/court/
Sponsor: Illinois. Courts
Description: Despite the name, this site links to all levels of the state court system and to the Administrative Office of the Illinois Courts. The full text of opinions from both the Illinois Supreme Court and Appellate Court are available from 1996.
Subject: Illinois

Local Governments

2679. Addison
http://www.addisonadvantage.org

2680. Algonquin
http://www.algonquin.org

2681. Aurora
http://www.ci.aurora.il.us

2682. Barrington
http://www.ci.barrington.il.us

2683. Barrington Hills
http://www.ci.barrington-hills.il.us

2684. Bartlett
http://www.village.bartlett.il.us

2685. Batavia
http://www.cityofbatavia.net

2686. Beach Park
http://www.villageofbeachpark.com

2687. Bellwood
http://www.vil.bellwood.il.us

2688. Bloomingdale
http://www.vil.bloomingdale.il.us

2689. Bloomington
http://www.cityhall.ci.bloomington.il.us

2690. Bolingbrook
http://www.bolingbrook.com

2691. Brookfield
http://www.brookfield-il.org

2692. Buffalo Grove
http://www.vbg.org

2693. Burr Ridge
http://www.burr-ridge.gov

2694. Carbondale
http://www.ci.carbondale.il.us

2695. Carol Stream
http://www.carolstream.org

2696. Cary
http://www.caryillinois.com

2697. Champaign
http://www.ci.champaign.il.us

2698. Chicago
http://www.ci.chi.il.us

2699. Chillicothe
http://www.ci.chillicothe.il.us

2700. Collinsville
http://www.ci.collinsville.il.us/

2701. Cook County
http://www.co.cook.il.us

2702. Crystal Lake
http://www.crystallake.org

2703. Decatur
http://www.ci.decatur.il.us

2704. Deerfield
http://www.deerfield-il.org

2705. DeKalb
http://www.cityofdekalb.com/

2706. Downers Grove
http://www.vil.downers-grove.il.us

2707. DuPage County
http://www.co.dupage.il.us

2708. DuQuoin
http://www.duquoin.org

2709. Elk Grove Village
http://www.elkgrove.com

2710. Elmhurst
http://www.elmhurst.org

2711. Elsah
http://www.elsah.org

2712. Freeport
http://www.ci.freeport.il.us

2713. Geneseo
http://www.geneseo.il.us/

2714. Geneva
http://www.geneva.il.us/

2715. Glendale Heights
http://www.glendaleheights.org

2716. Grayslake
http://www.ci.grayslake.il.us

2717. Gurnee
http://www.gurnee.il.us

2718. Harwood Heights
http://www.harwoodheights.org

2719. Henry County
http://www.henrycty.com

2720. Hoffman Estates
http://www.hoffmanestates.com

2721. Island Lake
http://www.villageofislandlake.com

2722. Jackson County
http://www.co.jackson.il.us

2723. Johnsburg
http://ci.johnsburg.il.us

2724. Joliet
http://www.ci.joliet.il.us

2725. Kane County
http://www.co.kane.il.us

2726. Kankakee
http://www.ci.kankakee.il.us

2727. Lake County
http://www.co.lake.il.us

2728. Lake Forest
http://www.cityoflakeforest.com/

2729. Lemont
http://www.lemont.il.us

2730. Libertyville
http://www.libertyville.com

2731. Lincolnshire
http://www.village.lincolnshire.il.us

2732. Lisle
http://www.vil.lisle.il.us

2733. Lombard
http://www.villageoflombard.org

2734. Madison County
http://www.co.madison.il.us

2735. Marion
http://www.ci.marion.il.us

2736. Mascoutah
http://www.mascoutah.com

2737. McHenry County
http://www.co.mchenry.il.us

2738. McLean County
http://www.mclean.gov

2739. Mendot
http://www.mendota.il.us

2740. Moline
http://www.moline.il.us

2741. Mount Prospect
http://www.mountprospect.org

2742. Mundelein
http://www.mundelein.org

2743. Murphysboro
http://www.murphysboro.com/city/

2744. Naperville
http://www.naperville.il.us

2745. Niles
http://www.vniles.com

2746. Normal
http://www.normal.org

2747. Northbrook
http://www.northbrook.il.us

2748. Oak Brook
http://www.oak-brook.org

2749. Palatine
http://www.palatine.il.us

2750. Palos Heights
http://www.palosheights.org

2751. Palos Park
http://www.palospark.org

2752. Peoria
http://www.ci.peoria.il.us

2753. Peoria County
http://www.co.peoria.il.us

2754. Piatt County
http://www.co.piatt.il.us

2755. Pontiac
http://www.pontiac.org

2756. Quincy
http://www.ci.quincy.il.us

2757. Rantoul
http://www.village.rantoul.il.us

2758. Rock Island County
http://www.co.rock-island.il.us

2759. Rockford
http://www.ci.rockford.il.us

2760. Rolling Meadows
http://www.ci.rolling-meadows.il.us

2761. Romeoville
http://www.romeoville.org

2762. Roselle
http://www.roselle.il.us

2763. Saint Charles
http://www.ci.st-charles.il.us

2764. Salem
http://www.ci.salem.il.us

2765. Sangamon County
http://www.co.sangamon.il.us

2766. Schaumburg
http://www.ci.schaumburg.il.us

2767. Skokie
http://www.skokie.org/

2768. Sleepy Hollow
http://www.sleepy-hollow.il.us

2769. Spring Valley
http://www.spring-valley.il.us

2770. Springfield
http://www.springfield.il.us

2771. Streamwood
http://www.streamwood.org/

2772. Vernon Hills
http://www.vernonhills.org/

2773. Villa Park
http://www.invillapark.com/

2774. Westmont
http://www.westmont.il.us

2775. Wheaton
http://www.wheaton.il.us/

2776. Will County
http://www.willcountyillinois.com

2777. Wilmette
http://www.wilmette.com

2778. Winnetka
http://www.villageofwinnetka.org

2779. Woodstock
http://www.woodstock-il.com

Indiana

2780. accessIndiana
http://www.in.gov/
Sponsor: Indiana State Government
Description: The Indiana Government site offers links to the executive, legislative, and judicial branches of the state government and to a state agency index and phone book. An Online Services section has links to numerous databases and forms.
Subject: Indiana

2781. Indiana General Assembly
http://www.in.gov/legislative/
Sponsor: Indiana. Legislature
Description: Featuring calendars, study committees, legislators, and full, current bill information, this is a substantial site. The Bills and Resolutions section has the latest information about bills, which includes introduced bills, current status, committee reports, amendments, fiscal impact statements, and an actions list. This site also contains online versions of the *Indiana Code* and the *Indiana Administrative Code.* Featured sections include Session Information, Legislators, Laws and Administrative Rules, Publications and Other Documents, and Session Rules, Journals, and Archive.
Subject: Indiana

2782. Indiana Judicial System
http://www.in.gov/judiciary/
Sponsor: Indiana. Courts
Description: Judicial information is presented under several headings, including Courts, Judges, Attorneys, Education, and Research. The Research section includes access to judicial opinions from the Supreme Court, Appellate Court, and Tax Court. It also includes the state statues, administrative code, and state constitution.
Subject: Indiana

Local Governments

2783. Anderson
http://www.cityofanderson.com

2784. Bloomington
http://www.city.bloomington.in.us

2785. Carmel
http://www.ci.carmel.in.us

2786. Clarksville
http://www.town.clarksville.in.us

2787. Dearborn County
http://www.dearborncounty.org

2788. Elkhart
http://www.elkhartindiana.org

2789. Fishers
http://www.fishers.in.us

2790. Fort Wayne
http://www.ci.ft-wayne.in.us

2791. Franklin
http://www.ci.franklin.in.us/

2792. Greenwood
http://www.cityofgreenwood.com

2793. Hamilton County
http://www.co.hamilton.in.us

2794. Hammond
http://www.ci.hammond.in.us

2795. Huntingburg
http://www.huntingburg.org

2796. Indianapolis
http://www.indygov.org

2797. Johnson County
http://www.co.johnson.in.us

2798. Kokomo
http://www.ci.kokomo.in.us

2799. Lafayette
http://www.city.lafayette.in.us

2800. Marshall County
http://www.co.marshall.in.us

2801. Michigan City
http://www.michigancity.org

2802. Mishawaka
http://www.mishawakacity.com

2803. Muncie
http://www.cityofmuncie.com

2804. Noblesville
http://www.cityofnoblesville.org/

2805. Portage
http://www.ci.portage.in.us

2806. Porter County
http://www.co.porter.in.us

2807. Richmond
http://www.ci.richmond.in.us

2808. South Bend
http://www.ci.south-bend.in.us

2809. Tippecanoe County
http://www.co.tippecanoe.in.us

2810. Valparaiso
http://www.ci.valparaiso.in.us

2811. Vigo County
http://www.vigocounty.org/

2812. Vincennes
http://www.vincennes.org

2813. Wayne County
http://www.co.wayne.in.us

2814. West Lafayette
http://www.city.west-lafayette.in.us

Iowa

2815. Iowa General Assembly
http://www.legis.state.ia.us/
Description: The General Assembly site carries the full text of bills, amendments, and committee reports back to 1995. There are multiple directories of legislators and legislative calendars, and a searchable lobbyist directory. The Legislative Reference Materials section has the current and previous versions of the state code.

2816. Iowa Judicial Branch
http://www.judicial.state.ia.us/
Alternate URL: http://www.judicial.state.ia.us/online_records/
Description: This site provides information about the courts in sections such as Supreme Court, Court of Appeals, District Court, About Our Courts, Our Judges, News, Attorney Regulation, Court Rules, and Court Administration. Full text slip opinions are available back to May 1988. Additional court and public records are available free of charge at the alternate URL listed above.

2817. State of Iowa
http://www.state.ia.us/
Sponsor: Iowa State Government
Description: The Iowa state Web site has alphabetical and topical access to state government information and online services. The site's search engine has an option to search all state documents online, and there is also a link to the Iowa Electronic State Documents Repository.
Subject: Iowa

Local Governments

2818. Adams County
http://www.co.adams.ia.us

2819. Algona
http://www.ci.algona.ia.us/

2820. Ames
http://www.city.ames.ia.us

2821. Ankeny
http://www.ci.ankeny.ia.us

2822. Black Hawk County
http://www.co.black-hawk.ia.us/

2823 Buena Vista County
http://www.co.buena-vista.ia.us

2824. Burlington
http://www.burlington.lib.ia.us/City/maincity/maincity.htm

2825. Cedar Falls
http://www.ci.cedar-falls.ia.us

2826. Clive
http://www.ci.clive.ia.us

2827. Council Bluffs
http://www.ci.council-bluffs.ia.us

2828. Des Moines
http://www.ci.des-moines.ia.us

2829. Fayette
http://www.fayetteia.com

2830. Iowa City
http://www.icgov.org/

2831. Indianola
http://www.cityofindianola.com

2832. Johnson County
http://www.johnson-county.com/

2833. Lee County
http://www.leecounty.org

2834. Linn County
http://www.co.linn.ia.us

2835. Lisbon
http://www.lisboniowa.com

2836. Marion
http://www.cityofmarion.org/

2837. Marshall County
http://www.co.marshall.ia.us

2838. Orange City
http://www.orangecityiowa.com/

2839. Ottumwa
http://www.ci.ottumwa.ia.us

2840. Polk County
http://www.co.polk.ia.us

2841. Pottawattamie County
http://www.pottco.org

2842. Sac County
http://www.saccounty.org

2843. Scott County
http://www.scottcountyiowa.com

2844. Shelby County
http://www.shco.org

2845. Sioux City
http://www.sioux-city.org

2846. Storm Lake
http://www.stormlake.org/city/pages/index.htm

2847. Urbandale
http://www.urbandale.org

2848. Washington County
http://co.washington.ia.us

2849. Waterloo
http://www.wplwloo.lib.ia.us/waterloo/

2850. Webster City
http://www.webstercity.com

2851. West Des Moines
http://www.city.west-des-moines.ia.us

2852. Wright County
http://www.wrightcounty.org/

Kansas

2853. accessKansas
http://www.accesskansas.org/

Sponsor: Kansas State Government
Description: The official Kansas Web site has an array of government services online, including tax filing and motor vehicle records. Other information services include a state government phone directory, a directory of elected officials, and links to state-level trade associations for Kansas.
Subject: Kansas

2854. Kansas Judicial Branch
http://www.kscourts.org/
Sponsor: Kansas. Courts
Description: In addition to providing information about the Kansas courts, the Kansas Judicial Council, and other parts of the judicial branch, this site features slip opinions from the Kansas Supreme Court and Court of Appeals. Access to the cases is by docket number, date, case name, and keyword searching. Cases are available back to October 1996.
Subject: Kansas

2855. Kansas Legislature
http://www.kslegislature.org
Description: This site offers bill tracking and the full text of bills for the current legislative session. Access to the bills is by bill number or keyword search. The state statutes and legislative calendars and journals are also online. A link to the Kansas Legislative Research Department leads to more information on legislative and budget activity.

Local Governments

2856. Allen County
http://www.allencounty.org/

2857. Arkansas City
http://www.arkcityks.org

2858. Barton County
http://www.bartoncounty.org/

2859. Chanute
http://www.chanute.org/

2860. Derby
http://www.derbyweb.com

2861. Dodge City
http://www.dodgecity.org

2862. Douglas County
http://www.douglas-county.com

2863. El Dorado
http://www.eldoradokansas.com

2864. Franklin County
http://www.co.franklin.ks.us

2865. Garden City
http://www.garden-city.org

2866. Gardner
http://www.gardnerkansas.com

2867. Hutchinson
http://www.ci.hutchinson.ks.us/

2868. Jefferson County
http://www.jfcountyks.com

2869. Johnson County
http://www.jocoks.com

2870. Kansas City
http://www.wycokck.org

2871. Labette County
http://www.labettecounty.com

2872. Lansing
http://www.lansing.ks.us

2873. Lawrence
http://www.ci.lawrence.ks.us

2874. Leavenworth
http://www.ci.leavenworth.ks.us

2875. Leawood
http://www.leawood.org

2876. Lenexa
http://www.ci.lenexa.ks.us

2877. Manhattan
http://www.ci.manhattan.ks.us

2878. Merriam
http://www.merriam.org

2879. Miami County
http://www.co.miami.ks.us

2880. Olathe
http://www.olatheks.org

2881. Overland Park
http://www.opkansas.org

2882. Paola
http://www.ci.paola.ks.us

2883. Pittsburg
http://www.pittks.org

2884. Riley County
http://www.co.riley.ks.us

2885. Salina
http://www.ci.salina.ks.us

2886. Sedgwick County
http://www.sedgwick.ks.us

2887. Shawnee
http://www.cityofshawnee.org

2888. Topeka
http://www.topeka.org

2889. Wichita
http://www.wichitagov.org/

2890. Winfield
http://www.winfieldks.org

2891. Wyandotte County
http://www.wycokck.org

Kentucky

2892. Kentucky Court of Justice
http://www.kycourts.net/
Sponsor: Kentucky. Courts
Description: This site offers links to the state courts and directory of justices for each. Kentucky Supreme Court opinions are available online in PDF format and go back to mid-1999.
Subject: Kentucky

2893. Kentucky Legislature
http://www.lrc.state.ky.us/
Sponsor: Kentucky. Legislature
Description: This site provides access to descriptive information about the legislature along with access to full text legislation. Featured sections include Schedules and Visitor Information, Organization and Administration, Legislation and Legislative Record, Public Services, and Legislative Resources. Bills are accessible by bill number. The full text of recent bills and their status is available along with summaries of older bills back to 1986.
Subject: Kentucky

2894. Kentucky.gov
http://kentucky.gov/
Sponsor: Kentucky State Government
Description: Kentucky.gov is the official Web site for Kentucky. The site features links for residents and businesses, with special links to information on homeland security and online government services. A Publications, Research, and Maps section has links to sites such as the State Data Center and the Kentucky Virtual Library.
Subject: Kentucky

Local Governments

2895. Bellevue
http://www.bellevueky.org

2896. Boone County
http://www.boonecountyky.org

2897. Bowling Green
http://www.bgky.org

2898. Covington
http://www.covingtonky.com

2899. Erlanger
http://www.friendshipcity.com

2900. Fayette County
http://www.lfucg.com

2901. Fort Thomas
http://www.ftthomas.org

2902. Hopkinsville
http://www.hoptown.org/

2903. Jefferson County
http://www.co.jefferson.ky.us

2904. Jenkins
http://www.ci.jenkins.ky.us

2905. Kenton County
http://www.kentoncounty.org

2906. Lexington
http://www.lfucg.com

2907. Louisville
http://www.louky.org

2908. Maysville
http://www.cityofmaysville.com

2909. Newport
http://www.cityofnewportky.org

2910. Owensboro
http://www.owensboro.org/

2911. Winchester
http://www.winchesterky.com

Louisiana

2912. InfoLouisiana
http://www.state.la.us/
Sponsor: Louisiana State Government
Description: InfoLouisiana is designed to be the entry point to state government information and services. The Government section has a state agency index and links to the judicial and legislative branch sites and to local governments. The site also has extensive sections on recreation and tourism, business, education, and employment.
Subject: Louisiana

2913. Louisiana Legislature
http://www.legis.state.la.us/
Sponsor: Louisiana State Government
Description: This site consists of information about the legislative process, current legislators, committee information, links to both houses, and bill information. The full text of legislation is online back to 1997. The Louisiana Laws section has the searchable full text of the state code and constitution, and the House and Senate rules.
Subject: Louisiana

2914. Supreme Court of Louisiana
http://www.lasc.org/
Sponsor: Louisiana. Supreme Court
Description: The Louisiana Supreme Court site has the text of opinions and dockets online, and features a Case Search page. The Law Library and Legal Resources section includes state court rules and library research guides. See the Links section for links to the Web sites of the other state courts.
Subject: Louisiana

Local Governments

2915. Alexandria
http://www.cityofalexandriala.com/

2916. Baton Rouge
http://www.ci.baton-rouge.la.us

2917. Bogalusa
http://www.bogalusa.org

2918. Bossier City
http://www.bossiercity.org

2919. Caddo Parish
http://www.caddo.org

2920. Calcasieu Parish
http://www.cppj.net

2921. Gretna
http://www.gretnala.com

2922. Hammond
http://www.hammond.org

2923. Iberville Parish
http://www.parish.iberville.la.us

2924. Jefferson Parish
http://www.jeffparish.net

2925. Kenner
http://www.kenner.la.us

2926. Lafayette
http://www.lafayettegov.org

2927. Lake Charles
http://www.cityoflakecharles.com/

2928. Monroe
http://www.ci.monroe.la.us

2929. New Iberia
http://www.cityofnewiberia.com/

2930. New Orleans
http://www.new-orleans.la.us

2931. Saint Bernard Parish
http://www.st-bernard.la.us

2932. Saint Charles Parish
http://www.st-charles.la.us

2933. Saint James Parish
http://www.stjamesla.com

2934. Saint John The Baptist Parish
http://www.sjbparish.com/

2935. Saint Tammany Parish
http://www.stpgov.org/

2936. Shreveport
http://www.ci.shreveport.la.us

2937. Terrebonne Parish
http://www.tpcg.org/

2938. Walker
http://www.walker.la.us

Maine

2939. Maine Legislature
http://janus.state.me.us/legis/
Sponsor: Maine. Legislature
Description: The Main Legislature site is a gateway to the Maine House and Senate Web sites. It also has direct links to Session Information (current bills, committees, schedules, and documents) and to the state constitution, code, and session laws.
Subject: Maine

2940. Maine State Government
http://www.state.me.us/
Sponsor: Maine State Government
Description: Maine's official Web site features a variety of online government services, and sections on Government, Living, Visiting, Working, Business, Education, and Facts and History. The Government section has links to state government offices as well as links to local and federal government sites.
Subject: Maine

2941. State of Maine Judicial Branch
http://www.courts.state.me.us/
Sponsor: Maine. Courts
Description: The Judicial Branch site for the state of Maine includes links to other state courts, opinions and orders, information for jurors, and court rules, forms, and fees. Supreme Court opinions are online back to 1997.
Subject: Maine

Local Governments

2942. Aroostook County
http://www.aroostook.me.us

2943. Auburn
http://www.auburnmaine.org

2944. Augusta
http://www.ci.augusta.me.us

2945. Bangor
http://www.bgrme.org/

2946. Bath
http://www.cityofbath.com

2947. Biddeford
http://www.biddefordmaine.com

2948. Brewer
http://www.brewerme.org

2949. Cape Elizabeth
http://www.capeelizabeth.com

2950. Cumberland County
http://www.cumberlandcounty.org

2951. Dexter
http://www.dextermaine.org

2952. Gorham
http://www.gorhammeusa.org

2953. Kennebunk
http://kennebunkmaine.org/

2954. Lewiston
http://ci.lewiston.me.us/

2955. Orono
http://www.orono.org

2956. Portland
http://www.ci.portland.me.us

2957. Rockland
http://www.ci.rockland.me.us

2958. Saco
http://www.sacomaine.org

2959. South Portland
http://www.southportland.org

2960. Standish
http://www.standish.org

2961. Topsham
http://www.topshammaine.com

2962. Waterville
http://www.ci.waterville.me.us

Maryland

2963. Maryland General Assembly
http://mlis.state.md.us/
Sponsor: Maryland. Legislature
Description: The Maryland General Assembly site has state legislative information back to 1996, including proceedings, the full text of bills, and multiple indexes of the legislation. The site also has a directory of legislators, schedules, and budget documents.
Subject: Maryland

2964. Maryland Judiciary
http://www.courts.state.md.us/
Sponsor: Maryland. Courts
Description: Providing a fair amount of descriptive information about the Maryland court system, this site offers sections for the Courts, Court Forms, Court Services, Administration, Appellate Opinions, and Court Information Office. Under Appellate Opinions, there full text opinions from the Court of Special Appeals and Court of Appeals from 1995. Note that Maryland's highest court is called the Court of Appeals.
Subject: Maryland

2965. Maryland.Gov
http://maryland.gov/
Sponsor: Maryland State Government
Description: Maryland.Gov, the state's portal Web site, features online services, a state agency index, an events calendar, and traffic information. State and other government information and services are organized by topics such as Education, Business, Taxes, and Travel and Recreation.
Subject: Maryland

Local Governments

2966. Aberdeen
http://www.aberdeen-md.org

2967. Allegany County
http://gov.allconet.org

2968. Annapolis
http://www.ci.annapolis.md.us

2969. Anne Arundel County
http://www.co.anne-arundel.md.us

2970. Baltimore
http://www.ci.baltimore.md.us

2971. Baltimore County
http://www.co.ba.md.us

2972. Bowie
http://www.cityofbowie.org

2973. Calvert County
http://www.co.cal.md.us

2974. Carroll County
http://ccgov.carr.org/

2975. Charles County
http://www.charlescounty.org

2976. Chestertown
http://www.chestertown.com

2977. Cumberland
http://www.ci.cumberland.md.us

2978. Dorchester County
http://www.commissioners.net

2979. Frederick
http://www.cityoffrederick.com

2980. Frederick County
http://www.co.frederick.md.us

2981. Frostburg
http://www.ci.frostburg.md.us

2982. Gaithersburg
http://www.ci.gaithersburg.md.us

2983. Garrett County
http://www.co.garrett.md.us

2984. Greenbelt
http://www.ci.greenbelt.md.us

2985. Hagerstown
http://www.hagerstownmd.org

2986. Harford County
http://www.co.ha.md.us

2987. Howard County
http://www.co.ho.md.us

2988. Laurel
http://www.laurel.md.us

2989. Montgomery County
http://www.co.mo.md.us

2990. Ocean City
http://www.ococean.com

2991. Prince George's County
http://www.goprincegeorgescounty.com/

2992. Rockville
http://www.ci.rockville.md.us

2993. Saint Mary's County
http://www.co.saint-marys.md.us/

2994. Salisbury
http://www.ci.salisbury.md.us

2995. Takoma Park
http://www.cityoftakomapark.org

2996. Taneytown
http://www.ci.taneytown.md.us

2997. Washington County
http://pilot.wash.lib.md.us/washco/

2998. Wicomico County
http://www.co.wicomico.md.us

2999. Worcester County
http://www.co.worcester.md.us

Massachusetts

3000. Mass.Gov
http://www.mass.gov/
Sponsor: Massachusetts State Government
Description: Mass.Gov is the official site of the Commonwealth of Massachusetts. Information is organized topically under the headings Home and Health, Doing Business, Work and Education, Having Fun, and Getting Around. A section called Your Government covers elected official and voting, cities and towns, working for the state, state agencies, and business with the government.
Subject: Massachusetts

3001. Massachusetts Court System
http://www.state.ma.us/courts/
Alternate URLs: http://www.masslaw.com/
http://www.socialaw.com/
Sponsor: Massachusetts. Courts

Description: The primary URL offers descriptive information on the Massachusetts court system, juror information, forms, and press releases. At this time, the site does not carry full text opinions. For Massachusetts Supreme Judicial Court and Court of Appeals decisions, see the alternate URLs.
Subject: Massachusetts

3002. The General Court
http://www.state.ma.us/legis/
Sponsor: Massachusetts. Legislature
Description: The General Court of the Commonwealth of Massachusetts, despite its name, is the legislature for the state. The site includes bill status and the full text of the current legislation, and the full text of enacted legislation back to 1997. The site also features legislator and district information, legislative documents, guides to the state legislative process, and the Massachusetts constitution.
Subject: Massachusetts

Local Governments

3003. Agawam
http://www.agawam.ma.us

3004. Amherst
http://www.town.amherst.ma.us

3005. Andover
http://www.town.andover.ma.us

3006. Attleboro
http://www.ci.attleboro.ma.us

3007. Barnstable County
http://www.barnstablecounty.org/

3008. Bellingham
http://www.bellinghamma.org

3009. Belmont
http://www.town.belmont.ma.us

3010. Beverly
http://www.ci.beverly.ma.us

3011. Blackstone
http://www.infotech-maine.com/blackstonema/

3012. Boston
http://www.ci.boston.ma.us

3013. Braintree
http://www.town.braintree.ma.us/

3014. Brookline
http://www.town.brookline.ma.us

3015. Burlington
http://www.burlington.org

3016. Cambridge
http://www.ci.cambridge.ma.us

3017. Chelmsford
http://townhall.chelmsford.ma.us

3018. Chelsea
http://www.ci.chelsea.ma.us/

3019. Chilmark
http://www.ci.chilmark.ma.us

3020. Concord
http://www.concordnet.org

3021. Dartmouth
http://www.town.dartmouth.ma.us

3022. East Longmeadow
http://www.eastlongmeadow.org

3023. Easton
http://www.easton.ma.us

3024. Everett
http://www.ci.everett.ma.us

3025. Falmouth
http://www.town.falmouth.ma.us

3026. Fitchburg
http://www.ci.fitchburg.ma.us/

3027. Franklin
http://www.franklin.ma.us

3028. Gloucester
http://www.ci.gloucester.ma.us

3029. Haverhill
http://www.haverhill.com

3030. Holyoke
http://www.ci.holyoke.ma.us

3031. Ipswich
http://www.town.ipswich.ma.us

3032. Lawrence
http://www.cityoflawrence.com

3033. Leicester
http://www.ci.leicester.ma.us/

3034. Leominster
http://www.ci.leominster.ma.us

3035. Lexington
http://ci.lexington.ma.us/

3036. Longmeadow
http://www.longmeadow.org

3037. Lowell
http://www.ci.lowell.ma.us

3038. Lynn
http://lynnma.virtualtownhall.net/

3039. Malden
http://www.ci.malden.ma.us

3040. Mansfield
http://www.mansfieldma.com

3041. Marblehead
http://www.marblehead.com/

3042. Medford
http://www.medford.org

3043. Melrose
http://www.cityofmelrose.org/

3044. Methuen
http://www.ci.methuen.ma.us/

3045. Milford
http://www.milford.ma.us

3046. New Bedford
http://www.ci.new-bedford.ma.us

3047. Newton
http://www.ci.newton.ma.us/main.htm

3048. Northampton
http://www.ci.northampton.ma.us

3049. Peabody
http://www.ci.peabody.ma.us

3050. Pittsfield
http://www.ci.pittsfield.ma.us/

3051. Provincetown
http://www.provincetowngov.org

3052. Quincy
http://www.ci.quincy.ma.us

3053. Reading
http://www.ci.reading.ma.us

3054 Scituate
http://www.town.scituate.ma.us

3055. Sheffield
http://www.town.sheffield.ma.us

3056 Shrewsbury
http://www.ci.shrewsbury.ma.us

3057. Somerville
http://www.ci.somerville.ma.us

3058. Southbridge
http://www.ci.southbridge.ma.us

3059. Springfield
http://www.ci.springfield.ma.us

3060. Taunton
http://www.ci.taunton.ma.us

3061. Tewksbury
http://www.tewksbury.info/

3062. Wakefield
http://www.wakefield.ma.us

3063. Waltham
http://www.city.waltham.ma.us/

3064. Wellesley
http://www.ci.wellesley.ma.us

3065. Westfield
http://www.ci.westfield.ma.us

3066. Williamstown
http://www.williamstown.net

3067. Worcester
http://www.ci.worcester.ma.us

3068. Yarmouth
http://www.yarmouthcapecod.org/

Michigan

3069. Michigan Courts
http://www.courts.michigan.gov/
Description: The Michigan Courts site links to the sites for the Supreme Court, Court of Appeals, Trial Courts, and Administration of the Courts. Supreme Court and Court of Appeals opinions released since January 2001 are available online. The Courts site also features judicial biographies, filing information, oral arguments schedules, and other legal and administrative resources.

3070. Michigan Legislature
http://www.michiganlegislature.org/
Description: The Michigan legislative site has the status and full text of legislation back to 1997. It can be searched and browsed in a variety of ways, including by category, day of activity, and law affected. Other basic documents online include legislative calendars, journals, and committee meeting information. The site also carries the *Michigan Compiled Laws* and the state constitution.

3071. Michigan.gov
http://www.michigan.gov/
Description: This official site for Michigan is a portal with links to the Web sites for the state executive, legislative, and judicial branches. Information from the state is arranged topically under: Education and Career Development; Family, Health, and Safety; Travel and Recreation; Business Services; and Licensing, Certification, and Permits.

Local Governments

3072. Ann Arbor
http://www.ci.ann-arbor.mi.us

3073. Auburn Hills
http://www.auburn-hills.org

3074. Battle Creek
http://www.battlecreek.org

3075. Bay City
http://www.baycitygovernment.com

3076. Belleville
http://www.belleville.mi.us

3077. Berrien County
http://www.berriencounty.org

3078. Big Rapids
http://www.ci.big-rapids.mi.us

3079. Birmingham
http://www.ci.birmingham.mi.us

3080. Brighton
http://www.brightoncity.org

3081. Cedar Springs
http://www.cedar-springs.mi.us

3082. Clawson
http://www.ci.clawson.mi.us

3083. Clinton County
http://www.clinton-county.org/

3084. Dearborn
http://www.cityofdearborn.org/

3085. Detroit
http://www.ci.detroit.mi.us

3086. East Lansing
http://www.cityofeastlansing.com/

3087. Eastpointe
http://www.ci.eastpointe.mi.us

3088. Eaton County
http://www.co.eaton.mi.us

3089. Escanaba
http://www.escanaba.org

3090. Farmington
http://www.ci.farmington.mi.us

3091. Flat Rock
http://flatrockmi.org/

3092. Flint
http://www.ci.flint.mi.us

3093. Franklin
http://www.franklin.mi.us

3094. Genesee County
http://www.co.genesee.mi.us

3095. Grand Rapids
http://www.grand-rapids.mi.us

3096. Grand Traverse County
http://www.grandtraverse.org

3097. Greenville
http://www.ci.greenville.mi.us

3098. Grosse Pointe Woods
http://www.ci.grosse-pointe-woods.mi.us

3099. Hancock
http://www.cityofhancock.com

3100. Hillsdale
http://www.ci.hillsdale.mi.us

3101. Hillsdale County
http://www.co.hillsdale.mi.us

3102. Holland
http://www.ci.holland.mi.us

3103. Houghton
http://www.cityofhoughton.com

3104. Huntington Woods
http://www.ci.huntington-woods.mi.us

3105. Ingham County
http://www.ingham.org

3106. Ionia
http://city.ionia.mi.us/

3107. Jackson
http://www.cityofjackson.org/

3108. Jackson County
http://www.co.jackson.mi.us

3109. Kalamazoo
http://www.ci.kalamazoo.mi.us

3110. Kalamazoo County
http://www.kalcounty.com

3111. Kent County
http://www.accesskent.com/

3112. Lansing
http://www.ci.lansing.mi.us

3113. Lapeer
http://www.ci.lapeer.mi.us

3114. Lathrup Village
http://www.lathrupvillage.org

3115. Ludington
http://www.ci.ludington.mi.us

3116. Madison Heights
http://www.ci.madison-heights.mi.us

3117. Marine City
http://www.marinecity.org/

3118. Marquette County
http://www.co.marquette.mi.us

3119. Marysville
http://www.cityofmarysvillemi.com

3120. Midland
http://www.midland-mi.org/welcome.htm

3121. Midland County
http://www.co.midland.mi.us

3122. Muskegon
http://www.ci.muskegon.mi.us

3123. Muskegon County
http://www.co.muskegon.mi.us

3124. Oak Park
http://www.oakpark-mi.com

3125. Oakland County
http://www.co.oakland.mi.us

3126. Ottawa County
http://www.co.ottawa.mi.us/

3127. Owosso
http://home.shianet.org/~owosso/

3128. Plymouth
http://www.ci.plymouth.mi.us

3129. Pontiac
http://www.pontiac.mi.us

3130. Port Huron
http://www.porthuron.org

3131. Rochester Hills
http://www.rochesterhills.org

3132. Roseville
http://www.ci.roseville.mi.us

3133. Saint Clair Shores
http://www.ci.saint-clair-shores.mi.us

3134. Saint Johns
http://www.ci.saint-johns.mi.us

3135. Saint Joseph
http://www.sjcity.com

3136. Saline
http://www.ci.saline.mi.us

3137. Sterling Heights
http://www.ci.sterling-heights.mi.us

3138. Sturgis
http://www.ci.sturgis.mi.us

3139. Taylor
http://www.cityoftaylor.com/

3140. Three Rivers
http://www.threeriversmi.org

3141. Traverse City
http://www.ci.traverse-city.mi.us

3142. Trenton
http://www.trenton-mi.com

3143. Troy
http://www.ci.troy.mi.us

3144. Walker
http://www.ci.walker.mi.us

3145. Washtenaw County
http://www.ewashtenaw.org/

3146. Wayne
http://www.ci.wayne.mi.us

3147. Wayne County
http://www.waynecounty.com

3148. Zeeland
http://www.ci.zeeland.mi.us

Minnesota

3149. Minnesota State Court System
http://www.courts.state.mn.us/
Sponsor: Minnesota. Courts
Description: This site links to the Minnesota Courts and State Law Library, and to court rules, forms, and related judicial Web sites. Supreme Court and Court of Appeals opinions are available back to 1996.
Subject: Minnesota

3150. Minnesota State Legislature
http://www.leg.state.mn.us/
Sponsor: Minnesota. Legislature
Description: The primary links on this site are the House of Representatives; Senate; Legislation and Bill Status; Schedules; Statutes, Session Laws, and Rules; and Joint Departments and Commissions. The Bill Status section includes both the bill status and the full text of bills back to the 1993 session. The Statutes, Session Laws, and Rules section includes the *Minnesota Statutes*, the state constitution, and access to the *Minnesota Session Laws* back to 1994.
Subject: Minnesota

3151. North Star: Minnesota State Government Online
http://www.state.mn.us/cgi-bin/portal/mn/jsp/home.do?agency=NorthStar
Sponsor: Minnesota State Government
Description: The North Star portal for the Minnesota state government features directories for the state agencies, state legislature, school districts, and higher education institutions. Other sections include All About Minnesota, Online Services, and a Tools of Democracy section with key state documents and public information.
Subject: Minnesota

Local Governments

3152. Aitkin County
http://www.co.aitkin.mn.us

3153. Apple Valley
http://www.ci.apple-valley.mn.us

3154. Austin
http://www.austin-mn.com

3155. Barnesville
http://www.barnesvillemn.com/

3156. Benson
http://www.bensonmn.org

3157. Biwabik
http://www.cityofbiwabik.com

3158. Blaine
http://www.ci.blaine.mn.us

3159. Bloomington
http://www.ci.bloomington.mn.us

3160. Blue Earth
http://www.be.blue-earth.mn.us

3161. Blue Earth County
http://www.co.blue-earth.mn.us

3162. Brainerd
http://www.ci.brainerd.mn.us

3163. Brooklyn Park
http://www.ci.brooklyn-park.mn.us

3164. Brown County
http://www.co.brown.mn.us

3165. Burnsville
http://www.ci.burnsville.mn.us

3166. Carver County
http://www.co.carver.mn.us

3167. Champlin
http://ci.champlin.mn.us/

3168. Chanhassen
http://www.ci.chanhassen.mn.us

3169. Chisago County
http://www.co.chisago.mn.us

3170. Cokato
http://www.cokato.mn.us

3171. Cook County
http://www.co.cook.mn.us

3172. Coon Rapids
http://www.ci.coon-rapids.mn.us

3173. Cottage Grove
http://www.cottage-grove.org

3174. Crow Wing County
http://www.co.crow-wing.mn.us

3175. Dakota County
http://www.co.dakota.mn.us

3176. Detroit Lakes
http://www.ci.detroit-lakes.mn.us/

3177. Douglas County
http://www.co.douglas.mn.us

3178. Duluth
http://www.ci.duluth.mn.us

3179. Eagan
http://www.ci.eagan.mn.us

3180. East Grand Forks
http://www.ci.east-grand-forks.mn.us

3181. Eden Prairie
http://www.ci.eden-prairie.mn.us

3182. Edina
http://www.ci.edina.mn.us

3183. Elk River
http://www.ci.elk-river.mn.us

3184. Eveleth
http://www.evelethmn.com

3185. Fairbault County
http://www.co.faribault.mn.us

3186. Fairmont
http://www.fairmont.org

3187. Farmington
http://www.ci.farmington.mn.us

3188. Fergus Falls
http://www.ci.fergus-falls.mn.us

3189. Fridley
http://www.ci.fridley.mn.us

3190. Goodhue County
http://www.co.goodhue.mn.us

3191. Hennepin County
http://www.co.hennepin.mn.us

3192. Hermantown
http://www.hermantownmn.com

3193. Hinckley
http://www.ci.hinckley.mn.us

3194. Howard Lake
http://www.howard-lake.mn.us

3195. Hoyt Lakes
http://www.hoytlakes.com

3196. Hutchinson
http://www.ci.hutchinson.mn.us

3197. Itasca County
http://www.co.itasca.mn.us

3198. Kandiyohi County
http://www.co.kandiyohi.mn.us

3199. Lakeville
http://www.ci.lakeville.mn.us

3200. Le Sueur County
http://www.co.le-sueur.mn.us

3201. Long Lake
http://www.ci.long-lake.mn.us

3202. Luverne
http://www.cityofluverne.org/

3203. Mankato
http://www.ci.mankato.mn.us

3204. Maple Grove
http://www.ci.maple-grove.mn.us

3205. Melrose
http://www.ci.melrose.mn.us

3206. Minneapolis
http://www.ci.minneapolis.mn.us

3207. Minnetonka
http://eminnetonka.com/

3208. Moorhead
http://www.ci.moorhead.mn.us

3209. New Brighton
http://www.ci.new-brighton.mn.us

3210. New Hope
http://www.ci.new-hope.mn.us

3211. Nicollet County
http://www.co.nicollet.mn.us

3212. Nobles County
http://www.co.nobles.mn.us

3213. North Mankato
http://www.city.north-mankato.mn.us

3214. Northfield
http://www.ci.northfield.mn.us

3215. Oak Park Heights
http://www.cityofoakparkheights.com

3216. Oakdale
http://www.ci.oakdale.mn.us

3217. Olivia
http://www.olivia.mn.us

3218. Olmsted County
http://www.olmstedcounty.com

3219. Owatonna
http://www.ci.owatonna.mn.us

3220. Park Rapids
http://ci.park-rapids.mn.us/

3221. Pelican Rapids
http://www.pelicanrapids.com

3222. Perham
http://www.cityofperham.com

3223. Pine City
http://www.ci.pine-city.mn.us

3224. Pine County
http://www.pinecounty.com

3225. Plainview
http://www.plainviewmn.com

3226. Plymouth
http://www.ci.plymouth.mn.us

3227. Prior Lake
http://www.cityofpriorlake.com

3228. Ramsey County
http://www.co.ramsey.mn.us

3229. Red Wing
http://www.ci.red-wing.mn.us

3230. Redwood Falls
http://www.ci.redwood-falls.mn.us

3231. Renville
http://www.ci.renville.mn.us

3232. Renville County
http://www.co.renville.mn.us

3233. Richfield
http://www.ci.richfield.mn.us

3234. Rochester
http://www.ci.rochester.mn.us

3235. Roseville
http://www.ci.roseville.mn.us

3236. Saint Cloud
http://ci.stcloud.mn.us

3237. Saint Louis County
http://www.co.st-louis.mn.us

3238. Saint Paul
http://www.ci.stpaul.mn.us

3239. Sartell
http://www.ci.sartell.mn.us

3240. Scott County
http://www.co.scott.mn.us

3241. Shakopee
http://www.ci.shakopee.mn.us

3242. Sherburne County
http://www.co.sherburne.mn.us

3243. Shoreview
http://www.ci.shoreview.mn.us

3244. Shorewood
http://www.ci.shorewood.mn.us

3245. Silver Bay
http://www.silverbay.com

3246. South Saint Paul
http://www.southstpaul.org

3247. Spring Valley
http://www.ci.spring-valley.mn.us

3248. Stearns County
http://www.co.stearns.mn.us

3249. Steele County
http://www.co.steele.mn.us

3250. Stillwater
http://www.ci.stillwater.mn.us

3251. Wadena
http://www.ci.wadena.mn.us

3252. Washington County
http://www.co.washington.mn.us

3253. White Bear Lake
http://www.ci.white-bear-lake.mn.us/

3254. Winsted
http://www.winsted.mn.us

3255. Woodbury
http://www.ci.woodbury.mn.us

3256. Wright County
http://www.co.wright.mn.us

3257. Wyoming
http://www.wyomingmn.org

Mississippi

3258. Mississippi Legislature
http://www.ls.state.ms.us/
Sponsor: Mississippi. Legislature
Description: This site links to the Mississippi House of Representatives and Senate, both of which provide member biographies, chamber rules, and committee membership information. The Bill Status section has the status and full text of legislation back to 1997.
Subject: Mississippi

3259. Mississippi Supreme Court
http://www.mssc.state.ms.us/
Sponsor: Mississippi. Supreme Court
Description: The Mississippi Supreme Court site features biographies of Supreme Court and Court of Appeals justices. Online court documents include court decisions, rules, and dockets. The site also has a database of Mississippi Bar attorneys.
Subject: Mississippi

3260. Mississippi.gov
http://www.ms.gov/
Sponsor: Mississippi State Government
Description: Mississippi.gov is the official Web site for the state. The Missippi Government section of the site includes links to: state agencies, the state legislature, and judicial offices; directories of federal and state elected officials; local government sites; and state economic information and statistics. The statistics section includes the full text of the *Mississippi Official and Statistical Register*, or "blue book," in PDF format.
Subject: Mississippi

Local Governments

3261. Biloxi
http://www.biloxi.ms.us/

3262. Canton
http://www.cityofcanton.net

3263. D'Iberville
http://www.cityofdiberville.org

3264. Gautier
http://gautier.ms.us/

3265. Greenville
http://www.greenville.ms.us

3266. Gulfport
http://www.ci.gulfport.ms.us

3267. Hattiesburg
http://www.hattiesburgms.com

3268. Hinds County
http://www.co.hinds.ms.us

3269. Jackson
http://www.city.jackson.ms.us

3270. Kosciusko
http://www.cityofkosciusko.com

3271. Madison
http://www.ci.madison.ms.us

3272. Meridian
http://www.meridianms.org/

3273. Moss Point
http://www.cityofmosspoint.mississippi.com/

3274. Natchez
http://www.natchez.ms.us

3275. Olive Branch
http://www.ci.olive-branch.ms.us

3276. Pascagoula
http://www.cityofpascagoula.com/

3277. Rankin County
http://www.rankincounty.org

3278. Raymond
http://www.raymondms.com

3279. Starkville
http://www.cityofstarkville.org

3280. Stone County
http://www.stonecounty.com

3281. Tupelo
http://www.ci.tupelo.ms.us

3282. West Point
http://www.wpnet.org

Missouri

3283. Missouri General Assembly
http://www.moga.state.mo.us/
Sponsor: Missouri. Legislature
Description: The General Assembly site features the following sections: House, Senate, Legislative Joint Committees, Calendars, Hearings, Journals, Joint Bill Tracking, Legislator Lookup, Missouri Constitution, Missouri Revised Statutes, and Virtual Missouri Capitol Tour. The site has the status and text of legislation back to 1995, with supplemental information such as bill summaries and fiscal notes.
Subject: Missouri

3284. Missouri Judiciary
http://www.osca.state.mo.us/
Sponsor: Missouri. Courts
Description: This site provides access to the Supreme Court, Missouri Court of Appeals, Office of State Courts Administrator, and Circuit Courts. Opinions for all Missouri appellate courts are available; they are listed by date and can also be searched by word.
Subject: Missouri

3285. Missouri State Government
http://www.state.mo.us/
Sponsor: Missouri State Government
Description: Missouri's official Web site is a portal including links to online government services and to the state statutes, regulations, and constitution. Topical sections include Living, Traveling, Learning, Working, Business, and News.
Subject: Missouri

Local Governments

3286. Albany
http://www.albanymo.net/

3287. Audrain County
http://www.audrain-county.org

3288. Ballwin
http://www.ballwin.mo.us

3289. Belton
http://www.belton.org

3290. Blue Springs
http://www.bluespringsgov.com/

3291. Boone Count
http://www.showmeboone.com/

3292. Buchanan County
http://www.co.buchanan.mo.us

3293. Cape Girardeau
http://www.cityofcapegirardeau.org/

3294. Chesterfield
http://www.chesterfield.mo.us

3295. Clayton
http://www.ci.clayton.mo.us

3296. Clinton
http://www.clintonmo.com

3297. Columbia
http://www.ci.columbia.mo.us

3298. Crestwood
http://www.ci.crestwood.mo.us

3299. Creve Coeur
http://www.creve-coeur.org/

3300. East Prairie
http://www.eastprairiemo.net

3301. Ellisville
http://www.ellisville.mo.us

3302. Eureka
http://www.eureka.mo.us

3303. Florissant
http://www.florissantmo.com

3304. Fulton
http://fulton.missouri.org

3305. Hale
http://www.cityofhale.net

3306. Harrisonville
http://ci.harrisonville.mo.us/

3307. Hazelwood
http://www.ci.hazelwood.mo.us

3308. Independence
http://www.ci.independence.mo.us

3309. Jackson County
http://www.co.jackson.mo.us

3310. Joplin
http://www.joplinmo.org

3311. Kansas City
http://www.kcmo.org/kcmo.nsf/web/home?opendocument

3312. Kirksville
http://www.kirksvillecity.com

3313. La Plata
http://www.cityoflaplata.org

3314. Laclede County
http://laclede.county.missouri.org

3315. Lebanon
http://www.lebanonmissouri.org/

3316. Liberty
http://www.ci.liberty.mo.us

3317. Manchester
http://www.ci.manchester.mo.us

3318. Marceline
http://www.marceline.org

3319. Maryland Heights
http://www.marylandheights.com/

3320. Nixa
http://www.nixa.com

3321. North Kansas City
http://www.nkc.org

3322. Piedmont
http://www.cityofpiedmont.com

3323. Platte County
http://www.co.platte.mo.us

3324. Raytown
http://www.raytown.k12.mo.us/city/

3325. Saint Charles
http://www.stcharlescity.com

3326. Saint Charles County
http://www.win.org/county/sccg.htm

3327. Saint John
http://www.cityofstjohn.org

3328. Saint Joseph
http://www.ci.st-joseph.mo.us

3329. Saint Louis
http://stlouis.missouri.org

3330. Saint Louis County
http://www.stlouisco.com

3331. Saint Peters
http://www.stpetersmo.net/

3332. Sedalia
http://ci.sedalia.mo.us

3333. Springfield
http://www.ci.springfield.mo.us/

3334. Sullivan
http://www.sullivan.mo.us

3335. University City
http://www.universitycitymo.org

3336. Wildwood
http://www.cityofwildwood.com/

3337. Wright City
http://www.wrightcity.org

Montana

3338. Montana Legislative Branch
http://leg.state.mt.us/
Sponsor: Montana. Legislature
Description: Montana's legislative site includes core legislative information, as well as featured links to working groups such as the Environmental Quality Council and the Legislative Audit Committee. The site has directories of legislators and committees and links to committee documents. The full text of legislation is available back to 1999.
Subject: Montana

3339. State Law Library of Montana
http://www.lawlibrary.state.mt.us/
Sponsor: Montana. State Law Library
Description: The Montana State Law Library's Web site serves as the central point for access to state judicial information. This includes Supreme Court opinions, the state code and constitution, legal forms, and a guide to Montana legal research.
Subject: Montana

3340. State of Montana
http://www.discoveringmontana.com/
Sponsor: Montana State Government
Description: The official State of Montana Web portal has state information in sections titled About Montana, Tourism and Recreation, Working and Living Here, Online Services, Doing Business, Government, and Education. Reference information includes state maps, Census data, and links to Montana newspapers. The Government section has directories of state agencies and officials, and links to information on Montana counties and cities and on tribal governments.
Subject: Montana

Local Governments

3341. Belgrade
http://www.ci.belgrade.mt.us/

3342. Billings
http://ci.billings.mt.us

3343. Bozeman
http://www.bozeman.net

3344. Cascade County
http://www.co.cascade.mt.us/

3345. Fort Benton
http://www.fortbenton.com/cityhall/

3346. Gallatin County
http://www.co.gallatin.mt.us

3347. Great Falls
http://www.ci.great-falls.mt.us/

3348. Helena
http://www.ci.helena.mt.us

3349. Hill County
http://co.hill.mt.us

3350. Lewis and Clark County
http://www.co.lewis-clark.mt.us

3351. Lincoln County
http://www.libby.org

3352. Missoula
http://www.ci.missoula.mt.us

3353. Missoula County
http://www.co.missoula.mt.us

3354. Philipsburg
http://www.philipsburgmt.com/

3355. Ravalli County
http://www.co.ravalli.mt.us/

3356. Yellowstone County
http://www.co.yellowstone.mt.us

Nebraska

3357. Nebraska Judicial Branch
http://court.nol.org/
Alternate URL: http://www.nol.org/home/ncpa/opinions.html
Sponsor: Nebraska. Courts
Description: The Nebraska Judicial Branch site has court opinions, rules, and forms, and links to information about each of the Nebraska courts. A jurors handbook, filing fees, a legal glossary, and other helpful background information is organized into sections for the public, the court community, the press, and students and teachers. Slip opinions from the Supreme Court and Court of Appeals issued during the last 90 days are online at the primary URL above. Archived opinions back to 1997 are available through the alternate URL.
Subject: Nebraska

3358. Nebraska Legislature Online
http://www.unicam.state.ne.us/
Sponsor: Nebraska. Legislature
Description: Nebraska's single-chamber legislature offers this site with the full text of bills and the state statutes. The site also features descriptive and historical information on the legislature. The Legislative Documents section includes bills, amendments, resolutions, slip laws, and other legislative documents. Under Laws of Nebraska, the site carries the full text of the *Nebraska Statutes*, the state constitution, and the rules of the state legislature.
Subject: Nebraska

3359. State of Nebraska
http://www.state.ne.us/
Sponsor: Nebraska State Government
Description: The Nebraska portal site includes sections on: Agriculture and Natural Resources; Business and Employment; Citizen Services; Education in Nebraska; Facts About Nebraska; Health and Safety; Moving to Nebraska; Visiting Nebraska; and Your Government. In addition, there is a link to a special portal site for government information of interest to businesses. The Facts About Nebraska section has an online Nebraska Blue Book and an extensive online Nebraska Databook.
Subject: Nebraska

Local Governments

3360. Beatrice
http://www.ci.beatrice.ne.us

3361. Bellevue
http://www.bellevue.net/

3362. Columbus
http://www.ci.columbus.ne.us/

3363. Douglas County
http://www.co.douglas.ne.us

3364. Geneva
http://www.ci.geneva.ne.us

3365. Gothenburg
http://www.ci.gothenburg.ne.us

3366. Grand Island
http://www.grand-island.com/

3367. Hastings
http://www.cityofhastings.org/

3368. Kearney
http://www.ci.kearney.ne.us/

3369. Kimball
http://www.ci.kimball.ne.us

3370. Lincoln
http://www.ci.lincoln.ne.us

3371. Madison County
http://www.co.madison.ne.us

3372. Norfolk
http://www.ci.norfolk.ne.us

3373. Omaha
http://www.ci.omaha.ne.us

3374. Papillion
http://www.papillion.ne.us

3375. Ralston
http://www.cityofralston.com

3376. Sarpy County
http://www.sarpy.com

3377. Scottsbluff
http://www.ci.scottsbluff.ne.us

3378. South Sioux City
http://www.cityofsouthsiouxcity.org/

Nevada

3379. Nevada State Legislature
http://www.leg.state.nv.us

Sponsor: Nevada. Legislature
Description: Nevada's legislative site includes the full text of bills back to 1995, calendar information, and legislative district maps. The Law Library section has the *Nevada Revised States*, *Administrative Code, Register*, and selected Nevada city charters. Links are also provided to information from the Senate and Assembly, the Research Library, and the Counsel Bureau.
Subject: Nevada

3380. State of Nevada
http://silver.state.nv.us/
Sponsor: Nevada State Government
Description: The official State of Nevada site links to information from the state governor, elected officials, and the various state agencies, departments, and commissions. A side panel features hot topics, and an alphabetical menu of State/Federal Programs leads to a wealth of program and benefits information.
Subject: Nevada

3381. State of Nevada Supreme Court
http://nvcourtaoc.state.nv.us/
Alternate URL: http://www.leg.state.nv.us/scd/OpinionListPage.html
Sponsor: Nevada. Courts
Description: This official site for the Nevada Supreme Court includes general background information on the Court, its annual report, and links to related sites. The Links section points to other state courts and federal courts in Nevada, as well as sources for the text of the Supreme Court's opinions. See the alternate URL, from the state's legislative site, for the text of opinions released in the past 90 days.
Subject: Nevada

Local Governments

3382. Boulder City
http://www.ci.boulder-city.nv.us

3383. Carson City
http://www.carson-city.nv.us

3384. Clark County
http://www.co.clark.nv.us

3385. Douglas County
http://www.co.douglas.nv.us

3386. Elko
http://www.ci.elko.nv.us/

3387. Henderson
http://www.ci.henderson.nv.us

3388. Las Vegas
http://www.ci.las-vegas.nv.us

3389. Mesquite
http://www.mesquitenv.com

3390. North Las Vegas
http://www.ci.north-las-vegas.nv.us/

3391. Reno
http://www.ci.reno.nv.us

3392. Sparks
http://www.ci.sparks.nv.us

3393. Washoe County
http://www.co.washoe.nv.us

New Hampshire

3394. New Hampshire General Court
http://gencourt.state.nh.us
Sponsor: New Hampshire. Legislature
Description: Despite its name, this is the site of New Hampshire's legislature. The site features member information, calendars, and journals for both the House and Senate. The full text of legislation is online back to 1989. State laws, lobbyist lists, legislative procedure guides and other information are included in a section called "Census, Redistricting, Ethics, State Laws, etc."
Subject: New Hampshire

3395. New Hampshire Judicial Branch
http://www.state.nh.us/courts/
Sponsor: New Hampshire. Courts
Description: This simple page links to the pages for New Hampshire's Supreme Court, Superior Court, Probate Court, Family Division Pilot Program, Administrative Office of the Courts, and Law Library. The Supreme Court page includes the full text of slip opinions since 1995. Access is by date in reverse chronological order.
Subject: New Hampshire

3396. WEBSTER: New Hampshire State Government Online
http://www.state.nh.us/
Sponsor: New Hampshire State Government
Description: The New Hampshire State site links to the executive, judicial, and legislative branches as well as to e-government services. Major sections are Living, Working, Visiting NH, Education, Doing Business, Taxes, Cities and Towns, Facts about NH, and NH Laws and Rules.
Subject: New Hampshire

Local Governments

3397. Amherst
http://www.town.amherst.nh.us

3398. Bedford
http://www.ci.bedford.nh.us

3399. Berlin
http://www.ci.berlin.nh.us/

3400. Bow
http://www.ci.bow.nh.us

3401. Cheshire County
http://www.co.cheshire.nh.us/

3402. Claremont
http://www.claremontnh.com

3403. Colebrook
http://www.colebrook-nh.com

3404. Concord
http://www.ci.concord.nh.us

3405. Derry
http://www.derry.nh.us/

3406. Dover
http://www.ci.dover.nh.us

3407. Dunbarton
http://www.ci.dunbarton.nh.us

3408. Durham
http://www.ci.durham.nh.us

3409. Epping
http://www.ci.epping.nh.us

3410. Goffstown
http://www.goffstown.com/

3411. Greenfield
http://www.greenfieldnh.org

3412. Hanover
http://www.hanovernh.org

3413. Hillsborough
http://www.town.hillsborough.nh.us/

3414. Hollis
http://www.hollis.nh.us

3415. Hooksett
http://www.hooksett.org/

3416. Hudson
http://www.ci.hudson.nh.us

3417. Laconia
http://www.cityoflaconianh.org

3418. Manchester
http://www.ci.manchester.nh.us

3419. Merrimack
http://www.ci.merrimack.nh.us

3420. Milford
http://www.ci.milford.nh.us

3421. Nashua
http://www.ci.nashua.nh.us/

3422. Pelham
http://www.pelham-nh.com

3423. Pembroke
http://www.pembroke-nh.com

3424. Peterborough
http://www.ci.peterborough.nh.us

3425. Portsmouth
http://www.cityofportsmouth.com

3426. Raymond
http://www.raymond-nh.com

3427. Rockingham County
http://www.co.rockingham.nh.us

3428. Salem
http://www.ci.salem.nh.us

3429. Somersworth
http://www.somersworth.com

3430. Warner
http://www.warner.nh.us

3431. Weare
http://www.town.weare.nh.us/

3432. Windham
http://www.town.windham.nh.us/

3433. Wolfeboro
http://www.wolfeboro.com

New Jersey

3434. New Jersey Judiciary
http://www.judiciary.state.nj.us
Sponsor: New Jersey. Courts
Description: This site provides detailed information about New Jersey courts down to the municipal level. The Legal Reference Desk has links to the text of opinions from the Supreme Court and appellate courts, and a link to trial court decisions.
Subject: New Jersey

3435. New Jersey State Legislature
http://www.njleg.state.nj.us
Sponsor: New Jersey. Legislature
Description: The New Jersey Legislature has the full text of legislation and the transcripts of public hearings online back to 1996. Major sections of the site include Members, Districts, Bills, Committees, Laws and Constitution, and Legislative Publications. A General Information section

has information about the legislative process, the history of the legislature, and a Kids Page with more educational information.
Subject: New Jersey

3436. State of New Jersey
http://www.state.nj.us
Sponsor: New Jersey State Government
Description: This site aims to help the public keep in touch with what's happening throughout the state of New Jersey and find information on government services. Featured sections include New Jersey People, New Jersey Open for Business, Government Information, and Hangout for NJ Kids. The Government Information section has links to state government offices and documents, and to local and federal government links as well.
Subject: New Jersey

Local Governments

3437. Atlantic County
http://www.aclink.org

3438. Barnegat
http://www.ci.barnegat.nj.us

3439. Bayonne
http://www.bayonnenj.org/

3440. Bergen County
http://www.co.bergen.nj.us/

3441. Burlington County
http://www.co.burlington.nj.us

3442. Camden County
http://www.co.camden.nj.us

3443. Cape May County
http://www.co.cape-may.nj.us

3444. Carteret
http://www.ci.carteret.nj.us

3445. Colts Neck
http://www.colts-neck.nj.us

3446. Cumberland County
http://www.co.cumberland.nj.us

3447. East Orange
http://www.ci.east-orange.nj.us

3448. Edison
http://www.edisonnj.org

3449. Elizabeth
http://www.elizabethnj.org

3450. Englewood
http://www.cityofenglewood.org/

3451. Essex County
http://www.co.essex.nj.us

3452. Gloucester County
http://www.co.gloucester.nj.us

3453. Hackensack
http://www.hackensack.org

3454. Hoboken
http://www.ci.hoboken.nj.us

3455. Hudson County
http://www.hudsoncountynj.org/

3456. Hunterdon County
http://www.co.hunterdon.nj.us

3457. Jersey City
http://www.cityofjerseycity.com/

3458. Longbranch
http://www.longbranch.org

3459. Monmouth County
http://www.shore.co.monmouth.nj.us

3460. Morris County
http://www.co.morris.nj.us

3461. Mount Arlington
http://www.ci.mount-arlington.nj.us

3462. New Brunswick
http://www.cityofnewbrunswick.org/

3463. Newark
http://www.ci.newark.nj.us

3464. Ocean County
http://www.oceancountygov.com

3465. Passaic
http://www.cityofpassaic.com

3466. Plainfield
http://www.plainfield.com/

3467. Princeton
http://www.princetonol.com/gov/

3468. Ridgefield Park
http://www.ridgefieldpark.org

3469. Salem County
http://216.155.54.158/

3470. Somerset County
http://www.co.somerset.nj.us

3471. Summit
http://www.ci.summit.nj.us

3472. Sussex County
http://www.sussex.nj.us/

3473. Trenton
http://www.ci.trenton.nj.us

3474. Union County
http://www.unioncountynj.org

3475. Vineland
http://www.ci.vineland.nj.us/

3476. Wyckoff
http://www.wyckoff-nj.com

New Mexico

3477. New Mexico Legislature
http://legis.state.nm.us/
Sponsor: New Mexico. Legislature
Description: The legislative pages for New Mexico feature links to the House, Senate, and Committees. The Bill Finder service provides access to state legislation back to 1996. The Bill Watcher service provides email notification on the status of current legislation. This legislative site also includes the state statutes and administrative code, a glossary of legislative terms and abbreviations, and an FAQ on using the site.
Subject: New Mexico

3478. New Mexico State Judiciary
http://www.nmcourts.com/
Sponsor: New Mexico. Courts
Description: Under the Judicial Sites heading, this site links to a Case Lookup service, a judicial branch directory, the full text of opinions from the New Mexico Supreme Court and Court of Appeals, and other court information. Under the Other Judicial Sites heading, the site links to New Mexico courts and to several federal judicial sites.
Subject: New Mexico

3479. State of New Mexico
http://www.state.nm.us/
Sponsor: Mexico State Government
Description: The New Mexico state government portal has major sections on education, living in NM, working in NM, and visiting the state. Government-specific sections include Government in NM, e-Services, and State Employees. The About New Mexico section has a wealth of reference information, including a link to the state's Online Blue Book.
Subject: New Mexico

Local Governments

3480. Albuquerque
http://www.cabq.gov

3481. Belen
http://www.belennm.com

3482. Bernalillo County
http://www.bernco.gov

3483. Clovis
http://www.cityofclovis.org

3484. Corrales
http://www.village.corrales.nm.us

3485. Dona Ana County
http://www.co.dona-ana.nm.us

3486. Farmington
http://www.fmtn.org

3487. Gallup
http://www.ci.gallup.nm.us

3488. Hobbs
http://hobbsnm.org

3489. Las Cruces
http://www.las-cruces.org

3490. Los Alamos County
http://www.lac.losalamos.nm.us

3491. Otero County
http://www.co.otero.nm.us

3492. Roswell
http://www.roswell-usa.com/city/

3493. San Juan County
http://www.co.san-juan.nm.us

3494. Santa Fe
http://www.ci.santa-fe.nm.us

3495. Santa Fe County
http://www.co.santa-fe.nm.us

3496. Silver City
http://www.townofsilvercity.org

3497. Tucumcari
http://www.cityoftucumcari.com

New York

3498. New York State
http://www.state.ny.us/
Sponsor: New York State Government
Description: The New York State site features information from the Office of the Governor along with a detailed Citizen Guide linking to government information and services. Other major sections include Doing Business, Working, Learning, Healthcare, Visiting, Government, and Government Agencies.
Subject: New York

3499. New York State Assembly
http://assembly.state.ny.us/
Alternate URL: http://www.senate.state.ny.us/
Sponsor: New York. Legislature
Description: The New York State Assembly and Senate each maintain separate Web sites. The Assembly site includes basic search interfaces for current state legislation and state laws. It also features legislative calendars, public hearings schedules, and press releases from the Speaker. A Minority Communications section has press releases and reports from the minority party. The alternate URL above leads to the Web site for the New York State Senate. The Senate legislation database features more search and display options and includes lists of links to current budget bills and the governor's veto and approval messages. The site also includes Senate reports, rules, schedules, and press releases.
Subject: New York

3500. New York State Unified Court System
http://www.courts.state.ny.us/
Sponsor: New York. Courts
Description: This main site for the New York courts provides central access to the various court decisions, rules, and Web sites. It has considerable legal information for citizens as well as forms and electronic services for attorneys. Note that while in most states the highest court is called the Supreme Court, New York's highest court is its Court of Appeals. Court of Appeals decisions are online back to 2000.
Subject: New York

Local Governments

3501. Albany County
http://www.albanycounty.com

3502. Allegany County
http://www.co.allegany.ny.us

3503. Auburn
http://www.ci.auburn.ny.us

3504. Binghamton
http://www.ci.binghamton.ny.us

3505. Buffalo
http://www.ci.buffalo.ny.us

3506. Canandaigua
http://www.ci.canandaigua.ny.us

3507. Cattaraugus County
http://www.co.cattaraugus.ny.us

3508. Cayuga County
http://www.co.cayuga.ny.us

3509. Cheektowaga
http://www.town.cheektowaga.ny.us

3510. Chemung County
http://www.chemungcounty.com

3511. Clinton
http://www.townofclinton.com

3512. Cohoes
http://www.cohoes.com

3513. Cortland
http://www.cortland.org

3514. Eastchester
http://www.eastchester.com

3515. Erie County
http://www.erie.gov

3516. Esperance
http://www.townofesperance.org

3517. Genesee County
http://www.co.genesee.ny.us

3518. Geneva
http://www.geneva.ny.us

3519. Hempstead
http://www.townofhempstead.org

3520. Irondequoit
http://www.irondequoit.org

3521. Irvington
http://www.ci.irvington.ny.us

3522. Ithaca
http://www.ci.ithaca.ny.us

3523. Kingston
http://www.ci.kingston.ny.us

3524. Larchmont
http://www.ci.larchmont.ny.us

3525. Livingston County
http://www.co.livingston.state.ny.us

3526. Madison County
http://www.madisoncounty.org

3527. Malta
http://www.malta-town.org

3528. Massapequa Park
http://www.ci.massapequa-park.ny.us

3529. Middletown
http://www.ci.middletown.ny.us

3530. Monroe County
http://www.co.monroe.ny.us

3531. Montgomery County
http://www.co.montgomery.ny.us/

3532. Mount Vernon
http://www.ci.mount-vernon.ny.us/mv/index.htm

3533. Nassau County
http://www.co.nassau.ny.us

3534. New York City
http://www.ci.nyc.ny.us

3535. Niagara Falls
http://niagarafallsusa.org/

3536. Olean
http://www.cityofolean.com

3537. Onondaga County
http://www.co.onondaga.ny.us

3538. Ontario County
http://www.co.ontario.ny.us

3539. Orange County
http://www.co.orange.ny.us

3540. Orleans County
http://www.orleansny.com

3541. Oswego
http://www.oswegony.org

3542. Oswego County
http://www.co.oswego.ny.us

3543. Palmyra
http://www.palmyrany.com

3544. Pelham
http://www.townofpelham.com

3545. Pleasant Valley
http://www.ci.pleasant-valley.ny.us

3546. Poughkeepsie
http://www.cityofpoughkeepsie.com/gov/govset.html

3547. Putnam County
http://www.putnamcountyny.com

3548. Queens
http://www.queens.nyc.ny.us

3549. Queensbury
http://www.queensbury.net

3550. Rensselaer County
http://www.rensco.com

3551. Rochester
http://www.ci.rochester.ny.us

3552. Rockville Centre
http://www.ci.rockville-centre.ny.us

3553. Rye
http://www.ci.rye.ny.us

3554. Saint Lawrence County
http://www.co.st-lawrence.ny.us

3555. Saratoga County
http://www.co.saratoga.ny.us/

3556. Saratoga Springs
http://www.saratoga-springs.org

3557. Schenectady County
http://govt.co.schenectady.ny.us

3558. Southampton
http://www.town.southampton.ny.us

3559. Steuben County
http://www.steubencony.org

3560. Suffolk County
http://www.co.suffolk.ny.us

3561. Sullivan County
http://co.sullivan.ny.us

3562. Syracuse
http://www.syracuse.ny.us

3563. Tompkins County
http://www.tompkins-co.org

3564. Tonawanda
http://www.ci.tonawanda.ny.us

3565. Webster
http://www.ci.webster.ny.us

3566. Westchester County
http://www.westchestergov.com

3567. White Plains
http://www.ci.white-plains.ny.us

3568. Woodbury
http://www.ci.woodbury.ny.us

3569. Yonkers
http://www.cityofyonkers.com/

North Carolina

3570. North Carolina
http://www.ncgov.com
Sponsor: North Carolina State Government
Description: This official North Carolina site presents government information for three audiences: Citizens, Business, and State Employees. Each section has a selection of subject categories linking to state or federal government resources. The site also links to the Governor's Page and to news releases from the state's executive branch.
Subject: North Carolina

3571. North Carolina Courts
http://www.nccourts.org/
Sponsor: North Carolina. Courts
Description: The site features a broad range of information from the North Carolina courts. The Citizens section has a legal glossary and explanations of court procedures. The Courts section provides access to opinions, calendars, dockets, and directories of court officials. The Supreme Court and Court of Appeals slip opinions are available back to 1997.
Subject: North Carolina

3572. North Carolina General Assembly
http://www.ncga.state.nc.us/
Sponsor: North Carolina. Legislature
Description: The General Assembly site links to the House and Senate pages, each of which provides information on the chamber's members, committees, and calendars. The Bill Information section provides a number of different ways to access legislation, with the text available back to 1997.
Subject: North Carolina

Local Governments

3573. Alexander County
http://www.co.alexander.nc.us

3574. Anson County
http://www.co.anson.nc.us

3575. Apex
http://www.ci.apex.nc.us

3576. Asheboro
http://www.ci.asheboro.nc.us/

3577. Asheville
http://www.ci.asheville.nc.us

3578. Belmont
http://www.ci.belmont.nc.us/

3579. Buncombe County
http://www.buncombecounty.org

3580. Burke County
http://www.co.burke.nc.us

3581. Burlington
http://www.ci.burlington.nc.us

3582. Cabarrus County
http://www.co.cabarrus.nc.us

3583. Caldwell County
http://www.co.caldwell.nc.us

3584. Cary
http://www.ci.cary.nc.us

3585. Catawba County
http://www.co.catawba.nc.us

3586. Chapel Hill
http://www.ci.chapel-hill.nc.us

3587. Charlotte-Mecklenburg
http://www.charmeck.nc.us

3588. Chatham County
http://www.co.chatham.nc.us

3589. Clemmons
http://www.newsdirectory.com/go/?f=&r=nc&u=www.clemmons.org

3590. Cleveland County
http://www.co.cleveland.nc.us

3591. Columbus County
http://www.columbus.nc.us

3592. Concord
http://www.ci.concord.nc.us

3593. Cornelius
http://www.cornelius.org

3594. Craven County
http://www.co.craven.nc.us

3595. Cumberland County
http://www.co.cumberland.nc.us

3596. Currituck County
http://www.co.currituck.nc.us

3597. Dare County
http://www.co.dare.nc.us

3598. Davidson County
http://www.co.davidson.nc.us

3599. Davie County
http://www.co.davie.nc.us

3600. Dunn
http://www.dunn-nc.org

3601. Durham
http://www.ci.durham.nc.us

3602. Durham County
http://www.co.durham.nc.us

3603. Eden
http://www.ci.eden.nc.us

3604. Elizabethtown
http://www.elizabethtownnc.org

3605. Fayetteville
http://www.cityoffayetteville.org/

3606. Forest City
http://www.townofforestcity.com

3607. Forsyth County
http://www.co.forsyth.nc.us

3608. Greensboro
http://www.ci.greensboro.nc.us

3609. Greenville
http://ci.greenville.nc.us/

3610. Guilford County
http://www.co.guilford.nc.us

3611. Halifax County
http://www.halifaxnc.com

3612. Harnett County
http://www.harnett.org

3613. Havelock
http://www.cityofhavelock.com

3614. Henderson
http://www.ci.henderson.nc.us

3615. Henderson County
http://www.henderson.lib.nc.us/county/

3616. Hickory
http://www.ci.hickory.nc.us

3617. High Point
http://www.high-point.net

3618. Huntersville
http://www.huntersville.org

3619. Iredell County
http://www.co.iredell.nc.us

3620. Jacksonville
http://www.ci.jacksonville.nc.us

3621. Johnston County
http://www.co.johnston.nc.us

3622. Kannapolis
http://www.ci.kannapolis.nc.us

3623. Kitty Hawk
http://www.townofkittyhawk.org

3624. Laurinburg
http://www.laurinburg.org

3625. Lenoir
http://www.ci.lenoir.nc.us

3626. Lenoir County
http://www.co.lenoir.nc.us

3627. Lincoln County
http://www.co.lincoln.nc.us

3628. Monroe
http://www.ci.monroe.nc.us

3629. Moore County
http://www.co.moore.nc.us

3630. Mooresville
http://www.ci.mooresville.nc.us

3631. Morganton
http://www.ci.morganton.nc.us

3632. New Hanover County
http://www.co.new-hanover.nc.us

3633. Northampton County
http://www.northamptonnc.com/

3634. Onslow County
http://www.co.onslow.nc.us

3635. Orange County
http://www.co.orange.nc.us

3636. Pasquotank County
http://www.co.pasquotank.nc.us

3637. Person County
http://www.personcounty.net

3638. Pitt County
http://www.co.pitt.nc.us

3639. Polk County
http://www.co.polk.nc.us

3640. Raleigh
http://www.raleigh-nc.org

3641. Randolph County
http://www.co.randolph.nc.us

3642. Reidsville
http://www.ci.reidsville.nc.us

3643. Richmond County
http://www.co.richmond.nc.us

3644. Rockingham County
http://www.co.rockingham.nc.us/

3645. Rocky Mount
http://www.ci.rocky-mount.nc.us

3646. Rowan County
http://www.co.rowan.nc.us

3647. Rutherford College
http://www.ci.rutherford-college.nc.us

3648. Salisbury
http://www.ci.salisbury.nc.us

3649. Sanford
http://www.sanfordnc.net/

3650. Smithfield
http://www.smithfield-nc.com

3651. Stanly County
http://www.co.stanly.nc.us

3652. Stokes County
http://www.co.stokes.nc.us

3653. Tarboro
http://www.ci.tarboro.nc.us

3654. Topsail Beach
http://www.topsailbeach.org

3655. Union County
http://www.co.union.nc.us

3656. Valdese
http://www.ci.valdese.nc.us

3657. Wake County
http://www.co.wake.nc.us

3658. Washington
http://www.ci.washington.nc.us

3659. Wayne County
http://www.esn.net/waynecounty/

3660. Wilmington
http://www.ci.wilmington.nc.us

3661. Wilson
http://www.wilsonnc.org

3662. Wilson County
http://www.wilson-co.com

3663. Winston-Salem
http://www.ci.winston-salem.nc.us

North Dakota

3664. DiscoverND - North Dakota State
http://discovernd.com/
Sponsor: North Dakota State Government
Description: DiscoverND is the official state Web site for North Dakota. The Government section of the site includes links to state agencies, local governments, public records, and state elected officials. Other sections include Business, Education, Employment, e-Government, and Visiting North Dakota.
Subject: North Dakota

3665. North Dakota Legislative Branch
http://www.state.nd.us/lr/
Sponsor: North Dakota. Legislature
Description: Offering information on past, present, and future legislative sessions, this site provides basic information about the Legislative Assembly as well as State Laws, Agency Rules, and the Legislative Council. The text of legislation in online back to 1995.
Subject: North Dakota

3666. North Dakota Supreme Court
http://www.court.state.nd.us/
Sponsor: North Dakota. Supreme Court
Description: The Supreme Court Web site offers information on the whole state court system. Supreme Court opinions are online back to 1984, organized by year, topic, title, and by Justice name. A Courts section includes Supreme Court documents as well as links to information on the other state courts. A Guide section includes guides to the North Dakota judicial system.
Subject: North Dakota

Local Governments

3667. Bismarck
http://www.bismarck.org

3668. Burleigh County
http://www.co.burleigh.nd.us/

3669. Cass County
http://www.co.cass.nd.us

3670. Dickinson
http://www.dickinsonnd.com/

3671. Fargo
http://ci.fargo.nd.us

3672. Grand Forks
http://www.grandforksgov.com

3673. Minot
http://web.ci.minot.nd.us

3674. Renville County
http://www.renvillecounty.org

Ohio

3675. Ohio General Assembly
http://www.legislature.state.oh.us/
Sponsor: Ohio. Legislature
Description: The General Assembly site has links to information from the Senate, House of Representatives, and legislative agencies. A Search for Legislative Information section searches current legislation but also features links to search the *Ohio Revised Code*, *Ohio Administrative Code*, and databases of legislators and lobbyists.
Subject: Ohio

3676. Ohio Government Information and Services
http://www.state.oh.us/
Sponsor: Ohio State Government
Description: Ohio's site includes pages designed for residents, business, visitors, and state employees. Links to online services are featured on the home page, along with links to the Governor's Office.
Subject: Ohio

3677. Supreme Court of Ohio
http://www.sconet.state.oh.us/

Sponsor: Ohio. Supreme Court
Description: This site focuses on the Supreme Court; the Related Web Sites section links to all other state courts. Supreme Court opinions are online back to 1992. The site also features background information on the Ohio Supreme Court and the state judicial system.
Subject: Ohio

Local Governments

3678. Akron
http://www.ci.akron.oh.us

3679. Allen County
http://www.co.allen.oh.us

3680. Alliance
http://www.cityofalliance.com

3681. Athens
http://www.athensohio.info

3682. Avon
http://www.cityofavon.com

3683. Batavia
http://www.batavianewyork.com/

3684. Beavercreek
http://www.ci.beavercreek.oh.us

3685. Bedford
http://www.bedfordoh.gov/

3686. Bellevue
http://www.cityofbellevue.com

3687. Bentleyville
http://www.vil.bentleyville.oh.us

3688. Blue Ash
http://www.blueash.com

3689. Brook Park
http://www.cityofbrookpark.com

3690. Brunswick
http://www.brunswick.oh.us

3691. Butler County
http://www.butlercountyohio.org

3692. Cambridge
http://www.cambridgeoh.org

3693. Canton
http://www.cityofcanton.com

3694. Centerville
http://www.ci.centerville.oh.us

3695. Cheviot
http://www.cheviot.org

3696. Cincinnati
http://www.rcc.org/

3697. Clermont County
http://www.co.clermont.oh.us

3698. Cleveland
http://www.cleveland.oh.us

3699. Cleveland Heights
http://www.clevelandheights.com

3700. Columbus
http://www.ci.columbus.oh.us

3701. Coshocton County
http://www.co.coshocton.oh.us

3702. Cuyahoga County
http://www.cuyahoga.oh.us

3703. Cuyahoga Falls
http://www.ci.cuyahoga-falls.oh.us

3704. Dayton
http://www.ci.dayton.oh.us

3705. Delaware County
http://www.co.delaware.oh.us

3706. Dublin
http://www.dublin.oh.us

3707. Eastlake
http://www.eastlakeohio.com/home.htm

3708. Elyria
http://www.ci.elyria.oh.us

3709. Erie County
http://www.erie-county-ohio.net

3710. Euclid
http://www.ci.euclid.oh.us

3711. Fairborn
http://ci.fairborn.oh.us/city/

3712. Findlay
http://www.ci.findlay.oh.us

3713. Forest Park
http://www.forestpark.org

3714. Fostoria
http://www.ci.fostoria.oh.us

3715. Franklin County
http://www.co.franklin.oh.us

3716. Gahanna
http://www.gahanna.org

3717. Garfield Heights
http://www.garfieldhts.org/

3718. Germantown
http://www.ci.germantown.oh.us

3719. Girard
http://www.cityofgirard.com

3720. Grandview Heights
http://www.grandviewheights.org

3721. Granville
http://www.granville.oh.us

3722. Green
http://www.cityofgreen.org

3723. Greene County
http://www.co.greene.oh.us

3724. Grove City
http://www.ci.grove-city.oh.us

3725. Groveport
http://www.groveport.org/Selection.htm

3726. Hamilton
http://www.hamilton-city.org

3727. Hamilton County
http://www.hamilton-co.org

3728. Hubbard
http://www.cityofhubbard.com

3729. Huber Heights
http://www.ci.huber-heights.oh.us

3730. Kettering
http://www.ci.kettering.oh.us

3731. Lake County
http://www.co.lake.oh.us

3732. Lakewood
http://www.ci.lakewood.oh.us/

3733. Lancaster
http://www.ci.lancaster.oh.us

3734. Lima
http://www.cityhall.lima.oh.us

3735. Logan County
http://www.co.logan.oh.us

3736. Lorain
http://www.ci.lorain.oh.us

3737. Lorain County
http://www.lorcnty.org/

3738. Mahoning County
http://www.mahoningcountygov.com

3739. Mansfield
http://www.ci.mansfield.oh.us/

3740. Massillon
http://www.massillonohio.com

3741. Maumee
http://www.maumee.org

3742. Medina County
http://www.co.medina.oh.us

3743. Mentor
http://www.cityofmentor.com/

3744. Miamisburg
http://www.ci.miamisburg.oh.us

3745. Middletown
http://www.ci.middletown.oh.us

3746. Montgomery County
http://www.co.montgomery.oh.us

3747. Moraine
http://www.ci.moraine.oh.us

3748. Newark
http://www.ci.newark.oh.us/

3749. North Olmsted
http://www.ci.north-olmsted.oh.us

3750. North Ridgeville
http://www.ci.north-ridgeville.oh.us

3751. Oakwood
http://www.ci.oakwood.oh.us

3752. Orange Village
http://www.orangevillage.com

3753. Oregon
http://www.ci.oregon.oh.us

3754. Orrville
http://www.orrville.com

3755. Oxford
http://www.cityofoxford.org

3756. Painesville
http://www.painesville.com

3757. Pickerington
http://www.ci.pickerington.oh.us

3758. Port Clinton
http://www.ci.port-clinton.oh.us

3759. Reynoldsburg
http://www.ci.reynoldsburg.oh.us

3760. Rocky River
http://www.rrcity.com

3761. Scioto County
http://www.sciotocountyohio.com

3762. Shaker Heights
http://www.shakeronline.com

3763. Sharonville
http://www.ci.sharonville.oh.us

3764. Sidney
http://www.sidneyoh.com

3765. Springboro
http://www.ci.springboro.oh.us

3766. Springdale
http://www.springdale.org

3767. Springfield
http://www.ci.springfield.oh.us

3768. Stow
http://www.stow.oh.us

3769. Strongsville
http://www.strongsville.org

3770. Summit County
http://www.summitoh.net

3771. Sylvania
http://www.cityofsylvania.com

3772. Tallmadge
http://www.tallmadge-ohio.org

3773. Toledo
http://www.ci.toledo.oh.us

3774. Trotwood
http://www.trotwood.org

3775. Trumbull County
http://www.co.trumbull.oh.us

3776. Tuscarawas County
http://www.co.tuscarawas.oh.us/

3777. Upper Arlington
http://www.ua-ohio.net/

3778. Vandalia
http://www.ci.vandalia.oh.us

3779. Warren County
http://www.co.warren.oh.us

3780. West Carrollton
http://www.westcarrollton.org

3781. Westerville
http://www.ci.westerville.oh.us

3782. Wickliffe
http://www.cityofwickliffe.com

3783. Williams County
http://www.co.williams.oh.us

3784. Willoughby
http://www.willoughbyohio.com

3785. Wood County
http://www.co.wood.oh.us

3786. This entry intentionally left blank.

3787. Xenia
http://www.ci.xenia.oh.us

Oklahoma

3788. Oklahoma Legislative Service Bureau
http://www.lsb.state.ok.us/
Sponsor: Oklahoma. Legislature
Description: This page points directly to the House and Senate sites along with links to the online legislative information system. Legislative information includes the text of bills from the current and previous sessions, the state statutes and constitution, and a glossary of legislative terms.
Subject: Oklahoma

3789. Oklahoma State Courts Network
http://www.oscn.net
Sponsor: Oklahoma. Courts
Description: The Oklahoma State Courts Network provides unified access to the appellate and district courts of the state. One section presents the courts' dockets and another compiles state legal research resources such as cases, court rules, and opinions of the Attorney General. The legal research section has extensive current and historical materials and features sophisticated search and browse capabilities.
Subject: Oklahoma

3790. Your Oklahoma
http://www.state.ok.us/
Sponsor: Oklahoma State Government
Description: Oklahoma's state site links to the Governor's Web site and to a list of state agency sites. The front page features quick links to online services and topical information.
Subject: Oklahoma

Local Governments

3791. Ada
http://www.adaok.com

3792. Altus
http://www.cityofaltus.org

3793. Ardmore
http://www.ardmore.org/

3794. Bethany
http://www.ci.bethany.ok.us

3795. Bixby
http://www.bixby.com

3796. Broken Arrow
http://www.city.broken-arrow.ok.us

3797. Canadian County
http://www.canadiancounty.org/county/

3798. Chickasha
http://www.chickasha.org

3799. Del City
http://www.cityofdelcity.com

3800. Enid
http://www.enid.org

3801. Kay County
http://www.courthouse.kay.ok.us/home.html

3802. Lawton
http://www.cityof.lawton.ok.us

3803. Lexington
http://www.cityoflexington.com

3804. Moore
http://www.ci.moore.ok.us

3805. Muskogee
http://www.ci.muskogee.ok.us

3806. Norman
http://www.ci.norman.ok.us

3807. Oklahoma City
http://www.okc-cityhall.org

3808. Oklahoma County
http://www.oklahomacounty.org

3809. Owasso
http://www.cityofowasso.com/

3810. Ponca City
http://www.poncacity.com/ponca/

3811. Purcell
http://www.cityofpurcell.com

3812. Sand Springs
http://www.ci.sand-springs.ok.us

3813. Shawnee
http://www.shawneeok.org/

3814. Stillwater
http://www.stillwater.org

3815. Tecumseh
http://www.tecumsehok.com

3816. Tulsa
http://www.ci.tulsa.ok.us

3817. Tulsa County
http://www.tulsacounty.org

3818. Washington County
http://www.co.washington.ok.us

3819. Weatherford
http://www.cityofweatherford.com

Oregon

3820. Oregon Judicial Department
http://www.ojd.state.or.us/
Sponsor: Oregon. Courts
Description: This site features information on the courts and access to full-text cases. The News and Appellate Opinions link leads to the text of Oregon Supreme Court, Court of Appeals, and Tax Court decisions. They are arranged chronologically by year of decision. More state legal documentation can be found under the link to the State of Oregon Law Library's Internet Legal Resources.
Subject: Oregon

3821. Oregon State Legislature
http://www.leg.state.or.us/
Description: Major links for the Oregon legislative site lead to information from the House, Senate, and committees, as well as to databases for laws and legislation. The full text of legislation is online back to 1995. The site features a citizen's guide to the Oregon legislative process and a Kids' Page explaining the work of the state government and legislature.

3822. Oregon.gov
http://www.oregon.gov/
Sponsor: Oregon State Government
Description: Oregon's state government portal is organized by topic, such as Visiting, Working, Business, and Education. A Spanish-language section also directs citizens to services. An OnLine section offers licensing information, motor vehicle forms, a business registry database, and more. The Government section covers state, local, national, international, and Oregon tribal governments. The *Oregon Revised Statutes*, administrative rules, and other documents are also included in the Government section.
Subject: Oregon

Local Governments

3823. Albany
http://www.ci.albany.or.us

3824. Ashland
http://www.ashland.or.us

3825. Beaverton
http://www.ci.beaverton.or.us

3826. Bend
http://www.ci.bend.or.us

3827. Benton County
http://www.co.benton.or.us

3828. Canby
http://www.ci.canby.or.us

3829. Central Point
http://www.ci.central-point.or.us

3830. Clackamas County
http://www.co.clackamas.or.us

3831. Columbia County
http://www.co.columbia.or.us

3832. Coos Bay
http://www.coosbay.org

3833. Coos County
http://www.co.coos.or.us

3834. Corvallis
http://www.ci.corvallis.or.us

3835. Cottage Grove
http://www.cottagegrove.org

3836. Deschutes County
http://www.co.deschutes.or.us

3837. Douglas County
http://www.co.douglas.or.us

3838. Eagle Point
http://www.cityofeaglepoint.com

3839. Eugene
http://www.ci.eugene.or.us

3840. Gresham
http://www.ci.gresham.or.us

3841. Hillsboro
http://www.ci.hillsboro.or.us

3842. Jackson County
http://www.co.jackson.or.us

3843. Josephine County
http://www.co.josephine.or.us

3844. Junction City
http://www.ci.junction-city.or.us

3845. Keizer
http://www.keizer.org

3846. Klamath County
http://www.co.klamath.or.us

3847. Lake Oswego
http://www.ci.oswego.or.us

3848. Lane County
http://www.co.lane.or.us

3849. Lebanon
http://www.ci.lebanon.or.us

3850. Lincoln County
http://www.co.lincoln.or.us

3851. Linn County
http://www.co.linn.or.us

3852. Malheur County
http://www.malheurco.org

3853. Marion County
http://www.co.marion.or.us/

3854. McMinnville
http://www.ci.mcminnville.or.us

3855. Medford
http://www.ci.medford.or.us

3856. Multnomah County
http://www.co.multnomah.or.us

3857. Newberg
http://www.ci.newberg.or.us

3858. Oregon City
http://www.orcity.org/

3859. Pendleton
http://www.pendleton.or.us

3860. Philomath
http://www.ci.philomath.or.us

3861. Portland
http://www.ci.portland.or.us

3862. Redmond
http://www.redmond.or.us

3863. Roseburg
http://roseburg.rosenet.net/

3864. Salem
http://www.ci.salem.or.us

3865. Sherwood
http://www.ci.sherwood.or.us

3866. Springfield
http://www.ci.springfield.or.us

3867. Tigard
http://www.ci.tigard.or.us

3868. Tillamook County
http://www.co.tillamook.or.us

3869. Troutdale
http://www.ci.troutdale.or.us

3870. Union
http://www.cityofunion.com

3871. Wallowa County
http://www.co.wallowa.or.us

3872. Washington County
http://www.co.washington.or.us

3873. West Linn
http://www.ci.west-linn.or.us

3874. Wilsonville
http://www.ci.wilsonville.or.us

3875. Yamhill County
http://www.co.yamhill.or.us

Pennsylvania

3876. Pennsylvania General Assembly
http://www.legis.state.pa.us/
Sponsor: Pennsylvania. Legislature
Description: House, Senate, and Session are the three main sections of this state assembly site. The Session section includes a link to the Electronic Bill Room where one can find the text and history of legislation back to 1975, searchable by bill number, word, or topic. A separate Welcome Center page links to Pennsylvania legislature, government, and history guides.
Subject: Pennsylvania

3877. Pennsylvania State Government: PAPowerPort
http://www.state.pa.us/
Sponsor: Pennsylvania State Government
Description: The Pennsylvania state government portal packs a wealth of information under the basic categories of Business, Government, Learning, Living, Technology, Visiting, Working, and About Pennsylvania. The site, called PAPowerPort, also features links to regional newspapers, radio, and TV, along with lottery results, on its home page. A keyword search, subject search, and site map help with finding information on this large site.
Subject: Pennsylvania

3878. Pennsylvania Unified Judicial System
http://www.courts.state.pa.us/
Sponsor: Pennsylvania. Courts
Description: This site illustrates the state judicial system as a pyramid, with the Supreme Court at the top and the municipal and traffic courts along the bottom. Each part of the pyramid is linked to information on that state court. An Opinions link on the home page leads to opinions from the Supreme Court, Superior Court, and Commonwealth Court of Pennsylvania.
Subject: Pennsylvania

Local Governments

3879. Allegheny County
http://www.county.allegheny.pa.us

3880. Allentown
http://www.allentownpa.org

3881. Beaver County
http://www.co.beaver.pa.us

3882. Bethlehem
http://www.cityofbethlehem.org

3883. Bucks County
http://www.buckscounty.org

3884. Butler County
http://www.co.butler.pa.us

3885. Cambria County
http://www.co.cambria.pa.us

3886. Camp Hill
http://www.camphill-pa.org/

3887. Carrolltown
http://www.carrolltown.pa.us

3888. Centre County
http://www.co.centre.pa.us

3889. Chester
http://www.chestercity.com

3890. Chester County
http://www.chesco.org

3891. Clearfield County
http://www.clearfieldco.org

3892. Columbia County
http://www.columbiapa.org

3893. Cranberry
http://www.twp.cranberry.pa.us

3894. Cumberland County
http://www.co.cumberland.pa.us/

3895. Dauphin County
http://www.dauphinc.org

3896. Delaware County
http://www.co.delaware.pa.us

3897. Downingtown
http://www.downingtown.org

3898. Doylestown
http://www.doylestownpa.org

3899. Easton
http://www.easton-pa.com

3900. Elk County
http://www.co.elk.pa.us

3901. Erie County
http://www.eriecountygov.org

3902. Greene County
http://county.greenepa.net

3903. Greensburg
http://www.city.greensburg.pa.us

3904. Hazleton
http://www.hazletoncity.org

3905. Indiana County
http://www.indianacounty.org

3906. Jenkintown
http://www.jenkintown.com

3907. Juniata County
http://www.co.juniata.pa.us

3908. Lackawanna County
http://www.lackawannacounty.org

3909. Lancaster
http://www.cityoflancasterpa.com/

3910. Lancaster County
http://www.co.lancaster.pa.us

3911. Lehigh County
http://www.lehighcounty.org

3912. Lower Merion Township
http://www.lowermerion.org/

3913. Lycoming County
http://www.lyco.org

3914. Malvern
http://www.malvern.org

3915. Media
http://www.mediaborough.com/

3916. Mercer County
http://www.mcc.co.mercer.pa.us

3917. Mifflin County
http://mifflincounty.lcworkshop.com

3918. Monroe County
http://www.co.monroe.pa.us

3919. Monroeville
http://www.monroeville.pa.us

3920. Montgomery County
http://www.montcopa.org

3921. Mount Joy
http://www.mountjoypa.org

3922. Mount Lebanon
http://mtlebanon.org

3923. Murrysville
http://www.murrysville.com

3924. Norristown
http://www.norristown.org

3925. Penn Hills
http://www.pennhills.org

3926. Philadelphia
http://www.phila.gov

3927. Pittsburgh
http://www.city.pittsburgh.pa.us

3928. Reading
http://www.ci.reading.pa.us

3929. Saint Marys
http://www.cityofstmarys.com

3930. Schuylkill County
http://www.co.schuylkill.pa.us

3931. Shippensburg
http://www.borough.shippensburg.pa.us

3932. Somerset
http://www.somersetborough.com

3933. Union County
http://www.unionco.org

3934. Upper Darby Township
http://www.upperdarby.org

3935. Venango County
http://www.co.venango.pa.us

3936. Washington County
http://www.co.washington.pa.us

3937. West Chester
http://www.west-chester.com

3938. Westmoreland County
http://www.co.westmoreland.pa.us/index.shtml/

3939. Wormleysburg
http://www.borough.wormleysburg.pa.us

3940. York
http://www.yorkcity.org

3941. York County
http://www.york-county.org

Puerto Rico

3942. Government of Puerto Rico
http://www.gobierno.pr/
Sponsor: Puerto Rico. Government
Description: The official site of the government of Puerto Rico is a Spanish-language site. It organizes access to other government Web services and portals, such as links to government agencies, Puerto Rican municipalities, and cultural and economic information.
Subject: Puerto Rico

Rhode Island

3943. Rhode Island General Assembly
http://www.rilin.state.ri.us/
Sponsor: Rhode Island. Legislature
Description: Most documents on this site can be found in the General Assembly Legislative Information section. The text of legislation is available back to 1997, and House and Senate Journals are online back to 1998. This section also includes the current state statutes, legislative calendars, committee information, and guides to the state legislature. The House and Senate sections have Assembly member lists and biographies.
Subject: Rhode Island

3944. Rhode Island Government
http://www.ri.gov/
Sponsor: Rhode Island State Government
Description: The Rhode Island state government site includes a personalization feature called MyRhodeIsland and a feature for sending reminders from the site to your PDA called MyRI-Direct. Major sections of the site include State Agencies, Government, Business, Education, Rhode Island Facts and History, and Recreation and Travel.
Subject: Rhode Island

3945. Rhode Island Judiciary
http://www.courts.state.ri.us/

Sponsor: Rhode Island. Courts
Description: This central site for the state judicial branch has links to each court or functional level: Supreme, Superior, Family, District, Workers' Compensation, and Traffic Tribunal. The Supreme Court's published opinions are online back to 1999. Published decisions from Superior Court are online back to 2000.
Subject: Rhode Island

Local Governments

3946. Barrington
http://www.ci.barrington.ri.us

3947. Bristol
http://www.onlinebristol.com/

3948. Cranston
http://www.cranstonri.com

3949. East Greenwich
http://www.eastgreenwichri.com

3950. East Providence
http://www.eastprovidence.com

3951. Johnston
http://www.johnston-ri.com

3952. Newport
http://www.cityofnewport.com

3953. Pawtucket
http://www.pawtucketri.com

3954. Portsmouth
http://www.portsmouthri.com

3955. Providence
http://www.providenceri.com

3956. Scituate
http://www.scituateri.org

3957. Warwick
http://www.warwickri.com

3958. Woonsocket
http://www.ci.woonsocket.ri.us

South Carolina

3959. MySCgov.com
http://www.myscgov.com
Sponsor: South Carolina State Government
Description: This central site for the state links to Governor, Education, Commerce and Tourism, Government, State Agencies, and South Carolina State Jobs. The Government section points to a

variety of state government information areas, including Elected Officials, State Agencies, Legislature, Boards and Commissions, and State Telephone Directory. The State Agencies page offers an hierarchical list of the major state agencies that have an Internet presence.
Subject: South Carolina

3960. South Carolina Judicial Department
http://www.judicial.state.sc.us/
Sponsor: South Carolina. Supreme Court
Description: The Judicial Department site provides a consistent interface for accessing information from the state's Supreme Court, Court of Appeals, and Trial Courts. Supreme Court and Court of Appeals opinions are online going back to 1997. The site's calendar compiles schedules for all of the courts.
Subject: South Carolina

3961. South Carolina Legislature Online
http://www.scstatehouse.net/
Sponsor: South Carolina. Legislature
Description: This site offers one-click access to South Carolina House and Senate calendars, journals, committees, and members' biographies. The Legislation, Research, and Publications sections each present documents and resources. Legislation for the current session can be searched by various criteria. Some special services, such as printer-ready reports on legislation going back to 1975, require registration. The site also offers a Palm Pilot Service and an electronic legislation tracking service with email alerts.
Subject: South Carolina

Local Governments

3962. Aiken County
http://www.aikencounty.net

3963. Anderson
http://www.cityofandersonsc.com

3964. Beaufort
http://www.cityofbeaufort.org/

3965. Beaufort County
http://www.co.beaufort.sc.us

3966. Bennettsville
http://www.bennettsvillesc.com

3967. Charleston
http://www.ci.charleston.sc.us

3968. Charleston County
http://www.charlestoncounty.org

3969. Columbia
http://www.columbiasc.net

3970. Edgefield County
http://www.edgefieldcounty.org

3971. Florence
http://www.cityofflorence.com

3972. Goose Creek
http://www.cityofgoosecreek.com

3973. Greenville County
http://www.greenvillecounty.org

3974. Greenwood County
http://www.co.greenwood.sc.us

3975. Hilton Head Island
http://www.ci.hilton-head-island.sc.us

3976. Horry County
http://www.horrycounty.org

3977. James Island
http://www.townofjamesislandsc.org

3978. Lexington County
http://www.lex-co.com

3979. Mount Pleasant
http://www.townofmountpleasant.com

3980. Myrtle Beach
http://www.cityofmyrtlebeach.com

3981. Newberry
http://www.cityofnewberry.com

3982. North Augusta
http://www.northaugusta.net

3983. North Charleston
http://northcharleston.org

3984. Orangeburg
http://www.orangeburg.sc.us

3985. Pickens County
http://www.co.pickens.sc.us

3986. Port Royal
http://www.portroyal.org

3987. Richland County
http://www.richlandonline.com

3988. Rock Hill
http://www.cityofrockhill.com

3989. Spartanburg County
http://www.co.spartanburg.sc.us

3990. Springdale
http://www.springdalesc.com

3991. Sumter
http://www.sumter-sc.com

South Dakota

3992. South Dakota Legislature
http://legis.state.sd.us/
Description: South Dakota's legislative Web site is managed by the assembly's Legislative Research Council. The site has the full text of the state statutes and constitution online and searchable. The full text of legislation is online back to 1997. Current and archived administrative rules and notices are also online.

3993. South Dakota Unified Judicial System
Alternate URL: http://www.sdjudicial.com
Description: This site features information on the structure, history, and procedures of the Unified Judicial System for South Dakota. The Supreme Court opinions are available back to 1996, and a search page allows for searching opinions or calendars. Other sections include a legal glossary and information on the state bar exam.

3994. State of South Dakota
http://www.state.sd.us/
Description: Major sections of South Dakota's state site are Government, Business, Education, Employment, Family/Health, and Travel/Parks. The site features over a thousand state forms online, links to major state-sponsored email news and alert services, and a searchable database of state publications.

Local Governments

3995. Aberdeen
http://www.aberdeen.sd.us/

3996. Deadwood
http://www.cityofdeadwood.com/

3997. Lawrence County
http://www.lawrence.sd.us

3998. Madison
http://www.madison.sd.us

3999. Pennington County
http://www.co.pennington.sd.us

4000. Rapid City
http://www.rcgov.org

4001. Sioux Falls
http://www.sioux-falls.org

4002. Spearfish
http://www.city.spearfish.sd.us

Tennessee

4003. Tennessee Administrative Office of the Courts
http://www.tsc.state.tn.us/
Sponsor: Tennessee State Government
Description: This site provides unified access to information from the state judicial system. There are opinions going back 2 years, current dockets, and biographies of the justices for the Appellate Courts: the Supreme Court, Court of Appeals, and Court of Criminal Appeals. For each of the trial courts, the assigned judges are listed.
Subject: Tennessee

4004. Tennessee General Assembly
http://www.legislature.state.tn.us/
Sponsor: Tennessee. Legislature
Description: The Assemby site has separate sections for the Senate, House, joint chamber activities, and bills. The House section has PDF copies of the *Legislative Manual*, *House Chamber Book*, and a weekly legislative research review. Both chambers publish information on their members, committees, calendars, and staff. The Bills section has legislation from the current and previous sessions.
Subject: Tennessee

4005. TennesseeAnytime
http://www.state.tn.us/
Sponsor: Tennessee State Government
Description: TennesseeAnytime is the official Web site for the state of Tennessee. Information is arranged by topic, such as Business, Education, and Employment. A Facts And Records section leads to reference material on the state, including the state blue book, history and genealogy resources, maps, and state publications and statistics. The Government section has links to state agencies and Web sites for the three branches of the state government.
Subject: Tennessee

Local Governments

4006. Bartlett
http://www.cityofbartlett.org

4007. Brentwood
http://www.brentwood-tn.org

4008. Bristol
http://www.bristoltn.org/

4009. Chattanooga
http://www.chattanooga.gov

4010. Clarksville
http://www.cityofclarksville.com

4011. Columbia
http://www.columbiatn.com

4012. Cookeville
http://www.ci.cookeville.tn.us

4013. Dickson
http://www.cityofdickson.com

4014. Fairview
http://www.fairview-tn.org

4015. Farragut
http://www.townoffarragut.org

4016. Fayetteville
http://www.fayettevilletn.com

4017. Franklin
http://www.franklin-gov.com

4018. Germantown
http://www.ci.germantown.tn.us

4019. Hamilton County
http://www.hamiltontn.gov

4020. Hendersonville
http://www.hvilletn.org

4021. Jackson
http://ci.jackson.tn.us

4022. Johnson City
http://www.johnsoncitytn.com

4023. Kingsport
http://ci.kingsport.tn.us

4024. Knox County
http://www.korrnet.org/knox/

4025. Knoxville
http://www.ci.knoxville.tn.us/

4026. LaVergne
http://www.lavergne.org

4027. Macon County
http://www.maconcountytennessee.com

4028. Manchester
http://www.manchestertn.org

4029. Maryville
http://www.ci.maryville.tn.us

4030. Memphis
http://www.ci.memphis.tn.us

4031. Milan
http://www.cityofmilantn.com

4032. Millington
http://www.ci.millington.tn.us

4033. Morristown
http://www.morristowncityhall.com

4034. Murfreesboro
http://www.ci.murfreesboro.tn.us

4035. Nashville
http://www.nashville.gov

4036. Oak Ridge
http://www.ci.oak-ridge.tn.us

4037. Rutherford County
http://www.rc.state.tn.us

4038. Sevierville
http://www.seviervilletn.org

4039. Shelby County
http://www.co.shelby.tn.us

4040. Smyrna
http://www.smyrnatn.org

4041. Troy
http://www.troytn.com

4042. Washington County
http://www.washingtoncountytn.com

4043. Williamson County
http://www.williamson-tn.org

Texas

4044. Texas Judiciary Online
http://www.courts.state.tx.us/
Sponsor: Texas. Courts
Description: This site offers links to the Supreme Court, Court of Appeals, Court of Criminal Appeals, Trial Courts, Court Rules, and Judicial Agencies. Supreme Court opinions are available back to 1997. They are accessible by date.
Subject: Texas

4045. Texas Legislature Online
http://www.capitol.state.tx.us/
Sponsor: Texas. Legislature
Description: The Texas Legislature Online site has a straightforward design with links to the House, Senate, legislative process information, the state statutes, and legislative support agencies. A side panel provides multiple ways to access to bills back to 1995. The Search Bills section allows searching by multiple facets and features a sophisticated advanced search mode.
Subject: Texas

4046. TexasOnline
http://www.state.tx.us/
Sponsor: Texas State Government
Description: The Texas state Web site is in English with an option to view the entire site in Spanish. The site includes a wealth of information organized into categories such as About Texas, Online Services, Government, Education and Training, Laws and Criminal Justice, and Regional and Community Resources. A number of online resources are available through the category Licenses, Permits, Registration, and Public Records. The TexasOnline home page also links directly to the Texas Records And Information Locator (TRAIL) database hosted by the state library.
Subject: Texas

Local Governments

4047. Abilene
http://www.abilenetx.com

4048. Addison
http://www.ci.addison.tx.us

4049. Allen
http://www.ci.allen.tx.us

4050. Alvin
http://www.alvin.tx.citygovt.org/

4051. Amarillo
http://www.ci.amarillo.tx.us

4052. Angleton
http://www.angleton.tx.us

4053. Arlington
http://www.ci.arlington.tx.us

4054. Austin
http://www.ci.austin.tx.us

4055. Austin County
http://www.austincounty.com

4056. Balch Springs
http://www.balchspringscity.com

4057. Beaumont
http://www.cityofbeaumont.com

4058. Bedford
http://www.ci.bedford.tx.us

4059. Bellaire
http://www.ci.bellaire.tx.us

4060. Benbrook
http://www.ci.benbrook.tx.us

4061. Bexar County
http://www.co.bexar.tx.us

4062. Blanco County
http://www.moment.net/~blancoco/

4063. Boerne
http://www.ci.boerne.tx.us

4064. Brazoria County
http://www.brazoria-county.com

4065. Brazos County
http://www.co.brazos.tx.us

4066. Brownwood
http://www.ci.brownwood.tx.us

4067. Bryan
http://www.ci.bryan.tx.us

4068. Burleson
http://www.burlesontx.com

4069. Carrollton
http://www.ci.carrollton.tx.us

4070. Cedar Hill
http://www.cedarhilltxgov.org

4071. Cedar Park
http://www.ci.cedar-park.tx.us

4072. Chambers County
http://www.co.chambers.tx.us

4073. Cleburne
http://www.ci.cleburne.tx.us

4074. College Station
http://www.ci.college-station.tx.us

4075. Colleyville
http://www.colleyville.com

4076. Collin County
http://www.co.collin.tx.us

4077. Converse
http://www.conversetx.net

4078. Coppell
http://www.ci.coppell.tx.us

4079. Corpus Christi
http://www.ci.corpus-christi.tx.us

4080. Corsicana
http://www.ci.corsicana.tx.us

4081. Dallam County
http://www.dallam.org

4082. Dallas
http://www.dallascityhall.com

4083. Dallas County
http://www.dallascounty.org

4084. Deer Park
http://www.ci.deer-park.tx.us

4085. Del Rio
http://www.cityofdelrio.com

4086. Denison
http://www.ci.denison.tx.us

4087. Denton
http://www.ci.denton.tx.us

4088. Denton County
http://www.co.denton.tx.us

4089. DeSoto
http://www.ci.desoto.tx.us

4090. Duncanville
http://www.ci.duncanville.tx.us

4091. Eagle Pass
http://www.cityofeaglepass.com

4092. El Paso
http://www.ci.el-paso.tx.us

4093. El Paso County
http://www.epcounty.com

4094. Ennis
http://www.ennis-texas.com

4095. Euless
http://www.euless.org

4096. Farmers Branch
http://www.ci.farmers-branch.tx.us

4097. Flower Mound
http://www.flower-mound.com

4098. Fort Worth
http://ci.fort-worth.tx.us

4099. Freeport
http://www.freeport.tx.us

4100. Friendswood
http://www.ci.friendswood.tx.us

4101. Frisco
http://www.ci.frisco.tx.us

4102. Galveston
http://www.cityofgalveston.org

4103. Galveston County
http://www.co.galveston.tx.us

4104. Garland
http://www.ci.garland.tx.us

4105. Gatesville
http://www.ci.gatesville.tx.us

4106. Georgetown
http://www.georgetown.org

4107. Grand Prairie
http://www.ci.grand-prairie.tx.us

4108. Grapevine
http://www.ci.grapevine.tx.us

4109. Grayson County
http://www.co.grayson.tx.us

4110. Greenville
http://www.ci.greenville.tx.us

4111. Guadalupe County
http://www.co.guadalupe.tx.us

4112. Haltom City
http://www.ci.haltom-city.tx.us

4113. Hamilton
http://www.ci.hamilton.tx.us

4114. Harlingen
http://enterprise.ci.harlingen.tx.us

4115. Harris County
http://www.co.harris.tx.us

4116. Harrison County
http://www.co.harrison.tx.us

4117. Hays County
http://www.co.hays.tx.us

4118. Hidalgo County
http://www.co.hidalgo.tx.us

4119. Houston
http://www.ci.houston.tx.us

4120. Huntsville
http://www.ci.huntsville.tx.us

4121. Hurst
http://www.ci.hurst.tx.us

4122. Irving
http://www.ci.irving.tx.us

4123. Jefferson County
http://www.co.jefferson.tx.us

4124. Katy
http://ci.katy.tx.us

4125. Keller
http://www.cityofkeller.com

4126. Kerrville
http://www.kerrville.org

4127. Kilgore
http://www.ci.kilgore.tx.us

4128. Lampasas
http://www.ci.lampasas.tx.us

4129. Lancaster
http://www.ci.lancaster.tx.us

4130. Laredo
http://www.cityoflaredo.com

4131. League City
http://www.ci.league-city.tx.us

4132. Levelland
http://www.ci.levelland.tx.us

4133. Lewisville
http://www.cityoflewisville.com

4134. Longview
http://www.ci.longview.tx.us

4135. Lubbock
http://www.ci.lubbock.tx.us

4136. Lucas
http://www.ci.lucas.tx.us

4137. Lufkin
http://www.ci.lufkin.tx.us

4138. Mansfield
http://www.mansfield-texas.com

4139. Marshall
http://www.ci.marshall.tx.us

4140. McAllen
http://www.mcallen.net/

4141. McKinney
http://www.mckinneytexas.org

4142. McLennan County
http://www.co.mclennan.tx.us/

4143. Mesquite
http://www.cityofmesquite.com

4144. Midland
http://www.ci.midland.tx.us

4145. Missouri City
http://www.ci.mocity.tx.us

4146. Montgomery County
http://www.co.montgomery.tx.us

4147. Mount Pleasant
http://www.mpcity.net

4148. Nacogdoches
http://www.ci.nacogdoches.tx.us

4149. Nassau Bay
http://www.nassaubay.com/

4150. New Braunfels
http://www.ci.new-braunfels.tx.us

4151. North Richland Hills
http://www.ci.north-richland-hills.tx.us

4152. Nueces County
http://www.co.nueces.tx.us

4153. Odessa
http://www.ci.odessa.tx.us

4154. Orange County
http://www.co.orange.tx.us

4155. Overton
http://www.ci.overton.tx.us

4156. Palacios
http://www.cityofpalacios.com

4157. Pasadena
http://www.ci.pasadena.tx.us

4158. Pearland
http://www.cityofpearland.com

4159. Pflugerville
http://www.cityofpflugerville.com

4160. Pharr
http://www.cityofpharr.org

4161. Plano
http://www.planotx.org

4162. Port Arthur
http://www.portarthur.net

4163. Richardson
http://www.cor.net

4164. Richland Hills
http://www.richlandhills.com

4165. Rosenberg
http://www.ci.rosenberg.tx.us

4166. Round Rock
http://www.ci.round-rock.tx.us

4167. Rowlett
http://www.ci.rowlett.tx.us

4168. Rusk
http://www.rusktx.com

4169. San Angelo
http://www.sanangelotexas.org

4170. San Antonio
http://www.ci.sat.tx.us

4171. San Marcos
http://www.ci.san-marcos.tx.us

4172. Schertz
http://www.ci.schertz.tx.us

4173. Seguin
http://www.ci.seguin.tx.us

4174. Southlake
http://www.ci.southlake.tx.us

4175. Southside Place
http://www.ci.southside-place.tx.us

4176. Stephenville
http://www.ci.stephenville.tx.us

4177. Sugar Land
http://www.ci.sugar-land.tx.us

4178. Tarrant County
http://www.tarrantcounty.com

4179. Taylor
http://ci.taylor.tx.us/taylorcity/homepage.html

4180. Temple
http://www.ci.temple.tx.us

4181. Texarkana
http://www.txkusa.org/tx/

4182. Tom Green County
http://www.tgcl.co.tom-green.tx.us/county/

4183. Travis County
http://www.co.travis.tx.us

4184. Tyler
http://www.tylertexas.com/city/

4185. Waco
http://www.waco-texas.com

4186. Watauga
http://www.ci.watauga.tx.us

4187. Waxahachie
http://www.waxahachie.com

4188. Webb County
http://webbcounty.com

4189. West Lake Hills
http://www.westlakehills.org

4190. West University Place
http://www.ci.west-university-place.tx.us/

4191. Westlake
http://www.westlake-tx.org

4192. White Oak
http://www.cityofwhiteoak.com

4193. Wichita Falls
http://www.ci.wichita-falls.tx.us

4194. Williamson County
http://www.williamson-county.org

4195. Wills Point
http://www.cityofwillspoint.com

4196. Woodway
http://www.woodway-texas.com

4197. Wylie
http://www.ci.wylie.tx.us

4198. Yoakum
http://www.cityofyoakum.org

Utah

4199. Utah State Courts
http://courtlink.utcourts.gov/
Sponsor: Utah. Courts
Description: The Utah judicial site links to information from the state courts and provides a number of online services. Users may get email notification when appellate opinions are posted. An Online Court Assistance Program prepares individual court filings online for landlord-tenant and uncontested divorce cases through a series of online questions and forms. Appellate court opinions are online back to 1997.
Subject: Utah

4200. Utah State Legislature
http://www.le.state.ut.us/
Sponsor: Utah. Legislature
Description: House and Senate links on this site lead to current membership, organizational, and legislative information from those chambers. More complete legislative records are available through the unified home page. The full text of bills going back to 1991 is available online, although more complete information is available for bills from 1997 forward.
Subject: Utah

4201. Utah.gov
http://www.utah.gov/
Sponsor: Utah State Government
Description: The official site for the state of Utah is organized topically, with special sections for Utah news, online services, and featured government Web sites. Topical sections are for information relating to citizens, education, business, employment, and tourism. The Government section has state, local, and federal links.

Local Governments

4202. American Fork
http://www.afcity.com

4203. Bountiful
http://www.ulct.org/bountiful/home.html

4204. Carbon County
http://www.co.carbon.ut.us

4205. Cedar City
http://www.cedarcity.org

4206. Davis County
http://www.co.davis.ut.us

4207. Draper
http://www.draper.ut.us

4208. Duchesne County
http://www.duchesnegov.net

4209. Ivins
http://www.ci.ivins.ut.us

4210. Juab County
http://www.co.juab.ut.us

4211. Logan
http://www.ci.logan.ut.us

4212. Midvale
http://www.midvalecity.org

4213. Murray
http://www.ci.murray.ut.us

4214. North Logan
http://www.ci.north-logan.ut.us

4215. North Salt Lake City
http://www.ci.north-salt-lake.ut.us

4216. Ogden
http://www.ogdencity.com

4217. Orem
http://www.orem.org

4218. Park City
http://www.parkcity.org

4219. Provo
http://www.provo.org

4220. Richfield
http://www.richfieldcity.com

4221. Saint George
http://www.sgcity.org

4222. Salt Lake City
http://www.ci.slc.ut.us

4223. Salt Lake County
http://www.slco.org

4224. Sandy
http://www.sandy-city.net

4225. Spanish Fork
http://www.spanishfork.org/sfc/default.htm

4226. Taylorsville
http://www.ci.taylorsville.ut.us

4227. Tooele County
http://www.co.tooele.ut.us

4228. Utah County
http://www.co.utah.ut.us

4229. Wasatch County
http://www.co.wasatch.ut.us

4230. Weber County
http://www.co.weber.ut.us

4231. West Jordan
http://www.wjordan.com

4232. West Valley
http://www.ci.west-valley.ut.us

4233. Woods Cross
http://www.woodscross.com

Vermont

4234. State of Vermont
http://www.state.vt.us/
Sponsor: Vermont State Government
Description: This state Web site provides a basic alphabetical index to state government offices and services, followed by links to related Vermont sites. The top of the site's main page highlights links to major government sites, education information, Vermont localities, state procurement and contracting opportunities, and state maps and ski conditions.
Subject: Vermont

4235. Vermont Judiciary
http://www.vermontjudiciary.org
Description: For each of the Vermont state courts, this site includes brief descriptive information, a court calendar, and a link to opinions if they are available. For the Supreme Court, slip opinions are available back to 1993. The site also has information on court forms and fees, and on representing oneself in court.

4236. Vermont Legislature
http://www.leg.state.vt.us/
Sponsor: Vermont. Legislature
Description: The full text of bills and state statutes are available on this site. The Legislative Bill Tracking System provides access to bills back to 1987. The Vermont Statutes Online provides browsing access to the statutes in HTML format. Other sections include a legislative directory, House and Senate rules, legislative reports and publications, and historic information on the Vermont State House.
Subject: Vermont

Local Governments

4237. Barre
http://www.ci.barre.vt.us

4238. Bennington
http://www.bennington.com/government/

4239. Burlington
http://www.ci.burlington.vt.us

4240. Essex Junction
http://www.essexjunction.org

4241. Montpelier
http://www.montpelier-vt.org

4242. Rutland
http://www.rutlandtown.com

Virginia

4243. Commonwealth of Virginia
http://www.vipnet.org/cmsportal/
Sponsor: Virginia State Government
Description: The Official Commonwealth of Virginia Home Page emphasizes online services for citizens, businesses, and users of wireless devices. The Government section of the site links to state agency and employee directories, state forms, press releases, and local Virginia governments.
Subject: Virginia

4244. Virginia General Assembly
http://legis.state.va.us/
Sponsor: Virginia. Legislature
Description: The Senate and House of Delegates sections of the Virginia assembly site offer lists of members, committees, and daily floor minutes. The site has the full text and status information for bills and resolutions going back to 1994. The state code and administrative code are also online and searchable. A fee-based service called Lobbyist-in-a-Box tracks selected bills and sends updates to subscribers.
Subject: Virginia

4245. Virginia's Judicial System
http://www.courts.state.va.us/
Sponsor: Virginia. Courts
Description: The Virginia Courts Web site features full-text opinions and information on the court system, individual courts, and judges. The Opinions section provides access to the Synopsis of Opinions from the Supreme Court of Virginia as well as the full text of opinions from both the Supreme Court and the Court of Appeals.
Subject: Virginia

Local Governments

4246. Accomack County
http://www.esva.net/~accomack/

4247. Albemarle County
http://www.albemarle.org

4248. Alexandria
http://www.ci.alexandria.va.us

4249. Altavista
http://www.ci.altavista.va.us

4250. Amherst County
http://www.amherstva.com

4251. Arlington County
http://www.co.arlington.va.us

4252. Augusta County
http://www.co.augusta.va.us

4253. Bedford
http://www.ci.bedford.va.us

4254. Bedford County
http://www.co.bedford.va.us

4255. Blacksburg
http://www.blacksburg.va.us

4256. Bluefield
http://town.bluefield.va.us

4257. Botetourt County
http://www.co.botetourt.va.us

4258. Bristol
http://www.bristolva.org

4259. Caroline County
http://www.co.caroline.va.us

4260. Carroll County
http://www.co.carroll.va.us

4261. Charles City County
http://www.co.charles-city.va.us/

4262. Charlottesville
http://www.charlottesville.org/

4263. Chesapeake
http://www.chesapeake.va.us

4264. Chesterfield County
http://www.co.chesterfield.va.us

4265. Clarke County
http://www.co.clarke.va.us

4266. Culpeper County
http://www.co.culpeper.va.us

4267. Danville
http://www.ci.danville.va.us

4268. Dickenson County
http://www.dickensonctyva.com

4269. Emporia
http://www.ci.emporia.va.us/

4270. Fairfax
http://www.ci.fairfax.va.us

4271. Fairfax County
http://www.co.fairfax.va.us

4272. Falls Church
http://www.ci.falls-church.va.us

4273. Fauquier County
http://www.co.fauquier.va.us

4274. Franklin
http://www.franklinva.com

4275. Franklin County
http://www.franklincountyva.org

4276. Frederick County
http://www.co.frederick.va.us

4277. Gloucester County
http://www.co.gloucester.va.us

4278. Goochland County
http://www.co.goochland.va.us

4279. Hampton
http://www.hampton.va.us

4280. Hanover County
http://www.co.hanover.va.us

4281. Harrisonburg
http://www.ci.harrisonburg.va.us

4282. Henrico County
http://www.co.henrico.va.us

4283. Henry County
http://henrycounty.neocomm.net

4284. James City County
http://www.james-city.va.us

4285. King William County
http://www.co.king-william.va.us

4286. Lancaster County
http://www.lancova.com

4287. Leesburg
http://www.leesburgva.org

4288. Loudon County
http://www.co.loudoun.va.us

4289. Lynchburg
http://www.ci.lynchburg.va.us

4290. Manassas Park
http://www.ci.manassas-park.va.us

4291. Martinsville
http://www.ci.martinsville.va.us

4292. Middlesex County
http://www.co.middlesex.va.us

4293. Newport News
http://www.newport-news.va.us

4294. Norfolk
http://www.norfolk.va.us

4295. Norton
http://www.nortonva.org

4296. Orange
http://www.townoforangeva.org

4297. Page County
http://www.co.page.va.us

4298. Petersburg
http://www.petersburg-va.org

4299. Poquoson
http://www.ci.poquoson.va.us

4300. Portsmouth
http://www.ci.portsmouth.va.us/

4301. Prince William County
http://www.co.prince-william.va.us

4302. Purcellville
http://www.purcellvilleva.com

4303. Richmond
http://www.richmondgov.com

4304. Roanoke
http://www.roanokegov.com

4305. Roanoke County
http://www.co.roanoke.va.us

4306. Shenandoah County
http://www.co.shenandoah.va.us

4307. Smithfield
http://www.co.smithfield.va.us

4308. Smyth County
http://www.smythcounty.org

4309. Spotsylvania County
http://www.spotsylvania.va.us

4310. Staunton
http://www.ci.staunton.va.us

4311. Suffolk
http://www.city.suffolk.va.us

4312. Tazewell County
http://www.tazewellcounty.org

4313. Urbanna
http://www.urbanna.com

4314. Vienna
http://www.ci.vienna.va.us

4315. Virginia Beach
http://www.city.virginia-beach.va.us

4316. Warrenton
http://www.townofwarrenton.com

4317. Washington
http://www.town.washington.va.us

4318. Washington County
http://www.washcova.com

4319. Westmoreland County
http://www.co.westmoreland.va.us

4320. Williamsburg
http://www.ci.williamsburg.va.us

4321. Winchester
http://www.ci.winchester.va.us

4322. Wise County
http://www.wisecounty.org

4323. York County
http://www.yorkcounty.gov

Washington

4324. Access Washington
http://access.wa.gov/
Sponsor: Washington State Government
Description: Access Washington presents information on Washington state's government and its services. It features Public Services, Business, Education, Government, and Technology section. The Government page offers an alphabetical State Agency Index, a State Subject Index, and information on tribal and local governments.
Subject: Washington

4325. Washington State Courts
http://www.courts.wa.gov/
Sponsor: Washington. Courts
Description: This state judicial site brings together information from the Supreme Court, Court of Appeals, Trial Courts, and Administrative Office of the Courts. Opinions from the appellate courts issued within the past 90 days are searchable online. The site also has court forms and a court personnel directory that can be searched by name.
Subject: Washington

4326. Washington State Legislature
http://www.leg.wa.gov/wsladm/default.htm
Sponsor: Washington. Legislature
Description: The Washington State Legislature site has sections for the House, Senate, Legislative Agencies, Legislative and Bill Information, Laws and Agency Rules, a Kids Page, and directories of the state's legislators and its U.S. congressional delegation. Legislation is online back to 1997. The *Revised Code of Washington* and *Washington Administrative Code* are also online in full.
Subject: Washington

Local Governments

4327. Adams County
http://www.co.adams.wa.us

4328. Anacortes
http://www.cityofanacortes.org

4329. Auburn
http://www.ci.auburn.wa.us

4330. Bainbridge Island
http://www.ci.bainbridge-isl.wa.us

4331. Bellevue
http://www.ci.bellevue.wa.us

4332. Bellingham
http://www.cob.org/

4333. Benton County
http://www.co.benton.wa.us

4334. Blaine
http://www.ci.blaine.wa.us

4335. Burien
http://www.ci.burien.wa.us

4336. Burlington
http://www.ci.burlington.wa.us

4337. Camas
http://www.swwcn.org/clark/camas/home.htm

4338. Carnation
http://www.ci.carnation.wa.us

4339. Chelan
http://www.cityofchelan.com

4340. Cheney
http://www.ci.cheney.wa.us

4341. Clallam County
http://www.clallam.net/

4342. Clark County
http://www.co.clark.wa.us

4343. Colfax
http://www.ci.colfax.wa.us

4344. Columbia County
http://www.columbiaco.com

4345. Covington
http://www.ci.covington.wa.us

4346. Cowlitz County
http://www.cowlitzcounty.org

4347. Des Moines
http://www.ci.des-moines.wa.us

4348. Duvall
http://www.cityofduvall.com

4349. Edgewood
http://www.ci.edgewood.wa.us

4350. Edmonds
http://www.ci.edmonds.wa.us

4351. Ellensburg
http://www.ci.ellensburg.wa.us

4352. Enumclaw
http://www.ci.enumclaw.wa.us

4353. Ephrata
http://www.ephrata.org

4354. Everett
http://www.everettwa.org/

4355. Federal Way
http://www.ci.federal-way.wa.us

4356. Fife
http://www.ci.fife.wa.us

4357. Friday Harbor
http://www.fridayharbor.org

4358. Gig Harbor
http://www.harbornet.com/gigharbor/index.html

4359. Grant County
http://www.grantcounty-wa.com

4360. Grays Harbor County
http://www.co.grays-harbor.wa.us

4361. Hoquiam
http://www.ci.hoquiam.wa.us

4362. Island County
http://www.islandcounty.net

4363. Issaquah
http://www.ci.issaquah.wa.us

4364. Jefferson County
http://www.co.jefferson.wa.us

4365. Kalama
http://www.cityofkalama.com

4366. Kelso
http://www.kelso.gov

4367. Kenmore
http://www.cityofkenmore.com

4368. Kennewick
http://www.ci.kennewick.wa.us

4369. Kent
http://www.ci.kent.wa.us

4370. King County
http://www.metrokc.gov

4371. Kirkland
http://www.ci.kirkland.wa.us

4372. Kitsap County
http://www.kitsapgov.com

4373. Kittitas County
http://www.co.kittitas.wa.us

4374. Lacey
http://www.wa.gov/lacey/

4375. Lakewood
http://www.ci.lakewood.wa.us

4376. Lewis County
http://www.co.lewis.wa.us

4377. Longview
http://www.ci.longview.wa.us

4378. Lynden
http://www.lyndenwa.org

4379. Lynnwood
http://www.ci.lynnwood.wa.us

4380. Marysville
http://www.ci.marysville.wa.us

4381. Mercer Island
http://www.ci.mercer-island.wa.us

4382. Mount Vernon
http://www.ci.mount-vernon.wa.us

4383. Mukilteo
http://www.ci.mukilteo.wa.us

4384. Newcastle
http://www.ci.newcastle.wa.us

4385. Normandy Park
http://www.ci.normandy-park.wa.us

4386. North Bend
http://ci.north-bend.wa.us

4387. Oak Harbor
http://www.oakharbor.org

4388. Okanogan County
http://www.okanogancounty.org

4389. Olympia
http://www.ci.olympia.wa.us

4390. Pacific County
http://www.co.pacific.wa.us

4391. Pasco
http://www.ci.pasco.wa.us

4392. Pierce County
http://www.co.pierce.wa.us/PC/

4393. Port Angeles
http://www.ci.port-angeles.wa.us

4394. Poulsbo
http://www.cityofpoulsbo.com

4395. Pullman
http://www.ci.pullman.wa.us

4396. Puyallup
http://www.ci.puyallup.wa.us

4397. Redmond
http://www.ci.redmond.wa.us

4398. Renton
http://www.ci.renton.wa.us

4399. Richland
http://www.ci.richland.wa.us

4400. San Juan County
http://www.co.san-juan.wa.us

4401. SeaTac
http://www.seatac.wa.gov

4402. Seattle
http://www.ci.seattle.wa.us

4403. Shelton
http://www.ci.shelton.wa.us

4404. Shoreline
http://www.cityofshoreline.com

4405. Snohomish County
http://www.co.snohomish.wa.us

4406. Snoqualmie
http://www.ci.snoqualmie.wa.us

4407. Spokane
http://www.spokanecity.org

4408. Spokane County
http://www.spokanecounty.org

4409. Steilacoom
http://www.ci.steilacoom.wa.us

4410. Stevens County
http://www.co.stevens.wa.us

4411. Sumner
http://www.ci.sumner.wa.us

4412. Tacoma
http://www.cityoftacoma.org

4413. Thurston County
http://www.co.thurston.wa.us

4414. Tukwila
http://www.ci.tukwila.wa.us

4415. University Place
http://www.ci.university-place.wa.us

4416. Vancouver
http://www.ci.vancouver.wa.us

4417. Whatcom County
http://www.co.whatcom.wa.us

4418. Whitman County
http://www.whitmancounty.org/

4419. Yakima
http://www.ci.yakima.wa.us

4420. Yakima County
http://www.co.yakima.wa.us

West Virginia

4421. State of West Virginia
http://www.state.wv.us/
Sponsor: West Virginia State Government
Description: The West Virginia state Web site features links to elected officials and state agencies, as well as to information and services in such areas as education, employment, taxes, motor vehicles, workers' compensation, health, recycling, state contracts, and maps and travel.
Subject: West Virginia

4422. West Virginia Legislature
http://www.legis.state.wv.us/
Sponsor: West Virginia. Legislature
Description: Major sections of this site include Senate, House, Leadership, West Virgina Code, Acts of the Legislature, Bill Tracking, Kids, and Brochures and Photos. Both the House and Senate sections feature searching and browsing for each chamber's bills.
Subject: West Virginia

4423. West Virginia Supreme Court of Appeals
http://www.state.wv.us/wvsca/
Sponsor: West Virginia. Supreme Court

Description: Despite the name, this site has information on all levels of the state courts: the Supreme Court of Appeals, circuit courts, magistrate courts, and family courts. Supreme Court opinions are online back to 1991. The Supreme Court section also features live Internet broadcasting of the Supreme Court proceedings and an email alert service for news of decisions. Other sections include a court system overview and legal reference.
Subject: West Virginia

Local Governments

4424. Beckley
http://www.beckley.org

4425. Berkeley County
http://www.berkeleycountycomm.org

4426. Bridgeport
http://www.bridgeportwv.com

4427. Charleston
http://www.cityofcharleston.org

4428. Clarksburg
http://www.clarksburg.com

4429. Fairmont
http://www.cityoffairmontwv.com

4430. Huntington
http://www.cityofhuntington.com

4431. Kanawha County
http://www.kancocomm.com

4432. Monongalia County
http://www.co.monongalia.wv.us

4433. Morgantown
http://www.morgantown.com

4434. Parkersburg
http://www.parkersburg-wv.com

4435. Pocahontas County
http://www.neumedia.net./~pocahontascc/

4436. Weirton
http://www.cityofweirton.com

Wisconsin

4437. Wisconsin Court System
http://www.courts.state.wi.us/
Sponsor: Wisconsin. Courts
Description: The Wisconsin court system site includes links to all levels of the state court system and direct links to opinions, forms, online court records, and court telephone directories. Wisconsin appellate opinions released since the summer of 1995 can be searched online.
Subject: Wisconsin

4438. Wisconsin State Legislature
http://www.legis.state.wi.us/
Sponsor: Wisconsin. Legislature
Description: The Wisconsin Legislature site links to the Senate, Assembly, Legislative Service Agencies, Legislation, Wisconsin Law, Wisconsin Blue Book, and Who Are My Legislators?. The text and status of legislation can be searched back to 1995. The Wisconsin Law section includes the state statutes, constitution, acts, and the administrative code and register.
Subject: Wisconsin

4439. Wisconsin.gov
http://www.wisconsin.gov/
Sponsor: Wisconsin State Government
Description: The official state Web site features an agency index and an extensive subject index. Major topical areas include Government, Public Services, Business, Education, and Wisconsin Facts. In addition to state government directories, the Government section has links to federal, local, and tribal governments.
Subject: Wisconsin

Local Governments

4440. Appleton
http://www.appleton.org

4441. Barron County
http://www.co.barron.wi.us

4442. Beloit
http://www.ci.beloit.wi.us

4443. Bloomer
http://www.ci.bloomer.wi.us

4444. Brookfield
http://www.cityofbrookfield.com

4445. Brown County
http://www.co.brown.wi.us

4446. Buffalo County
http://www.buffalocounty.com

4447. Chippewa County
http://www.co.chippewa.wi.us

4448. Cudahy
http://www.ci.cudahy.wi.us

4449. Dane County
http://www.co.dane.wi.us

4450. De Pere
http://www.ci.de-pere.wi.us

4451. Eau Claire County
http://www.co.eau-claire.wi.us

4452. Fitchburg
http://www.city.fitchburg.wi.us

4453. Fond du Lac
http://www.ci.fond-du-lac.wi.us

4454. Franklin
http://www.ci.franklin.wi.us

4455. Germantown
http://www.village.germantown.wi.us

4456. Grant County
http://grantcounty.org/

4457. Green Bay
http://www.ci.green-bay.wi.us

4458. Greendale
http://www.greendale.org

4459. Howard
http://www.village.howard.wi.us

4460. Iowa County
http://www.iowacounty.org

4461. Jackson County
http://www.co.jackson.wi.us

4462. Janesville
http://www.ci.janesville.wi.us

4463. Kenosha
http://www.kenosha.org

4464. Kenosha County
http://www.co.kenosha.wi.us

4465. La Crosse County
http://www.co.la-crosse.wi.us

4466. Lincoln County
http://www.co.lincoln.wi.us

4467. Madison
http://www.ci.madison.wi.us

4468. Manitowoc
http://www.manitowoc.org

4469. Marathon County
http://www.co.marathon.wi.us/

4470. Marinette
http://www.marinette.wi.us

4471. Marshfield
http://www.ci.marshfield.wi.us

4472. Mayville
http://www.mayvillecity.com

4473. Menasha
http://www.town-menasha.com

4474. Merrill
http://www.ci.merrill.wi.us

4475. Middleton
http://www.ci.middleton.wi.us

4476. Milton
http://www.ci.milton.wi.us

4477. Milwaukee
http://www.ci.mil.wi.us

4478. Milwaukee County
http://www.co.milwaukee.wi.us

4479. Monona
http://www.monona.wi.us

4480. Mosinee
http://www.mosinee.wi.us

4481. Muskego
http://www.ci.muskego.wi.us

4482. Neenah
http://www.ci.neenah.wi.us

4483. New Berlin
http://www.newberlin.org

4484. New London
http://www.newlondonwi.org

4485. Oconto County
http://www.co.oconto.wi.us

4486. Outagamie County
http://www.co.outagamie.wi.us

4487. Ozaukee County
http://www.co.ozaukee.wi.us

4488. Platteville
http://www.ci.platteville.wi.us

4489. River Falls
http://www.rfcity.org

4490. Rock County
http://www.co.rock.wi.us

4491. Shawano County
http://www.co.shawano.wi.us

4492. South Milwaukee
http://www.ci.south-milwaukee.wi.us

4493. Stevens Point
http://www.ci.stevens-point.wi.us

4494. Suamico
http://www.suamico.org

4495. Sun Prairie
http://www.ci.sun-prairie.wi.us

4496. Superior
http://www.ci.superior.wi.us

4497. Two Rivers
http://www.ci.two-rivers.wi.us

4498. Verona
http://www.ci.verona.wi.us

4499. Village of Hartland
http://www.villageofhartland.com/

4500. Walworth County
http://www.co.walworth.wi.us

4501. Washington County
http://www.co.washington.wi.us

4502. Waukesha
http://www.ci.waukesha.wi.us

4503. Waukesha County
http://www.waukeshacounty.gov

4504. Wausau
http://www.ci.wausau.wi.us

4505. Wauwatosa
http://www.ci.wauwatosa.wi.us

4506. West Allis
http://www.ci.west-allis.wi.us

4507. West Bend
http://www.ci.west-bend.wi.us

4508. West Salem
http://www.westsalemwi.com

4509. Whitefish Bay
http://www.village.whitefish-bay.wi.us

4510. Winnebago County
http://www.co.winnebago.wi.us

Wyoming

4511. State of Wyoming
http://www.state.wy.us/
Sponsor: Wyoming State Government
Description: Wyoming's state site presents separate pages for links of interest to citizens, business, and visitors. A Government section has links to the Governor's Office, state agencies, and local government Web sites. It also features a list and detailed subject index of government services.
Subject: Wyoming

4512. Wyoming Judicial Branch
http://courts.state.wy.us/
Sponsor: Wyoming. Courts
Description: This central site covers the Wyoming Supreme Court, District Courts, Circuit Courts, and Justice of the Peace Courts. It also links to court rules, the state law library, and the Wyoming State Bar. Supreme Court opinions from the past 2 years are available online.
Subject: Wyoming

4513. Wyoming State Legislature
http://legisweb.state.wy.us/
Sponsor: Wyoming. Legislature
Description: This site has legislative information, including bills, for the current session and for sessions going back to 1998. The current state statutes and constitution can be browsed online. The site also has legislative manuals, a guide to compiling legislative histories of Wyoming laws, and a *Citizen's Guide to the Wyoming Legislature*.
Subject: Wyoming

Local Governments

4514. Campbell County
http://ccg.co.campbell.wy.us

4515. Casper
http://www.cityofcasperwy.com

4516. Cheyenne
http://www.cheyennecity.org

4517. Gillette
http://www.ci.gillette.wy.us

4518. Jackson
http://www.ci.jackson.wy.us

4519. Laramie County
http://webgate.co.laramie.wy.us

4520. Lincoln County
http://www.co.lincoln.wy.us

4521. Sheridan
http://www.city-sheridan-wy.com

4522. Sweetwater County
http://www.co.sweet.wy.us

4523. Torrington
http://www.city-of-torrington.org

4524. Uinta County
http://www.uintacounty.com

CHAPTER 18

International

This last chapter describes international resources, Web sites for intergovernmental organizations and for non-U.S. national governments. While the bulk of this book focuses on the U.S. federal government, the Web sites in this chapter can provide a starting point for international research.

The Featured Sites and General sections highlight Web sites that serve as directories to the sites of foreign governments and parliaments, international organizations, and foreign embassies in the United States. A brief and selective International Organizations section follows. The final section lists the primary Web sites of other nations. Short descriptions indicate the language or languages of the sites, many of which have English-language content.

Bookmarks & Favorites

International Organizations
- International Governmental Organizations,
      http://www.library.northwestern.edu/govpub/resource/internat/igo.html
- United Nations, http://www.un.org/english/

Country Links
- Embassy.org, http://www.embassy.org
- Foreign Government Resources on the Web,
      http://www.lib.umich.edu/govdocs/foreign.html

Featured Sites

4525. Foreign Government Resources on the Web
`http://www.lib.umich.edu/govdocs/foreign.html`
Sponsor: University of Michigan. Library
Description: This site from the University of Michigan Documents Center features links to the Web sites from the governments of countries around the world. Access is available by country, world region, and subject. The site also links to quality Web sites providing international reference information. Available subject categories include Embassies, Flags, News, Statistics, and Treaties.
Subjects: Foreign Governments; Reference — International; Finding Aids

4526. International Governmental Organizations
`http://www.library.northwestern.edu/govpub/resource/internat/igo.html`
Sponsor: Northwestern University
Description: Northwestern University Library's Government and Maps section provides this alphabetical list of links to intergovernmental organizations. The list includes over 150 links to Web sites from organizations such as the African Development Bank, the Convention of Biological Diversity, the International Atomic Energy Agency, the Organization of American States, and the World Bank Group. There are special sections for links to pages from the United Nations and the European Union.
Subjects: Finding Aids; International Organizations

The international government resources in this chapter are divided into three sections, spanning the entry numbers indicated here:

General	*4527–4534*
Intergovernmental Organizations	*4535–4561*
Other Countries	*4562–4776*

General

4527. Embassy.org
http://www.embassy.org/embassies/
Alternate URL: http://www.state.gov/misc/10125.htm
Sponsor: TeleDiplomacy Inc.
Description: Embassy.org is a directory of foreign governments' embassies located in Washington, DC. It provides addresses and phone numbers. When available, it also provides Web and email addresses. The alternate URL above is for the State Department's list of Web sites for foreign embassies in the United States. This is a simple list of links. Users need to consult the individual web sites to obtain addresses or phone numbers.
Subject: Embassies

4528. Geneva International Forum: Directory Guide of International Institutions, Missions, Consulates, and Companies
http://geneva.intl.ch/gi/egimain/edir.htm
Sponsor: Inter-Survey Consultants
Description: The Geneva International Forum Directory focuses on international organizations located in Geneva, Switzerland. This site is a directory that covers hundreds of UN organizations, international institutions, permanent missions, nongovernmental organizations, and companies located in Geneva. Access to the database is by thematic, keyword, and geographic searches along with access by type of organization (for example, United Nations organizations and agencies, intergovernmental organizations, public and private institutions). The institutions included in the Geneva International Database cover a wide range of social, technical and scientific themes.
Subject: Reference — International

4529. Governments on the Web
http://www.gksoft.com/govt/
Sponsor: Gunnar Anzinger
Description: This is one of the most extensive lists of international, national, regional, and local governmental and government-related Web servers. Its database covers governmental institutions on the Web including parliaments, ministries, agencies, law courts, embassies, councils, broadcasting institutions, central banks, multigovernmental institutions, and political parties. It contained more than 17,000 entries from more than 220 countries and territories as of May 2002. Available in English and German, it is arranged in a hierarchical index organized by continent, country, and then by smaller divisions. It also has thematic groupings including heads of states, parliaments, political parties, elections, statistics, and currency.
Subjects: Foreign Governments; Finding Aids

4530. International Agencies and Information
http://www.lib.umich.edu/govdocs/intl.html
Sponsor: University of Michigan. Library
Description: The frames version of this Web site provides pointers to many lists of international and intergovernmental Web sites. Access to international agencies is by three categories: agencies, related Web sites, and subject. The Agencies section is an alphabetical listing by acronym in the frame or by an alphabetical listing of agencies in the full window. Within the UN section, there are links to official UN records. In addition to the links to international and intergovernmental sites, there are sections for international treaties and simulations and other international-related information.
Subject: International Organizations

4531. International Documents Task Force
http://www.library.uiuc.edu/doc/idtf/home.htm
Sponsor: Government Documents Round Table (GODORT)
Description: This site features annotated Web links to excellent collections of international government Web sites, including International Governmental Organizations (IGO's) and Non-governmental Organizations (NGO's). Sections of the site are relevant only to the professional library group

sponsoring the site, the Government Documents Roundtable's International Documents Task Force. However, the Web Links and Topical Guides sections present selective lists of online resources for foreign and international research that will be of use to others.

The IDTF Web site is sparse in terms of design, yet it excels in information content both as a finding aid for intergovernmental organization sites and for sites of other countries. It also contains substantial information for international documents librarians.

Subject: Government Information — International

4532. Inter-Parliamentary Union

`http://www.ipu.org/`

Sponsor: Inter-Parliamentary Union (IPU)

Description: The IPU is an international organization of parliaments from different countries. The IPU Web site features two databases and links to parliamentary Web sites around the world. The two databases are PARLINE and PARLIT. For all countries with a national legislature, the PARLINE (parliaments online) database provides general information on each parliament's chambers, a description of the electoral system, the results of the most recent elections, and information on the working of the presidency of each chamber. PARLIT (parliaments and literature) is a bibliographical database covering parliamentary law and legislative elections throughout the world. The database contains literature since 1992. Other sections include Functioning and Documents, Main Areas of Activity, Publications, Women in Parliaments, and Press Releases.

For anyone interested in the legislative bodies of other countries, this is an information-rich site to visit.

Subjects: Foreign Governments; Parliaments — International

Publication: *World of Parliaments: IPU Quarterly Review*

4533. Web Sites of National Parliaments

`http://wc.wustl.edu/parliaments.html`

Sponsor: Washington University

Description: This page presents a simple list of links to more than 60 Web sites from, supported by, and relating to parliamentary bodies from different countries. The entries range from the Estonian Riigikogu to the Nicaraguan National Assembly and the Israeli Knesset. At the end of the alphabetical country lists is another section entitled International and Regional Parliamentary Institutions.

Subject: Parliaments — International

4534. Yahoo! Government: Countries

`http://dir.yahoo.com/Government/countries/`

Sponsor: Yahoo! Inc.

Description: This section of the well-known Yahoo! directory of Internet resources covers government sites from over 140 other countries. Under a country's name, the links may include such sections as Agencies; Government Officials; Embassies and Consulates; Executive, Legislative, and Judicial Branches; Law; Military; Ministries; and Politics.

While this site is not as comprehensive as Governments on the Web, it is a useful adjunct that occasionally has links not found on Governments on the Web.

Subjects: Foreign Countries; Finding Aids

Intergovernmental Organizations

4535. African Union

`http://www.africa-union.org/en/home.asp`

Description: The African Union is the successor to the Organization of African Unity. The site includes news, leadership information, and a map of member countries with basic information about each one.

Subject: Africa

4536. ASEAN Web
`http://www.asean.or.id/`
Sponsor: Association of Southeast Asian Nations (ASEAN)
Description: This intergovernmental body established to promote economic cooperation includes the governments of Brunei Darussalam, Cambodia, Indonesia, Laos, Malaysia, Myanmar, Philippines, Singapore, Thailand, and Viet Nam. Its Web site features sections on Economic Integration, Human and Social Development, and Transnational Issues. A Statistics section has economic indicators for the region, such as Gross Domestic Product (GDP), interest rates, trade volume, and inflation. The Publications section includes a publications list and online versions of *Business ASEAN* and ASEAN annual reports.
Subjects: International Economic Relations; Asia

4537. Asia-Pacific Economic Cooperation
`http://www.apecsec.org.sg/`
Sponsor: Asia-Pacific Economic Cooperation (APEC)
Description: The Asia-Pacific Economic Cooperation (APEC) is an international forum promoting open trade and economic cooperation. Established in 1989 in response to the growing interdependence among Asia-Pacific economies, its members are located in the Pacific Rim and include the United States. The APEC Secretariat in Singapore hosts the central APEC Web site. The site's sections are About APEC, Member Economies, APEC Activities, Business and Investment, Community Interest, Publications and Library, Databases, and News and Events.
Subjects: International Economic Relations; Asia

4538. Europa
`http://europa.eu.int/`
Sponsor: European Union (EU)
Description: Available in multiple languages, Europa is the European Union's (EU) official Web site, with links to the Parliament, the Council, the Commission, the Court of Justice, the Court of Auditors, and more. The News section provides access to press releases, "press packs" on key issues, and information on the Europe by Satellite TV news. The Institutions section links to various EU agencies. The section Activities provides key subject access to the many common EU activities such as agriculture, energy, and public health. EU At A Glance links to reference material, such as the main government Web sites of member countries and maps of EU and applicant countries. Official Documents has links to European Union law (the EUR-Lex service); the European Parliament, the Council, and the Commission; the annual general report; and the *Bulletin of the European Union*. The Information Sources section has a variety of links to sites that provide information about various aspects of the EU, links to information sources of EU institutions, and links to the publications and statistics pages.

Europa includes an excellent overview of the European Union, a central finding aid for component agencies, and a substantial amount of official documents. This is an excellent starting point for those searching for governmental and intergovernmental information on Europe.
Subjects: International Economic Relations; Europe

4539. Food and Agriculture Organization (FAO) of the United Nations
`http://www.fao.org/`
Sponsor: United Nations — Food and Agriculture Organization (FAO)
Description: The FAO is a specialized agency within the United Nations, focused on improving nutrition, agricultural productivity, and the standard of living in the world's rural areas. Featured sections include Statistical Databases, Agriculture, Economics, Fisheries, Forestry, Economics and Nutrition, Sustainable Development, Technical Cooperation, Legal Office, Decentralized Offices, Publications, and Events Calendar. The Publications page provides access to an interactive catalog of publications and ordering information.
Subjects: Agriculture — International; Nutrition — International; Rural Development — International
Publications: *State of Food and Agriculture*
State of Food Insecurity in the World
State of the World's Forests
State of World Fisheries and Aquaculture

4540. G8 Information Centre, University of Toronto
http://www.g8.utoronto.ca/
Sponsor: University of Toronto
Description: This site organizes and provides access to materials and sites related to the G8 (formerly the G7), its summits, and other meetings. The G8 refers to a group of eight major market-oriented democracies. Categories include G8 in the News, Scholarly Writings and Policy Analyses, Other G8-Related Sites and Documents, and Summits, Meetings, and Documents of the G7 and G8. Documents within the G8 Information Centre site can be retrieved by country, year, subject, and other search options.

This should be a starting point for any search of G8-related material. Coverage is excellent, and the site is well organized and easy to navigate.
Subject: International Economic Relations

4541. Inter-American Development Bank
http://www.iadb.org/
Sponsor: Inter-American Development Bank (IDB)
Description: The Inter-American Development Bank was established to help accelerate economic and social development in Latin America and the Caribbean. Its Web site features four main categories entitled Projects, Resources, Inside the IDB, and Featured Pages. The Projects is one of the more substantial sections with details on the many IDB projects. Under Resources, there are the sections Statistics, Publications, and Press. The Statistics section offers several databases, statistical tables and graphs, country data and regional reports, and hemispheric links. With these resources, data is accessible for income distribution, hemispheric trade, population, prices, and national accounts for countries in South and Central America. The Press and Publications sections include press releases, newest releases from the IDB, ordering information, and the newsletter *IDB América*. The site has Spanish, French, Portuguese, Japanese, and English versions.
Subjects: International Economic Development; South America; Caribbean
Publication: *IDB América*

4542. International Bureau of Education
http://www.ibe.unesco.org/
Sponsor: United Nations — United Nations Educational, Scientific, and Cultural Organization (UNESCO)
Description: The International Bureau of Education (IBE) is a UNESCO center for information and research in the field of education, focusing currently on the management of curricula change for the 21st century. This Web site features International Activities, Regional Programmes, and Country-level Activities. Under the International section is a Databanks page, with links to Innodata, a database of educational innovations at the primary and secondary level, and a list of country dossiers. It also includes access to World Data on Education, a full-text database describing the structure of the education systems and educational developments in IBE member countries.
Subject: Education Research — International

4543. International Court of Justice—Cour internationale de Justice
http://www.icj-cij.org/
Sponsor: United Nations — International Court of Justice (ICJ)
Description: The International Court of Justice is the principal judicial organ of the United Nations. Its Web site features English and French versions with sections such as What's New, Docket, Decisions, General Information, Basic Documents, and Publications. The Decisions section includes selected recent cases with some sections available in full text. The Publications page connects to five series: *Yearbook*; *Bibliography* (annual); *Acts and Documents*; *Judgments, Advisory Opinions, and Orders*; and *Pleadings, Oral Arguments, and Documents.*
Subject: International Law

4544. International Labour Organization
http://www.ilo.org/
Sponsor: United Nations — International Labour Organization (ILO)
Description: The International Labour Organization is a United Nations agency that formulates international labor standards setting minimum standards of labor rights such as the right to organize,

collective bargaining, and abolition of forced labor. Its Web site features sections including Standards and Fundamental Principles and Rights at Work, Employment, Social Protection, and Social Dialogue. A Resources page includes recent publications, lists of books titles by subject and CDROMs, databases, and selected full-text articles from the *International Labour Review* as well as online access to the ILO magazine, *World of Work,* available in PDF. This site is available in English, French, and Spanish.
Subject: Labor-Management Relations — International
Publication: *International Labour Review*

4545. International Monetary Fund (IMF)
http://www.imf.org/
Sponsor: International Monetary Fund (IMF)
Description: The International Monetary Fund is an international organization established to promote international monetary cooperation, exchange stability, and economic growth. Its Web site features sections such as About the IMF, News Releases, Publications, IMF Finances, IMF At Work, and Country Information. The IMF Finances section provides exchange rates for selected currencies and for the current month, in addition to other financial resources. The Publications page provides search and browse access to IMF print and online publications. A fair number of publications are accessible online.
Subjects: International Economic Relations; Monetary Policy — International

4546. Interpol
http://www.interpol.int/
Sponsor: International Criminal Police Organization (Interpol)
Description: The official Web site for the International Criminal Police Organization includes general information about Interpol's principles, structure, and members. It also features topical sections on current issues in international law enforcement, including Terrorism, Children and Human Trafficking, DNA Profiling, Drugs, Information Technology Crime, Soccer Hooliganism, and more.
Subjects: International Crimes; Law Enforcement — International

4547. NATO Official Home Page
http://www.nato.int/
Sponsor: North Atlantic Treaty Organization (NATO)
Description: The North Atlantic Treaty Organization is an alliance of independent nations committed to each other's defense. The NATO Web site features news, speeches, and videos on current NATO activities. The Organization section features information on the structure of NATO and links to the national information servers of member countries. The Issues section covers such topics as terrorism, operations in the Balkans, and the military expenditures of member nations. The Services section includes several email update services available. Online publications include the quarterly *NATO Review.*

While only a small subset of their printed publications are available, the Web site provides a significant collection of documents from and about NATO. It is an excellent source of information on the organization.
Subject: Military Forces — International
Publications: *NATO Handbook*
NATO Review

4548. Organisation for Economic Co-operation and Development (OECD) Online
http://www.oecd.org/
Sponsor: Organisation for Economic Co-operation and Development (OECD)
Description: OECD Online contains descriptive information about the OECD, its activities, and its member countries. Major categories include About OECD, Themes, Documentation, Statistics, News, Country Information, Bookshop, and Online Services. A list of topical links to OECD resources appears on the home page. The Bookshop section includes ordering information and a list of publications. The home page also provides online access to a revolving selection of publications under the heading Editor's Choice. Press releases are available under the News section, and under Documentation, there is free access to many online documents including *OECD Policy Briefs, OECD Observer, OECD in Figures,* and the *Annual Report.*

The site contains useful descriptive information about the OECD and a useful collection of free online publications and statistics.
Subject: International Economic Development
Publications: *OECD in Figures*
OECD Policy Briefs
The OECD Observer

4549. Organization of American States
http://www.oas.org/
Sponsor: Organization of American States (OAS)
Description: The OAS Web site features information on the organization and its involvements. Major sections include Latest News, About the OAS, General Assembly, Organizational Structure, Publications, Documents, Library, Museum, Webcast, and Inter-American Agency for Cooperation and Development. A drop-down menu on the home page (OAS Issues) leads to information on such issues as Against Terrorism, Civil Society, Culture, Drug Control, Gender Equality, Democracy, and more. The Publications page includes ordering information and links to online books. The site is available in English, Spanish, French and Portuguese.
Subjects: South America; Caribbean
Publication: *Américas*

4550. Organization of the Petroleum Exporting Countries (OPEC)
http://www.opec.org/
Sponsor: Organization of the Petroleum Exporting Countries (OPEC)
Description: OPEC is an organization of oil-exporting nations dedicated to the stability and prosperity of the petroleum market. The OPEC Web site features sections such as About OPEC, News and Info, Member Countries, Meetings, OPECNA (News Agency), Publications, and FAQs. The Publications section highlights major print publications available for ordering and since March 2001, current online versions of *OPEC Annual Report* (1998 and 1999), *OPEC Bulletin* (2001 archives), *OPEC Annual Statistical Bulletin* (1998 and 1999), *Monthly Oil Market Report* (2001 archives), and *OPEC Statute.*
Subject: Petroleum — International
Publications: *Monthly Oil Market Report*
OPEC Annual Report
OPEC Annual Statistical Bulletin
OPEC Bulletin
OPEC Statute

4551. UNESCO (United Nations Educational, Scientific, and Cultural Organization)
http://www.unesco.org/
Sponsor: United Nations — United Nations Educational, Scientific, and Cultural Organization (UNESCO)
Description: As the primary United Nations agency dealing with education, science, culture, and communication between countries on such topics, the UNESCO Web site features sections such as Current Events, Publications/Audiovisual, Documents, Information Services, Fields of Activity, Legal Instruments, and Statistics. The Statistics has news on statistics reported in the areas of education, literacy, culture, science, and technology.
Subjects: Culture — International; Education — International; Science and Technology Policy — International
Publication: *The UNESCO Courier*

4552. United Nations
http://www.un.org/
Sponsor: United Nations
Description: This main United Nations site features information and documents about the UN. Aside from organization and program information, the site includes an extensive news center, UN Webcast section, and the educational CyberSchoolBus section. Other sections link to the main bodies of the UN, such as the General Assembly, Security Council, and Economic and Social Council.

A section called Issues on the UN Agenda organizes UN resources by topic, such as AIDS Climate Change, Disarmament, Human Rights, Peace and Security, Sustainable Development, and Terrorism. The Member States section includes a list with date of admission to the UN, as well as links to Permanent Missions and to non-member states maintaining Permanent Observer Missions at UN Headquarters. The Publications, Stamps, and Databases section of the site includes sales publications and online versions of popular UN publications. The Documentation and Maps section has meeting records, Security Council resolutions, *Journal of the United Nations*, press releases, and other documents.

Subject: International Relations
Publications: *Africa Recovery*
Development Update
Image and Reality
UN Chronicle

4553. United Nations Children's Fund Works for Children Worldwide (UNICEF)

http://www.unicef.org/
Sponsor: United Nations — United Nations Children's Fund (UNICEF)
Description: UNICEF presents a site filled with information on international children's rights, the health and well-being of children, the abuse of children, and other material related to children. The site features the following main categories: UNICEF in Action; Highlights; Information Resources; Donations, Greeting Cards, and Gifts; Press Centre; Voices of Youth; and About UNICEF. Information Resources includes such sections as Publications, Catalogues, Executive Speeches, Statistics, and more. Many publications are available online, including *The State of the World's Children, The Progress of Nations,* and the *UNICEF Annual Report.* Additional resources are located under Press Centre, which includes the sections Press Releases (latest and archived), UNICEF in the News, and Statistical Data. UNICEF programs are listed under UNICEF in Action.

The UNICEF sites are a treasure trove of information about children and UNICEF's activities on behalf of children.
Subject: Child Welfare — International
Publications: *The Progress of Nations*
The State of the World's Children
UNICEF Annual Report

4554. United Nations Scholars' Workstation

http://www.library.yale.edu/un/
Sponsor: Yale University. Library
Description: The Yale University's United Nations Scholars' Workstation gives access to a collection of texts, finding aids, data sets, maps, and pointers to electronic and print information. The site covers United Nations studies including disarmament, economic and social development, environment, human rights, international relations, international trade, peacekeeping, and population and demography. Some sections are subject to access restrictions in accordance with Yale University's licensing agreements.

Unlike so many Internet sites, the Scholars' Workstation refers to both print and electronic resources. The great advantage to this is that users can be directed to appropriate information resources regardless of format. Because the Workstation is aimed at serving users at Yale, there is a definite slant toward resources accessible at Yale and detailed information on the UN Studies Program at Yale. However, the other sections can be useful to others interested in the United Nations as well.
Subject: International Relations

4555. United Nations System

http://www.unsystem.org/
Sponsor: United Nations
Description: This site is the official Web site locator for the UN system of organizations. It includes an Alphabetic Index of all United Nations Organizations (UNOs) with their abbreviations and the city where the headquarters is located. Other resources available are a UN System Chart, UN System Highlights, the UN News Service, Missions to the UN, and UN Information Centers. The site is available in English and French.

For finding component UN organizations' Web sites, this should be the first site to check. The listings are easy to browse, and they clearly denote which agencies have a presence on the Internet.
Subject: International Relations

4556. World Bank Group

http://www.worldbank.org/
Sponsor: World Bank
Description: This site concentrates on information about the World Bank, its programs, and constituent organizations. Sections include Data and Statistics, Documents and Reports, News and Media, Projects and Policies, Publications, and Topics in Development. A Countries and Regions section provides detailed data on countries of the world. The site also links to pages for World Bank agencies: International Bank of Reconstruction and Development, International Development Association, International Finance Corporation, Multilateral Investment Guarantee Agency, and International Centre for Settlement of Investment Disputes.
Subject: International Economic Development

4557. World Health Organization (WHO)

http://www.who.int/
Sponsor: United Nations — World Health Organization (WHO)
Description: The World Health Organization (WHO) is a UN agency focusing on global health issues. The WHO site features the major categories: Countries, Health Topics, Emergencies, Disease Outbreaks, Press Releases, Publications, Research Tools, and General WHO Information. The Countries section gives a health profile of member nations. Health Topics is an A to Z index of WHO programs, publications, and contacts. The Press section links to a long list of backgrounders and fact sheets on global health topics such as the major causes of blindness, childhood diseases in Africa, dengue, malaria, and tobacco use.
Subject: Health and Safety — International
Publications: *WHO Weekly Epidemiological Record*
World Health Report

4558. World Intellectual Property Organization

http://www.wipo.int/
Sponsor: United Nations — World Intellectual Property Organization (WIPO)
Description: This central WIPO Web site features English, French, Spanish, and Arabic versions. The site includes sections such as About WIPO, About Intellectual Property, News and Information Resources, and Activities and Services. Sections such as Documents, Pressroom, Intellectual Property Digital Library, Electronic Bookshop, and Conferences, Meetings, and Seminars can be accessed under News and Information Resources. Under Activities and Services are links to the Patent Cooperation Treaty (PCT) System, the Madrid System, and the Hague System. On the PCT System page, the site links to an online version of the *PCT Gazette,* which is available back to 1998 and is available in English and French.
Subject: Intellectual Property — International
Publication: *PCT Gazette*

4559. World Meteorological Organization

http://www.wmo.ch/
Sponsor: United Nations — World Meteorological Organization (WMO)
Description: The World Meteorological Organization is a United Nations agency that promotes the effective use worldwide of meteorological and hydrological information, notably in weather and water resource prediction and in climatology. This site features pages for each of the major WMO Programmes and such categories as Hot Topics, Major Issues, Publications, and About Us.
Subject: Meteorology — International

4560. World Trade Organization (WTO)

http://www.wto.org/
Sponsor: World Trade Organization (WTO)
Description: The WTO Web site feature Trade Topics, The WTO, Resources, Documents, and

Community/Forums. Under Trade Topics, the page organizes information under the headings Goods, Services, Intellectual Property, and Dispute Settlement. Under the Resources page, there are links to Documents Online, Publications, Statistics, Economic Research and Analysis, and a page to download material, such as brochures, reports, guides, and video clips. The Publications section includes an Online Bookshop, Documents Online, Trade Policy Reviews, and the newsletter *Focus*. Users can also download annual reports and the annual *International Trade Statistics* publication.

Subject: International Trade
Publications: *Focus*
International Trade Statistics
WTO Annual Report

4561. Worldatom: International Atomic Energy Agency (IAEA)
http://www.iaea.or.at/worldatom/
Alternate URL: http://www.iaea.org
Sponsor: United Nations — International Atomic Energy Agency (IAEA)
Description: This site is designed as an IAEA public information service. After the featured stories on the home page, the site has links to such sections as About the IAEA, Meetings, Programmes, Documents, Periodicals, Reference Centre, Press Centre, and Books. The Focus Series section has subject access to current IAEA efforts and programs, covering topics such as combatting nuclear terrorism, depleted uranium, power plant safety, radioactive waste, and water management. The Programmes area links to Nuclear Safety, Nuclear Sciences and Applications, Nuclear Energy, and Safeguards and Physical Protection.
Subjects: Nuclear Power Plants — International; Nuclear Waste — International; Nuclear Weapons — International

Other Countries

Afghanistan

4562. Islamic Transitional State of Afghanistan
http://www.af/
Sponsor: Afghanistan. Government
Description: This is the Web site for the post-Taliban transitional government of Afghanistan. The site includes presidential speeches, policy documents, and links to several government ministries. It also includes United Nations documents and material related to the reconstruction process.

Albania

4563. Kuvendi
http://www.parlament.al/
Sponsor: Albania. Parliament
Description: This Web site for the Kuvendi, the Albanian Parliament, is in Albanian with an English version option and includes sections for the structure of the parliament, parliamentary groups and committees, a bulletin of the parliament, and a section for the constitution.

4564. President of the Republic of Albania
http://www.president.al/
Sponsor: Albania. Government
Description: The president's site includes some English information about the presidency and the government.

Algeria

4565. Council of Nation
http://www.majliselouma.dz/
Sponsor: Algeria. Parliament
Description: The Council of Nation is the upper chamber of Algeria's parliament. Their Web site is available in Arabic and French versions. It includes information on the Council's members, organization, and documents.

4566. People's Democratic Republic of Algeria
http://www.el-mouradia.dz/
Sponsor: Algeria. Government
Description: This is the Web site for the Algerian Presidency. It is available in Arabic and French versions. It includes information on the president, presidential documents, and the presidential building. Background information on the country, its government, and national symbols is also included.

Andorra

4567. General Council, Principality of Andorra
http://www.consell.ad/micg/webconsell.nsf?Open
Sponsor: Andorra. Parliament
Description: While most of the content is available only in Catalan, this parliamentary Web site has navigational options in English, Spanish, and French. It includes information on the legislature, lists of laws passed going back to 1993, the parliamentary schedule, and official publications.

4568. Government of Andorra
http://www.govern.ad/
Sponsor: Andorra. Government
Description: In Catalan, this site includes news, links to information on government officials and the ministries, and links to other government Web sites.

Angola

4569. National Assembly
http://www.parlamento.ao/index_sf.htm
Sponsor: Angola. Parliament
Description: In Portuguese, this is the site for the National Assembly of Angola. It includes lists of laws and resolutions approved, going back to 1993. It also includes links to committees, information on political parties, and background information on the Assembly itself.

Antigua and Barbuda

4570. Government of Antigua and Barbuda
http://www.antiguagov.com/
Sponsor: Antigua and Barbuda. Government
Description: Antigua's government Web site includes basic information on chief government officials and government news.

Argentina

4571. Argentina National Congress
http://www.congreso.gov.ar/
Sponsor: Argentina. Parliament
Description: The congressional Web site, in Spanish, links to the sites for both the Senate and the Chamber of Deputies. Each offers information on members, committees, news, and legislation.

4572. Presidency of the Nation of Argentina
http://www.presidencia.gov.ar/
Sponsor: Argentina. Government
Description: The Spanish-language site for the Argentine presidency offers information on issues, presidential speeches and activities, and the cabinet, and includes links to other government Web sites.

Armenia

4573. Government of Armenia
http://www.gov.am/
Sponsor: Armenia. Government
Description: This site currently offers Armenian and English versions of its Web site. The main categories are the Government, the Press Center, and the Reforms Center, with links to other sections as Formation of the Government and Government Activities Program. Under the Government, there are links to pages for the prime minister, Cabinet members, government structure, and staff of the government.

4574. National Assembly of Armenia
http://www.parliament.am/
Sponsor: Armenia. Parliament
Description: This site of the Parliament of Armenia offers Armenian, Russian, and English versions. It features a historical overview of the Armenian parliament, information on members, the rules of procedure, and current news.

Australia

4575. Fed.gov.au
http://www.fed.gov.au/KSP/
Sponsor: Australia. Government
Description: The Australian national government portal site provides a full index of links to government Web sites, links to items of current interest, links to the most popular Australian government Web pages, and a government search engine. It also has channels for students, businesses, citizens, and non-residents, and a topical index to Australian government information on the Web.

4576. Parliament of Australia
http://www.aph.gov.au/
Sponsor: Australia. Parliament
Description: The Australian Parliament's site includes links to the Senate, House of Representatives, Committees, Legislation, Publications, and the Hansards of the Senate and the House. The Information and Research section includes procedural guides and issue analysis from the Parliamentary Library, the House, and the Senate.

Austria

4577. Austrian Parliament
http://www.parlament.gv.at/
Sponsor: Austria. Parliament
Description: The Austrian Parliament's Web site is primarily in German but has some English content. The site includes information on members, committees, and current schedules. It includes texts of constitutional laws and parliamentary organization and procedure.

4578. Federal President of the Republic of Austria
http://www.hofburg.at/
Sponsor: Austria. Government
Description: This site offers content in both German and English. It includes information about the office of the president, the president's speeches, and election information, and has contact information for upper-level staff.

Azerbaijan

4579. Milli Mejlis of the Republic of Azerbaijan
http://www.meclis.gov.az/
Sponsor: Azerbaijan. Parliament
Description: The Azerbaijan parliament site includes information on the history and structure of the parliament and the national constitution and laws. The site can be viewed in English or Azerbaijani.

4580. President of the Republic of Azerbaijan
http://www.president.az
Sponsor: Azerbaijan. Government
Description: This English-language site offers information on the president, the country, and the office of the president.

Bahamas

4581. Commonwealth of the Bahamas
http://www.bahamas.gov.bs/bahamasweb/home.nsf
Sponsor: Bahamas. Government
Description: The Bahamian government site includes information on all branches of government and links to the Web sites for government agencies. Major sections are About the Bahamas; The Government; Business, Finance, and E-Commerce; Visiting the Bahamas; and News and Publications.

Bahrain

4582. State of Bahrain
http://www.bahrain.gov.bh/english/index.asp
Sponsor: Bahrain. Government
Description: The State of Bahrain Web site has links to information on the Royal Family, the government, ministries, statistics and services, and general information about the country and business and the economy. The URL above is for the English language version of the site.

Bangladesh

4583. Bangladesh Parliament Legislative Information Centre
http://www.parliamentofbangladesh.org/indexeng.html
Sponsor: Bangladesh. Parliament
Description: This site offers an English-language version with information on the parliament, the Bangladesh constitution, and rules of procedure.

4584. Government of the People's Republic of Bangladesh
Alternate URL: http://www.bangladeshgov.org
Sponsor: Bangladesh. Government
Description: This English-language site has links to the sites for the Prime Minister and each of the ministries. It also includes the constitution, maps, and links to Bangladesh newspapers online.

Barbados

4585. Government of Barbados Information Network
http://www.barbados.gov.bb/
Sponsor: Barbados. Government
Description: This site offers links to government agencies and ministries and is in English.

Belarus

4586. Council of Ministers of Republic of Belarus
http://www.government.by/eng/sovmin/index.htm
Sponsor: Belarus. Government
Description: This site has background information on the Council and links to some of the ministerial Web sites.

4587. President of the Republic of Belarus
http://www.president.gov.by/eng/
Sponsor: Belarus. Government
Description: This site is in English and Russian and includes sections on the president, news, and the Republic. The presidential section has documents and speeches.

Belgium

4588. Belgian Federal Government Online
http://belgium.fgov.be/
Sponsor: Belgium. Government
Description: The Belgian Federal Government Online is available in Dutch, French, English, and German. The site features information about a variety of subjects including the government, the country, art and culture, tourism, and statistics. The Official Belgian Sites section links to federal and other government Web sites.

4589. Chamber of Representatives of Belgium
http://www.dekamer.be/
Sponsor: Belgium. Parliament
Description: The lower house of the Belgian parliament hosts this site, which also links to the Senate's site. It includes information on members and committees, and links to publications from both chambers. Most legislative documents are in PDF format. A limited amount of information is available in English.

Belize

4590. Government of Belize
http://www.belize.gov.bz/
Sponsor: Belize. Government
Description: The Belize Web site features links to information from the office of the prime minister and the Cabinet. A Press Office section has press releases and a Library section has the full text of selected publications.

Bhutan

4591. Bhutan
http://www.kingdomofbhutan.com/
Sponsor: Bhutan. Government
Description: This English-language site from the Bhutan Tourism Corporation has basic information on Bhutan including some sections on the government.

Bolivia

4592. National Congress of Bolivia
http://www.congreso.gov.bo/
Sponsor: Bolivia. Parliament
Description: This Bolivian parliamentary site is in Spanish and includes sections on the presidency of the Congress, both chambers, the constitution, the library and archives, and a database of laws back to 1979.

Botswana

4593. The Republic of Botswana—The Government of Botswana
http://www.gov.bw/home.html
Sponsor: Botswana. Government
Description: This page offers an index of ministries, information about business and investments in Botswana, and economics and budget information.

Brazil

4594. Brazilian Legislature
http://www.camara.gov.br/
Alternate URL: http://www.senado.gov.br/
Sponsor: Brazil. Parliament
Description: These pages, in Portuguese, are the official sites for the two houses of parliament for Brazil.

4595. República Federativa do Brasil
http://www.brasil.gov.br/
Sponsor: Brazil. Government
Description: The Brazilian federal government site, in Portuguese, has news and information on all three branches of government, government programs, issues, statistics, and news. It also links to the Web sites for the ministries.

Brunei

4596. Government of Brunei Darussalam
http://www.brunei.gov.bn/
Sponsor: Brunei. Government
Description: This site, available in an English version, features sections on the Sultan, the Crown Prince, the national constitution, cabinet, and ministries.

Bulgaria

4597. Government of the Republic of Bulgaria
http://www.government.bg/
Sponsor: Bulgaria. Government
Description: This official site provides basic information on the government and is in Bulgarian and English. There are links to the prime minister, council of ministers, press releases, and the Web sites of the individual ministries.

4598. National Assembly of Republic of Bulgaria
http://www.parliament.bg/
Sponsor: Bulgaria. Parliament
Description: The National Assembly's site offers an English language version. It includes information about the current members and committees, the constitution, and an introduction to legislative procedure.

Burkina Faso

4599. Presidency of Burkino Faso
http://www.presidence.bf/
Sponsor: Burkina Faso. Government
Description: In French, this site provides information on the president and his Cabinet, and has the full text of basic documents such as the constitution. A links section includes the sites for major ministries.

Cambodia

4600. National Assembly of the Kingdom of Cambodia
http://www.cambodian-parliament.org/
Sponsor: Cambodia. Parliament
Description: The Cambodian assembly site offers an English language version and a brief history of the assembly, which held its first session in 1993. Major sections of the site cover the leadership, committees, daily summaries of legislative activities, a directory of members, and press releases.

Cameroon

4601. Republic of Cameroon - Prime Minister
http://www.spm.gov.cm/
Sponsor: Cameroon. Government
Description: The Prime Minister's site, in English and French, includes his biography, speeches, and information on his activities. It also includes sections on the major government departments, laws and regulations, education, tourism, embassies and consulates, and Cameroon itself.

Canada

4602. Canada's Parliament
http://www.parl.gc.ca/
Sponsor: Canada. Parliament
Description: The main Canadian Parliament site also has English and French versions, both of which provide extensive information on the Canadian legislative bodies. The site features an A-Z index and has the full text, summaries, and status of legislation.

4603. Government of Canada
http://www.gc.ca/
Sponsor: Canada. Government
Description: This site offers a French and English version both of which provide detailed information and links to government agencies, programs, services, and publications.

Cape Verde

4604. Republic of Cape Verde
http://www.governo.cv/
Sponsor: Cape Verde. Government
Description: The official Web site for the Cape Verde government is in Portuguese and features information on the structure of the government and biographies of its leaders. It includes the text of speeches and government announcements and links to other national sites.
   A fourth link to the page for the legislature is currently not in operation.

Chad

4605. Embassy of Chad
http://www.chadembassy.org/
Sponsor: Chad. Government
Description: While not the official government site, this well designed English-language site from the Chad embassy in Washington, DC, includes information about the government, government officials, and the country in general.

Chile

4606. Gobierno de Chile
http://www.gobiernodechile.cl/
Sponsor: Chile. Government
Description: In Spanish, the site for the government of Chile has current news and information about the president, his Cabinet, ministries, and country of Chile. The site links to all three branches of government and to the various ministries.

4607. National Congress of Chile
http://www.congreso.cl/
Sponsor: Chile. Government
Description: This parliamentary site for Chile links to both the sites for both chambers as well as to the national parliamentary library. The site is in Spanish.

4608. Presidency of the Republic of Chile
http://www.presidencia.cl/
Sponsor: Chile. Government
Description: This Spanish-language site provides news and information from the president of Chile and has sections for the Cabinet and the constitution.

China

4609. Chinese Government Online Project
http://www.gov.cn
Sponsor: China. Government
Description: This government project site is almost entirely in Chinese, with one index of selected government agencies in English.

Colombia

4610. Presidency of the Republic of Colombia
http://www.presidencia.gov.co/
Sponsor: Colombia. Government
Description: This site, in Spanish, includes current government news, information about government programs, official documents and laws, links to information on the ministries, and a directory of Colombian embassies abroad and foreign embassies in Bogota.

4611. Senate of the Republic of Colombia
http://www.senado.gov.co/
Sponsor: Colombia. Parliament
Description: The site for the Senate in the Colombian parliament is in Spanish and includes the constitution, background information on the parliament, and a database of laws.

Congo (Brazzaville)

4612. Republic of Congo - Brazzaville
http://www.congo-site.cg/
Sponsor: Congo (Brazzaville). Government
Description: This site for the Republic of the Congo is in French. It includes government news items and announcements organized by topic, such as Economy, Politics, and Diplomacy.

Costa Rica

4613. Government of Costa Rica
http://www.casapres.go.cr/
Sponsor: Costa Rica. Government
Description: This Spanish-language site provides presidential news releases, speeches, and links to the ministries. Some documents also have an English version.

4614. Legislative Assembly - Republic of Costa Rica
http://www.racsa.co.cr/asamblea/
Sponsor: Costa Rica. Parliament
Description: The Costa Rican parliament site includes information on its leadership and schedule, laws, press releases, and the national budget. It is in Spanish.

Croatia

4615. Croatian Parliament
http://www.sabor.hr/
Sponsor: Croatia. Parliament
Description: This site for the Croatian parliament is in Serbo-Croatian with some documents translated into English.

4616. Government of the Republic of Croatia

http://www.vlada.hr/

Sponsor: Croatia. Government

Description: This general Croatian government site offers both a Serbo-Croatian version and an English version. Both link to information about the government, government documents and sessions, and the current edition of the *Croatian Government Bulletin*. Archived editions from 1998 are also available.

Cyprus

4617. The Republic of Cyprus

http://www.pio.gov.cy/

Sponsor: Cyprus. Government

Description: Major sections of this site include About Cyprus, The Cyprus Issue, and Government. The site is in both English and Greek. The Government section includes information on executive branch agencies and on elections results. The Reference section lists addresses and contacts for many government departments and for Cyrus missions abroad.

Czech Republic

4618. Office of the Czech Republic Government

http://www.vlada.cz/

Sponsor: Czech Republic. Government

Description: This Czech Republic government Web site is in Czech and English. It includes biographies of leaders and a directory of addresses and Web links for the president, parliament, ministries, and other Czech institutions.

4619. Parliament of the Czech Republic

http://www.psp.cz/

Alternate URL: http://www.senat.cz/

Sponsor: Czech Republic. Government

Description: The primary URL is for the Chamber of Deputies and the alternate URL points to the Senate. Each site has an English language version.

Denmark

4620. Folketinget

http://www.folketinget.dk/

Sponsor: Denmark. Parliament

Description: The Folketinget is the Danish parliament. Its Web site is primarily in Danish, but there is an English-language version.

4621. Statsministeriet - Prime Minister's Office

http://www.statsministeriet.dk/Index/mainstart.asp?o=1&n=3&s=1

Alternate URL: http://www.stm.dk/Index/mainstart.asp?o=1&n=3&s=1

Sponsor: Denmark. Government

Description: This is the Danish Prime Minister's Web site, in Danish with an alternate English language page.

Dominican Republic

4622. Presidency of the Dominican Republic

http://www.presidencia.gov.do/

Sponsor: Dominican Republic. Government
Description: The president's Web site includes speeches, a biography, and bulletins. It also has information on the National Palace, the structure of the government, and links to the ministries and agencies. The Web site is in Spanish with an English language version.

East Timor

4623. Easte Timor
http://www.gov.east-timor.org/
Sponsor: East Timor. Government
Description: East Timor become an independent state in May 2002. The government's Web site provides background information and links to documents such as the official gazette, the constitution, laws, and presidential directives. Some information is in English; official documents are in Portuguese.

Ecuador

4624. Presidency of the Republic of Ecuador
http://www.presidencia.gov.ec/
Sponsor: Ecuador. Government
Description: This Spanish-language presidential site has information on the current president and presidential palace, and a list of past presidents. It also carries current government news and information about the ministries.

Egypt

4625. Egyptian Presidency
http://www.presidency.gov.eg/
Sponsor: Egypt. Government
Description: This English-language site has information on the president, news releases, a profile of Egypt, and an archive of presidential addresses. There is little additional information on the rest of the government.

4626. Egyptian Shoura Assembly
http://www.shoura.gov.eg/
Sponsor: Egypt. Parliament
Description: The Shoura Assembly is the upper house of the Egyptian parliament. This site is in Arabic with an English language option. It has information on current members and committees, and a brief history of the Shoura Assembly.

El Salvador

4627. Presidency of El Salvador
http://www.casapres.gob.sv/
Sponsor: El Salvador. Government
Description: This Web site includes basic information on the president, vice president, and government of El Salvador. The Government section has biographies of the ministers and links to their ministry sites, as well as links to independent agencies. The site is in Spanish.

Estonia

4628. Estonia - Official State Web Center
http://www.riik.ee/et/
Sponsor: Estonia. Government
Description: This government portal site is in Estonian, English, and Russian. It provides information on Estonian government, parliament, the president (including press releases and speeches), the supreme court, and various ministries and offices.

4629. Parliament of Estonia
http://www.riigikogu.ee/
Sponsor: Estonia. Parliament
Description: The site for the Riigikogu, Estonia's parliament, is available in Estonian, English, and Russian. It has information on procedure, members, and committees. The Chancellery section contains policy studies, the parliamentary journal in Estonian, and other research information.

Ethiopia

4630. Federal Democratic Republic of Ethiopia Spokesperson
http://www.ethiospokes.net/
Sponsor: Ethiopia. Government
Description: This site is in English and generally has press releases and information about the Ethiopian Eritrean Conflict. Some basic information on the government and the economy is also available.

Federated States of Micronesia

4631. Congress of the Federated States of Micronesia
http://www.fsmcongress.org/
Sponsor: Federated States of Micronesia. Parliament
Description: This well-organized site includes the full text of pending bills and approved laws in PDF format. Press releases, committee information, and daily schedules and hearing notices are also included.

4632. Information on the Federated States of Micronesia
http://www.fsmgov.org/info/
Sponsor: Federated States of Micronesia. Government
Description: This portal site has sections for the national government, congress, and state governments. It also provides topical access under headings such as History, People, Health, Economy, Investment, and Foreign Affairs.

Fiji

4633. Fiji Government Online
http://www.fiji.gov.fj/
Sponsor: Fiji. Government
Description: In English, this portal site offers a variety of sections including Press Releases, President, Cabinet, Parliament, Judiciary, Missions and Departments, Fiji Links, and Fiji Missions Overseas.

Finland

4634. Finnish Government
http://valtioneuvosto.fi/liston/base.lsp
Alternate URL: http://www.vn.fi/
Sponsor: Finland. Parliament
Description: This Web site of the government of Finland links to a wide variety of news, information, and Web sites for the Finnish government and ministries. It has an English version and a text-only version.

4635. Suomen Eduskunta - Parliament of Finland
http://www.eduskunta.fi/
Sponsor: Finland. Parliament
Description: This site provides basic information about the Finnish parliament and has an English version. Sections include Members, Committees, Library of Parliament, and History of the Finnish Parliament.

France

4636. French National Assembly
http://www.assemblee-nat.fr/
Sponsor: France. Parliament
Description: The French national parliament site has extensive information on the sessions, schedules, documents, and activities of the assembly, including the option to view sessions on streaming video. An English language version offers top and second level pages in English but many substantive pages are not translated.

4637. Office of the French President
http://www.elysee.fr/ang/
Sponsor: France. Government
Description: This is the English language version of the Web site for the president of the French republic. The Institutions section includes the constitution and historical documents, and Web sites for the major executive offices. There are also sections for presidential speeches and communiques of the council of ministers.

Gambia

4638. Republic of The Gambia
http://www.gambia.gm/
Sponsor: Gambia. Government
Description: This official Gambian Web site is in English and is maintained by the Gambian Department of State for Trade, Industry, and Employment. Its focus is on business and investment in The Gambia.

Georgia (Republic)

4639. Parliament of Georgia
http://www.parliament.ge/
Sponsor: Georgia (Republic). Parliament
Description: This English language version has information about Georgia, the parliament, its structure, information about the laws, and activities of the current session.

4640. Press Office of the President of Georgia
http://www.presidpress.gov.ge/
Sponsor: Georgia (Republic). Government
Description: This English-language site features the president's biography, speeches, messages, and interviews. It also includes the state constitution.

Germany

4641. Bundesregierung Deutschland
http://www.bundesregierung.de/
Sponsor: Germany. Government
Description: This central site for the government of Germany links to recent news, press releases, ministries and the cabinet, and government policies and programs. It is in German with versions also available in English, Spanish, and French.

4642. Deutscher Bundestag—German Parliament
http://www.bundestag.de/
Sponsor: Germany. Government
Description: The Bundestag's site includes information about the organization of the parliament; the legislative process; member biographies; election information, calendar of sessions, and information for visitors; and some databases. The site is in German, with English and French versions.

Ghana

4643. Republic of Ghana
http://www.ghana.gov.gh/
Sponsor: Ghana. Government
Description: This Ghana government portal site organizes information under topical sections such as Investing, Governing, and Visiting, and has an A–Z index. The Governing section links to the ministries, council of state, legislature, and judiciary.

Greece

4644. Hellenic Parliament
http://www.parliament.gr/
Sponsor: Greece. Parliament
Description: Available in Greek and English, this site presents descriptive information including the organization and history of the Parliament.

4645. Hellenic Republic The Prime Minister's Office
http://www.primeminister.gr/
Sponsor: Greece. Government
Description: In Greek with an English mirror, this is the official page from the prime minister's office. Sections include Prime Minister, Cabinet, and Speeches and Releases.

Guatemala

4646. Congress of the Republic of Guatemala
http://www.congreso.gob.gt/
Sponsor: Guatemala. Parliament
Description: This site for Guatemala's unicameral legislature is in Spanish. It includes information on members, procedures, and legislation.

Guinea

4647. République de Guinée
http://www.guinee.gov.gn/
Sponsor: Guinea. Government
Description: In French, this site features links for the president, the National Assembly, other government bodies, and other political and economic topics, as well as information about the country.

Guyana

4648. Government Information Agency, Guyana
http://www.gina.gov.gy/
Sponsor: Guyana. Government
Description: The Government Information Agency site carries the text of presidential speeches and statements, government news, and links to the ministries and other institutions.

4649. Parliament of Guyana
http://www.sdnp.org.gy/parliament/
Sponsor: Guyana. Parliament
Description: This site provides general information on the parliament and its members, and lists Acts of Parliament back to 1993.

Haiti

4650. Embassy of Haiti
http://www.haiti.org/
Sponsor: Haiti. Government
Description: The Haitian Embassy to the United States provides this site. The Government section, in English, has basic information on the president, executive branch, and other government institutions.

Holy See (Vatican City)

4651. Vatican: The Holy See
http://www.vatican.va/
Sponsor: Holy See (Vatican City). Government
Description: This site, available in English and other languages, includes news and press announcements and information on the Vatican City State, as well as information about the papacy and the Catholic church.

Honduras

4652. National Congress of Honduras
http://www.congreso.gob.hn/
Sponsor: Honduras. Parliament
Description: This site provides extensive information about and from the congress, in Spanish.

4653. Presidency of the Republic of Honduras
http://www.casapresidencial.hn/
Sponsor: Honduras. Government
Description: The Presidency offers a well organized site with a wealth of information, in Spanish. The site includes news releases, a Cabinet directory, biographies of past presidents, links to government sites, and topical sections such as Health, Agriculture, and Education.

Hungary

4654. Hungarian National Assembly
http://www.mkogy.hu/
Sponsor: Hungary. Parliament
Description: In Hungarian, this site provides a basic overview and information on the Hungarian National Assembly's factions and parliamentary organizations. The English version has limited information, with links to the NATO Information Center and EU Integration Web sites.

4655. Prime Minister's Office, Hungary
http://www.meh.hu/
Sponsor: Hungary. Government
Description: This site offers information on the Prime Minister and the government ministries of Hungary. It is available in English and Hungarian.

Iceland

4656. Althingi
http://www.althingi.is/
Sponsor: Iceland. Parliament
Description: The Althingi is the parliament of Iceland. Primarily in Icelandic, the site includes some pages available in English and Danish.

4657. Government Offices of Iceland
http://www.stjr.is/interpro/stjr/stjr.nsf/pages/index.html
Alternate URL: http://iceland.org/
Sponsor: Iceland. Government
Description: The Web site of the Icelandic Government includes information about the prime minister, government ministries, and news and policy statements. It also links to the legislative and judicial branches. It is in Icelandic with an English version. The alternate URL is the official Web site of the Icelandic Foreign Service, an English-language site featuring information about Iceland and links to government Web sites.

India

4658. Government of India—Directory of Official Web Sites
http://goidirectory.nic.in/
Sponsor: India. Government
Description: This directory Web site provides links to Web sites of ministries, departments, states, organizations, and other government institutions and bodies. The site is in English.

4659. Indian Parliament
http://parliamentofindia.nic.in/
Sponsor: India. Parliament
Description: This site features information on the Parliament with links to the Council of States (Rajya Sabha) and the House of the People (Lok Sabha) as well as links to the government and the President.

Indonesia

4660. Indonesian Parliament
http://www.dpr.go.id/
Sponsor: Indonesia. Parliament
Description: This is the site of the Parliament of Indonesia and is only in Indonesian.

Iran

4661. Presidency of the Islamic Republic of Iran
http://www.president.ir/
Sponsor: Iran. Government
Description: This official site provides information on the Iranian President, members of his Cabinet, speeches, and news. This is an English-language version with a link to the Farsi page.

Iraq

4662. Iraqi Presidency
http://www.uruklink.net/iraq/
Sponsor: Iraq. Government
Description: The Web site for Iraqi President Saddam Hussein includes presidential speeches and summaries of the council of ministers meetings. There is an English-language version.

Ireland

4663. Ireland - Information on the Irish State
http://www.irlgov.ie/
Sponsor: Ireland. Government
Description: This portal site for the Irish government organizes links to government information by agency and by topic. It links to special portals for citizens and for businesses, and has general information about Ireland. The site has both Gaelic and English versions.

4664. Parliament of Ireland
http://www.irlgov.ie/oireachtas/
Sponsor: Ireland. Parliament
Description: This English language page for the Oireachtas, the Irish parliament, offers information and links to both chambers, committees, debates, members, and more.

Israel

4665. State of Israel Government Gateway
http://www.info.gov.il/eng/mainpage.asp
Sponsor: Israel. Government
Description: This gateway site provides links to government information by ministry and subject headings. It includes a keyword search engine and has Hebrew and English versions.

4666. The Knesset—The Israeli Parliament
http://www.knesset.gov.il/index.html
Sponsor: Ireland. Parliament
Description: In Hebrew, Arabic, and English, this site provides information from and about the Israeli Knesset including its powers and functions, laws, membership, parties, elections, and documents.

Italy

4667. Governo Italiano
http://www.palazzochigi.it/
Sponsor: Italy. Government
Description: The Italian Prime Minister's site provides government news and information on the ministries and departments. The site is in Italian.

4668. Parlamento Italiano
http://www.parlamento.it/
Sponsor: Italy. Parliament
Description: This site links to pages for the Camera dei Deputati and the Senato della Repubblica. The site is in Italian with the option to view pages in English and other languages.

Jamaica

4669. Government of Jamaica, Cabinet Office
http://www.cabinet.gov.jm/
Sponsor: Jamaica. Government
Description: The Jamaican government site has sections for the Cabinet Ministers, Press Briefings, Important Documents, Speeches, and government Web site links.

Japan

4670. National Diet of Japan
http://www.sangiin.go.jp/eng/index.htm
Alternate URL: http://www.shugiin.go.jp/itdb_main.nsf/html/index_e.htm
Sponsor: Japan. Parliament
Description: Available in both Japanese and English, the Sangiin (House of Councillors) site offers information on this chamber of the National Diet of Japan. The alternate URL is for the Shugiin (House of Representatives), the second chamber of the National Diet, and is also available in Japanese and English.

4671. Prime Minister of Japan
http://www.kantei.go.jp/foreign/index-e.html
Sponsor: Japan. Government
Description: This English counterpart to the Japanese original provides information on the prime minister; his activities, speeches, and policy initiatives; and the Cabinet. The Governmental Framework section includes an organization chart with links to the ministry sites.

Jordan

4672. Jordan National Information System
http://www.nic.gov.jo/
Sponsor: Jordan. Government
Description: This government portal site has links to the parliament and ministry Web sites. It also links to government information by topic. There is an English and an Arabic version of the site.

Kazakhstan

4673. Official Kazakhstan
http://www.president.kz/
Sponsor: Kazakhstan. Government
Description: Major sections of this site include State, Economy, and Culture. The State section has background information on the structure and individual components of the Kazakh government. The site has both English and Kazakh versions.

Kenya

4674. State House, Kenya
http://www.statehousekenya.go.ke/
Sponsor: Kenya. Government
Description: This site of the president of Kenya mainly provides information about the president and his activities and staff. The Government section has links to the National Assembly, ministries, government offices and departments.

Korea, South

4675. Korea.net: Korean Government
http://www.korea.net/
Alternate URL: http://www.kois.go.kr/
Sponsor: Korea, South. Government
Description: This portal site, available in English, is maintained by the government's Korean Information Service. The Government section has information on all branches of government, and a section for laws and regulations. Other major sections include Economy, Culture, and Issues. Patience is required when accessing these sites because of the significant download time for the many images.

4676. National Assembly of the Republic of Korea
http://www.assembly.go.kr/
Sponsor: Korea, South. Parliament
Description: Almost entirely in Korean, this is the official site for the National Assembly of the Republic of Korea. There is a reduced-content English version also, which gives general information about the assembly, the laws, and the members.

Kuwait

4677. Kuwait National Assembly
http://www.alommah.gov.kw/
Sponsor: Kuwait. Parliament
Description: The English language version of this site has information on the Kuwaiti Constitution, assembly elections, and democratic principles.

Kyrgyz Republic

4678. Kyrgyz Republic
http://www.gov.kg/cgi-bin/page.pl
Sponsor: Kyrgyzstan. Government
Description: In Russian only, this site features news and information on the Kyrgyzstan Republic.

Laos

4679. Lao Embassy to USA
http://www.laoembassy.com/
Sponsor: Laos. Government
Description: This English-language site presents brief information on government officials and members of the National Assembly and links to the Foreign Affairs Ministry page.

Latvia

4680. Chancery of the President
http://www.president.lv/
Sponsor: Latvia. Government
Description: The Chancery of the President of Latvia offers this site, available in an English version, with information on the president, speeches, and news and press conferences. A Links section covers state agencies and related sites.

4681. Latvijas Republikas Saeima
http://www.saeima.lv/
Sponsor: Latvia. Parliament
Description: The Parliament of Latvia site is available only in Latvian. It presents information on the structure, proceedings, and history of the Saeima.

Lebanon

4682. Lebanese Parliament
http://www.lp.gov.lb/
Sponsor: Lebanon. Parliament
Description: This site provides basic information on the Parliament of Lebanon, its members, and its committees. It is in Arabic with an English version also available.

4683. Lebanese President
http://www.presidency.gov.lb/
Sponsor: Lebanon. Government
Description: The Lebanese presidential site has an English language option and basic information on the president and the presidency. Under Presidency, the Links section includes Web sites for the ministries, agencies, and other institutions.

Lesotho

4684. Lesotho Government Official Website
http://www.lesotho.gov.ls/
Sponsor: Lesotho. Government
Description: The Lesotho government Web site has a portal structure, with current government news, official documents, links to the ministries, and topical links such as Politics, Tourism, Economy, and Health.

Liechtenstein

4685. Principality of Liechtenstein
http://www.fuerstenhaus.li/
Sponsor: Liechtenstein. Government
Description: In German with an English language option, this site presents government information under the State section which covers the executive, judicial, and legislative branches. Other sections cover the economy and business, community profiles, and the Liechtenstein noble family.

Lithuania

4686. Government of the Republic of Lithuania
http://www.lrvk.lt/
Sponsor: Lithuania. Government
Description: In Lithuanian with an English version, this site includes information on the prime minister, links to the ministries, and the policy agenda of the government.

4687. Parliament of the Republic of Lithuania
http://www.lrs.lt/
Sponsor: Lithuania. Parliament
Description: The Web site of the Parliament of Lithuania is in Lithuanian with an English mirror. It includes information on the parliament's structure, procedures, and history, and the full text of important laws.

Luxembourg

4688. Le Gouvernement Luxembourgeouis
http://www.gouvernement.lu/
Sponsor: Luxembourg. Government
Description: In French, this site includes detailed information on the government and its program and budget. Publications can be viewed or purchased online.

4689. Luxembourg Chamber of Deputies
http://www.chd.lu/default.jsp
Sponsor: Luxembourg. Parliament
Description: The Chamber of Deputies site is in French. It includes information on leadership, members, and schedules, and has an option to view sessions online. Information on bills, parliamentary questions, and laws can be found under Portail Documentaire.

Macedonia (Former Yugoslav Republic)

4690. Government of the Republic of Macedonia
http://www.gov.mk/
Sponsor: Macedonia (Former Yugoslav Republic). Government
Description: This site, available in Macedonian and English, features information on government bodies, Cabinet members, national symbols, and links to other government sites.

Madagascar

4691. Malagasy National Assembly
http://www.assemblee-nationale.mg/en/index.htm
Sponsor: Madagascar. Parliament
Description: The Madagascar parliamentary site is in French with an English-language version.

Malawi

4692. Government of the Republic of Malawi
http://www.malawi.gov.mw/
Sponsor: Malawi. Government
Description: This central site organizes links to the ministries under the headings General Administration, Social and Community Services, and Economic Services.

Malaysia

4693. Parliament of Malaysia
http://www.parlimen.gov.my/
Sponsor: Malaysia. Parliament
Description: This parliamentary site has an English-language version. It covers both the Senate and the House of Representatives and includes bills, laws, and proceedings. Official documents are in Malay.

4694. Prime Minister's Office of Malaysia
http://www.smpke.jpm.my/
Sponsor: Malaysia. Government
Description: This site features sections on the Prime Minister, the Prime Minister's Office, the Government, News, Referral Information, and Links. The pages are in English.

Maldives

4695. President's Office, Republic of Maldives
http://www.presidencymaldives.gov.mv/v3/
Sponsor: Maldives. Government
Description: This site has an English-language version and provides the president's speeches, an overview of the government, and sections on national development and environmental protection.

Malta

4696. Gov.mt
http://www.gov.mt
Sponsor: Malta. Government
Description: Gov.mt, the Maltese government's official portal site, has an English-language version. The site includes topical access to government information under such headings as Education, Health, and Housing. Each topical section includes links to the relevant institutions.

Marshall Islands

4697. Republic of the Marshall Islands
http://www.rmiembassyus.org/
Sponsor: Marshall Islands. Government
Description: This Marshall Islands site is hosted by the government's embassy in the United States. It includes information on the current government and has sections on the economy, tourism, and the history of nuclear testing.

Mauritania

4698. Site officiel du gouvernement
http://www.mauritania.mr/
Sponsor: Mauritania. Government
Description: This site is in French; a link to an English version is not functional at this time. It includes sections such as Economy, News, Administration, Tourism, and Culture.

Mauritius

4699. Government of Mauritius
http://ncb.intnet.mu/govt/house.htm
Sponsor: Mauritius. Government
Description: This English-language site features sections entitled Our Constitution, Ministers, Ministries, Governmental Bodies, and Parliament Members among others.

Mexico

4700. Mexico Legislature
http://www.cddhcu.gob.mx/
Alternate URL: http://www.camaradediputados.gob.mx/
Sponsor: Mexico. Parliament
Description: The primary URL above is for the Cámara de Diputados site. For the Senado de la República, see the alternate URL. Each contains a wealth of news and information about their schedule, members, committees, and laws in Spanish.

4701. Presidency of the Republic of Mexico
http://www.presidencia.gob.mx/
Sponsor: Mexico. Government
Description: The site for the president of Mexico features information on the president, his Cabinet, agenda, and government news, in Spanish.

Mongolia

4702. Parliament of Mongolia
http://www.parl.gov.mn/
Sponsor: Mongolia. Parliament
Description: This site is in Russian with an English version. Major sections include Sessions, Standing Committees, Who's Who, and Law Library.

Morocco

4703. Kingdom of Morocco—Royaume du Maroc
http://www.mincom.gov.ma/
Sponsor: Morocco. Government
Description: This Morocco site features detailed news and information about the country and its government. See the Government section for links to the ministries. The site has Arabic, French, English, and Spanish versions.

Mozambique

4704. Página Oficial de Moçambique
http://www.mozambique.mz/
Sponsor: Mozambique. Government
Description: This site offers basic facts about the country and has links to such sections as Government, Parliament, Economy, Health, and Environment. The site is available in Portuguese and English.

Myanmar

4705. Myanmar - The Golden Land
http://www.myanmar.com/
Sponsor: Myanmar. Government
Description: This site offers general information on the country and links to government information such Ministry Home Pages and Press Releases.

Namibia

4706. Namibian Parliament
http://www.parliament.gov.na/default.asp
Sponsor: Namibia. Parliament
Description: The Parliament of Namibia site includes information from both houses, the National Assembly and the National Council. Overview information and information on bills, acts, and publications is in a shared Parliament section.

Nepal

4707. Nepali Congress
http://www.nepalicongress.org.np/index.php
Sponsor: Nepal. Parliament
Description: This site has news, information, a history, and documents regarding the Nepali Congress. The site is in Nepali but sections can be viewed in English.

Netherlands

4708. Het Parlement - The Dutch Parliament
http://www.parlement.nl/
Sponsor: Netherlands. Parliament
Description: The Dutch Parliament Web site links to both the Eerste Kamer (Upper House) and the Tweede Kamer (Lower House). The sites are in Dutch.

New Zealand

4709. Govt.nz - New Zealand Government Online
http://www.govt.nz/
Sponsor: New Zealand. Government
Description: This government portal has an A–Z index to government agencies and their Web sites, news, and information on government services. The site is in English.

4710. New Zealand Parliament
http://www.parliament.govt.nz/
Sponsor: New Zealand. Parliament
Description: The New Zealand Parliament Web site features links to House and Committees, Ministers, Politics and News, Visiting Parliament, Parliamentary Agencies, and Executive Government Agencies. The site is in English.

Nicaragua

4711. National Assembly of the Republic of Nicaragua
http://www.asamblea.gob.ni/
Sponsor: Nicaragua. Parliament
Description: In Spanish, the Nicaraguan National Assembly site has information on its members, committees, and legislative documents. The links section includes links to government agencies, news sources, and other sites.

4712. Presidency of the Republic of Nicaragua
http://www.presidencia.gob.ni/
Sponsor: Nicaragua. Government
Description: In Spanish, this site has information on the president and his Cabinet, and executive publications.

Nigeria

4713. Presidency of Nigeria
http://www.nopa.net/
Alternate URL: http://www.nigeria-consulate-atl.org/
Sponsor: Nigeria. Government
Description: This Web site from the president of Nigeria features information about the government and the president in such sections as Rebuilding Nigeria, Remarkable Speeches, Useful Information, and Government Websites. The alternate URL features additional news and information about the government from the consulate in Atlanta.

Norway

4714. ODIN
http://odin.dep.no/
Sponsor: Norway. Government
Description: ODIN is the central Web site for the Norwegian Government, the Office of the Prime Minister, and the ministries. It has pages in Norwegian and English with a few available in French and German as well.

4715. Stortinget - The Norwegian Parliament
http://www.stortinget.no/
Sponsor: Norway. Parliament
Description: In Norwegian with an option to view some English-language pages, this site has information on the members, constitution, rules of procedure, committees, and parties.

Oman

4716. Sultanate of Oman, Ministry of Information
http://www.omanet.com/
Sponsor: Oman. Government
Description: Maintained by the Ministry of Information, this site includes sections on the government, culture, economy, and history of Oman. It links to other ministries and to other government and non-government sites. The site is in Arabic with an English-language version.

Pakistan

4717. Islamic Republic of Pakistan
http://www.pak.gov.pk/
Sponsor: Pakistan. Government
Description: This official Web site is in English with sections on the government, economy, president, and chief executive.

Panama

4718. Presidency of the Republic of Panama
http://www.presidencia.gob.pa/
Sponsor: Panama. Government
Description: This site features basic information on the president, the government structure, and the Presidential Palace. It is in Spanish.

Papua New Guinea

4719. Prime Minister's Office of Papua New Guinea
http://www.pm.gov.pg/pmsoffice/PMsoffice.nsf
Sponsor: Papua New Guinea. Government
Description: In English, this site offers press releases, archives, and a photo gallery on the prime minister.

Paraguay

4720. Portal Paraguay Gobierno
http://www.paraguaygobierno.gov.py/
Sponsor: Paraguay. Government
Description: In Spanish, this government portal links to the executive, legislative, and judicial branches, and presents the official gazette and other documents.

Peru

4721. Congress of the Republic of Peru
http://www.congreso.gob.pe/en/index.asp
Sponsor: Peru. Parliament
Description: This site is subtitled "Parliamentary Portal of Peru and the World." In addition to the legislative information, it includes information about Peru and links to government Web sites. The default language is Spanish. Most top-level pages are available in English, but documents and most substantive, updated content has not been translated.

4722. Portal of the Peruvian Government
http://www.perugobierno.gob.pe/
Sponsor: Peru. Government
Description: This Spanish-language government portal links to information from the executive, legislative, and judicial branches. It includes an alphabetical list of links to government agencies and a topical index to government services for the citizen.

Philippines

4723. Office of the President Network
http://www.opnet.ops.gov.ph/
Sponsor: Philippines. Government
Description: This English-language page features information about the executive branch of government and has links to such sections as Press Releases, Speeches, and Directives and Issuances.

4724. Philippine House of Representatives
http://www.congress.gov.ph/
Sponsor: Philippines. Government
Description: This English-language page features extensive information from the Philippine House of Representatives including sections on legislation, schedules, and publications.

Poland

4725. Official Web Site of Poland
http://www.poland.pl/
Sponsor: Poland. Government
Description: This portal site, in English with a Polish mirror version, covers news and information related to all aspects of Polish life. The State and Government section has an extensive directory of links to Polish and international government sites.

Portugal

4726. Parliament of Portugal
http://www.parlamento.pt/
Sponsor: Portugal. Parliament
Description: The Portuguese Parliament site includes extensive information about the parliament, its members, committees, and activities. Some pages have been translated into English but most of the site is only available in Portuguese.

4727. Portugal Government Portal
http://www.portugal.gov.pt/
Sponsor: Portugal. Government
Description: This Portuguese government site includes an English-language version, although many of the sections have not yet been translated. The site provides government information and links, focusing on the executive branch.

Qatar

4728. Amiri Diwan - State of Qatar
http://www.diwan.gov.qa/
Sponsor: Qatar. Government
Description: The Qatar government site is in Arabic with an English-language version. The site includes the speeches of the Amir and the Prime Minister and a directory of executive support offices.

Romania

4729. Government of Romania
http://www.gov.ro/engleza/index.html
Sponsor: Romania. Government
Description: The English version of this government portal site offers links to government press releases and policy information, directory listings and Web links for the ministries, and links to the parliamentary Web sites.

Russia

4730. Russian Duma
http://www.duma.ru/
Sponsor: Russia. Parliament
Description: This is the official Web site for the Duma, the Russian Parliament. The site is in Russian and includes sections on the Duma history, members, laws, and parliamentary library.

4731. Russian Government
http://www.gov.ru/
Sponsor: Russia. Government
Description: This is the Web site of the Russian Federation administration. It features official information and documents from the Russian president and links to other official government Web sites. It is in Russian.

Rwanda

4732. Republic of Rwanda
http://www.gov.rw/
Sponsor: Rwanda. Government
Description: In English, this site provides information about the country and government of Rwanda. It links to the Web sites for the president and the transitional national assembly. Other sections cover the issue of reconciliation and reconstruction after the 1994 genocide.

Saint Kitts and Nevis

4733. Government of St. Kitts and Nevis
http://www.stkittsnevis.net/
Sponsor: Saint Kitts and Nevis. Government
Description: This English-language site includes a government directory for access to contact information to the ministries, information on the current budget, a legislative agenda, and general information on this twin-island nation. There are links to other St. Kitts and Nevis-related Web sites.

Saint Lucia

4734. Government of Saint Lucia
http://www.stlucia.gov.lc/
Sponsor: Saint Lucia. Government
Description: The portal site for this West Indies country includes links to all branches of government, the official gazette, speeches, and press releases.

Saudi Arabia

4735. Royal Embassy of Saudi Arabia
http://www.saudiembassy.net/
Sponsor: Saudi Arabia. Government
Description: The Royal Embassy of Saudi Arabia in Washington, DC, hosts this English-language site. The site offers major government news or statements, and its country profile section includes descriptive information about the Saudi government.

Senegal

4736. Republic of Senegal
http://www.gouv.sn/
Sponsor: Senegal. Government
Description: This official site for the Republic of Senegal includes links to all major agencies and branches of government, news, publications, and featured topics such as investing in Senegal and Senegalese international relations. It is in French.

Serbia and Montenegro

4737. Serbia and Montenegro
http://www.gov.yu/
Sponsor: Yugoslavia. Government
Description: Serbia and Montenegro, recently renamed from the Federal Republic of Yugoslavia, has not established Web content for its new identity. This site is largely under construction at the time of this writing.

Singapore

4738. Parliament House of Singapore
http://www.gov.sg/parliament/
Sponsor: Singapore. Parliament
Description: The official site for the Parliament of Singapore includes information about the Parliament, bills introduced, parliamentary committees, members, and speeches. The Web site is in English.

4739. Singapore Government Online Portal
http://www.gov.sg/
Sponsor: Singapore. Government
Description: This portal site links to government news, information, and online services. It includes a search engine and list of links for government agencies.

Slovakia

4740. National Council of the Slovak Republic
http://www.nrsr.sk/
Sponsor: Slovakia. Parliament
Description: This site of the National Council of the Slovak Republic is available in Slovak with a smaller English language version. The English-language version is largely descriptive, with background information on the Council and its structure.

4741. Slovak Republic Government Office
http://www.government.gov.sk/
Sponsor: Slovakia. Government
Description: The Government Office site is in Slovak with an English-language version. It includes government news, policy, speeches, and documents.

Slovenia

4742. Republic of Slovenia
http://www.sigov.si/
Sponsor: Slovenia. Government
Description: This is the official site of the Republic of Slovenia. It offers parallel versions in Slovene and English and links to information from the president, prime minister, parliament, and judiciary.

South Africa

4743. Parliament of South Africa
http://www.parliament.gov.za/
Sponsor: South Africa. Parliament
Description: This English-language site of the Parliament of South Africa features links to the National Assembly, committees, parliamentary papers, bills, acts, public hearings, and publications.

4744. South African Government Online
http://www.gov.za/
Sponsor: South Africa. Government
Description: The South African government site features links to departments, ministers, the government system, local and provincial governments, reports, documents, and forms. The site is in English.

Spain

4745. La Moncloa Web
http://www.la-moncloa.es/
Sponsor: Spain. Government
Description: Named for the presidential palace, this site includes extensive information on the ministries and links to major state institutions such as the royal household, the congress, and the judiciary. It is in Spanish with English and French versions.

4746. Senate of Spain
http://www.senado.es/
Alternate URL: http://www.congreso.es/
Sponsor: Spain. Government
Description: The Spanish Senate's site features information on the Senate, its procedures and bills, publications, definitions and rules, and other documents. The main site is in Spanish but some of the content is mirrored in English. The alternate URL connects to the Web site of the Congreso de los Diputados and is primarily in Spanish.

Sri Lanka

4747. Sri Lanka—Official Web Site of the Government
http://www.priu.gov.lk/
Sponsor: Sri Lanka. Government
Description: This official site of the government of Sri Lanka, sponsored by the Presidential

Secretariat, has links to various sections including Government, President, Prime Minister, Parliament, and Ministries. The site features contact information for all Sri Lankan ministries and institutions and has links to other government Web sites. The site is in English.

Swaziland

4748. Swaziland Government
http://www.swazi.com/government/
Sponsor: Swaziland. Government
Description: In English, this official Web site of the Swaziland government offers information on government ministries, the prime minister, speeches, and a link to the government newsletter, *Swaziland Today.*

Sweden

4749. Riksdag - Swedish Parliament
http://www.riksdagen.se/
Sponsor: Sweden. Parliament
Description: In Swedish with an English version, the Sveriges Riksdag (Swedish Parliament) site features information about members, news, and documents.

4750. Swedish Government
http://www.regeringen.se/
Sponsor: Sweden. Government
Description: In Swedish with an English version, the site offers such sections about the Swedish government as Members of Government, Ministries, Legislation, System of Government, and Government Agencies.

Switzerland

4751. Federal Authorities of the Swiss Confederation
http://www.admin.ch/
Sponsor: Switzerland. Government
Description: With an English language version, this Swiss government site links to the major government officers and agencies as well as to the legislative and judicial sites. It also links to the Web sites for each of the cantons of Switzerland.

Syria

4752. Syrian Arab Republic - The Parliament
http://www.syria-people-council.org/english/
Sponsor: Syria. Parliament
Description: The English-language version of this site includes sections on the history of the parliament, the legislative process, members, committees, and documents. It also links to other government Web sites.

Taiwan

4753. Legislative Yuan
http://www.ly.gov.tw/
Sponsor: Taiwan. Parliament
Description: The Legislative Yuan is the parliamentary body of Taiwan. Its Web site is in Chinese with an English language version.

4754. The Executive Yuan of the Republic of China
http://www.ey.gov.tw/web/index.htm
Sponsor: Taiwan. Government
Description: The Executive Yuan is the highest administrative agency for the Taiwan government. Its Web site is in Chinese with a mirror site in English. The English site has such sections as Organization of the Executive Yuan and Its Functions, Members of the Cabinet, Premier, Web Sites of the Executive Yuan, and National Statistics.

Thailand

4755. Royal Thai Government
http://www.thaigov.go.th/
Sponsor: Thailand. Government
Description: In both English and Thai, this site features information in the following sections: the Prime Ministers, Government House, the Cabinet, Government Policies, and Press Releases and Speeches.

4756. Thai Parliament
http://www.parliament.go.th/
Sponsor: Thailand. Parliament
Description: This official Web site of the Thai National Assembly has versions available in Thai and in English. It includes information in such sections as the National Assembly, the Library of Parliament, and Political Parties.

Togo

4757. Republic of Togo
http://www.republicoftogo.com/
Sponsor: Togo. Government
Description: Available in French and English, this site includes a government directory and features information on foreign affairs, the economy, and domestic politics.

Trinidad and Tobago

4758. Government of Trinidad and Tobago
http://www.gov.tt/
Sponsor: Trinidad and Tobago. Government
Description: The Trinidad and Tobago Web site features information on the economy, government news and speeches, and the government's agenda. The Government section of the site features links to the president, prime minister, the Senate and Parliament, and the judiciary.

4759. Parliament of the Republic of Trinidad and Tobago
http://www.ttparliament.org/
Sponsor: Trinidad and Tobago. Parliament
Description: This English-language site features information about the Parliament of the Republic of Trinidad and Tobago. It offers the following sections: Notable Offices, Senate, House of Representatives, Committees, Hansard, and Legislation.

Tunisia

4760. Site du Gouvernement Tunisien
http://www.ministeres.tn/
Sponsor: Tunisia. Government
Description: This site offers information on the Tunisian government and its ministries along with some country information and government publications. The site is in French.

Turkey

4761. Turkish Grand National Assembly
http://www.tbmm.gov.tr/
Sponsor: Turkey. Parliament
Description: The official site of the Turkish Parliament features links to a few pages in English, which offer information on the Turkish constitution and the text of several publications.

4762. Turkish Presidency
http://www.cankaya.gov.tr/
Sponsor: Turkey. Government
Description: This is the official Web site of the Presidency of Turkey. It is only available in Turkish.

Uganda

4763. Government of Uganda
http://www.government.go.ug/
Sponsor: Uganda. Government
Description: This site features information about the structure of the Uganda Government, government news, offices and addresses of the officers in ministries, and links to the executive, judiciary, parliament, and the constitution. The page is in English.

4764. Parliament of the Republic of Uganda
http://www.parliament.go.ug/
Sponsor: Uganda. Government
Description: This site features information about the structure of the Ugandan Parliament. The site is under construction, and only the following sections are available: History, Constitution, MPs, Administration, and Parliamentary Updates. The page is in English.

Ukraine

4765. Ukrainian Government Portal
http://www.kmu.gov.ua/
Sponsor: Ukraine. Government
Description: In Ukrainian with an English version, this portal links to the government agencies and the legislature and has a search engine. Other sections provide information on the country, the economy, and government services.

United Arab Emirates

4766. Federal National Council
http://www.almajles.gov.ae/
Sponsor: United Arab Emirates. Government
Description: This site is in Arabic with an English-language version. It has information on the role, members, and documents of the council.

4767. United Arab Emirates Government Gateway
http://www.uae.gov.ae/
Sponsor: United Arab Emirates. Government
Description: In Arabic and English, this site links to the ministries and provides quick links to types of information, such as statistics, available from the ministries. A section called UAE 2000 provides information by topic, such as political systems, the economy, and oil and gas.

United Kingdom

4768. Houses of Parliament
http://www.parliament.uk/
Sponsor: United Kingdom. Parliament
Description: This site features information about and direct links to the House of Commons and the House of Lords. The content includes the Hansard reports of debates, information on bills before Parliament, a directory of members, links to committee Web pages, and parliamentary publications and archives.

4769. UK online
http://www.ukonline.gov.uk/
Sponsor: United Kingdom. Government
Description: This central site for the government of the United Kingdom offers current government news, a search engine, and A to Z indexes to national and local government Web sites. Other sections include links to government services online and a newsroom.

Uruguay

4770. Legislature of the Republic of Uruguay
http://www.parlamento.gub.uy/
Sponsor: Uruguay. Parliament
Description: This Spanish-language site from the Parliament of Uruguay provides basic information about the Parliament with links to legislation, legislators and both houses, new developments, and current activities.

4771. Presidency of the Republic of Uruguay
http://www.presidencia.gub.uy/
Sponsor: Uruguay. Government
Description: This central government page features general information, history, government organizations, a guide to state services, and a link to the Web site of the president. The site is in Spanish.

Uzbekistan

4772. Press Service of the President of the Republic of Uzbekistan
http://www.press-service.uz/
Sponsor: Uzbekistan. Government
Description: The Press Service site is in English and Russian. It includes presidential news, speeches, and documents.

Vanuatu

4773. Government of the Republic of Vanuatu
http://www.vanuatugovernment.gov.vu/
Sponsor: Vanuatu. Government
Description: This English-language site includes information on the country, its government structure, the president and prime minister, and government news.

Venezuela

4774. Presidency of the Republic of Venezuela
http://www.venezuela.gov.ve/
Sponsor: Venezuela. Government
Description: In Spanish, this site offers information on the president and his Cabinet, government ministries, the branches of government, the official gazette, and the government agenda.

Vietnam

4775. National Assembly of the Socialist Republic of Vietnam
http://www.na.gov.vn/
Sponsor: Vietnam. Parliament
Description: This official Vietnamese site has an English-language version. It includes basic background information on the assembly and Vietnamese government.

Yemen

4776. Republic of Yemen House of Representatives
http://www.parliament.gov.ye/
Sponsor: Yemen. Parliament
Description: In Arabic, this site offers basic information on the heads of state and the Yemen House of Representatives, including members, activities, and the constitution.

Sponsor Name/Site Name Index

This index lists Web site names by the sponsoring government department, company, or organization. The numbers refer to entry numbers. Excluded from this index are entries for the Web sites of members of Congress, states, localities, and countries; these exclusions are covered by the Master Index at the end of this book.

Publication Index

This index covers many of the online publications available from the sites listed in this book. This index lists the documents by their publication title. See the SuDoc Index for access by the Superintendent of Documents (SuDoc) number associated with the publication. Note that the numbers refer to entry numbers and not to page numbers.

SuDoc Index

This index covers many of the online publications available from the sites listed in this book. This index lists the documents by their Superintendent of Documents (SuDoc) number for those that have a SuDoc number. For access by publication title, see the preceding index. Note that the numbers refer to entry numbers and not to page numbers.

Master Index: Subjects, Sponsors, and Site Names

This index includes entries for the Subjects, Sponsors, and Site Names listed in this directory. Where the Site Name duplicates a Sponsor, the index entries are merged. Note that the numbers refer to entry numbers and not to page numbers.

Project MUSE®